DATE DUE

FE1 5 '95			

DEMCO 38-297

THE STUDY
OF AMERICAN
FOLKLORE

An Introduction

SECOND EDITION

THE STUDY OF AMERICAN FOLKLORE

An Introduction

SECOND EDITION

Jan Harold Brunvand

UNIVERSITY OF UTAH

W·W·NORTON & COMPANY·INC·

NEW YORK

SECOND EDITION

Library of Congress Cataloging in Publication Data

Brunvand, Jan Harold.
  The study of American folklore: An Introduction

  Includes bibliographical references and index.
   1. Folk-lore—United States.   I. Title.
GR105.B7   1978   398.'07   77–13707
ISBN 0-393-09048-5

          1 2 3 4 5 6 7 8 9 0

Contents

I. INTRODUCTION

II. ORAL FOLKLORE

III. CUSTOMARY FOLKLORE

IV. MATERIAL FOLK TRADITIONS

APPENDICES

Preface to the Second Edition

Since its publication in 1968, *The Study of American Folklore* has been widely used not only as a college-level survey introduction, but also as a standard reference work for folklore teachers, scholars, and enthusiasts alike, including librarians, fieldworkers, archivists, high school students and teachers, state and local historians, and many others. While the book was not intended for some of the uses to which it has been put—such as a questionary for collecting folklore or a source of airtight definitions and final categories for all folklore genres—it has, reportedly, served them well. Considering its broad scope and the vigorous growth of American folklore studies in the past decade, it is gratifying how well this textbook has succeeded both in and beyond the classroom.

The revision is aimed at enhancing both its pedagogic and reference uses by adjusting this product of my late 1950s study and early 1960s writing to the dimensions of folkloristics in the 1970s. During this time span, American folklore scholarship changed as much as in all the years since its turn-of-the-century founding in such ways as the development of new theories, more attention to modern and urban folk traditions, increased interest in customary and material folklore (folklife), continuing mass popularity of folklore materials, and even some redefining of the term "folklore" itself. All of these aspects are reflected in the revision without alteration in the original strategy of organizing the discussion in terms of the types and subtypes of traditional materials which folk transmit in varying versions and which scholars have studied.

The most obvious changes in the book are the reorganization of chapters so as to juxtapose the discussion of music with the folksong and ballad chapters, grouping all customary traditions in one section, adding short section introductions, and splitting each of the two original chapters on material folk traditions to accommodate their doubled size. A major supplement to the book is a new sample study, the essay (Appendix D) by David Evans on Afro-American blues tradition. Another highly significant addition is the introduction of theoretical advances in folkloristics since 1968 in general terms to the introductory chapters and in specific applications to the genre chapters. The Bibliographic Notes are updated through 1975, and entries now include book publishers' names and have the journal volume numbers in arabic numerals. Several minor discrepancies and shortcomings of the original text pointed out by readers have been cleared up, and the entire contents were subjected to a review that resulted in a multitude of small changes, deletions, or additions on virtually every page. Professors Toelken and Glassie similarly revised and corrected their appended studies.

The result is "An Introduction" (still the subtitle) which is more timely, comprehensive, and pragmatic, but also, it is hoped, which represents the various points of view about American folklore in a fair and non-polemic way. Rather than adopting any specific contemporary approach, such as performance-centered analysis, my goal was to give beginning students an eclectic overview of modern theories and then guide their further reading in the ongoing study of American folklore.

Salt Lake City, Utah
July 1977

Preface

The fact that there is no completely satisfactory, modern, and authoritative basic guidebook to the types of folklore found in the United States has not impeded the growth (in one sense) of either American folklore scholarship or popular interest in the subject. Professional folklore societies and publications are proliferating in this country, college folklore courses flourish as never before, and, as somebody said recently, all anyone seems to need to become an overnight success as a folk singer is a guitar and a cold in the head. But this apparent harmony masks confusion. The fact is that there are damaging gaps in understanding between academically trained folklore specialists at one end of the scale, devoted but self-taught amateurs in the middle, and the general public at the other end. When members of these three groups discuss "American folklore" among themselves, the words may have a variety of meanings, and when the untrained enthusiasts give courses or write articles on American folklore, misinformation is spread and confusion is worse confounded.

In one form or another, the question frequently asked is: "What constitutes the subject matter of American folklore?" There is no single reference work, however, that gives a reliable answer. Richard M. Dorson's *American Folklore* (Chicago, 1959), for instance, is an excellent historical survey of the development of the major folk traditions, but it does not attempt to define "folklore" itself in all of its varieties except in general terms or by means of examples. Dorson's accompanying anthology, *Buying the Wind* (Chicago, 1964), contains further examples from seven regional groups, as well as an excellent introductory essay on folklore collecting in the United States, but it offers no basic definitions or categories. Using the bibliographies in these works, one might educate himself in basic matters, but it would be a long path, and one partly traced through a thicket of out-of-print books and obscure journals. At the end many kinds of American folklore that are vigorously alive in oral tradition would still be left unmentioned, for print has not kept up with word of mouth.

A trustworthy guidebook is needed, of course, for folklore generally. Kenneth S. Goldstein's *A Guide for Field Workers in Folklore* (Philadelphia, 1964) illustrates this. Goldstein declines "getting involved further in the problem of definition." Instead, he assumes that his readers will already know "the essentials of folklore" (genres and basic theory), and he advises those who do not to take a good college course in folklore and make use of such works as Sean O'Sullivan's *A Handbook of Irish Folklore* (Dublin, 1942. Reprinted Hatboro, Pa., 1963). Another writer who recently faced the same problem is Alan Dundes, who in the introduction to his anthology, *The Study of Folklore* (Englewood Cliffs, N.J., 1965), briefly criticizes existing definitions, enumerates typical materials of folklore, and then expresses hope that these matters will be clearer to his readers after they have studied the anthologized articles.

It is obvious that an Irish handbook has limited value outside of Ireland, and that a collection of previous studies is limited by the range of topics that has already been treated in reasonably concise essays. But more general survey volumes on folklore have never been completely successful. Alexander H. Krappe's *The Science of Folklore* devoted chapters to individual categories, but Krappe emphasized folk literature of Europe and ignored both American folklore and the folklore of material culture entirely. Moreover, his book has not been revised since it was published in 1930. Recent general handbooks have tended to be overwhelmingly American in orientation, but are not inclusive or fully reliable even for this country.

I am not bold enough to attempt another comprehensive survey of world folklore. As a matter of fact, I have narrowed my scope further even than "American folklore"—down to the folklore of this country that is transmitted in the English language. Thus, the qualification "Anglo-American" should be understood in all chapter titles. Anglo-American folklore is a coherent and manageable body of material that one might hope to define and organize. Once controlled, this material is a logical basis for further studies of folklore either in other countries or among different ethnic groups in the United States.

It should not be inferred by my focus on Anglo-American materials that these are purely native traditions to be understood solely in the context of American culture. On the contrary, very little that is discussed here does not have its counterparts, if not its origin, in the Old World. So far as space permitted, I have departed from time to time in my survey of types of folklore to show how these items of "American folklore" are anchored in other traditions of other places. Although this is obvious in the lore of ethnic groups in America (see Chapter 3), it is fully as true of Anglo-American folklore, and by following the general methods outlined in Chapter 2, and using the bibliographic notes, the student will be able to reveal for himself some further roots of American folk tradition abroad.

The purpose of this book, then, is to pave the way for such deeper studies by presenting systematically the types of folklore found in the United States, indicating briefly some analyses that have been made and others that are needed, and suggesting some of the links between American folklore and its parent traditions. I have written with academic folklore beginners in mind, but anyone interested in American folklore for any reason should find the book useful. Professional folklorists will find that I have generalized freely from their studies, citing my sources in the text or the bibliographic notes. I have attempted not to cite the same works more times than necessary, although certainly many items have a bearing on more than one kind of folklore. For ease of reference, the major terms that are introduced appear in boldface or italicized type, both where they occur in the text and in the index.

Levette J. Davidson's *A Guide to American Folklore* (Denver, 1951) comes closer than any other previous work to the present one, but I have organized my subjects in a different way, treated them in much greater detail, and drawn on the folklore scholarship that has appeared in the years since Davidson wrote his book. I have included my suggestions for further studies in the chapters themselves, instead of listing them separately, as Davidson did, at the end of the chapters. I have also tried to emphasize currently circulating examples of American folklore rather than rare or extinct ones, not only because these apparently ephemeral examples are those most likely to be recognized by readers, but also because they can often be shown to have had a long history in folk tradition. I hope I will be forgiven for some undue emphasis on texts from Indiana, Idaho, and Illinois. This should not suggest any preference on my part for states beginning with "I," rather it was simply the result of my living and collecting in these states while this book was being planned and written.

Like Davidson's *Guide*, this one deals largely with materials of folklore and not with theoretical concepts. But the three introductory chapters provide some background for the study of these materials, while the bibliographic notes suggest further readings. In the appendix are three original studies in American folklore presented as samples of the sort of analysis that may be made of each of the three basic types.

Abbreviations Used in the
Bibliographic Notes

AA	American Anthropologist		of the [English] Folklore Society)
AFFWord	(Journal of "Arizona Friends of Folklore")	GR	Geographical Review
		HF	Hoosier Folklore
AQ	American Quarterly	IF	Indiana Folklore
ArQ	Arizona Quarterly	IMH	Indiana Magazine of History
AS	American Speech		
BJA	British Journal of Aesthetics	IY	Idaho Yesterdays
		JAF	Journal of American Folklore
CA	Current Anthropology		
CFQ	California Folklore Quarterly	JAMS	Journal of the American Musicological Society
CL	Comparative Literature	JEGP	Journal of English and Germanic Philology
EM	Ethnomusicology		
FF	Folklore Forum	JFI	Journal of the Folklore Institute
FFemC	Folklore Feminists Communication		
		JGLS	Journal of the Gypsy Lore Society
FFC	Folklore Fellows Communications (Helsinki)	JIFMC	Journal of the International Folk Music Council
FFMA	The Folklore and Folk Music Archivist		
		JOFS	Journal of the Ohio Folklore Society
Folk Life	(Full title of the journal of the [English] Society for Folk Life Studies)	JPC	Journal of Popular Culture
		JSP	Journal of Social Psychology
Folklore	(Full title of the journal		

KF   *Keystone Folklore*
      (Until 1973, *KFQ*)
KFQ   *Keystone Folklore*
      Quarterly (After
      1973, *KF*)
KFR   *Kentucky Folklore*
      Record
KR   *Kenyon Review*
LFM   *Louisiana Folklore*
      Miscellany
MF   *Midwest Folklore*
MFR   *Mississippi Folklore*
      Register
MH   *Minnesota History*
MJLF *Midwestern Journal of*
      Language and
      Folklore
MLN   *Modern Language*
      Notes
MLQ   *Modern Language*
      Quarterly
MLW   *Mountain Life and*
      Work
MP   *Modern Philology*
MQ   *Musical Quarterly*
MSF   *Mid-South Folklore*
NCF   *North Carolina Folklore*
      (After 1973, *NCFJ*)
NCFJ *North Carolina Folklore*
      Journal (Until 1973,
      NCF)
NEF   *Northeast Folklore*
NEQ   *New England Quarterly*
NH   *Nebraska History*
NJF   *New Jersey Folklore*
NMFR *New Mexico Folkore*
      Record

NWF   *Northwest Folklore*
NYF   *New York Folklore*
      (Until 1975, *NYFQ*)
NYFQ *New York Folklore*
      Quarterly (After
      1975, *NYF*)
OFB   *Oregon Folklore*
      Bulletin
PADS *Publications of the*
      American Dialect
      Society
PF   *Pennsylvania Folklife*
PMLA *Publications of the*
      Modern Language
      Association
PTFS *Publications of the*
      Texas Folklore
      Society
SFQ   *Southern Folklore*
      Quarterly
TAW   *The American West*
TFSB *Tennessee Folklore*
      Society Bulletin
TQ   *Texas Quarterly*
TSL   *Tennessee Studies in*
      Literature
TSLL *Texas Studies in*
      Literature and
      Language
UHQ   *Utah Historical*
      Quarterly
UHR   *Utah Humanities*
      Review
WAL   *Western American*
      Literature
WF   *Western Folklore*

Basic Bibliography:
Collections Cited in Notes by Title Only

Beck, Horace P., ed. *Folklore in Action: Essays for Discussion in Honor of MacEdward Leach*. Philadelphia: American Folklore Society Bibliographical and Special Series, vol. 14, 1962.

Dorson, Richard M., *American Folklore and the Historian*. Chicago: University of Chicago Press, 1971.

Dorson, Richard M., *Folklore: Selected Essays*. Bloomington: Indiana University Press, 1972.

Dundes, Alan. *Analytic Essays in Folklore*. The Hague and Paris: Mouton, 1975.

Dundes, Alan. *The Study of Folklore*. Englewood Cliffs, N.J.: Prentice-Hall, 1965.

Pound, Louise. *Nebraska Folklore*. Lincoln: University of Nebraska Press, 1959.

Richmond, W. Edson. *Studies in Folklore*. Bloomington: Indiana University Folklore Series, no. 9, 1957.

Acknowledgments

To my dear wife Judith belongs the major credit for convincing me that I could write this book, sustaining me when the going got rough, and criticizing my work when it needed criticism. Our children—Erik, Amy, Dana, and Karen—all behaved themselves "while Daddy was making his book," with the understanding that their names would appear in it.

I stand in great debt for my own introduction to folklore to all of my instructors at Indiana University, especially Professors Richard M. Dorson, Warren E. Roberts, and W. Edson Richmond. I was also privileged to get to know Stith Thompson, Indiana University Professor Emeritus, and to study with Archer Taylor of the Univerisity of California and Katharine Luomala of the University of Hawaii when they were visiting professors at Indiana University in the summer of 1958. All of these folklorists, and others, will recognize many of their ideas in this book. I hope they are fairly represented.

Students in my folklore classes at the University of Idaho (1961–1965), Indiana University (Summer, 1965), and Southern Illinois University at Edwardsville (1965–1966) heard early versions of many of these chapters in lecture form, and they aided greatly by forcing me to revise and clarify numerous points that were still obscure to beginners in folklore. I was supported in the last stages of preparing the manuscript by the granting of released time and funds for secretarial assistance from Southern Illinois University. My two student typists, Kathleen M. Evans and Gail E. Schulze, did an exemplary job of turning a chaotic final draft into a neatly finished manuscript. The library staff of Southern Illinois University at Edwardsville, while in the throes of consolidating several far-flung operations into a brand new one in a half-finished building, did a heroic job of finding sources for me. Professors William H. Jansen of the University of Kentucky and Wayland D. Hand of UCLA provided final critical readings of the manuscript and offered several useful suggestions for its improvement.

For many specific suggestions on preparing the revised edition, I am grateful to Madeleine and Daniel Barnes, John A. Burrison, William H. Jansen, Kenneth L. Ketner, Roger L. Welsch, and John O. West.

I · INTRODUCTION

❖❭❖❭❖❭❖❭❖❭❖❭❖

1

The Field of Folklore

Folklore comprises the unrecorded traditions of a people; it includes both the form and content of these traditions and their style or technique of communication from person to person. The study of folklore (or "folkloristics") attempts to analyze these traditions (both content and process) so as to reveal the common life of the human mind apart from what is contained in the formal records of culture that compose the heritage of a people. Only by turning to the folklore of peoples, probing into its meanings, patterns, and functions, and searching for links between different bodies of tradition may we hope to understand the intellectual and spiritual life of humanity in its broadest dimensions. This type of research has been a respected academic specialty in Europe for generations. In the United States, however, the field of folklore is relatively new, and it tends to be narrowly understood by many people who may have been attracted to it through treatments in the popular media, where the word "folklore" is very loosely applied, or who may know the word only with reference to children's literature or in the sense of rumor, hearsay, or error. However, it is in the scholarly sense of "oral and customary tradition" that we are employing the word "folklore" here. The American folklorist Archer Taylor put it succinctly in 1948: "Folklore is the material that is handed on by tradition, either by word of mouth or by custom and practice."

The chief difficulty in defining "folklore" more completely and scientifically is that the word has acquired varying meanings among the different people who use it. The word was coined by a nineteenth-century English scholar, W. J. Thoms, to supply an Anglo-Saxon word to replace the Latinate term "popular antiquities," or the intellectual "remains" of earlier cultures surviving in the traditions of the peasant class. Modern folklorists have tried to avoid the peasant connotations of the term, but they still use it partly in the original sense to signify that portion of any culture that is passed on in oral or customary tradition. Folklorists tend to exclude as spurious or contaminated any supposed folklore that is transmitted largely by print, broadcasting, or other commercial and organized means. American folklorists sometimes use the term "fakelore" (coined by Richard M. Dorson in 1950) to disparage the professional writers' contrived inventions and rewritings—like many Paul Bunyan stories—which are foisted on the public as genuine examples of native folk traditions, but which have only a thin basis of real tradition underlying them.

"Folk" is a somewhat misleading term in an academic context, which has led some folklorists to suggest substitutes for "folklore" such as "hominology" or simply "lore." But "hominology" is just another word for "anthropology" and has achieved no currency; the term "lore" itself is no improvement, since it is hard to justify including behavioral and material data under that heading, and it is still necessary to differentiate *traditional* "lore" from other aspects of culture. The anthropological terms "folk culture" and "verbal arts" have also been proposed as better names for folklore, but neither seems adequate for the purpose; furthermore, "folk culture" implies specific social and economic conditions that are not found in most of the settings folklorists study. The best approach, still, for understanding the scholarly field of American folklore seems to be to state as clearly as possible the concepts folklorists themselves hold, for, as one frustrated definer of the term finally put it, "Folklore is what folklorists study."

Folklore is the traditional, unofficial, non-institutional part of culture. It encompasses all knowledge, understandings, values, attitudes, assumptions, feelings, and beliefs transmitted in traditional forms by word of mouth or by customary examples. Many of these habits of thought are common to all human beings, but they always interact with and are influenced by the whole cultural context that surrounds them. Folklore manifests itself in many oral and verbal forms ("mentifacts"), in kinesiological forms (customary behavior, or "sociofacts"), and in material forms ("artifacts"), but folklore itself is the whole traditional complex of thought, content, and process which ultimately can never be fixed or recorded in its entirety; it lives only in its performance or communication as people interact with one another. It is instructive to represent these generalizations and terms as a chart, with typical labels for the supposed levels of culture (or behavior) on one axis and the kinds of traditional materials (or products) on the other. The result is as follows:

	Products:		
	ORAL	CUSTOMARY	MATERIAL
Levels:	(Mentifacts)	(Sociofacts)	(Artifacts)
Elite (academic, progres- sive, etc.)			
Normative (popular, mass, mainstream, etc.)			
Folk (conservative, tradi- tional, peasant, etc.)			
Primitive (nonliterate, uncivilized, etc.)			

In general, the elite and normative traditions are transmitted in print or by other formal means, while folk and primitive traditions rely on oral or customary circulation, although there are always exceptions. If we try now to isolate one specific human need or desire for each level and its typical products, we arrive at a set of samples like this:

	ORAL (entertainment)	CUSTOMARY (cure)	MATERIAL (housing)
Elite	novel	doctor's care	architect's design
Normative	television serial	patent medicine	tract development house
Folk	tall tale or joke	home remedy	log cabin or saltbox house
Primitive	tribal myth	witch doctor	igloo

Such a chart and samples, of course, are oversimplifications of very complex phenomena, and an important part of many research projects in folklore is sorting out the various threads of influence and the interweavings in one level from another. For example, while most movies are popular art, some serious works of "cinema" tend to be elite; musical comedy would seem to be a mass-culture variant of opera. Similarly, bluegrass music has roots in folk music but most of its development is in popular music, and Paul Bunyan stories span the same two categories. In general, the movement of ideas tends to be from top to bottom, as when Greek Revival architecture became a popular style for banks and survived later as a traditional decorative style on houses. Other materials and ideas, however, have stayed in place (many barn types), or moved upward ("folk" clothing becoming "fashionable"), or skipped steps ("primitive" poetry or arts appealing to "elite" critics). The study of folklore itself is, of course, "elite." Most important to bear in mind is that any individual may be aware of, influenced by, and participate in any level of culture during his lifetime, or even during the course of a particular day.

The materials and manifestations of folklore are extremely wide ranging and diverse; their genres may be identified as either *ethnic* (or *native*) *categories,* those of the people themselves (like "old-wive's tales"), or *analytical categories,* those of research scholars (like "Child ballads"). For the purpose of an orderly presentation of American folklorists' practices, we will treat the types of folklore here, using typical analytical categories, in three groups, according to their modes of existence: *oral, customary,* or *material.*

Oral folklore, the type most commonly studied until recently in the United States, may be conveniently arranged and listed from the simplest to the most complex varieties. At the level of the individual word is *folk speech,* including dialect and naming. Traditional phrases and sentences make up the area of folk *proverbs* and *proverbial sayings,* while traditional questions are folk *riddles.* Next are folk *rhymes* and other traditional poetry, then folk *narratives* of all kinds, and finally *folksongs* and folk *ballads* with their *music.*

Customary folklore, which often involves both verbal and nonverbal elements, includes folk *beliefs* and *superstitions,* folk *customs* and *festivals,* folk *dances* and *dramas, gestures,* and folk *games.*

Material folk traditions include folk *architecture, crafts, arts, costumes,* and *foods.*

These categories and subcategories overlap, of course, but such a three-part classification emphasizes elements that go into folklore and shows how individual items and performances may be roughly sorted on the basis of their major modes of existence. Placing a folk singer's lyrics in one category, his guitar-playing style and melody in another, and the call and figures of a dance done to the same song in a third is not intended to lead to fragmentation either of the tradition involved or the study of it. The classification is only a means of clarifying and organizing the processes and materials that are to be observed and analyzed. Without an awareness of these elements of a traditional performance, there would be a tendency simply to tape-record "the song" without capturing its context or the nonverbal nuances. Similarly, because folktales are basically verbal folklore, folklorists should not overlook collecting and studying such nonverbal elements as facial expressions, gestures, and audience reactions while tales are being told. The ideal study is one that takes into account the entire traditional event, which is what we are referring to as a "performance."

The foregoing discussion identifies mainly the *materials* that circulate in folk tradition; we can extract from these materials some common qualities that will provide us with a good general *definition* of the subject. Anyone who has tried to investigate the scholarly conception of folklore has probably soon discovered that scholars themselves do not always agree on the details of an acceptable definition. The most obvious demonstration of this disagreement is in the twenty-one separate definitions published in the *Standard Dictionary of Folklore* found on many library shelves. But despite these semantic disagreements, most folklorists actually are in accord on the essentials of their field of study, whatever the wording of their individual definitions. Folklorists generally associate five qualities with true folklore: (1) its content is oral (usually verbal), or custom-related or material; (2) it is traditional in form and transmission; (3) it exists in different versions; (4) it is usually anonymous; (5) it tends to become formularized. Each of these terms is used in a fairly broad sense, and the first three qualities are the primary ones to be considered in arriving at a definition.

Folklore is oral or custom-related; that is, it passes by word of mouth and informal demonstration or imitation from one person to another and from one generation to the next. Much folklore is "aural," reaching the ear either from voices or from musical instruments. While written folklore (such as graffiti or autograph rhymes) is verbal without being oral, its transmission is customary, not institutionalized. The same is true for learning to produce or use folk artifacts, such as whittled wooden chains, hand-sewn quilts, or traditional log cabins. Folklore is never transmitted *entirely* in a formal manner through printed books, phonograph records, school classes, church sermons, or by other learned, sophisticated, and commercial means.

Folklore is traditional in two senses: it is passed on repeatedly in a relatively fixed or standard form, and it circulates among members of a particular group. Traditional form or structure allows us to recognize corresponding bits of folklore in different guises. The characters in a story, the setting, the length, the style, even the language may vary, but we can still call it the "same" story if it maintains a basic underlying form. Think, for example, of "Cinderella," which is recognizable even in a comic-strip parody if the characters are made modern teen-agers, or in the movies if the parts are acted by Hollywood stars in a big-city setting.

Comic strips and movies are not folklore, of course, and this leads to the observation that the first two qualities must be found together to define folklore. For example, some things, like conversations, are oral, but not traditional. (Entire conversations are not passed on between members of a group in a relatively fixed or standard form and repeated over and over again.) Other things, like legal processes, are largely traditional, but not oral. (The proceedings in courts of law are preserved in print, not by word of mouth. Law precedents must be followed precisely, but folk informants seldom refer to printed collections of folklore.) Only those aspects of culture that are both oral or customary and traditional may be folklore; thus, there may be traditional folk stories, proverbs, or gestures passed on either in conversations or in courtroom arguments and testimony. These items are legitimate examples of folklore. The American "folk groups" that support major bodies of tradition are discussed in Chapter 3. Much controversy has centered on the meaning of the "folk" in "folklore," but it is sufficient to say here that one should not think only of quaint, rustic tradition-bearers, but rather of any group that has distinctive oral traditions, which is to say, just about *any* group.

Oral transmission invariably creates different versions of the same text, and these versions or "variants" are the third defining character-istic of folklore. Folklorists often speak of individual recordings of folklore as either "texts" or "versions," reserving the term "variants" for texts that deviate more widely from the common standard. A story, proverb, or other text is living folklore only as long as it con-tinues to circulate orally in different traditional variations. "The Three Bears," for instance, except in oral parodies, has always been a liter-ary tale; "Home on the Range" was collected as an oral folksong but, after the influence of wide reprint, is now learned from books or sheet music in a standardized form.

Generally speaking, then, folklore may be defined as *those mate-rials in culture that circulate traditionally among members of any group in different versions, whether in oral form or by means of cus-tomary example, as well as the processes of traditional performance and communication.*

Although oral or customary tradition and the presence of different versions serve to define folklore, the two other qualities, anonymity and formularization, are important enough to belong in a complete description. Folklore is usually anonymous simply because authors' names are seldom part of texts that are orally transmitted, and folk ar-tifacts are seldom signed, although occasionally a ballad may contain the supposed name or initials of its composer in the last verse, and sometimes local tradition preserves the name of a notable folk com-poser or artisan. On occasion, too, research has unearthed the iden-tity of a creator of folklore, but the majority of folklore bears no trace of its authorship, and even the time and place of its origin may be a mystery.

Most folklore tends to become formularized; that is, it is expressed partly in clichés. These may range in complexity from simple set phrases and patterns of repetition to elaborate opening and closing devices or whole passages of traditional verbal stereotypes. Further-more, there are different bodies of formularized language in different countries and for different kinds of folklore, so that we can distinguish English and American ballads, for example, partly on the basis of the different formulas used in each. Nonverbal folklore too makes use of stereotyped habits, gestures, patterns, designs, and the like. One interesting area of folklore research is the identification and attempted explanation of this recurring formularization.

The boundaries of the field of folklore laid out in this chapter do not take in all of the various recent uses to which the terms "folk" and "lore" have been put. They do, however, delimit rather broadly the scholarly area that folklorists have staked out for their studies. It bears repeating that this area is one of prime significance for our fuller understanding of human behavior and culture. Certainly the current popularization and sometimes banalization of folklore, the appearance of fakelore, and even utter misapplication of the term "folklore," also reveal important things about culture and behavior, and these deserve study, too. But this is subject matter for another kind of book, one for which a survey like the present one is probably a necessary prerequisite.

In this book, after brief discussions of the study of folklore and of the major bearers of American folk traditions, specific types of oral, customary, and material folk tradition from American sources are presented in the context of scholarly studies and theories.

BIBLIOGRAPHIC NOTES

The Victorian gentleman-scholar W. J. Thoms suggested the term "folklore" in a letter to *The Athenaeum* in 1846; see Duncan Emrich, " 'Folk-Lore': William John Thoms," *CFQ* 5 (1946), 355–74. The twenty-one definitions by modern folklorists are gathered in *Funk & Wagnalls Standard Dictionary of Folklore, Mythology, and Legend,* 2 vols. (New York: Funk & Wagnalls, 1949; rev. 1 vol. edn., 1972). The Thoms letter and a discussion of the dictionary definitions are reprinted in Dundes's *The Study of Folklore,* which contains other important articles, including Archer Taylor's quoted in this chapter, on the problem of defining folklore. Richard M. Dorson introduced the word "fakelore" in an article in *The American Mercury* 70 (March 1950), 335–43, and he furnished the background for his coinage in an article in *Zeitschrift für Volkskunde* 65 (1969), 56–64.

Three addresses by former presidents of the American Folklore Society are important statements on the field of folklore. They are: Herbert Halpert's "Folklore: Breadth Versus Depth," *JAF* 71 (1958), 97–103; Wayland D. Hand's "American Folklore After Seventy Years: Survey and Prospect," *JAF* 73 (1960), 1–11; and William Bascom's "Folklore, Verbal Art, and Culture," *JAF* 86 (1973), 374–81. Three professional assessments of the state of American folklore studies are Tristram P. Coffin's "Folklore in the American Twentieth Century," *AQ* 13 (1961), 526–33; Francis Lee Utley's "The Academic Status of Folklore in the United States," *JFI* 7 (1970), 110–15; and Richard M. Dorson's "Is Folklore a Discipline?" *Folklore* 84 (1973), 177–205.

For statements on the discipline, made two decades apart by the dean of American folklore scholars, see Stith Thompson's "American Folklore after Fifty Years," *JAF* 51 (1938), 1–9, and "Folklore at Midcentury," in *MF* 1 (1951), 5–12. Jan Harold Brunvand reviewed Thompson's evaluations in the light of another twenty years' progress in "New Directions for the Study of American Folklore," *Folklore* 82 (1971), 25–35. A politically oriented critique by John Alexander Williams titled "Radicalism and Professionalism in Folklore Studies: A Comparative Perspective" was published in *JFI* 11 (1974 [Misdated, 1975]), 211–34, and answered by Richard M. Dorson in the same journal, 235–39.

One can gain a clear impression of older European attitudes toward folklore from *The Handbook of Irish Folklore* and Krappe's *The Science of Folklore* (see the Preface), and also from *The Handbook of Folklore* published by the [English] Folk-Lore Society in 1890 and revised and enlarged in 1957. Especially pertinent in the *Handbook* is the first chapter, "What Folklore Is," in which it is declared that folklore is "the expression of the psychology of early man" and comprises "the traditional Beliefs, Customs, Stories, Songs, and Sayings current among backward peoples, or retained by the uncultured classes of more advanced peoples." A grudging nod toward "folklife" was inserted in an addendum to the 1913 edition of the *Handbook*, but this was qualified by the insistence that "by no stretch of definition can the word *lore* be taken to include the material objects to which it may be attached." To redress the balance at last, the Society for Folk Life Studies was formed in England in 1961, and their yearbook, *Folk Life*, first appeared in 1963.

Alan Dundes has presented "The American Concept of Folklore" in *JFI* 3 (1966), 226–45, repr. in *Analytic Essays in Folklore*, pp. 3–16. Taking a comparative approach, Américo Paredes discussed "Concepts About Folklore in Latin America and the United States" in *JFI* 6 (1969), 20–38. An important exegesis is Paulo de Carvalho Neto's *Concepto de Folklore* (Montevideo, Uruguay, 1955) first translated into English as *The Concept of Folklore* (Coral Gables, Fla.: University of Miami Press, 1971).

That North American folklorists have widened their characteristic view of folklore as oral literature and are embracing the Continental concept of folklore as "folklife," or the totality of traditional life, is indicated by such developments as the establishment of a master's degree program in American folk culture by the State University College, Oneonta, New York, at The Farmer's Museum at Cooperstown. Henry Glassie, a holder of this degree and a leading American folklife scholar, wrote the study presented in Appendix C of this book. His general appraisal of the cultural roles of handmade things appears in "Artifacts: Folk, Popular, Imaginary, and Real," published in Marshall Fishwick and Ray B. Browne's *Icons of Popular Culture* (Bowling Green, Ohio: Bowling Green University Popular Press, 1970), pp. 103–22.

The theoretical problems in trying to distinguish folklore types and categories are taken up in a "Symposium on Folk Genres" conducted by Dan Ben-Amos in the journal *Genre* 2 (1969), i–301; of particular importance is Ben-Amos's own essay there, "Analytical Categories and Ethnic Genres," pp. 275–301. These essays were reprinted in book form as *Folklore Genres*, ed. Dan Ben-Amos, American Folklore Society Bibliographic and Special Series, no. 26 (Austin, Texas, 1976). Alan Dundes identifies "Some Minor Genres of American Folklore" (envelope sealers, evasive answers, feigned apologies, etc.) in *SFQ* 31 (1967), 20–36. A good example of how the social context in which a folkloric item is communicated determines its genre is Ronald L. Baker's note " 'Hogs are Playing with Sticks—Bound to be Bad Weather': Folk Belief or Proverb?" *MJLF* 1 (1975), 65–67.

Probably the most influential publication directed to the strong current desire to redefine "folklore" along contextual or behavioristic lines is Dan Ben Amos's "Toward a Definition of Folklore in Context," pp. 3–15, in "Toward New Perspectives in Folklore," ed. Américo Paredes and Richard Bauman, *JAF* 84 (1971), iii–172 and in the American Folklore Society Bibliographic and Special Series, no. 23 (1972). This essay, originally a paper delivered orally at an AFS meeting, was debated in print even before it reached print itself; see Roger L. Welsch, "A Note on Definitions," *JAF* 81 (1968), 262–64; Richard Bauman, "Towards a Behavioral Theory of Folklore: A Reply to Roger Welsch," *JAF* 82 (1969), 167–70; Roger D. Abrahams, "On Meaning and Gaming," *JAF* 82 (1969), 268–70; and Jan Harold Brunvand, "On Abrahams' Besom," *JAF* 83 (1970), 81.

Folklore Forum devoted its "Bibliographic and Special Series" no. 12 to fourteen articles on "Conceptual Problems in Contemporary Folklore Study"; the most lucid of these (despite its title) was Gerald Cashion's "Folklore, Kinesiological Folklore, and the Macro-Folklore Complex," pp. 24–35. An equally well-written and clarifying essay is Kay L. Cothran's "Participation in Tradition," *KF* 18 (1973), 7–13. Identifying "folklore about folklore" as a traditional practice worthy of more study, Alan Dundes proposed "Metafolklore and Oral Literary Criticism," a concept quickly seized upon by folklorists, in *The Monist* 50 (1966), 505–16; repr. in *Analytic Essays in Folklore*, pp. 50–58.

2

The Study of Folklore

Folklore is fascinating to study because people are fascinating creatures. It is a diversified and complex subject because it reflects the whole intricate mosaic of the rest of human culture. Folklore is part of culture, but it is elusive, flowing along separately from the mainstream of the major intellectual attainments of humanity. In traditional lore, however, there are counterparts for literary and representational art, philosophical speculations, scientific inquiries, historical records, social attitudes, and psychological insights. Thus, the study of folklore is a subdivision of the broader study of people and their works, and as such folklore research has much in common with both the humanities and the social sciences.

From the humanistic point of view folklore research has tended to emphasize the "lore," usually taking a literary approach to the recorded "texts" of verbal traditions; from the social science point of view folklore research has emphasized the "folk," taking an anthropological approach to the full cultural significance of traditions. Thus, to a humanist, proverbs may be "folk philosophy," riddles may be "traditional metaphorical questions," and folktales may be "oral literature," but to an anthropologist these forms may be considered as educational tools, social controls, or status markers. Taken from either viewpoint, the materials of folklore afford the unique opportunity of studying what exists and persists in culture largely without the support of established learning, religion, government, and other formal institutions. Folklore represents what people preserve in their culture by custom and word of mouth when few other means exist to preserve it. The discovery of the historical depth and the geographical breadth of some of these traditional "survivals" (as they were once called) is what first gave the study of folklore much of its fascination. Nowadays, however, there is much more interest in the *present* functions and meanings of folk traditions, and the literary and anthropological approaches to folklore study are merging as a new "folkloristic" study develops.

What humanists and social scientists shared when they studied folklore was an interest in finding out how, why, and which traditional cultural mentifacts, sociofacts, and artifacts developed, varied, and were passed on. From observations and records of these materials they hoped to reconstruct something of the unrecorded intellectual life of people of the past and present. The findings of such folklore research are applicable to many fields. Some literary scholars are interested, for instance, in the folk roots of epic and other narrative poetry and in the stylistic or thematic use of folklore in literature. Students of the fine arts may similarly consider the background of their subjects in folk music and folk art. Historians find that oral traditions, although seldom factually accurate, furnish unusual insights into grass-roots attitudes toward historical events. Psychologists have long held that folklore, in common with dreams and other manifestations of fantasy, contains clues to the subconscious. Sociologists may study folklore (especially protest lore) along with other data on group life and behavior. While such applications of folklore study to other fields (such as the natural sciences) are still in an early stage, other and new applications (such as studying the efficacy of folk medicine) are also emerging. In fact, probably every field of study involving people and their works will in some way eventually make use of evidence from folklore as folklorists continue to refine and publicize their work. And the more unified approach of recent folklore research holds even more promise for the application of findings to other fields.

Modern folkloristics embraces oral, customary, and material aspects of tradition equally, and it makes eclectic use of theoretical and methodological approaches from anthropology, linguistics, communications, psychology, and other relevant areas. The hope is to develop a viable approach to studying the whole phenomenon that is known as "folklore" (behavior, texts, performances, effects, etc.), whenever and wherever it occurs, and from a point of view that is uniquely "folkloristic." While several distinct theoretical approaches and schools of thought have developed within folklore studies (some of which are discussed in more detail in later chapters), most folklore research may still be thought of as an attempt to answer only a few of the fundamental questions *definition* (what folklore is)

classification (what the genres of folklore are)

source (who "the folk" are)

origin (who composed folklore)

transmission (how folklore is carried, how fast, and how far)

variation (how folklore changes and for what reasons)

structure (what the underlying form of folklore is and the relation of form to content)

function (what folklore means to its carriers and how it serves them)

meaning and *purpose* (what the performer intends to convey and the intended effect)

use and *application* (what should be done with folklore and in what other areas of study it is useful).

Ideally, no folk product or performance would be considered fully understood until answers had at least been suggested for all such questions. In practice, however, because past folklorists have tended to be specialists in one genre or region or technique, studies seldom considered more than one or two of these matters at a time, and very few aspects of folklore have been subjected to more comprehensive research. It is perhaps best to survey published folklore scholarship according to the traditional three stages of such research: *collection*, *classification*, and *analysis*.

The raw materials of oral folklore research are texts (or "records of mentifacts"). It is axiomatic that these texts must be called verbatim from oral sources; editorial additions to or "improvements" in the texts have no part in honest research. Most folklorists today seek out promising informants and use tape recorders to collect their exact words, practicing a variety of interview techniques to achieve a re- laxed atmosphere and a natural response. Not only the most skilled "active" informants are sought, but also the relatively "passive" infor- mants who may remember interesting lore, although they impart it only in garbled or fragmentary form. Often collectors will make sev- eral visits to their best informants, sometimes over a long span of time, re-recording familiar material and asking for new items.

Besides verbatim texts, folklorists record data about the informants themselves (age, occupation, national origin, etc.) and gather back- ground on their families and communities. An informant's gestures and facial expressions should be described as an integral part of the performance, and these may be captured in candid photographs. In the most penetrating studies, informants may even be asked to discuss or interpret their texts, and experiments have been attempted with some informants and their audiences.

Questionnaires are successfully used for folklore collecting in Europe, generally with trained semiprofessional field workers asking the questions of residents in their own region. Mailed questionnaires allow researchers to cover a wider area than they might conveniently visit in person, but this technique also limits the inquiry to a specific subject and eleminates the free association that is often the most productive part of direct collecting. Only a few studies of American folklore have thus far made use of questionnaires, but they seem to hold great promise, particularly for accurate distributional and variation studies of folk customs and folk artifacts.

Folklore texts or descriptions of customs and artifacts may sometimes be collected from handwritten sources, such a diaries, letters, and notebooks, or from printed matter, either books, magazines, or newspapers. Some Civil War folksongs, for instance, survived in soldiers' writings, and many Colonial "divine providences" collected and printed by Puritan writers were probably old popular beliefs and superstitions. American regional newspapers in the nineteenth century preserved much traditional native humor that has not been fully explored. Current popular periodicals also occasionally print items of folklore that have been reported as actual events.

A beginning folklore collector can learn much about field problems and techniques by reading accounts of fieldwork by veteran collectors. For example, the works of Richard M. Dorson, one of the most active and successful American collectors, are rich in anecdotes and suggestions. In his *Negro Folktales in Michigan* (Cambridge, Mass., 1956) two prefatory chapters analyze the communities and informants visited and include several photographs of narrators in action. He recalls that it was the leather patches on his jacket sleeves that convinced one informant that he was really a "writer feller" and not, as some others in the town thought, an FBI agent.

In *Bloodstoppers and Bearwalkers* (Cambridge, Mass., 1952) Dorson describes how he pieced together the Upper Peninsula legend of "The Lynching of the McDonald Boys" from numerous incomplete reports and offhand allusions. "Old-timers have spun the grisly yarn . . . to pop-eyed youngsters for more than sixty years . . . [but] no two granddads tell quite the same story, for this is strictly a family tradition, never frozen in print, and unceasingly distorted with the vagaries that grow from hearsay and surmise." The Ozark collector Vance Randolph is as industrious and successful in the field as Dorson, but more casual in his approach; he generally includes in his books a prefatory note something like the following from his collection of Ozark jokes, *Hot Springs and Hell* (Hatboro, Pa., 1965):

> Some of these items were recorded on aluminum discs, but most of them were set down in longhand and typed a few hours later while the details were still fresh in my mind. They are not verbatim transcripts, but every one of them is pretty close to the mark. They are not literary adaptations. I did not add any characters or incidents, or try to improve the narrator's style. I did not combine different versions, or use material from more than one informant in the same tale. Many backwoods jokes are nonverbal anyhow, and some folk humor is too subtle for print, just as certain folk tunes cannot be compassed by the conventional notation. I just set down each item as accurately as I could and let it go at that.

Unorthodox collecting methods sometimes yield good results when conventional approaches fail. Some folklorists, for instance, have tried rocking an empty rocking chair, opening an umbrella in the house, or violating some other superstitious taboo in order to elicit a response about bad luck. Others have had success singing a song or telling a tale in garbled form so that intended informants will correct them. Kenneth S. Goldstein once devised a field experiment that led two Scottish women unselfconsciously to tell their versions of a previously tape-recorded family legend in the presence of the other. He later asked them to retell the legend on the pretense that he had accidentally erased the tape. He discovered that each storyteller had somewhat modified her own telling, influenced by what she had heard from the other narrator. An excellent collection of Norwegian tall tales was made by a paint company through a contest advertised in popular periodicals. Similarly, I found a rich stock of shaggy-dog stories that had been collected by a network radio program devoted to answering listeners' questions. A student based a fascinating term project on the following topic, presented with teachers' cooperation to several classes of elementary-school children: "Write down your favorite jump-rope rhyme and tell why you like it." (Some specific hints on tape-recorder technique are included in Chapter 12, and on collecting with camera or sketch pad in Chapter 18.)

Whatever the collecting methods employed, and however ingenious or well prepared the collector may be, persistence and a willingness to adapt to the informants' habits and moods will pay off in the long run. The following quotation from John A. Lomax's autobiographical *Adventures of a Ballad Hunter* (New York, 1947) is illustrative:

> It was cowboy songs I most wished. . . . These I jotted down on a table in a saloon back room, scrawled on an envelope while squatting about a campfire near a chuck wagon, or caught behind the scenes of a broncho-busting outfit or rodeo. To capture the cowboy music proved an almost impossible task. The cowboys would simply wave away the large horn I carried and refused to sing into it! Not one song did I ever get from them except through the influence of generous amounts of whiskey, raw and straight from the bottle or jug.

An important, but often neglected, aspect of fieldwork in folklore is the ethical dimension—the responsibilities and liabilities of a folklorist with regard to his informants and their material, especially when embarrassing, antisocial, or illegal material is involved. Unless clear legal limits of access to and liability for collected information are established (and this is seldom done), the folklorist would do well to code or to give pseudonyms to his human sources of questionable lore. Such material might concern drug use, moonshining, telephone or machine fraud, tax evasion, and the like. But even less criminal subjects may raise ethical questions, such as whether informants should be compensated for their cooperation, by whom collected material may be used and for what purposes, and whether published material should be specifically credited to informants. In general, it is never a good idea to record folklore surreptitiously unless the informants are advised of the act later and allowed to review the material, and archives should always insist upon some kind of informants' and collectors' release forms accompanying any filed material and clearly outlining any conditions to be imposed on it.

Collected folklore texts, descriptions of customs, or artifacts are of little use to a scholar until identified by category and arranged systematically in an archive (or museum) or published. Classification of the myriad forms of folklore facilitates their study just as classification systems do for the natural sciences: without standardized terminology and arrangement, scholars could not communicate effectively or gather data from archives and published collections. The difficulty, of course (as pointed out in Chapter 1), is that ethnic or "native" categories differ a great deal from culture to culture or even from person to person. The more abstract "analytical" categories devised by scholars have not always yielded mutually exclusive systems, nor have they won universal scholarly acceptance. Any classification, it should be borne in mind, is always for a purpose; and, for the purpose of organizing data for analysis, certain traditional categories have become established in the voluminous reference works for motifs, tales, ballads, superstitions, riddles, proverbs, and other forms. These classification systems, whatever their shortcomings, have yet to be superseded in folkloristics; they structure the balance of this book and are cited in the appropriate bibliographic notes.

Since much American folklore has been collected by university folklorists or by their students, the largest folklore archives in this country are on campuses. Although there is no national folklore archive in the United States, nor even a uniform archiving system in use, individual archivists can still consult the standard reference works to arrange and annotate their materials. Folklore journals and other publications rely on the same indexes. Most archivists and editors also make some attempt to cross-index materials by region and by ethnic background and sometimes even by collector, but since no one can anticipate all the possible research needs future users of an archive may have, the chief frustration of archivists is probably locating among their varied holdings all the materials potentially useful for a particular project. Some archives have tried to increase their flexibility and usefulness by publishing catalogs of their holdings or by attempting to computerize materials. Folk museums must add to their tasks of acquisition, cataloguing, storage, and retrieval, the challenges of display and interpretation for the public which few folklore archives even attempt to meet.

In the past it was assumed that only when folklore had been collected in some quantity, classified in considerable detail, and made generally available to scholars could any significant analysis take place. In general, for historical and transmission studies, this still holds true. The oldest and perhaps still the most common technique of folklore analysis is comparison, usually of different versions of the same item. Such a comparative approach requires relatively many recorded examples arranged in workable categories by type.

Another avenue of comparative research followed by some American folklorists is to bring their folkloristic viewpoint to bear on other closely related scholarly fields. For example, such material traditions in the United States as homemade cabins, houses, and barns have been investigated for some time by American folklorists and cultural geographers, the former concerning themselves mainly with the survival and variation of traditional patterns, and the latter with regional distribution and the explanations for it. To some degree, architectural historians have also been involved, fitting "vernacular" styles in with the sequence of high or academic design. An eclectic American folklorist such as Henry Glassie (See Chapter 18 and Appendix C), has some acquaintance with all three fields, plus solid field experience; he attempts to frame a unified explanation for certain kinds of traditional buildings.

Even a beginning student not specializing in folklore might study comparatively some common attitudes toward geography and such other fields as journalism, law, business, or politics, as found in folk speech, proverbs, place names, legends, tall tales, jokes, folksongs, or other genres. A student might consider the cartographic suggestions of such expressions as "*up* North" and "*down* South," the historical suggestions of "*out* West," and the difference between "*back* East" and "*down* East"); then one might assemble variant folk sayings referring to geographic features—"to be sold down the *river*" as opposed to "to cross that *river* when we come to it"; and "as old as the *hills*" versus "over the *hill*." Such an approach could be revealing of regional culture in relation to physical geography. Other geographic lore would seem to derive from old schoolroom drills. There is one orally collected song, for instance, that describes numerous geographic features of oceans and shorelines, always returning in the refrain to "Green Little Islands." Another song, collected in the Ozarks, names and accurately characterizes thirteen Texas rivers and streams. Also likely from the schoolroom are several variants of a sentence for remembering how to spell the word "geography" itself: "*G*eorge *E*lliot's *o*ld *g*randmother *r*ode *a* *p*ig *h*ome *y*esterday."

While students' own research in folklore may be limited by time or unavailability of published references, the folklore student should at least become aware of the range and diversity of recent research as it extends far beyond collection, classification, and comparative analysis. Other effective techniques of folklore study include linguistic analysis, psychological interpretation, structural dissection, and examination of folklore's role in culture. Some scholars concern themselves mainly with the inventor, composer, and creator of folk material; others are preoccupied with the interplay between folk and popular culture. Efforts have been made recently to put folklore research on a more scientific basis with clearer statements of beginning hypotheses and better control of variables and findings. Theoretical models of human behavior, used in social science research, have been proposed for some areas of folklore study. Linguistic structuralism (the analysis of grammar according to patterns of speech) has flowered into several approaches toward a true folkloristic structuralism. Most folklorists now agree that "folklore" exists not as a fixed set of abstract genres, verbal or otherwise, but as traditional patterns of thought and behavior manifested in various ways during acts of communication between people; an entire new approach, variously called "contextual," "rhetorical," "behavioral," or "performance-oriented" folkloristics is taking shape around these concepts. The specific application of all such analytical methods is taken up in this book in connection with specific categories of folklore discussed in the following chapters. However, more general theoretical works are listed in the bibliographic notes to this chapter, and all references in the book to a single approach may be gathered by using the index.

The study of American folklore, either in its own rather vague boundaries or as applied to outside subjects, is still a relatively young and flexible academic discipline. Almost every new folklore journal or conference suggests some new approaches or theories for future research, and even the categories of folklore themselves are being continually expanded. The history of American folklore studies has only begun to be compiled, and the dimensions of such fields as urban folklore, obscene folklore, and women's folklore have barely been sketched out. The appointment of several "State Folklorists" (in Tennessee, Minnesota, and Maryland most recently) holds great promise for future regional research, just as the passage of the American Folklife Preservation Act in 1976 does for national study. To keep abreast of such developments, the reader may follow current publications and use the bibliographic tools listed following these chapters.

BIBLIOGRAPHIC NOTES

E. J. Lindgren's essay "The Collection and Analysis of Folk-Lore," although outdated, is still worth reading; see *The Study of Society*, ed. F. C. Bartlett and others (London: Routledge and Kegan Paul, 1939), pp. 328–78. Discussions by an international group of folklore scholars on the collecting, archiving, publicizing, and study of folklore were edited by Stith Thompson in *Four Symposia on Folklore;* the talks were held at Indiana University in 1950 and published as No. 8 in the I. U. Folklore Series (Bloomington, 1953). Martha Warren Beckwith's *Folklore in America: Its Scope and Method* (Poughkeepsie, N.Y.: Vassar College Folklore Foundation, 1931) was an early survey of the field. In *Our Living Traditions: An Introduction to American Folklore* (New York: Basic Books, 1968) Tristram P. Coffin gathers twenty-five essays by American folklorists which cover a wide variety of approaches; the chapters were originally written as Voice of America broadcasts.

Richard M. Dorson surveyed "Current Folklore Theories" in *CA* 4 (1963), 93–112. His essay is updated and expanded as the introduction to the excellent general textbook *Folklore and Folklife: An Introduction* (Chicago: University of Chicago Press, 1972) which contains specialized chapters by folklorists mostly associated somehow with the graduate program at Indiana University. In Dorson's *Folklore: Selected Essays* (Bloomington: Indiana University Press, 1972) are gathered eleven journal articles on folklore theory, methodology, oral style, and similar subjects. Thirteen articles by another major American folklorist are included in *Mody Boatright: Folklorist. A Collection of Essays*, ed. Ernest B. Speck (Austin: University of Texas Press, 1973). A somewhat idiosyncratic but intriguing approach is taken by Munro S. Edmonson in *Lore: An Introduction to the Science of Folklore and Literature* (New York: Holt, Rinehart and Winston, 1971); the author identifies his subject matter as "connotative semantics and analogic systems of thought" and pursues it widely through world literature and oral tradition.

Archer Taylor outlined "The Problems of Folklore" in *JAF* 59 (1946), 101–7. Louise Pound's thorough survey, "The Scholarly Study of Folklore," from *WF* 11 (1952), 100–8, was reprinted in *Nebraska Folklore*, pp. 222–33. Stanley Edgar Hyman defined the questions of origin, structure, and function in folklore studies and criticized some popularized anthologies in "Some Bankrupt Treasuries," *KR* 10 (1948), 484–500. Other general discussions of approaches to folklore are reprinted in Dundes's *The Study of Folklore*.

Techniques of collecting folklore are expertly treated in the Introduction to Richard M. Dorson's *Buying the Wind* and in Kenneth S. Goldstein's *Guide* (see the Preface). Rosalie H. Wax's *Doing Fieldwork: Warnings and Advice*

(Chicago: University of Chicago Press, 1971), although written for anthropologists, offers good examples and advice for folklorists as well. William R. Ferris, Jr., takes up some special problems in "The Collection of Racial Lore: Approaches and Problems," *NYFQ* 27 (1971), 261–79. Two fieldwork guides which may be useful even outside the regions they deal with are Jan Harold Brunvand, *A Guide for Collectors of Folklore in Utah* (Salt Lake City: University of Utah Press, 1971) and Edward D. Ives, *A Manual for Field Workers*, published as no. 15 of *Northeast Folklore* (Orono, Me.: University Press, 1974). An extremely detailed and useful survey is Eleanor Fein Reishtein's "Bibliography on Questionnaires as a Folklife Fieldwork Technique," *KFQ*, 13 (1968), 45–69, 121–66, 219–32.

The field experiences of two folksong collectors are preserved in W. Roy Mackenzie's *The Quest of the Ballad* (Princeton, N.J.: Princeton University Press, 1919) and John A. Lomax's *Adventures of a Ballad Hunter* (New York: Macmillan, 1947). The results of many years of devoted collecting in the Ozarks are gathered in the numerous books edited by Vance Randolph, in the prefaces and notes to which are many insightful comments on the art of unobtrusive collecting.

The chief example of a comprehensive American regional collection, fully classified and annotated, is the seven-volume *The Frank C. Brown Collection of North Carolina Folklore*, edited by a committee of specialists (Durham, N.C.: Duke University Press, 1952–64). Analyses of folklore in a specific regional tradition are found in such books as Emelyn E. Gardner's *Folklore from the Schoharie Hills* (Ann Arbor: University of Michigan Press, 1937); and Richard M. Dorson's *Negro Folktales in Michigan* (Cambridge, Mass.: Harvard University Press, 1956). The last, for instance, contains not only the verbatim texts, classified and fully identified with background data, but also chapters on "The Communities and the Storytellers" and "The Art of Negro Storytelling," and four pages of photographs.

From 1958 to 1968, *The Folklore and Folk Music Archivist*, published by Indiana University, provided a quarterly forum for articles on collecting, documenting, indexing, and cataloguing folklore. The editor, George List, published "A Statement on Archiving" in *JFI* 6 (1969), 222–31. A finding list, *Folklore Archives of the World*, ed. Peter Aceves and Magnus Einarsson-Mullarký constituted the first number of the *Folklore Forum* "Bibliographic and Special Series" (Bloomington, Ind., 1968). One model for catalogs of folklore archival holdings is Florence Ireland's "The Northeast Archives of Folklore and Oral History," *NEF* 13 (1972). Important legal questions were raised in an American Folklore Society symposium of 1971 published as "Folklore Archives: Ethics and the Law" *FF* 6 (1973), 197–210. Directions for modernizing archival techniques are discussed by Robert A. Georges, Beth Blumenreich, and Kathie O'Reilly in "Two Mechanical Indexing Systems for Folklore Archives: A Preliminary Report," *JAF* 87 (1974), 39–52.

A necessary skill of the folklorist is demonstarated in George G. Carey's "Folklore from the Printed Sources of Essex County, Massachusetts," *SFQ* 32 (1968), 17–43. An important methodological essay is Alan Dundes's "The

Study of Folklore in Literature and Culture: Identification and Interpretation," *JAF* 78 (1965), 136–42, repr. in *Analytic Essays in Folklore*, pp. 28–34. MacEdward Leach surveyed "Folklore in American Regional Literature" in *JFI* 3 (1966), 376–97; but Roger D. Abrahams found the "lore-in-literature" approach insufficient and proposed other kinds of analysis in "Folklore and Literature as Peformance," *JFI* 9 (1972), 75–94. Essays on folklore in individual American authors abound in the journals; two examples are Karl P. Wentersdorf's "The Element of Witchcraft in *The Scarlet Letter*," *Folklore* 83 (1972), 132–53; and Sandra Bennett's "Thurber and Traditional Comic Modes," *JOFS* 2 (1973), 1–11. A book-length study admirable for its sound approach and full details is Ronald L. Baker's *Folklore in the Writings of Rowland E. Robinson* (Bowling Green, Ohio: Bowling Green University Popular Press, 1973). Two attempts at a wider synthesis are Daniel Hoffman's *Form and Fable in American Fiction* (New York: Oxford University Press, 1961; Norton Paperback edn. 1973) and Gene Bluestein's *The Voice of the Folk: Folklore and American Literary Theory* (Amherst: University of Massachusetts Press, 1972).

Richard M. Dorson suggests projects involving "Folklore and Cultural History" in *Research Opportunities in American Cultural History*, ed. John Francis McDermott (Lexington: University of Kentucky Press, 1961), pp. 102–23. An important theoretical discussion of folklore and history, citing mostly African examples, is Jan Vansina, *Oral Tradition*, translated by H. M. Wright (Chicago: Aldine Publishing Co., 1965). Articles on folklore and history appeared in *JFI* 1 (1964). Richard M. Dorson collected a dozen of his essays from journals in *American Folklore and the Historian* (Chicago: University of Chicago Press, 1971) including the important "A Theory for American Folklore" from 1959 and his thoughts on the "Theory . . . Reviewed" from 1969, both originally published in *JAF*. William A. Wilson takes a Western perspective in "Folklore and History: Fact Amid the Legends" *UHQ* 41 (1973), 40–58. Two exemplary books on the subject are William Lynwood Montell's *The Saga of Coe Ridge: A Study in Oral History* (Knoxville: University of Tennessee Press, 1970) and Gladys-Marie Fry's *Night Riders in Black Folk History* from the same publisher (1975).

The history of folklore study itself and how it bears on ongoing research was taken up in the special "American Folklore Historiography" issue of *JFI* 10 (June/August 1973), 1–128. Important backgrounds are contained in Richard M. Dorson's book *The British Folklorists: A History* (Chicago: University of Chicago Press, 1968). Individual folklorists' works are evaluated in such studies as Dudley C. Gordon's "Charles F. Lummis: Pioneer American Folklorist," *WF* 28 (1969), 175–81; and Dorson's "Elsie Clews Parsons: Feminist and Folklorist," *AFFword* 1 (1971), 1–4, reprinted in *FFemC* 2 (1974), 4 ff. Doubtless of great future interest for historians of American folkloristics will be *Roads into Folklore*, no. 14 in the *Folklore Forum* "Bibliographic and Special Series" (Bloomington, Ind.: 1975), which contains anecdotal accounts of how they got into folklore by forty of Richard M. Dorson's students with a bonus of one parody entry credited to "Gregor Isomotif."

Kenneth S. Goldstein described his innovative research methods in "Experimental Folklore: Laboratory vs. Field," *Folklore International*, ed. D. K. Wilgus (Hatboro, Pa.: Folklore Associates, 1967), pp. 71–82. Theoretical backgrounds for such studies are given in Kenneth Laine Ketner's "The Role of Hypotheses in Folkloristics," *JAF* 86 (1973), 114–30; an opposing view appears in Anne and Norm Cohen, "A Word on Hypotheses," *JAF* 87 (1974), 156–60. Alan Dundes pointed to what he saw as a limiting mind-set for research in "The Devolutionary Premise in Folklore Theory," *JFI* 6 (1969), 5–19; reprinted in *Analytic Essays in Folklore*, pp. 17–27. Responses to this have come from Ronald Grambo in *FF* 3 (1970), 57–58; William M. Clements in *NYFQ* 29 (1973), 243–53; and Elliott Oring in *WF* 34 (1975), 36–44, among others.

David J. Hufford provides an overview of another analytic approach in "Psychology, Psychoanalysis, and Folklore," *SFQ* 38 (1974), 187–97. Paulo de Carvalho-Neto's *Folklore and Psychoanalysis*, originally published in 1956, was issued in its first English translation in 1972 (Coral Gables, Fla.: University of Miami Press) with a foreword by Alan Dundes, a leading North American advocate of psychoanalytic interpretations of folk tradition. A representative psychological analysis is illustrated in Eric Berne's "The Mythology of Dark and Fair: Psychiatric Use of Folklore," *JAF* 72 (1959), 1–13. A sociopsychological study is Brian Sutton-Smith's "A Formal Analysis of Game Meaning," *WF* 18 (1959), 13–24. A sociological approach is *Water Witching U.S.A.* by Evon Z. Vogt and Ray Hyman (Chicago: University of Chicago Press, 1959).

Two pacesetting early treatments of folklore in its cultural context were by William Hugh Jansen, "A Culture's Stereotypes and their Expression in Folk Clichés," *Southwestern Journal of Anthropology* 13 (1957), 184–200; and "The Esoteric-Exoteric Factor in Folklore," *Fabula* 2 (1959;, 205–11, which was reprinted in *The Study of Folklore*, pp. 43–51. A chief advocate of this "contextual" or "behavioral" approach to folklore is Roger D. Abrahams, three of whose influential articles are the following: "Folklore in Culture: Notes Toward an Analytic Method," *TSLL* 5 (1963), 98–110; "Introductory Remarks to a Rhetorical Theory of Folklore," *JAF* 81 (1968), 143–58; and "A Rhetoric of Everyday Life: Traditional Conversational Genres," *SFQ* 32 (1968), 44–59. Abrahams's pioneering study *Deep Down in the Jungle: Negro Narrative Folklore from the Streets of Philadelphia* appeared in 1964 (Hatboro, Pa.: Folklore Associates) and in a revised edition in 1970 (Chicago: Aldine Press). Another representative study from this viewpoint is Richard Bauman's "Verbal Art as Performance," *AA* 77 (1975), 290–311. A group of articles on folklore and culture appeared in *JFI* 2 (1965).

A useful general discussion of the structural approach is Butler Waugh's "Structural Analysis in Literature and Folklore," *WF* 25 (1966), 153–64. In *Structural Models in Folklore and Transformational Essays* (The Hague: Mouton, "Approaches to Semiotics" 10, 1971) Pierre and Elli [Köngäs] Maranda provide a systematic presentation of an important structural theory and method. This is a revised version of an essay first published *MF* (1962) supplemented by new studies of myth and riddle. The Marandas' anthology *Structural Analysis of Oral Tradition* (Philadelphia: University of Pennsylvania Press, 1971) contains eleven essays by various scholars analyzing myth, ritual, drama, folktale, ridde, and folksong. The contributors include most of the leading contemporary structuralists who are doing folklore studies.

An imaginative application of the oral-formulaic theory to American materials is found in Bruce A. Rosenberg's *The Art of the American Folk Preacher* (New York: Oxford University Press, 1970). A related analytic approach is found in Bennison Gray's "Repetition in Oral Literature," *JAF* 84 (1971), 289–303; and another is William M. Clements's "The Rhetoric of the Radio Ministry," *JAF* 87 (1974), 318–27.

Brief notes on traditional "Geographic Sayings from Louisiana" were published in *JAF* 67 (1954), 78 by Fred Kniffen. He distinguished those sayings that "attribute qualities to specific areas" ("the ozone belt") from those "based on a striking natural process in geography" ("My grandfather crossed there on a plank."). One is reminded of numerous sayings elsewhere in the United States that fall into the same classes, "the banana belt," for instance, for unusually mild climates in northern regions, and "You can set your watch by it" referring to Old Faithful. Two discussions of general relationships for cooperation are Roger T. Trindell's "American Folklore Studies and Geography," *SFQ* 34 (1970), 1–11; and W. F. H. Nicolaisen's "Folklore and Geography: Towards an Atlas of American Folk Culture," *NYFQ* 29 (1973), 3–20. An excellent example of a specific application of geographic and folkloristic methods is E. Joan Wilson Miller's study "Ozark Superstitions as Geographic Documentation," *The Professional Geographer* 24 (1972), 223–26.

A groundbreaking panel, "Folk Literature and the Obscene," sponsored by the American Folklore Society, was published in a special issue of *JAF* (75, 1962, 189–282) edited by Frank A. Hoffmann; speakers included Herbert Halpert, Horace Beck, Alan Dundes, and Gershon Legman. *The Horn Book: Studies in Erotic Folklore and Bibliography* (New Hyde Park, N.Y.: University Books, 1964) by Legman is a basic scholarly reference in this area. Kenneth S. Goldstein discusses a process common to handling of obscene folk materials in "Bowdlerization and Expurgation: Academic and Folk," *JAF* 80 (1967), 374–86; and Mac E. Barrick presents some traditional erotic materials that appear in written form as "The Typescript Broadside," *KFQ* 17 (1972), 27–38.

The interrelations of folklore with mass culture have begun to be discussed by scholars. Priscilla Denby surveys "Folklore in the Mass Media" in *FF* 4 (1971), pp. 113–25. Alan Dundes's "Advertising and Folklore," *NYFQ* 19 (1963), 143–51, may be compared with Tom E. Sullenberger's "Ajax Meets the Jolly Green Giant: Some Observations on the Use of Folklore in American Mass Marketing," *JAF* 87 (1974), 53–65. Other mass-cultural studies are Tom Burns's "Folklore in the Mass Media: Television," *FF* 2 (1969), 90–106, and John T. Flanagan's "Grim Stories: Folklore in Cartoons," *MJLF* 1 (1975), 20–26.

Dick Sweterlitsch edited nine "Papers on Applied Folklore" in *FF*, Bibliographic and Special Series, no. 8 (1971). See also Mary Ellen B. Lewis's "The Feminists Have Done It: Applied Folklore," *JAF* 87 (1974), 85–87.

The invaluable bibliographic notes in Richard M. Dorson's *American Folklore* (pp. 282–300) should be supplemented in any search for references to a particular topic in folklore by the analytic indexes to folklore journals (*JAF*, *WF*, *PTFS*, etc.) and the annual AFS bibliography published in the Supplement to *JAF* until 1963, when it was shifted to the new journal *Abstracts of Folklore Studies*. When *Abstracts* ceased publication in 1969 its important bibliographic function was filled by the expanded folklore section of the huge Modern Language Association bibliography appearing annually in *PMLA*. Perhaps the most important American folklore bibliography was that published annually in *SFQ* from 1937 to 1973 (continued in book form thereafter by Merle E. Simmons and published by the Folklore Institute, Bloomington, Indiana); its founder, Ralph Steele Boggs, also published the useful *Bibliography of Latin American Folklore* (New York: H. W. Wilson Co., 1940). Charles Haywood's *A Bibliography of North American Folklore and Folksong* is unusual in that it includes much North American Indian material; originally published in 1951, it was reprinted in two volumes by Dover Books in 1961, but unfortunately none of the numerous factual errors in citations of the first edition were corrected.

3

Folk Groups: Bearers of
American Folk Tradition

Depending upon how it is defined, "American" folklore may be pictured as nonexistent, relatively rare, or extremely common. As late as 1930 Alexander H. Krappe, a prominent American folklorist, was still European-oriented enough to take the extreme position that there was no such thing as American folklore, but only a few importations that eventually lost themselves in our mechanized age. The American Folklore Society itself was formed in 1888 partly to collect the "fast-vanishing relics" of foreign (including Negro) folklore in the United States; as for the phrase *American Folklore*, that referred to the Indians, or to the nationality of members of the society. Published collections of American folklore still appear prefaced with gloomy essays about disappearing traditions and the rapid loss of our meager folklore. The other extreme is reached by the many popular books and records that try to boost every scrap of Americana in sight—old or new—as another example of our profuse national folklore. Most of these publications are very heavy on fakelore—that is, imitation folklore attributed to a group that never possessed it.

Whether American folklore exists in abundance is a question that one should not be dogmatic about until the terms "American" and "folklore" are explained. Our criteria for "folklore" are "oral customary, and material tradition," while for "American" an inclusive definition would be *"found* in the United States," and a restrictive one, *"originated* in the United States." Most American folklorists incline toward the inclusive view, as far as theory is concerned, although their field-collecting emphasizes older native American, or at least Americanized, material. For example, while some American folklore collectors have realized that there exist traditional native songs (most of them relatively recent) of protest, industries, parodies, pornography, and the like, what even they have collected most vigorously are old British traditional ballads and lyrical songs.

American folklore research has amply demonstrated that there is a substantial body of oral, customary, and material tradition circulating in the United States, some of it native, and some transplanted from other cultures. Of course individual folk practices do fade away, but new ones are constantly appearing, so that the report of the demise of American folklore, as Mark Twain said about the report of his own death, "has been greatly exaggerated." In a general sense we can say that some types of folklore (such as folk drama) are nearly extinct in the United States; some types survive vigorously in quite ancient forms (such as superstitions); some types have been revived for a popular audience (folk dances and songs); and some types are still being invented along contemporary lines (jokes).

To assert that folklore is regularly being created and transmitted in modern American culture is to suggest that "the folk" must now exist in a modern guise. While most attempts to characterize the sources of folklore have emphasized isolation, lack of sophistication, and groups with relative homogeneity, judging from the materials that folklorists collect and study, such qualities are certainly not essential to fostering folklore. On the contrary, folklore flourishes among some of the most sophisticated and mobile Americans—teen-agers, entertainers, athletes, professors, and members of the armed forces. Strict preconceived notions of who "the folk" are have led to much disputing in folklore research when energy might better have been devoted to fieldwork and comparative studies to learn just how folklore actually is developed and put into circulation. For such studies, no better definition of the "folk" would seem necessary than "anyone who has folklore."

On the broad general level four basic theories have been offered to explain who the folk are and how their lore originates. The **communal theory** holds that the folk are unsophisticated peasants who compose folklore as a group effort. The **survivals theory** pushes the origin of folklore back to a "savage stage" of civilization and maintains that modern folklore is an inheritance or "survival" from the past. The theory of **gesunkenes Kulturgut** ("debased elements of culture") reverses the direction of diffusion—folklore has sunk from a high origin, such as "learning," to become tradition among the common people. Finally, the theory of **individual origins and communal re-creation** holds that an item of folklore has a single inventor at any level of society, but that it is repeatedly made over as it is transmitted by word of mouth. Each of these theories has been applied to specific types of American folklore, and each has some validity in particular cases, as is pointed out in later chapters.

The focus on specific creators and performers of traditions usually involves identifying these individuals with what have been called **folk groups.** The acceptance of traditions by these groups usually implies some degree of conformity with group tastes and values. (There are exceptions, however, both in individual traditional creators with no strong group affiliation, and in lore that is subversive of group values.) While some such groups may be identified simply in terms of obvious social, political, or geographic factors, they are often identified for folklore purposes first by their distinctive folk speech and other traditions—the lingo and lore which set one group apart from others. Thus, among themselves, loggers talk about "widow makers" (dangerous dangling limbs) and may sing ballads about woods disasters; children playing independently from adult supervision may cry "King's-X" (a "truce term" in a game like "Tag") and play a game like "Anthony Over" (a ball game played around a garage or other small building); residents of southern Illinois speak of themselves as living in "Egypt" and giving varying legendary explanations for the name based on supposed parallels to the history of the old-world country in Biblical times; and Finns in America tell stories from both the old country and the new, mixing their native tongue with English into "Finglish." These examples suggest four major kinds of American folk groups—*occupational groups, age groups, regional groups,* and *ethnic or nationality groups.* Sometimes it is also possible to distinguish folk groups that are set apart by religion, education, hobbies, neighborhood, or even family. Viewed from this point of view, it is clear that folk groups need not be composed only of hillbillies, and that a person may also belong to several folk groups at the same time. A Polish steelworker in Gary, Indiana, for instance, may know distinct types of ethnic, industrial, and regional lore at the same time, and if he happens to be a second-generation American he may also know immigrant lore unknown to his own parents. The first test of a folk group is the existence of shared folklore; then the background of this conformity can be investigated.

Among **occupational groups** in the United States, we immediately associate the old rugged callings with vigorous oral traditions: ax logging, raft and barge freighting, sailing before the mast, and running cattle were all activities rich in folklore. The long exposure of small bands of toughened men to the elements led them all to fall back on their stocks of stories and songs for entertainment, and the dangers inherent in the work produced superstitions like the "Flying Dutchman" and the "ghost herd." But the present has its comparable groups too with their own folklore, as studies of mining, railroading, oil pumping, and other industries have shown. The modern armed forces retain typical traditions of the older all-male labor groups, but physical strain is no necessary accompaniment to occupational folklore; jet pilots, journalists, even clergymen (including seminarians) have esoteric oral traditions of language and lore that are little known outside these groups. So quick is folklore to develop around a new job that there is already a considerable cycle of exoteric oral stories circulating about electronic computers and their programmers. The folklore of many other modern occupations has barely been recognized; this includes most factory lore of assembly and processing plants, folklore of government service, of science, and of academic life. Merely to suggest the possibilities of the latter, there are the ubiquitous campus stories of eccentric and absent-minded professors, of master cheaters in the student body, of prudish deans of women, and of administrators and their vagaries. These topics and others are discussed by Dr. Toelken in Appendix B, "The Folklore of Academe."

The distinctive folklore of different **age groups** is another area that is little understood, beyond the general notion of children growing from one stage to another, shedding layers of folklore as they go and acquiring new ones. Probably the study of this material will have to consider the differing folklore of sexes at the same time, for the rigid patterns of child behavior (who plays which games when or tells which stories to whom or uses which terms) are bounded by both age and sex. Girls seldom play marbles and boys usually do not jump rope, although both activities are popular in the springtime, as is kite flying with either sex. Children's folklore offers a particularly interesting field for research, for here we have almost a pure field situation in which some items are transmitted completely by word of mouth in an atmosphere of great textual conservatism, as any adult who has changed the wording of a bedtime story or tried to instruct a child in the "right way" to play a game like "Kick the Can" knows. While American children's folklore has been collected in some quantity, little analysis has been made until recently of such factors as its distribution, variants, or function. Even the collecting tends to be from grownups recalling their youth instead of from the youths themselves, and it tends to be spotty: we have the singing games, but few of the jokes of small children, the jargon but little of the sexual or alcoholic lore of teen-agers, and so forth. Probably beyond adolescence people cease to have much significant age-group lore and instead participate in other folk groups, but even this is a supposition that has never been systematically examined.

Regional groups have yielded some of the most bountiful harvests of folklore material in this country because geographic features tend to create relative isolation and encourage a community spirit that sustains long-standing traditions. The major folklore regions that American folklorists have described so far are New England, the southern Appalachians, the Midwest, the Ozarks, and the Southwest. Some folkloristic sub-regions that have been identified are Schoharie county, New York; Brown county, Indiana; the Upper Peninsula of Michigan, and the Mormon-settled Great Basin. State and other political boundaries have little effect on the types of folklore and its distribution, although many state collections have been brought together, mostly as a convenience for publishing. Studies of regional folk groups offer an excellent chance for cooperative projects by folklorists working with historians, geographers, linguists, and others; certainly a thorough understanding of settlement history and the national backgrounds of immigrants should underlie any study of their folklore. Although such cross-disciplinary research has been unusual in this country, it has been done for some time in Europe. Soviet folklorists, in particular, have organized collective expeditions to gather the lore of one region or of one craft in depth. The results have been far richer than the random gatherings of pre-Revolutionary fieldworkers, but they have contained the predictable overlay of propaganda applications as well.

Several American folklorists began working at the regional level and later branched out to broader comparative studies, just as some regional folklore journals have expanded their coverage. Thus *Midwest Folklore* (1951), formerly *Hoosier Folklore Bulletin* (1942), and *Hoosier Folklore* (1946), became the more international *Journal of the Folklore Institute* (1964); in 1968 a new journal, *Indiana Folklore*, began. The *California Folklore Quarterly* (1942) became *Western Folklore* (1947), and *Southern Folklore Quarterly* (1937) no longer has any particular southern slant. On the other hand, new regional journals have sprung up: *Northeast Folklore* (1958) and *Mid-South Folklore* (1973), for example.

Ethnic or nationality groups have a folklore as rich and varied as the American population itself. Again, only a fraction of it has been recorded or studied. The folktales, songs, proverbs and other folklore of American Indians, however, have been intensively studied for generations, partly by folklorists, but mostly by anthropologists with special linguistic and ethnographic training. There has been very active folklore collecting and research among American blacks, both in the Deep South and in the northern ghettos and other settlements, as black folk music, then tales and other lore have interested scholars. The early studies were concerned mainly with tracing African survivals in America, but now folklorists are increasingly dealing with the psychological and sociological functions of folklore among blacks. The best-documented nationality group in the United States is also an important regional group—the so-called "Dutch" of German Pennsylvania about whom there are numerous articles and books. Fewer studies are available about the folklore of such other groups as the Jews in big cities, the Spanish in the Southwest, the Cajuns in Louisiana, and the Scandinavians in the Midwest. Some other urban nationality groups that have been approached are the Greeks in Tarpon Springs, Florida, the Finns in Astoria, Oregon, the Poles in Hamtramck, Michigan, and the Spanish in Denver, Colorado. All these and many other groups await more attention; to mention only four more, consider the Basques in the Far West, the Puerto Ricans in New York City, the Norwegians in the Northwest (including Alaska), and the Bohemians in Nebraska.

Often the study of immigrant folklore has resulted from the devoted work of a scholar who is himself a fairly recent arrival. One such notable collector is the Lithuanian-American Jonas Balys. Another is the Hungarian-American Linda Dégh. In other groups an American-born descendant of immigrants takes up folklore collecting such as Warren Kliewer among Low-German speaking Mennonites, and Robert Georges among Greeks. Non-European groups have been very little studied, but they could be; one good possibility is in the "Chinatowns" of several cities, and another is the Japanese of California. In a sense, the United States is the world's greatest meeting ground of foreign folklores and an ideal arena for observing the survival of old traditions and the assimilation of new ones. American Christmas customs, for example, are a curious blend of several European sources, while immigrant folksong repertoires tend to be influenced by hillbilly, Tin Pan Alley, blues, and even cowboy songs. The scope of possibilities can be imagined when the largest nationality groups of all are considered—Irish, Italian, German, Scandinavian, and especially the most prominent group, the Anglo-Americans.

This chapter has only sketched in rough outline some few American folk groups, and it has only referred to a fraction of their folklore. To treat fully the oral traditions of even one such group would require at least a book in itself, preceded by extensive field work. Essentially, the following chapters should be regarded as only a survey of English-language folklore in America. Most of it, naturally, is Anglo-American in character, if not in origin, but all the groups mentioned above have occasionally been referred to and their traditions sampled.

BIBLIOGRAPHIC NOTES

Alexander H. Krappe discussed " 'American' Folklore" in *Folk-Say: A Regional Miscellany* in 1930 (Norman: University of Oklahoma Press), pp. 291–97, but he strongly denied that there really was any; Krappe maintained that there were only imported traditions in this country and that the culture of the immigrant was lost to the folklorist shortly after they arrived and began to become Americanized.

Three studies of contemporary individual creators of folk traditions (from New York, Maine, and Newfoundland) are printed in *Folksongs and their Makers* (Bowling Green, Ohio: Bowling Green University Popular Press, 1970). Two fine examples of dictated life stories from folk sources have been published by *Northeast Folklore;* they are "Fleetwood Pride, 1864–1960: The Autobiography of a Maine Woodsman" (9, 1967); and "Me and Fannie: The Oral Autobiography of Ralph Thornton of Topsfield, Maine" (14, 1973). Five studies of "Creativity in Southern Folklore" constituted a special issue of

Studies in the Literary Imagination (3, April 1970, 1–107) compiled by John A. Burrison. Gregory Gizelis discussed the same point, namely, real individual creation as an aspect of folk tradition, in his note "A Neglected Aspect of Creativity of Folklore Performers," *JAF* 86 (1973), 167–72.

American folklore arranged in an occupational group context is collected in Tristram Potter Coffin and Hennig Cohen's *Folklore from the Working Folk of America* (New York: Doubleday, 1973; Anchor paperback, 1974). The "occupational folklore" issue of *JOFS* is 3 (1974), 1–67. Following are some representative recent articles on the folklore of specific occupations: Marcello Truzzi, "The American Circus as a Source of Folklore: An Introduction," *SFQ* 30 (1966), 289–300; Joyce Gibson Roach, "Diesel Smoke & Dangerous Curves: Folklore of the Trucking Industry," *PTFS* 35 (1971), 45–53; Lois A. Monteiro, "Nursing-Lore," *NYFQ* 29 (1973), 97–110; William R. Ferris, "Railroad Folklore: An Overview," *NCFJ* 22 (1974), 169–76; and Mary C. Fields, "The View from the Water Table: Folklore of the Offshore Oilfield Workers," *MSF* 2 (1975), 63–76. Book-length studies of the lore of occupational groups are Mody C. Boatright's *Folklore of the Oil Industry* (Dallas: Southern Methodist University Press, 1963), George Korson's *Black Rock: Mining Folklore of the Pennsylvania Dutch* (Baltimore: Johns Hopkins Press, 1960), and Horace Beck's *Folklore and the Sea* (Middletown, Conn.: Wesleyan University Press, 1973).

American children's lore is gathered mostly in journal articles, such as Nancy C. Leventhal and Ed Cray, "Depth Collecting from a Sixth-Grade Class," *WF* 22 (1963), 159–63, and 231–57. (Articles dealing with individual genres of childlore are listed in the appropriate bibliographic notes that follow.) An excellent book-length treatment drawn from research among English children reveals many parallels in American lore. See Iona and Peter Opie's *The Lore and Language of Schoolchildren* (New York: Oxford University Press, 1959); for a comparison based on the Opies' work see Loman D. Cansler, "Midwestern and British Children's Lore Compared," *WF* 27 (1968), 1–18. Brian Sutton-Smith, who has published many good studies of children's games, discusses "Psychology of Childlore: the Triviality Barrier," in *WF* 29 (1970), 1–8. An interesting analysis based on a verbatim ninety-minute tape-recorded storytelling session with five boys is given in Steve Bartlett's "Social Interaction Patterns of Adolescents in a Folklore Performance," *FF* 4 (1971), 39–67. In "Teaching and Collecting Folklore at a Boys' Prep School," *KFQ* 15 (1970), 55–113, the folklore of adolescents was collected and studied by themselves, and edited by Angus K. Gillespie.

A good example of how the data of cultural geography is used to differentiate a regional folk group is found in E. J. Wilhelm, Jr., "Folk Settlement Types in the Blue Ridge Mountains," *KFQ* 12 (1967), 151–74. The Ozarks, a prime American folk enclave, is discussed in E. Joan Wilson Miller's "The Ozark Culture Region as Revealed by Traditional Materials," *Annals of the Association of American Geographers* 58 (1968), 51–77. The riches of material already collected there are indexed in Vance Randolph's *Ozark Folklore: A Bibliography*, Folklore Institute Monograph Series, vol. 24 (Bloomington: Indiana University Press, 1972); it extends only up to 1964 and yet lists 2,489 items.

One model study of a region and its folk groups, prefaced by a discussion of "the folk" in the United States, is Richard M. Dorson's *Bloodstoppers and Bearwalkers: Folk Traditions in the Upper Peninsula* (Cambridge, Mass.: Harvard University Press, 1952; paperback repr., 1972). A fine Western counterpart is Austin and Alta Fife's *Saints of Sage and Saddle: Folklore Among the Mormons* (Bloomington: Indiana University Press, 1956).

There are many large popularized anthologies of American folklore, most of them either arranged or cross-indexed by regional groups, and many of them probably trading on the success of B. A. Botkin's inclusive but somewhat unscholarly *A Treasury of American Folklore* (New York: Crown Publishers, 1944) and Botkin's several regional "treasuries." Tristram P. Coffin and Hennig Cohen's *Folklore in America* (Garden City, N.Y.: Doubleday, 1966; Anchor paperback, 1970) draws all of its examples from *JAF*, but often without the annotations or analyses originally provided there. Duncan Emrich's *Folklore on the American Land* (Boston: Little, Brown and Company, 1972) includes some extraneous editorializing by the compiler, but the sources and bibliography are clearly stated, and the illustrative photographs of Americans from the 1930s and '40s are excellent.

A popularized anthology from one important region is Richard Chase's *American Folk Tales and Songs . . . as Preserved in the Appalachian Mountains . . .* (New York: New American Library, 1956; Dover Books repr., 1971). John Greenway's *Folklore of the Great West* (Palo Alto, Calif.: The American West Publishing Co., 1969) is drawn from the pages of *JAF* but presented in an essentially nonscholarly format. Similarly, Jan Harold Brunvand's "Folklore of the Great Basin," *NWF* 3 (1968), 17–32, is written for a nonprofessional audience, although based on scholarly sources and fieldwork. Perhaps the best introduction to regional American folklore is Dorson's *Buying the Wind,* which presents folklore from seven regions to illustrate the corresponding discussion in Chapter 3 in his *American Folklore.*

Supplementary to Frank C. Brown's collection of North Carolina folklore mentioned in the notes to Chapter 2 is Charles Bond's article "Unpublished Folklore in the Brown Collection," *NCF* 20 (1972), 11–20, which catalogs and offers a few samples from materials on file in the Duke University Library. Other state anthologies include Earl J. Stout's *Folklore from Iowa,* American Folklore Society Memoir vol. 29 (New York, 1936); Harold W. Thompson's *Body, Boots and Britches* (on New York State) (Philadelphia: J. P. Lippincott, 1940); George Korson's *Pennsylvania Songs and Legends* (Philadelphia: University of Pennsylvania Press, 1949); Samuel J. Sackett's *Kansas Folklore* (Lincoln: University of Nebraska Press, 1961); Roger L. Welsch's *A Treasury of Nebraska Pioneer Folklore* (Lincoln: University of Nebraska Press, 1966); and three works by George G. Carey, *Maryland Folklore and Folklife* (Cambridge, Md.: Tidewater Publishers, 1970); *Maryland Folk Legends and Folk Songs* (Cambridge, Md.: Tidewater Publishers, 1971); and *A Faraway Time and Place: Lore of the Eastern Shore* (on Chesapeake Bay) (Washington,

D.C., and New York: Robert B. Luce, 1971). In *Sang Branch Settlers: Folksongs and Tales of a Kentucky Mountain Family*, American Folklore Society Memoir, vol. 61 (Austin, Tex.; 1974) Leonard Roberts presents a family tradition within a regional context.

A useful index to *HFB* (1942–45) and *HF* (1946–50) was published by *FF* as their Bibliographic and Special Series, no. 10 (1973). Other regional folklore journals are *Tennessee Folklore Society Bulletin* (1934) *New York Folklore Quarterly* (1945–74, *New York Folklore* thereafter), *Keystone Folklore Quarterly* (1956–73, *Keystone Folklore* thereafter), *Kentucky Folklore Record* (1955), *New Mexico Folklore Record* (1946), *AFFWord* ("Arizona Friends of Folklore," 1971), *Journal of the Ohio Folklore Society* (new series begun in 1972), *Louisiana Folklore Miscellany* (1960), *Midwestern Journal of Language and Folklore* (1975), *Northwest Folklore* (1965–68), and *North Carolina Folklore* (1952–72, *North Carolina Folklore Journal* thereafter). The *Publications of the Texas Folklore Society* have appeared in annual volumes since 1924, and there were sporadic folklore journals in Illinois, New Hampshire, Wisconsin, and several other states. For information about these, see an article in yet another regional journal: William J. Griffin's "The *TFS Bulletin* and Other Folklore Serials in the United States: A Preliminary Survey," *TFSB*, 25 (1959), 91–96.

Publications on American Indian folklore, especially in the anthropological literature, are far too numerous and varied to be represented here by a few citations. One might begin with the folktale by reading Stith Thompson's *Tales of the North American Indians* (Cambridge, Mass.: Harvard University Press, 1929; paperback repr., Bloomington: Indiana University Press, 1966). Judith C. Ullom's *Folklore of the North American Indians* (Washington, D.C.: Library of Congress, 1969) is a concise but useful guide to sources; and Barre Toelken's review article "The Native American" in *WF* 29 (1970), 268–78, discusses recent publications from a folkloristic viewpoint.

For backgrounds to Afro-American folklore see Ruth Finnegan's comprehensive survey *Oral Literature in Africa* (New York: Oxford University Press, 1970). Papers of the African Folklore Conference held at Indiana University in 1970 were published in *African Folklore*, ed. Richard M. Dorson (Bloomington: Indiana University Press, 1972). A particularly valuable collection that places Afro-American folklore in a historical context is Bruce Jackson's *The Negro and His Folklore in Nineteenth-Century Periodicals*, American Folklore Society Bibliographic and Special Series, vol. 18 (Austin, Tex., 1967). Roger D. Abrahams's *Positively Black* (Englewood Cliffs, N.J.: Prentice-Hall, 1970) offers interpretive social and cultural comments on his own and others' recent studies. Alan Dundes's *Mother Wit from the Laughing Barrel: Readings in the Interpretation of Afro-American Folklore* (Englewood Cliffs, N.J.: Prentice-Hall, 1973) anthologizes many important essays on the subject. An often unappreciated cross-ethnic pattern of borrowing is treated in Alan Dundes's "African Tales Among the North American Indians," *SFQ* 29 (1965), 207–19.

The distinguished Canadian folklorist C. Marius Barbeau discussed "The

Field of European Folk-Lore in America" in *JAF* 32 (1919), 185–97; Reidar Th. Christiansen, while Professor of Folklore at the University of Oslo, wrote "A European Folklorist Looks at American Folklore," *PTFS* 28 (1958), 18–44. Christiansen's full discussion, *European Folklore in America*, was published as Number 12 of *Studia Norvegica* (Oslo, 1962). W. John Rowe placed more emphasis on material traditions than verbal folklore in "Old-World Legacies in America," *Folk Life* 6 (1968), 68–82. *The Folklore of Texas Cultures*, ed. Francis Edward Abernathey, *PTFS* 38 (1974), is a good compilation of lore from two dozen groups found in the Lone Star State with illustrations drawn from both old and recent photographs of each group.

The only older book-length work on an immigrant group's folklore to be recommended is Phyllis H. Williams's *South Italian Folkways in Europe and America* (New Haven, Conn.: Yale University Press, 1938); a worthy recent counterpart is Carla Bianco's *The Two Rosetos* (Bloomington: Indiana University Press, 1974), a comparison of folkways in Roseto Valfortore, Italy, and Roseto, Pennsylvania. Representative journal articles on immigrant folklore are Henry R. Lang, "The Portuguese Element in New England," *JAF* 5 (1892), 9–18; Jay K. Ditchy, ed., "Early Louisiana French Life and Folklore from the Anonymous Breaux Manuscript," *LFM* 2 (May 1966); Robert A. Georges, "Matiasma: Living Folk Belief [Greek]," *MF* 12 (1962), 69–74; Warren Kliewer, "Collecting Folklore Among Mennonites," *Mennonite Life* 14 (July 1961), 109–12; Arthur L. Campa, "Spanish Folksongs in Metropolitan Denver," *SFQ* 24 (1960), 179–92; Rosan Jordan DeCaro, "Language Loyalty and Folklore Studies: The Mexican-Americans," *WF* 31 (1972), 77–86; Pat Bieter, "Folklore of the Boise Basques," *WF* 24 (1965), 263–70; Alixa Neff, "Belief in the Evil Eye Among the Christian Syrian-Lebanese in America." *JAF* 78 (1965), 46–51; and Erik Wahlgren, "Scandinavian Folklore and Folk Culture in the Trans-Mississippi West," *NWF* 3 (1969), 1–16.

Theoretical and methodological matters underlying immigrant folklore studies are taken up in Elli Kaija Köngäs, "Immigrant Folklore [Finnish]: Survival or Living Tradition?" *MF* 10 (1960), 117–23; and Linda Dégh, "Approaches to Folklore Research Among Immigrant Groups," *JAF* 79 (1966), 551–56.

An aural anthology of Indian, Immigrant, and Anglo-American folk music from one state is the record *Folk Voices of Iowa*, collected and edited by Harry Oster (Iowa City: University of Iowa Press, 1965).

The long tradition of folklore studies among Canada's diverse ethnic and regional groups has been continued and consolidated lately in the Canadian Centre for Folk Cultural Studies at the National Museum of Man in Ottawa. A useful introduction to their research is provided by Carmen Roy in Paper No. 7 of their "Mercury Series" (Ottawa, 1973); a representative commissioned report is Jan Harold Brunvand, *Norwegian Settlers in Alberta*, Mercury Series, Paper No. 8 (Ottawa, 1974). Robert B. Klymasz's *An Introduction to the Ukranian-Canadian Immigrant Folksong Cycle* (Ottawa: National Museums of Canada, Bulletin no. 234, Folklore Series no. 8, 1970) is a model study with texts in two languages, music, illustrations, and three small discs of recorded examples. An essay with implications for the future of this research is Klymasz's "From Immigrant to Ethnic Folklore: A Canadian View of Process and Tradition," *JFI* 10 (1973), 131–39.

Until very recently American folklore continued to be thought of only in a rural or small-town setting; a special issue of *JAF* devoted to "The Urban Experience and Folk Tradition" (83, no. 328, April–June, 1970; Bibliographical and Special Series no. 22, 1971), ed. Américo Paredes and Ellen J. Stekert, indicated changes in attitude that were developing. Richard M. Dorson's contribution to this publication, "Is there a Folk in the City?" 185–228, elicited much discussion along with the eventual expansion of his thesis in Bruce E. Nickerson's "Is there a Folk in the Factory?" *JAF* 87 (1974), 133–39. A revealing case in point is Mac E. Barrick's collectanea titled "Folktales from the Institute at Duke," *NCFJ* 23 (1975), 75–81, which contains traditional material heard from some fifty scholars assembled for the Sixth Southeastern Institute of Medieval and Renaissance Studies. That modern and urban folklore is by no means exclusively an American phenomenon is indicated by Stewart Sanderson's article "The Folklore of the Motor-car," in *Folklore* 80 (1969), 241–52. A useful reference is Camilla Collins's "Bibliography of Urban Folklore," *FF* 8 (1975), 57–125.

Modern technology spawns folklore rather than replacing it or rendering it obsolete. Among others, Michael J. Preston has published examples of "Xerox-lore" in *KF* 19 (1974), 11–26; and in *JOFS* 3 (1975), pp. 27–30. A definitive (temporarily, no doubt) collection and commentary is offered in Alan Dundes and Carl R. Pagter, *Urban Folklore from the Paperwork Empire*, American Folklore Society Memoirs, vol. 62 (Austin, Tex.:, 1975).

Contemporary social concerns reflected in folklore are the subjects of such essays as Norine Dressen's, " 'The Boys in the Band is Not Another Musical': Male Homosexuals and their Folklore," *WF* 33 (1974), 205–18; Eve Mitchell's, "Folklore of Marijuana Smoking," *SFQ* 34 (1970), 127–30; and many others listed in the bibliographic notes to subsequent chapters. An important landmark is the "Women and Folklore" issue of *JAF* (88, no. 347, Jan.–Mar., 1975), edited by Claire R. Farrer.

Folklore collected from the folk group of folklorists themselves makes one wonder where it all will end; see Richard A. Reuss, " 'That Can't Be Alan Dundes! Alan Dundes Is Taller Than That!' The Folklore of Folklorists," *JAF* 87 (1974), 303–17.

II · ORAL FOLKLORE

❂❂❂❂❂❂❂❂❂❂❂❂

The lore that circulates from person to person by word of mouth includes the majority of the types originally associated with the term "folklore." Most of it is *oral* (one may quibble about exactly how human speech is produced, and we make an exception, of course, for instrumental music); a good part of it is *verbal*. All of it is *aural*. Calling it all "oral folklore" is something of a simplification, but to do so has been traditional for a long time in folklore studies. In an analogy with literary and language studies these types of mostly-oral folklore are set up in collections, archives, and studies usually in terms of their relative linguistic or stylistic complexity—from words, names, phrases, and sentences, to questions, rhymes, stories, songs, and ballads. While beginning students should find this a convenient approach (especially as they peruse older folklore studies), they should always bear in mind that any given folklore performance is more than the automatic transmission of "text," more even than text-in-context, but is in fact a complex communicative event in which "oral folklore" is only one conspicuous component.

Music is included in this section rather arbitrarily because so often in American folk tradition it coexists and interacts with words. Instead of separating for discussion purposes purely instrumental tradition, Chapter 12 sketches out the whole topic.

4

Folk Speech and Naming

The simplest level of verbal folklore is the traditional word, expression, usage, or name that is current in a folk group or in a particular region. When a Southerner says "y'all", or a Missourian pronounces his state name ending in "uh"[məzə́rə],* or an Easterner differs with a Midwesterner over what a *soda* and a *cruller* are, or a child names a puppy *Rex, Prince,* or *Queenie,* we have instances of what the folklorist calls **folk speech.** Strictly speaking, these subjects are in the domain of *linguistics* (especially dialect study or "linguistic geography") and of *onomastics* (the study of names), but the folklorist has a legitimate and somewhat specialized interest in them, too.

Dialect—the traditional deviation from standard speech—includes variations in *grammar* (both morphology and syntax), *pronunciation,* and *vocabulary.* While only trained linguists have the special ability and techniques needed to collect and study dialect in a rigorously scientific manner, they usually focus their attention on typical informants in one region who are interviewed on the basis of a formal questionnaire. Then "isoglosses" or dialect boundaries may be mapped to show the distribution of certain usages, and these maps are potential guides for folklore collecting. But a "linguistic atlas" does not serve all the needs of research in folk speech. For one thing, some distinction should be made between standard regional dialects and special regional or social folk dialects.

Folklorists also must concern themselves with the dialects of different groups, and they usually encounter deviations from standard speech only as they are embedded in folktales, songs, rhymes, and other traditional texts. They are interested in the use of dialect within groups, the retention of outmoded dialect forms in folklore texts, and

---

* The International Phonetic Alphabet (IPA) spelling to indicate pronunciation.

in the linguistic changes that take place as texts are transmitted orally. Similarly, the *naming* that a folklorist studies is that which is traditional and which appears in the context of other folklore. Whatever their separate specialties, then, folklorists should be aware of some terms and techniques for collecting and studying folk speech, while students of dialect or names may benefit from an awareness of folklore research methods and of folk materials.

Variations of grammar in folk speech may consist of nonstandard word forms (morphology) or word order (syntax); collectors of folklore should carefully record both kinds without exaggerating their occurrence. Also they should note whether some expressions used in folklore are missing in everyday speech. There are countless variations possible, but space permits illustrating only a few. The past tense of verbs, for instance, is frequently nonstandard in regional folk speech, so that informants may say "It *snew* yesterday," "I *seen* him," or "He *drownded*"; the past tense of *climb* may be *clim* or *clum*, and such distinctions as *hung/hanged* or *lay/laid* made in polite speech may be disregarded. Some speech forms such as *boughten, enthused, being as*, or *different than* have become so common as to be almost respectable now, while others such as *fotch* (past of *fetch*) and *hit* (for *it*) linger only in isolated regions like the Southern Appalachians. Many modern folk expressions like *I could care less* and *Tell it like it is*, although "ungrammatical," are heard in daily usage.

Dialect forms may be coined to fit a familiar pattern: the Ozark hillman has his combined verbs *house-clean, target-practice*, and many others like them, while the college student has *proficiency-out* (to substitute a proficiency examination for a course) and *brown-nose* (to flatter an instructor). The combinations with *-ify* follow another favorite pattern; they range from *prettify* and *speechify* to *rectify* (to correct school homework) and *witchify* (to apply witchcraft to). Accounts of children's talk may qualify as folklore when they achieve oral circulation as part of a family's anecdotes: "It's *winding*" (on the analogy of *raining* and *snowing*), "I *hood* it from you (nonstandard past tense of *hide*), and "We're *undusting*," (i.e., removing the dust).

Syntactical variations are often heard in the speech of nonnative-speaker groups, such as the Pennsylvania Germans, who are credited with sentences like "Make the window up," "Don't eat yourself done, there's a pie back," "the off is on" (i.e., "the vacation has begun"),

"Throw Mama from the train a kiss," and "Outen the lights." Often vocabulary plus word form or syntax vary simultaneously, as shown in the last example and in a sentence based on the word *liver-out* for "hired girl"—"Is your liver-out in?" Anecdotes based on such expressions as these are a form of folklore themselves, and they are more likely traditional tales than authentic incidents. Nevertheless, such speech does occur, and even in relatively sophisticated American circles, one may occasionally hear syntactical oddities learned by imitation, not classroom instruction, such as "I can't remember things like I used to could." (The author once heard a professor shout, "Where you stayin' at, Jack?" in an elevator that was crowded with delegates to a national Modern Language Association convention.)

For a folklore collector untrained in linguistics, the phonetic transcription of **dialect pronunciations** may be too demanding, but a satisfactory substitute for most purposes is the use of rhyming words. Thus, for local community names, the pronunciation of *Moscow* [máskow] in Idaho may be reported as rhyming with *toe; Spokane* [spowkǽn] in Washington rhymes with *can* rather than *cane;* residents of Indiana call their city of *Brazil* [bréyzəl] by a name rhyming with *hazel* (which may be closer to *gray zeal,* with almost no syllable accent), and *Versailles,* Indiana, (also Kentucky) rhymes with *curtails.* Berlin, New Hampshire, is accented on the first syllable, and the Thames River in Connecticut is pronounced *Thayms,* not *Temms.* The people of Utah speak of *Zion's Park* instead of Zion National Park. Such pronunciations as these for place names may prove useful for defining the boundaries of folk regions.

Sometimes a dialect pronunciation may creep into spelling, as in the sign painted by a southerner peddling "Red Haven" peaches who wrote *"Raid Haven* Peaches." Or the college freshman frequently must be taught not to spell *athlete* as he carelessly pronounces it— *athalete.* Especially when the point of a folk story turns on a certain pronunciation, it is important for the collector to record sounds carefully; such texts indicate folk recognition of dialect. Examples of this are jokes about Swedes confusing *jail* with *Yale,* or Finns praising the two American cars that begin with *P*—"the *Puiks* and the *Packards."* (The last instance might also be dated by the demise of the Packard.)

Regional variations in **dialect vocabulary** such as *earthworm, angleworm, night crawler, night walker, mud worm,* and *fish worm* have been extensively mapped by linguistic geographers; but folklorists tend to concern themselves less with the language of regions than with that of occupational and social folk groups. As a result, numerous glossaries have been compiled from such groups as actors, children, construction workers, homosexuals, jazz musicians, miners, railroad workers, and truck drivers, to name but a few. Euphemisms (for diarrhea or pregnancy, for instance) are a form of folk speech, as are intensifiers like *hogwash, tarnation,* and *oh fudge,* or such sham-swearing expressions as "Cheese and rice got damp in the cellar."

The easiest test of a folk group's existence is a specialized vocabulary, and an important early step in any fieldwork project is to compile a glossary of the distinctive terminology of the group under study. By way of example, consider college students, who may at first appear not to have any significant oral traditions, but from whom in a short time one might easily collect such terms (heard in the Northwest in 1961–63) as *high school Harry, pasture function* (night picnic with beer), *pig pot* (money collected for the escort of the ugliest partner at an "exchange party"), *troll* (plain or ugly girl), and *wimp* (coward). Traditional terminology of drug use includes *turn on, trip, speed, grass, pot,* and *roach-clip* (a holder for a marijuana cigarette). Folk language of space flight already includes *A-OK, blast off* (or *lift off*), *cherry picker, gantry, docking,* and nicknames for crewmen, rockets, and moon-exploration vehicles.

Military servicemen in general quickly learn to converse in the terms traditional in their group, such as *KP* ("Kitchen Police"), *SOP* (standard operating procedure), *no sweat, deuce and a half* (for a two-and-a-half ton truck), and *the old man.* When folk jokes based on a specialized vocabulary occur, we again have the phenomenon of folk commenting on their own distinctiveness. One such GI (Government Issue) story concerns a USO (United Service Organizations) entertainer who was asked whether she preferred "to *mess* with the officers or the men"; she responded, "Makes no difference, but can I eat first?"

Among nationality groups in the United States a whole conglomerate dialect language sometimes develops in the first generation. Norwegians tell about an emigrant joyfully greeting his mother back in the old country with "How's my *gamle mor?*" ("my old mother"). Another Norwegian-American is supposed to have remarked, describing a disastrous drought, *"Jeg luse hele kroppen,"* meaning, to him, "I lost my whole crop"; but in Norwegian the sentence sounds more like "I have lice on my entire body." In "Finglish" the word *nafiksi* frequently occurs—nonexistent in native Finnish, but derived in the United States from the English "enough." A Finnish-American storyteller might also end a text with the sentence *"Ne sanot että se oli tosi stori"* ("They said it was a true story"), using the final English word in an otherwise Finnish context. In the "Tex-Mex" spoken in the bilingual Southwest, one might hear *"Dame mi pokebuk"* ("Give me my pocketbook") or *"Es un eswamp"* ("It's a swamp").

"Pig Latin" and other secret languages of children deserve study. These include "backwards talk," "Double Dutch," "G-Talk," "King Tut," sign languages, and certain orthographic codes for writing secret messages. Even more peculiar is a regional "slanguage" discovered in Boonville, California, and dubbed "Boontling." Here a language of apparently nonsensical words was invented by children, but later spread to adults of the community. At first, the parents picked up the expressions in an attempt to understand and communicate with their children. Then others found in them a way to express what they felt was the uniqueness of Boonville, unrecognized and unappreciated by outsiders. The language includes many nouns, such as *gannow* ("apple"), *beemsh* ("show") and *higg* ("money"); verbs such as *dehigg* ("spend money") and *deek* ("learn"); and a few adjectives, such as *ball* ("fine"). The "Boontling" terms, together with local nicknames, are used in oral communication only and intermixed with otherwise conventional English. The following passage is typical:

> We have *ball gannows* here in *Boont*. Why don't we *dehigg* ourselves and have a *beemsh* so people will *deek* how *ball* our *gannows* are?

Folklorists' studies of American folk speech have usually been mere collections, although sometimes these have been rather imaginative ones. George W. Boswell extracted folk etymologies from folksong diction, finding such onomatopoetic terms as *trinkling* (Her life's blood came *trinkling* down"), oral mistakes like "He dressed himself in *a tie* [for *attire*] of blue," and irregular verb forms: "I *tuck* her by her yellow hair/ I *drug* her 'round and 'round." In a closer analysis of traditional speech patterns, Alan Dundes recognized three kinds of reduplicative phrases, identical (*din din* or *goody goody*), ablaut (*zig zag*), and rhyming (*mumbo jumbo*) with a marked preference in American English for the third type. The "Henny Penny phenomenon" of initial consonant alternation appears in many verbal folk forms, often as /h/:/p/ (*henpecked*), or /t/:/l/ (*Turkey Lurkey, toodleloo*), and even in such commercial brand names as Hotpoint and Hush Puppies (already a folk term).

Folk naming practices present a broad field for collecting as well as some interesting possibilities for interpretation, since there are certain traditional names or nicknames for almost anything that can be given a name, ranging from family members and domestic animals to vacation cottages, apartment houses, family cars, and hot rods, rifles, and elusive game fish. As in some primitive cultures in which one's "real" name is earned by a great deed, or perhaps even a shortcoming, American folk practice is to name children for some notable man or woman, to give names of positive connotation, to avoid giving names thought inappropriate for the child's sex, or to award one's nickname because of his appearance, behavior, or background.

Place names—both for geographic features and for communities—have been more thoroughly researched than any other branch of name-lore, but even here vast areas remain unexplored. From the folklorist's point of view (but not the historian's or the cartographer's) the legendary folk etymologies for place names are of prime concern. Thus the folk imagination can be counted on to concoct a story about gnawing on bones to explain a town name like *Gnawbone* [Ind.], whereas the likely origin is a corruption of the displaced French name *Narbonne.* Also having traditional roots are regional nicknames like *Hoosier, Sooner,* or *Webfoot.*

Studies have been made of such subjects as folk names for cats (*Tabby, Tom,* etc.), for plants (*piss fir, spear grass,* etc.), for pioneer foods (*hush puppies, hoe cakes, pluck and plunder stew,* etc.), and even for teen-ager's automobiles (*Blue Boy, Magnificent Six, Little White Dove, Travellin' Man,* etc.). Traditional variations in a folk name are demonstrated in those used for a favorite picnic dessert made from toasted marshmallows, graham crackers, and a chocolate bar: *some-mores, Brownie Delights, angels on horseback, angels with dirty faces, heavenly hoboes,* and *heavenly hash.* (The latter is also sometimes applied to a whipped-cream and fruit-cocktail salad.) In using traditional names like these, people are sometimes only following tradition or habit (*Tabby*); other times they may be rendering judgment (*piss fir*), alluding to a legend (*hush puppies*), revealing a mood (*Blue Boy*), or creating metaphysical images (*angels with dirty faces*).

Names play a traditional role—though not always an apparent one—in such folk sayings as "robbing *Peter* to pay *Paul*," "every *Tom, Dick and Harry*," and "quicker than you can say '*Jack Robinson*.' " Certain names recur in folk ballads (*Pretty Polly*), folktales (*Jack*), and legends (*Old Scratch*), while other names creep into everyday usage in remarks like "sign your *John Hancock*" (or, unreasonably, "your *John Henry*") and in sample addresses to *John Doe* or *John Q. Citizen*. Finally, ethnic and place names are employed as slurring adjectives in such terms as *Dutch treat, Mexican credit card* (a hose for stealing gasoline), *Indian giver, Puerto Rico Pendleton* (an old work shirt), *French Screw Driver* (a hammer), *Jewish Penicillin* (chicken soup), and *Vatican Roulette* (the "rhythm" birth control method).

The vocabulary and traditional naming habits of one folk group can be a fascinating subject for a limited folklore study; Northwest loggers offer a convenient example. Nearly every aspect of their life and work has acquired a distinctive folk term. There are terms for pieces of equipment (*A-frame, bells and buttons, gut wrappers*), terms for particular jobs (*cat skinner, choker setter, pond monkey*), terms for trees and logs (*widow maker*—a dangerously leaning or hanging tree or limb, *barber chair*—a split-cut stump), and even special terms for some foods (*saddle blankets* for hotcakes, *chokum* for cheese, *excelsior* for noodles, *bear sign* for blackberry jam).

Some of these loggers' terms have either penetrated to more general usage by other groups, or have acquired specialized meanings in the woods, and it is often impossible to tell which way a term has gone. *Haywire,* for instance, has long been used by loggers to refer to any lightweight wire (also called *straw wire*), and when such wire was frequently used for general camp repairs, it became a *haywire outfit*—a patched-together and mixed-up camp. This may be either the origin of or only an offshoot of the generally used expression "to go haywire." Similarly, the logger uses *hoosier* not for a resident of Indiana, necessarily, but for any greenhorn in the woods. A *gypo outfit* in loggers' parlance is not a company that "gyps" customers, but simply a company, especially a small one, that logs on contract. The term *skid road* used originally for a log-skidding road, then for the tough streets in West Coast towns, has been altered to *skid row* in general usage. (The loggers consider the term as phony as *lumberjack*, the term applied to the loggers by almost everyone but themselves.)

Names and naming contribute further to the flavor of woods terminology. Corn bread may be designated *Arkansaw wedding cake;* a homemade lantern is a *Palouser* (from the "Palouse" region of eastern Washington and northern Idaho); the Chinook word *Potlatch* (a gift-exchange festival) appears in the company name "Potlatch Forests Incorporated" (called *P.F.I.* or "Pin Feathers, Inc." locally), as well as in place names and in such terms as *Potlatch turkey* (crow) and *Potlatch tram* (a type of logging tramway). The American loggers' *peavey,* used all over the country, supposedly was developed by J. H. Peavey of Bangor, Maine, while a *Jacob's staff* and a *Johnson bar* are other tools not clearly traceable to sources. Loggers have christened their trucks and other modern equipment with such nicknames as *The Monster, Old Asthma, Road Runner,* or *Widow Maker,* just as fellow workers bear such descriptive nicknames as *White Pine Joe, The Galvanized Swede, Cruel-Jimmy Holmes,* or *Greasy Pete.*

A similar collecting project might successfully focus on any occupational group. Thus, the house painter's "haywire outfit" is a *Joe McGee rig,* although just why this name refers to makeshift equipment is unclear. (From the term come the verbs *Joe McGee it,* or simply *McGee it.*) Paint cans are always *pots;* thinner of any kind is *turps;* the last coat of paint applied is *the third coat,* and so forth. With the popularity of Citizens' Band two-way radios spreading from truckers to the general public, the esoteric "CB" language became better known: the *dirty side* refers to the eastern United States, *clean side* to the West. A highway patrolman is *Smokey the Bear,* and when he is checking traffic speeds, "Smokey's in the woods taking pictures." Furniture trucks are *bedbug haulers,* and a truck load of new cars is a *future junk yard.* In the folk language of some college students the course names may be humorously replaced: Abnormal Psychology becomes *Nuts and Sluts;* Introductory Geology is *Rocks for Jocks;* Military History is *Tanks and Jeeps;* and *Play a Day* refers to English Drama.

Every trade, every hobby, every age group, and every region has a dialect of its own, mostly still awaiting the thorough collector of folk speech. When such linguistic strayings from the presumed standard speech are purely ephemeral or technical, they may be regarded as *slang* or *jargon* respectively; but when such language is longer lived and more generally used, it becomes traditional speech of prime interest to the folklorist.

BIBLIOGRAPHIC NOTES

Linguistic, onomastic, and folkloristic studies of folk speech are scattered through the professional books and journals of all three disciplines. A good general survey of the subject is Raven I. McDavid's chapter, "The Dialects of American English," in W. Nelson Francis's *The Structure of American English* (New York: Ronald Press, 1958), pp. 480–543. McDavid also provides a comprehensive view of the two related disciplines in "Linguistic Geography and the Study of Folklore," *NYFO* 14 (1958), 242–62. From the folklorist's point of view, see Louis Pound's "Folklore and Dialect," *CFQ* 4 (1945), 146–53, reprinted in *Nebraska Folklore*, pp. 211–21.

Two useful general reference works are *A Dictionary of Americanisms On Historical Principles*, edited by M. M. Mathews (Chicago: University of Chicago Press, 1951) and *Dictionary of American Slang*, edited by Harold Wentworth and Stuart Berg Flexner (New York: Crowell, 1960; reissued with supplement, 1967). The basic background study for all such research is H. L. Mencken's *The American Language*, first published in 1919, issued in a rewritten and enlarged edition in 1936, with supplements added in 1945 and 1948, and subsequently many times reprinted (New York: Alfred A. Knopf).

Linguistic geographer Frederic G. Cassidy reviews the history of a proposed "Dictionary of American Regional English" in "The ADS Dictionary— How Soon?" *PADS* no. 39, (1963), 1–7 (The *DARE* project was accepted in 1964 as a cooperative research project of the Department of Health, Education, and Welfare; the American Dialect Society; and the University of Wisconsin.) James W. Hartman summarizes "Some Preliminary Findings from *DARE*" in *AS* 44 (1969), 191–99. Technical and detailed studies of the kind that will feed into such a project include Gary N. Underwood, "Midwestern Terms for the Ground Squirrel," *WF* 29 (1970), 167–74; James E. Spears, "Southern Folk By-Words, Intensifiers, and Reinforcement Phrases," *MFR* 6 (1972), 115–17; and a thorough study in one state, E. Bagby Atwood's *The Regional Vocabulary of Texas* (Austin: University of Texas Press, 1962).

Most folk speech studies by folklorists concern vocabulary; three exceptions are Gordon Wilson's "Some Folk Grammar," *TFSB* 33 (1967), 27–35; George W. Boswell's "The Operation of Popular Etymology in Folksong Diction," *TFSB* 39 (1973), 37–58; and Alan Dundes's "The Henny Penny Phenomenon: A Study of Folk Phonological Esthetics in American Speech," *SFQ*

38 (1974), 1–9. An imaginative study by Howard Wight Marshall and John Michael Vlach demonstrates the relationship between folk dialect and folk architecture; see "Toward a Folklife Approach to American Dialects," *AS* 48 (1973), 163–91

The best dialect survey of an American folklore region is Vance Randolph and George P. Wilson's *Down in the Holler: A Gallery of Ozark Folk Speech* (Norman: University of Oklahoma Press, 1953). Ramon Adams's three books on western folk speech *Cowboy Lingo* (Boston: Houghton Mifflin, 1936), *Western Words* (Norman: University of Oklahoma Press, 1944; rev. edn., 1968), and *The Cowboy Says it Salty* (Tucson: University of Arizona Press, 1971) are authoritative and highly readable. On Western American folk speech see also Richard Poulsen, "Black George, Black Harris, and the Mountain Man Vernacular," *Rendezvous* 8 (Summer 1973), 15–23.

For a discussion of "Spanglish" in Puerto Rico see Rose Nash in *AS* 45 (1970), 223–33; the same author discusses "Englañol" [Spanishized English] in *AS* 46 (1971), 106–22.

Children's folk speech, a neglected subject, is treated in Rochele Berkovits's "Secret Languages of Schoolchildren," *NYFQ* 26 (1970), 127–52; her examples include sign languages, bop talk, pig Latin, girl talk, boy talk, and an orthographic code traceable back to sixteenth-century Italian practice. Mary and Herbert Knapp discuss "Tradition and Change in American Playground Language" in *JAF* 86 (1973), 131–41; they analyze truce terms, terminology in games of tag, and a ceremony when children accidentally say the same thing and shout "jinx."

"Boontling," first reported in a folklore journal in the 1940s, has been widely discussed since. Charles C. Adams gathers most references and presents a detailed study in *Boontling: An American Lingo* (Austin: University of Texas Press, 1971), which should be supplemented with E. N. Anderson, Jr., and Marja C. Anderson, "The Social Context of a Local 'Lingo'," *WF* 29 (1970), 153–65.

Fully documented historical studies of individual expressions are well represented by Allen Walker Read's "The Folklore of O.K.," *AS* 39 (1964), 5–25; and Peter Tamony's "'Hootenanny': the Word, its Content and Continuum," *WF* 22 (1963), 165–70. The general language of American labor is glossed in an appendix to Archie Green's article "John Neuhaus: Wobbly Folklorist," *JAF* 73 (1960), 189–217. The following works are only a few of the many that deal with vocabulary in a particular occupation: Walter F. McCulloch, *Woods Words: A Comprehensive Dictionary of Loggers' Terms* (Portland: Oregon Historical Society, 1958); Roberta Hanley, "Truck Drivers' Language in the Northwest," *AS* 36 (1961), 271–74; John F. Runice, "Truck Drivers' Jargon," *AS* 44 (1969), 200–9; Terry L. McIntyre, "The Language of Railroading," *AS* 44 (1969), 243–62; T. G. Lish, "Word List of Construction Terms," *PADS* no. 36 (1961), 25–31; Barbara P. Harris and Joseph F. Kess, "Salmon Fishing Terms in British Columbia," *Names* 23 (1975), 61–66; Gerald E. Warshaver, "*Schlop* Scholarship: A Survey of Folkloristic Studies of Lunchcounter and Soda Jerk Operatives," *FF* 4 (1971), 134–45; and two by

Kelsie B. Harder: "The Vocabulary of Hog-Killing," *TFSB* 25 (1959), 111–15; and "Hay-Making Terms in Perry County," *TFSB* 33 (1967), 41–48.

Further references suggest some folk speech topics outside of strictly regional or labor terminology: S. J. Sackett, "Marble Words from Hays, Kansas," *PADS* no. 37 (1962), 1–3; R. T. Prescott, "Calls to Animals," *SFQ* 2 (1938), 39–42; Gertrude Churchill Whitney, "New England Bird Language," *WF* 20 (1961), 113–14; C. Douglas Chrétien, "Comments on Naval Slang," *WF* 6 (1947), 157–62; Richard K. Seymour, "Collegiate Slang: Aspects of Word Formation and Semantic Change," *PADS* no. 51 (1969), 13–22; Paul A. Eschholz and Alfred F. Rosa, "Course Names: Another Aspect of College Slang," *AS* 45 (1970), 85–90; and Julia P. Stanley, "Homosexual Slang," *AS* 45 (1970), 45–59.

Names, published quarterly as the journal of the American Name Society, since 1953, is the major organ for onomastic activities and studies in this country. The society's pamphlet publication, *Theory of Names*, by Ernst Pulgram (Berkeley, 1954), is a solid introduction to the field.

George R. Stewart's frequently reprinted book *Names on the Land* (New York: Random House, 1945) is the basic introduction for American place-name studies, many of which have been carried out in great detail for individual states; two good ones that have been recently revised are Lewis A. McArthur's *Oregon Geographic Names* (1928), 3rd edn. (Portland: 1952), and Will C. Barnes's *Arizona Place Names* (1935), revised and enlarged by Byrd H. Granger (Tucson: University of Arizona Press, 1960). E. Joan Wilson Miller, a geographer with folkloristic training, discusses "The Naming of the Land in the Arkansas Ozarks: A Study in Cultural Processes" in *Annals of the Association of American Geographers* 59 (1969), 240–51. Terry L. Alford's article "An Interesting American Place-Name" in *MFR* 2 (1968), 76–78, concerns the name "Indianola," seventeen examples of which in the United States he attributes to the origin in Texas, renamed from "Powderhorn" in 1849 and *not* because of an Indian maiden named "Ola," as sometimes reported. Robert M. Rennick discussed in general "The Folklore of Place-Naming in Indiana" in *IF* 3 (1970), 35–94, while Ronald L. Baker discusses the Indiana place named "Monsterville" in *Names* 20 (1972), 186–92. Audrey R. Duckert identifies eight varieties of "Place Nicknames" in *Names* 21 (1973), 153–60. An article by Hazel E. Mills, "The Constant Webfoot," in *WF* 11 (1952), 153–64, traces the history of Oregon's state nickname.

The general role of names and naming in folklore is taken up by Robert M. Rennick in "The Folklore of Curious and Unusual Names (A Brief Introduction to the Folklore of Onomastics)," *NYFQ* 22 (1966), 5–14, and by Jan Harold Brunvand in the introduction to the special issue of *Names* devoted to names in folklore: 16 (Sept. 1968), 197–206. Byrd Howell Granger surveys a sub-area in her article "Naming: in Customs, Beliefs, and Folktales," *WF* 20 (1961), 27–37. See also Robert M. Rennick, "Successive Name-Changing: A Popular Theme in Onomastic Folklore and Literature," *NYFQ* 25 (1969), 119–28 O. Paul Straubinger, Names in Popular Sayings," *Names* 3 (1955), 157–64; and Archer Taylor, "The Use of Proper Names in Wellerisms and

Folktales," *WF* 18 (1959), 287–93. Nicknames (among Amish) are the subject of studies by Maurice A. Mook in *Names* 15 (1967), 111–18; and (among prison inmates) by Bruce Jackson in *WF* 26 (1967), 48–54.

J. L. Dillard's *Black Names* (Contributions to the Sociology of Language, 13; The Hague and Paris: Mouton, 1976) traces patterns of African usage in black American naming. He considers personal names, musical-group names, church names, vehicle names, and names in trade and business.

A miscellany of name studies for specific subjects might include: *blooming plants*—Lalia Phipps Boone in *SFQ* 19 (1955), 230–36; *cats*—Wendell S. Hadlock and Anna K. Stimson in *JAF* 59 (1946), 529–30, and Archer Taylor in *JAF* 60 (1947), 86; *cars*—Jan Harold Brunvand in *Names* 10 (1962), 279–84, and *WF* 23 (1964), 264–65; *apartment houses*—Elli Kaija Köngäs in *JAF* 77 (1964), 80–81; *tobacco*—Kathrine T. Kell in *JAF* 79 (1966), 590–99.

House painters' jargon of the kind quoted at the end of this chapter is collected by Donald M. Hines in *AS* 44 (1969), 5–32; and by John Michael Bennett in *SFQ* 33 (1969), 313–16.

Ed Cray discusses "Ethnic and Place Names as Derisive Adjectives" and gives numerous examples in *WF* 21 (1962), 27–34. David J. Winslow takes a more specialized approach in "Children's Derogatory Epithets," *JAF* 82 (1969), 255–63. George Monteiro's examples are "Chinese Fire Drill," "French Screw Driver," (a hammer) and "Jewish Penicillin" (chicken soup) in his note published in *WF* 34 (1975), 244–46. The best summary of scholarship and most systematic approach to this whole subject is found in Alan Dundes's "Slurs International: Folk Comparisons of Ethnicity and National Character," *SFQ* 39 (1975), 15–38.

5

Proverbs and Proverbial Lore

One notch up from folk speech on the scale of complexity in verbal folklore is the proverb—the popular *saying* in a relatively *fixed form* which is, or has been, in *oral circulation*. Many attempts have been made to define proverbs more precisely than this, usually in terms of their origin ("the wisdom of many, the wit of one"), their nature (sayings that "sum up a situation . . . characterize its essence"), or their function (". . . to provide an argument for a course of action which conforms to community values"); but the three qualities italicized above are basic to all. First, the proverb must be a saying, not merely a traditional word like "fiddlesticks" or "phooey." Second, the proverb exists in a somewhat standardized form; "sour grapes" is proverbial, but not "bitter grapes," or "acid grapes," or "sweet grapes." Third, a proverb must have had some oral vitality as distinguished from the written clichés of poetry, advertising, sports reporting, and the like. Thus, for not quite fully explainable reasons, some authored epigrams, like "I'd rather be right than be President" or "History is bunk," have never become proverbial, while many others, like "Pride goeth before a fall" or "Something is rotten in Denmark," have, though generally misquoted. Four major categories of proverbs with several subdivisions, plus a broad classification of miscellaneous sayings might easily be distinguished in American traditon, and most of these are paralleled in folk sayings the world over.

The **true proverb** is always a complete sentence, never varies more than slightly in form, and usually expresses some general truth or wisdom. Some true proverbs are simple sententious comments such as "Live and let live," "Absence makes the heart grow fonder," and "Accidents will happen." A few of these leave part of the sentence unstated but understood: "No fool like an old fool," "Penny-wise and pound-foolish," etc. Other true proverbs are based on Aesop's fables or similar old stories; for example, "Don't count your chickens before they hatch," and "Don't kill the goose that lays the golden egg." But the majority of true proverbs are metaphorical descriptions of an act or event applied as a general truth; examples are numerous—"A burnt child dreads the fire," "A new broom sweeps clean," "A rolling stone gathers no moss."

Proverbial phrases, on the other hand, are never complete sentences, regularly vary in form as they are used, and seldom express any generalized wisdom; furthermore, nearly all of them are metaphorical. Proverbial verb phrases vary in number and tense and permit the addition of adverbial modifications. Such traditional phrases are often anthologized as infinitives ("to be in hot water," "to raise the roof," "to cut off one's nose to spite one's face"), although they do not occur in speech that way ("He's in hot water now!" or "You're going to get in hot water doing that!"). Phrases without a verb are equally common, such as "behind the eight ball," "from A to Z" (a modernization of "from Alpha to Omega"), "a song and dance."

While proverbial phrases are traditional metaphors, **proverbial comparisons** are traditional similes, usually expressed in the "like" or "as" form. A proverbial comparison may be logical and direct ("red as a beet," "go like blazes," "greedy as a pig"), or it may be ironical ("as clear as mud," "a face like a can full of worms," "as little chance as a snowball in Hell"). Often there is humorous particularization or exaggeration in American proverbial comparisons; "go like blazes," for instance, becomes "go like *blue* blazes," or a person's luck is described in terms of the chances of "a celluloid cat chased by an asbestos dog in Hell." Sayings may be stated in comparative form ("tighter than a drum," "lower than a snake's belly," "blacker than a stack of black cats") or in the "so . . . that" or "more . . . than" pattern: "so tight he screaks," "so slow you have to set a stake to see him move," "more nerve than Carter has Little Liver Pills," "more troubles than you can shake a stick at," and so on. Doubtless there are further typical patterns yet to be identified, for the collection and classification of proverbial comparisons is still in a pioneer stage.

The **Wellerism** (or "Quotation Proverb"), named for Charles Dickens' Sam Weller in *Pickwick Papers*, who often used them, is a fourth major kind of proverb. Wellerisms—actually much older than their nineteenth-century namesake—are easy to identify, but they are hard to imagine from their definition—"a saying in the form of a quotation followed by a phrase ascribing the quotation to someone who has done something humorous and appropriate." For example: " 'Everyone to his own taste,' [quotation] as the old lady said [ascription] when she kissed the cow [action]." Other familiar Wellerisms are " 'Neat but not gaudy,' said the Devil, as he painted his tail blue," and " 'It won't be long now,' as the monkey said when he backed into the electric fan." Some Wellerisms involve puns, sometimes with grammatical change (" 'I see,' said the blind man, as he picked up his hammer and saw"), and a few of them are completely obscure in meaning (" 'Aha!" she cried, as she waved her wooden leg and died.") Another curious fact about Wellerisms is that the speaker in them is frequently an old woman, the Devil, a monkey, or a blind man.

Variations of **miscellaneous proverbial sayings** seem to be innumerable, and they tend to come in and go out of fashion rather quickly. A few long-term popular types may be represented as follows: *Insults, retorts, and wisecracks* (sometimes called "slam sayings")—"He's all right in his place, but that hasn't been dug yet," "You make a better door than you do a window," and "He couldn't be elected dogcatcher in a ward full of cats." *Sarcastic interrogatives*— "Does a dog have fleas?" "Is the Pope a Catholic?" *Euphemisms*— "It's snowing down south." (Meaning, "Your slip is showing.") "There's a star in the East" (Meaning, "Your fly is unzipped.") *National and ethnic slurs*—"The British have taken to Scotch; the French have taken to cognac; the Italians have taken to port." *Authors and titles*—"*School Dinners*, by Major Sick." (A related category is *Records and artists*—" 'On the Sunken Side of the Street,' by the Earthquakes.") *Confucius say*—"Girl in stretch pants get stern look." *She was only*—"the stableman's daughter, but all the horsemen knew her." *Tom Swifties* (Wellerism-like often-adverbial puns based on a familiar expression in the old *Tom Swift* boys' books)—" 'Only seven more days,' Tom said weakly."

Because they are short, pithy, common, and extremely varied, proverbs offer many interesting possibilities for analysis which often lead to better understanding of other aspects of culture. The contents of proverbs, for instance, which may suggest their origin, are wide ranging. There are proverbs based on beliefs ("Rats leave a sinking ship"), proverbs based on weather signs ("All signs fail in a dry season"), proverbs based on medical lore ("An apple a day keeps the doctor away"), proverbs based on business ("Out of debt, out of danger"), proverbs based on folk law ("Two wrongs don't make a right"), proverbs deriving from historical events or slogans ("Old soldiers never die; they just fade away") and many proverbs referring to household or farm tasks ("A watched pot never boils," "Make hay while the sun shines," etc.). America's pioneer past is suggested by such proverbs as "to come down like Davy Crockett's coon," "to see the elephant" (a popular frontier expression meaning "to see everything worth seeing"), "dry as a powder horn," "to play possum," "to go on the warpath," and "The only good Indian is a dead Indian."

Numerous proverbs are really familiar quotations, usually misquoted, especially from the Bible, from Shakespeare, or from other literary sources. These are called *geflügelte Worte* or "winged words" in German, and they often are used by people without reference to any source. Biblical proverbs include "Money is the root of all evil" (misquoted from *I Tim.* 6:10) and the phrase "to cast bread upon the waters" (from *Eccles.* 11:1). Shakespeare has given us "What's in a name?" "The wish is father to the thought," and scores of other proverbs, while other important literary sources include Pope ("Fools rush in where angels fear to tread"), Congreve ("Hell hath no fury like a woman scorned"), Samuel Johnson ("Patriotism is the last resort of a scoundrel"), and Wordsworth ("The child is father to the man"). The extent to which our daily speech may be colored by such literary borrowings, often with some traditional variation, is indicated by the following common sayings, all of which gained their currency from *Hamlet,* and probably take their origin from that play as well: "A method in his madness," "brevity is the soul of wit," "to know a hawk from a handsaw," "suit the action to the words," "sweets to the sweet."

Many proverbs come from classical Greek and Roman sources ("Love is blind," "The die is cast," "Many men, many minds") or they contain references to classical mythology and history ("to cross the Rubicon," "as rich as Croesus," "Rome was not built in a day"). Similarly, there are proverbs which refer to Biblical or legendary characters, including "Adam's off ox," "poor as Job's turkey," "'round Robin Hood's barn," and "as bare as Mother Hubbard's cupboard." However, many personal references in proverbs are irretrievably lost in history; who, we may wonder, are "Sam Hill," "Jack Robinson," "George" (as in "Let George do it"), and the trio "Tom, Dick, and Harry." ("George" may refer to the tradition of calling railroad conductors by this name.) There may be an echo of saints' names in expressions such as "for the love of Mike," "for Pete's sake," and "rob Peter to pay Paul," but conclusive evidence for such origins has yet to be presented.

Proverbs exhibit most of the stylistic devices of poetry. They have *meter* ("You can leád a horse to wáter, but you cán't máke him drink"), *rhyme* ("Haste makes waste"), *slant rhyme* ("A stitch in time saves nine"), *alliteration* ("Live and let live"), *assonance* ("A rolling stone gathers no moss"), *personification* ("Necessity is the mother of invention"), *paradox* ("No news is good news"), *parallelism* ("Man proposes; God disposes"), and several other poetic characteristics. Many figures of speech occur not only in proverbial phrases and proverbial comparisons, but also in true proverbs.

The philosophy expressed in proverbs introduces yet another area of inquiry. In the first place, it is easy to think of proverbs that contradict one another, yet are current simultaneously: "Look before you leap" versus "He who hesitates is lost." Many proverbs offer conservative advice such as "Don't bite off more than you can chew" or "Experience is the best teacher," while others are more cynically inclined, such as "It's not what you know, but who you know" or "If you can't be good, be careful." On the whole, judging from several representative collections, the subjects of well-known American proverbs tend to come from homey, simple, familiar, natural, and domestic topics. Nouns like "dog," "man," "cat," "bird," "wind," "bear," and "day" appear more frequently than any others; a somewhat contradictory fact, however, is that references to the Devil in American proverbs usually outnumber those to God in collections by about four to one. The most popular individual proverbs in American sayings tend to create a picture of optimism and a rather Puritanical social code; in nineteenth-century Indiana novels, for instance, the chief favorites were "to build castles in the air," "Honesty is the best policy," and "to turn over a new leaf."

Although all of these topics, and many more, challenge the student of proverbs, most past studies have consisted only of collecting, and too often only from literary or other printed sources. Gradually, oral proverbs are also being collected, sometimes to be printed in regional folklore journals or for eventual use in the American Dialect Society's proposed *Dictionary of American Proverbs.* Oral collections are important for several reasons. They help to validate supposed proverbs from print, they are the only way to include off-color proverbs, they show which ancient proverbs still live in tradition, and they allow us to capture the process of proverb-making as it occurs.

Fully documented collections both from print and from oral tradition are needed before folklorists will be able to evaluate the numerous and often highly imaginative explanations that have been proposed for some proverbs. The expression "Mind your P's and Q's," for example, has had at least five different explanations; it is said to refer to penmanship, typesetting, measurements ("pints and quarts"), dancing instruction ("*pied et queue,*" that is, "foot and pigtail"), and religion (Puritan and Quaker). Without full collections of dated texts, it is impossible to evaluate such etymologies.

One such puzzle, a proverbial saying with internal rhyme, containing a national slur, has now been identified as an immigrant-American coinage. The saying is "Ten thousand Swedes ran through the weeds, chased by one Norwegian." Norwegian-American informants associated the saying with a seventeenth-century military engagement against Sweden, but, significantly, they never quoted the rhyme in Norwegian; as a matter of fact, the saying would not form a rhyme in Norwegian. One scholar concluded that most likely the rhyme was invented in the United States by Norwegians carrying on the traditional Old-World rivalry with Swedes; they probably patterned it after the similar Anglo-Irish rhyme, "Ten thousand micks [Irishmen] got killed with picks, at the Battle of Boyne Water."

Individual English proverbs may be traced through several historical dictionaries of them, sometimes even back to the Middle Ages. A sampling of these shows how deceptively "modern" an old saying might sound; "penny-wise and pound-foolish," for example, still very current, was recorded already in the seventeenth century. "The coast is clear" and "beggars cannot be choosers" were both known in the sixteenth century, "to eat one out of house and home," in the fifteenth, "a short horse is soon curried" and "look before you leap" in the fourteenth, and the proverb about leading a horse to water in the late twelfth century.

Other dictionaries of proverbs allow us to compare the sayings of different cultures concerning the same theme. S. G. Champion's *Racial Proverbs*, for instance, lists these, among others, under *celibacy:* "old maids lead apes in Hell" (English), "old maids and young dogs should be drowned" (Romanian), "a bachelor and a dog may do everything" (Polish), "an old spinster is not worth more than an unposted letter" (Hungarian), "a bachelor is never sent as a 'go-between' " (Russian), "no man too old for old maid " (black Jamaican), and "an old bachelor compares life to a shirt-button, because it so often hangs by a thread" (Chinese).

Even without going abroad for analogues, a comprehensive study of the interest of American authors in proverbs and their use of them would provide some new insights into American literature. From the beginning, American authors have cited proverbs; William Bradford, in *Of Plymouth Plantation*, begun in 1630 and chronicling the Pilgrims' first settlement, used "last and not least," "tide stops for no man," "one swallow makes no summer," and others. Benjamin Franklin was famous for the proverbs he employed in *Poor Richard's Almanack* and *The Way to Wealth*, although he seems to have coined only one that passed into oral circulation on its own—"Three removes [that is, *moves* to a new household] is worse than a fire." James Fenimore Cooper's novels were rich in proverbs; Ralph Waldo Emerson quoted proverbs, altered them, and even tried to invent them; and Carl Sandburg wove proverbs, wisecracks, and other folk speech into *The People Yes*.

Alan Dundes advocates study of the "folkloristic structure" of proverbs (as distinguished from the linguistic structure of their grammar). Such patterning is independent of the various languages in which a proverb may appear, and its analysis should allow eventually for a true structural definition of the proverb and its subtypes. Dundes begins with the observation that all proverbs contain a topic (A) and a comment (B), so that simple equational proverbs such as "Boys will be boys," "Business is business," or "Coffee boiled is coffee spoiled" might all be represented as an $A = B$ equation. Other proverbs are oppositional, asserting a contrast or a lack of equivalence, such as "A fair exchange is no robbery," "One swallow does not make a summer," or "Two wrongs don't make a right," all of which suggest the $A \neq B$ formula. Still other patterns are possible: "His eyes are bigger than his stomach" is $A>B$; "Half a loaf is better than no bread" might be $\frac{A}{2} >(B)$, and "Two heads are better than one" $2A>B$, although *essentially* both are still $A>B$. Many multi-descriptive element proverbs (whether oppositional or nonoppositional) are based on traditional semantic contrastive pairs (few-many, young-old, before-after, etc.): "Like father, like son" is a nonoppositional example, and "Man works from sun to sun, but woman's work is never done" is oppositional. Apparently a limited number of such structural types exist, with some types being more popular in one culture than in another.

The functions or uses of proverbs, although seldom studied in American folklore, would offer a fruitful field for research. As Roger Abrahams has pointed out, "The strategy of the proverb . . . is to direct by appearing to clarify; this is engineered by simplifying the problem and resorting to traditional solutions." The philosophy of a single prolific informant might be investigated by means of his proverbial stock. The use of proverbs in advertising ("When it rains it pours," etc.) could be studied. Parodies of proverbs are specially popular nowadays, either as separate utterances ("Absence makes the heart go wander," "Don't enumerate your fowl until the process of incubation has materialized," "Familiarity breeds attempt," "A stitch in time gathers no moss," "You've buttered your bread, now lie in it") or as the punch lines of so-called Shaggy Dog Stories ("People who live in grass houses shouldn't stow thrones"). Even international relations and political tensions might be better understood, one scholar has suggested, through *paremiology*—the study of proverbs. One recalls that the former Soviet Premier Nikita S. Khrushchev was inclined to pass judgment on events in terms of proverbs; his belief in peaceful coexistence with the United States, for instance, was once expressed with the Russian proverb "When you live with a goat, you must get used to the bad smell."

Bibliographic Notes

An excellent introduction to the nature and study of proverbs is Margaret M. Bryant's "Proverbs and How to Collect Them," *PADS* no. 4 (1954), a handbook prepared for the collectors in the ADS project to compile a *Dictionary of American Proverbs*. It is instructive to compare Archer Taylor's older survey, "Problems in the Study of Proverbs," *JAF* 47 (1934), 1–21, with his new foreword to the second edition of his 1931 classic, *The Proverb* (Hatboro, Pa.: Folklore Associates, 1962). Taylor, the chief American authority of proverbs, also outlined "The Study of Proverbs" in *Proverbium* no. 1 (1965), 1–10. This new bulletin is distributed free by the Society of Finnish Literature, Halituskatu 1, Helsinki, Finland, to libraries, institutes, and active proverb scholars. Archer Taylor's other contributions to *Proverbium* include "The Collection and Study of Proverbs" in no. 8 (1967), 161–76; and "Method in the History and Interpretation of a Proverb" in no. 10 (1968), 235–38. The fifteenth number of *Proverbium* (1970) was "Essays in Honor of Archer Taylor on his 80th Birthday" with a bibliography of Taylor's writings on proverbial lore.

The basic American proverb dictionary is Archer Taylor and Bartlett Jere Whiting's *A Dictionary of American Proverbs and Proverbial Phrases, 1820–1880* (Cambridge, Mass.: Harvard University Press, 1958); the introduction to this work is very useful, and the reference bibliography includes all of the important American collections in book or periodical form at the time of publication. Three inclusive state collections are B. J. Whiting's "Proverbs and Proverbial Sayings," in *The Frank C. Brown Collection of North Carolina Folklore*, vol. I (Durham, N.C.: Duke University Press, 1952), pp. 331–501; Jan Harold Brunvand's *Proverbs and Proverbial Phrases from Indiana Books Published before 1890*, Indiana University Folklore Series no. 15 (Bloomington, 1961); and Frances M. Barbour's *Proverbs and Proverbial Phrases of Illinois* (Carbondale and Edwardsville: Southern Illinois University Press, 1965). The bibliographies in these works may now be supplemented with F. A. DeCaro and W. K. McNeil's *American Proverb Literature: A Bibliography*, Bibliographic and Special Series no. 6, *Folklore Forum* (1970).

Proverbs circulating in the United States in languages other than English may be found in such journal articles as Rubén Cobos, "New Mexican Spanish Proverbs, *NMFR*, 12 (1969–70), 7–11; and Anna Mary Boudreux, "Proverbs, Metaphors and Sayings of the Kaplan Area [Vermillion Parish, Louisiana]," *LFM*, 3 (April 1970), 16–24.

The only book-length collection of proverbial comparisons is Archer Taylor's *Proverbial Comparisons and Similes from California*, Folklore Studies no. 3 (Berkeley, 1954). More California comparisons are printed in *WF* 17 (1958), 12–20. James N. Tidwell discusses the special language of American proverbial comparisons in "Adam's Off Ox: A Study in the Exactness of the Inexact," *JAF* 66 (1953), 291–94.

C. Grant Loomis gathered various miscellaneous kinds of nineteenth-century proverbial sayings in three articles in *Western Folklore*: Wellerisms and Yankeeisms are in *WF* 8 (1949), 1–21; epigrams and perverted proverbs in *WF* 8 (1949), 348–57; and such types as definitions, literal clichés, naming, and occupational punning are in *WF* 9 (1950), 147–52. Wayland D. Hand lists more perverted proverbs in *WF* 27 (1968), 263–64: "Familiarity breeds attempt," "A stitch in time gathers no moss," and so forth. In Charles Clay Doyle's "Title-Author Jokes, Now and Long Ago," *JAF* 86 (1973), 52–54, this minor proverbial genre is related to a mid–seventeenth-century English fashion for book title jokes. The same author comments on "Sarcastic Interrogative Affirmations and Negatives ["Is the Pope a Catholic?" or "Does a chicken have lips?"]," in *MJLF* 1 (1975), 33–34.

Besides sources of proverbs described in Taylor's *The Proverb*, Frances M. Barbour gave examples of three more in *MF* 13 (1963), 97–100; these are from songs (i.e., "Babes in the Woods"), from echoes of other proverbs (i.e., "easy as falling off a diet"), and from advertising (i.e., "good to the last drop"). C. Grant Loomis discussed other "Proverbs in Business" in *WF* 23 (1964), 91–94. In *Names* 6 (1958), 51–54, Archer Taylor concluded that the phrase "Tom, Dick, and Harry" was an Americanism of the early nineteenth century based upon antecedents reaching back three centuries; later, however, he found the same expression in earlier sources from England.

The relationships of proverbs to poetry are analyzed in detail by S. J. Sackett in "Poetry and Folklore: Some Points of Affinity," *JAF* 77 (1964), 143–53. B. J. Whiting extracted the proverbial material from the popular ballads for an article in *JAF* 47 (1934), 22–44. The unraveling of the background of "Ten Thousand Swedes" was accomplished by the Norwegian-American sociologist Peter A. Munch, who published his findings in *MF* 10 (1960), 61–69.

Two good reference works for tracing English proverbs are G. L. Apperson's *English Proverbs and Proverbial Phrases. A Historical Dictionary* (London: J. M. Dent, 1929; repr. Detroit: Gale Research Co., 1969) and W. G. Smith and J. E. Heseltine's *The Oxford Dictionary of English Proverbs* (Oxford, England: Oxford University Press, 1935, 3rd edn. revision by F. P. Wilson, 1970). S. G. Champion's *Racial Proverbs* (London: Routledge, 1938; rev. 1950) is perhaps the most reliable of several similar compilations of proverbs from many lands to be found in most large libraries.

On proverbs in literature, see Wolfgang Mieder, "The Essence of Literary Proverb Studies," *NYFQ* 30 (1974), 66–76 (also published in *Proverbium* no. 23 [1974], 888–94). Mieder surveyed "The Proverb and Anglo-American Literature" in *SFQ* 38 (1974), 49–62. Four good individual studies are Stuart A. Gallacher's "Franklin's *Way to Wealth:* A Florilegium of Proverbs and Wise Sayings," *JEGP* 48 (1949), 229–51; Warren S. Walker's "Proverbs in the Novels of James Fenimore Cooper," *MF* 3 (1953), 99–107; J. Russell Reaver's "Emerson's Use of Proverbs," *SFQ* 27 (1963), 280–99; and Joseph Moldenhauer's "The Rhetorical Function of Proverbs in *Walden*," *JAF* 80 (1967), 151–59.

Structural analysis of proverbs was suggested by Alan Dundes in *MF* 12 (1962), 31–38, in a review of *Trends in Content Analysis* (1959), ed. Ithiel de Sola Pool. Another approach was taken by G. B. Milner in "Quadripartite Structures," *Proverbium* no. 14 (1969), 379–83; Dundes subsequently reconsidered the matter and expanded upon his own proposal in "On the Structure of the Proverb," *Proverbium* no. 25 (1975), 961–73, reprinted in *Analytic Essays in Folklore*, pp. 103–18.

The majority of past studies of proverbs by literary folklorists have been collections or source searches, an exception that deals with functions being Joseph Raymond's "Tensions in Proverbs: More Light on International Understanding," in *WF* 15 (1956), 153–58. Representative of the functional or communications approach taken by some anthropological folklorists is E. Ojo Arewa and Alan Dundes's "Proverbs and the Ethnography of Speaking Folklore," in *AA* 66 (1964), 70–85. Recent studies with more attention paid to the contexts of proverbs' uses and meanings are Richard Bauman's and Neil McCabe's "Proverbs in an LSD Cult," *JAF* 83 (1970), 318–24, and James P. Leary's " 'The Land Won't Burn': An Esoteric American Proverb and its Significance," *MJLF* 1 (1975), 27–32.

6

Riddles and Other Verbal Puzzles

Folk riddles are traditional questions with unexpected (albeit traditional) answers—verbal puzzles (only a few involve writing) that demonstrate the cleverness of the questioner and challenge the wit of his audience. The practice of riddling can be traced to the dawn of literary expression; it is referred to in the most ancient Oriental and Sanskrit writings, in the Bible, in classical legends and myths, in European folktales and ballads, and in some of the earliest manuscripts of Medieval literature. Compilations of riddles were among the first printed books in the Middle Ages, and books of literary riddles remained a popular diversion well into the Renaissance. Since the beginning of professional interest in folklore in the nineteenth century, massive collections of folk riddles have been published in most European countries and in many countries outside Europe. Riddles have been found in the native cultures of all peoples, even the American Indians, who until recently were thought to possess only a few that had been borrowed from Europeans.

Not only is riddling widespread, but the variety of actual riddles in collections is dazzling. Yet the basic forms that riddles take seem to be relatively limited, and many individual riddles have persisted with little essential change for centuries. A striking example is the "Sphinx riddle" from the Greek legend of Oedipus—"What walks on four legs in the morning, on two in the afternoon, and on three in the evening?" This riddle, with the answer "man" (who crawls in infancy, walks upright in adulthood, and leans on a cane when aged), is only the best known of many with the same answer based on related puzzling questions that are common in Western tradition and scattered through the rest of the world. Literature has helped to keep the riddle of the Sphinx alive from the beginning, but its oral circulation has never ceased. It has been found in English in Great Britain,

Canada, the United States, and the West Indies. One collected from a fifteen-year-old schoolgirl in Scotland is rendered in rhyme without the metaphor of times of day, but with the added detail of man's decreasing vigor; yet it is still clearly recognizable as the same enigma that challenged Oedipus on the outskirts of Thebes:

> Walks on four feet
> On two feet, on three.
> The more feet it walks on,
> The weaker it be.

Folkloristic studies of riddles date from the late eighteen-hundreds in European languages, and emerged in English with the pioneering work of the American folklorist Archer Taylor, which began in the 1930s and culminated in the publication of his *English Riddles from Oral Tradition* in 1951. Taylor has given us the bibliography and methodology for riddle studies, as well as the important distinctions between the "true riddle" and others and an ingenious scheme of classification.

The **true riddle** is essentially a comparison between the unstated answer and something else that is described in the question. This description usually has two parts, a rather general and straightforward part, such as "Little Nancy Eddicote, in a white petticoat, and a red nose," followed by a more precise, but apparently contradictory part: "The longer she stand, the shorter she grows." The answer to this common English riddle is "a candle," and the riddle can be regarded as a *comparison* of a candle to a little girl, or a *description* of a candle in terms of a little girl. An American variant of this riddle adds a further contradictory detail but retains the same descriptive method:

> Little Miss Etticoat in a white petticoat
> Shorter and shorter she grows.
> Oh how she suffers while we with the snuffers
> Are nipping her little red nose.

These two basic parts of a true riddle are called by Taylor the *description* and the *block*, and they may be observed in a great variety of texts. Many riddles have only these two parts, plus an answer, as in the following:

Robbers came to our house and we were all in; [description]
The house leapt out the windows and we were all taken. [block]
    Answer: Fish in a net (The "house" is the water; "windows" are
        holes in the net.)

It is possible for a true riddle to have fully six distinct parts which may
be designated this way:

Introduction	As I went over London Bridge
Description	I met my sister
Name	Jenny;
Block	I broke her neck and drank her blood
	And left her standing empty.
Close	Answer me if you can.
Answer	A bottle of wine.

Few riddles collected from oral tradition, however, have all six parts.

Attempts to classify true riddles by their answers long frustrated
folklorists because the answers may vary considerably from text to
text and quite different riddles may have the same answers. Instead,
Archer Taylor's system classifies riddles by the nature of the item described in the question, using seven general categories:

    I. Comparisons to a Living Creature (e.g., the Sphinx riddle)
    II. Comparisons to an Animal
    III. Comparisons to Several Animals
    IV. Comparisons to a Person (e.g., "Little Nancy Eddicote,"
            "Sister Jenny," and "Humpty Dumpty")
    V. Comparisons to Several Persons (e.g., the fish in the net
            riddle)
    VI. Comparisons to Plants
    VII. Comparisons to Things

There are four further categories in Taylor's classification in which
the principle behind the puzzling question is an enumeration of details rather than the description of a recognizable item. With examples for each, these are:

    VIII. Enumerations of Comparisons
            Round as a hoop, deep as a cup; all the king's oxen
            can't pull it up.—A well.
    IX. Enumerations in Terms of Form or of Form and Function
            Patch on patch and has no seams.—Cabbage. [form]

X.   Enumerations in Terms of Color
Throw it up green, comes down red.—A watermelon.
XI. Enumerations in Terms of Acts
With what vegetable do you throw away the outside,
then cook the inside, then eat the outside, and throw
the inside away?—Corn.

Most English true riddles are very old, and their counterparts may
be found somewhere among Taylor's 1749 individual types, but occasionally a new one will be invented, such as the following:

What is round and has squares [the *block*]; it lived once upon a
time. You see it every day, and most every home has it?—A roll of
toilet paper.

One riddle based on comparisons (category VIII) refers to a unique
American animal, and so far has been reported only from the state of
Mississippi:

Hands like a man, ears like a bat, tail like a rat; guess what it is and
I'll give you my hat.—An opossum.

One peculiar American riddle describes the answer in terms of nonsense syllables that suggest its sound when in use:

My mother went over to your mother's house to borrow a wim
babble, wam bobble, a hind body fore body, whirl-a-kin nibble.—A
spinning wheel.

Two special categories, sometimes included with true riddles,
should be distinguished. The **neck riddle** is so called because it is
usually attributed in folktales and legends to a condemned prisoner
who, to "save his neck" must pose a riddle that no one can solve. His
riddle refers to a scene which he, and he only, has observed and can
identify from the cryptic description given. Samson's riddle in the
Bible (Judges 14:14) is a neck riddle:

Out of the eater came forth meat,
And out of the strong came forth sweetness.
—Honey comb in a lion's carcass.

One desperate prisoner—a Confederate captive in the Civil War, according to the story—declared:

Corn et corn in a high oak tree,
If you guess this riddle, you kin hang me.

The Union captors, however, could not guess that his name was Corn and he had been eating parched corn in a tree top before being captured.

The **pretended obscene** riddle is another special subtype, often of the comparative or enumerative type. Here the description suggests something risqué, usually sexual, but the correct answer is quite tame. For example, the question "What is a man called who marries another man?" has the bland solution, "a minister." Other pretended obscene riddles seem to be describing sexual intercourse, but actually refer to scrubbing clothes, chewing gum, picking fruit, making a bed, and other innocuous acts. Compare, too, this attempt to lead a listener into speaking a taboo word: "What has four letters, starts with an *F*, gives old folks a backache and young folks pleasure?"—A Ford [car].

In all of the riddle types presented thus far, the facts for answering are rather well contained within the questions themselves; when one understands how true riddles operate, he can learn to solve them. But there are many traditional riddles that do not follow such a predictable pattern, and they can only be solved by means of special knowledge or wit. These can be placed in several distinct categories.

The **riddling question** (or "clever question") is the general type of nonpredictable riddle. The "Riddle Song" of British balladry is made up of these: the first question in it "How can there be a cherry without a stone?" is answered, "A cherry when it's blooming, it has no stone." There are countless other such riddles: "How deep is the ocean?—A stone's throw"; "Where was Moses when the lights went out?—In the dark"; "What do they call little black cats in England?—Kittens"; and so forth. One riddling question is answered with a sound rather than a word: "What makes a horse go, a dog come, and a man stay?" For the answer, the sound of a kiss is made.

The **conundrum** is based on punning or other wordplay. The pun may occur in the answer ("When is a ship not a ship?—When it's *afloat.*") or in the question ("What has four wheels and *flies?*—A garbage truck.") Often the conundrum asks why one thing is like another—"Why is a thief in the attic like an honest man?—Because he's above doing a mean thing." Some conundrums develop double or larger multiple puns: "What's the difference between a ball and a prince?—One is thrown in the air; the other is heir to the throne." Or, "What would happen, geographically speaking, if a black waiter dropped a roasted turkey?—The fall of Turkey, the destruction of China, the overthrow of Greece, and the humiliation of Africa." A few that form a spoonerism * in the answer may be termed *spooneristic conundrums:* "What's the difference between the clown at the circus and a guilty conscience?—One is a cute amuser, the other a mute accusor."

The general terms **puzzle** or **problem** may be applied to a host of traditional questions involving special Biblical, arithmetical, genealogical, or practical knowledge for an answer. These may be posed seriously for an attempted solution, or they may be completely whimsical. For example, there are serious arithmetical riddles involving weights and measures, ages, or monetary figures that can be solved by an acute mind, but the following Ozark text is pure whimsy:

> If it takes a peckerwood eight months t' peck a four-inch hole in a gum-tree that would make 250 bundles o' good shingles, how long would it take a wooden-legged grasshopper t' kick all th' seeds out'n a dill pickle seven inches long an' an inch and a quarter thick?
> —There ain't no answer, you fool!

Some problems involve the practical enigmas of transporting incompatible creatures across a river in a small boat, or picking a matched set of socks out of a drawer in the dark, and the like. But one is a sort of anagrammatic problem, requiring the solver to find four letters that will make five words to fill the blanks:

> An _____ old woman of _____ intent
> Put on her _____ and away she went.
> "Come _____ my son," she was heard to say.
> "We'll _____ on the fat of the land today."

Some traditional questions are really not intended to be answered at all; they are merely **catch questions,** designed to embarrass the

---

* Named for Rev. W. A. Spooner (1844–1930), an Englishman famous for unintentionally interchanging the sounds of words in sayings.

unwary. A boy asks a girl, "Do you know what virgins eat for break-fast?" and all she need do is respond "No, what?" to bring his laugh and her blush. A child asks "What comes after seventy-five?" and if one is gullible enough to say "seventy-six," he gleefully shouts, "That's the spirit!"

A prolific modern form of riddle, usually just termed a "joke," is the **riddle joke;** these come and go in fad cycles, usually centering on a single theme while they last; they are always inane. Most familiar, probably, are the so-called *moron jokes* with their outrageous puns: "Why did the little moron cut a hole in the rug?—To see the floor-show." A favorite cycle dwelt upon foods—grapes, pickles, bananas, etc. ("What's purple and conquers continents?—Alexander the Grape." "What's green, bumpy, and floats around in the ocean?— Moby Pickle.") A Mormon variant asks, "What's purple and has twenty-seven wives?" the answer being, "Brigham Plum." Another group of riddle jokes centers on elephants, and still others are *sick jokes* (macabre humor); there are many based on personalities in the news. Not all of these are strictly speaking *riddles*, but since most of them do involve the questioning form, and they function as jokes do in oral tradition, they might conveniently be classified as riddle jokes.

Two special kinds of riddles are "non-oral," involving as they do either gestures or drawings. The **non-oral riddle** itself (or sometimes "facial droodle") has only the question "What's this?" accompanied by a gesture, such as waving the hand and snapping fingers (a butterfly with hiccups), or holding fingertips of both hands together palm-to-palm with fingers flexing (a spider doing pushups on a mirror). The *droodle*, which was briefly syndicated in many newspapers, but was initially derived from folklore asks "What's this?" about sketches like these:

—A man
practicing his
trombone in a
telephone booth.

—A girl with a pony
tail in a bubble bath
practicing the trumpet.

—A bear climbing
a tree. (Variant:
a giraffe's neck.)

As in most oral riddles, the droodle basically involves seeing something from an unusual point of view. The persistence of this principle in droodle-art across a span of some 300 years is illustrated in the two examples below, the right-hand one from an Italian source of 1678, and the left-hand one from the United States about 1950:

—A soldier and his dog,
just disappearing around
a corner.

—A blind beggar with cup
and stick, just coming around
a corner.

Even the complicated riddle-like *question guessing* game that John F. Kennedy's aides reportedly played during dull moments in the 1960 Presidential campaign is based on taking an unusual viewpoint. Here the quizzer gave an *answer* and the players tried to find a question to match. To the answer, "9-W," for example, the proper question was, "Is your name spelled with a 'V,' Mr. Wagner?" The answer—*"Nein,* 'W'."

There are several other types of traditional verbal puzzles and tricks, some of which require a written rather than purely oral presentation. The **palindrome** is a sentence that reads the same backward or forward, such as "Madam, I'm Adam" (what Adam said to Eve), "Able was I ere I saw Elba" (referring to Napoleon), and "A man, a plan, a canal: Panama" (an allusion to Theodore Roosevelt's backing for the Panama Canal). The **all-letter sentence** is just what its name implies—a sentence containing all the letters of the alphabet, such as "William F. Jex quickly caught seven dozen Republicans." Such sentences are used by teletype operators and typewriter repairmen to test their equipment, and many people immediately rap out "The quick brown fox jumps over the lazy dog" when trying out a new typewriter. A sentence that contains all the letters only once each is "J. Q. Vandz struck my big fox whelp." The **over-and-under sentence** depends upon written position for its meaning; the following, allegedly used as an address, is translated, "John Underwood, Andover, Massachusetts."

Wood
John
Mass.

Analogous to this are the following two over-and-under renderings of traditional phrases:

Well   Once
My word   4 P.M.
 ("Well upon my word")   ("Once upon a time")

Other written puzzles employ different positional clues:

("Laying it on the line")

("Grapes in season")

One very curious traditional item is based on the following numbers and letters written on a sheet of paper: 3909 Ǝ H T. The question is then asked, "If this many nuns went to Rome, who would be the happiest?" The answer is discovered by holding the paper up to the light backwards and reading through it—"The Pope."

The **tongue-twister** is a verbal puzzle requiring agility in *pronouncing* difficult sounds, rather than in providing answers. The best known is probably "Peter Piper picked a peck of pickled peppers," which is only the sentence for "p" from a whole tongue-twister alphabet once popular in elocutionist handbooks. Many tongue-twisters have a kind of surrealistic quality: "Seven slick slimy snakes sliding slowly southward," or "Two toads totally tired tried to trot to Tadbury." Campus favorites are those tongue-twisters that may lead the unwary into uttering an off-color word or expression: "She slit a sheet, a sheet she slit, and in her slitted sheet she'd sit." There are also tongue-twister songs of this type.

Finally, the traditional **mnemonic device** might be considered a verbal puzzle; these are rhymes, sayings, words, or other devices intended to aid the memory of difficult facts. There are mnemonic devices for remembering spellings, geographic facts, scientific principles, navigational rules, and many other matters. Some are very simple, such as the acronym "Roy G. Biv" for remembering the colors in the spectrum in order (*R*ed, *O*range, *Y*ellow, *G*reen, *B*lue, *I*ndigo and *V*iolet), while some are more complex, as in the sentences used for remembering the twelve cranial nerves from "olfactory" to "hypoglossal" ("*O*n *o*ld *O*lympus' *t*owering *t*ops, *a* *F*inn *a*nd *G*erman *v*iewed *s*ome *h*ops") or for the scale of hardness for geological analysis from "talc" to "diamond" ("*T*roy girls *c*an *f*lirt *a*nd *o*ther *q*ueer *t*hings *c*an *d*o").

Many English and American riddles of all varieties have been collected and published, providing rich possibilities for analysis. One interesting observation that can be verified simply from the index of answers in Taylor's classification is that the subjects of true riddles tend to come from the world of a farm woman looking out of her kitchen window; thus, the most characteristic answers to riddles are berries, fruits, garden vegetables, the stars and the moon, the well, a needle and thread, cooking utensils, clothing, and the like. Furthermore, in common with many proverbs, riddles are essentially metaphorical, and they exhibit other stylistic features of poetry, especially meter and rhyme. Sometimes, too, archaic words and expressions are preserved in riddle texts.

The structure of true riddles interested folklorists Robert Georges and Alan Dundes, who pointed out that the same basic "topic-comment" form exists in them as in some proverbs. They defined the riddle structurally as containing "one or more descriptive elements . . . the referent [to which] is to be guessed." They determined that the description may be either *oppositional* or *nonoppositional* (that is, may or may not contain the "block" element), and either *literal* or *metaphorical*. Riddles with blocks (oppositional) are almost always metaphorical, and may exhibit one of three kinds of opposition, *antithetical* (only one part can be true), *privational* (the second part denies a logical or natural attribute of the first), or *causal* (the first part consists of an action that is denied by the second). To this Roger Abrahams has added the identification of three techniques employed in riddling, *incomplete detail* (not enough information provided for the parts to fit together clearly), *too much detail* (inconsequential details that bury the important traits), and *false Gestalt* (commonly leading to off-color answers in catches and pretended obscene riddles). These approaches (and others have extended them) help to tie up loose ends of earlier definitions, furnishing more concrete and specific descriptions of what riddles really are.

The symbolism and functions of riddles in folk tradition raise further questions. Do riddles mask meanings not immediately apparent in their literal wording? How can these meanings be discovered? What roles do riddles play in folk groups as entertainment and as educational devices? Are riddles primarily children's folklore, and how long do *they* circulate them? What are the favorite times for asking riddles, besides parties, dances, "bees," wakes, and other social occasions during which they have previously been observed? Is riddling usually engaged in as a "concert" (one riddler performing for the others) or as a "contest" (riddlers taking turns and matching question for question)? What are the usual practices of guessing riddles? Do these matters all vary from region to region, family to family, period to period? Do the uses of riddles in folktales and ballads reflect their earlier functions in courtship, initiation, legal processes, and the like?

One study of the riddles included in British and Anglo-American traditional ballads concluded that there is thinly veiled sexual symbolism in all of them. The sequence of answers in the widely known "Riddle Song," for instance—cherry, egg, ring, baby—suggests impregnation, an interpretation also supported by both context and variants of the ballad. Another pioneering field study carried out in the United States and Scotland resulted in the first systematic observations of riddling customs in these areas. While riddles in American tradition tended to occur only incidentally, the riddle session or contest was still occasionally discovered in Scotland; in one such session the collector recorded sixty-five riddles from five persons during an evening. Such studies begin to answer questions about riddles and riddling, and they point the way for many other possible analyses of these eternally fascinating enigmas.

BIBLIOGRAPHIC NOTES

Archer Taylor surveyed "Problems in the Study of Riddles" in *SFQ* 2 (1938), 1–9; and he compiled "A Bibliography of Riddles" in *FFC* no. 126 in 1939. His *English Riddles from Oral Tradition* was published in 1951 (Berkeley: University of California Press) and established the basic corpus of English and Anglo-American true riddles. A succinct essay on the types of riddles is Taylor's "The Riddle" in *CFQ* 2 (1943), 129–47. A similar statement is his "The Riddle as a Primary Form" published in *Folklore in Action*, pp. 200–7. An article in a popular vein that incorporates folkloristic concepts is Duncan Emrich's "Riddle Me, Riddle Me, What is That?" in *American Heritage* 7 (Dec. 1955), 116–19.

The supposed nonexistence of American Indian riddles was challenged in three articles in *JAF*: Archer Taylor's "American Indian Riddles" in 57 (1944), 1–15; Charles T. Scott's "New Evidence of American Indian Riddles" in 76 (1963), 236–41; and David P. McAllester's "Riddles and Other Verbal Play Among the Comanches," in 77 (1964), 251–57.

The riddles themselves from collections in English up to 1951 are all included in Archer Taylor's classification, but three representative articles from mid-America might be listed for reference to their original publication with notes. Vance Randolph and Isabel Spradley published "Ozark Mountain Riddles" in *JAF* 47 (1934), 81–89; Randolph and Taylor published more "Riddles in the Ozarks" in *SFQ* 7 (1944), 1–10; and Paul G. Brewster published "Riddles from Southern Indiana" in *SFQ* 3 (1939), 93–105. A group of 143 items of riddling lore, including forty-eight true riddles, from the state of Mississippi was analyzed in George W. Boswell's "Riddles in the WPA-Collected Folklore Archives," *MFR* 3 (1969), 33–52.

Various riddle types are often intermixed in the published collections such as Catherine Harris Ainsworth's "Black and White and Said All Over" in *SFQ* 26 (1962), 263–95, containing 535 miscellaneous texts collected by mail from ninth-grade and tenth-grade students in seven states. The conundrum alluded to in Ainsworth's title is discussed in many different contexts, variants, and offshoots in Mac E. Barrick's note "The Newspaper Riddle Joke," *JAF* 87 (1974), 253–57. Another large riddle collection from schoolchildren is Meryl Weiner's "The Riddle Repertoire of a Massachusetts Elementary School," *FF*

3 (1970), 7–38, in which about 260 students from first through fifth grades contributed examples.

Two recent articles have explored the dynamics of the so-called "pretended obscene" riddles with particular attention to what a culture senses as being obscene and how a particular folklore genre operates with these assumptions; see Jan Hullum, "The 'Catch' Riddle: Perspectives from Goffman and Metafolklore," *Folklore Annual* 4–5 (1972–73), 52–59; and Waln K. Brown, "Cognitive Ambiguity and the 'Pretended Obscene Riddle'," *KF* 18 (1973), 89–101. Use of pretended obscene riddles in a prank or initiation context is discussed by Richard Bauman in "The Turtles: An American Riddling Institution," *WF* 29 (1970), 21–25.

Conundrums from nineteenth-century American newspapers were compiled by Archer Taylor in *CFQ* 5 (1946), 273–76; and by C. Grant Loomis in *WF* 8 (1949), 235–47. Donald M. Hines culled 230 examples from regional newspaper files in "Rare Blooms from a Rude Land: Frontier Riddles from the Inland Pacific Northwest," *IF* 6 (1973), 205–40; he discovered only nineteen that were "true riddles."

The faddish elephant riddle-jokes were published in a number of journal notes and articles, perhaps the largest selection being Ed Cray and Marilyn Eisenberg Herzog's "The Absurd Elephant: A Recent Riddle Fad," *WF* 26 (1967), 27–36. Roger D. Abrahams and Alan Dundes offered interpretive suggestions in "On Elephantasy and Elephanticide," *The Psychoanalytic Review* 56 (1969), 225–41, repr. in *Analytic Essays in Folklore*, pp. 192–205.

A small collection largely of arithmetical puzzles gathered by a radio station in Lafayette, Indiana, was annotated by Ray B. Browne for *MF* 11 (1961), 155–60. A page of short written "Verbal Puzzles" appeared in *NCFJ*, 23 (1975), 112. Sixteen examples of what some people call "logic problems," short puzzling narratives with cryptic solutions, were published by Danny W. Moore in "The Deductive Riddle: An Adaptation to Modern Society," *NCFJ* 22 (1974), 119–25.

Non-oral riddles were printed in *WF* 17 (1958), 279–80, and *WF* 19 (1960), 132–133. David Bowman asks the questions "Whatever Happened to Droodles? Whatever Happened to Roger Price?" in *JPC* 9 (1975), 20–25. He provides useful information about their popularization in the United States during the early 1950s by Roger Price's publications, but he fails to identify the droodle itself (not the name) as a much older form. Four examples of "pictorial riddles" drawn for amusement by seventeenth-century Italian painters are reproduced as Figure 55 and mentioned on pp. 54–55 in Donald Posner, *Annibale Carracci*, vol. I (London: Phaidon Press, Ltd., 1971). These were originally published by Carlo Cesare Malvasia in Bologna in 1678.

Tongue-twisters are sometimes printed as fillers in folklore journals or in general folklore anthologies; one specialized article, however, is Maurice A. Mook's "Tongue Tanglers from Central Pennsylvania," *JAF* 72 (1959), 291–96; the article is followed by a tongue-twister song from collegiate tradition (pp. 296–97). Another popular article, by Duncan Emrich, is "The Ancient Game of Tongue-Twisters," *American Heritage* 6 (Feb. 1955), 119–20. A children's book of tongue-twisters, but with a useful bibliography, is Alvin Schwartz's, *A Twister of Twists, a Tangler of Tongues* (Philadelphia and New York: J. B. Lippincott, Co., 1972). A richly annotated article on mnemonic devices was published by Alan Dundes in *MF* 11 (1961), 139–47.

A structural analysis of true riddles was made by Robert A. Georges and Alan Dundes and published in *JAF* 76 (1963), 111–18, reprinted in *Analytic Essays in Folklore*, pp. 95–102. Dundes and Roger D. Abrahams survey riddles from a structural and typological viewpoint in their chapter "Riddles" in Dorson's textbook *Folklore and Folklife: An Introduction*, pp. 129–43.

J. Barre Toelken examined the riddle ballads in "Riddles Wisely Expounded," *WF* 25 (1966), 1–16. "Riddling Traditions in Northeastern Scotland" were described by Kenneth S. Goldstein in *JAF* 76 (1963), 330–36.

7

Rhymes and Folk Poetry

Rhyme is a basic stylistic device of verbal folklore, and it occurs in many types beside the rhyming proverbs and riddles already mentioned. There are some rhymes in folktales—the dialogues in "The Three Little Pigs" and the giant's threats in "Jack and the Beanstalk" for example. Folk beliefs may be expressed in rhyme, for instance:

> Mole on the neck, trouble by the peck,
> Mole on the face, suffers disgrace.

or the card players' rule:

> Cut 'em thin, sure to win,
> Cut 'em deep, sure to weep.

A traditional rhyme may serve as a characterizing or mnemonic device:

> Low and lazy,
> Broad and hazy,
> High and crazy.

This refers to the Episcopal Church services, "low" (no kneeling, hence "lazy"), "high" (formal and full of symbolism), and "broad" (a "hazy" mixture of low and high).

A belief-rhyme that is regarded as having magical power is called a *charm*, the best known being the "Star light, star bright" verse used for wishing on a star. Many charms are intended to affect the transference of some ailment:

> Sty, sty, leave my eye;
> Take the next one passing by.

Other charms may make butter come in a churn, remove warts, stop bleeding in a wound, or drive the rain away to "come again another day." Good advice is sometimes transmitted in a rhyme, such as the following one for hours of sleep:

> Nature needs but five.
> Custom gives thee seven.
> Laziness takes nine,
> And wickedness eleven.

Besides such uses of rhyme in other kinds of folklore, there are numerous independent rhymes, largely circulated by children, that are chanted, whined, sung, shouted, muttered, or otherwise recited as suitable occasions appear. These bits of fluid folklore are highly elusive and have not been systematically collected or arranged on a large scale in the United States; thus, this chapter can only indicate some basic types of folk rhymes and suggest a few possible sub-divisions. In general, there are four major categories of American folk rhymes—*nursery rhymes; rhymes of play, games, and fun* (including "the dozens" or "jiving"); *rhymes of work;* and *written traditional rhymes.* A few longer rhymed texts (including epic toasts or "toasties") qualify for the rather vague title *folk poetry.*

Nursery rhymes, although usually British in origin and often printed in their transmission, still play a role in American oral folk-lore. Parents may read "Mother Goose" to children out of books, but book-versions tend to vary significantly from text to text, and children alter them further as they repeat them.

At first, as children learn the rhymes by heart, they will rebel at any variation that is introduced into their favorites. Later, however, they delight in **parodies of nursery rhymes,** which range from such innocent humor as the spider saying to Miss Muffet, "Pardon me, is this seat taken?" or "Mary Mary, quite contrary" finding in her gar-den "one lousy petunia," all the way to such obscene parodies and grotesqueries as:

> Little Jack Horner
> Sat in a corner
> Eating his sister.

What may be the best-known verse in the English language, "Mary Had a Little Lamb," is also probably the most often parodied. It was composed by Mrs. Sarah Josepha Hale of Boston in 1830. It appeared by 1871 in the United States and by 1886 in England in journalistic parodies—a sure sign that readers were expected to be familiar with it. The themes of printed parodies clustered around subjects like Mary having different pets, or new clothes, desiring special food or drink, and the like; only a few suggested the risqué twist that oral parodies have taken. The following, for example, is from a college humor magazine of 1928:

> Mary had a little dress
> It was so light and airy;
> It never showed a speck of dust,
> But it showed just lots of Mary.

This has its counterpart in the oral parody:

> Mary had a little lamb,
> She also had a bear;
> I've often seen her little lamb,
> But I've never seen her bear.

Persistence of tradition is illustrated in the "Mary" parodies. The earliest recorded reference to the rhyme was a note in *Harper's Weekly* in 1869, discovered by folklorist C. Grant Loomis in which a child was reported to be confused about the "fleas as white as snow." Still known in oral tradition is the parody:

> Some folks say that fleas are black,
> But I'm not sure they know.
> 'Cause Mary had a little lamb,
> Whose fleas were white as snow.

A full collection of children's oral parodies of "Mary" would reveal some of their preoccupations. For instance, delight in wordplay and a dawning awareness of the facts of life are suggested in:

> Mary had a little lamb
> (Boy was the doctor surprised!)

Or, observe the abrupt shift from playing with a pet at home to the real business of going off to school (initiated by the domineering figure of a parent and supported by vigorous vernacular language) in this one:

> Mary had a little lamb,
> Her father shot it dead.
> Now Mary takes her lamb to school,
> Between two hunks of bread.

The contents of Mother Goose rhymes, as Archer Taylor has pointed out, are extremely broad, reflecting a great range of traditional sources that include lullabies (*Bye Baby Bunting*), finger rhymes (*Pat a Cake*), bouncing rhymes (*To Market, to Market, to Buy a Fat Pig*), story rhymes (*Old Mother Hubbard*), games (*Here We Go 'round the Mulberry Bush*), riddles (*Humpty Dumpty*), limericks (*Hickory Dickory Dock*), and even such types as charms, street cries, mnemonic devices, and traditional prayers. Ingenious and sometimes fantastic theories and interpretations have been offered for the origin and meaning of nursery rhymes, but about all that might be safely said is that many of them are very old, and some of them were certainly used (and perhaps invented) for political and social satire in Great Britain.

Most of the "explanations" offered for English nursery rhymes turn out to be what the best authorities on the genre (Iona and Peter Opie) characterize as "the work of the happy guessers." For instance, "Mary, Mary, quite contrary" is said to refer to Mary, Queen of Scots, and her ladies-in-waiting (the "four Marys" of balladry); the "cockleshells" are said to be decorations on a particular dress of the Queen's. One problem with this theory is that no version of the rhyme was found until some 150 years after Mary's beheading. On the other hand, there are some examples of "political squibs" in nursery rhymes, such as the use of "Jack Spratt" to ridicule an Archdeacon Pratt in the seventeenth century, and a popular rhyme that emerged in 1914 as a political cartoon with this text:

> Kaiser, Kaiser-gander, where do your men wander?
> Upstairs, downstairs, in my lady's chamber,
> Burning their cathedrals till they couldn't say their prayers,
> Then there came the British troops who flung them down the stairs.

Play rhymes begin a baby's social life with such highly amusing (to infants) activities as bouncing, finger and toe counting, and tickling to the accompaniment of chants such as "This is the Way the Farmer

Rides," "Here is the Church; Here is the Steeple," "This Little Piggy," and

> Ticklee, ticklee on the knee,
> If you laugh, you don't love me.

All these rhymes are performed in connection with gestures or other actions, thus combining simple motor activity with a rhythmic verse. The parent chants, "Round a bit, round a bit, like a wee mouse," while circling his finger in baby's palm; then he says, "Up a bit, up a bit, into the house," while running his fingers up baby's arm to tickle him under the chin. Later, the baby learns to perform the rhyme on himself or others. Another favorite group of rhymes assigns comical names to the features of the face—"chinchopper" and "eye-winker." In finger-and-toe counting rhymes, with their simple narrative plots, the child probably is expected to identify with the smallest digit, who not only "cried 'wee, wee, wee,' all the way home," but in other versions and other lands may be chastised as a glutton, a cry-baby, a tattletale, a prig, or a noisy nuisance who wakes up the big, strong thumb. As children grow more adept in their motions they master the more complex gestures that accompany rhymes like "Pease Porridge Hot," "Two Little Blackbirds," or "Eensy Weensy Spider."

Next, what one collector has called, "the *ars poetica* of children" manifests itself in **game rhymes.** Simplest is the basic trochaic beat of a bounce-ball-catch rhyme. ("Ĭvorў sóap/Seé ĭt flóat . . ."), followed in complexity by the rhymes that involve both bouncing and patting the ball, then making leg movements ("O Leary") and pantomime gestures or bouncing the ball to another child. When competitive games begin, the **counting-out rhyme** appears for choosing "it." The one beginning 'Eeny, meeny, miney, mo" is at once the most common and the most obscure in meaning of all counting-out rhymes; it may derive from the number system of some lost or minor language, but no convincing origin for it has yet been proposed. The rhyme has changed to suit the times, so that the offensive word "nigger" has yielded to "chigger," "tiger," "froggy," or "lawyer," who is caught by the toe. Children of many countries know variants fully as complicated as this American one:

> Eentery, meentery, cutery corn
> Apple seed and apple thorn
> Wire, briar, limber lock,
> Three geese in a flock.
> One flew east, and one flew west.
> One flew over the cuckoo's nest.
> **O-U-T** spells "out goes she!"

Jump-rope rhymes exhibit astonishing variety within a limited number of basic forms, and they frequently contain perceptive commentaries from a child's-eye view of the world. The simplest pattern is the *plain jump* game in which a child simply chants a rhyme to the rhythm of her jumping. More demanding is the *endurance jump* based on an open-end rhyme which continues until the jumper misses:

> I love coffee; I love tea,
> How many boys are stuck on me?
> One, two, three, four . . .

Endurance jumps frequently use *prophetic rhymes*, as above, or end "Yes-no-maybe," or with a series of colors, or with the alphabet. Social comment is specific in the following example in which the young jumper is watching her older sister primp:

> Grace, Grace, dressed in lace,
> Went upstairs to powder her face.
> How many boxes did she use?
> One, two, three, four . . .

The game of *speed jump* is set off by such words as "pepper," "hot," or "fire" in a rhyme; then the rope is twirled with ever-increasing speed until the jumper misses. Most complicated of all are *action rhymes* which require the jumper to imitate the behavior of the subject of the verse—usually "Teddy Bear"—as he touches the ground, turns around, goes upstairs, says his prayers, and so forth. Finally, there are *call-in, call-out rhymes* to signal changing jumper during a group game.

The list of characters frequently mentioned in jump-rope rhymes is peculiar. While "Mickey Mouse" and "Teddy Bear" (or sometimes "Yogi Bear") seem suitable for the context, what is the reason for the continuing popularity of "Shirley Temple," "Betty Grable," and that shadowy figure in popular rhymes, "the lady with the alligator purse"? Several past motion picture stars and other historical personages, too early for most of today's rope-jumpers to remember in action, live on in their rhymes:

> Charlie Chaplin went to France,
> To teach the ladies how to dance;

It is clear that "Teddy Bear," originally referring to Theodore Roosevelt, is now to the jump-rope rhymes what the littlest pig is to the toe-counting verse. The child sees himself and his beloved stuffed toy suppressed in a world that is tyrannically ruled by harsh adults, in a rhyme like the following:

> Teddy on the railroad, pickin' up stones,
> Along came a train and broke Teddy's bones.
> "Oh," said Teddy, "that's not fair!"
> "Oh," said the engineer, "I don't care!"

And for a nutshell summary of the course of life, what could be clearer than this:

> First comes love, then comes marriage,
> Then comes Judy with a baby carriage.

Rhymes too numerous to list accompany other games and recreations; they are usually gathered and studied in connection with the games themselves. A typical game of "Hide and Seek" illustrates this. First there is a counting-out rhyme to select "it." The designated child then covers his eyes and counts in a formula manner to a specified number before calling out "Bushel of wheat, bushel or rye/Who's not ready holler 'I' " or "Bushel of wheat, bushel of clover/Who's not ready can't hide over." When he tags a hider, "it" calls out one saying or rhyme, but if a hider slips in safely, he can cry a rhyme of his own, calling the others in "free." Other games may have more or less rhyme content than this, but nearly all active folk games have some rhyme attached to them; amusements like the following are little more than a rhyme followed by appropriate behavior:

> Order in the courtroom, monkey wants to speak,
> First one to speak is a monkey for a week.

A vast number of rhymes have no connection with organized play or games at all, but are simply recited for the pure fun of it. Even so, there may be some underlying sense to the most nonsensical of them:

> I sent my boy to college,
> With a pat on the back.
> I spent ten thousand dollars,
> But I got a quarterback.
>
> *
>
> Marriage for me in '73
> Marriage for sure in '74
> Anything alive in '75

Many are **topical rhymes:**

> Roosevelt's in the White House
> Waiting to be elected.
> Wilkie's in the garbage can,
> Waiting to be collected.

Some fun rhymes are **parody rhymes,** often of religious texts such as prayers, hymns, and blessings:

> Good food, good meat,
> Good God, let's eat!
>
> *
>
> Now I lay me down to sleep,
> Bedbugs all around me creep.
> If they bite before I wake,
> I pray the Lord their jaws will break.

Some parodies of old school recitations are in rhyme:

> The boy stood on the burning deck,
> Melting with the heat.
> His big blue eyes were full of tears,
> And his shoes were full of feet.

Other rhymed recitations are pure nonsense rather than parodies:

> Ladies and gentlemen, hoboes and tramps,
> Crosseyed mosquitoes, bowlegged ants,
> I now tell you something I know nothing about.
> Last night about 3 o'clock this morning,
> An empty truck load of bricks drove up my front back alley,

And ran over my poor dead cat and half killed her.
I rushed her to the hospital as slow as I could go,
And there I saw Gene Autry eating vinegar with a pitchfork.

But most **nonsense orations** are composed in a sort of surrealistic free verse:

Ladies and jellyfish, I come here not to dress you.or undress you,
but to address you as to how Christopher Cockeyed Cucumber
crossed the Missisloppi River with the Declaration of Indigestion in
one hand and the Star Speckled bannaner in the other. . . .

Athletic cheers form a pattern for further parodies, such as this effete revision of a popular one, "Retard them, retard them/Make them relinquish the ball," or this bilingual gem from Wisconsin:

Lutefisk, lefse,
Takk skal du ha.
Soughton High School
Rah! Rah! Rah!

Many fun rhymes reflect nothing more than pure boredom, day-dreaming, and release:

Spring is sprung, the grass is riz,
I wonder where the birdies is.

*

Squirrel, squirrel on the ground,
You don't make a single sound
I know why so still you are,
You've been flattened by a car.

*

If I was the President of the United States
I'd eat molasses candy and swing on all the gates.

*

Said Aaron to Moses,
"Let's cut off our noses."
Said Moses to Aaron,
"It's the fashion to wear 'em."

Other nonsense rhymes are **circular rhymes;** among the best known are the dialect pieces beginning "My name is Yon Yonson," and "Where do you worka John?" which advance a story for a few lines that lead right back to the opening line and repetitions *ad infinitum*.

A curious form of nonsense rhyme is the so-called **spelling-riddle,** really only another fun rhyme. "How do you spell 'snapping turtle'?"

> Snopey, snappin'
> Fat an' tickin'
> Tortle, tortle,
> Snappin' turtle.

Rhymes of derision may be classified as fun rhymes, fun at least for the ones who chant them against fat kids, skinny kids, weak kids, foreign kids, kids who wear glasses, sissies, tattle-tales, and all the other unfortunates of a child's world. Let a youngster acquire a sweetheart, and someone is sure to amuse himself with "Johnny's got a girl-friend" sung to a well-known tune, or the rhyme:

> Johnny's mad, and I'm glad,
> And I know what'll please him.
> A bottle of ink to make him stink
> And _____ to squeeze him.

Similarly, **rhymed retorts** are delivered:

> What's your name?
> —Puddin-tane
> Ask me again and I'll tell you the same.
> *
> Do you like Jelly?
> —I'll punch you in the belly.
> *
> See my finger?
> See my thumb?
> See my fist?
> You better run!

Ritualized **rhymed insults,** usually directed at another's mother, are nearly restricted to the black tradition of "sounding" or "playing the dozens." Mild examples of dozens, which are often quite obscene (the "dirty dozens"), are:

> I can tell by your eyes,
> You've been eatin' welfare pies.
> *

I can tell by your hair,
Your father was a grizzly bear.

*

Fee, fie, fo, fum,
Your mother's a bum.

*

I can tell by your toes,
Your mother wears brogues.

A second type of mostly black folk verse is the "toast," not primarily a drinking stanza or compliment as much as a longer narrative or editorial rhymed recitation.

What might be called **work rhymes** are gradually disappearing from American life, and they have always tended to shade off into folksongs. This category includes various rhymes associated with a particular trade, craft, or calling; they function as advertising, or for retaining useful information, for maintaining the rhythm of work, or simply to ease strain and weariness.

Peddlers' cries (or "street cries") and newsboys' calls—chanted or sung—were once heard regularly on many American streets from fresh fruit and vegetable men, rag and bone collectors, fish mongers, refreshment dispensers, and other wandering hawkers; but now most street vendors, except for ice cream salesmen, have been replaced by supermarkets; even the "Good Humor Man" now relies on bells or recorded music to announce his arrival. Old-time peddlers' cries are rarely heard, or an occasional informant may recall how they used to sound. The words were generally very simple—mere lists of the goods offered:

Green corn and tomatoes
Sweet and Irish potatoes.

*

Blackberries, blackberries,
Fresh and fine,
Just off the vine.

The rhymes were often imperfect, the form loose and the words improvised from a stock of commonplaces. Sometimes a claim for the product's qualities was included in the cry:

> Hot tamales, floatin' in gravy,
> Suit your taste and I don't mean maybe.
>
> *
>
> Watermelons, come and see,
> Every one sold with a guarantee.
>
> *
>
> Ice cold lemonade!
> Freeze your teeth, curl your hair,
> Make you feel like a millionaire.

In Texas, and perhaps elsewhere, the story was told of an Italian street peddler who was weak in English and so followed an American hawker around calling out, "Same-a-ting! Same-a-ting!"

Planting rhymes have also been driven aside by automation; no powered corn drill needs anyone to chant "One for the blackbird/One for the crow . . ." or any of its numerous continuations and variants. Other such rhymes contained the traditional dates for planting certain crops, information now secured from a government bulletin or a county farm adviser:

> Plant pumpkin seeds in May,
> And they will all run away.
> Plant pumpkin seeds in June,
> And they will come soon.

Verses for rhythmic group work—sea chanteys, chain-gang hollers, chopping and pounding songs, and so forth—usually were delivered in a two-part call-and-response pattern, with a leader initiating the call or song and the community of workers chorusing back the response. One Afro-American rhyme for shifting railroad ties went:

> Oh, shove 'em up solid,
> Up solid and sound,
> So the big Nine-Hundred, boys,
> Cannot whop him down.

Although many of these types are dead or dying now, circus roustabouts used them until recently when hoisting the big tops, and one such practice remains vigorous in **military cadence chants:**

> *Leader:* You had a good home but you left.
> *Chorus:* You're right!

> *Leader:* Jody was there when you left.
> *Chorus:* You're right!

The "left-rights," of course, must fall on the proper feet for the march; the name "Jody," which occurs frequently, represents the civilian men back home who enjoy the good life that paratroops secure for them. Comments on army life and discipline are also popular:

> Ain't no need in lookin' down,
> Ain't no discharge on the ground.

(A more recent version, heard in Joseph Wiseman's film *Basic Training:*

> Uncle Dicky, drop the bomb—
> I don't want to go to "Nam.")

*

> Airborne, airborne, where you been?
> Round the world and gone again.
> What you gonna do when you get back?
> Run again with a full field pack.

Some traditional admonitions in rhyme (often incorporating folk beliefs) might simply be termed **rhymed advice:**

> If he has one white foot, buy him,
> If two, try him,
> Three, deny him,
> Four white feet and a white nose,
> Take off his hide and feed him to the crows.
>   —(Advice for buying horses)

Although they are seldom transmitted orally, certain **written rhymes** qualify as folklore on the grounds of traditionality, variation, and anonymity. For example, verses found carved on old powder horns often turn out to be variants of this one:

> I powder with my brother ball,
> A hero like I conquer all.
> The rose is red, the grass is green,
> The years are past which I have seen.

Other powder-horn rhymes commemorate the designer or owner of the horn, and may advertise the latter's prowess:

The man who steals this horn,
Will go to Hell, so sure as he is born.
I James Fenwick of Ogdensburg
Did the year of 1817 kill 30 wolf,
10 bear, 15 deer
And 46 partridges.

Similar traditional verses are sometimes found on hope chests, jewel boxes, snuff boxes, and the like.

Epitaphs, especially humorously facetious or ironical ones, may be traditional, as is the following:

Pass on stranger, don't waste your time,
O'er bad biography or bitter rhyme,
For what I am this crumbling clay insures,
And what I was is no concern of yours.

The flyleaves of old textbooks are another source of written traditional rhymes; **flyleaf inscriptions** may be simple statements like: "In case of flood, stand on this; it's dry," but often they are traditional admonitions in rhyme:

If by chance this book should roam,
Box its ears and send it home.

*

Don't steal this book
My little lad,
For fifty cents,
It cost my dad;
And when you die
The lord will say,
"Where is that book,
You stole one day?"
And when you say,
You do not know,
The lord will say,
"Go down below!"

One curious inscription found written over the ten commandments in a school book dated 1832 reveals its rhymed message when a letter "e" is inserted for each dot:

P.RS.V.R.Y.P.RF.CTM.N
.V.RK..PTH.S.PR.C.PTST.N

Graffiti—writings on public walls—are frequently traditional, sometimes rhymed, but most often take the form of witty prose commentaries:

> Death is nature's way of telling you to slow down.
>
> *
>
> Ask God in prayer and she will answer.

A related form, **desk-top inscriptions** (or "horizontal graffiti") may comment on the school or college situation:

> I came, I saw, I laughed.
>
> *
>
> Professional absentee sits here.

or involve some whimsical trick writing:

THGUAC M'I PLEH
REDNU GNIHTEMOS NO
KSED SIHT

Autograph rhymes (or "Friendship verses") constitute the largest, most varied, and most enduring category of written American folk rhymes. Enjoying a great vogue in the late nineteenth century, autograph books then were elegant; the writings in them tended to be pious and sentimental:

> Remember well and bear in mind,
> A constant friend is hard to find,
> But when you get one, kind and true
> Forsake not the old one for the new.
>
> *
>
> Our lives are albums written through,
> With good or ill, with false or true,
> And as the blessed Angels turn,
> The pages of your years,
> God grant they read the good with smiles,
> And blot the bad with tears.

But even then whimsical verses began to appear—often comments on the writing of such verses, or on marriage:

Some write for pleasure,
Some write for fame,
But I write simply,
To sign my name.

*

When you get married and cannot see,
Put on your specks and think of me!

*

As you slide down the bannister of life,
I hope you don't get a splinter in your career.

The "When you get married" verse with the "Yours 'til . . ." sign-off is still a favorite autograph gimmick, rivaled recently by such novelty inscriptions as these:

Two sat in a hammock
About to kiss,
When all of a sudden,
It went like sıɥʇ.

*

Don't be ♯
Don't be ♭
Just be ♮

*

Y Y U R
Y Y U B
I C U R
Y Y 4 Me

The enduring long-term favorite autograph-book rhyme, whether "straight" or in parody, is "Roses are red/Violets are blue. . . ."

Folk Poetry is a term that has been very broadly applied, ranging from a description of the proverb as "A one-line folk poem" to consideration of lengthy folksong texts as poems. A reasonable limitation of the term might be to use it for "longer" folk rhymes (usually more than one stanza), especially those that are not connected with a specific game or work, such as many Afro-American toasts which, like "Shine," or "The Titanic" reach nearly epic proportions. The traditional *limerick*, which is usually off-color and hence circulated orally, is a familiar example of folk poetry:

There was an old lady from Kent,
Whose nose was most awfully bent.
She followed her nose,
One day I suppose,
And nobody knows where she went.

The Spanish-American *memoria*—newspaper verses memorializing the dead—have been considered to be folk poetry, leading folklorist T. M. Pearce, an investigator of this and other local verse, to propose this definition of a folk poet:

> He writes often of community events and personalities associated with them and of manifestations of natural forces with effects upon society. He writes of the experiences of individuals when such happenings offer occasion for joy or sorrow to groups of relatives and friends or acquaintances. His poetic forms (metrical and stanzaic) are traditional, sometimes irregular or modified in the direction of informal and freer communication. His poetic idiom is stamped with expressions describing group feeling and thought.

This definition could embrace the soldiers of the First World War who composed rhymed chronicles of their experiences, such as the following fragments of a long piece written in a notebook by a retired Indiana railroad man:

In the year of 1918, April the 26th day,
I joined the American army to help whip Germany.
I spent four weeks at camp Taylor in the city of Louisville,
There they dressed me in khaki and taught me how to drill.

*

In fourteen days I had eight meals,
And most of them, I fed the seals.
Most of the way it was very cool.
July the 10th we arrived at Liverpool.

*

There we seen hard fighting, also done our bits,
Sending over three-inch shells, making each one a good hit.
For two weeks we advanced continually through the Hindenburg line,
And our intentions were very great for reaching the River Rhine.
The huns made no resistance, they knew they couldn't win.
They kept right on retreating away from us fighting men.

*

The 11th of November we had them on the hop
When they gave us orders at eleven o'clock to stop.
But we were not sorry, a happy bunch were we,
To know the war was over and we had won the victory.

One long poetic text—the Twenty-third Psalm—has inspired many full-length parodies. Certainly there is a traditional process operating when so many different versions of this verse circulate around themes such as the Model-T Ford ("The Ford is my auto, I shall not want another/ It maketh me to lie down in mud puddles . . .") and the Great Depression ("Mr. Roosevelt is my shepherd, I am in want/ he maketh me to lie down on park benches . . ." or "The Welfare Board is my shepherd, I shall not want another/ It maketh me work in the road ditches . . .") and so forth. Most of the twenty-third Psalm parodies are conservative, pious, and anti-big government in tone; several of them are commentaries on recent American presidents.

Clearly the folk poets of our culture, whoever they are, in common with the recognized art poets, respond to both personal emotions and social conditions in their works. And at the present time in history, when formal poetry has discarded nearly every restraint of the past masters, and Tin Pan Alley composers may touch upon the most serious and immediate problems—often employing folksong forms— it becomes virtually impossible to draw hard and fast lines around art, popular, or folk poetry.

BIBLIOGRAPHIC NOTES

There is no book-length collection of general American folk rhymes to compare with Thomas Talley's specialized work *Negro Folk Rhymes* (New York: Macmillan, 1922). Duncan Emrich's *American Folk Poetry* (Boston: Little, Brown, 1974) is really an anthology of the lyrics of American folksongs. Interesting popular collections are Carl Withers's *A Rocket in My Pocket: The Rhymes and Chants of Young America* (New York: Henry Holt, 1948), Lillian Morison's *A Diller A Dollar: Rhymes and Sayings for the Ten O'clock Scholar* (New York: Crowell, 1955), and Ian Turner, *Cinderella Dressed in Yella: Australian Children's Play-Rhymes* (Melbourne: Heinemann Educational Publications, 1969) which has a good introduction, thorough annotation, and a surprising number of parallels to American rhymes.

Some general compendiums of folklore have sections of rhymes; Paul G. Brewster edited them for the *Frank C. Brown Collection of North Carolina Folklore*, vol. I (Durham, N.C.: Duke University Press, 1952), pp. 160–219.

Kansas Folklore (Lincoln: University of Nebraska Press, 1961), ed. Samuel J. Sackett and William E. Koch, has two chapters of folk verse (pp. 116–37). A representative special collection is Ruth Ann Musick and Vance Randolph's "Children's Rhymes from Missouri," *JAF* 63 (1950), 425–37.

Iona and Peter Opie's *The Oxford Dictionary of Nursery Rhymes* (New York: Oxford University Press, 1951) is the standard work on that genre, providing bibilography and evaluations of the many interpretations of Mother Goose. Archer Taylor's succinct and useful survey "What is 'Mother Goose'?" appeared in *NMFR* 2 (1947–48), 7–13. Nursery rhyme parodies are discussed by C. Grant Loomis in "Mary Had a Parody: A Rhyme of Childhood in Folk Tradition," *WF* 17 (1958), 45–51; and by Joseph Hickerson and Alan Dundes in "Mother Goose Vice Verse," *JAF* 75 (1962), 249–59.

Sam M. Shiver's "Finger Rhymes" in *SFQ* 5 (1941), 221–34, presents an interesting comparative survey of foreign, mostly German, and some English texts. Marian Hansen gathers "Children's Rhymes Accompanied by Gestures" in *WF* 7 (1948), 50–53. Dorothy Howard has written many fine articles on children's folklore, among them "The Rhythms of Ball-Bouncing and Ball-Bouncing Rhymes," *JAF* 62 (1949), 166–72.

Counting-out rhymes held the interest of some early folklorists in America, among them Henry Carrington Bolton, who published a classic book, *The Counting-Out Rhymes of Children* (New York: Appleton, 1888; repr. Detroit: Singing Tree Press, 1969); Bolton published an article with the same title during the same year in Volume 1 of *JAF* (31–37). Later notes on counting-out rhymes appeared in *JAF* 2 (1889), 113–16, and *JAF* 10 (1897), 313–21. Still later, an important Midwestern collector, Emelyn E. Gardner, published "Some Counting-Out Rhymes in Michigan," *JAF* 31 (1918), 521–36.

Roger D. Abrahams's *Jump-Rope Rhymes: A Dictionary* (Austin, Texas: AFS Bibiographic and Special Series, vol. 20, 1969) gathers numerous examples and compiles a thorough bibliography of previously published sources which need not be listed here again. The classification of jump-rope rhymes used in this chapter was suggested by Bruce R. Buckley in *KFO* 11 (1966), 99–111. Ed Cray includes previously unpublished variants (which, therefore, are not listed in Abrahams's work) in "Jump-Rope Rhymes from Los Angeles," *WF* 29 (1970), 119–27.

Paul G. Brewster collected " 'Spelling Riddles' from the Ozarks," in *SFQ* 8 (1944), 301–3. Kenneth W. Porter collected references from earlier published notes, and he classified various texts of "Circular Jingles and Repetitious Rhymes" in *WF* 17 (1958), 107–11; George Monteiro performed the same service for "Parodies of Scripture, Prayer, and Hymn," in *JAF* 77 (1964), 45–52. See also Kenneth W. Porter, "Humor, Blasphemy, and Criticism in the Grace Before Meat," *NYFQ* 21 (1965), 3–18.

The game of playing the dozens is discussed by Roger D. Abrahams in *JAF* 75 (1962), 209–20, and by Guy Owen in *NCFJ* 21 (1973), 53–54. Some similar material from white informants was included in Anna K. Stimson's "Cries of Defiance and Derision, and Rhythmic Chants of West Side New York City, 1893–1903," *JAF* 58 (1945), 124–29, and in Millicent R. Ayoub and Stephen

A. Barnett's "Ritualized Verbal Insult in White High School Culture," *JAF* 78 (1965), 337–44. The publications dealing with toasts are listed in the bibliography of Bruce Jackson's collection and study titled *Get Your Ass in the Water and Swim Like Me: Narrative Poetry from Black Oral Tradition* (Cambridge, Mass.: Harvard University Press, 1974). Jackson wrote a negative response to the article by Dennis Wepman, Ronald B. Newman, and Murray B. Binderman, "Toasts: The Black Urban Folk Poetry" in *JAF* 87 (1974), 208–24, which appeared in the next volume of *JAF* along with a rejoinder by the original authors.

Street cries have been published in numerous scattered sources; among them are Elizabeth Hurley's Texas collection "Come Buy, Come Buy" in *PTFS* 25 (1953), 115–38; Edward Pinkowski's "Philadephia Street Cries" in *KFQ* 5 (1960), 10–12; Laurilynn McGill's "The Street Cry as an Artistic Verbal Performance," *Folklore Annual* 3 (1971), 17–25; and Richardson L. Wright's *Hawkers and Walkers in Early America* (New York: F. Ungar Publishing Co., 1927, repr. 1965), Chapter XV.

Kenneth Porter discusses the familiar "Corn-Planting Rhyme" ["One for the blackbird . . ."] in *WF* 17 (1958), 205–7. A collection of Afro-American work chants is William R. Ferris, Jr., "Railroad Chants: Form and Function," *MFR* 4 (1970), 1–14. George G. Carey, himself a former paratrooper, prepared "A Collection of Airborne Cadence Chants" for *JAF* 78 (1965), 52–61.

Rhymes from old powder horns were illustrated and discussed by W. M. Beauchamp in *JAF* 2 (1889), 117–22, and *JAF* 5 (1892), 284–90. Epitaphs were discussed by D. P. Penhallow in *JAF* 5 (1892), 305–17; northern California epitaphs were printed by Kennth W. Clarke in *WF* 20 (1961), 238, and *WF* 21 (1962), 146. An interesting chapter on "Flyleaf Scribblings" was included in Clifton Johnson's *Old-Time Schools and School-Books* (New York: Macmillan, 1904, reissued in paperback by Dover Publications in 1963); the chapter was also reprinted in *What They Say in New England*, edited from Clifton Johnson's various folklore publications by Carl Withers (New York: Columbia University Press, 1963), pp. 196–206. An early note on the same subject was Fanny D. Bergen's "Flyleaf Rhymes and Decorations," *New England Magazine*, n.s. 23 (1901), 505–11, which contains variants of several references quoted by Johnson. A more recent discussion is Robert H. Woodward's "Folklore Marginalia in Old Textbooks," *NYFQ* 18 (1962), 24–27.

Graffiti have recently been the subject of both scholarly and popularized treatments. A casual survey of much typical wall writing is Norton Mockridge's *The Scrawl of the Wild: What People Write on Walls–and Why* (Cleveland and New York: World Publishing Co., 1968). A lavish production with examples in color and an interpretation written by Norman Mailer is *The Faith of Graffiti* (New York: Praeger, 1974). Alan Dundes studied just toilet graffiti, coining a new term for them, in "Here I Sit—A Study of American Latrinalia," *Kroeber Anthropological Society Papers* no. 34 (Spring 1966), 91–94, reprinted in *Analytic Essays in Folklore*, pp. 177–91. In "The Growth of Graffiti," 7 (1974), 273–75, Mac E. Barrick analyzes thirty-two additions to a single graffito written in a men's room of the Duke University library; further campus examples are discussed in Patricia A. Mastick, "The Function of Political Graffiti as Artistic Creativity," *NYFQ* 27 (1971), 280–96. Terrance L. Stocker, Linda W. Dutcher, Stephen M. Hargrove, and Edwin A. Cook present a comprehensive bibliography of studies and a most ambitious analysis in their article "Social Analysis of Graffiti" in *JAF* 85 (1972), 356–66. Introducing a category of graffiti neither obscene nor humorous is Sylvia Ann Grider, "*Con Safos:* Mexican-Americans, Names and Graffiti," *JAF* 88 (1975), 132–42.

Alan Dundes has thoroughly surveyed the bibliography of friendship verses in "Some Examples of Infrequently Reported Autograph Verse," *SFQ* 26 (1962), 127–30. Two representative older collections are Vance Randolph and May Kennedy McCord's "Autograph Albums in the Ozarks," *JAF* 61 (1948), 182–93, in which a useful classification of these rhymes is offered; and Lelah Allison's "Traditional Verse from Autograph Books," *HF* 8 (1949), 87–94, in which Gay Nineties and modern verse are compared. W. K. McNeil has recently published three important articles on the subject: "The Autograph Album Custom: A Tradition and Its Scholarly Treatment," *KFQ* 13 (1968), 29–40; "From Advice to Laments: New York Autograph Album Verse: 1820–1850," *NYFQ* 25 (1969), 175–94; and the continuation of the latter article to 1850–1900 in *NYFQ* 26 (1970), 163–203. Stephen Stern reports on interviews with those who write in and collect autograph books in his article "Autograph Memorabilia as an Output of Social Interaction and Communication," *NYFQ* 29 (1973), 219–39. A related area of tradition is described in Steven J. Zeitlin's "As Sweet As You Are; the Structural Elements in the Signed High School Yearbook," *NYFQ* 30 (1974), 83–100.

The quotation from T. M. Pearce in this chapter comes from his "What is a Folk Poet?" published in *WF* 12 (1953), 242–48; Rubén Cobos supplemented some of Pearce's assertions in "The New Mexican *memoria,* or In Memoriam Poem," in *WF* 18 (1959), 25–30. Further examples of Mexican-American folk poetry appear in Inez Cardozo-Freeman, "Arnulfo Castillo, Mexican Folk Poet in Ohio," *JOFS* 1 (1972), 2–28, and John Donald Robb, "H. V. Gonzales: Folk Poet of New Mexico," *NMFR* 13 (1973–74), 1–6.

The passages quoted above from the World War I rhymed chronicle were collected by me from Clarence E. ("Old Hickory") Pierson in Bloomington, Indiana, on August 8, 1959; Elsie Clews Parsons discussed similar folk poems in her note, "War Verses," in *JAF* 47 (1934), 395. Américo Paredes reviewed the concept of folk poetry in his article "Some Aspects of Folk Poetry" in *TSLL* 6 (1964), 213–25; he saw the subject as ranging from the proverb to the folksong and drew comparisons between "The Maid Freed from the Gallows" and Shakespeare's Sonnet 73 ("That time of year thou mayst in me behold") to illustrate his points. Two studies of individual folk poetry composers are Edward D. Ives's *Laurence Doyle, The Farmer Poet of Prince Edward Island* (Orno, Me.: University of Maine Studies, no. 92, 1971), and Steven A. Schulman, "Howess Dewey Winfrey: The Rejected Songmaker," *JAF* 87 (1974), 72–84. An example of the traditional recitation, a neglected genre of folk poetry, is given in *AFFword* 2 (1972), 38–39; the piece is titled "The Volunteer Organist."

G. Legman published his essay "The Limerick: A History in Brief" in *The Horn Book* (New Hyde Park, N.Y.: University Books, 1964), pp. 427–53. Legman's definitive collection *The Limerick: 1700 Examples, With Notes, Variants, and Index,* originally published in France and long a rare book, was reprinted recently (New York: Bell Publishing Co., 1974). A most engagingly written popular survey is William S. Baring-Gould's *The Lure of the Limerick: An Uninhibited History* (New York: Clarkson N. Potter, 1967).

The presidential parody of the Twenty-third Psalm appears in Ed Cray, "The Quadrennial Perennials" *WF* 24 (1965), 199–201. Further examples appear in Gray Alan Fine, "In Search of the Quadrennial Perennials," *FF* 7 (1974), 203–5, and in Mac E. Barrick, "The Presidential Psalm," *FF* 8 (1975), 357–60.

8

Myths and Legends

Traditional prose narratives—that is, oral stories—often loosely termed "folktales," constitute one of the largest and most complex branches of folklore. These narratives include stories that are regarded as true, called "myths" and "legends," and stories that are regarded as fictional, properly called by the term "folktales." Myths are distinguished from legends (as anthropologist William Bascom has formulated it) by the attitudes of storytellers toward them, the settings described in them, and their principal characters. Myths are regarded as sacred, and legends as either sacred or secular; myths are set in the remote past in the otherworld or an earlier world, and legends in the historical past; myths have as their principal characters gods or animals, while legends generally have humans in the major roles.

Myths, then, may be defined as traditional "prose narratives, which, in the society in which they are told, are considered to be truthful accounts of what happened in the remote past." Typically they deal with the activities of gods and demigods, the creation of the world and its inhabitants, and the origins of religious rituals. Whenever myths purport to explain such matters as origins of geographic features, animal traits, rites, taboos, and customs, they are known as *explanatory* or *etiological* narratives.

There is some difficulty in using these terms and distinctions since "myth" has acquired other specialized meanings among literary critics, historians, and philosophers. Furthermore, it is not always possible to establish absolutely whether a given narrative is a folktale, legend, or myth. Another problem arises with religious narratives in our own culture; are such biblical stories as those of the Creation, the Flood, the Last Supper, and the Resurrection, *myths?* According to the definition, they seem to be; they also display the basic folklore quality of having variants in other cultures. But the biblical narratives of printed scripture cannot meet all of the tests for folklore since they do not circulate in oral tradition, and they are sustained by formal in-doctrination. Thus, we may say that modern Americans—or any liter-ate people with an unvarying scriptural basis for their religion—have no myths, in the folkloristic sense. The only true American myths are the native Indian religious narratives, which were orally transmitted and which developed variant forms. Also, ironically, some Christian stories were picked up by the Indians and retold in varying forms, sometimes joining with native myths.

There are good reasons for American folklorists to be concerned with myths, whether the so-called *primitive myths* of prehistoric cul-tures and modern preliterate peoples, the *oriental myths* of India and the Far East, or the familiar *occidental myths* of the classical world and ancient northern Europe. Among these three bodies of world myth there are certain themes that recur again and again, raising dif-ficult questions of origin and dissemination. Fantastic and grotesque elements that have widespread distribution in myths are especially puzzling. Another enigma is the relatively limited number of distinct *forms* of myths, the texts of which may vary greatly in their specific *details*.

These points may be illustrated by turning to one of the most comprehensive general reference works in folklore studies, Stith Thompson's *Motif-Index of Folk-Literature*. The contents and the broad scope of this encyclopedic six-volume work are indicated in its subtitle, "A Classification of Narrative Elements in Folktales, Ballads, Myths, Fables, Mediaeval Romances, Exempla, Fabliaux, Jest-Books and Local Legends." A **motif,** or "narrative element," from these traditional texts is any striking or unusual unit recurring in them; it may be an object (such as a magic wand), a marvelous animal (such as a speaking horse), a concept (such as a taboo, or forbidden act), an ac-tion (such as a test or a deception), a character (such as a giant, an ogre, or a fairy godmother), a character-type (such as a fool or a prophet), or a structural quality (such as formulistic numbers or cu-mulative repetition). Thousands of such elements are arranged in the *Motif-Index* according to a systematic plan, along with bibliographic references to their occurrences in collected texts. (A fair number, however, exist as separate oral narratives, sometimes termed one-motif tales.) Use of the work is facilitated by detailed synopses before each of the twenty-three chapters, numerous cross-references throughout it, and an alphabetical "index to the *Index*" in the sixth volume. Although the *Motif-Index* is primarily used in studies of folktales, it has applications for analyzing myths and the other forms that were excerpted for it as well.

Motifs from myths are scattered throughout the *Index*, but the predominantly mythological motifs are contained in Chapter "A" under the following broad divisions:

Ao—A99.	Creator
A100—A499.	Gods
A500—A599.	Demigods and culture heroes
A600—A899.	Cosmogony and cosmology
A900—A999.	Topographical features of the earth
A1000—A1099.	World calamities
A1100—A1199.	Establishment of natural order
A1200—A1699.	Creation and ordering of human life
A1700—A2199.	Creation of animal life
A2200—A2599.	Animal characteristics
A2600—A2699.	Origin of trees and plants
A2700—A2799.	Origin of plant characteristics
A2800—A2899.	Miscellaneous explanations

These thirteen general categories of mythological motifs are subdivided into numerous specific categories that are numbered in groups of tens. For example, A1200—A1299. "Creation of man," is broken down as follows in the synopsis:

A1210.	Creation of man by creator
A1220.	Creation of man through evolution
A1230.	Emergence or descent of first man to earth
A1240.	Man made from mineral substance
A1250.	Man made from vegetable substance
A1260.	Mankind made from miscellaneous materials
A1270.	Primeval human pair
A1290.	Creation of man—other motifs

As can be seen above between A1270. and A1290., Thompson sometimes skipped numbers in the *Motif-Index* to allow for adding further groups of motifs. Also, within each chapter (which in this in-

stance contains 279 pages of closely printed motif entries) the sub-
divisions are made infinitely expandable by a system of "points." Thus
motif A1266. is "Man created after series of unsuccessful experiments," and A1226.1. is the more specific motif "Creator makes man
out of butter first; it would not stand up and melted." If a new myth
were discovered in which man were made out of margarine first,
then, considering this as a variant of butter, the number * A1226.1.1.
could be added; but if a new material, say chocolate, were used for a
succession of creations, number * A1226.2. would be appropriate.
(Whenever a new motif number is created, it is designated with a
"star" until it appears in a revised edition of the master index.) It
might also be noted that two cross-references appear under A1226.,
numbers A630. "Series of creations," and A1401. "Culture originated
by previous race of man." Thompson's bibliographic references indicate that the concept of a series of unsuccessful experiments to
create man is found in myths from Greece, Latin America, and the
Banks Islands in the Pacific New Hebrides; the unsuccessful creation
out of butter is found in a myth from India. These references do not
establish, of course, that there is any historical relationship between
these similar myth-motifs, although further research may suggest that
there is.

The varied and sometimes fantastic nature of mythological motifs is
shown in the *Motif-Index* in the materials out of which man is said to
have been made. The mineral substances include sand sprinkled with
water, earth reddened with animal blood, stones, ice, shells, and
metals. Vegetable substances indexed include trees and wood, fruit,
nuts, seeds, sugar-cane stalks, ears of corn, herbs, and grass. In some
mythological explanations of the creation of man the raw material
comes from the body of the creator himself—his sweat (the Lithuanians); his spittle (the Lithuanians and in Oceanic myths); or even a
broken-off toenail (the Indians of Brazil). The *Motif-Index* lists parallels for the Judaic-Christian explanation that man was made from clay
or other earth in Hindu, Babylonian, Greek, Irish, Siberian, Chinese, Polynesian, Indonesian, Australian, Eskimo, North and South
American Indian, and Aztec mythology. Again, it must be borne in
mind that listing such parallels does not presuppose any necessary
historical connection between these bodies of mythology. Some of
these particular parallels, in fact, must predate Judaism and Chris-

tianity, while others were probably influenced directly by missionaries.

Although certainly questions of oral tradition are being considered in them, the many studies of primitive myths made by anthropologists do not directly relate to a survey of Anglo-American folklore; nor do most of the literary, linguistic, psychoanalytical, or structural studies of myths. But a direct connection between the study of primitive or literary myths and of modern folklore lies in the elements these narratives share with folktales, and in the theories that were derived from early studies investigating the origin of myths and their relationship to tales.

The history of theories of myth origins is essentially the history of attempts to account for similar elements in different bodies of mythology and similarities between myths and folktales. In story after story—whether myth or tale—heroes are set difficult tasks to perform, they slay monsters, and they receive royal gifts as rewards; women sometimes marry animals that often turn out to be transformed humans; food or other necessities are magically provided, and characters go on long voyages and sometimes return unrecognized. Basically only two explanations are possible for such parallels: they may be the result of *polygenesis*, the independent invention of the same materials in different places, or of *diffusion*, the single invention at one place of an item that was then transmitted to other regions.

It is noteworthy that those pioneer folktale scholars, Jakob and Wilhelm Grimm of nineteenth-century Germany, perceived both possibilities and selected diffusion, which still has more favor among folklorists, as the better explanation. The Brothers Grimm theorized that folktales, such as those they collected in Germany, were *broken-down myths* that had originated among the prehistoric Indo-European tribes and had been disseminated during their migrations throughout Europe. The difficulty of supporting the theory, of course, is that Indo-European is entirely a hypothetical language, as are its supposed speakers and their culture.

A second nineteenth-century theory drew further on the advancing study of comparative linguistics for its evidence. It was championed by another German "philologist," or what we would now call a linguist, Max Müller, an Oxford University professor. When Sanskrit came to be recognized as the key language of the Indo-European family, Müller compared the names of gods in various bodies of mythology with the names of heavenly bodies in Sanskrit; he concluded that all of the principal gods' names had originally stood for solar phenomena. His theory, which came to be called *Solar Mythology* (or "The Philological School") regarded myths as essentially accounts of the recurrence of day and night; the European folktales presumably were descended from myths and conveyed the same symbolism.

Followers of Max Müller, both in England and in the United States, carried solar (and also lunar) explanations of myths to great lengths, applying them to texts from around the world. Similar research also produced a "zoological" interpretation that read animal symbolism into myths, and a sweeping "Indianist" theory that traced all European folktales back to India.

The solar mythologists were opposed by the so-called *English Anthropological School* of comparative mythologists. Their theoretical foundation was the idea of *cultural evolution,* patterned on the biological evolution which Charles Darwin had described in *The Origin of Species* in 1859. Assuming that all cultures, like plants and animals, had evolved in stages from lower to higher forms, these anthropologists postulated that the primitive and peasant cultures of today retain "survivals" of the "savage stage" of modern civilization. E. B. Tylor's landmark book *Primitive Culture* (1871) articulated this *theory of survivals,* and the following passage from Andrew Lang's *Custom and Myth* (1884) describes the method by which it was applied.

> The student of folklore is led to examine the usages, myths, and ideas of savages, which are still retained, in rude enough shape, by the European peasantry. . . .
>
> The method is, when an apparently irrational and anomalous custom is found in any country, to look for a country where a similar practice is found, and where the practice is no longer irrational and anomalous, but in harmony with the manners and ideas of the people among whom it prevails. . . . Folklore represents, in the midst of a civilised race, the savage ideas out of which civilisation has been evolved.

With Andrew Lang as their standard-bearer, the English anthropologists waged a devastating campaign against the solar mythologists, even to the extent of using Max Müller's own method to prove that Müller himself was a sun god. One monument of Victorian scholarship, Sir James G. Frazer's *The Golden Bough* (first published in 1890 and expanded to twelve volumes by its final revision in 1915) was essentially a massive assemblage of evidence of the world-wide persistence of folk beliefs, myths, and customs that was taken by some readers to support the theory of survivals in culture.

The suggestion of several nineteenth-century German scholars that the fantasy world of dreams might have given rise to myths anticipated the *psychoanalytical approach to myths* introduced by Sigmund Freud. This school, like that of the English anthropologists, assumed that polygenesis explained widespread myth parallels. The Freudian explanation drew on the study of dreams, neuroses, and complexes to unravel the workings of the unconscious and subconscious minds with their Oedipal, phallic, and other symbolism. Carl Jung, who introduced the term "collective unconscious" for generalized human patterns of culture, and Otto Rank, author of *The Myth of the Birth of the Hero* (1914), made major contributions to this type of interpretation.

As early as the fourth century B.C. the idea arose that myths are actually based on historical traditions, and myth heroes were real people. The theory was known as *Euhemerism* after the Sicilian philosopher Euhemerus who proposed it; he held, in effect, that man had made gods in his own image. A kind of "new euhemerism" constituted the *Heroic Age Theory* set forth by H. M. and N. K. Chadwick in their work *The Growth of Literature* (3 volumes, 1932–40). They asserted that mythical heroes such as England's Beowulf, Germany's Siegfried, France's Roland, and Ireland's Cuchulain were based on actual chieftains who had led roving bands of warriors across prehistoric Europe; historical accounts of their deeds had been passed down as heroic legends and myths. Recently the theory was applied to the American frontier, and Davy Crockett was nominated as a heroic-age figure.

Exactly the opposite basic assumption—that the basis of myth is *never* history—underlies the *Myth-Ritual Theory* advanced by Lord Raglan in his work *The Hero* (1936). Like Otto Rank and others before him, Lord Raglan schematized a large number of mythical biographies into a *monomyth*. Raglan's analysis then held that no myth, legend, or folktale that significantly matched this pattern could preserve any history. Instead, religious ritual was the source of all myths, and myths preceded all genuine folklore. The myth-ritual theory has been strongly criticized in the United States, but has also had a vigorous defense in the writings of Stanley Edgar Hyman.

Although all of these theories of myth origins once had their firm adherents, most of them claim only a few serious advocates among folklorists today. But the theories introduced in these early studies continue to influence folklore scholarship. The question of polygenesis versus diffusion must still be dealt with; the concepts of folktales as "broken-down myths," or of all folklore as cultural "survivals," are far from dead. Psychoanalytical theory has gained recent disciples among professionally trained folklorists, as has euhemerism. Many terms introduced in the nineteenth-century studies are still employed by writers. And several anthropological-folklorists have tried to combine what they consider to be the best features of several schools of analysis and interpretation into new, more comprehensive explanations of myths. Prominent efforts of this nature include M. J. and F. S. Herskovits's *Dahomean Narrative* (1958), Melville Jacobs's *The Content and Style of an Oral Literature* (1959), and Joseph Campbell's series *The Masks of God* (1959 and following).

Most contemporary American folklorists are concerned more with legends than myths, for American folk tradition, though lacking true myths, is rich in legendary lore, much of it European in background. Legends, like myths, are prose narratives regarded by their tellers as true; unlike myths, they are generally secular and are set in the less-remote past in a conventional earthly locale. Legends are sometimes referred to as *folk history*, although history is soon distorted by oral transmission. Because many legends reflect folk beliefs, the term *belief tale* is also applied to them; and just as myths serve the function of validating religious rites in a primitive culture, legends are often used to validate superstitions in modern folklore. Since the spread of legends is analogous to the dissemination of rumors, some sociological rumor theories have been applied to legends as well.

Legends are usually *migratory*—widely known in different places—but when texts become rooted and adapted to a particular place, they are said to be *localized*, or *local lengends*. Often legends are circulated in *cycles*, or groups of narratives relating to one event, person, or theme. In any case, the classification of legends has been a vexing matter; as the folklorist Wayland D. Hand, who has wrestled with the problem recently, writes, "For the systematizer, folk legends seem endless in bulk and variety, and they are often so short and formless as to defy classification." For discussion purposes, however, four groups of legends may be established on the basis of their primary concern with religion, the supernatural, individual persons, or localities and their histories.

Religious legends include the narratives to which the term "legend" originally applied exclusively—stories of the lives of Christian saints. Such stories belong to religious literature when they have been attested by an official investigation (known as "hagiography") and are entered in printed accounts, but they remain folklore while they circulate orally in traditional versions. Even the sanctioned "lives of saints" in print contain numerous traditional motifs from folk sources, and saintly influences continue to be manifested, according to folk accounts both from Europe and the United States, in many cases never validated by the Church. A counterpart tradition in a native-American sect is that of the miraculous appearances of the three "Nephites" who have aided Mormons in time of need by bringing them food, comforting them, rescuing them, and sometimes healing them.

"Legend" now refers to many more kinds of stories than just *saints' legends*, and even the term "religious legends" includes other types. Traditional stories about miracles, revelations, answers to prayers, marvelous icons, and blessings bestowed upon the faithful may all be called religious legends if their dissemination is largely oral and some of their motifs are traditional. To say that such stories are legendary is not necessarily to say that they are of doubtful veracity, for folklore may be true as well as false. Thus, such a legend as that about a group of nuns who retreat to prayerful sanctuary before an advancing forest fire and emerge later to find that the fire has miraculously bypassed them may be believed, but unprovable, or it may be supported by historical record. In either case, however, it is a religious legend as long as traditional oral versions continue to circulate.

A third category of religious legends is "the bible of the folk"—a cycle of stories which fill the blanks of, or extend, biblical narratives. For example, the term "Adam's Apple" refers to legendary accounts of the apple sticking in Adam's throat when he took it from Eve and ate. The dog is said to have a cold nose because he was late coming to the Ark and had to ride next to the rail. Gypsies are allowed to roam the whole earth, according to legend, because one of them stole the nail forged for Christ's heart when He was nailed to the cross. Various animals or plants are rewarded or formed as they are because of some legendary connection with the life of the Saviour. Flies which gathered on the body of Christ at His crucifixion looked like nails and prevented more nails from being driven—therefore they may dine at kings' tables—while various trees (the aspen, poplar and others) are said to be "cursed" for supplying wood for His cross. (All of these examples, it should be noted, are etiological legends, and to many tellers may even function as myths.) The folklorist Francis Lee Utley has referred to this area of religious legends as "an uncharted wilderness" that requires the use of numerous sources, both written and oral, for its successful exploration.

Supernatural legends generally take the form of supposedly factual accounts of occurrences and experiences which seem to validate superstitions. For the simplest of these, a kind of prelegend that is merely a "narrative of a personal happening," the useful term *memorate* was coined by the Swedish folklorist C. W. von Sydow. The Hungarian-American folklorists Linda Dégh and Andrew Vázsonyi have isolated the concept they call the *proto-memorate,* referring to any "credibility-seeking utterance like folk belief itself" which may precede or provide background for legend formation. The true legend must be a traditional rather than just a personal narrative. These stories might logically be called "belief tales," for their usual effect is to give credence to folk beliefs; yet, as Patrick B. Mullen points out, sometimes the "basic narrative value" of a legend may keep it alive in tradition long after anyone seriously believes it. Supernatural legends may be grouped according to such categories of superstition as beliefs in supernatural creatures, in returning spirits of the dead, in magic, and in supernatural signs.

European legendry is full of stories of supernatural creatures, both evil ones, such as vampires, werewolves, trolls, and other monsters; and the partly helpful ones, such as elves, brownies, fairies, *nisser,* and other "little people." But it may be said that very few of these creatures migrated to the New World; we can collect legends of "bearwalkers" and other shape-shifters, and of occasional zombies and other monsters, but only in relatively isolated pockets of folk culture, especially where Indian, Afro-American, or certain immigrant tradition is strong. It is true that legends of witchcraft are not uncommon in the United States, but these too, linger mostly in the backwoods and among special groups. Supernatural legends concerning the returning spirits of the dead, however, are just as common and as varied in the United States as they are abroad.

The term *ghost stories* suggests blood-curdling scare tales about white-sheeted or invisible spooks who are out to destory humankind. But most ghosts in American legends are lifelike in appearance, and come back from the dead only to set right an error or finish a task. A better term for these creatures is *revenants,* or "returners"—those who return from the world of the dead, usually only temporarily. Their reasons for coming back are numerous, and harmless to anyone with a clear conscience. Only a few spirits return for revenge, and they always have justification; more commonly they return for such a purpose as to reveal hidden treasure, to ask that a crooked limb in the coffin be straightened, or to reveal the cause of death. A common motif in these legends is E402: "Mysterious ghostlike noises heard." These sounds include calls, moans, snores, sobs, sighs, footsteps, and sometimes even that old standby of Hollywood horror films, chain-rattling. Often a brave person can communicate with the spirit by means of these noises, asking for one for "yes," and two for "no" to discover the reason for the haunting. Besides humans, even the ghosts of animals may come back to torment the living, but more often they come to assist. The ways by which ghosts may be summoned, the reasons they come, their appearance, the attempts to placate them, and the variants of tales about encounters with them can make up a fascinating study within a region or for a particular folk group, but only a few such studies have been completed.

An approach to legend research suggested by John M. Vlach is to distinguish from actual supernatural belief tales the *humorous antilegends* which are told mostly by children and adolescents to evoke simultaneous fear and laughter. Serving a more sinister purpose were the *stories of "Night Riders" and "Night Doctors"* which were told by Southern whites to intimidate their black slaves by encouraging superstitious fear of ghosts and bogies. A study by Gladys-Marie Fry based on ex-slave narratives and oral history interviews reveals how actual mounted white patrols and the Ku Klux Klan served to lend credence among blacks to the rumors spread by whites about ghostly spirits and human body-snatchers who would capture them if they ventured forth after dark. Thus a cycle of created legends was used for social control and racial suppression.

Memorates of supernatural signs and magic are probably much more common than full-scale legends concerning them, although memorates have not been collected as frequently as legends by American folklorists. Yet, one often hears first-person accounts of folk cures that worked, wishes that came true, warnings of death that were fulfilled, bad luck that followed a traditional omen, prophetic dreams, and so forth. As one analysis has described the legend-forming sequence, "primary stimuli," such as folk superstitions (i.e., "Bad luck comes in threes") encounter the "releasing stimuli" involved in an actual situation (three unlucky things happen to someone); the event is interpreted ("That saying is *true!*"), and the happening is narrated to others as a memorate. Repeated transmissions of the memorate support the folk belief, and may eventually produce a traditional legend.

The most convenient subject in which the student might observe the growth of modern legends is the *urban belief tale*—contemporary stories in a city setting which are reported as true individual experiences, but which have traditional variants that indicate their legendary character. Most urban belief tales contain supernatural, or at least highly unnatural, motifs, but this fact shakes popular belief not a whit; people from all walks of life credit the tales, and publications including *Time, Reader's Digest*, and local newspapers reprint them frequently as gospel truth. One of the commonest of these tales is "The Vanishing Hitchhiker" (Motif E332.3.3.1.), in which the spirit of a young girl returns annually on the anniversary of her death and tries to hitchhike home; another favorite concerns "The Death Car," a late-model automobile selling for a song because the smell of a corpse cannot be eradicated from it. Such tales may spring from verifiable history (Richard M. Dorson traced "The Death Car" to 1938 in Mecosta, Mich.), but the facts get lost, and new localizations are provided. For example, the story of the lady's dead cat wrapped up in a package for burial, which is then pilfered by a shoplifter while she pauses in a department store on the way to a vacant lot or a friend's yard, has been reported as factual and recent by newspapers in different cities for at least twenty-five years; possibly such an event *did* happen somewhere once, but certainly not all the times and in all the places to which it has been attributed. A variation on the dead cat theme involves guests at a dinner party who are sent to a hospital to have their stomachs pumped when the family pet cat, earlier caught nibbling at the fish course, is found dead on the back porch. The next day a neighbor confesses that he ran over the cat in the driveway and left the corpse on the porch. Another updating is the story of the child who accidentally sprinkles the cat with a hose and puts it into a microwave oven to dry out, whereupon the cat explodes.

Several themes are especially popular in urban belief tales and they reflect some basic anxieties of our time. In stories involving a grisly accident, such as a decapitation in an elevator accident, Motif F1041.7, "Hair turns gray [or white] from terror" often occurs. A favorite tale about a girl who sickens and sometimes dies because black widow spiders have infested her hairdo (see Appendix B) has counterparts in tales of insects living under plaster casts or in the sinus cavities. A similar story describes a girl embalmed alive in a "poisoned dress" which had been taken from a corpse and resold. Foreign matter in food is another frequent motif—a mouse tail in a Pepsi-Cola bottle, a finger in the restaurant chop suey, a dead rat floating in a chocolate company's vats, a Kentucky-Fried rat, and so forth. Defective or accidentally released experimental products crop up repeatedly in stories—the bathing suit that becomes transparent, the economical carburetor, a light bulb that never burns out, a tin-can speedometer casing on a Japanese car, and so forth. Sometimes a well-known business concern (such as Pepsi-Cola above) may become associated with a particular legend. The Waldorf Astoria, for example, is frequently named as the place where a secret recipe for "Red Velvet Cake" was once sold to a customer for an outrageous price. In revenge, she distributed the "secret" ("Add one-quarter cup of red food coloring to a standard cake recipe") widely among her friends. The management of the Waldorf cannot explain why, but the legend has stuck to them for upwards of ten years now, and no such cake was ever featured on their menus; furthermore, customers are never charged for recipes from the Waldorf kitchens.

Anxiety about being caught in the nude or being otherwise embarrassed is projected in several migratory legends of wide circulation in the United States. In a railroading version a traveling businessman wearing only his pajamas is enticed into a young woman's Pullman compartment where he awakens alone the next morning, his clothes and luggage now back on his own Pullman car which had been cut out from the train during the night. In a house-trailer variation, the man is napping nude in the trailer while his wife drives; at a sudden stop for a traffic light he groggily arises and steps outside, only to be left behind when the light changes. A cycle of "nude surprise party" stories describes a serviceman or businessman misunderstanding the secretive arrangements of his girlfriend or secretary for a dinner party at her home; he removes his clothes in anticipation of lovemaking only to discover that the event is really a surprise welcome-home party or an office party in his honor. Another surpriser-surprised tale describes a housewife caught doing the laundry nude by the gas-meter reader, or a baby sitter and her boyfriend caught frolicking in the nude. There is a flatulent form of the theme in which a girl breaks wind in the front seat of her date's car, unaware that the couple they are double-dating with are already in the back seat.

The distances over which such stories disseminate before becoming localized are remarkable, even with print and broadcasting to assist the folk process. The legend about a grandmother's or step-mother's corpse stolen from the car-top when a vacationing family was driving her back home for burial was collected in England only about a month before it showed up, also as a "true" story, in the United States. Also quickly rooted was the tale about a man who returned to his parked car to find a dent in the fender and this note under the windshield wiper: "The people who are watching think I'm writing my name and address on this note, but I'm not." This one was printed, in each instance as a local occurrence, in the San Francisco *Chronicle* in July 1963, and in the London *Daily Mirror* in September 1963. The legend about the husband who fills a Cadillac parked in front of his house with cement, thinking that the owner is in the house seducing his wife, now has international circulation. The folk-lorist Louie W. Attebery found reliable corroborative evidence of such an event reported in a Denver, Colorado, newspaper in 1960; the vehicle in this instance was a 1946 DeSoto. The same story, however, was heard in Texas some four months earlier, suggesting that life may at times imitate lore.

Personal legends are stories attached to individuals and told as true. In Old World tradition, cycles of ancient *hero legends* described an impressive catalog of national champions such as Roland, Charlemagne, St. Patrick, King Arthur, and Robin Hood; in American folklore the hero legend has been manifested first in such frontier figures as Davy Crockett and the keelboatman and scout Mike Fink, later in regional characters like Johnny Appleseed and Billy the Kid, and in the twentieth century in the largely fakelore elaboration of Paul Bunyan and the characters created in imitation of him. Scattered narratives, sometimes heroic, also circulate about gangsters (John Dillinger), sports stars (Babe Ruth, John L. Sullivan, Jim Thorpe), martyrs (Martin Luther King, John F. Kennedy), and military leaders (Generals Doolittle, Patton, MacArthur) as well as others. But the stories concerning such figures do not correspond in number and national folk circulation to the European heroic legend cycles, and no greater misconception exists about American folklore than the notion that we are a people who have continually created and celebrated epic folk heroes. The vaunted "heroes" of juvenile literature and chamber-of-commerce boosting are inventions of professional writers and public-relations men, not of the folk groups to which they are attributed. The typical hero of genuine indigenous *oral* tradition in the United States is not the brawling frontier trailblazer or the giant mythical laborer, but rather the local tall-tale specialist who has gathered a repertoire of traditional exaggerations and attached them all to his own career. Figures like John Darling of New York State, Abraham "Oregon" Smith of southern Indiana and Illinois, and Len Henry of northern Idaho were famous yarnspinners in their own regions, but unknown elsewhere. They have been the subjects of study by folklorists, but have no popular reputations beyond their own communities, where they were celebrated fondly as "the biggest liars in seven counties." These figures might, like John Darling, be pictured mainly as powerful men or great hunters, or they might possess a special repertoire, like Oregon Smith's travel yarns. Smith also had a reputation as a folk doctor, hence his other nickname, Sassafras, from his favorite source of a curative potion. Almost invariably the story is told about someone approaching the local liar to ask him to "Tell the biggest lie you know!" The vaunted liar, however, says he is too busy to tell a lie; "old man so-and-so just died and I have to go order a coffin for him."

When people call on the widow, they discover that the liar has indeed told them a big one, for there is old so-and-so, rocking on the front porch. Although this story is reported as a tribute to the yarnspinner's quick wit, actually it is a traditional tale that has been widely collected both in Europe and America.

First-person reminiscences and *family stories* have long puzzled American folklore collectors and scholars. How many repetitions are needed, or how widely must a tradition be spread for it to qualify as folklore? How can we draw distinctions between unstructured musings, polished retellings of events, memorates, and personal legends? Every folklorist who has tape-recorded good informants has had to deal with such questions. It has been asserted, with some convincing examples, that family traditions constitute a traditional category including misfortune stories, personal experience stories, favorite anecdotes about eccentric relatives, often-repeated—and somewhat embellished—experiences, nicknames and expressions of a family group, and the like. Jimmy Durante's famous sign-off, for intance, "Good night, Mrs. Calabash, wherever you are!" is said to refer to a pet name he used for his first wife. In one family a whining child was always called "Ransey Sniffle." In some Texas families, the folklorist Mody Boatright has reported, members cherish traditional accounts of how their pioneer forebears behaved and why they came to Texas. Richard M. Dorson suggests the term "sagaman" for the old-timer who spins long, fantastic yarns about his own exploits, in which "he plays an heroic role, overmastering the hazards and outwitting the dangers presented by vicious men, ferocious beasts, and implacable nature." Personal reminiscences of these kinds furnish background for the other folklore texts of gifted informants, and for this reason also they ought to be collected.

The *anecdote* is a short personal legend, supposedly true but generally apocryphal, told about an episode in the life of either a famous individual or a local character. George Washington and the cherry tree seem promising anecdotal material, but somehow Parson Weems' little vignette has never varied one iota in traditional retellings. It is always "I cannot tell a lie; I did it with my little hatchet." The anecdote about the famous intellectual and the chorus girl has better folk credentials. In one version it is George Bernard Shaw who is propositioned thus: "You have the greatest brain in the world.

I have the most graceful body. Let us then produce the perfect child." Shaw responded, "But suppose the child had my body and your brain!" In other accounts Albert Einstein is the man named, but the episode has ultimately been found in an Old French manuscript dated 1319, and it was reprinted several times in the eighteenth and nineteenth centuries. Another persistent anecdote deals with John Philip Sousa's name being derived from his initials "S. O." (for "Siegfried" or "Sigismund Ochs," presumably a German) and the "U.S.A." stenciled on his baggage when he traveled to (or from) the United States; another version claims that "John Phillipso USA" was the baggage marking. Sousa was actually born in Washington, D.C., and the family name was Sousa (a Portuguese name) from the start. Tales of this sort circulate especially about political figures, scientists, gangsters, show-business personalities, professional athletes, and military men. They should be distinguished carefully from *jokes* about personalities, which are obviously false, though revealing of popular attitudes toward public figures; anecdotes always have the air of truth about them, and they supposedly demonstrate how people have revealed their own personalities.

Anecdotes of local characters emphasize supposed character and personality traits of their subjects in stories presumed to be true by the local populace, but they are often made up of motifs found in other regions as well. The local miser pays his son a penny for going to bed without supper, and then charges him a penny for breakfast; the town's laziest man wins a load of corn in a contest, and asks "Is it shelled?" The village dolt is eating his first banana on a train ride; the train goes through a tunnel, and he cries out that the fruit has blinded him. The clever rascal, on the other hand, plays dumb and always picks the big coin (nickel) instead of the little one (dime) because, "Otherwise those smart alecks would quit asking me to choose." The absent-minded professor is a frequent target of local-character anecdotes of college campuses. He forgets that he has driven to the campus and walks home; when he gives a speech, he sometimes reads both the original and the carbon-copy of each page; and when he reaches into his pocket for the frog he caught for dissection class, he finds instead the sandwich he thought he had eaten for lunch. (Such academic anecdotes are among the material discussed in Appendix B.)

The comical Indian, sometimes foolish but more often shrewd, was the subject of a long cycle of anecdotes from early American history that still echoes through modern jokebooks and in oral folklore. The white man shivers in his heavy winter clothing while the Indian is comfortable in only a blanket, because, as he explains it, "Me all face." (This story has been traced to a late classical Greek source which came via French and English literary versions to the United States.) In other anecdotes Indians turn the tables on whites by using their own law and their religion against them, or the white settler may frighten the Indians by removing his wig, wooden leg, glass eye, or other artificial members. A common theme in these anecdotes is feeding the Indians; the redskins arrive at a farm or ranch to beg for food, and the settler watches in dismay as a whole platter of fried eggs disappears down the gullet of one brave, while all of the others demand the same size serving. The Indians may stand around the molasses barrel, dipping their fingers into it and licking off the sweet. One brave is said to have eaten a whole pot of half-cooked beans one day; he was found dead the next day with his stomach distended. An anecdote about Indians offering to trade many horses or other valuables for a blond white girl is related as true in several accounts of early Western travel, but an historian's study of them indicates that "Goldilocks on the Oregon Trail" is a legendary story stemming from traditional sources rather than from first-hand experience. An old Navajo living on the tribal reservation in Arizona is the subject of a recent local-character anecdote. He walks to town to pick up his monthly government check, stopping overnight at several hogans of kinsmen on the way. By the time he has gone in and back, it is time to begin going in again for the next check.

Local legends are those which are closely associated with specific places, either with their names, their geographic features, or their histories. Presumably these legends are unique regional creations, but in reality many of them are simply localized versions of migratory legends; even one that originates from a local feature or event tends to spread outward, changing and being localized as it moves. A good example of the transplanted migratory legend is the Maine woods story of "The Man Who Plucked the Gorbey" (Canada Jay), who later was plucked of his own hair while he slept. This tale evidently goes back to a Scottish and North-Country English legend about plucking a sparrow, but it has become solidly entrenched in Maine and New Brunswick, being locally credited there to some thirty different characters. The continually varying and radiating local-historical legend is illustrated by the tale from Carrollton, Alabama, about the black prisoner, the image of whose face was engraved by lightning onto a window or mirror while he awaited trial in 1878 for burning a courthouse. The name of the prisoner, the date, and the facts of his crime are a matter of historical record, but the oral legend developed numerous variations of detail as it circulated in and around Carrollton; the lightning-image motif now appears with other local legends elsewhere in Alabama, Kentucky, and Georgia (as well as in an Agatha Christie mystery story).

Sometimes stories that seem to be reliable accounts of local incidents, even being carried by newspapers, have legendary plots with a long history in tradition. A good example is the legend, first reported from Syria in the fifth century, about Jews torturing and ritually murdering a Christian child. This accusation, generally false, was common in the Middle Ages, and it has been revived frequently ever since. (The British-American traditional ballad "Little Sir Hugh" is one variant.) In Nazi Germany it was a common piece of anti-Semitic propaganda, and by 1933 it had turned up in American hate literature. In the 1960s the legend took a new twist when an assault upon a white child was attributed either to blacks or Mexicans. Reports of the story, often detailed as to supposed time, place, and result, are circulated by print and word of mouth; they serve to reinforce prejudice and encourage persecution of the falsely accused minority group.

Local place-name etymologies, which were mentioned in Chapter 4, often have their parallels and close variants in other places. Numerous puzzling town names, for example, are explained as being made up on the basis of early settlers' initials, or as coming from some final-desperation act like pointing out a name from a map of Europe while blindfolded or taking a name from the side of a provisions box. Also, folk etymologies often disagree about the origin of the same name. One version may try to make sense out of the name spelled backwards, while another maintains that United States Post Office officials either misread the handwritten name that townspeople submitted or made an error while taking it down.

Several of these processes are illustrated in Idaho place-name stories collected by students. *Emida* is said to be derived from the names of three early settlers, *E*ast, *Mi*ller, and *Da*wson, but other informants point out that "It's 'a dime' spelled backwards, and that's about what it's worth!" *Moscow* is usually assocated with the Russian capital, leading to the mistaken notion that many Russians settled that part of Idaho, but sometimes stories are developed around phrases such as "Ma's cow," or "the moss cow." *Tensed,* Idaho, is near the old *Desmet* mission, named for its founding father; one folk etymology maintains that spelling the mission name backwards for the village name was not acceptable to the Post Office department, so officials in Washington changed the "m" to "n" on their own. Other people say that a telegraph operator or a writer mistook the letter while sending the name in for registry. Stories like these abound in every region, and the collector can usually assume that hardly any oral explanation for a place name will actually convey historical truth.

Striking geographical features are frequently the subjects of local legends. Scores of deep, dark, cold lakes are supposed to be bottomless, and a number of them are also said to have monsters lurking in them. Some lakes have underground connections with other lakes, complete with currents strong enough to pull a drowned person from one to the other. Most large caves were robber hideouts and have treasure stashed away inside somewhere; or else someone was trapped there once and starved to death before rescuers arrived. Western deserts are said to contain hidden oases, known to early explorers, but never found since. Mountain ranges are sprinkled liberally with "lost mines," or in California and the Southwest with lost Spanish missions that are represented as being crammed with treasure.

Even outstanding man-made features like bridges, tunnels, dams, and mountain highways acquire legendary lore about such things as their designers' methods ("His six-year old son really drew the original plans") or accidents during construction ("There's a workman's body inside that concrete!"). The "haunted house" tradition, which includes many other kinds of buildings besides houses, is a good example of a migratory supernatural motif which becomes localized in regional legends; another is "The Graveyard Wager" (Motif N384.2. "Death in the graveyard; person's clothing is caught; Tale Type 1676B, "Clothing caught in graveyard"), which is generally attached to a specific local cemetery. In the vicinities of mental institutions, legends often circulate concerning maniac escapees who were never recaptured, but who still live as wild men in a woods or swamp.

Local *historical legends* are a largely still-uncollected aspect of American narrative folklore, although folk ballads based on historical events have long interested folksong scholars. Such occurrences as lynchings, feuds, sensational crimes, scandals, fires and other natural disasters, Indian massacres, and labor disputes have generated legends that become formularized in characteristic ways as they pass in oral tradition and that eventually accumulate supernatural and other motifs. Probably because of their preoccupation with other forms of folklore, or because such legends may seem to be simply garbled local history of little value, few collectors have awarded them the attention, for example, that Dorson did in the Upper Peninsula of Michigan with "The Lynching of the McDonald Boys," and "How Crystal Falls Stole the Courthouse from Iron River," or that William Ivey did in the same region with "The 1913 Disaster," a legend from the community of Calumet. Countless other legends based on local history could be collected and studied elsewhere.

Cycles of national legends tend to cluster around the most dramatic events in the country's history. Thus, in Norway for example, the most numerous historical legends are about the miracles of St. Olaf, the medieval Great Plagues, the wars with Sweden, and the Nazi occupation. In the United States, legend cycles have developed about the Revolution, the Civil War (particularly in the South), the Indian Wars, and the settlement of the frontier.

BIBLIOGRAPHIC NOTES

J. R. Rayfield's "What Is a Story?" in *AA* 74 (1972), 1085–1106, establishes criteria by which listeners accept or reject a telling as conforming to their idea of what constitutes a story. William Bascom's formulation of definitions for "The Forms of Folklore: Prose Narratives" appeared in *JAF* 78 (1965), 3–20. Stith Thompson's *The Folktale* (New York: Dryden Press, 1946) is a basic older survey of traditional prose narratives and their study; his *Motif-Index* has been published in a revised edition (Copenhagen and Bloomington, Ind.: Indiana University Press, 1955–58). J. L. Fischer's survey article "The Socio-psychological Analysis of Folktales," *CA* 4 (1963), 235–95, is important, with a valuable bibliography and comments by seventeen anthropologists and folklorists; like Thompson, Fischer and others use the general term "folktale" for all traditional prose narratives.

The introduction by Bødker in *European Folk Tales*, ed. Laurits Bødker, Christina Hole, and G. D'Aronco (Copenhagen: Rosenkilde and Bagger; and Hatboro, Pa.: Folklore Associates, 1963) compares similar motifs in folktales and myths. Richard M. Dorson surveys recent publications concerning "Mythology and Folklore" in *Annual Reviews of Anthropology* 2 (1973), 107–26.

"Myth: A Symposium," edited by Thomas A. Sebeok for *JAF* (October–December 1955), reprinted in 1958 by Indiana University Press, contains nine important articles on theories of myth including Richard M. Dorson's "The Eclipse of Solar Mythology," and Thompson's "Myths and Folktales." William Bascom discussed "The Myth-Ritual Theory" in *JAF* 70 (1957), 103–14, and set off a wave of responses, favorable and hostile, in the following issues of the *Journal*. Two later important contributions to evaluating the myth-ritual and other monomyth theories are Archer Taylor's "The Biographical Pattern in Traditional Narrative," *JFI* 1 (1964), 114–29; and Herbert Weisinger's "Before Myth," *JFI* 2 (1965), 120–131. Two other good anthologies of myth studies are "Myth and Mythmaking," ed. Henry A. Murray in *Daedalus* (Spring 1959); and the January–March 1966 special issue of *JAF*, ed. Melville Jacobs, and called "The Anthropologist Looks at Myth." Jacobs's methods of myth-analysis were criticized in a review of *The People Are Coming Soon: Analyses of Clackamas Chinook Myths and Tales* (Seattle, 1960), by Sven Liljeblad in *MF* 12 (1962), 93–103. In "Five Interpretations of a Melanesian Myth," *JAF* 86 (1973), 3–13, Elli Köngäs-Maranda subjects the same text to analysis in terms of 1) Myth and Ritual, 2) Reflection of Culture, 3) Charter of Society, 4) Freudian and Jungian Symbolism, and 5) Structure.

For nearly one hundred examples of native American traditional prose narratives see Stith Thompson's *Tales of the North American Indians* (Cambridge, Mass.: Harvard University Press, 1929; paperback edn., Bloomington: Indiana University Press, 1966). Alan Dundes's "The Morphology of North American Indian Folktales," in *FFC* no. 195 (1964) discusses the structural approach to myths and establishes some basic forms of Indian narratives. Levette J. Davidson quotes some interesting examples of "White Versions of Indian Myths and Legends" in *WF* 7 (1948), 115–28. Links between Asiatic and American Indian mythology were considered in Gudmund Hatt's monograph *Asiatic Influences in American Folklore*, Det. Kgl. Danske Videnskabernes Selskab, Historisk-Filologiske Meddelelser, 31:6 (Copenhagen, 1949). Another specific case is taken up in E. Adamson Hoebel's "The Asiatic Origin of a Myth of the Northwest Coast," *JAF* 54 (1941), 1–9. I make reference to an Old Norse myth to explain a recent American joke in a note "Thor, the Cheechako and the Initiates' Tasks: A Modern Parallel for an Old Jest," *SFQ* 24 (1960), 235–38.

For legends, a basic survey is Wayland D. Hand's "Status of European and American Legend Study," *CA* 6 (1965), 439–46. Fourteen important papers from a conference on legends were edited by Hand as *American Folk Legend: A Symposium* (Berkeley and Los Angeles: University of California Press, 1971). Richard M. Dorson gathered American legends in a historical context in his anthology *America in Legend: Folklore from the Colonial Period to the Present* (New York: Pantheon Books, 1973).

Reidar Th. Christensen proposed a list of international legend types and catalogued the Norwegian variants in his work "The Migratory Legends," *FFC* no. 175 (1958). Another important classification of widespread legends is Barbara Allen Woods's *The Devil in Dog Form: a Partial Type-Index of Devil Legends* (University of California Folklore Studies no. 11: Berkeley, 1959). A specific European story that appears as both folktale and legend is studied in terms of its special American adaptations in Butler H. Waugh's, "The Child and the Snake in North America," *Norveg* 7 (1960), 153–82.

Frederic C. Tubach's "Index Exemplorum: A Handbook of Medieval Religious Tales," in *FFC* no. 204 (1969), is a basic reference work on religious legends and tales with some 5400 examples identified in thirty-seven central collections. *White Magic: An Introduction to the Folklore of Christian Legend* (Cambridge, Mass.: Harvard University Press, 1948), by C. Grant Loomis is a good folkloristic discussion of saints' legends; Loomis also wrote on "Legend and Folklore" in *CFQ* 2 (1943), 279–97. A Jewish-American folk group is studied largely in terms of its legendry in Jerome R. Mintz's *Legends of the Hasidim* (Chicago: University of Chicago Press, 1968). An international religious-legend complex is traced in George K. Anderson's *The Legend of the Wandering Jew* (Providence, R.I.: Brown University Press, 1965). A distinctly American religious-legend cycle is the subject of such studies as Hector Lee's *The Three Nephites: The Substance and Significance of the Legend in Folklore* (University of New Mexico Publications in Language and Literature, no. 2: Albuquerque, 1949), and William A. Wilson's, "Mormon Legends of the Three Nephites Collected at Indiana University," *IF* 2 (1969), 3–35; and "The Vanishing Hitchhiker Among the Mormons," *IF* 8 (1975), 80–97. F. L. Utley's "The Bible of the Folk" appeared in *CFQ* 4 (1945), 1–17.

Louis C. Jones analyzed "The Ghosts of New York" in *JAF* 57 (1944), 237–54. The same was done for California ghosts by Rosalie Hankey in *CFQ* 1 (1942), 155–77. Jones's anthology *Things That Go Bump in the Night* (New York: Hill and Wang, 1959), presents ghost beliefs and legends from New York and includes a chapter on "The Vanishing Hitchhiker." Recent studies of this enduring modern legend are Douglas J. McMillan, "The Vanishing Hitchhiker in Eastern North Carolina," *NCF* 20 (1972), 123–28, and Katharine Luomala, "Disintegration and Regeneration, the Hawaiian Phantom Hitchhiker Legend," *Fabula* 13 (1972), 20–59.

Another anthology of ghost stories from one state is Ruth Ann Musick's *The Telltale Lilac Bush and Other West Virginia Ghost Tales* (Lexington, Ky.: University of Kentucky Press, 1965). A good collection of Canadian ghost legends is Helen Creighton's *Bluenose Ghosts* (Toronto: Ryerson Press, 1957). Ghost stories told by juveniles held in correctional facilities are found in Bess Lomax Hawes's "La Llorona in Juvenile Hall," *WF* 27 (1968), 153–70, and Craig Soland's two-part article "Ghost Stories from Cottage II," *AFF-Word* 3 (July 1973), 1–24; 3 (January 1974), 1–33.

Roger E. Mitchell studies a woodsman alleged to have sold his soul to the Devil in *George Knox: From Man to Legend*, no. 11 of *NEF* (1969). In a related vein, Christine Goldberg compiled a catalog of "Traditional American Witch Legends" published in *IF* 7 (1974), 77–108.

An important analysis of the formation of legendary narratives is Lauri Honko, "Memorates and the Study of Folk Beliefs," *JFI* 1 (1964), 5–19, which should be supplemented by Linda Dégh and Andrew Vázsonyi's article "The Memorate and the Proto-Memorate," *JAF* 87 (1974), 225–39. Patrick B. Mullen made two important contributions to the study of legend forms: "The Relationship of Legend and Folk Belief," *JAF* 84 (1971), 406–13, and "Modern Legend and Rumor Theory," *JFI* 9 (1972), 95–109. On rumor itself, see Tomotsu Shibutani, *Improvised News: A Sociological Study of Rumor* (Indianapolis: Bobbs-Merrill, 1966). A fascinating and unique study of legend-formation is Helen Gilbert's "The Crack in the Abbey Floor: A Laboratory Analysis of a Legend," *IF* 8 (1975), 61–78.

The journal *Indiana Folklore* began with a volume devoted to studies of current legends (1 [1968], 9–109); this interest continues with regular publication of such articles as John M. Vlach's "One Black Eye and Other Horrors: A Case for the Humorous Anti-Legend, *IF* 4 (1971), 95–140. Other studies of the legendary lore of American adolescents are Danielle Roemer, "Scary Story Legends," *Folklore Annual* 3 (1971), 1–16, and Kristie Harling, "The Grunch: An Example of New Orleans Teen-Age Folklore," *LFM* 3 (April 1971), 15–20. For the use of rumor and legend to control black slaves, see Gladys-Marie Fry, *Night Riders in Black Folk History* (Knoxville: University of Tennessee Press, 1975).

Dorson gives his evidence for the history of "The Death Car" in *American Folklore* (Chicago: University of Chicago Press, 1959), pp. 250–52. Louie W. Attebery documents the urban tale sometimes called "The Solid Cement Cadillac" as having involved a 1946 DeSoto in Denver, Colorado, in 1960: "It Was a DeSoto," *JAF* 83 (1970), 452–57. Other studies of urban belief tales are J. Russell Reaver's "'Embalmed Alive': A Developing Urban Ghost Tale," *NYFQ* 8 (1952), 217–20; my own note on "Red Velvet Cake" in *OFB* 2 (1963), 5–7; Wayland D. Hand's "Migratory Legend of 'The Cut-Out Pullman': Saga of American Railroading," *NYFQ* 27 (1971), 231–35; William Hugh Jansen's "The Surpriser Surprised: A Modern Legend," *FF* 6 (1973), 1–24; and Andrea Greenberg, "Drugged and Seduced: A Contemporary Legend," *NYFQ* 29 (1973), 131–58. "The Stolen Corpse" is given in an English version and annotated in *Folktales of England*, edited by Katharine M. Briggs and Ruth L. Tongue (Chicago: University of Chicago Press, 1965), pp. 99–100. Some folkloristic "Tales of Nieman-Marcus" were gathered by James Howard in *PTFS* 25 (1953), 160–70.

Hero legends of European traditional literature are surveyed in Jan deVries's *Heroic Song and Heroic Legend* (paperback edition, London and

New York: Oxford, 1963). The authentic versus the ersatz aspects of American heroic legendry have been discussed thoroughly in many publications, which are referred to in Dorson's *American Folklore*, pp. 199–243. The basic story of Paul Bunyan's origins is detailed in Daniel G. Hoffman's study *Paul Bunyan, Last of the Frontier Demigods* (Philadelphia: University of Pennsylvania Press, 1952; reissued by Columbia University Press, 1966). Howard W. Marshall documents the invention of a farmer's hero on the Paul Bunyan model in "The Heroic Urge in Kansas: The Creation of Johnny Kaw," *AFFWord* 1 (Oct. 1971), 11–21.

Older traditional aspects of the frontier boast are discussed in two articles in *AS*, one by Dorothy Dondore in 6 (1930–31), 45–55, and the other by William F. Thompson in 9 (1934), 186–99. An article of mine describes a local liar, "Len Henry: North Idaho Münchausen," *NWF* 1 (1965), 11–19. Roger D. Abrahams surveys "Some Varieties of Heroes in America" in *JFI* 3 (1966), 343–62, and Michael Owen Jones suggests a formula for the development of a heroic figure, using it as his title: "(PC + CB) × SD (R + I + E) = Hero," *NYFQ* 27 (1971), 243–60. Bruce A. Rosenberg views the mythologizing of a character in history in his *Custer and the Epic of Defeat* (University Park, Pa.: Pennsylvania State University Press, 1974). William E. Lightfoot investigates a modern hipster hero in "Charlie Parker: A Contemporary Folk Hero," *KFQ* 17 (1972), 51–62.

Few collections of American local legends are fully representative of the genuine oral lore of a vicinity. The most complete regional collection of legends is volume 3 in the *Publications of the Texas Folklore Society*, J. Frank Dobie, editor, *Legends of Texas* (1924; repr. 1964). Florence H. Ridley traces the history of the legend of Jews ritually murdering a Christian child in "A Tale Told Too Often," *WF* 26 (1967), 153–56. Ronald L. Baker discusses "The Role of Folk Legends in Place-Name Research" in *JAF* 85 (1972), 367–73. Richard M. Dorson's *Bloodstoppers and Bearwalkers* (Cambridge, Mass.: Harvard University Press, 1952; repr. in paperback, 1972) contains personal and local legends from the Upper Peninsula of Michigan: "sagemen" are discussed on pp. 249–72. Family legends are studied by Kim S. Garrett in "Family Stories and Sayings," *PTFS* 30 (1961), 273–81; Mody Boatright in the title essay of *The Family Saga and Other Phases of American Folklore* (Urbana, Ill.: University of Illinois Press, 1958), pp. 1–19; Patrick B. Mullen, "Folk Songs & Family Traditions," *PTFS* 37 (1972), 49–63; and Stanley H. Brandes, "Family Misfortune Stories in American Folklore," *JFI* 12 (1975), 5–17.

The Anatomy of the Anecdote (Chicago: University of Chicago Press, 1960), by Louis Brownlow, journalist, public servant, and educator, contains an informative discussion of the form and some good examples from the author's rich repertoire of family and political stories; the book was edited from tape-recorded talks by Brownlow. "Professor Einstein and the Chorus Girl" was traced by Jerah Johnson in *JAF* 73 (1960), 248–49. Sousa-name anecdotes were discussed by several correspondents, including Sousa's daughter, Helen Sousa Abert, in the letters to the editor columns of *Popular Mechanics* in July

1959. Other studies primarily of anecdotes are Wendy D. Caesar's " 'Asking a Mouse Who His Favorite Cat Is': Musicians' Stories about Conductors," *WF* 84 (1975), 83–116; Henry E. Anderson's "The Folklore of Draft Resistance," *NYFQ* 28 (1971), 135–50; and Harry Joe Jaffe's "The Welfare Letter," *WF* 34 (1975), 144–48. Sandra K. D. Stahl provides an illuminating discussion in "The Local Character Anecdote," *Genre* 8 (1975), 283–302.

A general survey of "Comic Indian Anecdotes" by Richard M. Dorson appeared in *SFQ* 10 (1946), 113–28; see also Rayna D. Green, "Traits of Indian Character: The 'Indian' Anecdote in American Vernacular Tradition," *SFQ* 39 (1975), 233–62. The "Me All Face" story was traced in a note by Cecily Hancock in *JAF* 76 (1963), 340–42, and the *"Membra Disjuncta"* story was the subject of a note by Austin E. Fife in *WF* 22 (1963), 121–22. Colorado characters were treated in Levette J. Davidson's " 'Gassy' Thompson—and Others: Stories of Local Characters," *CFQ* 5 (1946), 339–49. Anecdotes about a Utah Mormon local character are collected in Thomas E. Cheney's *The Golden Legacy: A Folk History of J. Golden Kimball* (Salt Lake City: Peregrine Smith, 1974). Francis Haines published his study "Goldilocks on the Oregon Trail" in *IY* 9 (Winter 1965–66), 26–30.

Dorson collected New England local legends of Indian tragedies, haunts, buried treasure, and place names in *Jonathan Draws the Long Bow* (Cambridge, Mass.; Harvard University Press, 1946), pp. 138–98. The Upper Peninsula historical legends appeared in Dorson's *Bloodstoppers and Bearwalkers*. See also William Ivey's " 'The 1913 Disaster': Michigan Local Legend," *FF* 3 (1970), 100–14. "The Man Who Plucked the Gorbey" was studied by Edward D. Ives in *JAF* 74 (1961), 1–8; and "The Face in the Window" was analyzed by Mildred Barnett Mitcham in *SFQ* 12 (1948), 241–57, and Mildred M. Nelson in *SFQ* 15 (1951), 254–61. Other articles on local legends include Gerard T. Hurley's "Buried Treasure Tales in America," *WF* 10 (1951), 197–216; Peter Gerhard's "The 'Lost Mission' of Baja California," *WF* 17 (1958), 97–106; Austin E. Fife's "The Bear Lake Monster," *UHR* 2 (1948), 99–106; and Henry A. Person's "Bottomless Lakes in the Pacific Northwest," *WF* 19 (1960), 278–80.

9

Folktales

If legends are folk history, then **folktales** are the short stories of oral literature. Folktales are traditional prose narratives that are strictly fictional and told primarily for entertainment, although they may also illustrate a truth or point a moral. Folktales range in length and subject matter from some European stories about fantastic wonders and magical events that take hours—even days—of narration, to brief American topical jokes with concentrated plots and snappy punchlines that are told in minutes. The term "folktale" usually connotes the complex, so-called fairy tale, familiar in children's literature. But there is no valid justification for ignoring recent tales that may have more realistic plots. Not only have these recent types of folktales replaced fairy tales in most American and many foreign oral traditions, but also, more often than not, these contemporary tales turn out upon investigation to have quite ancient parallels.

The folktales of the world, like the myths and legends, encompass a great variety of different narrative elements contained in a fairly limited array of basic forms, and both the details and the general outlines of specific folktales appear in widespread cultures and through great reaches of time. The recognition of these similarities spurred attempts in Europe in the early nineteenth century to organize comparative folktale research and to trace tales back to the most likely origins. By the late nineteenth century a standard methodology had emerged, along with the first of several important reference publications; since analogous folktale *materials* and similar *methods* of study are found in the United States, it is appropriate to begin with this European background.

A suitable general term for the "ordinary folktale" of broad Indo-European distribution is a basic problem, even though the characteristic style and form of such tales are easily recognized. Formularized openings and closings set off the items in this category from other folktales; in English, they frequently begin with "Once upon a time . . ." and end "They lived happily ever after." The setting is often some unnamed kingdom in a remote age; the characters usually include royalty, the structure of the tales tends to be based on threefold repetition, and some of the typical motifs are imaginary creatures (ogres, dragons, and giants), transformations, magic objects, helpful animals, and supernatural powers or knowledge. The hero in these tales is frequently a poor stepchild who rises to wealth, power, and authority through a combination of supernatural aid, good luck, and his own ingenuity and perseverance.

"Fairy tale" is a poor term for such folktales, since they almost never are concerned with the "little people," or fairies, of legendary narratives. The expression "nursery tales" is equally inappropriate, since mostly adults have circulated them. "Wonder tales" is a reasonable term that has some currency among folklorists, but the German word *"Märchen"* is the most widely adopted scholarly term. That is the name that the Brothers Grimm used for their famous collection, first published in 1812, the *Kinder- und Hausmärchen*, or "Children's and Household Folktales."

As the collection of *Märchen* and other folktales spread, encouraged by nationalism, and as the study of these tales progressed, it became increasingly desirable to devise a uniform system of referring to individual tale plots. In the beginning, "catch-word titles" alone were sufficient—"Cinderella," "Puss in Boots," "Jack the Giant Killer," "Rumpelstiltzchen." In some early studies the numbers of the tales in the Grimm collection were used for reference purposes. But as large numbers of folktales were collected, serious drawbacks appeared in these systems. Titles vary greatly from country to country, or even within an individual country. For instance, Cinderella is often a boy in Scandinavian tales with the nickname "Askeladden," or "the ash lad." The helpful dwarf Rumpelstiltzchen is "Tom-Tit-Tot" in English folktales, and has a different local name in each of the many countries from which that tale has been collected. Most tales are collected from oral tradition without any titles at all being given them by informants, and often several distinct tale plots are intermixed in one oral text. The use of the Grimm numbers for classification, obviously, was limited solely to the tale types that the Grimms had collected.

In Denmark, by the second half of the nineteenth century, the ballad scholar Svend Gruntvig had worked out a classification system for archiving the Danish folktales for his own convenience in consulting them, but this was too narrow for general use. However, in Finland in the late nineteenth century a folklorist devised a catalog based on most of the then-published European texts that introduced what has become the standard reference and classification system for *Märchen* and for some other kinds of European folktales as well. Kaarle Krohn, a founding father of modern folktale research, recognized the great need for an index of European folktale types when he experienced difficulties gathering from many countries variants of stories about the competition of a bear and a fox. He posed the problem to his student Antti Aarne, who undertook to solve it, producing in 1910 a catalog called *Verzeichnis der Märchentypen* (*Folklore Fellows Communications* no. 3), which was translated and enlarged in 1928 by the American folklorist Stith Thompson as *The Types of the Folktale* (*FFC*, no. 74). In its present second revision (*FFC*, no. 184; 1961), the *Type-Index* is an essential tool for any collecting, archiving, or comparative analysis of Indo-European folktales throughout their present worldwide distribution.

The *Type-Index* should not be confused with the *Motif-Index*, introduced in Chapter 8. The two works are cross-indexed in great detail, but they are distinctly different references. The *Type-Index*, theoretically, classifies only whole plots, while the *Motif-Index* is an index of narrative elements—actions, actors, objects, settings, and the like. ("Cinderella" is *Type* 510A, but "Identification by fitting of slipper" is *Motif* H36.1., and merely one narrative element of some versions of that tale.) In reference to the scholars who developed the *Type-Index*, tales catalogued therein are frequently cited as "Aarne-Thompson" types (or simply "AT" or "AaTh" types, and sometimes "MT" for "*Märchentypus*"). The *Motif-Index* was Thompson's creation alone, and was separately compiled; motifs are simply cited by their lettered chapters in Thompson's system, and with their individual numbers. Both indexes may be used to identify tales and their elements, to arrange archives, and to collect bibliographic references. But the *Type-Index* deals mainly with Indo-European folktales, especially *Märchen*, while the *Motif-Index* is completely international in its scope and contains narrative elements from many kinds of texts besides folktales. There is some overlapping of the two indexes in the area of one-motif tales, which properly seem to belong in the *Type-Index*. The most important basic distinction between the two indexes is that while the designation of a "type" in the folktale catalog implies that all of the items listed there are historically related, *Motif-Index* entries make no such implication. To put it differently, it is assumed in the *Type-Index* that polygenesis of whole tales is impossible; in the *Motif-Index* it is assumed that polygenesis does explain parallels between some individual narrative elements that are widely known.

Before going beyond the cataloguing of types and motifs to actual studies of folktales, it is necessary to define the basic kinds of tales that are found, especially in Anglo-American folk tradition. For this purpose, the *Type-Index* furnishes a convenient outline:

    I.   Animal Tales (Types 1 to 299)
    II.   Ordinary Folktales (Types 300 to 1199)
    III.   Jokes and Anecdotes (Types 1200 to 1999)
    IV.   Formula Tales (Types 2000 to 2399)

Animal tales have as their main characters domestic or wild animals (mammals, birds, reptiles, fish, insects, etc.) that speak, reason, and otherwise behave like human beings. Usually these animals correspond to certain stock character types, such as the clever fox or rabbit, the stupid bear, the faithful dog, and the industrious ant. Frequently these tales describe conflicts between different animals or between animals and men. A few animal tales are etiological, for example Type 2, "The Tail-Fisher," which explains that the bear now has a short tail because he was once tricked by the fox into fishing through the ice with his original long one. Several of the favorite stories printed in children's books are traditional animal tales. "The Bremen Town Musicians," for example, is Type 130, "The Animals in Night Quarters"; and "The Three Little Pigs" is Type 124, "Blowing the House In." Genuine oral versions of such tales, however, usually differ markedly from printed ones. For instance, in a Kentucky Mountain text of Type 124 the pigs are named "Mary, Martha, and Nancy" and they build their houses out of chips and clay, chips and hickory bark, and "steel and arn." When the wolf comes, he threatens "to get up on the house and fiddy, fiddy, faddy your house all down."

It must be conceeced that popular adapted versions, at least in this country, now outnumber oral-traditional texts of animal tales, as well as of many other folktales. The best-known examples of animal tales in the United States come from southern blacks, and even these have been publicized mainly in the semi-literary renderings of Joel Chandler Harris (the creator of "Uncle Remus") and in the cartoon treatments of Walt Disney. Both of these adaptations are somewhat removed from the actual oral specimens of such tales as Type 175, "The Tarbaby and the Rabbit," which has a wide international distribution.

Fables are often regarded as a special subtype of animal tales, even though some fables have only human characters in them. A better term for fables might be *moral tales*, for their distinguishing quality is an explicit or implied lesson, often expressed as a proverbial moral to the story. Of the roughly five hundred to six hundred Greek and Indic fables that are known in literature, only about fifty have been collected from oral tradition. Such popular phrases as "the lion's share," "sour grapes," and "belling the cat" refer to such tales, these particular ones bearing the type numbers AT 51, 59, and 110 respectively.

Famous literary imitations of animal tales that have become children's classics should not be confused with stories in the oral tradition. Hans Christian Andersen's "The Ugly Duckling," for example, is not a folktale, although it might loosely be called a "fairy tale" in the popular sense of the term. Similarly, "The Three Bears" was written by Robert Southey, the English Poet Laureate (1813–43), probably in imitation of a folktale, and went through various literary revisions rather than oral changes. Parodies of "The Three Bears," however, do exist in modern folklore; in one of these, Mother Bear responds to the others' requests for their porridge, "Gripe, gripe, gripe, and I haven't even made breakfast yet!"

The **ordinary folktales** in part II of the Aarne-Thompson index include most of the *Märchen* proper, although the German term is sometimes used to refer to the entire contents of the *Type-Index*. But as Thompson writes in the preface of his latest revision, "There are certainly many things in the index which are by no means *Märchen*," The "ordinary folktales," a poorly named category, constitute about one-half of the entire type catalog, and include almost all of the *Märchen* that are in it. Their characteristic features, as earlier stated, are formularized language and structure, supernatural motifs, and sympathy for the underdog or commoner.

All of the European immigrant groups in the United States, to some extent, carried their *Märchen* here with them, but these were seldom translated by the folk into English, and thus have not usually persisted as oral tales in the second generation. The British wonder-tale tradition, however, with no language barrier to cross, became well established in this country, especially in the Southern Appalachian and Ozark mountains. There, distinctive American adaptations took place, and the collected texts sometimes seem almost like native stories. Type 313, "The Girl as Helper in the Hero's Flight," became "The Devil's Pretty Daughter" in the Ozarks. In Kentucky, Type 425A, "The Monster as Bridegroom," was collected as "The Girl that Married a Flop-Eared Hound-Dog," and Type 326, "The Youth Who Wanted to Learn What Fear Is," was collected as "Johnny That Never Seen a Fraid." A North Carolina text that is a combination of Type 330, "The Smith Outwits the Devil," and Type 332, "Godfather Death," is locally titled "Whickety-Whack, Into My Sack." One cycle of Southern tales clustered around three brothers—Jack, Will, and Tom—with emphasis on the clever youngest one; these are known as "The Jack Tales." In urban parts of the United States, where the influence of printed collections of European folktales has been strong, wonder tales like these are usually not well known in oral tradition.

Although the plots of Americanized *Märchen* may contain such unlikely motifs as royal characters, magical transportation, giants, ogres, and even unicorns, the language of the tellings is full of regional dialect. Expressions such as "bedads" (an exclamation), "bless me," "lit out," and "I reckon," are common; and terms such as "ash cake" (bread baked directly in fireplace ashes), "poke" (for a bag or sack), "riddle" (for a sieve), and "house plunder" (for the necessities of housekeeping) are freely introduced. As in the European versions of *Märchen*, the home life of royalty is described in very folksy terms; the hero may go down to "the king's house" and "holler him out"; and when the king summons the women in his family, he may call out, "Hey, old woman and girls! Come on over here." As was shown for animal tales, parodies of *Märchen* circulate among sophisticated modern folk, who base them on book-versions they know; for example, Type 440, "The Frog King," (the first tale in the Grimm collection) ends in a parody version with a college coed saying to the prince in her room who has been transformed from a frog, "What is my house-mother going to say?" The adaptation of one European folktale, "The Taming of the Shrew" (Type 901), is analyzed in the study appearing here as Appendix A.

The **jokes and anecdotes** section of the *Type-Index* also has a somewhat misleading title; no real difference between the two categories is established, and, as we have seen, the term "anecdotes" belongs to a subclass of personal legends. Also, only a few of the countless jokes told in modern tradition are included here. This section of the index is essentially a classification of the older European *jests*, or *merry tales*—humorous stories characterized by short and fairly simple plots, and by realistic settings. Some typical characters in the older jests were numskulls, married couples, and parsons; stories that may be found in the *Type-Index* about such character-types are still popular today in the United States.

Numskull stories, also called *noodle tales*, attribute absurd ignorance to people, often to a particular group. In Denmark, for example, the traditional fools are the *Molbos*; in England they are the "Wise Men of Gotham," and in the United States they may be two stupid Irishmen named "Pat and Mike." Some old favorite examples that have been collected frequently in this country are Type 1240, "Man Sitting on Branch of Tree Cuts it Off"; Type 1278, "Marking the Place on the Boat [Where an Object was Lost Overboard]"; and Type 1319, "Pumpkin Sold as Ass's Egg."

Stories about married couples frequently deal with competition between husbands and their wives. For example in Type 1351, "The Silence Wager," a man and his wife become so angry that they refuse to speak to one another, even during a grave crisis. In Type 1365A, "Wife Falls into a Stream," the obstinate wife drowns, and her husband looks for the body upstream where he believes she would have drifted against the current. In a subtype of that tale the man and wife had been arguing about whether to cut something with a knife or with scissors; the man throws his wife into the stream, and as she drowns, she lifts her fingers out of the water and makes a clipping motion in order to be able to give the last opinion in the dispute.

Jokes about parsons and religious orders make fools of churchmen. In Type 1791, "The Sexton Carries the Parson," one of the most popular anticlerical tales brought to the United States, thieves are overheard dividing their loot in a graveyard, and the two foolish listeners believe it is the Devil and the Lord dividing souls. In American versions, however, the listeners are not always specified as churchmen. In Type 1833, "The Boy Applies the Sermon," a parson's rhetorical question in a sermon receives a literal and absurd answer from someone in the congregation. For example, an American version has this dialogue:

> Parson: "How shall we get to heaven?"
> Baseball Player (just waking up): "Slide!"

Only a fraction of the oral jokes in American folk tradition are to be found in the Aarne-Thompson *Type-Index*. A few of them can be identified with Thompson's motif numbers, but the majority have not been entered in any catalog of its type. Some may be original American jests, but most of them probably have foreign parallels or counterparts. The histories of these stories cannot be written until workable reference systems are published. Thus, the indexing of jokes is a major future task for American folktale scholars. However, not even the basic framework for a classification has been developed. One possibility, employed in some college archives, is to arrange texts according to their general subjects under such headings as "Jokes about Religions," "Jokes about Nationalities," "Jokes about Sex." Another system is to group stories according to stock character types: "Jokes about Hillbillies," "Jokes about Musicians," "Jokes about Politicians." The difficulty with such plans is obvious: many jokes will fit several categories, for instance, a sexy joke about a hillbilly, or a joke about an Irish politician.

The immigrant *dialect story* has been identified as a distinctive American folk creation, and these might easily be grouped by nationalities or languages. The humorous point of such jokes is the immigrant's broken English and his resulting mistakes in using the language. The impetus for their circulation is not necessarily prejudice, for immigrants themselves are the best raconteurs, but generally a humorous recital of some of the group's problems in acculturation. Some dialect stories reproduce the actual linguistic quirks of a nationality group, such as the "l"-"r" confusion among Japanese speaking English. Other tales adhere to different groups, as does the story of the newly wealthy immigrant who orders a home built containing a "Halo Statue." He finally explains, "You know. It rings: you pick it up; you say, 'Halo, statue?' "

The *Jewish-American dialect story* is a particularly interesting sub-type, involving as it does both the humorous crystallization of the eso-teric and exoteric attitudes of Jews and Gentiles toward themselves and each other (and also attitudes toward the others' attitudes toward *themselves*), as well as the dialect flavoring of an exaggerated form of Yiddish-American speech. The best informants, usually American-born offspring of European Jewish immigrants, become masters of the nasalized accent, stylized gesture, and dramatic role-playing typi-cal of the form. The Jewish-American businessman in a joke asks the headmaster of Eton College, "Mine Jake, he's speaking de King's En-glish now?" Then the narrator assumes the part of the headmaster to deliver the punchline. He hunches his shoulders, spreads his up-turned palms wide, and whines, "Netchally, vat else?"

A study of the development of the *Negro dialect story* in America would yield insights into the psychology involved in the changing relationships between races. One group of jokes, now dying out, pic-tures the black as a comical old darky—slowmoving, dull-witted, usually named something like "Rastus" or "Liza," and always drawl-ing in a thick southern accent. (In the protest jokes of southern blacks' own biracial folk humor, the same type of character—often "John," the slave or hired man—manages to outsmart the white man.) An-other cycle of urban white stories creates a vicious stereotype of the black as a crude, oversexed, automobile-loving maniac. The latest de-velopment has been the *integration story* in which the effects of the civil rights movements are directly mirrored. In these jokes the white man seems to be jolted into a belated recognition of new patterns in American life. In one such story a white librarian refuses to censor books containing the word *nigger,* pointing out that offensive words like *bastard* appear in books, too. The black responds, "Yes, but us niggers is organized, and you bastards ain't." Another highly reveal-ing story concerns the football coach in a southern college who is forced to try out a black player. When the boy smashes through the team's best linemen, the coach shouts excitedly, "Will you look at that Mexican boy run!"

The whole complex of ethnic, religious, and racial folk humor in the United States deserves more investigation, but even separate studies of individual groups would not point up all of the interrela-tionships. For example, a Jewish dialect joke concerns the Jew con-verted to Catholicism who is put upon at once by his family and friends. He grumbles, "I've only been a Gentile for twenty minutes, and already I hate those Jews." The same story is told as a black dialect joke. Here a little black boy has smeared his face with flour or cold cream, and he runs home shouting, "I's white! I's white!" He is criticized by his family, and he declares that he already hates blacks. This theme of role-shifting is also found in the integration story about a southern black boy allowed the join a white gang. When their hot rod has a blowout, he is the first to complain, "There's not a nigger for miles around to change it for us." The sometimes absurd basis for racial pride is illustrated in the joke about an Indian boy and a black boy arguing over who comes from the most notable race. The Indian wins the dispute when he points out that little white boys never play "cowboys and niggers." A related joke pits a white child in debate against a child from a black family that has just moved into the neighborhood. The black wins this round when he declares, "At least we don't live next door to no niggers."

The **joke fads** of recent years have attracted some folklorists' attention, although often merely as material to collect and then to publish in simple subject-matter classifications. These fad cycles are generally made up of riddle-jokes (see Chapter 6) rather than narrative jokes, and thus they might logically be compared to other riddle forms and perhaps analyzed in terms of riddling themes and structures. The riddle form (question and answer) is characteristic of "elephant jokes," "grape jokes," many "sick jokes" and "wind-up doll jokes," as well as the older "moron jokes," and "knock-knocks." "Polack jokes" follow the same pattern: Question—"How do you tell the groom at a Polish wedding?" Answer—"He's the one with a clean bowling shirt on." A few Polack jokes have some narrative content (becoming noodle tales), and some are based on a sketch or diagram, such as the "Polish Computer System" for "output processing," an elaborate drawing which folds down to a picture of a simple toilet. All such jokes cycles, although they appear and disappear much more rapidly than old traditional folklore, and despite the boost that mass communication gives them, clearly belong to the field of folklore and deserve the folklorist's study.

Two minor categories of American jokes about children await more than token notice by folklorists. One is the stories involving children's misunderstandings of religious and patriotic texts; these may well demonstrate a basic joke-making process. First a child's inadvertent error is related as an anecdote by his amused parents, but eventually it is repeated often enough to become an anonymous jest. This sequence, at least, would seem to explain the origins of such stories as that about a child who wants to name his teddy bear "Gladly," because the people sing at church, "Gladly, the Cross-Eyed Bear"; or the one about the child's recitation in the Pledge of Allegiance to the Flag, ". . . one nation, indigestible, with liver and juices for all." The second minor subtype is what might be called the *"pictorial* joke." Here children in grade school are asked to add a line to a drawing on the blackboard. The last child adds a line which converts the innocent sketch into an obscene picture. Another kind of pictorial folktale is usually told to children by adults. The storyteller illustrates his tale with a simple sketch map of the locale of the tale. The last line which is added turns it into a picture of the animal being described or hunted in the story—a wildcat, a duck, or other animal.

A detailed classification has been published for one modern joke type, the *shaggy dog story.* Some 700 texts were secured from both printed and oral sources, including the entries mailed in response to a radio program's nationwide contest. The following definition, based on the stories' humorous twists, was worked out for their classification into three major groups and some 200 types and subtypes: "A nonsensical joke that employs in the punchline a psychological non sequitur, a punning variation of a familiar saying, or a hoax, to trick the listener who expects conventional wit or humor." On the basis of style, it was found that shaggy dog stories "usually describe ridiculous characters and actions, and often are told (to heighten the effect of the final letdown) in a long drawn-out style with minute details, repetitions, and elaborations." The whole classification was lettered and numbered after the manner of the *Motif-Index* so that new materials could be added at any point; but like the *Type-Index,* it provided a brief summary of each plot, a list of known versions, cross-references, and bibliographic and comparative notes. For example, the joke about a midget knight mounted on a large shaggy dog, which has the punchline, "I wouldn't send a knight out on a dog like that!" was classified as C425. "The Midget Knight and his Mount," in a category with other stories that end with punning variations of popular sayings. Twenty-eight versions of the tale were reported, fifteen from the radio contest, six from a folklore archive, two from *Boys' Life* magazine, one each from a joke book, a mail-order catalog, a comic strip, *Today's Health* magazine, and a newspaper political cartoon. Other jokes in the index were related to literature; to historical persons; to traditional myths, tale types and motifs; to popular poems and songs; and one even to a Sumerian fable that is possibly 5,000 years old.

Types 1875 to 1999 in the Aarne-Thompson index are *tales of lying*, commonly called **tall tales** or "windies" in the United States; this section is supplemented by a portion of Chapter "X" (Humor) in the *Motif-Index*, Motifs X900. to X1899., "Humor of Lies and Exaggerations." Americans think of the tall tale as a peculiarly American product, just as the Turk, the German, and the Scandinavian each thinks of it as peculiarly *his* national invention, all of them forgetting that there were tall tales before any of their nations was thought of.

Some of the best-known American windies are found in the *Type-Index*, among them Type 1889F, "Frozen Words Thaw"; Type 1889L, "The Split Dog"; Types 1890A through F, "The Wonderful Hunt"; and Type 1920B, often called "Too Busy to Tell a Lie." Even though a good number of lying tales are included in the *Type-Index*, they have never been considered to be very numerous in most European countries. In the Norwegian standard type catalog, for example, which was published in 1921, only four such tales were listed, but when a marine paint company in Norway offered prizes in 1959 for good "skipper tales," some 100 tall tale texts were among the entries that sailors submitted. Some were Aarne-Thompson lying tales previously unlisted in the Norwegian catalog; others could be identified with motif numbers, and most of the new discoveries are known in some form in American folklore as well.

Tall tales may not be original with Americans, but they are certainly very popular in the United States and fully characteristic of American folklore. Mody Boatright has written that they represent a sort of reverse bragging about the hardships of settling the continent, and an exaggeration of natural features of the frontier. They flourished among frontiersmen, Boatright suggested, as a buoyant reaction to the wilderness itself and against the Eastern-tourists' version of what life out West was like. Men *were* tough there, though not as tough as the Eastern emphasis on eye-gouging fights made them seem, and the tall tales made men even tougher. Danger and death *were* familiar, so the tales laughed at death. Westerners *did* love to gamble, and in tall tales gambling was pictured as mania. A folk story about how a cowboy went about reporting a man's death to the bereaved wife indicates the proper climate for tall tales. He: "Howdy, widow Jones." She: "I'm not a widow." He: "Bet you ten dollars you are!"

That illustration is really a local-character story, not a tall tale, but it is just that sort of narrator—the laconic, poker-faced, hardened, regional character—who specialized in telling tall tales (or "talking trash") to his cronies, youngsters, and tourists. Vance Randolph expresses the tone very well in the title of his book of Ozark tall tales: *We Always Lie to Strangers.* The success of tall tales does not depend on belief in the details of the story, but rather on a willingness to lie and be lied to while keeping a straight face. The humor of these tales consists of telling an outrageous falsehood in the sober accents of a truthful story. The best tall tales are only improvements upon reality: smart animals are made smarter, big mosquitoes are made bigger, bad weather is made worse, huge crops are made even larger. There is the smart dog that hunts all kinds of game and even starts to dig worms when its master gets out a fishing pole one morning. There are the mosquitoes that eat a team of horses and pitch horseshoes for the harness. There is the wind that blows a suspended log chain out straight and snaps links off the end. And there is the strawberry that is so big that the cook won't cut one for only two orders of strawberry shortcake. (Tall-tale humor of this kind is often captured in postcard art created by using pasteups or trick photography.)

Although these and numerous other tall tales have been frequently collected and printed, they retain an appeal in oral transmission that quickly fades in reading printed versions. The art of the tall tale, like the art of the anecdote and the joke, is primarily a verbal one, deriving from the skill of the teller rather than from the originality of his material. When stretching the truth becomes second nature with a yarnspinner, he may become truly inspired on the spur of the moment. One noted local liar once got a jolt from a sparkplug when an automobile engine was running. Someone asked, "Did it shock you, Len?" "Nope," the old-timer shot back, "I was too quick for it."

The **formula tales** in the last section of the *Type-Index* represent a very ancient category of folktales, those based on a strict pattern of development, usually involving repetition. Both old formula tales in several subclasses, and new tales based on old formulas are known in the United States.

Cumulative tales, or "chains" (Types 2000 to 2199) are often based on the device of adding a further detail with each repetition of the plot. Familiar examples are Type 2030, "The Old Woman and her Pig," and Type 2035, "House that Jack Built." Another group contains a series of alternate responses, as in Type 2014, "Chains Involving Contradictions or Extremes." A popular American collegiate example that has not been catalogued in any index of types contains sequences like the following, with the audience furnishing the responses:

> "We've just built a new fraternity house!" (Yay!)
> "With only one bar." (Boo!)
> "A mile long!" (Yay!)

Catch tales (Types 2200 to 2205), like catch questions in riddling tradition, lead the listener on to be hoaxed; in this instance the trick consists of causing him to ask a question to which the storyteller returns a foolish answer. A favorite catch tale in the United States is Type 2205, "Teller is Killed in His Own Story," sometimes with the following variation, in a story about being surrounded by Indians— Listener: "What did you do?" Storyteller: "What could I do? I bought a blanket." Another recent favorite, not specifically listed in the *Type-Index,* is a long, boring story involving the repeated line "Patience, little burro, patience." When an exasperated listener finally demands the point of the story, the narrator admonishes him, "Patience, little burro, patience."

Endless tales (Type 2300) are formula tales which might continue indefinitely if the narrator had the will and the breath for it. These stories set up an action that is then repeated ad infinitum—sheep jumping over a fence, geese quacking, locusts carrying corn from a barn one grain at a time. *Rounds* (Type 2320) are endless stories that come back to their own starting points and then begin again. Often the situation is a tale within a tale within a tale, theoretically without any ending. One example is: "I laughed so hard I thought I'd die. I did die. They buried me, and a flower grew on my grave. The roots grew down and tickled me. I laughed so hard I thought I'd die. I did die. . . ."

One final tale form does not appear in the Aarne-Thompson index as a separate type, although several different animal tales and *Märchen* display its characteristic device—a song or rhyme that is interspersed with the prose narration. This is the so-called *cante fable,* or "singing tale." The narratives in which neck riddles are embedded suggest the *cante fable* form. Two of the best-known examples are often printed as nursery tales—"The Three Little Pigs" (Type 124), and "Jack and the Beanstalk," (Type 328). Another European-American tale frequently collected as a *cante fable* is Type 1360C, "Old Hildebrand." In some versions a man bets his fiddle against a ship-captain's cargo that his wife can resist seduction for two hours; the man sings:

> Be true, my lover, be true, my lover
> Be true for just two hours;
> Be true, my lover, be true, my lover,
> The cargo will soon be ours.

But the wife, from inside the captain's cabin, sings back:

> Too late, my lover, too late, my lover,
> He grabbed me round the middle;
> Too late my lover, too late my lover,
> You've lost your damned old fiddle.

An especially popular *cante fable* in the United States has to do with a man invited to supper who sees some very plain food replaced by better fare when the minister or other important guests arrive unexpectedly. The man then chants something like:

> The Lord be praised,
> But I'm amazed,
> To see how things are mended.
> Applesauce and pumpkin pie,
> When pudding and milk were intended.

Or a prairie preacher, subtly protesting the sameness of all his meals out, may pray:

> For rabbit roasted and rabbit fried,
> For rabbit cooked and rabbit dried,
> For rabbit young and rabbit old,
> For rabbit hot and rabbit cold,
> For rabbit tender and rabbit tough,
> We thank thee, Lord, that we have enough.

The identification of different classes and subclasses of folktales, and the cataloguing of types and motifs, are only preliminary steps in the study of these narratives. The *Type-* and *Motif-Indexes* do not analyze tales, interpret them, or trace them to their origins; they simply organize the collected material in a systematic fashion, outline the usual forms, and provide bibliography. The two indexes used together render the tasks of identifying narratives, gathering variants, and analyzing them immeasurably easier than the process would be without such reference works. Thus, any folklorist working with traditional prose narratives should become thoroughly familiar with these indexes. To illustrate their use, we might examine a verbatim entry from the *Type-Index:*

660 *The Three Doctors.* The hog's heart, the thief's hand, the cat's eye. The three doctors make a trial of their skill [H504.]. One removes one of his eyes, one his heart, and the other a hand [F668.1.]. They are to replace them without injury the next morning [E782.]. During the night they are eaten and others substituted [X1721.2. E780.2.], and one of the doctors thus acquires a cat's eye which sees best at night, one a thief's hand that wants to steal [E782.1.1.], and one a hog's heart that makes him want to root in the ground [E786.].

* BP II 552 (Grimm No. 118).—Finnish *50;* Finnish-Swedish *4;* Estonian *1;* Lithuanian *9;* Swedish *13* (Stockholm *2;* Göteborg *2,* Liungman *2,* misc. *7);* Norwegian *2;* Danish *3;* Irish *45;* French *7;* Flemish *3;* German: Ranke *6;* Czech: Tille Soupis II (2) 446f. *6;* Slovenian *3;* Polish *1;* Russian: Andrejev *1.*—Franco-American *4.*

Like all descriptions in the Aarne-Thompson index, this one begins with a numerical designation, a conventional title, and a condensed description of the tale type. The tale is summarized next, with the appropriate motif numbers indicated in brackets. (For the more complex tales, a separate motif list is used, and subtypes may be established.) Last come abbreviated bibliographic references, including the total numbers of variants contained in national folktale archives and collections. Turning to the motifs that are cited, we find the following entries in the *Motif-Index:*

H504.   Test of skill in handwork.
F668.1.   Skillful surgeon removes and replaces vital organs.
E782.   Limbs successfully replaced.
X1721.2.   Lie: man's organs replaced with animal's. He acts like animal.
E780.2.   Animal bodily member transferred to person or other animal retains animal powers and habits.
E782.1.1.   Substituted hand. Man exchanges his hand for that of another.
E786.   Heart successfully replaced.

For each of these motifs, cross-references to other related motifs and to Type 660 are provided; also further bibliography is listed under most of them, although not all references will necessarily be related to the tale type in question. To save space and avoid repetition, only the numbers and descriptions are given with the motifs above, but the bibliographic references quoted with the Type 660 entry are typical items: The "*BP" refers to the voluminous notes by Bolte and Polivka for the Grimm tales (asterisks are used throughout to mark the best reference sources); in this instance the tale is number 118 in Grimm. Then follow a list of sixteen countries or national groups in which this tale has been found (including Swedes in Finland and French in America) and, in italics, the totals for each country (*158 in all*). The full references for each abbreviated item in the list are given in a bibliography at the beginning of the index.

Equipped with such indexes, the folktale scholar is well prepared to identify and annotate the texts that he collects. Whether he begins searching for a whole tale plot, for a characteristic motif, or for details which may be in the alphabetical index to the *Motif-Index,* he will eventually be able to pin down parallels from narrative folklore that have already been identified and classified. To do this, however, he must not take type and motif entries too literally; the indexes work best when they are flexibly applied. After all, an indexer cannot furnish the details of every text he has examined. In fact, he cannot usually even personally examine all of the relevant texts. Instead, for many items he must rely on catalogs and indexes made by others using their own collected materials.

Bearing these points in mind, it is not difficult to see that the following tale heard orally in the West in 1961 is related to this complex of type and motifs:

A cowboy is injured badly during a round-up, and a medical student is flagged down on a nearby highway to administer first aid. Finding an internal organ destroyed, the student calls for a wandering sheep to be dragged in, killed, and cut open. From the sheep's insides he borrows the parts to patch up the man. A year later the same student drives down the same road and sees the same crew rounding up cattle again. Inquiring about the injured man, he is told, "He's all right now. Course he had quite a lot of trouble this spring. He brought a nice pair of twin lambs, and we sheared him—he sheared eight pounds." That this tale is traditional and is related to Type 660 is suggested by other variants. In 1965, for example, an informant in Maine said that his uncle had sheep's intestines substituted for his own in a hospital operation, and "every spring they had to shear the old devil." In a volume of Civil War reminiscences, a doctor is described as removing the liver of a soldier wounded in the field. A dog eats it, so the physician substitutes a sheep's liver. The soldier recovers, but he has a "hankering after grass." If it seems that these American tales deviate too far from the outlined type description, consider this summary of a version from a Medieval collection, the *Gesta Romanorum* (Tale LXXVI): Two physicians alternate in removing and replacing each other's eyes; a crow steals one, however, which must then be replaced with a goat's eye that thereafter persists in looking up at trees.

A typical form of folklore research is the gathering of all available variants of an international tale to try to discover, by means of comparative analysis, its most likely place of origin and its probable routes of dissemination. This approach is often called "The Finnish Method," in reference to the late nineteenth-century Finns (Krohn, Aarne, and others) who developed it, or **The Historic-Geographic Method,** in reference to the plan of tale arrangement employed in it. The ultimate goal of this method is to be able to write "life histories" of individual folktales, and to reconstruct an *archetype*, or hypothetical original form, for each tale. The method is based on the assumption that complex folktales had a single origin in one time and one place (rather than having resulted from polygenesis), and that each tale then spread throughout its present area of distribution by *auto-migration*, that is, from person to person, without needing large-scale folk migrations to carry it.

Although scholars employing the historic-geographic method are never able to make a definitive statement of exactly where a given tale began, their studies so far have pointed to India as probably the most important center of folktale dissemination.

In essence, the historic-geographic method involves the following steps:

1. Gather all available texts (using the indexes, corresponding with archives, field collecting, etc.)
2. Label all texts (usually a letter-code for the language group and a number for the specific text)
3. Arrange literary texts historically and oral texts geographically (often north to south within each country)
4. Identify the traits to be studied and make a master outline of all traits found in the texts.
5. Summarize the traits in each individual text, referring to the outline of traits.
6. Compare all traits in texts, one by one, in order to:
   a. Establish subtypes (regional subclasses)
   b. Formulate the archetype (hypothetical original)
7. Reconstruct the life history of the tale which best explains all of the present texts and their variations.

Comparing the traits in families of folktales and reconstructing archetypal forms represent only one possible approach to studying the folktale, although until recently it has been the most popular one. Another important method, the **structural approach to folktales,** seeks to establish a *synchronic* basis (viewed without reference to historical change) rather than a *diachronic* basis (viewed in terms of historical development) for comparing folktales. Following the method of structural linguistics, Alan Dundes, the chief proponent of this approach, would begin by defining *minimal units* of folktales that are distinct from the specific contents of the tales. Whether a tale is about animals, ogres, or numskulls should make no difference in a structural analysis, as long as the *form* of the narratives is parallel. (Several similar tale-forms are widely separated in the *Type-Index*, Dundes has pointed out, simply because their cast of characters and other details differ).

Borrowing terms from structural linguistics, and adapting them to the system of the Russian structuralist Vladimir Propp, Dundes further suggests that if the phonetic level of linguistic analysis is the equivalent of what he calls the "etic" (nonstructural) approach of motif-indexing, then the "emic" level would be reached by an index of the structural units, or *motifemes*. The Proppian approach, which leaves folktale elements in their original linear sequence as the tales are told, Dundes terms "syntagmatic," or analogous to the analysis of syntax in languages. A "paradigmatic" approach, akin to the use of paradigms (sample patterns) in language analysis, rearranges the folktale elements so as to reveal their underlying structure, usually as sets of oppositions: life/death, raw/cooked, good/evil, and so forth. The leading exponent of this method is the French anthropologist Claude Lévi-Strauss. Structural approaches, it is emphasized, would not eliminate the comparative approach or its long-established reference tools. Rather, both synchronic and diachronic studies are needed to fully explore folktale form and development.

As a counterbalance to the highly schematized and often largely statistical nature of both historic-geographic and structural analyses of folktale texts, there is a need for more studies of the oral style of tale narrators. For this to be done requires first that collectors record much more than just the text and the informant's background. We would need to know *where* tales are told, *how* they are told, *when* they are told, and *to whom*. Probably photographs—preferably motion pictures—are necessary to record gestures and facial expressions, and it is desirable to observe good informant's retelling tales to different audiences. We should take note of the dramatic role-playing of the teller, his use of repetitions and other verbal formulas, his personal or local references and other improvisations, and also the responses that come from his audience. When data of this sort are collected and have been analyzed, it is possible to differentiate the styles characteristic of a specific tale, of a tale-teller, or of an individual culture. Moving beyond even these concerns, and rejecting past studies of story texts and their contents, Robert A. Georges advocates instead a holistic analysis, not of "stories" but of "storytelling events"—which are "communicative events . . . social experiences, and . . . unique expressions of human behavior."

BIBLIOGRAPHIC NOTES

Stith Thompson's *The Folktale* (see Chapter 8) is the definitive survey of the field. Besides the *Type-* and *Motif-Indexes* discussed in Chapters 8 and 9, American folklorists should consult the satellite work by Ernest W. Baughman, *A Type and Motif-Index of the Folktales of England and North America* The Hague: Indiana University Folklore Series no. 20, 1966). Advanced study of the folktale requires use of several reference works in foreign languages, especially Johannes Bolte and Georg Polívka, *Anmerkungen zu der Kinder- und Hausmärchen der Brüder Grimm,* 5 vols. (Leipzig, 1913–32). An important article translated from German for Alan Dundes's book *The Study of Folklore* is Axel Olrik's *"Epische Gesetze der Volksdichtung" (Epic Laws of Folk Narrative,)* (1909). A good survey of older European folktale theories in English is in Emma Emily Kiefer's *Albert Wesselski and Recent Folktale Theories* (Bloomington: Indiana University Folklore Series no. 3, 1947).

European folktales in authentic texts, accurately translated and fully annotated, are available in the "Folktales of the World" series published under the general editorship of Richard M. Dorson by the University of Chicago Press. *Folktales of England,* edited for the series by Katharine M. Briggs and Ruth L. Tongue (Chicago, 1965) is of particular interest to American folklorists. Briggs also compiled the important new reference work titled *A Dictionary of British Folktales in the English Language;* Part A covers folk narratives, Part B folk legends (Bloomington: Indiana University Press, 1970, 1971, 2 vols. each part).

Some representative non-English tales collected in the United States may be found in the following: Joseph Médard Carrière's *Tales from the French Folk-Lore of Missouri* (Evanston and Chicago, Ill: Northwestern University Press, 1937); Thomas R. Brendle and William S. Troxell's *Pennsylvania German Folk-Tales, Legends, Once-Upon-a-Time Stories, Maxims, and Sayings* (Morristown, Pa.: Pennsylvania German Society Publications no. 50, 1944); Richard M. Dorson's "Polish Wonder Tales of Joe Woods," *WF* 8 (1949), 25–52 and 131–45; Rosemary Agonito's "Il Paisano: Immigrant Italian Folktales of Central New York," *NYFQ* 23 (1967), 52–64; Francine Pelly's "Gypsy Folktales from Philadelphia," *KFQ* 13 (1968), 83–102; Anthony Milanovich's "Serbian Tales from Blanford," *IF* 4 (1971), 1–60; and Elaine K. Miller's *Mexican Folk Narrative from the Los Angeles Area* (Austin, Tex.: AFS Memoir, vol. 56, 1973).

Robert B. Klymasz is only one field collector who has published non-English tales from Canada, in such works as *Folk Narratives Among Ukrainian-Canadians in Western Canada* (Ottawa: Canadian Center for Folk Culture Studies, Paper no. 4, 1973), and "The Ethnic Joke in Canada Today," *KFQ* 15 (1970), 167–73.

In 1957 (vol. 70), the *Journal of American Folklore* published "The Folktale: A Symposium" with important articles by Warren E. Roberts, "Collections and Indexes: A Brief Review" (pp. 49–52); Richard M. Dorson, "Standards for Collecting and Publishing American Folktales" (pp. 53–57); and Herbert Halpert, "Problems and Projects in the American-English Folktale" (pp. 57–62).

The Library of Congress published the useful bibliography by Barbara Quinnam, *Fables: from Incunabula to Modern Picture Books* (Washington, D.C., 1966). "Southey and 'The Three Bears' " was discussed by Mary I. Shamburger and Vera R. Lachman in *JAF* 59 (1946), 400–3.

There are many reliable book-length collections of American folktales. Richard Chase's two books, *The Jack Tales* (Cambridge, Mass.: Houghton Mifflin, 1943), and *Grandfather Tales* (Boston: Houghton Mifflin, 1948), are important Southern-Appalachian collections, especially the first with its notes by Herbert Halpert. All of Vance Randolph's Ozark collections, which contain a variety of folktale types and forms, are outstanding; these (all published by Columbia University Press) are *Who Blowed up the Church House?* (1953), *The Devil's Pretty Daughter* (1955), *The Talking Turtle* (1957)—all with notes by Halpert—and *Sticks in the Knapsack* (1958), with notes by Ernest W. Baughman. Marie Campbell's collection *Tales from the Cloud Walking Country* (Bloomington: Indiana University Press, 1958) contains folktales from Kentucky. Ruth Ann Musick's *Green Hills of Magic* (Lexington: University of Kentucky Press, 1970) is subtitled "West Virginia Folktales from Europe."

Leonard W. Roberts, an excellent collector of Kentucky folktales, has published numerous texts in journals such as *Mountain Life and Work, Kentucky Folklore Record*, and *Tennessee Folklore Society Bulletin*. His book, *South from Hell-fer-Sartin* (Lexington: University of Kentucky Press, 1955; reissued in paperback, Berea, Ky.: Council of the Southern Mountains, 1964), like his subsequent collections, is rendered in absolutely verbatim oral style and has complete notes for all tales. Roberts's *Old Greasybeard: Tales from the Cumberland Gap* (Detroit Folklore Associates, 1969) contains fifty tales; his *Sang Branch Settlers: Folksongs and Tales of a Kentucky Mountain Family* (Austin, Tex.: AFS Memoir, vol. 61, 1974) incorporates all the material previously published in book and microcard form as *Up Cutshin and Down Greasy* (Lexington: University of Kentucky Press, 1959).

Numerous folktales have been published in journal articles, only a few of which may be cited here. A double "Folk Narrative Issue" of *Midwest Folklore* (6, 1956, 5–128) is a good example of such publications. Another is Helen Creighton and Edward D. Ive's "Eight Folktales from Miramichi as Told by Wilmot MacDonald," *NEF* 4 (1962), 3–70, a model of editing and annotation. Jan Harold Brunvand's "Folktales by Mail from Bond, Kentucky," *KFR* 6 (1960), 69–76, describes an unusual collecting method and provides several annotated texts. An excellent variety of folk narrative types is represented in Donald Allport Bird and James R. Dow's "Benjamin Kuhn: Life and Narratives of a Hoosier Farmer," *IF* 5 (1972), 137–63. Horace P. Beck discussed

"The Acculturation of Old World Tales by the American Indian" with the example of a "Jack Tale" in *MF* 8 (1958), 205–16.

It is essential that folktales be heard, not just read, if they are to be fully appreciated. For this purpose two fine recordings of North Carolina storytellers are available: *Jack Tales Told by Mrs. Maud Long of Hot Springs, N.C.*, ed. Duncan Emrich (Washington, D.C.: Library of Congress Disc no. AAFS L47, 1957); and *Ray Hicks of Beech Mountain, N.C., Telling Four Traditional "Jack Tales,"* ed. Sandy Paton, texts transcribed by Lee B. Haggerty (Sharon, Conn.: Folk-Legacy Records no. FTA-14, 1964).

A good selection of older European jests, some of which have modern oral counterparts, is *A Hundred Merry Tales and Other Jestbooks of the Fifteenth and Sixteenth Centuries*, edited by P. M. Zall (Lincoln: University of Nebraska Press, Bison Books paperback edn., 1963). A fully annotated collection of oral American jests is Vance Randolph's *Hot Springs and Hell* (Hatboro, Pa.: Folklore Associates, 1965) containing 460 brief items from the Ozarks and 130 pages of notes and bibliography. Richard M. Dorson called attention to "Dialect Stories of the Upper Peninsula: A New Form of American Folklore" in *JAF* 61 (1948), 113–50.

Cycles of ethnic jokes have long interested American folklorists. Dorson discussed "Jewish-American Dialect Stories on Tape," in *Studies in Biblical and Jewish Folklore*, edited by D. Noy, R. Patai, and F. L. Utley (Bloomington: Indiana University Folklore Series no. 13, 1960), 111–74; further texts were published in *MF* 10 (1960), 133–46. The subclass of "Rabbi Trickster Tales" was the subject of an article by Ed Cray in *JAF* 77 (1964), 331–45. The following are analytical articles on Jewish dialect stories: Heda Jason, "The Jewish Joke: The Problem of Definition," *SFQ* 31 (1967), 48–54; Naomi and Eli Katz, "Tradition and Adaptation in American Jewish Humor," *JAF* 84 (1971), 215–20; and Dan Ben-Amos, "The 'Myth' of Jewish Humor," *WF* 32 (1973), 112–31.

The typical repertoire of Southern black folk narratives is surveyed by William R. Ferris, Jr., in "Black Prose Narrative in the Mississippi Delta," *JAF* 85 (1972), 140–51; a traditional vein of black jokelore is discussed by Harry Oster in "Negro Humor: John and Old Marster," *JFI* 5 (1968), 42–57. A brief discussion of some developments in dialect stories about blacks is in a note by Mac E. Barrick in *KFQ* 9 (1964), 166–68. Further study of black-white self-images and interrelationships as expressed in jokes may be found in such articles as Paulette Cross's "Jokes and Black Consciousness: A Collection with Interviews," *FF* 2 (1969), 140–61; Norine Dresser's "The Metamorphosis of the Humor of the Black Man," *NYFQ* 26 (1970), 216–28; and William R. Ferris, Jr.'s, "Racial Stereotypes in White Folklore," *KFQ* 15 (1970), 188–98. Two standard collections of black folk narratives with copious notes and bibliography are Richard M. Dorson's *Negro Folktales in Michigan* (Cambridge, Mass.: Harvard University Press, 1956), and *American Negro Folktales* (Greenwich, Conn.: Fawcett Premier Books, paperback, 1967), which incorporates part of the first-named collection.

In "American Numskull Tales: The Polack Joke," *WF* 26 (1967), 183–86,

Roger L. Welsch directed folklorists' attention to a new popular cycle of ethnic riddle-jokes. In 1969 William M. Clements published *The Types of the Polack Joke*, a comprehensive catalog, as Bibliographical and Special Series no. 3 of *FF* (a supplementary list appeared in *FF* 4 [1971], 19–29). Mac E. Barrick compared "Racial Riddles and the Polack Joke," in *KFQ* 15 (1970), 3–15; and Kathleen A. and Michael J. Preston discussed the "Visual Polack Joke" in *JAF* 86 (1973), 175–77.

Three articles which concentrate on interpretive analysis of more than one cycle of racial or ethnic joke are Jan Harold Brunvand, "Some Thoughts on the Ethnic-Regional Riddle Jokes," *IF* 3 (1970), 128–142; Nathan Hurvitz, "Blacks and Jews in American Folklore," *WF* 33 (1974), 301–25; and Alan Dundes, "A Study of Ethnic Slurs: The Jew and the Polack in the United States," *JAF* 84 (1971), 186–203.

Two folklorists have subjected the "sick joke" to some analysis; Brian Sutton-Smith published " 'Shut Up and Keep Digging': The Cruel Joke Series," *MF* 10 (1960), 11–22; and Roger D. Abrahams published "Ghastly Commands: The Cruel Joke Revisited," *MF* 11 (Winter 1961–62), 235–46. The first article in a folklore journal on another recent popular genre was Alan Dundes's "The Elephant Joking Question," *TFSB* 29 (1963), 40–42. More analysis was offered in Roger D. Abrahams's "The Bigger They are the Harder they Fall," *TFSB* 29 (1963), 94–102. A brief list of examples was printed in *WF* 23 (1964), 198–99; and a comprehensive gathering of them was made by Mac E. Barrick in "The Shaggy Elephant Riddle," *SFQ* 28 (1964), 266–90. Maurice D. Schmaier discussed "The Doll Joke Pattern in Contemporary American Oral Humor," in *MF* 13 (Winter 1963–64), 205–16. Robin Hirsch also treated this form in an article in *WF* 23 (1964), 107–10.

G. Legman, the leading authority on sexual folklore, is the author of a combined collection, classification, and (mostly Freudian) analysis titled *Rationale of the Dirty Joke: An Analysis of Sexual Humor* (First Series, New York: Grove Press, 1968); volume two, the "Second Series" is titled *No Laughing Matter* (New York: Breaking Point, Inc., 1975). Religious jokelore is studied in Jan Harold Brunvand's "As the Saints Go Marching By: Modern Jokelore Concerning Mormons," *JAF* 83 (1970), 53–60. In a third rich vein of modern oral humor, Michael J. Preston examines "A Year of Political Jokes (June 1973–June 1974); or, the Silent Majority Speaks Out," *WF* 34 (1975), 233–44.

My note on "Jokes About Misunderstood Religious Texts" appeared in *WF* 24 (1965), 199–200. A "pictorial folktale" was noted by Maud G. Early in *JAF* 10 (1897), 80. My own "Classification for Shaggy Dog Stories," appeared in *JAF* 76 (1963), 42–68.

Three recent essays dealing with studies of traditional jokes in a broad context are Francis Lee Utley and Dudley Flamm's "The Urban and the Rural Jest (With an Excursus on the Shaggy Dog)," *JPC* 2 (1969), 563–77; Jan Harold Brunvand's "The Study of Contemporary Folklore: Jokes," *Fabula* 13 (1972), 1–19; and Frank Hall's "Conversational Joking: A Look at Applied Humor," *Folklore Annual* 6 (1974), 26–45.

There are, of course, numerous recordings of professional comedians telling jokes, and only a few of folk jokesters; a folklorist recites some good examples on the record *Folklore of the Mormon Country: J. Golden Kimball Stories, Together with the Brother Petersen Yarns, Told by Hector Lee* (Sharon, Conn.: Folk Legacy Records, Inc., FTA-25, 1964). The record has anecdotes on side one, and dialect stories on side two.

The Norwegian tall-tale contest referred to in this chapter was described by Gustav Henningsen in *Vestfold-Minne* in 1961 and was translated by Warren E. Roberts as "The Art of Perpendicular Lying" in *JFI* 2 (1965), 180–219. Mody Boatright's theory of frontier tall tales is contained in *Folk Laughter on the American Frontier* (New York: Macmillan, 1949; Collier Books paperback edn., 1961). A stylistic study of tall tales based on 233 texts of "The Wonderful Hunt" selected from a manuscript archive of more than 2,000 American tall tales is reported in J. Russell Reaver's "From Realtiy to Fantasy: Opening-Closing Formulas in the Structures of American Tall Tales," *SFQ* 36 (1972), 369–82. Examining the tellers, contexts, and attitudes involved in traditional joking and lying, Kay Cothran wrote of "Talking Trash in the Okefenokee Swamp Rim, Georgia," *JAF* 87 (1974), 340–56.

Stan Hoig's *The Humor of the American Cowboy* (Caldwell, Idaho: Caxton Press, 1958; Signet paperback edn., 1960) contains a good selection of Western occupational tall tales. Mody Boatright's *Tall Tales from Texas* (Dallas: Southern Methodist University Press, 1934) selects examples from one state, as does Stephen Dow Beckham's *Tall Tales from Rogue River: The Yarns of Hathaway Jones* (Bloomington: Indiana University Press, 1974)—Oregon. Roger L. Welsch's *Shingling the Fog and Other Plains Lies: Tall Tales of the Great Plains* (Chicago: Swallow Press, 1972), the best annotated of this group, fills in part of the middle section of the West with tales from both oral and journalistic sources.

Vance Randolph's near-classic *We Always Lie to Strangers* was published in New York (Columbia University Press) in 1951. Lowell Thomas, who collected tall tales from his huge radio audiences by mail for many years, published *Tall Stories* in 1931 (Funk & Wagnalls) and it has been frequently reprinted. *Hoosier Tall Stories* in the American Guide Series (Federal Writers' Project in Indiana, 1937) is a rare book, but a comprehensive collection. More Indiana tall tales are in my article in *MF* 11 (1961), 5–14. Samuel T. Farquhar reprinted in a 1904 pamphlet of tall tales from Maine in *CFQ* 3 (1944), 177–84. An excellent collection from the same state is C. Richard K. Lunt's "Jones Tracy: Tall-Tale Hero from Mount Desert Island," *NF* 10 (1968), 1–75. An important older collection recently made available again is James R. Masterson's *Tall Tales from Arkansas* (Boston: Chapman and Grimes, 1942; republished as *Arkansas Folklore* by Rose Publishing Company, Little Rock, Ark., 1974). Roger L. Welsch explores an area of folk-popular overlapping in "Bigger'n Life: The Tall-Tale Postcard," *SFQ* 38 (1974), 311–24, adapted from the introduction to his book *The Tall-Tale Postcard: A Pictorial History* (New York: A. S. Barnes, 1976).

The *cante fable* in America has been collected and discussed in a series of articles, including two by Herbert Halpert in *SFQ* 5 (1941), 191–200, and *JAF*

55 (1942), 133–43; one by Leonard Roberts in *MF* 6 (1956), 69–88; and one by Edward D. Ives in *NEQ* 32 (1959), 226–37. Halpert provides rich annotation for one popular category of *cante fables* "The Humorous Grace" in *MSF* 3 (1975), 71–82.

The chief theoretical underpinning for the Historic-Geographic Method of folktale analysis, Kaarle Krohn's *Die Folkloristische Arbeitsmethode* (Oslo, 1926) was translated by Roger L. Welsch as *Folklore Methodology* (Austin, Texas: AFS Bibliographic and Special Series no. 21, 1971). Archer Taylor identified "Precursors of the Finnish Method of Folklore Study" in *MP* 25 (1927–28), 481–91. Taylor wrote that the method "is only common sense codified into a rigid procedure and not applied at random." He also published "The Black Ox," *FFC* no. 70 (1927)—a historic-geographic study of Finnish variants alone—as an exemplification of the method. A full-length study of worldwide distribution of a tale is Warren E. Roberts's "The Tale of the Kind and the Unkind Girls: Aa-Th 480 and Related Tales," in *Fabula, Supplement, Series B,* no. 1 (Berlin, 1958). Edwin C. Kirkland's "The American Redaction of Tale Type 922" in *Fabula* 4 (1961, 248–59, is a comparative study of what is known here as "Pat and Mike and the Three Questions." Bruce A. Rosenberg and John B. Smith discuss "The Computer and the Finnish Historical-Geographical Method," marrying their presentation with the questionable acronym FARTS (Folktale Analysis, Retrieval and Tabulating System) in *JAF* 87 (1974), 149–54.

Two older survey articles on folktale studies are Anna Birgitta Rooth's "Scholarly Tradition in Folktale Research," *Fabula* 1 (1958), 193–200; and Jan DeVries's "The Problem of the Fairy Tale," *Diogenes* no. 22 (1958), 1–15. Recent surveys that project sweeping changes in folktale studies are J. L. Fischer's "The Sociopsychological Analysis of Folktales," *CA* 4 (1963), 235–95; Melville Jacobs's "A Look Ahead in Oral Literature Research," *JAF* 79 (1966), 413–27; and Heda Jason's "A Multidimensional Approach to Oral Literature," *CA* 10 (1969), 413–26.

V. Propp's *Morphology of the Folktale,* first published in Russia in 1928, the background for much modern structuralism in folklore, should be consulted in the second revised English translation (introduction by Alan Dundes) published both as AFS Bibliographical and Special Series vol. 9 (Austin, Texas, 1968) and as Indiana University Research Center in Anthropology, Folklore, and Linguistics, Publication no. 10 (Bloomington, 1968). Alan Dundes proposed the application of Propp's system to the structural study of tales in the Aarne-Thompson catalog in an article in *JAF* 75 (1962), 95–105, reprinted in *Analytic Essays in Folklore,* pp. 61–72, and he demonstrated its application in "The Binary Structure of 'Unsuccessful Repetition' in Lithuanian Folktales," *WF* 21 (1962), 165–74. For other structural studies, refer to the Bibliographic Notes to Chapter 2 and to those for individual genre chapters. Alsace Yen offers a comparison "On Vladimir Propp and Albert B. Lord: Their Theoretical Differences" and criticizes the English translation of Propp's work in *JAF* 86 (1973), 161–66.

The importance of studying story*telling* rather than simply story *plots* is emphasized in Linda Dégh's important study (published first in German in 1962), *Folktales and Society: Story-Telling in a Hungarian Peasant Community* (Bloomington: Indiana University Press, 1969). Another useful European study of a folk narrator, Mark Azadovskii's *"Eine Sibirische Märchenerzählerin,"* FFC no. 68 (1926) has been translated by James R. Dow and published as "A Siberian Tale Teller" by the Center for Intercultural Studies in Folklore and Ethnomusicology, Monograph Series, no. 2 (Austin: University of Texas, 1974). The first influential and inclusive essay taking this approach by an American folklorist is Robert A. Georges's "Toward an Understanding of Storytelling Events," *JAF* 82 (1969), 313–28.

John Ball's thoughts on "Style in the Folktale" appeared in *Folklore* 65 (1954), 170–72. William Hugh Jansen considered the problems of "Classifying Performance in the Study of Verbal Folklore" in *Studies in Folklore,* pp. 110–18. Richard M. Dorson analyzed the styles of six storytellers in "Oral Styles of American Folk Narrators," *Style in Language,* ed. Thomas A. Sebeok (Cambridge, Mass., New York, and London: Technology Press of MIT, 1960), pp. 27–51; the article was reprinted in *Folklore in Action,* pp. 77–100 and again (with four additional text samples) in Dorson's *Folklore: Selected Essays,* pp. 99–146. Bruce A. Rosenberg considers the question of style in both written and oral storytelling in his essay "The Aesthetics of Traditional Narrative" in Stanley Weintraub and Philip Young's *Direction in Literary Criticism* (University Park, Pa.: Pennsylvania State University Press, 1973), pp. 7–22.

My Western text of Type 660, "The Two Doctors," with discussion of the variants that are mentioned in this chapter, appeared in "Some International Folktales from Northwest Tradition," *NWF* 1 (Winter 1966), 7–13. Luc Lacourcière studies nine French-Canadian texts of Type 660 in *"Les Transplantations Fabuleuses: conte-Type 660,"* *Cahiers d'Histoire* no. 22 (Québec: Archives de Folklore, Université Laval, 1970), pp. 194–204. A recent version from Italy retold as a sexy joke is reprinted in *European Anecdotes and Jests,* ed. Kurt Ranke (Copenhagen: Rosenkilde and Bagger, 1972), p. 10.

10

Folksongs

Folksongs have seemed peculiarly elusive before ventures at scholarly definition. The following attempt from A. H. Krappe's *The Science of Folklore* (1930) demonstrates the typical shortcomings of many others:

> The folksong is a song, i.e. a lyric poem with melody, which originated anonymously, among unlettered folk in times past and which remained in currency for a considerable time, as a rule for centuries.

Not only is the logic here neatly circular (folksong = song of the folk), but also the criteria of illiterate origins and "considerable" age will simply not apply to the greater part of the materials accepted as folksongs by folklorists of Krappe's time and later. American folksongs would be ruled out entirely; Krappe's own first example, named a few lines further on, does not fit:

> . . . the American *Kentucky Home*, though it is supposed to have originated in circles of a somewhat darker hue than is popular in certain sections of the country, is a genuine folksong of both coloured and white people.

Krappe's remark is a racist one, and "My Old Kentucky Home," of course, is a Stephen Foster composition that has never achieved any oral circulation in variants.

We have, on the one hand, the broad and vague popular concept that almost any folksy song performance is a folksong. On the other hand, we have narrow-minded antiquarian definitions such as Krappe's. But if we simply look at what folklorists have collected and studied, we will discover that **folksongs** consist of words and music that circulate orally in traditional variants among members of a particular group. Like other kinds of oral traditions, folksongs have come from various sources, have appeared in various media, and have sometimes been lifted out of folk circulation for various professional or artistic uses. But all of those which qualify as true *folk*songs have variants found in oral transmission.

The words and music of folksongs belong together and should be gathered and analyzed together; however, to facilitate a systematic survey of the kinds of American folksongs and ballads, their tunes are discussed separately in Chapter 12.

Folksongs are distinguished from non-folksongs by their fluidity of form and content. This is apparent in contrast to the two other basic bodies of song—art songs and popular songs. *Art songs* are learned from printed scores exactly as their composers originally wrote them. Professional singers are expected to perform art songs in a manner that is in keeping with the musical conventions of the composer's own time, and usually in the composer's own language. Such songs as Schubert's *Lieder;* "Drink to Me Only With Thine Eyes," "Ave Maria," favorite arias from operas, musical settings of well-known texts (including in the United States "The Lord's Prayer," "Trees" and Roy Harris's setting of Sandburg's "Fog,") are all familiar examples of art songs. They may follow any form the composer wishes to use, and they have a special, enduring, intellectual or emotional "highbrow" appeal.

Popular songs are also printed, or more often commercially recorded, and they, too, come from the pens of professional composers, sometimes more businessmen than artists. Professional singers are expected to sing popular songs as they were written and to pay royalties for their use. These songs are generally much more stereotyped in form than art songs are, tending either to fit a rigid ABA pattern (like that of "Sweet Sue") or following some current mode (like the AAB twelve-bar blues form and blues diction used for some rock pieces). Most popular songs enjoy only a short but a very intense existence, being enormously popular with a broad, mostly adolescent, audience for weeks or at most months, and then disappearing for good from the juke boxes and disk-jockey shows.

Folksongs as a group are even more widely accepted than art songs and popular songs, having circulated for generations, sometimes in different countries, among illiterate and semiliterate folk who had little knowledge of the other two bodies of song. Yet both middle-class and upper-class people know folksongs, too. Folksongs outlast most popular songs, and they may also be much older than art songs; for the latter generally go back to the eighteenth or nineteenth centuries at most, while some folksongs survive from the Middle Ages or earlier. Folksongs are unlimited in form and subject matter, ranging from very simple to relatively complex. But their chief distinction remains the manner by which they circulate and the resulting effect on their form: folksongs, unlike any other kind, are passed on mostly in oral tradition, and they develop traditional variants.

Since these song types are not defined primarily by their origin, folksongs may actually originate from either art songs or popular songs. As many scholars have emphasized, folksongs are *perpetuated* in oral tradition, but they need not have *originated* there. In fact, a song belonging to any one of the three groups may turn into one of the other two types, if we only apply our definitions a bit broadly.

Art songs, for instance, such as "O Promise Me" or the wedding march from *Lohengrin* reached a popular-song audience when they began to be regularly sung at weddings. The wedding march achieved oral circulation as a folksong when words like the following were fitted to it:

> Here comes the bride,
> Big, fat, and wide.
> See how she wobbles from side to side.

Similarly, the theme melody from a Rachmaninoff piano concerto became a popular song, "Full Moon and Empty Arms." The "Toreador Song" from *Carmen* is folksong when it is sung:

> Oh Theodora,
> Don't spit on the floor-a;
> Use the cuspidor-a,
> That's-a what it's for-a.

By the same token, some popular songs outlive their typical brief careers to survive for generations as "standards." This is true especially of songs closely associated with particular singers like Bing Crosby ("White Christmas") or Judy Garland ("Over the Rainbow"). Probably some popular songs also last because of the inherent high quality of their melodies and lyrics, and in a sense these are art songs in disguise. One thinks of "Stardust," "September Song," and "Smoke Gets in Your Eyes," all of which have somewhat unconventional tunes and lyrics for popular songs. Other popular song hits seem to cloy the public's taste eventually and are then cynically parodied in oral tradition, thus becoming folksongs: "Jealousy" turns into "Leprosy" (". . . is making a mess of me"), and "It's Magic" turns into "It's Tragic" ("You smile your teeth fall out;/Your hair looks just like sauerkraut . . ."). The popular song "Davy Crockett" spawned at least a dozen folk parodies, with lines like "Born on a table top in Joe's Cafe,/Dirtiest place in the U.S.A."

When folksongs are "arranged" and enter the repertoires of professional singers and singing groups, they cease to behave like folksongs and become art songs. This has been the case especially with Afro-American spirituals ("Go Down Moses," "Swing Low Sweet Chariot," etc.), with some folk lyrics ("Black is the Color of My True Love's Hair" and "Shenandoah"), and with many foreign folksongs, which like foreign art songs are generally sung in the parent language. When folksongs catch the ears of a broad sector of the public, they may become popular songs for a brief period. Such was the case with "Goodnight Irene," and "Tom Dooley." More recently popular songs called "The Riddle Song," and "Scarborough Fair" were derived from Anglo-American folk ballads.

It should be evident now why folklorists cannot answer immediately when asked if "Barbara Allen" (or "Tom Dooley," or "Blue-Tailed Fly,") is a *folksong*. The only response they can give is, "Which version?" Even knowing that, they might have to conclude, "Yes and no." The decision must ultimately rest on the singer's performance and source—in short, on the singer's folk tradition, if any—rather than on any features of text and tune themselves. If words and music were learned orally from other traditional singers, if the performance is natural, and if oral variants exist, then there is a likelihood that we are dealing with folksong. Thorny problems, of course, do exist—the city fad for singing country folksongs, for instance, or the deliberate composition of popular songs in the folk style, or a song like "Greensleeves" which is widely regarded as a folksong, but which was actually revived professionally from a non-folk tradition. Such problems, however, are legitimate ones for investigation by folklorists. An example of the findings of such a study is the case of

"Home on the Range." That song was first a piece of Kansas newspaper verse (in 1873), then an anonymous, somewhat fluid, cowboy folksong. It finally was tracked back to its written source, and now it is a "standard" that is invariably sung just as it is printed in songbooks.

The various ways by which folksongs have been transmitted are by no means limited solely to oral performance. Print, writing, sound recording, and broadcasting have all played a part in circulating folksongs among traditional singers. For example, many narrative songs now regarded as folksongs originated as *broadsides*—crudely printed single sheets containing the lyrics for a new song and the name of a familiar tune to which it might be sung. Broadsides flourished in England from about the sixteenth to the early nineteenth centuries. They were sold on the streets, usually for a penny. Broadsides were printed in the United States until somewhat later, and have occasionally been revived in the twentieth century for such gatherings as labor union rallies and pacifist or civil rights demonstrations. (The general nature of Anglo-American broadside ballads is taken up in the next chapter.) *Songsters*—pamphlets of printed songs—became popular in the nineteenth century, and some are still printed now and then; their contents were generally very miscellaneous, for they were compiled freely from all available sources, folk and otherwise. Songsters also were cheaply printed and sold, and like broadsides, they were not preserved with any care either by their buyers or by early libraries. Today, however, intact broadsides and songsters are treasured library acquisitions. Countless American folksongs were also circulated in print by means of *periodicals*, especially local newspaper columns of old songs and poems. Sometimes readers were asked to submit the full texts for incomplete songs sent in by others, thus creating an informal folklore-collecting project. Some readers kept clippings of old song columns, and a few newspapers retained files of submitted songs for reference use; both kinds of collections can still occasionally be discovered.

Handwritten *"ballet books"* (ballad books) constitute another good source of folksongs ready-collected by informants themselves. The term "ballet book" has been applied to any notebook or scrapbook of songs kept by an individual for his own use. Some are in old copy books or ledgers, while others are made out of printed books with blank paper pasted over the pages; the songs they contain usually were selected from all the songs that happened to be known to their compilers, some of whom even kept track of their own printed and oral sources.

Finally, *commercial recordings* have played an important role in folksong transmission. Beginning in 1923 when a recording company first put a "hillbilly" singer on a commercial 78 rpm disk, folksongs have been borrowed from oral tradition and then fed back into it through recordings. Other songs such as Vernon Dalhart's version of "The Death of Floyd Collins" or The Carter Family's "Worried Man Blues" originated from recording artists and their writers, and then passed on to an oral life.

All that we have been describing here represents a liberal, modern scholarly concept of American folksong. But such have not always been the accepted dimensions of the subject. In 1897, nine years after the American Folklore Society was founded, an early historian of American literature could write that we are a people "practically without folksongs." Nowadays, however, few anthologies of American literature do not contain a section devoted to native ballads and folksongs.

The first American folklorists in the late nineteenth century knew of almost no oral-traditional songs in the United States. Francis James Child, the great ballad editor, brought out his definitive edition of traditional British ballads at Harvard in the 1890s without doing any fieldwork and including only a handful of American versions that others had sent him. But the famous English collector Cecil J. Sharp found English folksongs of all kinds in abundance in the southern Appalachians beginning in 1917, and his writings encouraged others to seek them too.

Pioneering American collectors like Phillips Barry in the Northeast and John A. Lomax in the West and South began to publish native-American folksongs at about the same time, and gradually academic folklorists accepted their finds and had to revise their own ideas about folksong types and dissemination. Widely respected scholars such as Louise Pound of the University of Nebraska and H. M. Belden of the University of Missouri were instrumental in promoting a broad definition of American folksong, while such industrious collectors as George Korson, working among coal miners, and Vance Randolph among Ozark mountaineers gathered a widened spectrum of songs for

analysis. Recently, John Greenway has contended that American so-
cial-protest songs should be admitted into an inclusive definition of
folksong, such as his:

> . . . folksong is any song concerned with the interests of the folk
> and in the complete possession of the folk, who in turn are members
> of a homogeneous, unsophisticated, enclave living in but isolated
> from a surrounding sophisticated society by such features as geogra-
> phy, topography, race, religion, economic and educational depriva-
> tion, social inferiority, or even choice.

The latest historian of Anglo-American folksong studies, D. K.
Wilgus, along with Greenway and others, has taken a rationalistic
view of folksong tradition and emphasized the importance of the hill-
billy-record influence upon American folksongs.

So broad is the field of folksong, that Wilgus conceded in his history of its scholarship: "It is doubtful that there will ever be a complete, not to speak of a consistent, outline of the varieties of folksong."
Yet, classify we must, and if we borrow terms freely from many editions and studies, and invent a few new ones to fill gaps, we come up
with something like the following scheme, with the large divisions
based on form (arranged from simple to complex) and the subclasses
organized by subject matter or function.

Since folksongs consist of oral-traditional words and music, it is possible to imagine examples in which one element is stronger than the
other, or even exists without the other's presence at all. Such *proto-
folksongs* do in fact occur in folk tradition. Vocal music without
words—what we might call **wordless folksong**—is found in American
folklore in such traditions as "chin music," (or "Diddling", and in
Ireland, "lilting") when the voice imitates the sound of dance music
played on a fiddle. The sound effect is similar to the nonsense refrains
of some folk ballads, and it has a counterpart in jazz "scat singing."
Some jazz instrumental styles derive from the early use of such
partly-vocal instruments as the Jew's harp, the jug, and the kazoo, developing into muted and "growl" effects produced on conventional
band instruments. Yodeling, hollering, and Afro-American church
"moaning," "humming," or "groaning," as it is variously called, are all
further examples of wordless folksong. Another type, known either as
"eephing" or "hoodling," consists of breathy, grunting quasi-musical

noises that sound somewhat like animal imitations. Wordless songs need not even necessarily be vocal; the "Johnny is a sissy!" three-note melody may be sung, hummed, whistled, or played on an instrument with the same insulting effect. The "wolf whistle," has an unmistakable meaning without any vocalizing of melody or words for it. However, the seven-stroke rhythmic pattern of one simple four-note melody does have traditional words associated with it: "Shave and a haircut, two bits." There can be no doubt that these items live orally, for no songbooks contain them, yet everyone knows them. If you tap out the first five beats of "Shave and a haircut," someone will respond with "two bits"; if you hum "Johnny is a sissy" at a child, he will react. Similarly, the wolf whistle has no formal support as a greeting from etiquette books, but it speaks eloquently just the same because of its folk denotation.

When *words* predominate and melody is weak, we have what might be termed **near-songs.** The *cante fable,* as we have seen, is half-and-half, and the verse may either be chanted or sung. The peddlers' cries, discussed earlier as rhymes, are often delivered in a singsong chant, but sometimes are truly sung. Children's play-and-game rhymes fall into the same twilight zone between verse and song, as do many field hollers and work hollers. Square-dance calls, auctioneers' chants, and "talking blues" are all partly song, partly chant. For all of these materials, it could be said in general that the texts are fully traditional and formularized, but the tunes are improvised and free. They are *nearly* songs, but not quite.

The first group of true songs, with both traditional words and music, are those which closely match the rhythm of some special activity, and thus they have been called **functional songs.** Here we might classify *lullabies* that are smoothly rhythmical, peaceful, or repetitious ("Hush Little Baby" is all three) so that they will induce sleep. Bess Lomax Hawes, who analyzed the "peculiar melange" of songs used as lullabies, also identified "happy vocalizing . . . a chatty style" and especially "the spatial isolation of the baby" as typical traits of content and performance.

Work songs belong in the functional folksong category if they are regulated by the repeated pulses of chopping, hammering, marching, pulling on ropes, and so forth. Most American work songs are either Afro-American slave songs ("Take This Hammer," being the best-

known example) or sailor's "sea chanteys" (Hangman Johnny," "Away
to Rio"). A few still circulate as call-and-response songs or chants used
when circus workers hoist a tent:

> Every time (Heave it!)
> Ding, dong, ring (Heave it!)
> Look on the table (Heave it!)
> Same damn old thing!

Play-party songs, which could be classified as functional songs, are
discussed in Chapter 15 in connection with folk dancing. Children's
game songs belong in this category, for they are never sung apart from
the playing of the game, and the words and melody closely follow the
action of the game. A few songs are *mnemonic songs* used for remembering such lists as the Presidents of the United States, the capitals of
the states, or basic geographical terms. A Utah example simply ver-
sifies the names of all the state's counties to the tune of "Reuben and
Rachel":

> Utah Train
> Beaver, Carbon, Davis, Morgan,
> Dagget, Millard, and Duchesne,
> Iron, Uinta, Rich, and Summit,
> Garfield, Cash, Piute, and Kane.
>
> Wasatch, Washington, and Weber,
> San Pete, San Juan, Salt Lake, Wayne,
> Juab, Box Elder, Grand, Tooele,
> Sevier, Emery, Utah train.

These first three broad divisions—wordless folksongs, near-songs,
and functional folksongs—constitute clearly differentiated groups
with easily recognizable contents. However, the folksongs that fit into
them include only a small fraction of the whole. The last two divisions—lyrical folksongs and narrative folksongs—are much more
complicated groups and involve many more texts. Narrative folksongs
are discussed separately in the next chapter, leaving **lyrical folksongs**
(the usual meaning of the simple term "folksongs") for the remainder
of this one.

Some lyrical folksongs are true *folk lyrics*, that is, traditional songs
devoted to expressing a mood or a feeling without telling any con-

nected story. Many are expressions of despair for a lost or hopeless love and are sometimes developed as a series of impossible desires:

> Wisht I was a little fish,
> I'd swim to the bottom of the sea,
> And there I'd sing my sad little song,
> "There's nobody cares for me."
>
> *
>
> I wish I was a little sparrow,
> Had wings, and oh! could fly so high.
> I'd fly away to my false lover
> And when he'd ask, I would deny.

Other folk lyrics have the thread of a story implied in them, as in "Down in the Valley" and "On Top of Old Smokey," while others simply take the form of warnings to lovers about the wiles of the opposite sex. Apart from the joys and sorrows of love, some folk lyrics refer to death ("Bury Me Beneath the Willow"), homesickness ("The Indian Hunter," or "Let Me Go"), and general discontent ("Trouble in Mind"). One that is probably of literary origin complains about household toil:

> There's too much of worriment goes to a bonnet,
> There's too much of ironing goes to a shirt,
> There's nothing that pays for the time you waste on it,
> There's nothing that lasts us but trouble and dirt.
>
> Oh, life is toil and love is a trouble,
> And beauty will fade and riches will flee;
> And pleasures they dwindle and prices they double,
> And nothing is what I wish it to be.

A major category of American folk lyrical song is the Afro-American *blues,* a folk form based on field hollers and cries which developed countless fluid stanzas of emotional responses to life, entered a commercial and urban stage, and then profoundly influenced, both musically and textually, most of American popular music. In its classic form, the blues consist of a three-line twelve-bar pattern based on repeating one line of four musical bars twice and then rhyming a third line containing a complementary or responsive idea with it. A famous published example, based on a folk verse, goes:

> I hate to see that evening sun go down,
> I hate to see that evening sun go down,
> Because my baby, she done left this town.

The spirit of the blues is often, although not necessarily, melancholy:

> Woke up this morning, blues all 'round my bed,
> Woke up this morning, blues all 'round my bed,
> Picked up my pillow, blues all under my head.

The subject matter is commonly disappointed love:

> I want to know, why did my baby go,
> I want to know, why did my baby go,
> I love that woman, love her 'til it hurts me so.

And blues imagery is often frankly sexual, as shown in this Bessie Smith lyric, typical of folk blues, although from a commercial recording:

> Bought me a coffee-grinder, got the best one I could find,
> Bought me a coffee-grinder, got the best one I could find,
> So he could grind my coffee, 'cause he has a brand new grind.

A black prisoner's blues, as recorded in Louisiana, is grippingly phrased:

> Wonder why they electrocute a man at the one o'clock hour at night,
> Wonder why they electrocute a man at the one o'clock hour at night,
> The current much stronger, people turn out all the light.

Spirituals and other traditional *religious songs* may sometimes allude to a biblical story or religious legend, or allegorize a lesson, but their narrative content is subordinate to their expression of strong feeling; they may be considered lyrical folksongs except for the relatively few that are "religious ballads." There are "white spirituals" as well as black ones, and the controversy over origins and precedence has filled several books. Religious songs exhibit much more variety than may be illustrated briefly, but the basic simplicity of many is seen in a stanza like "Where, oh where are the good old patriarchs? [three times]/Safely over in the promised land." Some religious folksongs are infused with the imagery and fervor of revival meetings and fire-and-brimstone preaching. Frequent scenes depicted in others are crossing rivers, washing away sin, walking in heaven, and riding trains. Some folk hymns derive from English Protestant hymns, which later appeared in the old American "shape-note" collections like *The Sacred Harp* in which each tone of the scale was printed in a differently shaped note. The liveliest folk religious songs such as "That Old Time Religion," anticipate the "gospel songs" that are still commercial country-music or bluegrass favorites on phonograph records and on the radio.

In the same spirit as religious songs are the *homiletic songs* that dispense advice like "Paddle Your Own Canoe," or ask embarrassing questions like "Why Do you Bob Your Hair, Girls?" But for every song that criticizes a life of "Puttin' on the Style," there are a dozen more that we might call *songs of gamblers, drinkers, ramblers, and prisoners*. Here the dissolute life, if not directly recommended for others, is often at least gloried by the singer. Witness "Old Rosin the Beau," who for his funeral wants to have his six pallbearers line up at the graveside and have one last drink to him, their burden. Some temperance songs circulate orally, like "Lips that Touch Liquor Must Never Touch Mine" and "I'll Never Get Drunk Anymore," but the more numerous variety either describe the brewing process ("Moonshine" and "Mountain Dew") or revel in its product ("Pass 'Round the Bottle" and "Pickle My Bones in Alcohol"). The most common song of the group is variously titled "Jack of Diamonds," "Rye Whiskey," "On Top of Clinch Mountain," or sometimes just "A Card-Player's Song." Typical verses, which may occur in any order, include:

> Jack of diamonds, Jack of diamonds
> I know you of old,
> You robbed my poor pockets
> Of silver and gold.
>
> For the work I'm too lazy
> And beggin's too low,
> Train robbin's too dangerous
> So to gamblin' I'll go.
>
> I eat when I'm hungry,
> I drink when I'm dry,
> And when I get thirsty,
> I lay down and cry.

> I've played cards in England,
> I've played cards in Spain,
> I'll bet you ten dollars,
> I'll beat you next game.

Folksongs of courtship and marriage form a distinct group. These include songs that describe a courtship ("The Quaker's Wooing" and "The Old Man's Courtship" or "Old Boots and Leggings"), those that represent a courting dialogue ("I'll Give to You a Paper of Pins" and "Soldier, Soldier, Will You Marry Me?"); a few that express a desire for marriage ("I Love Little Willie, I Do" and "The Old Bachelor"), but many more that celebrate the single life ("Wish I was Single Again" and "I Am Determined to Be an Old Maid").

The logical sequel to songs of courting and marriage is the group of *nursery and children's songs,* many of which derive their appeal and their easy memorability from the use of a simple repeated pattern. This is true of "Go Tell Aunt Rhody," "The Barnyard Song" (or "I Bought Me a Cat"), "There Was an Old Woman had a Little Pig," "There's a Hole in the Bottom of the Sea," and a host of others. The last named is a *cumulative song,* analogous to the cumulative folktales, and others involve imitations of animal sounds, dramatic dialogues (as in "Billy Boy"), gestures ("John Brown's Baby Had a Cold Upon its Chest"), and "jump" (or "scare") endings ("Old Woman All Skin and Bones"). This is also the place to mention three bodies of modern folksongs of childhood and adolescence that have not been collected or studied systematically—*summer camp songs, high school songs,* and *college songs.* A few representative examples of school and college songs are given in Appendix B; camp songs (which are sentimental, religious, homiletic, or simply funny) may be suggested by these two samples, one a parody and the other pure nonsense:

> Let me call you sweetheart,
>   I'm in love with your machine.
> Let me hear you whisper
>   that you'll buy the gasoline.
> Keep your headlights burning,
>   and your hands upon the wheel.
> Let me call you sweetheart,
>   I'm in love with your automobile.
>   *

> One bottle of pop, two bottles of pop
> Three bottle of pop, four bottle of pop
> [up to seven bottles]

> Don't put your dust in my dustpan,
> My dustpan, my dustpan,
> Don't put your dust in my dustpan,
> My dustpan's full

> Fish and chips and vinegar,
> Vinegar, vinegar,
> Fish and chips and vinegar,
> Pepper, pepper, pepper pot!

Although many folksongs (and a few ballads) are humorous, there are at least three kinds of funny songs that might be separately noted. First, *dialect songs*, like dialect stories, derive their humor from an exaggeration of racial or national speech peculiarities. Those in southern black dialect often stem from blackface minstrel shows, while Chinese songs from the West and "Swede songs" from the upper Midwest reflect regional settlement patterns and local prejudices. Second, *nonsense songs* take their comedy from a stream of purely meaningless verbiage, often delivered at a rapid-fire pace. Examples include "The Barefoot Boy with Shoes On," "It Was Midnight On the Ocean, Not a Streetcar Was in Sight," "The Soft Side of a Brick," and "The Billboard Song." Third, *parody songs*, seldom collected and studied, seem to cluster to a few old popular numbers. "My Bonny Lies Over the Ocean" being the apparent favorite, and yielding versions like:

> My Bonny has tuberculosis;
> My Bonny has only one lung;
> She coughs up the blood and corruption,
> And rolls it around on her tongue.

Evidence for the folk status of "Happy Birthday" are the many parodies of the familiar words:

> Happy Birthday to you,
> Happy Birthday to you,
> You act like a baby,
> But you look ninety-two.
>
> *

Happy Birthday to you
You live in a zoo,
We're sure that you'll live there,
On your next birthday too.

Regional and occupational folksongs are numerous in this country and offer insights into the history of labor and of settlement that few other sources give. *Cowboy songs* are now well known, thanks largely to the early collecting efforts of N. Howard (Jack) Thorp and John A. Lomax, who first started to collect and publish them after 1908. There are also songs of loggers, railroaders, sailors, miners, military men, and other workers, and of such hobby groups as mountain climbers, skiers, and surfers.

Proof that the creation of occupational folksongs has not died out lies in a group collected from American fighter pilots in Southeast Asia in 1967 and 1968. Mostly parodies based on commercial hillbilly, folk, and popular songs, these were often heavy with technical jargon and social protest, as this set of words for two stanzas of "Wabash Cannonball" demonstrates:

"Hello, Cam Ranh Tower, this is Hammer 41;
My BLC light's glowing, I've just lost PC-1,
The engine's running roughly, the EGT is high,
Please clear me for a straight-in, this bird's about to die!"

"Hammer 41, this is Cam Ranh Tower here;
We'd like to let you in right now, but a senator is near;
He's here to please constituents, his plane is close at hand,
So please divert to Tuy Hoa, we can't clear you to land."

Verses from three songs of early American occupational groups demonstrate how the working conditions and workers' attitudes were mirrored in their singing then too, and how the general themes of songs, as well as details of texts, tended to be passed on westward. One whalers' song contains this verse:

Some days we're catching whalefish, boys, and more days we're getting
none,
With a twenty-foot oar placed in our hand from four o'clock in the morn.
But when the shade of night comes down we nod on our weary oar.
Oh, it's then I wished that I was dead, or back with the girls on shore!

A Northeast loggers' song describes similar conditions, even to the time of arising:

> At four o'clock in the morning the boss he will shout,
> "Heave out, my jolly teamsters; it's time to be on the route."
> The teamsters they jump up all in a frightened way,
> "Where is me boots? Where is me pants? Me socks is gone astray!"

And one cowboy song seems to be nothing more than a rewording of the above.

> Oh early every morning you will hear the boss say,
> "Get out boys, it's the breakin' of day."
> Slowly you rise with your little sleepy eyes,
> And the bright dreamy night's passed away.
>
> . . . The cowboy's life is a very dreary life,
> It's a ridin' through the heat and the cold.

The most prominent group of regional songs are those of early western travel and settlement, which, like tall tales, seem to laugh at hardships with an ironic tone. One song cheerfully concerns "Starvin' to Death on My Government Claim," another celebrates "The Dreary Black Hills'," and a third begins:

> I am looking rather seedy now,
> While holding down my claim,
> And my victuals are not always served the best;
> And the mice play slyly round me,
> As I nestle down to sleep
> In my little old sod shanty in the West.

One ubiquitous Western song, sung to the tune of the old hymn "Beulah Land," has variants for many states—"Kansas Land," "Dakota Land," "Nebraska Land," etc., all with verses like:

> I've reached the land of wind and heat,
> Where nothing grows for man to eat.
> The wind it blows with feverish heat,
> Across the plains so hard to beat.
>
> O Dakota land, sweet Dakota land,
> As on thy fiery soil I stand,

> I look away across the plains
> And wonder why it never rains,
> Till Gabriel blows his trumpet sound
> And says the rain's just gone around.

In the Northwest the same song appears as "Oregon, Wet Oregon" or "Webfoot Land."

It would be a gross understatement to say that American folksongs have been collected and published with more energy than has been devoted to their classification and study; as a matter of fact, they have hardly been analyzed at all. The few categories for folksongs suggested in this chapter have counterparts in almost every published collection, but the specific songs placed under them vary widely. One person's "regional song" may be another's "comical song" and a third's "satirical song." Different terms entirely—including "historical songs," "jingles," "martial and political songs," and "dance songs"— appear in some collections, and every system has its "miscellaneous" under which usually appear what one scholar has called "sentimental balladlike pieces"—songs like "In the Baggage Coach Ahead," "Christmas at the Poor House," "Little Rosewood Casket," and "The Dream of the Miner's Child." The situation for folksong *studies* is even worse; in two exceptional examples only one Anglo-American lyric, "Green Grows the Laurel," was the subject of an exhaustive scholarly article, and only one type of American folksong—the regional and occupational—was the subject of a broad distributional survey.

American folksongs, therefore, seem to offer a particularly promising area for future research. Hundreds of songs have been collected in possibly thousands of variants, and many of these are available in print. The broad outlines of a suitable classification system seem clear enough, but the details need to be worked out and published. Almost any song or song-type that might be selected for study exists in enough variants from enough different regions to yield fascinating data, and both texts and tunes are usually intrinsically appealing in themselves. Question of style, variation, function, and meaning would immediately present themselves in the study of any song. For all these reasons, and with the bibliographic aids and theoretical models now at hand and the many American folklorists interested in music, the study of American folksongs has the possibility of advancing quickly to the high level already achieved in the study of the Anglo-American ballad, which is discussed in the next chapter.

BIBLIOGRAPHIC NOTES

An excellent general introduction to the whole subject is George Herzog's essay "Song: Folk Song and the Music of Folk Song" in *Funk & Wagnalls Standard Dictionary of Folklore, Mythology, and Legend*, (1950) 2:1032–50. Two comparable articles limited to the United States are Louise Pound's "American Folksong: Origins, Texts and Modes of Diffusion," *SFQ* 17 (1953), 114–21; reprinted in *Nebraska Folklore*, pp. 234–43; and Bruno Nettl's chapter "Words and Music: English Folksong in the United States" in Nettl, Charles Hamm, and Ronald Byrnside's *Contemporary Music and Music Cultures* (Englewood Cliffs, N.J.: Prentice-Hall, 1975), pp. 193–221. Among book-length surveys, Russell Ames's small *The Story of American Folksong* (New York: Grosset & Dunlap, 1955) is interestingly keyed to history, but the discussion is often too sketchy. Bruno Nettl's *An Introduction to Folk Music in the United States* (Detroit: Wayne State University Studies no. 7, paperback edition, 1960; revised 1962; 3rd edn. rev. by Helen Myers, *Folk Music in the United States: An Introduction*, 1976) is comprehensive, though short, and well documented. Nettl and Myers consider both texts and tunes. Edith Fowke presents "Anglo-Canadian Folksong: A Survey" in *EM* 16 (1972), 335–50.

MacEdward Leach introduced a symposium of seven writers on folksong studies with a note, "Folksong and Ballad—A New Emphasis," *JAF* 70 (1957), 205–7. He identified the shift in interest from collecting to analysis. A second important collection of articles, originally in the *Texas Folklore Society Publications* (33, 1964), includes papers on the literary and esthetic approach, the anthropological approach, the comparative approach, and the rationalistic approach; see Roger Abrahams's *Folksong and Folksong Scholarship: Changing Approaches and Attitudes* (Dallas: Southern Methodist University Press, 1964). The definitive historical work is D. K. Wilgus's *Anglo-American Folksong Scholarship since 1898* (New Brunswick, N.J.: Rutgers University Press, 1959). Wilgus offered his assessment of folksong research and ventured a look ahead in two important articles: " 'The Text is the Thing,' " *JAF* 86 (1973), 241–52; and "The Future of American Folksong Scholarship," *SFQ* 37 (1973), 315–29.

Herzog and Nettl, cited above, discuss art, folk, and popular songs; see also Frank Howes's "A Critique of Folk, Popular, and 'Art' Music," *BJA* 2 (1962), 239–48; and Peter Stadlen's "The Aesthetics of Popular Music," *BJA* 2 (1962), 351–61.

Most folksong collections contain some texts from broadsides, songsters, clippings, "ballet books," and occasionally even phonograph recordings. An interesting separate publication from a manuscript source is Harold W. Thompson and Edith E. Cutting's *A Pioneer Songster* (Ithaca, N.Y.: Cornell

University Press, 1958); another is Ruth Ann Musick's "The Old Album of William A. Larkin," *JAF* 60 (1947), 201–51. In my article "Folk Song Studies in Idaho," *WF* 24 (1965), 231–48, a large Northwest newspaper collection of folksongs that goes back some thirty years is described.

Questions concerning the popularization and commercialization of folksongs have been discussed several times in folklore journals and meetings. William Hugh Hansen presented "The Folksinger's Defense" in *HF* 9 (1950), 65–75, in which he discussed the repertoires of three young Kentucky singers and their tastes and preferences in folksongs compared to folklorists' usual categories and theories. Sven Eric Molin touched off an exchange of opinions with his article "Lead Belly, Burl Ives, and Sam Hinton," in *JAF* 71 (1958), 58–79. Three folklorists criticized in the article replied with notes in the same issue, followed by a rejoinder by Molin and a "last word" by Sam Hinton. An amusing reaction to citybilly singing from a country singer is Eugene Haun's "Lares and Penates, Once Removed," *JAF* 72 (1959), 243–47. Oscar Brand, a popular performer of folksongs, has documented the rise of professional folksong-singing in his book *The Ballad Mongers* (New York: Funk & Wagnalls, 1962). In a related vein, see Norman Cohen's "Tin Pan Alley's Contribution to Folk Music," *WF* 29 (1970), 9–20. Those wishing to study this movement more closely should also consult such popular periodicals as *Caravan, Sing Out*, and *Broadside*.

John Greenway's thesis is backed by his *American Folksongs of Protest* (Philadelphia: University of Pennsylvania Press, 1953). It was attacked by Tristram P. Coffin in "Folksongs of Social Protest: A Musical Mirage," *NYFQ* 14 (1958), 3–9, with a brief rejoinder from Greenway, who then stated his position more fully in his article "Folksongs as Socio-Historical Documents," *WF* 19 (1960), 1–9; reprinted in *Folklore in Action*, 112–19. A book that deals with some of the same materials without calling them folksongs is Josh Dunson's *Freedom in the Air: Song Movements of the Sixties* (New York: Little New World Paperbacks, LNW-7, 1965). Richard A. Reuss discusses a major figure in the social uses of folk and folk-like music in his essay "Woody Guthrie and His Folk Tradition," *JAF* 83 (1970), 273–303; and provides an excellent historical survey in "American Folksongs and Left-Wing Politics: 1935–1956," *JFI* 12 (1975), 89–111. A good survey is in Jens Lund and R. Serge Denisoff's "The Folk Music Revival and the Counter Culture: Contributions and Contradictions," *JAF* 84 (1971), 394–405. The other side of the coin is exposed in Marcello Truzzi's "The 100% American Songbag: Conservative Folksongs in America," *WF* 28 (1969), 27–40.

Wilgus and Greenway as co-editors blazed a new trail with the "Hillybilly Issue" of *JAF* (77, July–September 1965), which contains important articles and discography. Shortly thereafter the American Folklore Society published Bill C. Malone's book *Country Music: U.S.A.* as Volume 54 in the Memoir Series (Austin, Texas, 1968). Another folklore journal issue devoted to "commercialized folk music in general, and hillbilly music in particular" was *WF* 30 (1971), 171–246. Two separate articles of particular interest are Howard Wight Marshall's " 'Keep on the Sunny Side of Life': Pattern and Religious

Expression in Bluegrass Gospel Music." *NYFQ* 30 (1974), 3–43 (expanded from a 1971 publication in *FF*); and Frederick E. Danker's "The Repertory and Style of a Country Singer: Johnny Cash," *JAF* 85 (1972), 309–29. A good general article on the whole subject of folksong mass popularity is Samuel P. Bayard's "Decline and 'Revival' of Anglo-American Folk Music" in *Folklore in Action*, pp. 21–29. Bayard describes how folksongs change musically into art or popular songs as they are reproduced by city singers in a synthetic atmosphere of folksiness.

There are far too many good general folksong collections to list them all, but Wilgus has a full bibliography. A few general collections and landmark volumes, however, may be mentioned. Cecil J. Sharp's *English Folksongs from the Southern Appalachians* first appeared in 1917 (New York and London: Oxford University Press) co-edited by Olive Dame Campbell. The two-volume edition, edited by Maud Karpeles, appeared in 1932 and was reissued in 1952. Louise Pound's anthology *American Ballads and Songs* (New York: Scribners, 1922) is a notable early book of native materials with a stunning introductory essay that manages to touch upon almost every important aspect of the pieces included. Midwestern states are well represented in collections such as Emelyn E. Gardner and Geraldine J. Chickering's *Ballads and Songs of Southern Michigan* (Ann Arbor: University of Michigan Press, 1939; repr. Hatboro, Pa.: Folklore Associates, 1967), Paul Brewster's *Ballads and Songs of Indiana* (Bloomington: Indiana University Folklore Series no. 1, 1940), and H. M. Belden's *Ballads and Songs Collected by the Missouri Folk-Lore Society* (Columbia: University of Missouri Studies vol. 15, 1940).

Vance Randolph's four-volume *Ozark Folksongs* (Columbia, Mo.: State Historical Society, 1946–50) is as indispensable as his many excellent folktale publications. The folksong texts in the *Frank C. Brown Collection of North Carolina Folklore* are edited in vol. 3 (1952) by H. M. Belden and Arthur Palmer Hudson; tunes are in vol. 5 (1962). Book-length collections published since Wilgus's history include two from the West, Lester A. Hubbard's *Ballads and Songs from Utah* (Salt Lake City: University of Utah Press, 1961); and Ethel and Chauncey O. Moore's *Ballads and Folk Songs of the Southwest* (Norman: University of Oklahoma Press, 1964).

The rich Afro-American folksong heritage has been well documented, earlier in such studies and anthologies as Dorothy Scarborough's *On the Trail of Negro Folksongs* (Cambridge, Mass.: Harvard University Press, 1925; repr. Hatboro, Pa.: Folklore Associates, 1963), and N. I. White's *American Negro Folksongs* (Cambridge, Mass.: Harvard University Press, 1928), and later in such works as Harold Courlander's *Negro Folk Music, U.S.A.* (New York: Columbia University Press, 1963). Social backgrounds of an important Afro-American musical form, the blues, are given in Frederic Ramsey, Jr.'s *Been Here and Gone* (New Brunswick, N.J.: Rutgers University Press, 1960), and George Mitchell's *Blow My Blues Away* (Baton Rouge: Louisiana State University Press, 1971). For tracing further developments, see Samuel B. Charters's *The Country Blues* (New York: Rinehart, 1959), Harry Oster's *Living Country Blues* (Detroit: Folklore Associates, 1969), and Charles Keil's *Urban*

Blues (Chicago: University of Chicago Press, 1966) and their discographies. Other aspects of blues tradition are discussed in William R. Ferris, Jr., "Racial Repertoires Among Blues Performers," *EM* 14 (1970), 439–49; and David Evans, "Techniques of Blues Composition Among Black Folksingers," *JAF* 87 (1974), 240–49. The popular-cultural effects of blues tradition are described in John M. Hellmann, Jr., " 'I'm a Monkey': The Influence of Black American Blues Argot on the Rolling Stones," *JAF* 86 (1973), 367–73. Another important aspect of black folksongs is treated by Bruce Jackson in articles and in his book *Wake Up Dead Man: Afro-American Worksongs from Texas Prisons* (Cambridge, Mass.: Harvard University Press, 1972).

Pioneering collections of American occupational and industrial folksongs were made by George Korson and published in such works of his as *Songs and Ballads of the Anthracite Miner* (New York: Grafton Press, 1927), *Minstrels of the Mine Patch* (Philadelphia: University of Pennsylvania Press, 1938; reissued Hatboro, Pa.: Folklore Associates, 1964), and *Coal Dust on the Fiddle* (Philadelphia: University of Pennsylvania Press, 1943; reissued Hatboro, Pa.: Folklore Associates, 1965). A companion work is Archie Green's *Only a Miner: Studies in Recorded Coal-Mining Songs* (Urbana: University of Illinois Press, 1972). Collections of sea songs include W. Roy Mackenzie's *Ballads and Sea Songs from Nova Scotia* (Cambridge, Mass.: Harvard University Press, 1928; reprinted Hatboro, Pa.: Folklore Associates, 1963), Elisabeth Bristol Greenleaf and Grace Yarrow Mansfield's *Ballads and Sea Songs of Newfoundland* (Cambridge, Mass.: Harvard University Press, 1933; reprinted Hatboro, Pa.: Folklore Associates, 1968), and Frederick Pease Harlow's *Chanteying Aboard American Ships* (Barre, Mass.: Barre Publishing Co., 1962). See also Elliott Oring, "Whalemen and their Songs: A Study of Folklore and Culture," *NYFQ* 27 (1971), 130–52.

The interplay between the songs of sailors and loggers is suggested in *Shantymen and Shantyboys* (New York: Macmillan, 1951) by William Main Doerflinger. For loggers' songs see Edith Fowke, *Lumbering Songs from the Northern Woods* (Austin, Texas: AFS Memoir Series vol. 55, 1970). Hardrock miners' folksongs were first discussed by Duncan Emrich in *CFQ* 1 (1942), 213–32. A collection of "Songs of the Butte Miner" supplemented that pioneering article in *WF* 9 (1950), 1–49, by Wayland D. Hand, Charles Cutts, Robert C. Wylder, and Betty Wylder. S. Page Stegner discussed "Protest Songs from the Butte Mines" in *WF* 26 (1967), 157–67. Other articles on occupational folksong traditions are Ann Miller Carpenter, "The Railroad in American Folk Song, 1865–1920," *PTFS* 36 (1972), 103–19; "Big Tops Bloom, But Chanteys Disappear" reprinted from *Billboard* in *WF* 17 (1958), 57–60; and Marcello Truzzi, "Folksongs of the American Circus," *NYFQ* 24 (1968), 163–75. These and several other traditions deserve further attention from folklorists.

Folksong collector John A. Lomax together with his son Alan produced some of the most widely read—and sometimes controversial—general anthologies of folksongs in this country. The publication of Alan Lomax's *The Folk Songs of North America in the English Language* (New York: Doubleday,

1960) was the occasion for several reviews in professional journals that variously damned and praised all of the Lomax books. See reviews by G. Legman and D. K. Wilgus in *JAF* 74 (1961), 265–69; by Gene Bluestein in *TQ* 5 (1962), 49–59; and by David P. McAllester in *EM* 6 (1962), 233–38.

John Lomax's *Cowboy Songs and Other Frontier Ballads* of 1910 (New York: Sturgis and Walton) has been reprinted and expanded several times. Jack Thorp's pamphlet *Songs of the Cowboys* of 1908, to which Lomax was indebted for several of his texts, was reprinted with variants, commentary, notes, and a lexicon by Austin E. Fife and Alta Fife (New York: Clarkson N. Potter, 1966). In "Jack Thorp and John Lomax: Oral or Written Transmission?" *WF* 26 (1967), 113–18, John O. West reviews the evidence that Lomax had used nineteen out of the twenty-three songs Thorp earlier printed without giving credit. Professor and Mrs. Fife have assembled at the Utah State University Library in Logan materials from print, recordings, and manuscripts for comprehensive analyses of most of the traditional songs of the cowboys. Two of their publications based on these data are *Cowboy and Western Songs: A Comprehensive Anthology* (New York: Clarkson N. Potter, 1969) with two hundred items, and *Heaven on Horseback: Revivalist Songs and Verse in the Cowboy Idiom* (Logan, Utah: Western Texts Society Series 1 1970).

In an essay titled "The Dying Cowboy Song," *WAL* 2 (1967), 50–57, John Barsness suggests that accounts of cowboy singing are greatly romanticized and that many collectors had little to do with real cowboys. The actual folksong repertoire of a real cowboy is given in Glenn Ohrlin's *The Hell-Bound Train, a Cowboy Songbook* (Urbana: University of Illinois Press, 1973). John I. White, the composer of the song, gives the background for the Western-tinged "Great Grandma" in *WF* 27 (1968), 27–31. J. D. Robb provides examples in Spanish and English of another type of western occupational song in " 'Whereof I Speak,' or Songs of the Western Sheep Camps," *NMFR* 12 (1969–70), 17–28.

Folksongs in scholarly journals are beyond counting, but some representative examples may be cited. Edward D. Ives has held to an exceptionally high standard of editing in his "Twenty-One Folksongs from Prince Edward Island," *NEF* 5 (1963), 1–87; and "Folksongs from Maine," *NEF* 7 (1965), 1–104. Another collection from this region is Richard M. Dorson, George List and Neil Rosenberg's "Folksongs of the Maine Woods: Annotated Transcriptions," *FFMA* 8 (1965), 1–33. From the Midwest and West come "Songs I Sang on an Iowa Farm," collected by Eleanor T. Rogers with notes by Tristram P. Coffin and Samuel P. Bayard, *WF* 17 (1958), 229–47; and Ben Gray Lumpkin, "Colorado Folk Songs," *WF* 19 (1960) 77–97. A small collection of items of a kind often ignored is given in Gloria Dickens's "Childhood "Childhood Songs from North Carolina," *NCFJ* 21 (1973), 4–9.

Edward D. Ives's book *Larry Gorman, The Man Who Made the Songs* (Bloomington: Indiana University Press, 1964) exhaustively traces and analyzes the work of a woods poet responsible for some of the best folksongs of the Northeast. Other studies that focus on the singer rather than the songs exclusively are Roger D. Abrahams's *A Singer and Her Songs: Almeda Riddle's Book of Ballads* (Baton Rouge: Louisiana State University Press, 1970), and Henry Glassie, Edward D. Ives, and John F. Szwed's *Folksongs and their Makers* (Bowling Green, Ohio: Bowling Green University Popular Press, 1970).

G. Legman deals with a long-neglected area of folksong in "The Bawdy Song In Fact and In Print" in *The Horn Book* (New Hyde Park, N.Y.: University Books, 1964), pp. 336–426. One such song is traced by Guthrie T. Meade, Jr., in "The Sea Crab," *MF* 8 (1958), 91–100; and Ed Cray has edited a sizeable anthology in *The Erotic Muse* (New York: Oak Publications, 1968).

Joseph Hickerson discusses college folksongs in two articles in *FFMA* 1 (1958), 2; and 6 (1963), 3–6. Some examples of camp songs are given by Linda Weaver in *NCFJ* 22 (1974), 75–79. Two nonsense songs ("The Soft Side of a Brick" and "She Was Built Like a Mississippi Shed") are given by Richard C. Poulsen in *AFFWord* 3 (1973), 11–15. Some military folksongs are given in an article by Gustave O. Arlt and Chandler Harris in *CFQ* 3 (1944), 36–40; and two by William Wallrich in *WF* 12 (1953), 270–82, and 13 (1954), 236–44. In the *FF* Bibliographic and Special Series no. 7 (1971), Major Joseph F. Tuso gathered thirty-three examples of "Folksongs of the American Fighter Pilot in Southeast Asia, 1967–68."

Good analytical studies of American folksongs (as opposed to studies of ballads) are still relatively uncommon. Some early ones by Phillips Barry are contained in the *Bulletin of the Folksong Society of the Northeast*, reprinted by the American Folklore Society with an introduction by Samuel P. Bayard (Philadelphia: Bibliographic and Special Series no. 11, 1960). An important work is Roger D. Abrahams and George Foss, *Anglo-American Folksong Style* (Englewood Cliffs, N.J.: Prentice-Hall, 1968). Levette J. Davidson first summarized the investigation of "Home on the Range" in *CFQ* 3 (1944), 208–11. John Lomax added his observations on the song in "Half-Million Dollar Song," *Southwest Review* 31 (1945), 1–8. Probably the definitive account is John I. White's article on it in *TAW* 12 (Sept. 1975), 10–15, a chapter from his book *Git Along Little Dogies: Songs and Songmakers of the American West* (Urbana: University of Illinois Press, 1975).

Tristram P. Coffin's "A Tentative Study of a Typical Folk Lyric: 'Green Grows the Laurel,' " *JAF* 65 (1952), 341–51, is unusual as a comparative study of a single nonnarrative song. Other approaches to specific genres of folksong are Peter T. Bartis's "An Examination of the Holler in North Carolina White Tradition," *SFQ* 39 (1975), 209–18; Bess Lomax Hawes, "Folksongs and Functions: Some Thoughts on the American Lullaby," *JAF* 87 (1974), 140–48; D. K. Wilgus and Lynwood Montell, "Clure and Joe Williams: Legend and Blues Ballad," *JAF* 81 (1968), 295–315; and Américo Paredes, "The *Décima* on the Texas-Mexican Border: Folksong as an Adjunct to Legend," *JFI* 3 (1966), 154–67.

Two uncommon studies of the nature of folksong variation are John Quincy Wolf's "Folksingers and the Re-Creation of Folksongs," *WF* 26 (1967), 101–11; and Tom Burns's "A Model for Textual Variation in Folksong," *FF* 3

(1970), 49–56. Norman Cazden's article "Regional and Occupational Orientations of American Traditional Song," *JAF* 72 (1959), 310–44, offers an unusual statistical analysis of folksong distribution for various regions.

Sources of recordings of authentic American folksongs are identified in the notes to Chapter 12.

11

Ballads

A traditional ballad is a narrative folksong—a folksong that tells a story. To carry the basic definition any further, as most ballad collectors and scholars have been inclined to do, is asking for trouble; every other quality that might be listed as characteristic of some ballads, requires a balancing list of other ballads that are exceptions to the rule. But because they *all* tell stories a traditional ballad *is* a narrative folksong.

We have defined "folksong" in Chapter 10, but how narrative is a "narrative?" At this point all folksong-versus-ballad distinctions become relative and arbitrary. For instance, the "folk lyric" called "On Top of Old Smokey," derived, in fact, from an English ballad "The Wagoner's Lad," still tells a reasonably clear story, in stanzas such as:

> Your parents are against me
> And mine are the same;
> So farewell, my true love
> I'll be on my way.

The same thing is true of "Careless Love," "The Dreary Black Hills," "Old Dan Tucker," and a host of other American folksongs. Conversely, some accepted ballads occur in many variants that have confusing story lines or extremely scant narrative content. Such ballads have often been reduced to an "emotional core" by the eroding or evolving effects of repeated oral transmissions.

Some 850-odd Anglo-American narrative folksongs have been arranged by scholarly indexers in three categories, *British traditional ballads, British broadside ballads,* and *native American ballads.* The idea that these ballad classifications are canonical has been exaggerated by some past scholars. Even in 1956 we find the noted Appalachian folklore collector Richard Chase declaring in his popular anthology *American Folk Tales and Songs,* that "The genuine *ballad* is only one type of folksong. Your 'ballad' is not a true *folk* ballad unless it is closely kin to one of the 305—no more, no less!—in Professor Child's great collection." (Italics in original.)

Francis James Child wrote in 1882 that he had gathered "every valuable copy of every known ballad," but this was a good forty years before field collecting of ballads in America had gotten well under way. All that the twentieth-century ballad indexer G. Malcolm Laws, Jr., claimed to offer was a "guide" and "bibliographical syllabus"; it is the users of these collections and indexes who have elevated them into canons and treated their rough groupings as if they were systematic classifications. All of which is preliminary to a warning that in the discussion that follows, the "three kinds of ballads," as well as generalizations offered about them, are merely to be regarded as convenient scholarly concepts of the past that facilitated description and analysis. The last word has certainly not been said on ballad definition or classification, although D. K. Wilgus seems to be making good progress toward an international Type Index with his proposal for a thematic catalog of the narrative units of traditional songs based on such events or actions as seductions, murders, punishments, and bereavements.

The **British traditional ballads** are usually known as "the Child ballads," not because they are sung by children or have any connection whatever with children's folklore, but because they were gathered from hundreds of manuscript and printed sources in the late nineteenth century by Professor Francis James Child of Harvard and published, together with voluminous notes, in his monumental work, *The English and Scottish Popular Ballads* (5 volumes, 1882 to 1898). They are called "Child ballads," of course, by scholars and not by folk informants, who would no more call them that than they would call "Jack, Will, and Tom tales" *Märchen*, or refer to such stories by their Aarne-Thompson type numbers.

The Child ballads have been the folksong collectors' prime finds and the literary anthologists' favorite set pieces. The collectors went to the extreme at one time in this country of periodically tallying-up, state by state and county by county, the Child ballad variants "recovered" from oral tradition, either in good or in fragmentary texts. The anthologists continue to reprint some eight or ten selected ballad versions from Child as examples of medieval popular poetry, notwithstanding the fact that most of these selections came from manuscript sources no earlier than the seventeenth century and were probably revised by ballad editors in the eighteenth century or later. The veneration that has surrounded the Child canon—the mystique of the 305 ballads that he included—is also seen in the typical "Child and other" arrangements of printed folksong collections.

The 305 Child ballads were granted a false exclusiveness by their editor's very choice of words in his title— *The* English and Scottish popular ballads—when there are many other British popular ballads that Child either would not admit on esthetic grounds or did not know. Yet there was considerable validity to his choices, too. These do constitute the oldest group of ballads in British tradition, and their basic *form* is found in medieval sources. These ballads are part of an international tradition in that they are related to corresponding narrative folksongs from the Continent, especially the Scandinavian ballads. The greatest influence upon Child was the edition of Danish ballads that came from the hand of Svend Grundtvig, beginning in 1853. Grundtvig's texts revealed numerous analogues to the English ballads. He also suggested the existence of early ballad exchanges that subsequent research validated. Furthermore, Grundtvig exerted direct influence on Child during an extended correspondence between them. Most important, these ballads serve as a norm against which other ballads are measured, for their treatments of subject matter, style, and narrative method are widely considered to be of a high poetic order, although within the limitations of a rigid set of traditional conventions.

The technique of comparing art songs and folksongs may be applied to literary poetry and ballad poetry. In literature we value originality—a fresh treatment of a universal theme, "What oft was thought, but ne'er so well expressed." But the traditional ballads, as Albert B. Friedman has written, are not literature, but "illiterature"; they exist only in different oral performances, not in fixed written texts, and thus they abound in features that oral transmission creates and sustains. They use only a few simple stanza forms; their rhyme and meter seem irregular compared to conventional poetry; their language is stereotyped and cluttered with clichés; they freely repeat phrases, lines, and sometimes whole stanzas, often as refrains; and their texts are full of dialect terms, archaisms, and garbled usage.

Despite all this, the best of the traditional ballads have a unique charm and force that have not been equaled in literary imitations. Although no amount of description can ever replace hearing ballads sung by traditional performers, the characteristic features of ballad poetry may at least be specifically illustrated.

The typical *ballad stanza* is the familiar one of many folk rhymes and jingles (including "Mary Had a Little Lamb") and of "common measure" in hymns. It is a quatrain rhyming "x,a,x,a" (that is, lines one and three are indeterminate) with lines measured "4,3,4,3" (counting strong beats only) as shown in this typical opening verse from the ballad that Child called "James Harris" or "The Demon Lover," and which is frequently collected in this country as "The House Carpenter." It is Child's number 243:

> "Well mét, well mét," said an óld true lóve,   (4,x)
> "Well mét, well mét," said hé;   (3,a)
> "I've júst retúrned from a fár foreign lánd,   (4,x)
> And it's áll for the lóve of thée."   (3,a)

Other ballads, regarded by some scholars as the oldest ones, have a two-line stanza of four strong beats each, usually with refrain lines filling out a quatrain, such as in the following opening stanza from the Scottish ballad "Willie's Lyke-Wake" (Child 25):

> "O Willie my són, what mákes you so sád?"
> As the sun shines over the valley
> "I lýe sarely síck for the lóve of a máid."
> Amang the blue flowers and the yellow.

There are other ballad stanzas, some critics say as many as a dozen, but the various forms cannot be fully established without reference to ballad music.

The *refrains* in ballads are often lyrical lines interspersed with story lines, as in the last example quoted, or they may involve both lyrical lines and repetition, as in this opening stanza from "The Two Sisters" (Child 10):

> There was an old man in the North Countree,
> Bow down!
> There was an old man in the North Countree,
> And a bow 'twas unto me

> There was an old man in the North Countree,
> And he had daughters one, two, three.
>   I'll be true to my love if my love be true to me.

Refrains like this suggest dance movements or directions. Others are lists of plants, such as "Parsley, Sage, Rosemary and Thyme" (which sometimes appears in forms like "Every rose grows merry in time"). A number of refrains sound like pure nonsense, being merely strings of syllables such as "hey nonny no," "derry, derry, down," and "lillumwham, lillumwham."

Repetition alone in ballads may provide a refrain, usually through having the last two lines of each quatrain repeated to form a six-line stanza, and there are numerous other instances of repetition as a structural device in the story lines themselves. Sometimes a question is repeated in an answer, or a command is repeated in action, with very little change in wording, as shown in these typical commonplace lines found in numerous ballads:

> "Who will shoe your pretty little foot,
> And who will glove your hand?"
> ". . . mother will shoe my pretty little foot,
> And father will glove my hand."
>
>   *
>
> "Go saddle me the black, the black,
> Go saddle me the brown,
> Go saddle me the fastest steed,
> That ever ran through town."
>
> She saddled him the black, the black,
> She saddled him the brown. . . .

The most typical form of ballad repetition is *incremental repetition*, in which several lines are repeated with a slight "increment" (addition or change). Some ballads like "The Maid Freed from the Gallows" (Child 95, also called "Hangman") and "Our Goodman" (or "Four Nights Drunk," Child 274) are developed entirely through this device. It is also seen in two stanzas from "The Bonny Earl of Murray" (Child 181):

> He was a braw [fine] gallant,
> And he rid at the ring;

And the bonny Earl of Murray,
Oh he might have been a king!

The next stanza is the same, except that the second line becomes
"And he played at the ba' [ball]," while the last is altered to "Was the
flower among them a' [all]."

The oft-repeated "shoe your foot," "saddle my horse," and other
stanzas ("Oh make my bed, mother . . ." and "Go dig my grave, father . . . ," etc.) are one kind of *commonplace*, or stereotyped diction, found in ballads. These are "commonplace stanzas," and there
are also repeated phrases. Wine is always "blood-red," steeds tend to
be "milk-white," knives are usually "wee penknives" (perhaps an alteration of "weapon knife"), and a frequent courtly servant is the
"little foot page." Child ballads often begin conventionally (" 'Twas in
the merry month of May . . .") and express times in commonplace
phraseology ("Two [or three] hours before it was day"). Such expressions certainly aid the ballad singer's memory, for he can fall back on
them easily if other words escape him, but whether they indicate the
spontaneous "formulaic composition" of ballads or simply are traditional poetic devices is debatable.

In the two opening stanzas of traditional ballads quoted, we can see
two other characteristic devices—ballads, like epics, often begin
abruptly, *in medias res,* (in the middle of the story) and they are
highly *dramatic*, being told largely in terms of dialogue and action. In
"The House Carpenter," for instance, we do not know who the "old
true love" is who has returned saying "well met, well met" (a greeting, like "welcome," apparently). But as the ballad progresses in the
dialogue of the next two stanzas, we can begin to piece the background together:

"Come in, come in, my old true love,
And have a seat with me.
It's been three-fourths of a long, long, year
Since together we have been."

"Well I can't come in or I can't sit down,
For I haven't but a moment's time.
They say you're married to a house carpenter,
And your heart will never be mine."

Two of the most popular ballads in literary anthologies, "Lord Randall" (Child 12) and "Edward" (Child 13), are told entirely in dialogue, as are several others. Most, however, have stanzas of dialogue alternated with stanzas of action, with an occasional bit of description. By this means ballads achieve the immediacy of real life, of plays, or, as one critic has suggested, of motion pictures. Another ballad characteristic that supports the film theory has been called *leaping and lingering*—the tendency to make abrupt scene changes and then "linger" in one place for several stanzas. The counterpart in film is the art of "montage," or selective cutting and splicing of long, middle, and close-up shots.

Perhaps the most striking aspect of traditional ballad style (or tone) is *impersonality*. Stories involving supernaturalism, stark tragedy, and bloody violence, often between lovers or family members, are narrated with little intrusion of editorial comment or sentimentality. Like modern newspaper stories, which often deal with the same kinds of subjects, the ballads tend to focus on the climax of an action and its result, relating the happenings in a straightforward, objective manner. Two examples must suffice. In "Mary Hamilton" (Child 173) a lady of the Scottish court disposes of her illegitimate child thus:

> She's tyed it in her apron
> And she's thrown it in the sea;
> Says, "Sink ye, swim ye, bonny wee babe!
> You'l neer get mair o me."

In "Little Musgrave and the Lady Barnard" (Child 81, often "Little Matty Groves" in the United States) a duel is described thus:

> The first stroke that Little Musgrave stroke,
> He hurt Lord Barnard sore;
> The next stroke that Lord Barnard stroke,
> Little Musgrave nere struck more.

All of the ballad characteristics described so far are typical of English and Scottish texts, although the stanzas of "The House Carpenter" and "The Two Sisters" actually came from American variants. When we look more closely at traditional ballads collected in this country, a pattern of alteration becomes apparent. American versions of Child ballads tend to lose details of their stories, to slough off super-natural motifs, to become subjective in tone, to acquire local references, and to change their language.

The longer that ballads are transmitted orally, the more they tend to be reduced to what the folklorist Tristram P. Coffin has aptly termed the "emotional core" of the narrative; the focus is always on the climax of the story. Long ballads, originally sprinkled with circumstantial details, may eventually become lyrical folksongs. "Sir Lionel" (Child 18), for example, in older versions telling a complicated tale about a knight slaying a wild boar and a giant, becomes in the United States "Old Bangum and the Boar," a comical song about a hunting expedition. "Little Sir Hugh" (Child 155), relating the same medieval legend as Chaucer's "Prioress's Tale," loses its anti-Semitic plot in American versions, and simply tells of a murder by a "Jewler's daughter" or "Gypsy lady." In "Mary Hamilton," Coffin's chief example of this process, the narrative is reduced to a five-stanza lament by the victim, and no story whatever is told.

Americans, presumably because they are hard-headed and practical, have tended especially to drop supernatural elements from British ballads. Little Sir Hugh no longer speaks miraculously after his murder, Sir Lionel faces no giant, James Harris is not a ghost (or the Devil) but merely a double-dealing sailor, and the ballad of "The Two Sisters" has lost its fascinating motif of a speaking harp being constructed from the dead girl's breastbone and strands of her hair. Ghosts, fairies, elves, and mermaids all drop out of most American texts. In the few variants in which the Devil still appears, he is a comic figure, not the Prince of Darkness.

American sentimentality and fundamentalist religion is credited with the alteration of the moral tone of many British traditional ballads. The most typical change is the addition of a concluding stanza that comments on the story. In "James Harris," the wife is persuaded to leave her husband and sail away with the returned lover. The ship sinks (in older British versions through magic), and this verse is then tacked on at the end:

> A curse be on the sea-faring men,
> Oh, cursed be their lives,
> For while they are robbing the House-Carpenter,
> And coaxing away their wives.

In some American versions of "Bonny Barbara Allen" (Child 84) the tragic heroine herself speaks:

> "Farewell ye virgins all," she said,
> "And shun the fault I've fell in;
> Henceforth take warning by the fall
> Of cruel Barbara Allen."

Unsavory subjects like incest are eliminated from the British ballads; cruel characters in them may return later and apologize for their behavior. In one of the most extreme examples of changed tone, the deeply moving British ballad "The Three Ravens" (Child 26, in Scotland "The Twa Corbies") became in the United States a rolicking nonsense song. The traditional British versions descend from one that was first printed in 1611, that began:

> There were three ravens sat on a tree,
>   Downe a downe, hay downe, hay downe
> There were three ravens sat on a tree,
>   With a downe
> There were three ravens sat on a tree,
> They were as blacke as they might be,
>   With a downe derrie, derrie, derrie, downe, downe.

The story continues as a dialogue between the ravens that reveals how a knight lying "slain under his shield" is guarded by his hawks and hounds, and finally carried off for burial by a fallow doe, "great with child," who perishes from the effort. The ballad ends with the comment:

> God send every gentleman,
> Such hawks, such hounds, and such a leman [sweetheart]

In the Scottish version the hawks and hounds desert the knight, his lady takes another mate, and the ravens feast on his corpse. However, the American versions ignore pathos entirely, so that the song begins:

> There were three crows sat on a tree,
>   Oh Billy Magee Magaw!
> There were three crows sat on a tree,
>   Oh Billy Magee Magaw!
> There were three crows sat on a tree,
> And they were black as crows could be;

And they all flapped their wings and cried,
  "Caw! Caw! Caw!"
And they all flapped their wings and cried,
  "Billy Magee Magaw!"

This time the two crows only pick out the eyes of an old dead horse, and the ballad sometimes ends:

O maybe you think there's another verse,
But there isn't.

Minor verbal variations in ballads may be the result of informants forgetting words, misunderstanding what they have heard, inserting a commonplace, or trying to improve on a story or expand it. A frequent result is the creation of near nonsense—"a parrot *sitting* on a willow tree" becomes "*exceeding* on a willow tree," or instead of characters calling out "*amain,* [vigorously] 'Unworthy Barbara Allen',," they do so "*amen.*" The first of these changes possibly came about as a result of misunderstood pronunciation, the latter from the use of an unfamiliar archaic word. Names in the British ballads are particularly subject to change in American tradition. In "The Gypsy Laddie" (Child 200), for example, many variants occur, including Gypsy Davey, Gypsum Davey, Black Jack Davey, and Harrison Brady.

In many instances, verbal changes in American versions of British traditional ballads serve to relocalize the setting. Thus, in a logger's version of the ballad called "The Farmer's Curst Wife" (Child 278), the subject is a "woodsman's wife"; and Lord Randall in Virginia may be "Johnny Randolph," picking up the name of a prominent local family. References to "deep blue sea" sometimes change to "Tennessee." One of the most amusing relocalizations has appeared in the commonplace stanza that attaches a "rose-briar" ending to a tragic love story:

One was buried in the old churchyard,
The other in the choir.
And out of her grave grew a red, red, rose,
And out of his a briar.

They grew and they grew to the old church top,
Til they couldn't grow any higher.

>And there they locked in a true-lover's knot,
>For all true lovers to admire.

A singer who did not recognize "choir" as a part of a church in which bodies might be interred changed it to "Ohio."

British broadside ballads are a more recent strain of balladry than the Child ballads, as noted in Chapter 10. Also, in contrast to Child's 305 ballads, the plots of broadsides are even more sensational, their attitudes are more subjective, their stanza forms are more varied, and their language is less poetic. Broadside diction tends even more heavily than that in Child ballads toward stereotypes, drawing both on the same commonplaces found in the older ballads and on some new ones. (The "Come all ye" opening stanza, for example, is frequent.) Broadsides not only are like newspapers in general style and narrative method, but also, in common with the most sensational modern tabloids, they often dwell upon murders, robberies, scandals, love triangles, and like subjects.

Many thousands of such topical ballads were composed, printed on tens of thousands of broadside sheets, and sold on the streets, in both England and America, to a public eager for their lurid stories. But only a very small number of these pieces passed into oral tradition and became folk ballads. The folk versions, in turn, continued to change in oral transmission in much the same way that Child ballads varied. Analysis of this whole process was greatly facilitated in 1957 when Professor G. Malcolm Laws, Jr., of the University of Pennsylvania published a classified bibliographic guide to some 290 common American ballads that had apparently derived from British broadsides, along with an illuminating discussion of their distribution, forms, and style. Laws's categories and some sample titles follow:

>(Letters "A" through "I" were reserved for the Laws native American ballad index, discussed next.)
>
>J. War Ballads (A small group with few American versions; "The Drummer Boy of Waterloo" is J 1.)
>K. Ballads of Sailors and the Sea ("The Sailor Boy" is K 12.)
>L. Ballads of Crime and Criminals ("The Boston Burglar" is L 16 B.)
>M. Ballads of Family Opposition to Lovers ("The Drowsy Sleeper" is M 4.)
>N. Ballads of Lovers' Disguises and Tricks ("Jack Monroe" is N 7.)

O. Ballads of Faithful Lovers ("Molly Bawn" or "The Shooting of
His Dear" is O 36.)

P. Ballads of Unfaithful Lovers ("The Butcher Boy" is P 24.)

Q. Humorous and Miscellaneous Ballads ("Father Grumble" is Q
1, and "The Babes in the Woods" is Q 34.)

Although ballads with broadside origins have not been so highly
regarded by folklorists as have Child ballads, most traditional singers
in America know more broadsides than any other kind of ballads. At
any rate, as Laws's analysis of the contents of six representative collections shows, in a total of more than 1,800 folksong and ballad texts,
broadsides outnumber either Child or native American ballads by
more than two to one. The fact that the collected *variants* of Child
ballads outnumber either of the other two types in the same books is
probably indicative of folklorists' rather than informants' preferences.
In one other large and diversified printed collection, Frank C.
Brown's *North Carolina Folklore,* a similar distribution among types
is maintained. Among some 184 identifiable texts here, forty-nine are
Child ballads, about seventy-five are broadsides, and about sixty are
native American ballads. Another revealing statistic about this collection is that the remaining printed texts—some 130 further ballads
from North Carolina folk tradition—do not appear in any of the three
published classifications of ballads in America, suggesting how incomplete these classifications still are.

Most other regional collections yield roughly similar figures. For
example, when a miscellaneous group of some 730 folksongs and
ballads (1,000 individual texts) from the Northwest was analyzed,
about one-quarter of them were found to be ballads, and these fell
into the following groups:

	INDIVIDUAL BALLADS	INDIVIDUAL TEXTS
Child	19	49
Laws Broadsides	41	71
(Other, prob. British)	12	36
Laws Native American	57	83
(Other, prob. American)	38	65

Such statistics suggest that non-Child ballads are more common
than Child ballads in American folk tradition, that many unclassified
Anglo-American ballads still exist, and that as a group ballads are out-

numbered in tradition by folksongs. Classifications, titles, and statistics, however, do not tell us anything about ballads themselves. Selected stanzas from the broadside ballads whose titles and Laws numbers were listed above, give some notion of their characteristics; the versions quoted are all from *The Frank C. Brown Collection of North Carolina Folklore.*

The broadside composers plodded rather grimly through their stories, getting the maximum pathos out of every possible situation, and always taking the easiest way out to provide the rhymes. The following stanza of Laws J 1, given in the informant's own spelling, is typical:

> And when [his] lips his mother pressed
> And bid her noble boy adue
> With ringing hands and aching breast
> Behold a march for Waterloo.

Even when the characteristic rhetoric of the older ballads appears, it does little to elevate the general tone. The following use of incremental repetition from Laws K 12, for instance, is undistinguished:

> "Oh, father, go build me a boat,
> That over the ocean I may float."
> The father built her a boat
> And over the ocean she did float.

Further repetition appears in one later stanza of this ballad, from the beginning of which an alternate title is sometimes taken:

> "Oh, captain, captain, tell me true,
> Does my dear sailor boy sail with you?"
> "No, no, he does not sail with me;
> I fear he's drowned in the sea."

Frequently broadsides are narrated in the first person, but not usually with any improved poetic art. The burglar from Boston in Laws L 16B merely begins with an obvious bid for sympathy (addressing himself directly to listeners) and then he reels out the sequence of events in a pedestrian manner:

> I was born in the town of Boston,
> A town you all know well,

Raised up by honest parents—
The truth to you I will tell—
Raised up by honest parents,
Raised up most tenderly,
Until I became a sporting man
At the age of twenty-three.

My character was taken
And I was sent to jail.
The people tried, but all in vain,
To keep me out on trail.
 [probably should be "out on *bail*"]
The juror found me guilty,
The clerk he wrote it down,
The judge he passed the sentence
To send me to Charlestown.

At times, however, the language becomes more inspired, as in the usual opening phrases of Laws M 4. In this particular version the first stanza is muddled, but the second one rescues the story. It should also be noted that, like many fine old traditional ballads, things begin *in medias res,* and they are carried on entirely in dialogue:

"Awake, arise, you drowsy sleeper!
Awake, arise; it's near about day.
Awake, arise; go ask your father
If you're my bride to be.
And if you're not, come back and tell me;
It's the very last time I'll bother thee."

"I cannot go and ask my father,
For he is on his bed of rest
And in his hand he holds a weapon
To kill the one I love the best."

This ballad often merges with the American "Silver Dagger," a kind of "climax of suicides" folksong:

And he taken up that silver dagger
And plunged it in his snowy white breast,
Saying "Farewell, Bessie, farewell, darling;
Sometimes the best of friends must part."

> And she taken up that bloody weapon
> And plunged it in her lily-white breast . . .

Among the love ballads, external complications mar most romances, and tragic endings are the rule, with few exceptions. But lovers bring some problems on themselves, often as the result of their own attempts at tricks and disguises. One favorite device is the long-lost lover coming back to his sweetheart in disguise. Another is the girl dressing in man's clothing to follow her lover into military service. From Laws N 7:

> She stepped into the tailor shop and dressed in men's array
> And enlisted with the captain to carry her away.
> "Before you get on board, sir, your name I'd like to know."
> She spoke with a pleasing countenance, "My name is Stephen
>   Monroe."
>
> "Your waist it is too slender, your fingers are too small,
> Your cheeks too red and rosy to face a cannon ball."
>
> "My waist is none too slender . . .

Generally the name in the above ballad is "Jack Monroe," and she is off to pursue "Jackie Frazier," from either of which characters the ballad may be named. Again in this passage, as well as the one quoted just before, we observe incremental repetition developing in the last partially-quoted line.

An unintentional disguise led to the death of Molly Bawn (or "Bond," Laws O 36), who is called "Polly Bonn" in the North Carolina version. She threw her apron over her head against the rain, with this result:

> With her apron pinned around her
> The rain for to shun;
> Jimmy Randall he saw her
> And shot her for a swan.

In British versions Molly's ghost may return to defend Jimmy at his murder trial, but American texts characteristically lose the supernaturalism.

Ballads of faithful lovers and unfaithful lovers run about even in Laws's index (forty to forty-one), but sometimes the classification of an individual piece is debatable. For instance, in Laws P 24 we have a faithful girl with an unfaithful sweetheart, and the ballad has been classified from her point of view:

> There lived a girl in that same town
> Where he would go and sit around.
> He'd take that girl upon his knee
> And tell her things that he wouldn't tell me.

Later she requests in her suicide note (using a commonplace stanza):

> "So bury me both wide and deep,
> Place a marble stone at my head and feet,
> And on my breast place a snow-white dove
> To show to the world that I died for love."

The saving grace of humor seems to raise some of the ballads in category "Q" a cut above most of the others in Laws's broadside index. "Devilish Mary" (Q 4) is a comical antifeminist (or at least antimarriage) piece; "The Love-of-God Shave" (Q 15) has some felicitous wording for a very funny situation; and "Finnegan's Wake" (Q 17) deserves the respectability and immortality it achieved from James Joyce's use of it. Another humorous success is Laws Q 1, in which a farmer, variously named, takes an ill-considered oath:

> Old Summerfield swore by the sun and the moon
> And the green leaves on the tree
> That he could do more work in one day
> Than his wife could do in three.

Teeny the cow has to be milked during the man's day at home, and she proves to be only one source of exasperation to him:

> Teeny inched and Teeny winced
> And Teeny curled her tail;
> She gave the old man such a kick in the face
> It made him drop his pail.

At the other extreme in the last category are some of the "miscellaneous" ballads—sad, trite, orphans with no home elsewhere in the index—like "The Babes in the Woods":

> Oh, don't you remember, a long time ago,
> Of two little children, their names I don't know.

They were *stole on the way* on a bright summer day
[probably *"stolen away"*]
And lost in the woods, I've heard people say.

And when it was night so sad was their plight
The moon went down and the stars gave no light.
They sobbed and they sighed and they bitterly cried;
Poor babes in the woods, they lay down and died.

And when they were dead the robins so red
Brought strawberry leaves and over them spread
And sang a sweet song the whole day long.
Poor babes in the woods, they lay down and died.

These three verses, all that usuallly remain in many American versions, are based on a long and highly circumstantial ballad. They show
that in broadside as well as Child ballads repeated oral transmission
tends to focus attention on the emotional core.

The broadsides have not stood up as very good poetry under close
examination, just as they did not under appraisal by Laws, who
wrote, "The average or below average broadside is not so much composed as patched together from the materials at hand." However, we
should bear in mind, as Laws also pointed out, that the poetic shortcomings of broadside ballads apply to them as printed literature only,
not as oral folksongs. Most of these texts can be surprisingly appealing
when they come from the lips of traditional singers. Such singers, at
any rate, make no distinctions themselves between Child and non-
Child ballads, but they sing either kind (or non-narrative folksongs)
interchangeably.

The **native American ballads** are the most recent strain of all, coming largely from the last half of the nineteenth century. In style they
are very similar to the British broadside ballads, and they have all of
their stereotypes of attitude and situation and most of their poetic
flaws. Current events, especially scandals and tragedies, still are common topics, but American history and development add new subjects, as the following summary of Professor Laws's categories shows
(from the 1964 revision of his *Native American Balladry*):

A. War Ballads ("The Texas Rangers" is A 8.)
B. Ballads of Cowboys and Pioneers ("Joe Bowers" is B 14.)

   C. Ballads of Lumberjacks ("Harry Bale" is C 13.)
   D. Ballads of Sailors and the Sea ("The *Titanic*" is D 24.)
   E. Ballads about Criminals and Outlaws ("Charles Guiteau" is E11.)
   F. Murder Ballads ("The Jealous Lover" is F 1.)
   G. Ballads of Tragedies and Disasters ("Springfield Mountain" is G16.)
   H. Ballads on Various Topics ("The Young Man Who Wouldn't Hoe Corn" is H 13.)
   I. Ballads of the Negro ("Frankie and Albert" is I 3.)

Laws had indexed 256 native American ballads by 1964, far too many to be discussed in detail here. But again we can survey their characteristics by examining a group of sample stanzas. This time all but one are quoted from H. M. Belden's *Ballads and Songs Collected by the Missouri Folk-Lore Society*.

According to Laws's count, only two native American war ballads have remained in tradition from the Colonial period, three from the Revolution, four from the War of 1812, two from the Indian wars, about a dozen from the Civil War, and none from World War I or other conflicts. This seems a very slim folk inheritance, but any valid generalization about American history in folk music would have to take folk*songs* into account as well; they survive in much greater numbers from all periods. A typical war ballad is a highly stereotyped account of some notable conflict, set off by patriotic sentiments or memories of mothers and sweethearts back home. The bare texts, as in the following stanzas from Laws A 8, convey little real sense of battle:

> I saw the Indians coming,
> I heard them give a yell.
> My feelings at that moment
> No human tongue can tell.
>
> Our bugle it was sounded,
> Our captain gave command.
> "To arms, to arms!" he shouted,
> "And by your horses stand."

The cowboy and pioneer ballads sometimes depict death and suffering in the Wild West, especially accidents in the cow camps—

"When the Work's All Done This Fall" (B 3), "Utah Carroll" (B 4), "Little Joe the Wrangler" (B 5), and so forth. But many of the Western pieces laugh at the dangers instead, and they picture a group of adventurers who are high-spirited and ready to tackle anything. Joe Bowers, for instance, risks security back East for the sake of his sweetheart Sally:

> "Oh Sally, dearest Sally,
> Oh Sally, for your sake
> I'll go to California
> And try to raise a stake."

> Says she to me, "Joe Bowers,
> You are the man to win;
> Here's a kiss to bind the bargain,"
> And she hove a dozen in.

Sally, however, proves false; when Joe next hears from her, she is married to a red-haired butcher, and she has a baby with red hair.

Missouri is a good state for Western subjects, but would seem an unlikely place for lumberjacks' ballads. Still, one does appear in Belden's collection (from an Arkansas informant), illustrating that the topics of ballads do not necessarily limit their distribution. In this example, the ballad about a logger named Harry Bahel, who was killed in a sawmill accident in Arcadia Township, Lapeer County, Michigan, appears as one about "Harry Dale," killed in "Arcadia, Laneer County," no state specified. As in all versions, the ballad begins with a commonplace "come all ye":

> Come all kind friends and parents,
> Come brothers one and all;
> Attention pay to what I say;
> 'Twill make your blood run cold.
> 'Tis about a poor unfortunate boy,
> Who was known both far and near.
> His parents raised him tenderly,
> Not many miles from here.

Then the story advances to a gory description of the tragic accident:

> In lowering the Vantle wheel [The reference is unclear.]
> He threw the carriage in its gear.

It drew him into the saw
And it sawed him all severe.

It sawed him through the shoulder blade
And half-way down his back,
And he fell upon the floor
As the carriage it rolled back.

Woods accidents dominate the lumberjack ballads as a group, the most typical ones being drownings or deaths by crushing during a river drive. Probably the best known of these is number C 1, "The Jam on Gerry's Rock" or "Foreman Young Monroe."

For a ballad of the sea, we must turn to another anthology, for Belden has none that are indexed in Laws. From the Frank C. Brown collection, however, come these typical stanzas and chorus of "The *Titanic*" (as written out by an informant):

It was on one Monday morning about one o'clock
When the great Titanic began to reel and rock.
All the people began to cry saying lord I have to die.
It was sad when that great ship went down.

Oh it was sad when that great ship went down.
There were husbands and their wives,
Little children lost their lives.
It was sad when that great ship went down.

You know it was ofel out on the sea.
The people were singing nearer my god to thee.
Some were homeward bound, sixteen hundered had to dround.
It was sad when that great ship went down.

The sinkings of many ships—both salt-water and Great-Lakes vessels—have been celebrated in balladry, but few have so gripped the folk imagination as did the sinking of the *Titanic* on her maiden voyage in 1912. Besides the serious version of the ballad, a comical version sung to a jolly tune still survives in American collegiate tradition, there are distinctive black variants, and there are at least four other *Titanic* ballads of more limited folk distribution.

Criminals and outlaws are the subjects of some of the most popular and widely distributed of the native American ballads. Their typical motifs include the Robin Hood tradition, the tenderhearted criminal, the regretful "boy gone wrong," and sometimes the defiant captive. Perhaps the best known is "Jesse James," about whom there are two distnct ballads (E 1 and 2), as well as one about his cohort "Cole Younger" (E 3). The assassin of President Garfield, like several other criminals of balladry, speaks for himself, using commonplace lines borrowed from older ballads and appealing for his listeners' sympathy.

> Come all ye Christian people,
> Wherever you may be,
> And likewise pay attention
> To these few words from me.
> For the murder of James A. Garfield
> I am condemned to die
> On the thirteenth day of June
> Upon the scaffold high.

> For my name is Charles Guiteau,
> And the name I'll never deny,
> Tho I leave my aged parents
> In sorrow for to die.
> Oh! little did they think
> While in my youthful bloom
> I'd be taken to the scaffold
> To meet my fatal doom.

The favorite American ballad topic is the murder of an innocent young girl. Naomi Wise, murdered in Randolph County, North Carolina, in 1808, has been described in Laws ballad number F 4. Pearl Bryan of Greencastle, Indiana, was murdered by her lover, Scott Jackson, in 1896, and is celebrated in Laws F 2 and 3. Leo Frank, according to folk tradition, beat little Mary Phagan to death as she walked home from working at The National Pencil Company factory in Atlanta, Georgia, in 1913, and that is the subject of number F 20. There are several other ballads associated with specific female victims, and many more that are generalized. Most of them, as a study by Anne B. Cohen shows, develop in stereotypic ways common also to sensational journalism. One of these ballads is about the killing of "fair Ellen," who is often called "Florella" or "Floella"; the ballad is usually titled "The Jealous Lover":

> One evening when the moon shone brightly
> There fell a gentle dew,
> When out of a cottage
> A jealous lover drew.
>
> Says he to fair young Ellen:
> "Down on the sparkling brook
> We'll wait and watch and wonder
> Upon our wedding day."

This unfortunate girl, like so many others, is most cruelly murdered; yet she forgives the killer with her last breath:

> "Oh Edward, I'll forgive thee,
> Though this be my last breath.
> I never was deceiving,
> Though I close my eyes in death."

The ballads in category "G" include those concerning railroad accidents (like "Casey Jones," G 1), mine fires and other subterranean tragedies (like "The Avondale Disaster," G 6 and 7), floods (like "The Johnstown Flood," G 14), fires, suicides, explosions, cyclones, and even a spelunking accident ("Floyd Collins," G 22). One more example of a characteristic development in American balladry—stemming from one of the oldest native ballads—is seen in "Springfield Mountain." This once-serious ballad describing an agricultural accident in New England in 1761 has turned into a funny song with a nonsense chorus, from which the following sequence is typical:

> "Oh, Mollie dear, do come and see
> What a venemous viper did bite me."
>   With a bumble bumble dick a ri dum
>   Able de dinctum day
>
> "Oh, Johnnie dear, why did you go
> Away down yonder in the field to mow?"
>
> "Oh, Mollie dear, I thought you knowed
> 'Twas Daddy's hay and it had to be mowed."

The miscellaneous classification includes ballads about wanderers, gamblers, and sportsmen, plus a few religious, romantic, and humorous pieces. One ballad (Laws H 13) even comments upon the unlikely poetic topic of hoeing corn. A lazy young man never hoes his corn, with this result:

> He went to the fence and he peeped in.
> The grass and the weeds were up to his chin.
> The careless weeds they grow so high
> Caused this young man for to sigh.

Even worse, he finds that his sweetheart will no longer have him:

> "Then what makes you ask me to wed
> When you can't raise your own corn bread?
> Single I am, single I'll remain.
> A lazy man I won't maintain."

In disgust—with *her* rather than with himself—the lazy farmer takes his leave:

> He picked up his hat and he went away,
> Saying, "Madam, you'll rue the day,
> Rue the day as sure as you're born,
> Giving me the mitten 'cause I didn't hoe my corn."

Finally, the ballads in category "I" were segregated because of their presumed Afro-American origin, or subject matter, although many of them have become generally familiar throughout the United States, including "John Henry" (I 1), "The Boll Weevil" (I 17), and "The Blue-Tailed Fly" (I 19). The best known of all is, of course, "Frankie and Johnny," (I 3, "Albert" in older versions) which has passed into literary drama, popular song, and jazz. Repeated attempts to identify the principals in the story with real-life figures have met with failure. The ballad, with its familiar "He done her wrong" chorus, is too common to need quoting at any length; Belden's text, however, is a somewhat unusual one, being a long composite of various stanzas known to his informant, interspersed with lines of commentary and explanation. The informant at one point said, "Then they go to the city, and for a while all is lovely. But Albert gets 'onery' and don't work and spends money on other women." Then follows:

> Frankie, she shot Albert,
> And I'll tell the reason why.
> Ever' dollar bill she give Albert,
> He'd give to Alice Blye. [also "Nelly Bly" and "Alice Frye."]

"Frankie and Johnny" has developed a group of near-commonplaces of its own; these are the chorus, Frankie's "forty-four" that goes "roota toot toot," and this "graveyard stanza":

> They took him to that cemet'ry
> In a rubber-tired hack,
> They took him to that cemet'ry
> But they did not bring him back.

In many versions ten men go to the funeral in that "rubber-tired hack," but only nine come back.

Ballads, especially the oldest British-American group, have attracted detailed and voluminous study since the beginning of British and American folklore research in the nineteenth century. Earlier surveys of this scholarship by Sigurd B. Hustvedt, and the recent books by D. K. Wilgus and Albert B. Friedman, eliminate the necessity to do any more here than sketch out trends and rough outlines and indicate some areas for future studies.

One curious fact about ballad scholarship is that a "final" publication, in the case of the Child ballads, came before collecting had been well established, or had even been begun in this country. Then a period of broad theorizing about ballad origins followed, with the "communalists" (led by F. B. Gummere) disputing with the supporters of individual origins (dominated by Louise Pound). The Pound group eventually prevailed, but it was in the skirmishes of this "ballad war" that it first became fully apparent how important it was for more collecting and classification of American materials to be carried out before analyses were further pursued. It was then, too, that Phillips Barry's useful term "communal re-creation" was coined. (See "theories of the folk" in Chapter 3.) Subsequently, many brilliant collectors and editors of ballads emerged in the United States.

Child's notes for *The English and Scottish Popular Ballads* were themselves international studies of individual ballads, and further such studies followed, notably of "Edward," "The Two Sisters," and "Lady Isabel and the Elf Knight." Another approach, popular for generations, was the isolation of one particular aspect of many ballads—superstitions, place names, proverbs, commonplaces, and the like. As American collecting progressed, comparative studies of British and American versions of ballads followed, with results like tracing the descendants of "The Unfortunate Rake," a British broadside, in such new forms as "The Young Girl Cut Down in Her Prime" (Laws Q 26) and "The Cowboy's Lament" (Laws B 1). In native American balladry, a favorite research topic has been searching for historical origins. Louise Pound, for instance, was able to show that John A. Stone, an early author of songster texts, probably composed "Joe Bowers." Austin E. Fife has traced the cowboy ballad "The Trail to Mexico" from a seventeenth-century broadside, "The Seaman's Complaint," to its later evolution into "Early, Early in the Spring" (Laws M 1), and finally to numerous versions and parodies in the American West.

Generally speaking, ballad studies in the beginning were oriented toward literature, and later were inclined to folkloristic and historic approaches. The strongest current trend is toward deeper studies of ballad music and the interdependence of texts and tunes (see Chapter 12). Interesting findings are also likely to come from the anthropological (or "functional") approach to ballads as "socio-historical documents" and from psychological or structural approaches to ballads. When these various possibilities are considered, along with the continuing need for better and more inclusive classifications of ballads, it is apparent that, despite voluminous ballad studies of the past, American folklorists may pursue their favorite subject for many years to come without running short of research topics. For the amateur or beginning folklorist, the history and the basic problems and broad approaches of ballad scholarship suggest many small-scale projects that are worth carrying out.

For example, students might teach themselves a great deal about ballad variation, and perhaps even make some original discoveries, by preparing an annotated edition of all readily available texts of a native or recent ballad. A good study of narrative method in ballads might also be done without any elaborate bibliographic materials. Another possibility is a full explication of the background, function, and meaning to the informant of a ballad that a student has collected from oral tradition. Psychological or structural discussions of ballads need not refer to every extant variant, but might be based on a fairly limited corpus from easily available library sources. There is also much to be learned from a close critical evaluation either of a ballad study, an old 78 rpm. "hillbilly" record of a ballad, or, perhaps, of a recent long-playing disk that purports to be reasonably "authentic" folk music.

BIBLIOGRAPHIC NOTES

General works on folksongs, cited in the notes to Chapter 10, by Herzog, Nettl, Pound, Ames, and Wilgus are all pertinent to ballads as well. The earlier history of ballad studies was treated in two books by Sigurd B. Hustvedt, *Ballad Criticism in Scandinavia and Great Britain during the Eighteenth Century* (New York: The American-Scandinavian Foundation, 1916), and *Ballad Books and Ballad Men* (Cambridge, Mass: Harvard University Press, 1930). Albert B. Friedman reviewed literary interest in ballads from the eighteenth century to the present in *The Ballad Revival* (Chicago: University of Chicago Press, 1961).

Two good general introductions are Gordon Hall Gerould's *The Ballad of Tradition* (Oxford: Oxford University Press, 1932; Galaxy paperback edn. 1957); and M. J. C. Hodgart's *The Ballads* (London: Hutchinson's University Library, 1950; Norton Library paperback edn. 1962).

MacEdward Leach and Tristram P. Coffin have edited *The Critics and the Ballad* (Carbondale, Ill: Southern Illinois University Press, 1961; paperback reprint, 1973), which contains fifteen articles (one a previously unpublished one by Phillips Barry) concerning ballad origins, definitions, meter and music, and the literary tradition of ballads. Two of the most important articles included here are Thelma G. James's "The English and Scottish Popular Ballads of Francis J. Child" and Coffin's " 'Mary Hamilton' and the Anglo-American Ballad as an Art Form," both originally published in the *Journal of American Folklore*.

The three basic American ballad syllabi were all published by the American Folklore Society in the "Bibliographic and Special Series"; Laws's *Native American Balladry* was volume 1 in the series (1950), revised in 1964; Coffin's *The British Traditional Ballad in North America* was volume 2 (1950), revised in 1963; and Laws's *American Balladry from British Broadsides* was volume 8 (1957). D. K. Wilgus outlines problems and progress in improving ballad classifications in "A Type-Index of Anglo-American Traditional Narrative Songs," *JFI* 7 (1970), 161–76.

There are many general anthologies of ballads. Three easily available ones all have excellent introductions. Bartlett Jere Whiting has edited *Traditional British Ballads* for "Crofts Classics" (paperback; New York, 1955), containing forty Child texts with notes. MacEdward Leach's *The Ballad Book* (New York: Harper, 1955), and Albert B. Friedman's *The Viking Book of Folk Ballads of the English Speaking World* (New York: Viking Press, 1956; Compass Books paperback, 1963) both contain many ballads, both Child and non-Child.

Folk ballads were gathered in volume 2 (1952) of the *Frank C. Brown Collection of North Carolina Folklore*, ed. H. M. Belden and Arthur Palmer Hudson. Ballad tunes are in volume 4 (1957). The Northwest ballad and folksong collection mentioned in this chapter was described in my article "Folk Song Studies in Idaho," *WF* 24 (1965), 231–48.

The thorny question of actual *oral* credentials for Child's selections is taken up in two recent articles: J. Barre Toelken, "An Oral Canon for the Child Ballads: Construction and Application," *JFI* 4 (1967), 75–101; and Kenneth A. Thigpen, Jr., "An Index to the Known Oral Sources of the Child Collection," *FF* 5 (1972), 55–69.

Literary aspects of the ballads have interested both folklorists and literary critics. Louise Pound examined the treatment of ballads in some popular anthologies of literature in her article in *SFQ* 6 (1942), 127–41. Arthur K. Moore took the literary point of view in an article in *CL* 10 (1958), 1–20. Holger Olof Nygard discussed a subject of importance to the question of literary ballad analogues in "Ballads and the Middle Ages," in *TSL* 5 (1960), 85–96. Central to the whole subject is Albert B. Friedman's book *The Ballad Revival: Studies in the Influence of Popular on Sophisticated Poetry* (Chicago: University of Chicago Press, 1961).

MacEdward Leach, an advocate of a literary approach to ballads, provided a good survey of the goals of such studies in "The Singer or the Song," *PTFS* 30 (1961), 30–45. His student, Tristram P. Coffin, has written many important articles from this point of view, including "The Folk Ballad and the Literary Ballad: An Essay in Classification," *MF* 9 (1959), 5–18; reprinted in *Folklore in Action,* 58–70; and "Remarks Preliminary to a Study of Ballad Meter and Ballad Singing," *JAF* 78 (1965), 149–53.

An important general introduction to the international body of ballads is W. J. Entwistle's *European Balladry* (Oxford: Oxford University Press, 1939). Archer Taylor discussed "The Themes Common to English and German Balladry" in *MLQ* 1 (1940), 23–35; and he published an important individual study of *"Edward" and "Sven i Rosengård"* (Chicago: University of Chicago Press, 1931). Paul G. Brewster studied "The Two Sisters" in *FFC* no. 147 (1953). The best study of "Lady Isabel" is by Holger Olof Nygard in *FFC* no. 169 (1958).

Three representative studies that draw material from many different ballads are L. C. Wimberly's *Folklore in the English and Scottish Ballads* (Chicago: University of Chicago Press, 1928); W. Edson Richmond's "Ballad Place Names," *JAF* 59 (1946), 263–67; and William E. Sellers's "Kinship in the British Ballads: The Historical Evidence," *SFQ* 20 (1956), 199–215.

There are a number of studies of variation in the American tradition of a particular ballad, including Foster B. Gresham's "The Jew's Daughter: An Example of Ballad Variation," *JAF* 47 (1934), 358–61; Frances C. Stamper and William Hugh Jansen's " 'Water Birch': An American Variant of 'Hugh of Lincoln,' " *JAF* 71 (1958), 16–22; Tristram P. Coffin's "The Problem of Ballad-Story Variation and Eugene Haun's 'The Drowsy Sleeper,' " *SFQ* 14 (1950), 87–96; Alisoun Gardner-Medwin's "The Ancestry of 'The House Carpenter': A Study of the Family History of the American Forms of Child 243," *JAF* 84 (1971), 414–27; and, a study that compares folk and popular traditions, Howard Wight Marshall's " 'Black Jack David' on Wax: Child 200 and Recorded Hillbilly Music," *KFQ* 17 (1972), 133–43.

A "formulaic improvisation" theory of ballad tradition was proposed by

James H. Jones in *JAF* 74 (1961), 97–112, and opposed by Albert B. Friedman in the same issue of the journal, 113–15.

Journalistic reporting of news was compared to broadside ballad style in Winifred Johnston's article "Newspaper Balladry," *AS* 10 (1935), 119–21. A longer and more detailed treatment of the same idea appeared in Helen MacGill Hughes's *News and the Human Interest Story* (Chicago: University of Chicago Press, 1940), pp. 126–49 and *passim*. For the developments based on the British broadside "The Unfortunate Rake" in American balladry, see references cited with the Folkways recording of the same title, edited by Kenneth S. Goldstein (FS 3805, 1960,) which contains twenty versions and parodies of that ballad. Two books which have treated broadsides in general are Leslie Shepard's *The Broadside Ballad: A Study in Origins and Meaning* (London: Herbert Jenkins, 1962), and Claude M. Simpson's *The British Broadside Ballad and Its Music* (New Brunswick, N.J.: Rutgers University Press, 1966).

Phillips Barry, the best early student of American folksongs, discussed "Native Balladry in America" in *JAF* 22 (1909), 365–73. Louise Pound, another pioneer in this area, published a landmark essay, "The Southwestern Cowboy Songs and English and Scottish Popular Ballads," *MP* 11 (1913), 195–207; reprinted in *Nebraska Folklore*, pp. 156–70. Austin E. Fife provides a detailed study of 147 known versions of a cowboy ballad in " 'The Trail to Mexico'," *MSF* 1 (1973), 85–102. Louise Pound's study of the composer of "Joe Bowers," originally published in *WF* 16 (1957), 111–20, was reprinted in *Nebraska Folklore*, pp. 171–83. A further study of the origin of that ballad was published by John Quincy Wolf in *WF* 29 (1970), 77–89. Two general articles of interest to the study of native balladry are Robert D. Bethke's "Narrative Obituary Verse and Native American Balladry," *JAF* 83 (1970), 61–68; and Tristram P. Coffin's "American Balladry: the Term and the Canon," *KF* 19 (1974), 3–10.

Geraldine J. Chickering in "The Origin of a Ballad," *MLN* 50 (1935), 465–68, reviewed the evidence for authorship of "Jack Haggerty" (Laws C 25). Arthur Field proposed some interesting interpretive answers to his question 'Why is the 'Murdered Girl' so Popular?" in *MF* 1 (1951) 113–19; but the definitive study in this genre has become Anne B. Cohen's book *Poor Pearl, Poor Girl! The Murdered Girl Stereotype in Ballad and Newspaper* (Austin, Texas: AFS Memoir Series, vol. 58, 1973). Further studies of American ballad origins are Daniel G. Hoffman's "Historic Truth and Ballad Truth: Two Versions of the Capture of New Orleans," *JAF* 65 (1952), 295–303; Peter R. Aceves's "The Hillsville Tragedy in Court Record, Mass Media, and Folk Ballads: A Problem in Historical Documentation," *KFO* 16 (1971), 1–38; Edward D. Ives's " 'Ben Deane' and Joe Scott: A Ballad and its Probable Author," *JAF* 72 (1959), 52–66; and two articles by Norm Cohen, " 'Casey Jones': At the Crossroads of Two Ballad Traditions," *WF* 32 (1973), 77–103; and "Robert W. Gordon and the Second Wreck of 'Old 97'," *JAF* 87 (1974), 12–38.

A few non-English ballad traditions in the United States have been sampled in such works as Américo Paredes, "*With His Pistol in His Hand*': *A Border Ballad and Its Hero* (Austin: University of Texas Press, 1958); and Joan B. Purcell, "Traditional Ballads Among the Portuguese in California," WF 28 (1969), 1–20 and 77–90.

For Recordings of American ballads see information in the notes to Chapter 12.

12

Folk Music

In 1898, when the publication of Francis James Child's edition of British traditional ballads was finally completed, the last section to leave the press (volume 5, part 10) contained the only reference in the entire work to folk music—a short index of published tunes for ballads, and fifty-five "Ballad Airs from Manuscript." No analysis whatever was made of these melodies, in contrast to Child's erudite and extremely detailed comments that had accompanied each group of ballad texts. This treatment of the music of ballads, and the proportion of space devoted to tunes as opposed to texts (20 pages out of about 2,500), are a good measure of the relative interest folklorists had in words versus music by the end of the nineteenth century.

In 1905, Phillips Barry, a forerunner of more diversified American folksong specialists of the twentieth century, delivered what he called later "the first shot fired in the thirty years' war for the rights of ballad music." He asserted then what has by now become a commonplace in folklore scholarship, that "the words constitute but one-half of a folksong; the air is no less an essential part." While this generalization has long since been accepted, the practice, especially of ballad editors, has changed but slowly. As late as 1944, Bertrand H. Bronson, one of the most thorough and systematic of musical folklorists himself, warned again, "If the student of the ballad is not prepared to give equal attention to the musical, as to the verbal, side of his subject, his knowledge of it will in the end be only half-knowledge."

Barry's metaphor proved inappropriate. There never was any protracted "ballad war" over the issue of the significance of music. Instead, most folklorists, while granting the importance of tunes, remained untrained either to collect or to study them. Editors of ballad and folksong collections continued to present mostly texts, and published very little tune analysis. Only as recently as 1950 had the study of traditional music become sufficiently advanced to justify a special term for it—**ethnomusicology.**

Detailed technical research in folk music is complex; to master it requires devoting much time to developing the skills of a specialist. But anyone who desires more than a superficial understanding of American folklore, and who wishes to avoid the kind of "half-knowledge" that Bronson cautioned against, should understand, in general terms at least, what the basic form and styles of American folk music are, how folk music is collected, and by what means it is analyzed.

In large part, American folk music is folk *singing*. Characteristically, in the oldest white tradition, it is solo singing, without accompaniment, of either lyrical or narrative matter (as "folksongs" or "ballads") by an amateur performer before a close-knit family or community audience. The songs are "strophic"—that is, arranged in stanzas—and the melody of the first stanza is used again and again with little conscious change until all the stanzas have been sung. A four-line stanza is common, but couplets, triplets, and stanzas of five, six or more lines also occur. Many folksongs, as we have already observed in Chapters 10 and 11, have "refrains," that is, regularly repeated independent elements attached to each stanza. The melodies to which folksongs are sung are not frozen to particular texts, so that one song-text may be sung to several melodies or one melody may be attached to various songs. Furthermore, the general tone of a folksong text may seem to clash with the melodies sometimes used for it, so that what strikes us as a "jolly" tune may be employed for a tragic ballad. Whenever American folksingers have been known to make up new song-texts, these generally have been sung to old folk tunes.

Singing style in Anglo-American tradition varies somewhat from region to region and group to group, but everywhere it differs radically both from concert-hall art-song style and popular singing. To the ear that is not accustomed to traditional singing, it may at first sound like merely an inept job of amateur vocalizing—the tone may be nasalized, the meter might not be maintained evenly, the pitch and tempo may waver in the first one or two stanzas or gradually shift from one point at the beginning of a song to another at the end. Unlike the professional singer, who tends to "act out" his material with appropriate facial expressions, gestures, and volume changes, the traditional white American folk singer usually maintains an even volume level and is quite passive, sometimes even to the extent of tilting his head back, staring into space, and holding his face mask-like. Black folk singers, in contrast, often perform in chorus and with instruments, may improvise more freely on the melodic or rhythmic base, introduce more personal feeling into their singing, and often slur words or notes and intersperse whoops, slides, or falsetto passages into the basic text.

A broad sampling of genuine traditional folksinging will reveal that most of these techniques and mannerisms (or lack of mannerisms), as well as others, are regular features of a definite folk style that has been maintained by oral transmission through unselfconscious imitation of other singers. The practice of speaking the last phrase in a ballad instead of singing it, for instance, which is common in the Northeast, is not just an individual habit or the result of the singer running out of breath; it is a distinct characteristic of the regional style—a kind of traditional local custom. Similarly, the way some singers "lead up" to a note, using a nasalized slur ("Nnnh-It was in the merry month of May . . .") is a device passed in oral transmission from person to person, possibly influenced by traditional fiddle-playing technique. In general terms, singers who hold closely to an even meter—often with one note for each syllable of text—and with very few musical ornaments, are said to have a *tempo-giusto* (strict-tempo) style, while those who deviate widely from an established meter, and who ornament the melody freely with trills, slurs, and glides, are said to be using a *parlando-rubato* (free, "speaking"-rhythm) style.

The melodies themselves of old traditional songs may seem peculiar to non-folk listeners. That is because their ears are used to hearing music based only on a "diatonic scale," that is, a series of tones separated by intervals of "seconds," or one-note jumps as represented by the white keys on the piano from C to C. Cultivated music, on the whole, is based on such scales in "major" and "minor" keys. But many old folksongs have melodies drawn from scales with larger intervals between some tones—the so-called "gapped scales"—or from scales with fewer than the usual seven tones ("do" to "do," as they are usually learned). These may be five-tone (*pentatonic*) or six-tone (*hexatonic*) scales. Even if a folksong is based on a seven-tone (*heptatonic*) scale, its intervals may be differently arranged so that its character is neither major nor minor, but "modal," or corresponding to the "Church modes" of the Middle Ages that are generally referred to by Greek names. (As it happens, the original Greek names became scrambled between the Classical period and the Middle Ages!) A folklorist without technical training in music may learn to recognize at least the general character of modal music by listening to the melodies of Gregorian chants or by playing the white keys of a piano as follows: C to C (*Ionian*, or "natural major"), D to D (*Dorian*), E to E (*Phrygian*), F to F (*Lydian*), G to G (*Mixolydian*), and A to A (*Aeolian*, or "natural minor").

The folksinging described so far has all been "monophonic," or single-toned, for in unaccompanied solo singing only one note of a melody can be produced at a time. But in group singing or when instruments are played to accompany songs there occurs what may loosely be termed "polyphony," or more than one tone at a time. (This is not to be confused with formal polyphony in art music.) In American tradition, for instance, listeners may join in singing the refrain of a song, or a whole group may sing work songs, game songs, or party songs together—usually in unison rather than in harmony. Traditional religious songs, especially in the South, may be rendered in harmony or unison by the congregation, with a leader to "line out," or recite, each line of the text in advance, a procedure sometimes referred to as "deaconing." Black congregations still sometimes call certain hymns that are regularly "lined out" by the term "Doctor Watts," a survival from the name Isaac Watts (1674–1748), the English author of many still-popular hymns. The typical accompanying instruments in American folk singing tradition are from the plucked-string family—the guitar, five-string banjo, and dulcimer—but sometimes the fiddle is also employed.

A bridge between vocal and purely instrumental music is formed by what were termed "wordless folksongs" in Chapter 10—"diddling" or chin music, nonsense chants, "scat singing," and so forth. From the other direction, we might think of clapping, "clogging" (rhythmic beating-time with the feet), and rattling spoons or "bones" as the simplest kind of instrumental folk music, closely followed by the near-vocal effects produced on instruments such as the kazoo, "Jew's harp," and mouth organ (or "French harp"). Highly complicated solo-instrumental music has developed in American folk tradition on the stringed instruments mentioned above, as well as, more recently, such others as the mandolin, the "Autoharp," and the electric guitar.

The student of instrumental American folk music should learn to approach the subject using its own terms and recognizing its own special techniques. For example, the "left-hand pizzicato" method of producing notes on a guitar or banjo by plucking strings with fingers of the upper, rather than the picking hand, has been called "pulling-off" in folk music, and its opposite is "hammering-on" or adding upper-hand notes by striking down sharply on selected strings. Folk guitar- and banjo-picking styles include patterns with names like "church lick," "lullaby lick," "Carter lick" (named for the Carter family's hillbilly guitar style heard on 1920s and 1930s records), "double thumbing," "Cotton picking," "frailing," "clawhammer" and "Scruggs." Most folk instrumentalists play in several tunings besides the standard one for their instruments, and these have acquired such names as "mountain minor," "natural flat," "cross key," and "discord." Stringed instruments may be grouped for playing dance music, but the traditional melodies that are played are often called simply "fiddle tunes." The names of these tunes are wildly diverse, but their typical form is quite regular. There are two sections of eight-measures each, with a "first and second ending" so that one part is played twice, then the other part twice, then the first, and so on until the musicians or the dancers are tired. Then some kind of concluding figure (often "shave and a hair cut") is used for a sign-off. Some fiddlers will refer to one part of a fiddle tune as the "coarse" (played on lower strings) and the other as the "fine" (played on upper strings). Some players have learned instruments left-handed or "upside down." A final matter that may be taken up with instrumentalists is how they learned to play and how long they practiced to master their first tune. To such an inquiry, answers from one large group of traditional fiddlers ranged from "just picked up the fiddle and played it" to "I can't do very good even now."

The collector of folk music must develop a few more skills than just the ability to thread a tape recorder and adjust its sound-level properly. Successful fieldwork, as the ethnomusicologist Bruno Nettl has remarked, sometimes resembles "a combination of public relations and mental therapy." As in any folklore field project, the collector must be able to identify and locate good informants, to put them at their ease, and to encourage them to perform for him naturally and without inhibitions. But folk-*music* collecting also involves some special problems and techniques.

Folklorists of the past had to be technically trained in musical transcription before they could collect folk music; then they simply wrote out the tones they heard while a performer repeated his material several times. However, since different listeners tended to hear slightly different things, and standard musical notation cannot adequately represent all of the effects that occur in folk music anyway, these field transcripts were of uneven quality. Furthermore, there was no way to go back and verify field notes after an informant died.

The tape recorder is the standard—and the ideal—tool for fieldwork in folk music, quickly replacing the cylinder, disk, and wire recorders that had preceded it. Modern high-fidelity recorders that operate from house current, batteries, or even from spring-wound motors are available today at prices that allow all folklorists either to have their own equipment or to have access to that belonging to universities, archives, and other institutions. But even the modern magnetic tape recorder has its quirks. Tapes may fade or the magnetic backing may crumble, destroying irreplaceable field data, and a tape-recorder that is improperly handled may yield results that are nearly useless.

Collectors must assume the responsibility for becoming thoroughly familiar with the specific equipment they will use *before* they get into the field to use it, but a few general techniques apply to any machines. The slow speeds of 1⅞ and 3¾ inches per second found on many home recorders are suitable for recording the speaking voice alone, but nothing slower than 7½ i.p.s. should ever be used for music because the faster speed reproduces a wider range of "cycles" or sound waves. A speed of 15 i.p.s., available on larger studio tape recorders, is even better for high-fidelity recording. The sound-level adjustment on the tape recorder should be set carefully for a trial recording at the normal volume for performance, and then checked periodically to assure that the results are "loud and clear," but not overrecorded so that interference is created. If it is possible to do so without upsetting the informant, the collector should "label" items by announcing the facts of the session at the beginning of each tape, and then identifying each selection with a title or description just before or after it is performed. To provide a reference point, a pitch-pipe A should be sounded just after each performance— *not* before, when it might predetermine an informant's choice of pitch. If instruments are played, the tuning of the individual strings should be recorded, with the order of strings announced as each one is played. It is also advisable to record an informant's actual tuning process from time to time. If the music is polyphonic, the microphone should be moved up to emphasize the role of each voice or instrument as a tune is repeated, keeping careful notes, of course, on where the microphone is situated at all times. Whenever possible, performers should be recorded several times on different days and perhaps before different audiences, in order to document their varying styles and techniques.

When the finished tapes are brought to an archive, copies should be made on separate reels of tape of any material that was recorded on "both sides" (really both "tracks") of tapes. In that way, cutting or splicing may be done without disturbing other items. Duplicate tapes might be "dubbed" for storage purposes, especially if one copy is to be played repeatedly for transcription or perhaps in the classroom. Some archives file disk-dubbings of all tapes to guard against tape-fading, but careful temperature and humidity control will assure reasonably long life for tape recordings if quality tapes are used at the start.

The transcription of the field tapes—that is, the writing-out of them in musical notation—is a long and complicated process involving hours of careful listening and a firm technical grasp of music. The basic problems may be merely physical to begin with. For instance, Professor Jan Philip Schinhan, editor of the more than 1,000 tunes in the Frank C. Brown collection from North Carolina, found that Brown had played his original wax cylinders over and over again for college classes until many of them were badly worn and scratched. Even the most sensitive job of dubbing retained all of the sound of scratches that had been engraved into the originals. In addition, during the copying process, a number of labels were mixed up. These were hard errors to compensate for because in some instances even the texts of songs were nearly inaudible, and the music was next to impossible to hear clearly.

The traditional folksinger's flexible style and unorthodox techniques make it difficult for even expert ethnomusicologists to reduce the sounds they hear to standard transcription. In order to stretch the possibilities of the system of notation, some special symbols have been introduced—a plus sign or arrow pointing upwards for a tone slightly higher than notated, a minus sign or downward arrow for slightly lower tone, small-head notes for indefinite pitches, and barring according to a melody's own internal structure rather than in a standard meter. There is the possibility of some aid to the transcriber from such mechanical devices as the oscillograph, which visually represents musical pitches on a graph, the stroboscope, which helps to identify individual pitches, and the "instantaneous musical notator," which produces a complete transcription from a sound recording, although a specially coded one that cannot substitute fully for standard notation.

Any folklorist can learn to record folk music clearly enough for study purposes, and any collector with some basic muscial ability and training can learn to produce a fair job of transcription from tapes. But when it comes to close technical analysis of folk music, we enter the true specialist's territory. Only the broad theoretical outlines need be sketched here. If collectors acquire some idea of what ethnomusicologists may wish to investigate, they can bring in the best possible field data for analysis.

Even preparing a complete transcription of a piece of folk music involves certain theoretical matters, such as how freely the modal scales should be interpreted, whether melodies should be transcribed to a common key signature, and how detailed a transcript need be for comparative purposes. Beyond such questions, the "first principles" of folk-musical analysis are generally as follows.

Tonality, determined by the kind of scale upon which a melody is based, may be indicated by a major or minor key signature or by one of the modal names, if applicable. "Gapped scales" are identified by the number of tones they contain—pentatonic, hexatonic, etc. The *range* of tones that occurs in a particular piece is sometimes indicated by the special terms "authentic" (all tones between the "tonic," or key-note, and the octave above) and "plagal" (some tones occur below the tonic). *Tempo* in a performance is represented in a transcription by the number of quarter-note beats per minute. *Meter* is stated as a standard "time signature" (4/4, 6/8, etc.) if appropriate, or simply by assigning time values to each tone, using the standard musical symbols, and then marking off musical phrases with bar lines. If the melody of a tune has been transcribed to a standard key, the original *pitch* of the tonic should be stated.

Once a tune has been carefully transcribed, the *phrasal pattern* of the melody may be determined, that is, the musical "statements" are counted and identified. (Some typical patterns in Anglo-American folksongs are AABA, AABB, ABAB, and ABBA.) The number of "bars" or measures in each melodic phrase is represented in parentheses, such as (4,3,4,3). Most ethnomusicologists have found it useful to go beyond this stage to define the *melodic contour* of a piece. This is done by removing all ornaments to the basic melody, then all repeated tones, until only a "skeletal melody" remains, which may be characterized (according to its shape on the page) as descending, ascending, arc (or "triangular"), undulating, or the like. From such skeletal abstracts of many melodies, combined with all of the other data, *tune families* may be recognized.

All of this technical data (which has been somewhat simplified above) lends itself perfectly to computer analysis, a technique that has been pioneered with the Child ballad melodies by Bertrand H. Bronson of the University of California. Bronson employs an IBM 5081 punch card, which provides twelve rows of eighty units each for data-storage, with extra space for printed information. He codes into each card—representing one variant melody—nine categories of musicological information, and he imprints on the cards certain bibliographic and historical notes. The cards may then be sorted in various ways, thus greatly speeding comparisons and analyses of melodies. Perhaps the opposite approach is represented by the ethnomusicologist Samuel P. Bayard, who urges that "The investigator must, by immersing himself in the tunes, have impressed on his mind the identifying features of various members of perhaps many different tune families." Yet even Bronson has written that "The essence of melodic identity [is] . . . almost a metaphysical idea."

Classifying Anglo-American folksongs into meaningful categories is still progressing. However, as George Herzog, one of the earliest American ethnomusicologists, wrote in 1937, "The study of a melody *begins* after it has been placed in some system or index; it does not end there." Probably the next logical step is a return to the text—

a close comparison of the "wedding" of folksong texts and tunes. But, as Herzog also wrote, "The marriage has often been rather modernistic; melodies as well as texts have frequently gone their own way."

Text-tune fit has already proved to be a fascinating subject for research, although few folklorists as yet have pursued it very far. Numerous questions suggest themselves. How much does verse-meter alter a melody, and in what ways? Is there a corresponding effect the other way? Do the phrasal patterns of words and music match, or does one sometimes cross-cut the other? Can the wandering tunes as well as the floating verbal stanzas of folksongs help to explain their histories? What kinds of symbolic functions, if any, do tunes contribute to their texts? What aspects of conscious creative art may be identified in the whole text-tune relationship in folksongs? The full explication of folksongs, comparable to what is done with art songs, depends upon securing answers to such questions.

The most revolutionary ideas in Anglo-American ethnomusicology have followed from Alan Lomax's proposal, backed by his years of field and editorial experience, for a "new science of musical ethnography." Lomax regards formal musical elements as merely one small and rather abstract segment of a total "folksong style," which, more importantly, includes such factors as the relationship between musicians and their audience, the physical behavior of musicians, the vocal timbre and pitch favored by different cultures, the social functions of music, and the psychological and emotional content of texts. Applying these criteria, Lomax first made a broad survey of world musical *styles* (in his enlarged sense of the term), listening to all available recordings of singers, until he could organize a rough grouping of musical families. From this background he listed fundamental factors in stylistic analysis, including the degree that singing is communal or individualistic in a culture, the quality of voice and the mode of production used, the prevailing mood of the music, the content of texts, and the social and emotional factors present in the culture. Lomax next made field observations of these criteria in Spain in 1953 and tested his hypothesis concerning the relationship between culture and singing styles in Italy in 1955. Finding a "positive correlation between the musical style and the sexual mores of the communities," Lomax studied the mechanics of this relationship in Italian lullabies, noting the relationships between mothers and children, the roles in society of women and children, and the customs surrounding the singing of lullabies. He concluded that "In those societies considered, the sexual code, the position of women, and the treatment of children seem to be the social patterns most clearly linked with musical style." He explored these ideas further in the Introduction and notes of his anthology *The Folk Songs of North America in the English Language* (1960). Here he asserted that "After many years of collecting in both countries, I am profoundly impressed by the comparative paganism and resignation of Britain, as contrasted with the Puritanism and free aggressiveness of America."

Perhaps the "last word" on this stage of Anglo-American ethnomusicology may be quoted from Charles Seeger, who has been one of the most specific critics of Lomax's proposal. Seeger suggests that for the present the task of studies might be to "refine music theory" and to "coarsen technological aids" until some kind of pragmatic middle ground is reached. So much, at least, is clear: from almost every point of view, the specialized study of folk music in America is still "wide open."

BIBLIOGRAPHIC NOTES

Many of the general works on folksongs and ballads cited fully in the notes to Chapters 10 and 11 contain discussions of music. The ballad anthologies edited by Leach and Friedman, for instance, treat ballad music briefly in their introductions. D. K. Wilgus surveys "Tune Scholarship" on pages 326 to 336 of his *Anglo-American Folksong Scholarship Since 1898*. In Bruno Nettl and Helen Myers's *Folk Music in the United States: An Introduction* the technical aspects of music are discussed throughout. Perhaps the best general survey of the subject is still George Herzog's article "Song: Folk Song and the Music of Folk Song" in *Funk & Wagnalls Standard Dictionary of Folklore, Mythology, and Legend*.

In Bruno Nettl's *Folk and Traditional Music of the Western Continents* (Englewood Cliffs, N.J.: Prentice-Hall, 1965), the most pertinent chapters are Chapter 2, "Studying the Structure of Folk Music" (pp. 15–32) and Chapter 3, "The General Character of European Folk Music" (pp. 33–52). Nettl has also authored the introductory textbook *Theory and Method in Ethnomusicology* (London: Free Press of Glencoe, 1964) wherein he discusses fieldwork, transcription, description of musical forms, style, instrumental music, and music in culture. He also provides guidance in bibliography and an appendix of exercises and problems designed for the reader with no advanced formal training in music.

Charles Seeger's essay "Professionalism and Amateurism in the Study of Folk Music" is recommended reading for any student embarking on such study for the first time. It appeared in *JAF* 62 (1949), 107–13, and was reprinted in *The Critics and the Ballad*, MacEdward Leach and Tristram P. Coffin (Carbondale: Southern Illinois University Press, 1961; paperback, Arcturus Books, 1973), pp. 151–60. Another good summary of studies and approaches is Samuel P. Bayard's essay, "American Folksongs and their Music," *SFQ* 17 (1953), 122–39.

A basis for studies of fiddle tunes is Ira W. Ford's collection *Traditional Music of America* (New York, 1940; reissued with an introduction by Judith McCulloh, Hatboro, Pa.: Folklore Associates, 1965). Vance Randolph listed "The Names of Ozark Fiddle Tunes" in *MF* 4 (1954), 81–86. Winston Wilkinson discussed some "Virginia Dance Tunes" in *SFQ* 6 (1942), 1–10. Samuel P. Bayard provided a detailed study of American fiddle tunes in his *Hill Country Tunes* (Philadelphia: AFS Memoir no. 39, 1944) and "Some Folk Fiddlers' Habits and Styles in Western Pennsylvania," *JIFMC* 8 (1956), 15–18. An interesting cross-genre analysis is Louie W. Attebery's article "The Fiddle Tune: An American Artifact," *NWF* 2 (1967), 22–29. A questionnaire survey of traditional fiddlers was reported by Marion Unger Thede in *EM* 6 (1962), 19–24. Thede also published *The Fiddle Book* (New York: Oak Publications, 1967), a self-instructor for would-be folk fiddlers containing music for 150 traditional fiddle tunes, a chatty discussion of fiddling, and some very fine photographs. Linda C. Burman's article "The Technique of Variation in an American Fiddle Tune," *EM* 12 (1968), 49–71, provides a detailed transcription and analysis of a 1926 recording of "Sail Away Lady," comparing the variations to those of Elizabethan virginalists. Eugene Wiggins discusses fiddlers' contests and folklore in literature in "Benéts' 'Mountain Whipoorwill': Folklore Atop Folklore," *TFSB* 41 (1975), 99–114.

Religious folk music in America has been studied by George P. Jackson, beginning with his *White Spirituals in the Southern Uplands* (Chapel Hill: University of North Carolina Press, 1933); see Wilgus for references to Jackson's other works as well as those of other scholars. Sacred harp shape-note singing has attracted the major attention in this area. Richard D. Wetzel, for example, treats "Some Music Notation Systems in Early American Hymn-Tune Books," *KFQ* 12 (1967), 247–60. A good description of sacred-harp singing in east Texas may be found in Francis Edward Abernethy's "Singing All Day & Dinner on the Grounds" in *PTFS* 37 (1972), 131–40. See also William H. Tallmadge, "Dr. Watts and Mahalia Jackson—The Development, Decline, and Survival of a Folk Style in America," *EM* 5 (1961), 95–99; and Joe Dan Boyd, "Negro Sacred Harp Songsters in Mississippi," *MFR* 5 (1971), 60–83.

For a useful recent assessment of the riches of black American folk music, long collected and published, see John F. Szwed, "Musical Adaptation Among Afro-Americans," *JAF* 82 (1969), 112–21. Robert Ladner, Jr., classifies the major types of black traditional music and traces its adaptation and imitation by whites in "Folk Music, Pholk Music and the Angry Children of

Malcolm X," *SFQ* 34 (1970), 131–45. Patrick B. Mullen describes "A Negro Street Performer: Tradition and Innovation" in *WF* 29 (1970), 91–103. The partially traditional music of the American minstrel show has been studied by Hans Nathan; see "The First Negro Minstrel Band and its Origin," *SFQ* 16 (1952), 132–44; and "Early Banjo Tunes and American Syncopation," *MQ* 42 (1956), 455–72.

Articles on the history and construction of folk instruments are listed in the notes to Chapter 19.

Few publications deal specifically with the field recording of traditional music. Bruno Nettl has a useful note, "Recording Primitive and Folk Music in the Field," in *AA* 56 (1954), 1101–2, from which several suggestions in the present chapter were taken. Maud Karpeles has prepared a small and useful manual called *The Collecting of Folk Music and Other Ethnomusicological Material* (London: International Folk Music Council, 1958). George List, director of the Indiana University Archives of Traditional Music, discussed "Documenting Recordings," in *FFMA* 3 (Fall 1960), 2–3; and "The Reliability of Transcription," in *EM* 18 (1974), 353–77. The latter is accompanied by a small disc recording of the examples presented. Charles Seeger evaluates the uses of an instantaneous music notator in "Prescriptive and Descriptive Music-Writing," *MQ* 44 (1958), 184–95.

Classic studies of American folk music are represented by the work of Cecil J. Sharp and Phillips Barry. Sharp's *English Folk-Song: Some Conclusions* (London: Simpkin and Co., 1907) still merits study, and Barry's approach may be seen in such articles as "Folk-Music in America," *JAF* 22 (1909), 72–81; "The Origin of Folk-Melodies," *JAF* 23 (1910), 440–45, and "American Folk Music," *SFQ* 1 (1937), 29–47.

An excellent summary of ethnomusicological approaches to analyzing American folksong is provided by George Foss in his essay "The Transcription and Analysis of Folk Music" in *Folksong and Folksong Scholarship*, edited by Roger D. Abrahams (Dallas: Southern Methodist University Press, 1964), pp. 39–71. In another valuable essay, Foss describes "A Methodology for the Description and Classification of Anglo-American Traditional Tunes," *JFI* 4 (1967), 102–26. Donald M. Winkleman's article "Musicological Techniques of Ballad Analysis," in *MF* 10 (Winter 1960–61), 197–205, provides a clear introduction by means of generalizations and examples. The individual approaches of two major scholars are seen in Samuel P. Bayard's "Prolegomena to a Study of the Principal Melodic Families of British-American Folk Songs," *JAF* 63 (1950), 1–44, reprinted in *The Critics and the Ballad*, 103–50; and Bertrand H. Bronson's "Some Observations about Melodic Variation in British-American Folk Tunes," *JAMS* 3 (1950), 120–34.

Bronson's theories and working methods may be traced through his important series of articles, eighteen of which are gathered in *The Ballad as Song* (Berkeley: University of California Press, 1969). The culmination of Bronson's work is appearing in his *The Traditional Tunes of the Child Ballads*, 4 vols. (Prentice, N.J.: Princeton University Press, 1959–72).

Two other folksong editions contain important technical studies of their music. Jan Philip Schinhan edited and analyzed "The Music of the Ballads" and "The Music of the Folksongs" for *The Frank C. Brown Collection of North Carolina Folklore* (4, 1957; 5, 1962). In Helen Hartness Flanders's *Ancient Ballads Traditionally Sung in New England*, 4 vols. (Philadelphia: University of Pennsylvania Press, 1960–65), the musical annotations are by Bruno Nettl.

An early discussion of the problems of folk music classification was George Herzog's "Musical Typology in Folksong," in *SFQ* 1 (1937), 49–55. A practical system is described by George List in "An Approach to the Indexing of Ballad Tunes," *FFMA* 6 (Spring 1963), 7–16.

Bronson discussed text-tune relationships in two articles, "The Interdependence of Ballad Tunes and Texts," *CFQ* 3 (1944), 185–207, reprinted in *The Critics and The Ballad*, pp. 77–102, and *The Ballad as Song* (see above); and "On the Union of Words and Music in the 'Child' Ballads," *WF* 11 (1952), 233–49, reprinted in his *The Ballad as Song* 112–32. A detailed individual study is found in George List's "An Ideal Marriage of Ballad Text and Tune," *MF* 7 (1957), 95–112. George W. Boswell provides a good general discussion of the subject in Chapter 23 of his and J. Russell Reaver's *Fundamentals of Folk Literature* (Oosterhout, The Netherlands: Anthropological Publications, 1962), pp. 188–95, and he has a closer study of the matter in his article "Reciprocal Controls Exerted by Ballad Texts and Tunes," *JAF* 80 (1967), 169–74.

Musical analysis of commercial and popularized folk music has advanced in such articles as Judith McCulloh's "Hillbilly Records and Tune Transcriptions," *WF* 26 (1967), 225–44; Neil V. Rosenberg's "From Sound to Style: The Emergence of Bluegrass," *JAF* 80 (1967), 143–50; and especially Anne and Norm Cohen's "Tune Evolution as an Indicator of Traditional Musical Norms," *JAF* 86 (1973), 37–47.

Alan Lomax proposed his concept of "Folk Song Style" in an article by that title published in *JIFMC* 8 (1956), 48–50. Charles Seeger offered a rebuttal and proposals of his own in "Singing Style," *WF* 17 (1958), 3–11. A more extended treatment of Lomax's ideas then appeared in his "Musical Style and Social Context," *AA* 61 (1959), 927–54, and in the introduction and notes to his anthology *The Folk Songs of North America in the English Language* (New York: Doubleday, 1960). Important reviews of that work are cited in the notes to Chapter 10. Alan Lomax's work in "cantometrics" yielded "The Good and the Beautiful in Folksong," *JAF* 80 (1967), 213–35 (an article replete with both field anecdotes and highly technical analysis of data), and the survey of world traditional song styles titled *Folk Song Style and Culture* (Washington, D.C.: American Association for the Advancement of Science, publication no. 88, 1968). For the background of this work and a concise summary of its method see William R. Ferris, Jr., "Folk Song and Culture: Charles Seeger and Alan Lomax," *NYFQ* 29 (1973), 206–18.

It is important that beginning students of folk music not confine themselves to studying printed materials alone, but also become familiar with recorded examples. A problem in this area, however, is caused by the great profusion of popularized or semi-original material on records, and the relative obscurity of companies that issue authentic recordings.

Several of the general books cited here and in Chapters 10 and 11 contain discographies. Wilgus offers an especially good annotated one on pages 365–82 of his work. The only catalog entirely devoted to authentic American folk music recordings offered for sale is published by the Library of Congress and may be obtained by mail from the Music Division, Recording Laboratory, LC Reference Department, Washington, D.C. 20402. Other companies with reliable folk music recordings include Folkways Records (available from Scholastic A-V Materials, 906 Sylvan Ave., Englewood Cliffs, N.J., 07632), Folk-Legacy Records (Sharon, Conn., 06069), Arhoolie Records (incorporating the important Folk-Lyric Records, Box 9195, Berkeley, Calif. 94719), and Rounder Records (186 Willow Avenue, Somerville, Mass., 02144).

Good individual recordings are far too numerous to list here in any detail, but a few representative examples that are especially well suited for teaching purposes deserve notice. Charles Seeger's production of *Versions and Variants of "Barbara Allen"* for the Library of Congress (AAFS L54) contains thirty renditions of this favorite ballad by American folksingers; Alan Jabbour's LC recording *American Fiddle Tunes from the Archive of Folk Song* (AFS L62) contains twenty-eight well-documented examples. On the Folk-Legacy label, one of the best examples available of a thoroughly annotated recorded collection is *Eleven Miramichi Songs Sung by Marie Hare* (FSC-9), which is accompanied by a booklet of background, textual, and musicological notes by Louise Manney and Edward Ives. An excellent two-record set from the same publisher is *The Traditional Music of Beech Mountain, North Carolina*, vol. 1, "The Older Ballads and Sacred Songs" (FSA-22) and vol. 2, "The Later Songs and Hymns" (FSA-23), both with notes by Sandy Paton. Among the numerous outstanding items in the Folkways catalog is the *Anthology of American Folk Music* (FA 2951, 2952, 2953), six LP recordings containing early folk-music items from commercial discs, plus identifying notes.

A record surveying folk music in one state is *Green Fields of Illinois* (CFC 201) published by the Campus Folksong Club, University of Illinois, Urbana. Two records that sample the rich folk music traditions of the state of Utah are *The New Beehive Songster*, vol. 1, "Early Recordings of Pioneer Folk Music" (OK 75003), vol. 2, recent Field recordings (OK 75004), published by Okehdokee Records and the University of Utah Press in Salt Lake City, Utah, 84112 (1976).

III · CUSTOMARY FOLKLORE

✿❀✿❀✿❀✿❀✿❀✿

While there is often an oral component to the folk traditions described in this section, and sometimes even a material component, customary folklore is essentially a matter of traditional *behavior*. Some customs are characteristically employed for communicating directly to other individuals (as when gesturing in greeting or leavetaking); some are practiced by vari-sized family or community groups (as in folk festivals); and some may involve set numbers of performers (as in most folk dances). The "audiences" for such traditional performances may be participants themselves (as in a game), the community (folk dramas), or even, perhaps, "the gods" (superstitions). Customary folklore is typically regarded as "just entertainment," but often it has overtones of magic, ritual, or traditional science.

In some past studies, behavioral lore has been treated much like oral lore (collecting game "texts," etc.), but special approaches and techniques are needed to do the job of analysis more fully. Therefore, each type presented here is put into the framework of the most reliable recent studies, whatever direction they have taken.

13

Superstitions

Superstitions are often thought of as naïve popular beliefs that are logically or scientifically untenable. Hence, the alternate term "folk belief" is often employed, carrying with it the equally negative connotations of unsophistication and ignorance that the word "folk" has in popular usage. Such a substitution seems mistaken on three counts. First, superstitions include not only belief, but also behavior and experiences, sometimes equipment, and usually sayings or rhymes. Second, no one is immune from the assumptions that underlie superstition, nor from holding or practicing superstitions to some degree. Third, the term "superstition" is now so well entrenched in folkloristics that it probably must continue to be tolerated, despite its traditional suggestions of ignorance and fear. While it may be more precise, as some folklorists have suggested, to speak of "folk (or 'traditional') science," "folk belief," or "conventional wisdom," rather than "superstition," it is under the latter name that most such items have been collected and published, and the habits of mind underlying them are the same in any case.

Superstitions involve beliefs, practices, and procedures based upon conscious or unconscious assumptions, usually concerned with the nature of cause and effect. Even though superstitions are not essentially just verbal statements, it is as such that they are usually transmitted and have often been collected by folklorists. Alan Dundes describes these characteristics in a typical compilation of "superstitious sayings": The sayings describe *conditions* (either *signs* or *causes*) and their supposed results: "If there's a ring around the moon (*sign*), it will rain (*result*)"; or, "Turn a dead snake belly up (*cause*), and it will rain soon (*result*)." Superstitions like the last example, in which deliberate human actions "*cause*" the *result*, are termed *magic*. Other superstitious sayings describe *conversions;* that is, when a *sign* is right, a certain act will *convert* the conventionally expected *result:* "If you break a mirror (*sign*), you'll have seven years bad luck (*result*), unless you gather up the pieces and throw them into running water (*conversion*)." Another example is, "If you see a shooting star (*sign*), you should say 'money' three times before it disappears (*conversion*), and then you'll have good luck (*result*)." Incorporating these characteristics into one description, Dundes proposes as a definition: "*Superstitions are traditional expressions of one or more conditions and one or more results with some of the conditions signs and others causes.*"

While this definition seems more satisfactory than many older ones that simply branded superstitions as nonreligious beliefs, bad logic, or (in Sir James G. Frazer's term) "false science," there are other objections to it. Mainly, it is a definition of the "expressions" of superstition, not of superstitious beliefs and practices themselves. As Michael Owen Jones points out, Dundes's approach merely to the published statements of superstition does not allow for considering "the meaning and function of the material or the nature of the folk mind." A better concept of superstition—much harder, however, to phrase in a concise description—would take account of the social contexts in which folk beliefs occur and also reflect the fact that informants themselves distinguish between useful traditional knowledge and harmful or foolish "superstitions." Dundes himself has suggested using the term *folk ideas* for simple statements of popular misconception that are neither signs, magic, or coversions, but which do appear in folklorists' collections of superstitions: "Lightning never strikes twice in the same place," or "Dragon flies feed [or cure] snakes," for example.

However unsound the assumptions underlying superstitious beliefs and behavior, they are generally couched in sound logic, and are remarkably widespread at every level of society. Recurrently since 1907 various American professors have investigated the degree of superstition found among their students. The published results of these surveys, which spanned the country geographically and reached students from a variety of backgrounds, indicated that many students are significantly superstitious, and that as a group they have become neither more nor less superstitious recently; only details of their belief and practice vary.

At the University of California at Berkeley, in 1907, 900 psychology

students were asked to list and comment upon their own superstitions. A total of 7,000 items was submitted: 4,000 were superstitions
known but not believed, 2,000 were recognized as superstitions but
still partly believed, and 1,000 were superstitions trusted fully. More
than one-half of the test group believed in some superstitions, the
most common being good and bad luck signs involving Friday the
thirteenth (or other occurrences of thirteen), breaking mirrors, opening an umbrella in the house, finding a horseshoe, hearing a dog
howl, seeing the moon over the left shoulder, or dropping silverware.

In 1923, forty-five students at Vassar College recorded 186 items of
superstitious belief and practice from their personal knowledge. Most
of the items had to do with good and bad luck, love and marriage, and
wishing. Some rather unusual examples turned up: "Say the word
'hare' last on the last day of one month, and the word 'rabbit' first the
next morning, and you will have good luck"; "A pause in conversation
that occurs twenty minutes before or after an hour signifies that an
angel is passing by"; "Count the cars in a passing freight train like
daisy petals, 'Loves me, loves me not' etc."

At about the same time as the Vassar collection, a Harvard professor of anthropology, who published his results in 1932, secured a
large number of superstitions from students at Harvard and elsewhere. By having the students write papers about their personal
superstitions, this investigator received comments as well as the
items themselves. The results suggested that 70 to 75 per cent of un-
dergraduates "carried out certain acts or refrained from carrying them
out in the hope that something good would follow or something evil
would be prevented." About one-quarter of those questioned owned
"fetishes"—lucky objects of some kind, such as coins, pens, clothing,
or amulets. A large number of superstitions were associated with examinations, athletics, and "games of chance." Although some of the
student writers strongly protested that superstition was dead in the
twentieth century, and some even complained that college students
should not be required to write such nonsense in an enlightened age,
others described elaborate personal rituals that they were convinced
had brought them luck. If they failed to practice these acts, the students suffered "a distinct feeling of uneasiness."

In 1950, an anthropologist at Indiana University submitted a questionnaire based on the Harvard study to 175 of his students and

analyzed the results in a rigorous statistical manner. His conclusions were the most scientifically controlled yet reported, and showed that students were just as superstitious as ever. Some believed firmly in fully one-half of the total list of thirty-three items, but the average number of items believed by an individual was 5.1. Women seemed to be generally more superstitious than men, and the freshman-sophomore group more superstitious than upperclassmen. Although the last finding seems to suggest that education erases superstition, the study also indicated that the more educated the parents the *more* superstitious the offspring. Furthermore, there was no significant relationship indicated between the number of superstitions believed by urban versus rural students, who presumably should be closer to the roots of "folk wisdom."

Fifty freshmen in English composition at the University of Idaho were assigned to write papers on their personal superstitions in 1961, and not a single student lacked for subject matter. Not only did many of them admit to certain irrational practices to assure themselves good luck in examinations, athletics, or dangerous situations, but also most of the writers could cite personal experiences that seemed to uphold the validity of their actions. The subjects included lucky items of clothing, ski accidents, wart cures, three on a match, logging and traffic dangers, farm and ranch work, and even a student wife's pregnancy, supposedly guaranteed by her residence in a lucky apartment and through the magic of the number three.

Surveys in many undergraduate folklore courses continue to yield the same kind of information about students' superstitions (see, e.g., Appendix B), but one need not have a captive experimental group of college students to show that modern educated people are superstitious. The popular press is rich in examples of the same sort of thing. Winners in contests and athletic events are frequently quoted in news stories describing their good luck charms; medical and advice columnists regularly answer queries about common superstitions; victims of serious diseases, when publicized, often are sent numerous folk cures, which are later reported back to the press. When President John F. Kennedy was suffering from his back ailment, for example, it was reported that someone had written to him, "Just get an old pair of shoes and put them under your bed upside down." In 1964, Mrs. Kathryn O'Hay Granahan, Treasurer of the United States, published a plea in a Sunday supplement magazine that had nationwide distribution, urging Americans to accept the two-dollar bill instead of rejecting it because of the bad luck that is supposed to attend that denomination, and not to tear off a corner to "let the bad luck drain out." In 1976 when printing and distribution of two-dollar bills was resumed, a spate of traditional and superstitious lore about them again appeared in the press. Just as this chapter was being first written the following statements appeared in the health column of the *St. Louis Post-Dispatch*: "My son is a year old and has asthma. Several people have told me that if I get a Chihuahua it will cure the asthma. My husband won't get the dog until you answer."

The survival of old superstitions, or at least the knowledge of them, is also apparent in some familiar contemporary practices. Hotel owners will skip thirteen when numbering floors, or use that floor for storage only. Manufacturers of billfolds sometimes put a piece of imitation money in each one so that it may safely be given as a gift, for, "Giving an empty billfold or purse will spoil your friendship." People who believe that spitting, in certain situations, is good luck, may only pretend to spit if the time and place happen to be wrong for the actual gesture. Other people, lacking a piece of wood to knock on, will playfully knock on their own heads if they happen to utter a statement that suggests some future good fortune. And otherwise perfectly sane and reasonable people will detour around a ladder, postpone business deals or trips that fall on the thirteenth of a month, or carefully date checks written on Sundays to the next day. The rationale for most superstitions such as these is that they may not help, but they won't hurt either. A news story about a sufferer from chronic hiccups, who was about to try hypnosis as a last resort, put the matter this way: "Desperate for relief, [she] already had tried surgery, shock therapy, more than 200 home remedies, chiropractic treatment, and prayer." Thus superstition thrives, side by side with modern medical science, psychology, and religion.

Many superstitions probably arose from faulty reasoning based on experiences. An event is assumed to be the cause of certain later happenings—the familiar logical fallacy of *post hoc, ergo propter hoc* ("after this, therefore because of this"). In a classic account of early travel on the Santa Fe Trail, Josiah Gregg's *Commerce of the Prairies* (1844), just such an instance was described:

There is but little rain throughout the year, except from July to October—known as the rainy season; and as the Missouri traders
usually arrive about its commencement, the coincidence has given
rise to a superstition, quite prevalent among the vulgar, that the
Americans bring the rain with them.

The line of reasoning is no different when modern students do well
on an examination, and then credit their "luck" to the T-shirt they
wore or the pen they used. Psychology favors them further when they
retain the same fetish for later examinations. But if their luck holds,
the superstition, rather than their understanding of how their own
minds work, is reinforced. Such practices are further encouraged by
the human tendency to want to believe in the supernatural, and to be
able to predict or control events.

Since individual superstitions may be generated by fallacious reasoning from personal experiences and reinforced by coincidences, it
is possible that there are countless private beliefs and practices that
never pass into folklore circulation at all. Nevertheless, even people's
personal superstitions tend to fall into traditional patterns involving
luck, divination, magic, dreams, colors, numbers, and so forth. This
largely explains why it is that while new collections of superstitions invariably contain many items previously unrecorded in printed collections, the existing classification schemes can readily accommodate
them. Frequently, older superstitions have simply been modernized:
a belief about a buggy, for example, is transferred to automobiles, or
one about farming is applied to home gardening.

There are numerous collections of American superstitions, and
some of them are voluminous. But although they have come from
widespread sources, there is still much to be collected from more
regions and more folk groups before a comprehensive study of American superstitions can be attempted. The basis for such a study is at the
University of California at Los Angeles in the files of Professor Wayland D. Hand, editor of the superstitions in *The Frank C. Brown
Collection of North Carolina Folklore* (volumes 6 and 7). Professor
Hand has assembled a master file of some 200,000 individual superstitions taken from all the presently published American collections and
arranged in one sequence in a systematic fashion. Individual folklorists in most states and in several provinces of Canada are pledged

to collect and publish superstitions in their own regions to broaden the base of Hand's data for his planned "Dictionary of American Popular Beliefs and Superstitions." Thus it is important to outline his classification system—as demonstrated in the North Carolina collection—as a guide to published and archived superstitions, even though much future work in the area is likely to put greater stress than Hand has on social contexts and functions.

The system contains fourteen major categories, which may be grouped under four broad headings: *the cycle of human life, the supernatural, cosmology and the natural world,* and *miscellaneous superstitions.*

Superstitions related to the cycle of human life fall into the first seven categories of Hand's system, as follows:

    I. *Birth, Infancy, Childhood*
    II. *Human Body, Folk Medicine*
    III. *Home, Domestic Pursuits*
    IV. *Economic, Social Relations*
    V. *Travel, Communication*
    VI. *Love, Courtship, Marriage*
    VII. *Death and Funereal Customs*

Many items in sections I, VI, and VII correspond in purpose to three of the four kinds of ceremonies to mark changes in the life cycle (*rites de passage,* or "rites of passage") commonly practiced in primitive cultures. By means of these rituals people "pass" safely from one stage of their existence to the next—from pre-life to life (at birth), from childhood to adulthood (at puberty), from a single to a married state (at marriage), and from life to the afterlife (at death). Such folk superstitions as putting an ax under the mother's bed to ease childbirth, having a bride wear or carry certain objects to ensure her future happiness, or guarding a corpse from cats at a wake are modern equivalents for the primitive's complex rituals at the same stages in life. For initiation to adulthood we have such formalized events as graduation, confirmation, and bar mitzvah, but very few folk superstitions. A rare exception is the traditional belief that the ribbon on a diploma must not be cut or broken, but must be slipped off whole to preserve one's luck.

Numerous current superstitions associated with *birth, infancy, and childhood* display concepts and habits of reasoning also associated with primitive cultures. Although it is unreasonable to adopt a "survivals" explanation for all such items, the origins of at least some of them may be so traced. The belief in pre-natal influence, for example, is essentially no different whether it exists among modern Americans or among aborigines: the pregnant mother's experiences are supposedly manifested in marks or habits of her child. If the mother is struck with something, the baby has a birthmark in the shape of that object; if she craves a particular food, that will turn out to be the baby's favorite food, too, or he may be "marked" in a related way. (So-called "strawberry birthmarks" are often explained from such events.) The term "harelip" for the deformity that looks like a hare's cleft lip hints at the superstition that the sight of a hare can cause a pregnant woman to bear a child with that mark. Similarly, personal names are frequently regarded with awe and surrounded with magic among primitives; modern people retain vestiges of the same attitude in such beliefs as that if an unnamed baby is sick, he will recover as soon as he is given a name, or that good luck attends a person whose initials spell a word.

Folk medicine is another area in which primitive practices may survive; in sickness, as during other crises, people almost instinctively rely on traditional cures, even if medical science has been consulted. Thus a person may secure a salve or ointment with a doctor's prescription, and then carefully apply it with the middle finger to improve its effectiveness; here magic and science combine, to the detriment of neither. Or, knowing that a nosebleed may be stopped by pressing a blood vessel, a traditionally inclined person chooses "brown paper" as the compress and "under the upper lip" as the pressure point. (In the nursery rhyme "Jack and Jill" it is "vinegar and brown paper" that Jack uses to "mend his head," and some people say a brown paper bag placed against the stomach is a cure or a preventative for car sickness.) The less that medical science knows about an ailment, the more likely it is that folk remedies will survive. For this reason, hiccups, sties, warts, fever blisters, rheumatism, cancer, and the common cold are among the ailments most frequently treated with folk cures.

Typical cures for warts illustrate some characteristic patterns in folk cures. "Measuring" as a curative device is demonstrated in superstitions requiring that the number of warts be represented by knots on a string or notches in a stick. "Plugging" is used when something that has been rubbed on the warts or pricked into them is driven into a hole in a tree or buried in the ground. "Transfer" is a common device for removing warts by passing them on by means of a ritual or a saying to someone else or even to an animal or object. The same devices appear in many cures for different ailments, and all of them are based on the principle that something may be invisibly removed from the infected area and magically disposed of somewhere else. (Since warts, like colds, appear and disappear with baffling illogic, folk cures for them seem destined to live on for many generations to come.)

"Faith healers," semiprofessional folk specialists in traditional medicine, usually employ a combination of personal and religious power, sometimes in combination with certain herbs or nostrums. Their concepts of diseases and cures may reflect popular writings on medicine of many decades earlier, and they generally also display folk attitudes held by their particular regional or ethnic group. For instance, the Mexican-American *curanderos* may be called upon to treat *mal puesto* (afflictions involving magic or witchcraft) or *mal naturales* (natural diseases, unknown among Anglo-Americans and not treated by physicians), such as *empacho* (a form of indigestion), *mal ojo* (evil eye), *susto* (fright sickness), and *caída de la mollera* (Fallen fontanel).

Superstitions associated with *home and domestic pursuits* usually have to do with cooking, clothing, housekeeping, and changing households. Many people, without considering themselves superstitious, will avoid such taboos as seating thirteen at a table, mending clothes while someone is wearing them, or allowing someone to enter the house, if accidentally locked out, through a window without exiting through the same route. Stirring cake batter clockwise, or eating the point of a wedge of pie last may seem simply to be meaningless habits, but to some informants they are lucky acts. Similar superstitions also survive as habits of thought in *economic and social relations*. Business people sense—even if they are not aware of a superstition—that if the first customer of the day buys nothing, they will have a bad day all day. People walking together will avoid allowing a post or tree to come between them, perhaps not realizing that some consider it a bad luck sign, or a condition that will allow wishes to come true after a dialogue is repeated that begins "Bread and butter—

Come to supper." The superstitions of games and sports also fall under category IV, and these constitute a rich area, especially when gambling is involved. Horse bettors are notoriously superstitious, but even hard-headed bridge players may think their luck is improved if they can manage to sit lined up with their partner the same way as the bathtub is positioned in the house.

Travel and communications is another "danger area," like birth, sickness, and gambling, for which superstition may provide a safeguard. These often take the form of auspicious days and times for beginning a trip, signs of future trips or of visitors to come, and procedures for traveling or for returning to fetch something forgotten at home. Recent superstitions about mail, telegrams, telephones, and the like conveniently fit into this category, too. These include items such as "If a letter falls to the ground when you mail it, bad luck will attend it"; or "Talking on the telephone during a storm may give you an electric shock."

Superstitions of *love, courtship, and marriage* concern aphrodisiacs and other love charms, divinations, and various practices to predict or insure marital or sexual happiness. Although few women probably believe in divination nowadays, many will still pretend anyway to determine their future mates by consulting objects ranging from buttons (which are counted, "doctor, lawyer, merchant, thief"), an apple peel pared in a whole strip (which is thrown over the left shoulder to fall in the shape of the man's initial), or a drinking straw (which is pinched into a pattern and then flattened until one of the initialed ends is intact and thus indicates the spouse's name). Anyone who has taken part in weddings knows the care that some brides will take to secure the required "Something old, something new, something borrowed, something blue." The suggestion that the bride might see the bridegroom shortly before the wedding is met with horror in some quarters. Other brides will even go to the extreme of being sure that they are not married while standing with their feet aligned at right angles to the floorboard in the church.

Superstitious *death and funeral customs* reflect our deepseated loathing for all things associated with our natural end. A bird flying into the house, a red spider, a dog howling at night, an empty rocking chair that is moving, a picture falling off the wall—these are only a few of the signs that were once widely regarded as sure omens of a coming death, and that still may occasion a good deal of anxiety. When there is a death in the house, people may stop the clocks, throw out water in flower vases, or perform other traditional acts for which there is no rational explanation, only the authority of traditional usage. Once it was bad luck to break through a funeral procession, while today it is merely bad manners (or, in many states, illegal). In any case, doing it accidentally leads one not only to a feeling of personal regret, but also to a definite twinge of uneasiness for offending the dead.

Superstitions concerned exclusively with the supernatural are gathered in category VIII of Hand's system, *Witchcraft, Ghosts, Magical Practices*. Although the Anglo-American witch is now mostly a semicomical figure of cartoons and Halloween decorations in the urban United States, it is unnecessary to go very far into the backwoods or among ethnic groups to find flourishing beliefs in midnight witch-riding, conjuring, hoodoo, cursing, casting spells, haunts, shape-shifting, and the like. Collections and studies of American superstitions are rich in supernatural lore, too voluminous to be summarized here. Ghost lore is still extremely active in the United States, despite the joshing that Americans reserve for British "ghost detectives" and dwellers in supposedly haunted castles. "Second sight" and other forms of supernatural communication through time or space are still trusted by some. Many people, perhaps most, engage in some aspects of "folk religion," which comprises, in Don Yoder's definition, ". . . views and practices of religion that exist among the people apart from and alongside the strictly theological and liturgical forms of the official religion." The modern Americans' habits of carrying lucky charms, knocking on wood, crossing their fingers, and cursing things that offend them, all point back to supernaturalism that is medieval, if not much more ancient.

Probably not best considered part of supernaturalism (although their popular name suggests that they *are*), are "water witches" who seek ground water sources by magical means. Such practitioners with their forked sticks or "doodle bugs" (for locating minerals) are a kind of traditional or folk scientist found in many rural counties in America, and in most urban ones as well.

Superstitions related to cosmology and the natural world fall into the following five categories in Hand's system:

Such *cosmic phenomena* as tides, winds, rainbows, and the movements of heavenly bodies have long been studied and regarded as possible portents, often of wars or of natural disasters. The more unusual the phenomenon, the more likely it will be read as an omen. As a result, eclipses, comets, and meteors ("shooting stars") occasion more superstitions than do phases of the moon, shifting patterns of stars, and bright colors of sunsets. General superstitions of this kind, as well as those dealing with *times, numbers, and seasons,* when they are unrelated to other areas of folk belief, fall into category IX. Examples include "Seeing the moon over the right [or left] shoulder is good luck"; "Sing before breakfast; cry before dinner"; "Trouble always comes in threes"; and "Nothing made of leather at Christmas time will last."

As Mark Twain pointed out, people talk about the weather, but they *do* very little about it—not even predict it with complete reliability—despite the science of meteorology with its orbiting weather satellites. The natural result is an enormous number of *weather superstitions.* Most items in category X are *signs*: "If you see a dog eating grass, it is going to rain soon"; or "If it snows on Christmas day, Easter will be green." Others are *magic*: "Sit in the middle of the room and hold a glass of water in your hand and you won't be struck by lightning during a storm"; or "Sleep with a flower under your pillow and the weather will be fair the next day." Only a few are *conversions,* such as, "Every flash of lightning is accompanied by a thunderbolt; if you can find one and keep it in your house, it will never be struck by lightning."

Superstitions concerning *animals and animal husbandry* (XI) or *plants and plant husbandry* (XIII) include all the beliefs and practices used to enhance agricultural success. Even in an age of farm advisors in every county, government bulletins to cover all problems, and technological advances for every need, many farmers still plant by the "signs," consult almanacs, treat sick animals with home cures, and follow countless other traditional usages. One of the most whimsical animal beliefs carried to the New World from the Old is that rats may be induced to leave a building by writing them a polite note that suggests another abode nearby, and stuffing it into a rat hole. Control of dangerous or threatening animals may be traditional. "Hold your breath and bees won't sting you"; "A rattlesnake won't cross a hair rope"; "Cut off the tip of a dog's tail and carry it with you and that dog will never harm you"; or "If you see a stray dog out on your lawn, cross your fingers and hold them tight and he won't defecate there." The familiar children's rhyme "Ladybug, ladybug, fly away home . . ." is said to have been used by hop growers to spare the useful little beetles when the vines were burnt off. The most common agricultural superstitions are those that deal with the best time to perform such farm work as planting, harvesting, dehorning, castrating, and slaughtering. Some farm traditions seem to have fairly logical explanations—such as the rules for animal surgery that correlate with the times of year naturally best suited for healing (i.e., months without an "R," that is, the summer months, are sometimes taboo for castration)—while others are strictly magic—such as the belief that thanking the giver will cause a gift plant to wither and die, or the belief that only if a hen is set on an even number of eggs will they all hatch.

Fishing and hunting superstitions exist because, like gambling, sports, sickness, crops, weather, and the like, success cannot be predicted or guaranteed. As a result, there are traditional signs for the good-luck days and places, and traditional magic for the best methodology of the hunt. Members of hunting or fishing parties may be excessively sensitive about such acts as sticking an ax into the ground (it will throw the dog's scent off), or stepping over a fishing pole (it will ruin the luck). Other sportsmen are convinced by years of experience that a big possum will always go up a little tree and vice versa, or that the behavior of a small fish kept in a tank at home will indicate how good the fishing will be that day. Commercial fishermen have many folk signs and practices associated both with increased production and better individual protection.

As in almost every classification in the study of folklore, there remains a group of very general items that may be no better labeled than simply "*Miscellaneous.*" This category contains the lore of wishing, general good and bad luck, and a small, but interesting, group of modern beliefs. One of the most persistent contemporary superstitions, for example, is that to save enough of an apparently worthless item will result in some kind of reward; the items saved may be ticket stubs, cigarette packages (or the red opening-tabs from the packages), beer-bottle labels, tea-bag tabs, or the red trademark tags from Levi's. Generally the assumption is that "a million of them" (or some other large number) will be good for some charitable gift such as a seeing eye dog for a blind person, a wheelchair for a cripple, or hospital care for a poor child. Probably the publicity given to recent prize contests has done much to keep such beliefs alive. Just as American children attach some significance to finding the words "Hershey Kisses" printed three times on an opening tab, or a whole Indian pictured on a Tootsie Pop wrapper, adults have traditions associated with the number of dots on an Olympia Beer label or the number of stars on a *Playboy* magazine cover. Other items for this miscellaneous category might be the beliefs that too much exposure to television may cause sterility, or that stones grow.

In this discussion of the persistence of superstitions and of their definition, classification, and folk rationalization, several theoretical aspects of superstitious behavior have also been introduced. These include faulty reasoning, coincidence, psychological predilection to believe in the supernatural, rites of passage, the theory of survivals, the uncertainty of some desired ends, fear of the abnormal or of the risky, fear of the dead, modernization of superstitions, and the power of magic to persist traditionally side by side with officially maintained science and religion. Two other important theories should be mentioned.

The famous theory of **sympathetic magic** proposed by Sir James G. Frazer in his twelve-volume work *The Golden Bough*, although discredited by modern anthropologists, provided terminology still in use for explaining some superstitions. Frazer believed that many primitive beliefs in magic were founded on the assumption of an inherent "sympathy" between unconnected objects. This could take the form either of *homeopathic magic* (magic of similarity), based on the idea that like objects may affect each other, or *contagious magic* (magic of touch), based on the idea that objects formerly in contact with each other continue to have an invisible connection. The theory was applied beyond primitive cultures to explain many superstitions, both ancient and modern. When the witches in *Macbeth* stir up waves in their kettle to make waves rise at sea, or when a primitive person fears that his likeness in a photograph will steal his soul away, or when planting lore implies a parallel between the crescent moon enlarging and crops increasing, *homeopathic magic* is said to be at work. In each instance an event *like* the desired one is involved. But when a nail or knife that caused a wound is treated along with the wound, or when a person's footprint may be molested to harm that person, or when the spittle of someone who has delivered the "evil eye" is used in the curative ritual, *contagious magic* is said to be at work. Here each event involves something formerly *in touch* with the subject of the magic. Both kinds of sympathetic magic are involved in such rites as a curse performed with a voodoo doll made as an image of the victim that also contains bits of his hair, nail parings, or clothing. In a wart cure, if a stolen dishrag is simply buried "to rot the wart away," only homeopathic magic is used; but if it must first be touched to the wart, contagious magic is at work also. Part of the difficulty in accepting wholly Frazer's "false science" approach is that when a magical act is followed by the desired result there may be nothing defective in either the logic or its application: some "superstitions," in other words, are true and useful. Conversely, the institutionalized religious "magic" of blessings, prayer, or good works may or may not prove effective, and thus may or may not (depending on one's belief) be accepted as "true." In other words, Frazer's explanation is rather ethnocentric, and most folklorists using his terminology do not completely accept his underlying theory.

The theory of **"gesunkenes Kulturgut"** proposed by the German scholar Hans Naumann, never gained much academic support after it was introduced in the nineteen-twenties. The theory held that some modern folklore may represent surviving fragments of learned traditions (rather than only "savage" ones) that have "sunken down" from a high stratum of society among the educated to a lower level in the peasant class. (The theory was the direct opposite of that held by the "survivals" school.) *"Gesunkenes Kulturgut,"* however, is an apt explanation for certain important bodies of superstition, mainly astrology and witchcraft. In each of these areas what were once the trusted beliefs of the best-educated people of earlier times have become present-day folk superstitions. Rulers of nations once consulted astrologers before making important decisions (some, in fact, still do!), and courts of law once seriously tried and condemned witches, but only traditional belief maintains these beliefs in the United States now.

Theories concerning superstitions, like all theories of folklore, should never be formulated too rigorously or applied too mechanically without full regard for the social contexts and field data on which they are based. In many instances it is obvious that more than one theory may apply. For example, the placing of an ax under the bed during childbirth might be alternately explained as part of a *rite of passage,* as the *survival* of primitive veneration for valuable tools, as an instance of *homeopathic magic* (the sharp edge "cutting" the pain), or as a safety precaution to counter the *fear of a dangerous situation.* An alert listener can detect the theoretical basis in explanations sometimes offered for common superstitions. "Three on a match" is usually explained as a fairly recent survival from a wartime safety measure; "step on a crack and break your mother's back" involves homeopathic magic; putting a piece of the desired mineral on a "doodle bug" (miner's divining rod) draws on contagious magic; and most personal validations for superstitions involve fallacious reasoning. It must also be borne in mind that explanations for superstitions, like those for proverbs, may themselves be traditional. Furthermore, when such explanations become sufficiently formularized, they are legends. It should also be remembered, as Toelken points out in Appendix B, that some statements of alleged folk belief are merely passed on because they appeal humorously or esthetically to the group; these are, in his terms, "artistic superstitions," not the more seriously-taken "religious superstitions."

Research approaches to superstitions have generally taken the form of collecting projects, classifications, attempts at better definitions, and theoretical studies. Another promising approach, so far only touched upon, is experimentation. An experiment with superstitions might be designed to field test a theoretical explanation, to determine the efficacy of a superstition, to study variations that occur in transmission, or for other purposes. An experiment on a very simple level that shows how coincidence reinforces belief was performed by the columnist Allan M. Trout of the *Courier-Journal* (Louisville, Ky.) in 1960. After hearing the first katydid on July 20th, Trout calculated by means of folk prognostication that the first frost would come ninety days later, on October 20th. He then proceeded to write his column for that date in advance, boldly predicting the weather that the katydids had promised. What did his readers find on the morning of October 20th? A light frost—the first of the season!

The katydid experiment, of course, was uncontrolled and unscientific; it demonstrated more about how superstitions arise through coincidence than about the natural causes that might underlie them. An experiment on a higher plane was reported in 1962 in the *Journal of American Folklore*. Pigeons were confined in boxes where food was delivered and colored lights were flashed in a random pattern. The birds, however, tended to react as if their own bodily movements or the appearances of the lights had a connection with the delivery of food. They learned to respond to the supposed light patterns, or to attempt to control the appearance of food by their movements; in short, they became what was term "superstitious." The experimenters concluded that the basic conditions that may lead to superstitions are deprivation and the uncertain appearance of a desired commodity, "accidental reinforcement" of behavior which supposedly leads to success, and the continued maintenance of such behavior even without much positive encouragement. Whether such stimulus-response experimentation tells us much about the psychological state of superstitions humans is open to question.

BIBLIOGRAPHIC NOTES

Alan Dundes compared definitions of superstitions and proposed the one quoted in this chapter in his "Brown County Superstitions," *MF* 11 (1961), 25–56; repr. in *Analytic Essays in Folklore*, pp. 88–94. In "Folk Beliefs: Knowledge and Action," *SFQ* 31 (1967), 304–9, Michael Owen Jones comments on Dundes's definition and suggests a need for an improved approach that will better account for meanings and functions of superstitions and for the workings of the "folk mind."

Dundes offers the term "folk ideas" for items of traditional attitude and assumption not easily included under "folk belief" or superstition; see "Folk Ideas as Units of World View," *JAF* 84 (1971), 93–103. He has collected examples of these ideas in such articles as "The Number Three in American Culture," in his anthology *Every Man His Way* (Englewood Cliffs, N.J.: Prentice-Hall, 1968), pp. 401–24 (repr. in *Analytic Essays in Folklore*, pp. 206–25); "Thinking Ahead: A Folkloristic Reflection of The Future Orientation in American Worldview," *Anthropological Quarterly* 42 (1969), 53–72 (repr. in *Analytic Essays in Folklore*, pp. 226–38); and in an article on the primacy of sight data in American folk speech and folk belief titled "Seeing is Believing," *Natural History* 81 (May 1972), 8–12, 86–87.

Studies of collegiate superstitions referred to in this chapter are as follows: Fletcher Bascom Dresslar's *Superstitions and Education,* University of California Publications in Education no. 5 (Berkeley, 1907); Martha Warren Beckwith's "Signs and Superstitions Collected from American College Girls," *JAF* 36 (1923), 1–15; Alfred Marston Tozzer's *Social Origins and Social Continuities* (New York: Macmillan, 1932), pp. 225–30, 242–66; Harold E. Driver's "A Method of Investigating Individual Differences in Folkloristic Beliefs and Practices," *MF* 1 (1951), 99–105; and Jan Harold Brunvand's "Folklore and Superstitions in Idaho," *IY* 6 (1962), 20–24 (see also a note in *WF* 22 [1963], 202–3).

Two other notes on student superstitions are Martin L. Wine's "Superstitions Collected in Chicago," *MF* 7 (1957), 149–59 (175 items from nineteen students at Austin High School); and Charles A. Huguenin's "A Prayer for Examinations," *NYFQ* 18 (1962), 145–48 (appeals to St. Joseph of Cupertino, "The patron saint of the stupid"). Gustav Jahoda reports several other studies of student superstitions in *The Psychology of Superstition* (Baltimore: Penguin Books, 1970), pp. 31—32.

Mark Graubard has compared ancient and modern attitudes toward superstitions in "Some Contemporary Observations on Ancient Superstitions," *JAF* 59 (1946), 124–33. A discussion of the truthfulness of some superstitions is E. H. Lucas's "The Role of Folklore in the Discovery and Rediscovery of Plant Drugs," *Cenntennial Review of Arts and Science* 3 (1959), 173–88. Bergen Evans's *The Natural History of Nonsense* (New York: Knopf, 1946; Vintage Books paperback edn., 1958) debunks many popular delusions. Ray B. Browne's "Superstitions Used as Propaganda in the American Revolution," *NYFQ* 17 (1961), 202–11 illustrates the appearance of such delusions in an earlier period.

Collections of American superstitions are listed in the bibliographies of both volumes of the North Carolina collection, and Wayland D. Hand's introduction in Volume 6 is a comprehensive survey of theories of superstitions and problems of research as they apply to the 8,569 items he has arranged and annotated here. Besides this invaluable work, a key European reference source is the *Handwörterbuch des deutschen Aberglaubens,* edited by Eduard von Hoffman-Krayer and Hanns Bächtold-Stäubli, 10 vols. (Berlin and Leipzig: W. deGruyter, 1927–42). Space permits listing only three other important American collections: Harry Hyatt's *Folklore from Adams County, Illinois* (New York: Alma Egan Hyatt Foundation, 1935; 2nd rev. edn., 1965); Vance Randolph's *Ozark Superstitions* (New York: Columbia University Press, 1947; Dover Books paperback edn., 1964); and Ray B. Browne's *Popular Beliefs and Practices from Alabama,* University of California Folklore Studies no. 9 (Berkeley and Los Angeles, 1958).

A good collection from Canada with bibliographic references to others is Helen Creighton's *Bluenose Magic: Popular Beliefs and Superstitions in Nova Scotia* (Toronto: Ryerson Press, 1968).

For study of the particular folk beliefs of Afro-American culture, begin with Newbell Niles Puckett's *Folk Beliefs of the Southern Negro* (Chapel Hill: University of North Carolina Press, 1926). An important early study is Zora Hurston's "Hoodoo in America," *JAF* 64 (1931), 317–417. The massive total field collection, mainly from black informants, of one dedicated collector is presented in Harry Hyatt's *Hoodoo-Conjuration-Witchcraft-Rootwork* (Hannibal, Mo.: Western Publishing Co. and Alma Egan Hyatt Foundation, vols. 1 and 2, 1970; vol. 3, 1973; vol. 4 forthcoming). See the detailed review of this work by Francis A. deCaro in *Louisiana Review*, 3 (Summer 1974), 29–38.

Confronting the vast materials available for classification and study, Samuel J. Sackett proposes "Using a Computer on a Belief Collection" in *WF* 29 (1970), 105–10. A reader offered a correction to Sackett's methodology in *WF* 30 (1971), 55.

In the folklore of childbirth, the curious practice of giving the husband medical care after his wife has given birth is discussed in historic and geographic perspective by Wayland D. Hand in "American Analogues of the Couvade," *Studies in Folklore*, pp. 213–29. Lucile F. Newman presents a large classified collection in "Folklore of Pregnancy: Wives' Tales in Contra Costa County, California," *WF* 28 (1969), 112–35.

A general approach to the subject of folk medicine may be made via the collection *American Folk Medicine: A Symposium* edited by Wayland D. Hand (Los Angeles, Calif.: UCLA Center for study of Comparative Folklore and Mythology, pub. 4, 1976).

Data on faith healing are contained in such articles as Terry M. Carbo, "The Faith Healing Beliefs of a New Orleans Family," *LFM* 2 (August 1968), 91–100; and Gopalan V. Gopalan and Bruce Nickerson, "Faith Healing in Indiana and Illinois, *IF* 6 (1973), 33–99. More analysis is given in Wayland D. Hand, "The Folk Healer: Calling and Endowment," *Journal of the History of Medicine and Allied Sciences* 26 (1971), 263–75; and Michael Owen Jones, *Why Faith Healing?* (Ottawa: Canadian Centre for Folk Culture Studies, paper no. 3, 1972). In an overview, Greg Johnson charts strategies of faith healing in "A Classification of Faith Healing Practices," *NYF* 1 (1975), 91–96.

Techniques of folk medicine are discussed in Wayland D. Hand's articles "Plugging, Nailing, Wedging, and Kindred Folk Medicinal Practices," in Bruce Jackson, ed., *Folklore and Society: Essays in Honor of Benj. A. Botkin* (Hatboro, Pa.: Folklore Associates, 1966), pp. 63–75; and " 'Passing Through': Folk Medical Magic and Symbolism," *Proceedings of the American Philosophical Society* 112 (1968), 379–402. Three further instances with photographs are given in Joseph D. Clark's note "Passing Through: A Folk Remedy," *NCFJ* 23 (1975), 11–15.

Occurrences of a curious belief concerning the human body are recorded in "Measuring for Short Growth," *HF* 7 (1948), 15–19. For instance, children may be considered undersized if their heights are not found to be seven times the length of their feet. For further data, see Barbara Ann Townsend and Donald Allport Bird, "The Miracle of String Measurement," *IF* 3 (1970), 147–62, with an additional account supplied in *IF* 4 (1971), 89–94.

Of particular interest in the general area of folk cures is Richard M. Dorson's "Blood Stoppers," *SFQ* 11 (1947), 105–18, which was reprinted with some additions as Chapter 7 of *Bloodstoppers and Bearwalkers* (Cambridge, Mass.: Harvard University Press, 1952). Another area of folk cures is presented in Frank M. Paulsen's "A Hair of the Dog and Some Other Hangover Cures from Popular Tradition," *JAF* 74 (1961), 152–68.

As background for a Spanish-American pattern of faith healing and folk medicine see Irwin Press, "The Urban Curandero," *AA* 73 (1971), 741–56. On the nature of ailments for which magical aid is sought, see Keith A. Neighbors, "Mexican-American Folk Diseases," *WF* 28 (1969), 249–59. A local study in this area is E. Ferol Benavides, "The Saints Among the Saints: A Study of Curanderismo in Utah," *UHQ* 41 (1973), 373–92.

Folk practices and beliefs concerning sex are discussed in three recent articles: Eleanor Long, "Aphrodisiacs, Charms, and Philtres," *WF* 32 (1973), 153–63; George W. Rich and David F. Jacobs, "Saltpeter: A Folkloric Adjustment to Acculturation Stress," *WF* 32 (1973), 164–79; and Lydia Fish "The Old Wife in the Dormitory—Sexual Folklore and Magical Practices from State University College," *NYFQ* 28 (1972), 30–36.

Folk beliefs and superstitions of various occupations constitute a fascinating but largely uncollected body of material. Actors' superstitions are found in Ralph Freud's "George Spelvin Says the Tag: Folklore of the Theater," *WF* 13 (1954), 245–50; Dan Gross's "Folklore of the Theater," *WF* 20 (1961), 257–63; and Wayland D. Hand's "Folk Beliefs and Customs of the American Theater: A Survey," *SFQ* 38 (1974), pp. 23–48. Other occupational studies include Lee Allen, "The Superstitions of Baseball Players," *NYFQ* 20 (1964), 98–109; Henry Winfred Splitter, "Miner's Luck," *WF* 15 (1956), 229–46; and two studies by Patrick B. Mullen, "The Function of Magic Folk Belief Among Texas Coastal Fishermen," *JAF* 82 (1969), 214–25; and "The Function of Folk Belief Among Negro Fishermen of the Texas Coast," *SFQ* 33 (1969), 80–91. Another study of fishermen's superstitions is John J. Poggie, Jr., and Carl Gersung, "Risk and Ritual: An Interpretation of Fishermen's Folklore in a New England Community," *JAF* 85 (1972), 66–72. An unusual study of urban black folk belief is David J. Winslow's "Occupational Superstitions of Negro Prostitutes in an upstate New York City," *NYFQ* 24 (1968), 294–301.

A body of European-American beliefs and practices is described by Aili K. Johnson in "Lore of the Finnish-American Sauna," *MF* 1 (1951), 33–39. Louis C. Jones traced "The Evil Eye Among European-Americans," in *WF* 10 (1951), 11–25, but found no evidence of survival among English or Scottish stocks.

A basic study of Anglo-American supernatural folklore is George Lyman Kittredge's book *Witchcraft in Old and New England* (Cambridge, Mass.: Harvard University Press, 1929; republished New York: Russell and Russell, 1956). Patricia K. Rickels collected "Some Accounts of Witch Riding" from a black college student who had been witch-ridden; see *LFM* 2 (August 1961), 1–17. On the basis of an interview with a "good" witch living in Philadelphia, Jane C. Beck published "A Traditional Witch of the Twentieth Century,"

NYFQ 30 (1974), 101–16. A catalog of American witch legends is cited in the notes to Chapter 8.

The practice of dowsing or "water witching" has attracted numerous studies; the most comprehensive is Evon Z. Vogt and Ray Hyman's *Water Witching U.S.A.* (Chicago: University of Chicago Press, 1959). A fascinating review of the book by a practicing "witch" is R. Carlyle Buley's "Water (?) Witching Can Be Fun," *IMH* 56 (1960), 65–77. Vogt also co-authored "Some Aspects of the Folklore of Water Witching in the United States" in *JAF* 71 (1958), 519–31 with Peggy Golde; and "The Urban American Dowser," *JAF* 82 (1969), 195–213, with Linda K. Barrett. A study of dowsing in a regional context is Hilda Webb's "Water Witching as Part of Folklife in Southern Indiana," *JFI* 3 (1966), 10–29.

A "Symposium on Folk Religion" edited by Don Yoder appeared in *WF* 33 (1974), 1–87. Steven M. Kane's "Ritual Possession in a Southern Appalachian Religious Sect," *JAF* 87 (1974), 293–302, deals with snake handling in a six-state area. Articles on Afro-American folk religion include David J. Winslow, "Bishop E. E. Everett and Some Aspects of Occultism and Folk Religion in Negro Philadelphia," *KFQ* 14 (1969), 59–80; James F. Byers, "Voodoo: Tropical Pharmacology or Psychosomatic Psychology?" *NYFQ* 26 (1970), 305–12; and Loudell F. Snow, " 'I Was Born Just Exactly with the Gift': An Interview with a Voodoo Practitioner," *JAF* 86 (1973), 272–81.

An early government publication, Edward B. Garriott's *Weather Folk-Lore and Local Weather Signs,* attempted to "segregate from the mass of available data the true sayings that are applicable to the United States." Material was drawn from two late-nineteenth-century collections; the work was published as U.S. Dept. of Agriculture, Weather Bureau, Bulletin No. 33—W.B. No. 294 (Washington, D.C., 1903; Superintendent of Documents Index No. A29.3:33). Another interesting older collection is W. J. Humphreys's *Weather Proverbs and Paradoxes* (Baltimore: Williams & Wilkins, 1923; 2nd. edn., 1934). Louise Pound surveyed the history of attempts to make rain on the Great Plains in her article "Nebraska Rain Lore and Rain Making," *CFQ* 5 (1946), 129–42, reprinted in *Nebraska Folklore*, 41–60. Background material from eighteenth-century New England for the study of a popular reference work on weather lore and other agricultural and domestic traditions is George Lyman Kittredge's *The Old Farmer and His Almanack* (Cambridge, Mass.: Harvard University Press, 1904).

Except that it becomes excessively ritualistic in its interpretations, W. W. Newell's "Conjuring Rats" in *JAF* 5 (1892), 23–32 is a good discussion of the old superstition concerning writing a note to rid a building of rats. Two items of recent folk belief are described in Michael J. Preston's "Olympia Beer Comes to Colorado: The Spread of a Tradition," *WF* 32 (1973), 281–83 (supposed significance of the dots on the backs of labels); and Harry Joe Jaffee's "The Stars of Playboy," *WF* 31 (1972), 122–23 (traditions about stars printed on the magazine cover).

Allan M. Trout's experiment was described in the *Courier-Journal* on October 20, 1960. The pigeon experiment was described by Arthur J. Bachrach in

"An Experimental Approach to Superstitious Behavior," *JAF* 75 (1962), 1–9. In "Superstitious Pigeons, Hydrophobia, and Conventional Wisdom," *WF* 30 (1971), 1–18, Kenneth Ketner with reference to such experiments asserts that notions of folk groups and their supposed beliefs are useless for defining superstition; instead he advocates study of the "psychological state of individuals" and prefers the term "conventional wisdom" to "superstition." An article that deals further with the habits of mind that permeate superstition is Eric Berne's "The Mythology of Dark and Fair: Psychiatric Use of Folklore," *JAF* 72 (1959), 1–13. Gustav Jahoda's *The Psychology of Superstition*, mentioned earlier in these notes, is the only book-length survey of modern psychological theories as they apply to folk beliefs.

14

Customs and Festivals

Possibly no other kind of American folklore has been so frequently referred to, yet so vaguely defined, so ill-classified, and so little understood or studied, as folk customs have been. While few proposed definitions of American folklore would exclude customs, nowhere is there
a comprehensive explication of the term, nor is it consistently employed. Tolerably rich materials are scattered through such sources as
state and local historical journals, but there is no definitive folklore
study of them. Customs are sometimes represented in folklore collections under such labels as "folkways," "usages," or "social institutions," or they are presented in collections together with superstitions
or material folklore. Some folklore anthologies that list "customs"
among their contents actually contain few or none, while others that
do include customs have no special terms for them. Indexers and bibli-
ographers of American folklore usually group customs with other
"minor areas" of traditional materials. Social historians and folklorists
who may be dealing with the same customs seem to be unaware of
each other's publications. For all of these reasons, this chapter is essentially an attempt toward integrating various points of view by ex-
tracting some generally useful terms and concepts.

To begin with, it is clear that customs are closely associated with
superstitions. Hence, the typical combination, "Beliefs and Customs," is used in *The Frank C. Brown Collection of North Carolina
Folklore* and other major collections. Like superstitions, customs involve both verbal and nonverbal elements that are traditionally applied in specific circumstances. But unlike superstitions, customs as
such do not involve faith in the magical results of such application.
Thus, the "customs" that incorporate traditional belief in the supernatural are usually classified as "superstitions."

A **custom** is a traditional *practice*—a mode of individual behavior or a habit of social life—that is transmitted by word of mouth or imitation, then ingrained by social pressure, common usage, and parental or other authority. When customs are associated with holidays they become *calendar customs*, and when such events are celebrated annually by a whole community they become *festivals*.

Transmitting folklore is itself customary. Storytelling, ballad-singing, riddle-posing, game-and-prank playing, and the like all depend for their survival on traditional performance and acceptance rather than on official control. Generally folklorists have not separated the customary contexts from folklore texts, except perhaps when studying something like quilting bees or barn raisings rather than quilt patterns or barns themselves, or searching for a "liars' contest" rather than merely for texts of tall tales. But there are more subtle behavioral patterns, integral parts of folklore performance situations, which folklorists are just beginning to study: "framing" devices that initiate and conclude folk transmissions, postural and gestural clues to meaning, audience-response codes, nonverbalized folk beliefs, and the like.

This expanded sense of the term "custom" involves the folklorist in what anthropologists term **ethnography**—the descriptive study of all traditions in a particular group or region. Ethnographic descriptions of different cultures make possible comparative studies, or **ethnology.** Since the terms "ethnography" and "ethnology" are sometimes used synonymously, especially in Europe, and both terms tend to be associated with studies of primitive cultures, the term "folklife" (from Scandinavian *"folk-liv"*) deserves the increased American usage it has had lately. **Folklife** refers to the full traditional lore, behavior, and material culture of any folk group, with emphasis on the customary and material categories. For verbal folklore the term **folk literature** has some currency, although whether "folklife" includes "folk literature" is not always clear. A safe generalization is that American folklorists have accepted the European concept of folklife as constituting their subject matter, and that they are borrowing from ethnography and ethnology for new field methods and theories. In both respects, customs are important data.

Not all customs are still living folklore. Those which have become a fixed part of national behavior and are practiced unvaryingly throughout a country (or sometimes several countries) are termed *manners* or *mores*, although their origins may lie in folklore and their sustaining power may still be that of tradition. The domestic manners that characterize Americans include switching the fork from hand to hand while eating, serving certain drinks iced, and maintaining a high degree of informality in social life. Manners may involve different levels of awareness, however; we switch fork hands as a matter of course; but icing drinks is a deliberate act, and social informality may be either studied or "natural."

Mores are defined as traditional modes of behavior that have achieved the status of moral requirements, often being institutionalized in laws. These include such practices as monogamous marriages, the patterns of family naming, and the age when adulthood begins. The attitude of *ethnocentrism* is the assumption that one's own customs, manners, and mores are the "right" ones, and that all others are scaled out in degrees of "wrongness" from this center. Ethnocentrism accounts for feelings among Americans, for example, that may range from intolerance of some other culture's religion (or lack of religion) to mild annoyance occasioned by having to drive on the "wrong" side of the highway in England, or being expected to bow as a greeting in Japan. That culture-contacts may lead to voluntary changes as well as to hostility is demonstrated by the spread of American courtship customs throughout much of the Old World.

National manners and mores, ethnocentrism, acculturation, and related subjects are the concerns of anthropologists, and especially sociologists; folklorists have been concerned mostly with customs that are both traditional and variable, being sustained informally in specific folk groups rather than nationally among the whole population. By the time traditional frontier hospitality evolved into the "Welcome Wagon," and the political barbecue became the "$100-a-Plate Dinner," these "folkways" had ceased to have much folkloristic significance, although they still might interest other students of American behavior.

Most true folk customs in the United States are associated with special events, especially those that require "rites of passage"—birth, marriage, and death. They begin at once when a child is born. Boy babies are customarily dressed in blue, and girls in pink, but sometimes only the first child of each sex in a family is so clothed, while later arrivals must make do with hand-me-down infantwear or may appear in other pastel shades. Father is expected to hand out cigars, a custom that may repeat itself after promotions in his occupation as well. (In Mormon-dominated Utah, and perhaps elsewhere from other influences, instead of cigars a new father passes out Tootsie Rolls or bubble-gum cigars.) None of these practices is required by any authority other than local custom, which varies from region to region or even from family to family. Some families have special clothes for the baby's homecoming or christening, or heirloom furniture for its room.

Celebrations of birthday anniversaries may begin as early as the first year in some families, and they may continue through one's entire life. More commonly, however, birthday parties are dropped at about high school age, sometimes to be revived once at the symbolic age of maturity (twenty-one years) and again as an annual celebration in later middle age. Children's birthdays almost invariably are the occasion for spanking—one spank for each year, with extras "to grow on," or "for good measure." Children in some regions maintain a fairly rigid schedule of extra-punishment days before and after the birthday anniversary—"pinch day," "hit day," "kiss day," and so forth. Blowing out birthday-cake candles and wishing are standard customs, sometimes varied by naming the candles for possible marriage partners and assuming that the last candle smoking marks the mate. Birthday gifts at a party may be held over the head of the celebrating child for him or her to guess the donor or to announce the use to which that gift is to be put. For each correct guess the child is granted a wish.

The loss of "baby teeth" is one of the few other non-holiday occasions in a child's life when customs are followed. The most common practice is for the child to sleep with the tooth under its pillow for the "tooth fairy" to buy for a quarter (prices vary). School customs (see also Appendix B) are practiced to some degree in most communities, often being channeled eventually by teachers and principals into well-regulated events. "Dress-up day" or "hillbilly day," under various names, are begun informally by students to vary the routine of regulated school dress, but eventually become sanctioned and controlled by school officials and are placed on the activities calendar. One school custom remains a folk one—the designation of a certain day (often Thursday) as "queer day," when the wearing of a certain color (often green, yellow, or purple) marks the "queers" (homosexuals). Many unsuspecting teachers have been ridiculed behind their backs for unwittingly violating the taboo. The hazing of freshmen, initiation into clubs, and "tapping" for honorary societies are further school occasions for which the establishment has forged ersatz "traditions" to supplant or forestall folk customs, although these seldom catch on as group traditions, and when they do the participants tend to modify them back in the direction of earlier folk behavior.

Courtship and engagement begin a new round of customs that may lead to marriage, the most tradition-regulated personal ceremony in American life, or, more recently, to other arrangements of living together that may have their own folk traditions. Here time has changed but not diminished the role of folklore. Couples formerly were granted the family parlor or porch swing for courting; today they have the automobile. Bundling as a courting custom gave way to "necking" or "petting" in the 1940s and '50s, "making out" and "scoring" later. Ice-cream socials or church "sings" were replaced by drive-ins (both movies and restaurants). Customs of "going Dutch," "blind dates," "double-dating," "study dates," and the like depended on individual finances and desires as well as on local practices. "Going steady" with one partner became a well-entrenched dating pattern surrounded with customary devices for signaling whether one is attached or free (exchanging rings, leaving certain buttons or buckles open, placement of jewelry, etc.). But under the influence of feminism by the late 1960s women were less often willing to display signs of "belonging" to a male, and they were as likely to initiate dates (or eschew them) as to wait to be asked. In some high schools and colleges a so-called "virgin pin" was worn, supposedly indicating by its position or shape whether a girl was or wasn't. Today the decline of a desire to "save one's virginity for marriage" has rendered the "virgin pin" obsolete; instead a lore of aphrodisiacs and folk birth-control methods circulates. Formally engaged couples still often have the time-payment diamond ring to advertise and seal their promises, but custom may decree the exchange of other special gifts as well.

Wedding customs begin with the "shower," often several of them, to emphasize different kinds of needed gifts. Shower parties are customarily for women only, although friends of the bridegroom may occasionally hold a gift "stag party" for him. Certain recreations are reserved exclusively for showers. A favorite is writing down the words of the future bride as she opens gifts. Her remarks are read aloud later as "what she will say to her husband on their wedding night."

Customs of the wedding itself are numerous, and largely regulated by tradition. They include the dress of participants, the seating of guests, the choice of attendants, kissing the bride, throwing rice, passing the bride's shoe around for money, playing pranks on the married couple, and decorating the car. Noisy harassment of brides and bridegrooms is an old custom in the United States. First it was the "shivaree," derived from the Old World word and custom of the "charivari." A crowd of friends and neighbors would awaken a bridal couple with "rough music" and shouting, subjecting them to various indignities, and pestering them until the husband surrendered and set up a treat. The shivaree was also known by such terms as "belling," "warmer," "serenade," "collathump," and "skimmilton." In 1946, a folklore journal reported, a recently married couple in Oregon were awakened and the husband dunked in a rainbarrel, then forced to push his wife around in a wheelbarrow while the celebrants threw firecrackers at him; afterward he was expected to treat the crowd to refreshments. Many Americans can describe similar customs firsthand, and shivarees still occur, but the typical custom today is to decorate and sabotage the honeymoon car. Crepe-paper decorations, signs on the car, additives to the gasoline, a note in the fuel-tank cap ("Help, I'm being kidnapped!") are among the usual tricks. Car inscriptions may include pictures, sayings, ribald rhymes, hearts and arrows (similar to tree carvings), and such formulas as "$1 + 1 = 3$". Sometimes pranks are directed at the newlyweds' home. A favorite is removing the labels from all of their canned goods or tying bells to their bedsprings.

Wedding customs, however rough, are essentially celebrations of a happy time. But customs associated with death are generally fraught with suggestions of fear or superstition. Pouring water out of vases, and stopping the clocks in a house in which death has occurred seem to mask some superstitious fear. Draping the furniture in the room in which a corpse lies, or leaving the digging tools by the grave for some days after the burial are marks of respect—or propitiation. Sometimes the disposal of the small personal belongings of the deceased is governed by custom rather than a formal will, and many families commemorate the anniversaries of a beloved's passing by printing annual poems or notices in the classified columns of a newspaper. In some communities the funeral is organized by a traditionally-appointed "arranger"; southern and southwestern writers have described family or community "decoration days," "memorial days," or days for "graveyard working" on which people gather at the cemetery for clean-up work, recreation, and to remember those who have passed away. Special foods may be served, and the names of those who died since the last memorial day are read aloud.

Apart from the cycle of life and the "rites of passage," customs tend to cluster around work, recreation, or social events. Family reunions (in Utah, also "missionary reunions"), "Old Home Weeks," and "Homecomings" may be structured around special customs, foods, or entertainments. Communal-labor parties, important to frontier survival, have largely disappeared from American life, except in recent experimental communities or among such religious sects as the Amish, who have deliberately maintained them. But in the past there was a great variety of work parties—quilting bees, apple-peelings, corn-shuckings, log-rollings, house-raisings, turkey drives, rabbit-drives (followed by a community "rabbit dance") and threshings. Nowadays, although neighbors may willingly "pitch in" to help others in emergencies, these are spontaneous and improvised occasions, usually not traditional ones. One such communal-aid tradition, still fairly common, in small-town neighborhoods, is the so-called "pound party" in which every participant brings a pound of some commodity to help set up housekeeping for a new neighbor or preacher. An urban counterpart is the Harlem "rent party." Certain occupations, such as auctioneering, livestock trading, rodeo work, and the like have rich traditional backgrounds and many continuing folk practices are associated with them.

Most traditional American frontier amusements were lost or greatly altered in later years. No longer do we enjoy the likes of "bear-baiting" or "gander-pulling" as recreations. Dog fighting and cock-fighting still persist illegally and in secret, while target-shooting matches ("turkey shoots," etc.) have changed their character and survived. Spelling bees, hay rides, taffy pulls, and ice-cream socials survive to some degree. Hunting and fishing are still very popular pursuits, and retain some customary traces, such as marking the forehead of the hunter with the blood of his first kill, or having the game divided among the participants of the hunt by a blindfolded outsider. Traditions have also developed in modern sports and children's games: choosing sides by odd or even fingers, choosing the server in tennis by spinning the racket, rallying for the serve in ping pong, deciding the order of play in baseball by placing hand over hand on the bat, tossing a coin for the kick-off in football.

Calendar customs in the United States cluster around a very few annual events, unlike those in Europe that are linked to many more occasions. (Large collections of British folklore have been devoted to descriptions of nothing but such customs.) American tradition has retained few Old World celebrations and has originated even fewer native ones. In chronological summary, the common American calendar customs may be listed as follows: *St. Patrick's Day,* wearing green; *April Fool's Day,* playing pranks; *Easter,* dyeing eggs and wearing new clothes; *May Day,* giving "May baskets"; *Independence Day,* shooting fireworks and giving patriotic speeches; *Halloween,* going "begging"; *Christmas,* caroling and hanging mistletoe; *New Year's Eve,* attending a "watch party" at which there is much noisemaking and general congratulations at the stroke of midnight. Other holidays on the American calendar—whether religious, patriotic, or folk in origin—tend to have only sporadic or commercially stereotyped customs associated with them. *Valentine's Day* card-exchanging is a good example, for without the elementary schools' and the merchants' emphasis of it, the custom would probably long since have died out. *Ground Hog Day* can hardly be thought of as an occasion for folk celebration, since practically the only observance of it nowadays is in newspaper feature articles. *Mother's Day* and *Father's Day* are officially established occasions only for further gift-giving, but another such holiday, *Labor Day,* has become the traditional time in some regions for "closing the summer cottage" or ending the season with one last beach party.

The most typical and original American holiday is certainly Thanksgiving—a combination of the traditional European peasant harvest festival with the first New England settlers' day of giving thanks to God. Really, the Pilgrims' "first Thanksgiving" so often depicted had more of the former character than the latter, while the special meal we eat on Thanksgiving Day nowadays is more Victorian than Colonial in its choice of foods and modes of preparation. The televised professional football games of today's holiday had their counterparts in the games and contests of early New England holidays.

There is little more to distinguish calendar customs from true **folk festivals,** perhaps, then the degree of community involvement in them and the elaboration of celebrations. Some of the most interesting American festivals are immigrant-group seasonal traditions uniquely developed in the United States. The commercialized Mardi Gras of New Orleans, for example, is much more elaborate and sophisticated than most Old-World carnival days or than the traditional celebration in some parts of rural Louisiana, where a party of masked riders travels from farm to farm singing and begging for food. The processions of the *penitente* brotherhood (carrying Christ's cross and receiving His whippings on their own backs), which originated in Spain centuries ago, differ markedly in the American Spanish Southwest, where they have evolved along new lines, even absorbing some Indian elements. The gradual change in the nature of Czech and Slovak harvest festivals as they were revived and sustained in the United States is typical of other such efforts at retention of Old World celebrations. Here, because the participants were no longer farmers, the spontaneous community ritual of Europe became a well-organized public drama with clearly defined actors and spectators. Whether there are any purely American festivals is uncertain, but probably the best case could be made for the rodeo. All others seem to have clear foreign prototypes: the county fair with harvest festivals, the circus with its ancient Roman ancestor, the family reunion with tribal and clan gatherings.

One unusual American celebration, probably derived from German festivals, is the "New Year's Shoot," as it is called in North Carolina, or the "New Year's Sermon" of Missouri. A party of riders travels from house to house, beginning at midnight of New Year's Eve, pausing at each one for the leader or "preacher" to deliver a set speech. Afterward, firearms are discharged and the party is invited into the house for a treat. The custom has elements in it common to English "mumming," which is still found in vigorous tradition in Nova Scotia, and resembles the customs of "belsnickles and shanghais" followed in the late nineteenth century in Virginia. The procedure is also very much like the country Mardi Gras of Cajun Louisiana, and has a dim parallel perhaps in the traditional Southern holiday greeting "Christmas gift!"

The observance of Passover by East European Jews in the United States is one of the few imported festivals that has been systematically compared to its original form. The changes are characteristic of America—the traditional "search for leaven," formerly conducted with a candle and a quill, is now performed with a flashlight and brush; shopping for new clothing replaces the "visit to the tailor"; the ritual cleansing of dishes and utensils is rendered unnecessary by ownership of a special set of them for exclusive holiday use, and the careful handwork in the baking of matzoh has been automated out of existence by the invention of the matzoh machine. New quasi-customs have appeared in the United States—the "Third Seder" (Passover meal) held outside the family circle, individual brand-preferences among the various commercially prepared Passover foods, new games played with the traditional old-country food (nuts), and songs sung in English (including the black spirtual "Go Down, Moses") after the Seder.

A further transplanting of holiday celebrations is exhibited in the Americanized Christmas customs that took root in Japan as early as the middle of the nineteenth century and flourished there, especially since the Allied Occupation following World War II. So pervasive is the celebration now that it is even marked on calendars issued by Shinto and Buddhist organizations, and there have been proposals either to make Christmas a new national holiday or to designate December 25 as "International Goodwill Day." Japanese merchants display Christmas decorations; families put up Christmas trees, or printed pictures of them; Christmas carols are played, parties held, and gifts exchanged. Lacking a fireplace chimney on which to attach their Christmas stockings, many Japanese children find presents placed near their pillows in the morning. Some, however, fasten their stockings on the pipe of the bathroom stove on Christmas Eve.

The term "folk festival" has been applied since the 1930s in the United States to annually sponsored public performances of folklore, generally folksongs and dances. Until recently, few of these revival efforts have received much support from professional folklore scholars, but folklorists are increasingly beginning to attend them, study them, join in planning them, and even take part in some of them. Only on the current folk festival stage have the folk, the folknik, and the folklorist all met face to face and begun to try to understand one another in some depth. The oldest consecutive folk festival is the "National Folk Festival," first held in St. Louis in 1934 with strictly American performers, but eventually branching out into all manner of immigrant and "ethnic" acts. Other festivals have sprung up (and some have died) faster than folklorists can make up their minds about how to regard them; these have ranged from glossy extravaganzas and their celebrity performers, to the rustic "Arkansas Folk Festival" in Mountain View, Arkansas, with its still largely home-grown talent and audience. Another development in the revivalist folk festival field, and a very promising one, is the appearance of university-sponsored annual events (at Chicago and the University of California at Los Angeles, for instance) where the enthusiastic collegiate folklore buff can rub elbows and share ideas with academic students of folklore and with practitioners of the genuine material itself. The Smithsonian Institution's "Festival of American Folklife" founded in 1967 has also very successfully combined education with entertainment by employing folklorists and folklore students to locate talented folk artisans and performers who are brought to Washington, D.C., for the annual event.

BIBLIOGRAPHIC NOTES

Funk & Wagnalls Standard Dictionary of Folklore, Mythology, and Legend, often a good guide for separate genres of folklore, has no general headings for either customs or festivals. The index to the *Journal of American Folklore* groups "Customs, Beliefs, and Superstitions," but the articles cited are mostly about superstitions. The annual bibliographies published by the American Folklore Society use the heading "Customs," placing under it "Festivals and Rites of Passage," but also "Social Relationships, Planting, etc." The Swiss folklorist and museum director Robert Wildhaber included a section on customs in his "Bibliographical Introduction to American Folklife," *NYFQ* 21 (1965), 259–302. He also discussed the European concept of "folklife" in his introduction.

William Graham Sumner introduced the term "folkways" in his classic book of that title (Boston, Mass.: Ginn and Co., 1907; Mentor Book paperback, 1960). He outlined the basic process of customs becoming "mores" (another term he coined), and mores becoming laws. Theodore Blegen urged historians' attention to "traditional beliefs, customs, folk art, ideas, and practices" in his *Grass Roots History* (Minneapolis, University of Minnesota

Press, 1947). His section on "Pioneer Folkways" (pp. 81–102) demonstrated the approach with data from Norwegian-American immigrant life.

Paul G. Brewster edited "Beliefs and Customs" for the *Frank C. Brown Collection of North Carolina Folklore* (vol. 1: pp. 221–82). However, not only beliefs, but also material folklore are described; most of the customs that appear here are related to superstitions. Wayland D. Hand seems to have used most of the same items plus many more in volumes 6 and 7 of the same collection, "Popular Beliefs and Superstitions," in some cases citing as the only comparative reference the identical item in volume 1. Hand's article "Anglo-American Folk Belief and Custom: The Old World's Legacy to the New," in *JFI* 7 (1970), 136–55, is a good example of thorough annotation of customary lore, using as examples mainly the "dumb cake" or "dumb supper" customs.

Three chapters in Everett Dick's *Sod-House Frontier, 1854–1890* (Lincoln, Neb.: Johnsen Pub. Co., 1954) illustrate the treasury of customs to be found in some social histories. They are chapter 20, "Sports"; chapter 26, "Amusements"; and chapter 35, "Crude Frontier Customs." A few special collections of customs exist: Afton Wynn's "Pioneer Folk Ways," *PTFS* 13 (1937), 190–238; Louise Pound's "Old Nebraska Folk Customs," *NH* 28 (1947), 3–31, reprinted in *Nebraska Folklore*, pp. 184–208; and "Customs," by S. J. Sackett, pp. 182–208 of *Kansas Folklore*, ed. Sackett (Lincoln: University of Nebraska Press, 1961). Norbert F. Riedl and Carol K. Buckles compiled a bibliography and an interesting study of "House Customs and Beliefs in East Tennessee" published in *TFSB* 41 (1975), 47–56. In "The Finlinson Family Reunion Tradition," *AFFWord* 4 (Spring 1974), 37–39, Jill Kelly describes a typical Mormon family celebration taking place in Oak City, Utah.

Allen Walker Read outlined the background of an American school custom in his article, "The Spelling Bee: A Linguistic Institution of the American Folk," *PMLA* 56 (1941), 495–512. Iona and Peter Opie in *The Lore and Language of Schoolchildren* (New York: Oxford University Press, 1959), give a "Children's Calendar" and describe British children's "Occasional Customs" (pp. 232–305), some of which have parallels among American children. Herbert Halpert discussed the custom of sending "chain letters" in *WF* 15 (1956), 287–89; Alan Dundes added a foreign reference and provided further examples in an article in *NWF* 1 (Winter 1966), 14–19.

Courtship and wedding customs in Utah were listed by Thomas E. Cheney in *WF* 19 (1960), 106, and some from the Ohio Valley were discussed by Lawrence S. Thompson in *KFR* 9 (1963), 47–50. Some modern campus courtship rituals of the kind discussed in Appendix B are the subject of Michael J. Preston's "The Traditional Ringing at Temple Buell College," *WF* 32 (1973), 271–74. Another aspect of wedding lore appears in Joyce Thompson and Phyllis Bridges, "West Texas Wedding Cars," *WF* 30 (1971), 123–26. One article on ethnic group customs is Philip V. R. Tilney, "The Immigrant Macedonian Wedding in Ft. Wayne," *IF* 3 (1970), 3–34. E. Bagby Atwood discussed "Shivarees and Charivaris: Variations on a Theme," in *PTFS* 32 (1964), 64–71. Other discussions of the history of the term and its variations appeared in *AS* 8 (1933), 22–26, and *AS* 15 (1940), 109–10. The 1946 Oregon shivaree was described by Rex Gunn in "An Oregon Charivari," *WF* 13 (1954), 206–7.

On the customary aspects of American funerals and cemeteries, see such works as Lawrence S. Thompson's "Rites of Sepulcher in the Bluegrass," *KFR* 9 (1963), 25–28; J. Frank Lee's "The Informal Organization of White Southern Protestant Funerals: The Role of the Arranger," *TFSB* 33 (1967), 36–40; and Donald B. Ball's "Social Activities Associated with Two Rural Cemeteries in Coffee County, Tennessee," *TFSB* 41 (1975), 93–98. Kentucky family memorial ceremonies have been described in Thelma Lynn Lamkin's "Spring Hill Decoration Day," *MF* 3 (1953), 157–60, and Harry Harrison Kroll's "Licking River Revisited," *SFQ* 26 (1962), 246–51. Similar traditions from other regions are found in Ted-Larry Pebworth's "Graveyard-Working: The Passing of a Custom," *LFM* 2 (August 1961), 44–49, and Robert Cowser, "Community Memorial Day Observances in Northeast Texas," *WF* 31 (1972), 120–21.

The following works treat various occupational customs: Henning Henningsen, *Crossing the Equator* (Copenhagen: Munksgaard, 1961); Wayland D. Hand, "The Folklore, Customs, and Traditions of the Butte Miner," *CFQ* 5 (1946), 1–25; and Donald J. Ward, "The 'Carny' in the Winter" [carnival concessions workers], *WF* 21 (1962), 190–92. Articles on traditional group work customs include William Marion Miller, "A Threshing Ring in Southern Ohio," *HF* 5 (1946), 3–13; Mrs. Arthur Turner, "Turkey Drives: South Mississippi, Greene County," *MFR* 3 (1969), 31–32; David Rhys Roberts, "Ice Harvesting," *NYFQ* 26 (1970), 114–26; and Celia M. Benton, "Corn Shuckings in Sampson County," *NCFJ* 22 (1974), 131–39. Auctioneer's traditions are collected in William Hugh Jansen's "Down Our Way: Who'll Bid Twenty?" *KFR* 2 (1956), 113–21; Anne Marsh and William Aspinall, Jr., "Harold E. Leightley: Portrait of an Auctioneer and His Craft," *KFQ* 16 (1971), 133–50; William R. Ferris, Jr., "Ray Lum: Muletrader," *NCFJ* 21 (1973), 105–19; and Mac E. Barrick, "The Folklore Repertory of a Pennsylvania Auctioneer," *KF* 19 (1974), 27–42.

Other aspects of occupational lore—still a largely unexplored field—are found in Don Boles, "Some Gypsy Occupations in America," *JGLS* 37 (1958), 103–10; Sandra Bennett, "Rodeo," *AFFWord* 2 (Sept. 1972), 1–10; and Albert B. Friedman, "The Scatological Rites of Burglars," *WF* 27 (1968), 171–79.

For two systematic and detailed presentations of a highly ritualized and illegal sporting event, see Gerald E. Parsons, Jr., "Cockfighting: A Potential Field of Research," *NYFQ* 25 (1969), 265–88, and Steven L. Del Sesto, "Roles, Rules, and Organization: A Descriptive Account of Cockfighting in Rural Louisiana," *SFQ* 39 (1975), 1–14.

The American Book of Days by George William Douglas (1938; revised edition by Helen Douglas Compton, New York: H. W. Wilson, 1948) is a useful reference source on American holidays, their origins and celebration. George R. Stewart's chapter on holidays (222–48) in his completely engaging book *American Ways of Life* (Garden City, N.Y.: Dolphin paperback, 1954) is the best single essay on the subject. Kelsie B. Harder's note "Just an April Fool,"

TFSB 27 (1961), 5–7 describes the custom of sending April Fool letters. On another holiday see Maurice A. Mook, "Halloween in Central Pennsylvania," *KFQ* 14 (1969), 124–29, and Catharine Harris Ainsworth, "Hallowe'en," *NYFQ* 29 (1973), 163–93. The best work on a single holiday is undoubtedly Venetia Newall's *An Egg at Easter, A Folklore Study* (Bloomington: Indiana University Press, 1971); while the best general essay on the larger topic is Robert J. Smith's chapter "Festivals and Celebrations," in *Folklore and Folklife: An Introduction*, ed. Richard M. Dorson (Chicago: University of Chicago Press, 1972), pp. 159–72.

The Louisiana Federal Writers Project publication *Gumbo Ya Ya* (Boston: Houghton Mifflin, 1945), ed. Lyle Saxon, Edward Dreyer, and Robert Tallant, has much interesting information on superstitions, customs, and festivals of that state. Two general books on foreign festivals in the United States do not carefully distinguish natural survivals from self-conscious revivals, but they are, nevertheless, informative: Allen H. Eaton's *Immigrant Gifts to American Life* (New York: Russell Sage Foundation, 1932); and Helen R. Coates's *The American Festival Guide* (New York: Exposition Press, 1956). The "Festival Issue" of *WF* was 31:4 (1972); it contains studies of four regions.

Articles on individual foreign festivals in the United States have appeared with some frequency in the journal of the California Folklore Society; these include Wayland D. Hand's "*Schweizer Schwingen:* Swiss Wrestling in California," *CFQ* 2 (1943), 77–84; William Hoy's "Native Festivals of the California Chinese," *WF* 7 (1948), 240–50; Charles Speroni's "California Fishermen's Festivals," *WF* 14 (1955), 77–91; and Father John B. Terbovich's "Religious Folklore Among the German-Russians in Ellis County, Kansas," *WF* 22 (1963), 79–88. In another journal, see Roslynn Plemer, "The Feast of St. Joseph," *LFM* 2 (Aug. 1968), 85–90. A similar subject treated in book-length form and fully illustrated with photographs is *The Amish Year* by Charles S. Rice and Rollin C. Steinmetz (New Brunswick; N.J.: Rutgers University Press, 1956).

Two original essays on Louisiana Cajun customary life were included in Richard M. Dorson's *Buying the Wind:* Harry Oster's "Country Mardi Gras" (pp. 274–81), and Calvin Claudel's "Folkways of Avoyelles Parish" (pp. 235–45). John Rowe described "Cronish Emigrants in America" and their traditions in *Folk Life* 3 (1965), 25–38. For another group's traditions see Norine Dresser, "'Is It Fresh?' An Examination of Jewish-American Shopping Habits," *NYFQ* 27 (1971), 153–60.

Penitente ceremonies are treated in George C. Barker's "Some Aspects of Penitential Processions in Spain and the American Southwest," *JAF* 70 (1957), 137–42; and Juan Hernandez's "Cactus Whips and Wooden Crosses," *JAF* 76 (1963), 216–24. Svatava Pirkova-Jakobson described "Harvest Festivals among Czechs and Slovaks in America," in *JAF* 69 (1956), 266–80.

The North Carolina "New Year's Shoot" is included in Brewster's chapter in *North Carolina Folklore* (vol. 1; pp. 241–43). H. M. Belden gave a partial text of the Missouri "New Year's Sermon" in *Ballads and Songs Collected by the Missouri Folk-Lore Society*, University of Missouri Studies 15 (Columbia,

1940), p. 514. Ruth H. Cline described "Belsnickles and Shanghais," in *JAF* 71 (1958), 164–65. For information on similar celebrations in various states see Walter L. Robbins's note "Christmas Shooting Rounds in America and Their Background," *JAF* 86 (1973), 48–52. On related traditions see Charles E. Welch, Jr., " 'Oh Dem Golden Slippers': The Philadelphia Mummers Parade," *JAF* 79 (1966), 523–36, and Herbert Halpert and G. M. Story, eds., *Christmas Mumming in Newfoundland* (Toronto: University of Toronto Press, 1969).

Beatrice S. Weinreich analyzed "The Americanization of Passover" in *Studies in Biblical and Jewish Folklore*, ed. Raphael Patai and others, Indiana University Folklore Series no. 13 (Bloomington, 1960), 329–66.

John E. Baur's *Christmas on the American Frontier, 1800–1900* (Caldwell, Idaho: Caxton Press, 1961) sketches a broad view of the adaptation of European customs in the American wilderness; Elizabeth Bacon Custer, widow of General Custer, described her own western army-camp Christmases in a manuscript edited by Walter F. Peterson as "Christmas on the Plains" and published in *TAW* 1 (Fall 1964), 52–57. David W. Plath studied "The Japanese Popular Christmas: Coping with Modernity" in *JAF* 76 (1963), 309–17. The November 1971 issue of *NCF* (19:4) contains several articles on Christmas customs and beliefs in North Carolina.

Sarah Gertrude Knott, a founder and leading force of the National Folk Festival, described her early problems and experiences with it in "The National Folk Festival After Twelve Yars," *CFQ* 5 (1946), 83–93. An address by Stith Thompson on "Folklore and Folk Festivals" delivered to the annual conference of the National Folk Festival Association in 1953 was published in *MF* 4 (1954), 5–12.

A local folk music festival and its folkloristic significance is analyzed in Barre Toelken's "Traditional Fiddling in Idaho," *WF* 24 (1965), 259–62. Gerald Weales wrote a humorous description of the 1952 Georgia Tech Homecoming Game as "an annual semi-religious festival" in his article "Ritual in Georgia," *SFQ* 21 (1957), 104–9. His observations on dress, symbols, decoration, the parade, cheers, and ecstatic responses to the game would apply easily to many other American sporting events.

15

Folk Dances and Dramas

Dances and dramas began in ritual and developed into entertainment. They have, in common with superstitions, customs festivals, and games, significant oral and customary elements. Both dance and drama are essentially performances in which participants assume certain active roles, but also utter the speeches and songs, or sometimes directions, which accompany the action. Dance has been associated with drama since their ancient origins, so it may not be stretching Aristotle's definition too far to suggest that the list of six elements he proposed for the drama could fit dance almost as well: action, character, thought, language, spectacle, and music. To some degree, the student of folk dances and dramas will be concerned with all of these elements, as well as with such other aspects as structure, function, dissemination, and variation.

American folk dances and dramas have always constituted a decidedly minor field of folklore research, for neither has exhibited much oral vitality since the nineteenth century. Folk dances in this country persist almost exclusively as a recent revival (even though a lively one), while folk dramas, replaced by commercial entertainments, are represented only in the barest survival. However, even with these limitations, there are questions that remain unanswered, reference works that should be compiled, theories awaiting better analysis, and even some further collecting that might be done in the Anglo-American field. Many more opportunities for research appear if the scope is broadened to include ethnic and immigrant dances in this country.

"The dance," wrote Curt Sachs, historian of the subject, "is the mother of the arts." In its basic form of a rhythmic, stylized pattern of individual or group movement performed with or without music in response to a religious or creative urge, dance has existed in every known culture, including the most primitive, and it occurs even among animals. From the movements of dancing, Sachs suggested, were derived the other means of artistic expression, all of which eventually drifted away from close involvement with worship and the cycle of life to their current connections largely with self-expression and entertainment. **Folk dances** are those dances that are transmitted in a traditional manner, whatever their origin, and that have developed traditional variants, whatever their other developments. Perhaps more than in any other field of folklore, such distinctions are extremely difficult to apply. Probably it is best, as Curt Sachs suggested, for ethnological purposes to treat all dances equally.

Gertrude P. Kurath, the leading American student of primitive dance, has distinguished primitive dance from folk dance in terms of the relationship of dancing to the rest of a given culture: "Natural cultures dance from the cradle to the grave; mechanized society, for sociability and diversion." Certainly this holds true in the United States, for although we still hold dances as a matter of custom at graduations, holidays, and weddings, all of our dancing, whether folk or not, is performed for "sociability and diversion," and not as ritual. Still, the potential student of folk dance has a good deal to learn from the authority on primitive dance.

Kurath has answered very specifically the questions, "What does a field worker record during the study of native dances?" and "What can a non-specialist do in the presence of unexpected festivities?" The three fundamental matters to observe, she said, are the *ground plan* (location, participants, arrangements, geometry, progression), the *body movements* (steps, posture, arms), and the *structure* (repetition, combination). Observations should be made in the above order, and the observer finally should participate in the dance he or she is describing, especially for the fullest understanding of its structure.

Complex systems of precise dance notation have been created, perhaps the most widely-accepted and elaborate being the "Labanotation" invented by Rudolf von Laban in 1920. For the nonspecialist collector the minimal technique required is simply the employment of camera or sketch pad whenever possible, and the consistent use of a standardized vocabulary for descriptions. As Kurath has shown, such a term as "step" is misleading and vague, unless the collector distinguishes such variations as the shuffle, run, trot, slide, gallop, skip, leap, jump, and hop. The last three terms can serve to illustrate just how precise dance descriptions should be, for a *leap* is springing from one foot to the other, a *jump* is springing up with both feet simultaneously and landing on both feet, and a *hop* is springing up on one foot and landing on the same foot again.

Given an interest in collecting folk dances, and having established a list of questions and a vocabulary for field use, what is there for the modern student of American folk dance to observe? Regrettably, there is very little in a purely traditional context. The two forms of Americanized folk dances—square dances and play-parties—had died out in most localities by the 1930s. A few dance *songs* were later popularized by professional folk singers, and square dancing has enjoyed a vigorous revival as an organized recreation, but neither of these developments is part of a true folk process. As a result, American folk dance scholars must often content themselves with investigating the nature of the revival movement itself, or devote themselves to discovering, analyzing, and classifying historic accounts of folk dancing. American Indians and immigrant groups still provide opportunities for fieldwork in dance ethnography, as do regional styles of social dancing. Even the lore of professional dance companies, which deals with dance rehearsal and performance, might be studied. None of these possibilities is without considerable folkloristic interest, and such studies ought not to be delayed longer even if other forms of folklore in the United States now seem more vigorous than dance. Much that is taken for granted or is simply ignored about American folk dancing might well be clarified by systematic research.

Both square dances and play-parties developed from British traditions, the former from "country dances," and the latter seemingly from children's games. The terminology of early forms is badly confused. English **country dances** were usually either *rounds* (dancers standing in a circle) or *longways* (dancers in two lines facing each other). But the French, who had similar folk dances, associated the English word "country" with their term *"contre"* ("against") to produce the name *"contredanse"* for the "longways" type. The term then became Anglicized as "contradance." The country dances throughout Europe probably all represent, at least in part, inheritances via *gesunkenes Kulturgut* of such popular nineteenth-century social dances as the spirited *cotillion,* in which partners were exchanged, and the *quadrille,* a dance for four couples. Neither rounds nor longways persisted in American folk dancing proper, although both formations are found in children's games, and the still-popular "Virginia Reel" is a longways.

The **square dance** is an authentic American folk development of the Old-World four-couple dance. The terms "New England Quadrille," "Kentucky Running Set," and "Cowboy Square Dance" indicate the principal centers of development—the Northeast, the Midwest and southern mountains, and the Far West. The three most distinctive features of the square dance are the shuffling-gliding-running step, the hand-clapping done by both dancers and bystanders, and the chanted or sung "calls" giving directions for the steps. New England square dancing was rather restrained and formal, but the shuffling step or *sashay* (from French *chassé,* "dance") was already present. In the Midwest hand-clapping was added, calls were formalized as part of the dance, and new figures such as "Birdy in the Cage," and "Grand Right and Left" became popular. The West introduced hybrid steps from other social dances for "sashaying," as well as the device of occasionally having boys lift their partners from the ground during the "swing." Eventually all of these movements backtracked and merged to a degree which renders it impossible to sort out the origins of such colorfully named figures as "Box the Gnat," "Georgia Rang Tang," "Dip for the Oyster," "Ocean Wave," "Shoot the Owl," "Grapevine Twist," and "Wring the Dishrag."

In communities where religious influences prohibited all forms of dancing, as well as the sinful fiddle music which accompanied them, the play-party became popular as a substitute, at least such is the often-repeated explanation of this recreation. **Play-parties** were usually organized as rounds rather than squares and were performed to songs sung by the participants themselves rather than to instrumental music and a caller. In most regions, waist-swinging was forbidden, and boys held their partners by the hand instead. By such means the ban against dancing was circumvented. The terms employed for the two kinds of activities were kept carefully separated. Play-parties were "plays," "games," or even "bounce-arounds," and they were always "played," never "danced." But square-dancing parties were "hoedowns," "barn dances," "house dances," "kitchen dances," "shindigs," or even "hog wrassles." It should be emphasized that both of these kinds of activities were part of the social life of adults or adolescents of courting age, but never until recently were they held for children.

As ballroom couple-dancing became more acceptable and popular among Americans, square dances nearly died out before there were any folklorists in the United States to collect them, and their organized revival, part of the general rise in folklore interest beginning in the late 1930s, was in full swing by the time scholars had begun to notice the form. But play-parties lasted longer in folk tradition and were not revived on a large scale. Also the play-party song leaves more of a text to be remembered and collected than does the square-dance call. The result is that there are many more play-party songs and descriptions available in reliable folklore sources than there are accounts of square dances. The most pressing need in square-dance studies is to uncover more published and unpublished early accounts of dances so that a better idea of historical development may be gained. But in play-party studies the time is ripe for a basic reference work to be compiled, along the lines of Child's great ballad anthology, to organize and facilitate comparisons of the numerous play-party texts already in print. Both endeavors would contribute to the verification or replacement of the unproven play-party origin theory mentioned earlier.

Play-party movements and songs may seem simple and rather repetitious, but they have been very popular in folk tradition and have evolved into both children's games and fiddle tunes of lasting popularity. The texts and formations themselves are not without interest. A careful classification of play-parties would have to take into account that a few of them are archway formations, longways, and even squares, as well as round games, and that not all of them require only skipping around and singing—some involve dialogue and dramatic action, choosing, kissing, and progressive figures. Sometimes dance directions are embedded literally in the song as in this one, called "Miller Boy":

> Happy is the miller boy, that lives by the mill;
> He takes his toll with a free good will.
> One hand in the hopper and the other in the sack,
> *The ladies step forward and the gents step back.*

After a close study of "Miller Boy"—text, tune, and dance—Keith Cunningham concluded that "the poetics fit the action of the game."

In other play-parties, such as "Go In and Out the Window" and "The Needle's Eye," the dance movement is metaphorically suggested. Some songs sketch a character type—"Captain Jinks," "Old Dan Tucker," or "Cincinnati Girls"—while others mirror frontier life—"Shoot the Buffalo," "Wait for the Wagon," or "Weevily Wheat." A number of puzzling, but strangely effective, lines and verses in old play-party songs have yet to be explained. These include:

> Water, water, wine-flower
> Growing up so high.
> We are all young ladies,
> And we are sure to die.
>> (An American play-party derived from
>> the British children's game "Wallflowers.")
>
> *
>
> Coffee grows in the white oak tree,
> The rivers run with brandy.
> My little gal is a blue-eyed gal,
> As sweet as any candy.
>> (The first line is the common title.)
>
> *
>
> The higher up the cherry tree,
> The finer grow the cherries;
> The more you hug and kiss the girls,
> The sooner will they marry.
>> (From "Weevily Wheat.")

For pure straightforward defiance of logic, however, nothing can beat the popular line from "Skip to My Lou" that goes, "Little red wagon painted blue."

Sometimes a play-party or other dance song will tell a story and thereby suggest an incipient ballad, or a dramatic game of children. In the "Hog Drivers" play party the players take the roles of various characters. First the hog drivers march in and sing to a tavern keeper:

> Hog drivers, hog drivers, hog drivers are we,
> A-courting your daughter so fair and so free.
> Can we get lodging, here, oh here?
> Can we get lodging here?

To which he responds:

> I have a fair daughter who sits by my side,
> But no hog driver can get her for a bride.
> You can't get lodging here, oh here;
> You can't get lodging here.

The hog drivers than angrily sing:

> Fair is your daughter, but ugly yourself;
> We'll travel on farther and seek better wealth.
> We don't want lodging here, oh here;
> We don't want lodging here.

The conclusion of the play is that the tavern keeper's daughter whispers her choice of husbands to her father, who then stops the hog drivers' march and allows the lucky young man to stay on. While this play party is certainly related to other dramatic courtship games such as "Three Knights from Spain," it also reflects social life of eastern Tennessee and western North Carolina during the heyday of hog raising and driving in the late nineteenth century.

Another good example of a dramatic dance song is the following text collected in Edwardsville, Illinois, from an elderly woman who said it was verses for "Old Joe Clark." She sang it in a spirited manner to the tune often used for the dance song, "Great Big 'Taters in Sandy Land," or "Sally Ann."

> "Hey, old man, where you been at?"
> "Down the mountainside shootin' craps."

> "I told you once, I told you twice,
> You can't make a livin' throwin' dice.

> "Get out of my house and go to town,
> Make that wooden leg jar the ground.

> "Sift your meal and save the bran,
> You can't make a livin' on rocky land."

The **dramatic element in folklore** has already been demonstrated several times in previous chapters. The Wellerism is a dramatic vignette containing both speech and action. Riddles involve two roles—the questioner's and the respondent's. In asking non-oral riddles, the poser adds a dramatic gesture to his question. Such riddle-jokes as the "knock-knocks" have separate speaking roles for each participant. The skillful narrator of folktales must impersonate many characters, and there are distinct dramatic techniques for narrating different kinds of tales—the deadpan of the tall-tale artist, the broken English of the dialect-joke raconteur, the imitative sounds of the animal-tale teller. One American fiddle tune, "The Arkansaw Traveler," has a dramatic skit associated with it. In this sketch, not to be confused with the ballad "An Arkansas Traveller" or "The State of Arkansaw" (Laws H 1), there is a dialogue between a man traveling through the Arkansas countryside and a hillbilly fiddler that includes exchanges such as:

> Traveller: Where does this road go to?
> Fiddler: I been livin' here twenty years, and it ain't gone nowhere
> yet.

Most traditional ballads are dramatic, and those that are based on incremental repetition are usually related entirely in dialogue. A remarkable fluidity of dramatic form is illustrated in the American versions of "The Maid Freed from the Gallows" (Child 95). Here a condemned girl is standing on the scaffold waiting to be hanged and repeatedly asking her relatives, and finally her sweetheart, if they have come to set her free or merely "to see me hanged on the gallow's tree." Tristram P. Coffin has observed:

> The story itself has taken a number of forms in America. It is, particularly with Negroes, popular as a drama and is also found as a children's game. It exists as a prose tale in the United States and West Indies and upon occasion has been developed as a cante fable.

Folk games too are often dramatic, as Chapter 17 shows. One game, "Mother, Mother, the Milk's Boiling Over," is a fairly complex playlet with ten distinct roles—mother, hired girl (or nurse), a thief (or witch), and seven children who are named for the days of the week. Each time the mother goes out the thief distracts the hired girl and steals a child; the mother is summoned repeatedly by the cry "The milk's boiling over!" and she contrives, when the last child is gone, to win them all back, one by one, from the thief. In common with most older dramatic games, this one goes back to an English prototype. "Charades" is a popular parlor game that is entirely dramatic, while "Poppy Show" is an old amusement of little girls which consisted of arranging poppy petals between small sheets of glass and then charging one pin for a look; the showman chants:

> Pinny, pinny, poppy-show,
> Give me a pin and I'll let you know.

Although the dramatic element in folklore is common, full-scale folk drama is rare in the United States. **Folk drama** includes plays that are traditionally transmitted, usually for regular performance at such occasions as initiations, seasonal celebrations, festivals, and religious holidays. Traditional transmission, as with some folk rhymes, may in this case include handwritten manuscripts. The folklore justification of such texts is that they are variable from region to region and generation to generation, and that they originate in an unselfconscious folk milieu rather than from a sophisticated artistic background.

One living tradition of folk drama in the United States is part of the religious pageantry of the Spanish Southwest, especially at Christmastime, but also at Easter. There are also some secular Spanish-American folkplays. The Christmas play of the shepherds (*Los Pastores*) exists in the Southwest in many versions, and it has been collected and studied by three generations of American folklorists.

The traditional English Christmas drama, *The Mummers' Play*, with its masked band of begging participants, was known in the New World in the eighteenth century. (It is related to the New Year's "shoots" and "belsnickles" described in the last chapter.) The drama itself, although still found in Canada, never became firmly established here as a folk custom; today's elaborate New Year's parade in Philadelphia is the only organized outgrowth of English mumming in the United States. The Philadelphia parade, which stems from traditional backgrounds, was granted official civic support in 1900. Only two instances of genuine mummers' *plays* have been recorded from American informants since then. In 1909, a text was collected in St. Louis from an immigrant from Worcestershire, England, who had taken part in it as a boy thirty-five years earlier.

The play had the familiar stock characters of the English tradition—Father Christmas, St. George, The Turkish Knight, The Italian Doctor, and others. The plot unfolds in the manner of a pageant, each grotesquely costumed character coming forth to announce himself before engaging in the simple ritualistic action, the sequence of which is suggested by the conventional identification of the parts as presentation, combat, lament, cure, and quête [the collection of a reward for the actors]. In 1930 a group of Kentucky mountaineers performed a mummers' play for folklorist Marie Campbell to show her how they had formerly been acted. The announcer began with this revealing notice:

> We air now aiming to give a dumb show for to pleasure the little teacher for not going off to level country to keep Christmas with her kin. Hit ain't noways perfect the way we act this here dumb show, but hit ain't been acted out amongst our settlement for upward of twenty or thirty year, maybe more. I reckon folks all knows hit air bad luck to talk with the dumb show folks or guess who they air.

No native American folk plays of any significance have developed. The use of the term for written dramas based on folk themes is misleading, but, beginning in the 1920s a so-designated "school of folk drama" centered around the Carolina Playmakers at the University of North Carolina. Outstanding among this group's work were the plays of Paul Green, set in a regional framework, such as *In Abraham's Bosom* (1927) and *The House of Connelly* (1931). These plays, however, are literature, not folklore. Another group of outdoor dramas or pageants are sometimes billed as "folk" productions; these include *Tecumseh!* in Ohio, *The Stephen Foster Story* in Kentucky, *Vicksburg* in Mississippi, and a pageant about Joseph Smith in Palmyra, New York.

A case might be made for the blackface minstrel show, vaudeville, or for the entertainments of some medicine shows, carnivals, and riverboats as American folk drama. But a better candidate is a now-obscure traveling tent comedy that still survives in some parts of the Midwest—the "Toby shows." Named for their stereotyped leader character, a red-haired, freckle-faced, country bumpkin named Toby, these shows appeal to a rural carnival audience with a play based on wholesome, homespun, slapstick humor. The Toby character had emerged by 1911, and Toby shows were common throughout the Mississippi Valley and the Southwest through the 1930s. Only a few, however, were revived after World War II. The texts for Toby shows were usually based on nineteenth-century popular drama, but extemporaneous dialogue and stage business were common. At least one Toby show was reported still traveling in 1964, providing folklorists with a rare example of native folk drama in action.

Popular juvenile skits, which may derive from vaudeville or other stage comedy, are the only other shreds of possible folk drama to be found in the United States. About a dozen of these playlets are popular at children's summer camps, Boy Scout and Girl Scout meetings, Sunday School picnics, and the like. The best known is probably "You Must Pay the Rent," a farcial melodrama involving the classic figures of villain, his victim (a beautiful girl), and the hero. Often this skit is performed as a monologue with the actor using a ribbon bow alternately as the girl's hair ribbon, the hero's bow tie, and the villain's drooping mustache. Another favorite skit, "Baby Can Spell," is based on the everyday humor of a small child understanding the words that adults spell out in conversations to keep secrets from him—"c-a-n-d-y," "b-a-b-y," and "s-e-x," for instance. A skit called "The Nut Buying Cider" embodies an old folk jest about a fool who tries to carry a beverage home in his hat. When the hat has been poured full, he flops it over to fill the other side. "The Balky Flivver" makes use of six children crouched down to represent an automobile's wheels, motor, and spare tire; while in "The Murder of the Lighthouse Keeper" a circular staircase is suggested simply by having all the actors run around the central figure several times—one way for up, the other for down. One of these skits, "The King of Beasts," resembles a traditional frontier prank. In the skit a group of brawny boys pull a long rope across the stage to which is supposed to be attached the "king." Instead a small child riding a kiddy-car finally emerges tied to the end of the rope. In the prank called "The Badger Fight," a greenhorn on the frontier would be given the honor of pulling the fierce badger out of his box to do battle with a dog. When the greeny pulled on the leash, a chamber pot slid into view.

BIBLIOGRAPHIC NOTES

Curt Sachs's *World of the Dance* (New York: Norton, 1937; Norton Library paperback, 1963) is a basic study with emphasis on the development of movements, themes, and forms from ancient to modern types of dance. The essay "Dance: Folk and Primitive" by Gertrude P. Kurath is a comprehensive survey and a scholarly article in itself, although it appeared in *Funk & Wagnalls Standard Dictionary of Folklore, Mythology, and Legend*, volume 1 (1949), pp. 276–96. The sketch of the development of square dances in this chapter is based largely on this article.

Kurath published "A Choreographic Questionnaire," in *MF* 2 (1952), 53–55, and her note "A Basic Vocabulary for Dance Descriptions," was in *AA* 56 (1954) 1,102–3. She dealt with another field technique in "Photography for Dance Recording," *FFMA*, 5 (Winter 1963), 1, 4. Labanotation as a folkloristic tool was discussed by Juana de Laban in "Movement Notation: Its Significance to the Folklorist," *JAF* 67 (1954), 291–95; and Nadia Chilkovsky in "Dance Notation for Field Work," *FFMA* 2 (Fall 1959), 2–3. A useful reference is Andrea Greenberg's "The Notation of Folk Dance: A Survey," *FF* 5 (1972), 1–10.

Kurath began a dance department in *Ethnomusicology* in 1956 (Newsletter No. 7); it is a valuable source for current bibliography. Her article "Panorama of Dance Ethnology," in *CA* 1 (1960), 233–54 is based on eighteen months of correspondence with scholars the world over; a bibliography is appended, along with a list of dance studies in progress and of dance films. An analytical article by Kurath demonstrates the possibilities of dance ethnology: "Dance Relatives of Mid-Europe and Middle America: A Venture in Comparative Choreology," *JAF* 69 (1956), 286–98.

Other professional students of folk dance are rare in the United States. The 1965 "Works in Progress" report published by the American Folklore Society listed only two besides Gertrude Kurath engaged in dance research, and both were writing historical studies. Such a work, with implications for folklore studies, is Marshall and Jean Stearns's *Jazz Dance: The Story of American Vernacular Dance* (New York: Macmillan, 1972). The situation in folk drama is no better. Five scholars are listed, but three are concerned with the use of folklore in literary drama, one is restricted to Spanish-American plays, and only one is studying general folk drama.

The American folk dance revival movement can be traced back to the English Folk Dance Society, founded by Cecil Sharp in 1911, which merged with the Folk Song Society (founded in 1898) in 1930. An American branch was organized in 1915 and later took the name the Country Dance Society of America. Ralph Vaughn Williams outlined the history of the English societies in an article in *EM* 2 (1958), 108–12; see also the similar article by S. R. S. Pratt in *JFI* 2 (1965), 294–99. Anyone interested in these movements should study the back numbers not only of *The Journal of the English Folk Dance and Song Society* and *English Dance and Song*, but also *The Folk Dancer* and *The Folklorist*, and the American periodicals *Folk Dance Guide* and *American Squares*. *Dance Magazine* also occasionally publishes articles on folk dancing.

Books associated with the revival of square dancing are too numerous to list in detail. A typical early one was Grace L. Ryan's *Dances of Our Pioneers* (New York: A. S. Barnes, 1939). Lloyd Shaw wrote two influential works,

Cowboy Dances: A Collection of Western Square Dances (rev. ed., Caldwell, Idaho: Caxton Press, 1952), and *The Round Dance Book: A Century of Waltzing* (Caldwell, Idaho: Caxton Press, 1950). A book that features a brief opening note by folklorist Louise Pound is Cornelia F. Putney and Jesse B. Flood's *Square Dance, U.S.A.* (Dubuque, Iowa: W. C. Brown Co., 1955). Most revivalist collections do not state their sources, but David S. McIntosh's *Singing Games and Dances* (New York, 1957) published by the National Board of Young Men's Christian Associations does—his own field work in southern Illinois. An account of folk dance revival and dance festivals in California is Virginia C. Anderson's, "It All Began Anew: The Revival of Folk Dancing," *WF* 7 (1948), 162–64.

There are no scholarly studies of square dances in American folklore journals, but an aid for such studies has been published in J. Olcutt Sanders' article "Finding List of Southeastern Square Dance Figures," in *SFQ* 6 (1942), 263–75. Sanders began by commenting on the meager list of reliable sources available for information on old-time square dancing, and the situation is little better years later. A type of needed historical work is represented by John Q. Wolf's "A Country Dance in the Ozarks in 1874," in *SFQ* 29 (1965), 319–21, and Robert D. Bethke's "Old-Time Fiddling and Social Dance in Central St. Lawrence County," in *NYFQ* 30 (1974), 164–84. The danger of an overenthusiastic folklore revival movement not having a solid background of scholarly knowledge was illustrated in an exchange published in *Western Folklore* in 1956 and 1957. A "Cowpuncher's Square Dance Call" was printed in one issue (15: 125–26) as a previously unpublished example of the "real thing," and a contrast to the "cheap imitations" of today. But folklorist Sam Hinton pointed out later (16: 129–31) that not only had the same stanzas been several times published earlier, but that they were not a dance call at all, but a poem by a known author describing a dance, and that the verses could not possibly function as a square-dance call.

The pioneering book on play-parties was Leah Jackson Wolford's *The Play-Party in Indiana* (Indianapolis, 1917). It was revised by W. Edson Richmond and William Tillson and republished as volume 20 of the *Indiana Historical Society Publications*, pp. 103 to 326, in 1959. The discussion on page 262 of the classification of play-parties is partly drawn from Wolford's introduction in the revised edition of her book. Wolford drew all her examples from Ripley County, Ind. B. A. Botkin collected Oklahoma play-parties for his study *The American Play-Party Song* (Lincoln: University of Nebraska, 1937; reissued, New York, 1963). A third collection is drawn entirely from another state— S. J. Sackett's *Play-Party Games from Kansas*, in *Heritage of Kansas* 5 (Emporia; Sept. 1961). The Sackett work should be supplemented by the chapter "Dances and Games" in the same author's *Kansas Folklore* (Lincoln: University of Nebraska Press, 1961), pp. 209–25, as well as by Alan Dundes's review in *JAF* 76 (1963), 251–52, which adds several Kansas references.

Numerous play-parties from other regions have been published in *JAF*, including texts from western Maryland—54 (1941), 162–66; eastern Illinois—32 (1919), 486–96; the Midwest generally—25 (1912), 268–73 and 28

(1915), 262–89; and Idaho—44 (1931), 1–26. Richard Chase includes some square dances and play-parties in his paperback anthology *American Folk Tales and Songs* (New York: New American Library of World Literature, 1956; Dover Publications Repr., 1971). The basic tool for bringing together many of the available texts is Altha Lea McLendon's, "A Finding List of Play-Party Games," *SFQ* 8 (1944), 201–34.

A good analytic review of publications on play-parties was published by Keith Cunningham in *AFFWord*, 2 (April 1972), 12–23. An excellent study of the historical background of a play-party is John Q. Anderson's " 'Miller Boy,' One of the First and Last of the Play-Party Games," *NCFJ* 21 (1973), 171–76. Some interesting contextual and comparative notes on another example, published by a non-folklorist, is Edmund Cody Burnett's "The Hog Drivers' Play-Song and Some of its Relatives," *Agricultural History* 23 (1949), 161–68.

The dramatic dance song on page 265 was collected from Mrs. Mary Jane Fairbanks, age 95, residing at the Anna Henry Nursing Home in Edwardsville, Illinois, on December 3, 1965. George Morey Miller discussed "The Dramatic Element in the Popular Ballad" in *University Studies of the University of Cincinnati*, Series 2, vol. 1, no. 1 (1905). The quotation from Tristram P. Coffin is from *The British Traditional Ballad in North America* discussed in Chapter 11. "Poppy Show" is described in W. W. Newell's *Games and Songs of American Children*, and in Lady Gomme's collection of English games, both cited in Chapter 17.

Richard M. Dorson discusses *Los Pastores* in his book *American Folklore* (Chicago: University of Chicago Press, 1959), pp. 103–7. He cites the basic bibliography of Spanish-American folk drama on page 293. A translation of some scenes of the shepherd's play is given in Dorson's *Buying the Wind* (Chicago: University of Chicago Press, 1964), pp. 466–79. To Dorson's list of sources should be added John E. Englekirk's two-part article "The Passion Play in New Mexico," *WF* 25 (1966), 17–33, 105–21.

Standard works on the English mummers' play are R. J. E. Tiddy's *The Mummers' Play* (Oxford: Oxford University Press, 1923); E. K. Chambers' *The English Folk-Play* (Oxford: Oxford Universtiy Press, 1933), and Violet Alford's *Sword Dance and Drama* (London: Merlin Press, 1962). Charles E. Welch, Jr., traced the history of the Philadelphia Mummers' Parade in *KFQ* 8 (1963), 95–106; related material is cited in the notes to the previous chapter. The mummers' texts collected in the United States were published in Antoinette Taylor's "An English Christmas Play," *JAF* 22 (1909), 389–94; and Marie Campbell's "Survivals of Old Folk Drama in the Kentucky Mountains," *JAF* 51 (1938), 10–24.

Information on the "school of folk drama" may be found in Robert E. Spiller *et al.*, *Literary History of the United States*, 4th edn., revised, (New York: Macmillan, 1974), pp. 722–24, and *Bibliography*, p. 200. Charles G. Zug III evaluates this material and its relationship to traditional folk drama in an article in *SFQ* 32 (1968), 279–94.

Larry Dale Clark submitted his story "Toby Shows: A Form of American Popular Theatre" as his Ph.D. dissertation at the University of Illinois in

1963; see *Dissertation Abstracts* 24 (May 1964), 4,858. Carol Pennepacker described "A Surviving Toby Show: Bisbee's Comedians," in *TSFB* 30 (1964), 49–52; and Jere C. Mickel published "The Genesis of Toby: A Folk Hero of the American Theater," in *JAF* 80 (1967), 334–40.

An interesting southern black religious drama is described in Redding S. Sugg, Jr., "Heaven Bound," *SFQ* 27 (1963), 249–66.

A collection of eleven popular skits was compiled by Norris Yates as "Children's Folk Plays in Western Oregon," *WF* 9 (1951), 55–62, but these playlets are by no means peculiar to that region, nor does this article exhaust the list of such skits.

16

Folk Gestures

Gestures are a silent language made up of movements of the body, or a part of it, used to communicate emotions or ideas. As such, they are an important aspect of informants' total performances, and, as Mac-Edward Leach emphasized in an essay on folklore collecting, we should try to record everything, the "voice—tone and inflection—gestures, facial expressions, [and] attitudes as well as words." To retain the fullest possible report, field collectors sometimes photograph the typical gestures informants use, or they describe them, as in the following passage from Richard M. Dorson's discussion of black storytellers:

> When the rabbit scoots away from the fox, or John runs from the Lord, the narrator slaps his hands sharply together, with the left sliding off the right palm in a forward direction—a manual trademark of the Negro raconteur.

Gestures that accompany folktales may be stylized, like these raconteurs', or like snapping the fingers to emphasize "Just like that!" They may also be introduced from everyday behavior—shrugging the shoulders to indicate doubt, flexing a bicep to show strength, shading the eyes when looking for something, raising an imaginary gun to shoot—whatever fits the action occurring in the tale. However, some folktale plots include specific gestures that are a necessary part of the performance. For example, Aarne-Thompson Type 924, "Discussion By Sign Language," and its subtypes concern manual-sign conversations that are sometimes mutually misunderstood, but still are finished to the complete satisfaction of both parties. In a riddle joke with gestures the question is asked why a stupid fellow has hunched shoulders and a dent in the middle of his forehead. The explanation is that when you ask him a question he "goes like this" (shrugging the shoulders), and when you explain it, he "does this" (slapping the palm of one hand to the forehead). The non-oral riddles described in Chapter 6 are other traditional questions involving gestures, and among children's chants, rhymes, and songs are further gesture pieces.

Superstitions, too, often involve traditional gestures. Crossing the fingers, tossing spilled salt over the left shoulder, and knocking on wood for good luck are familiar ones, as are the actions sometimes performed to seal a pact between children—crossing one's heart, raising the right hand in imitation of courtroom swearing, and spitting on the ground. When two Americans say the same words at the same time, they may hook little fingers and say "Needles-Pins," and make a wish; Spaniards hook the same finger, but say "Cervantes." Rituals of witchcraft make use of special gestures and symbols, and some body movements are believed to have the power to cast the "evil eye" on someone else, or to avert its power from oneself. An ancient one for the latter purpose is made by extending the forefinger and little finger of one hand and clenching the others—the "Devil's Horns." The sign of the cross is commonly made, outside of any formal religious context, to ward off bad luck.

A folk game involving gestures is "Rocks, Paper, and Scissors." Manual imitations of these three objects are given by several players sitting in a circle, gesturing in unison, and keeping time to a strict rhythmic beat. Penalties fall to players according to the formula that "paper covers rock, rocks break scissors, and scissors cut paper." Thus those who signed "paper" win over rock, rock over scissors, and scissors over paper. The punishment is a sharp slap on the wrist dealt by winners to losers, using the first two fingers of one hand held together, and dampened with the tongue before striking, and play continues until a player's wrist is too sore to go on.

Although gestures often accompany speech, a simple and familiar one by itself can communicate eloquently to those who know its customary meaning. Even animals employ such gestures—the friendly dog's wagging tail, for instance. Such use partly explains the long-term effectiveness of the famous United States Army recruiting poster that shows Uncle Sam pointing directly at the viewer. A profile representation of a pointing finger was once a common American direction sign, while the picture showing a forefinger laid across the lips, once posted in libraries, commanded, "Silence!" Advertisers, fashion photographers, and drama directors still make use of such well-known conventional gestures to convey desired feelings to their audiences. Many proverbial phrases contain references to gestures that have unambiguous meanings, such as "to turn up one's nose at" (scorn), "to keep a stiff upper lip" (courage), "to tear one's hair" (rage), and "to raise an eyebrow" (surprise, shock, or skepticism). The very word "supercilious" derives from the Latin terms for the gesture of raising eyebrows to denote haughtiness.

Any mannerism associated with passing on oral traditions may interest the folklore collector, but not all gestures are *folk* gestures. Some are merely **autistic, or nervous, personal gestures;** these include drumming with the fingers, jingling change, fussing with hair or clothing, biting the lips or fingernails, and cracking knuckles. Only a few of these—such as "twiddling" the thumbs, or stroking the chin or beard—may become stereotyped signs for certain attitudes, and then begin to circulate traditionally. Closely related to autistic gestures are **culture-induced gestures**—aspects of sitting, walking, hand movements, and stance which are learned unconsciously from one's cultural surroundings and employed as a symbolic code. Other movements belong to **technical gesture systems** that are usually taught by formal methods. The military salute is a good example of this: it is described precisely, with its proper use, in military manuals, and its correct form is instilled in every new member of the group. But a traditional mock version of the salute, which turns into the derisive gesture of "thumbing the nose," can be considered a folk gesture. The saying associated with this variation goes, "I salute the captain of the ship;/Pardon me, my finger slipped."

Complex systems of technical gestures are important for special uses, the best known being communication between deaf-mutes. American Indian sign language constitutes another highly developed system, as do religious gestures for prayer and worship, and gestures used for communication within certain monastic orders. Many occupations require that a special gesture language be flawlessly learned and consistently performed time after time. Umpires and referees of various sports have their strict systems, as do radio and television performers, land surveyors, music conductors, traffic and airport directors, auctioneers, and even surgeons, who use some hand signals during operations to request instruments from a nurse.

These occupational gestures that are learned from manuals or special instructors have their folk counterparts in others used in the same occupations that pass on through tradition. For example, the railroad worker's operating rulebooks show only a few official hand signals, but railroad men have other gestures of their own invention used for special purposes. If an inspector or other company authority is on a train, the signal may be given with the thumbs stuck into an imaginary vest. Another is the gesture of pretending to scratch one's head a few inches out in the air to indicate that the "big heads" are approaching. Similarly, truck drivers long used the two-finger "V" sign to signal between two trucks that a police patrol car is ahead. Automobile drivers picked up the same signal to warn oncoming cars of a radar speed-trap ahead.

Some systems of gesturing, such as those used for bidding in different kinds of auction sales, may have been folk gestures originally that were later regularized and formally adopted. Other systems, such as those used by a particular athletic team or coach to signal strategy, may be largely individual and secret. Whenever an occupation demands communicating in secrecy (as in professional baseball), or above the sound of loud noises (as in sawmills), or across a considerable distance (as when fencing a farm or ranch), then both systematized and informal gestures can be expected to develop.

A true **folk gesture** is one that is kept alive by tradition and that exhibits some variation in action or meaning. Most obscene gestures clearly qualify as "folk." Like customs, folk gestures tend to pattern themselves within national boundaries. An American waves goodbye with his palm out; Italians keep the palm turned in. Americans "thumb" a ride, while many Europeans wave the whole hand up and down when hitchhiking. Western peoples tend to point to themselves at chest level; Orientals point to their own noses. To signify that something is "just right," a Frenchman places his right index finger tip on the right thumb tip and kisses them both, while an American forms a circle with the same two fingers, holds that hand up, and gives it a little shake. In Sicily the same idea is conveyed by pinching the cheek, in Brazil by tugging on an ear lobe, and in Colombia by pulling down a lower eyelid. Kissing, considered as a gesture, displays several variations; *where* the kiss is applied is significant—the lips, cheek, forehead, back of hand, "blown" from the fingers or palm, and so forth. A greeting that consists of two kisses rapidly applied, one to each cheek, immediately seems to identify the performer as a Frenchman, though several other European cultures use this greeting too. Kissing a ring, a Bible, a piece of someone's clothing, or a photograph are widespread signs of extreme devotion.

An excellent example of a culturally significant gesture having a secret communications use was described in a news story during the Korean conflict. An American Air Force captain recounting his experiences as a prisoner in North Korea told how he was photographed with other prisoners in a mocked-up library, presumably to show the world how well they were being treated. To counter the propaganda value of the pictures, he made the sign of the "Devil's Horns" in each one, which to Americans is the "bull sign" or "baloney." To his captors, the gesture was innocuous, and the pictures were released to the press. In 1968 some members of the captured United States vessel *Pueblo* managed to repeat this trick, using an obscene gesture, when they too were photographed.

Gestures of greeting have become well established in different cultures and seldom change much, but the degree of formality in a social situation may allow for some variation in the greeting employed. Thus, a firm handshake is "correct" in some situations, while a hearty slap on the back or playful rumpling of the other's hair is better for others. Beginning with jazz musicians, and quickly spreading to other Americans, was an exaggerated handshake that began with a dramatic "windup" and the remark, "Give me some skin, man!" and culminated with the hands or fingers barely touching. Another playful American greeting is the manual imitation of shooting a revolver at someone else, usually accompanied by a wink, and sometimes by the expression, "Gottcha!" There are also mock handshakes, supposedly appropriate for different occupations; the "farmers' handshake" has the thumbs of one person turned down and being "milked" by the second person, and the "politicians' handshake" begins with great enthusiasm, and ends with the two parties reaching over each other's shoulders to pick each other's pockets. Many athletic teams and other groups (probably learning to do so from black members) use complicated little palm-slapping patterns as gestures of greeting.

No standard system of classifying folk gestures has been adopted. Some collectors have used the parts of the body as a basis for arrangement, while others classify in terms of meanings expressed. Some collections have not been put in any special order, but were simply published as random lists. A better possibility may lie in trying to establish categories based on the *nature* of different gestures. As has been shown, some are parodies of technical gestures or derivations from autistic gestures. Others imitate letters of the alphabet (forming a "C" with the hand to invite someone to have coffee with you), or they signify numbers (gestures to hot dog salesmen in grandstands). It might be noted that even the procedure for counting on the fingers is culturally determined. Germans begin counting with the thumb, so an American tourist holding up his index finger to order a beer is actually ordering *two*.

There are gestures borrowed for general folk use from a specialized application (the prizefighters' victory sign of hands joined over the head, wagging in jubilation and triumph). Some gestures come directly to the point, such as touching a wrist watch or cupping a hand behind the ear as signals to a speaker, or holding the nose as a reaction to an idea. Other gestures are more abstract, such as that of circling the forefinger around one ear to mean "crazy" (something loose in the head?), or rubbing one forefinger held at right angles against the other toward another person for "shame" (shedding the "dirt?"). A large group of folk gestures could be classed as pantomimic—that is, they are an acting out of the intended message. We gesture and say "Chalk one up" in the air with imaginary chalk against an invisible blackboard, as if keeping score of our "goofs"; and we pretend to slash the throat with a finger to show that a certain kind of trouble has occurred or is soon expected. Other pantomime gestures are those of playing an invisible violin, for mock sympathy; mopping the brow, for great exertion; breathing on and pretending to polish the fingernails, for self-pride; and smoothing an eyebrow with a dampened little finger, used by males to denote effeminacy in other males.

Gestures can be studied historically, geographically, comparatively, and structurally, like any other kind of folklore, although very few such investigations have been made. Most published studies of gestures are physiological, linguistic, or psychological, and thus beyond the scope of this survey. Two, however deserve mention.

In 1944 a psychologist published his detailed study of the "V for

Victory" campaign among the Allied nations, during World War II, an outstanding instance of morale boosting by means of symbolism. To anyone who remembers the war years, the image of Winston Churchill flashing the "V" gesture with his two fingers raised immediately comes to mind. But the sign was carried much further during the war in posters, advertising, the "dot-dot-dot-dash" of Morse code, and even through allusion to the code "V" by playing or humming the first phrase of Beethoven's *Fifth Symphony* (da,da,da,DA). The study traced the history of the campaign, schematized the communications process involved in it, analyzed the types of symbolism found, and described the degeneration of the symbol as it was widely applied apart from its original context. More recently, of course, the "V" sign, while retaining its "victory" meaning among athletes, politicians running for office, etc., has also become a sort of peace-and-pot greeting or recognition among young people, and it has an entirely separate function in the Cub Scouts organization, calling meetings to order and signifying ideals of the group.

Archer Taylor has produced the only full-length folkloristic study of a gesture in English in his work on the so-called "Shanghai Gesture," or thumbing the nose, also called "cocking a snook," "Queen Anne's fan," "taking a sight," and other names. After an exhaustive survey of the gesture in art, literature, news media, and oral tradition, Taylor concluded that it originated in Western Europe and had been known in Great Britain during the sixteenth century. It did not become faddish in England until early in the nineteenth century. In the United States it was first described by Washington Irving in *Diedrich Knickerbocker's History of New York* (1809), and it was well known by 1862 when Mark Twain made it the basis of his hoax in "The Petrified Man." Ezra Pound alluded to it in a poem in 1917, and since then numerous American writers and illustrators have continued to describe and picture it. Only recently, Taylor felt, has the gesture acquired an obscene connotation—the end result of its becoming increasingly more insulting as time passed.

Since 1956, when Taylor's study was published, the gesture has continued to be popular—*and* insulting. In 1959–60, for example, which was designated World Refugee Year, some sensitive English people became alarmed when postmarks depicting the symbol for that year—an outstretched, empty hand—occasionally became imprinted on canceled letters over stamps bearing Queen Elizabeth's picture so as to show Her Majesty delivering a perfect Shanghai Gesture.

BIBLIOGRAPHIC NOTES

There are a few small collections of American gestures but almost no studies of them, although groundwork for analysis as been laid. No "Gestures" heading exists in the index to *JAF* for volumes 1 to 70 (1888–1958), and no articles on gestures have appeared there since, but a key work appeared elsewhere in 1957: Francis C. Hayes's "Gestures: A Working Bibliography," *SFQ* 21, 218–317. Hayes's bibliography includes both foreign and English references, popular articles as well as scholarly ones, and some descriptions of specific gestures from literature and popular media. Obscure and unpublished items are included, and many entries are annotated, with their presence in four American libraries indicated.

Survey articles on gestures as folklore are rare. Charles Francis Potter's work in *Funk & Wagnalls Standard Dictionary of Folklore, Mythology, and Legend* (1, 451–53) is largely anthropological and religious in its orientation. A better survey is Levette J. Davidson's "Some Current Folk Gestures and Sign Languages," *AS* 25 (1950), 3–9; a more recent and more detailed one is Robert A. Barakat's "Gesture Systems" in *KFQ* 14 (1969), 105–21. Barakat also provides a very detailed discussion of more than two hundred "Arabic Gestures" in *JPC* 6 (1973), 749–93, which may serve as a model for similar surveys in other cultures.

MacEdward Leach's comment quoted at the beginning of this chapter is from "Problems of Collecting Oral Literature," *PMLA* 77 (1962), 335–40. Richard M. Dorson described gestures of black storytellers in *Negro Folktales in Michigan* (Cambridge, Mass.: Harvard University Press, 1956), p. 24. The gestures of Austrian storytellers are discussed and pictured in Karl Haiding's, *"Von der Gebärdensprache der Märchenerzähler,"* *FFC* no. 155 (1955).

A comprehensive treatment of gestures, written by a neurologist, is MacDonald Critchley's, *The Language of Gesture* (London: E. Arnold Co., 1939). Ernest Thompson Seton's book *Sign Talk* (Garden City, N.Y.: Doubleday, 1918) proposed an ingenious "universal signal code without apparatus" that borrowed gestures freely from various technical systems as well as from folk usage. An ambitious theoretical work, fully illustrated, that involves gestures in part, is Jurgen Ruesch and Weldon Kees's *Nonverbal Communication: Notes on the Visual Perception of Human Relations* (Berkeley and Los Angeles: University of California Press, 1961).

Francis C. Hayes distinguished technical, autistic, and folk gestures in his essay "Should We Have a Dictionary of Gestures?", in *SFQ* 4 (1940), 239–45. In addition, Professor Franz H. Bäuml of the University of California at Los Angeles has been working on a dictionary of gestures for several years.

Articles that present occupational folk gestures are Charles Carpenter's, "The Sign Language of Railroad Men," *American Mercury* 25 (Feb. 1932), 211–13; and C. Grant Loomis's "Sign Language of Truck Drivers," *WF* 15 (1956), 205–6.

Mario Pei discusses different nationalities and their typical gestures in *The Story of Language* (Philadelphia: Lippincott 1949). Some of his findings were illustrated with photographs of people performing the gestures in "Gesture Language," *Life* (January 9, 1950), pp. 79–81. An article in German by Lutz Röhrich contains thirty-seven plates illustrating historical gestures. See "*Gebärdensprache und Sprachgebärde,*" in *Humaniora: Essays in Literature, Folklore, Bibliography Honoring Archer Taylor on his Seventieth Birthday,* editors Wayland D. Hand and Gustave O. Arlt (Locust Valley, N.Y.: J. J. Augustin, 1960), pp. 121–49. Characteristic gestures of Spanish-speaking peoples were described in Walter Vincent Kaulfers's, "Curiosities of Colloquial Gestures," *Hispanica* 14 (1931), 249–64. The North Korean incident was reported in Captain Harold E. Fischer, Jr.'s "My Case as a Prisoner was Different," *Life* (June 27, 1955), pp. 147–60. A photograph of Fischer making the gesture (which *Life* termed "the whammy sign") is found on page 157 of that issue of *Life*.

Three lists of gestures from California have appeared: Charlotte McCord described thirty collected from the Berkeley campus of the University of California in *WF* 7 (1948), 290–92; William S. King added ten more in *WF*, 8 (1949), 263–64, and Jean Cooke published a strangely mistitled list of forty more gestures from Berkeley in "A Few Gestures Encountered in a Virtually Gestureless Society," *WF* 18 (1959), 233–37. None of these notes has bibliography. Many instances of gestures used by English children are cross-referenced under "gesture" in the index to Peter and Iona Opie's *The Lore and Language of Schoolchildren* (Oxford: Oxford University Press, 1959).

Edgar A. Schuler's article "V for Victory: a Study in Symbolic Social Control," appeared in *JSP* 19 (1944), 283–299. Further developments in the uses and meanings of the V-sign are illustrated in Jan Harold Brunvand, "Popular Culture in the Folklore Course," in Ray B. Browne and Ronald J. Ambrosetti, *Popular Culture and Curricula* (Bowling Green, Ohio: Bowling Green University Popular Press, 1970), pp. 59–72. Archer Taylor's "The Shanghai Gesture" was in *FFC* no. 166 (1956). Taylor added an English description of the gesture from shortly after 1810 in "The Shanghai Gesture in England," *WF* 23 (1964), 114. Wirephotos of canceled letters from England, with and without the embarrassing juxtaposition of open hand and royal nose, were distributed by the Associated Press in 1959 and printed in American newspapers.

17
Folk Games

Children's traditional games offer an ideal topic for folklore research. They are passed from child to child in almost pure oral tradition with no reference whatever to print, and probably with negligible influence from teachers, parents, or recreation leaders. The players are naturally conservative about their texts and will strive to maintain the "right way" of playing against all variations. Thus old games may survive, little altered, through many generations of children. Children's games also develop clear regional subtypes. When families change neighborhoods or move to other communities, the children will soon discover whether their old versions are played in the new home or whether they must adopt new ones, for seldom do newcomers succeed in converting their playmates to outside games. Finally, children are usually excellent informants—easy to locate, eager to perform, and uninhibited with their responses.

The folk games all people play, whether children, adolescents, or adults, may be based on the movements of the body (stepping, running, hopping, jumping, etc.), on simple social activities (chasing, hiding, fighting, dramatizing, etc.), on chance (the fall of dice, cards, bones, coins, etc.), or on elementary mathematics or mechanics (counting, sorting, balancing, throwing, handling equipment, etc.). These common foundation blocks may explain the similarity of certain games through long periods of time and in widespread cultures, or diffusion of folklore may better account for some similar forms. (It is the question once again of polygenesis versus diffusion from a single origin). Only detailed studies of many versions of different games can begin to suggest answers to such questions.

By their very nature as voluntary recreations with rules fixed only by custom and tradition, folk games reveal much about the societies in which they are played and about the individuals who play them.

Game preferences, the forms of games, local variations, attitudes toward play, and play behavior are all valuable cultural, sociological, and psychological data to be documented and analyzed. In such research, the nonverbal elements of games are significant along with such verbal ones as traditional sayings, rhymes, or songs associated with games. Good fieldwork in folk games requires that one describe the action clearly and logically; secure all variations in names, rules, and texts; sketch or photograph all diagrams or equipment; and collect the full social and contextual background of the game along with the text. Useful projects in game study would include collecting the games of one family, neighborhood, school class, or season.

It is not surprising that the first American folklorists were interested in collecting and studying folk games. For example, W. W. Newell, charter member of the American Folklore Society in 1888 and first editor of its journal, had already published a classic study, *Games and Songs of American Children,* five years earlier. But this early interest declined when folklorists assumed that children had abandoned folk games, resulting in only a scattering of articles and notes on folk games in this country until Paul G. Brewster's book *American Non-Singing Games,* appeared in 1953 to balance the picture Newell had given by describing the games without songs that Newell had ignored. Since then there has been increasing interest in game analysis among American scholars, and a comprehensive sociopsychological, anthropological, and folkloristic theory of play and games seems to be emerging as studies illuminate how role-playing and competition in games reveal underlying motives and reflect on other behavior.

The problem of classifying games, basic to further research, has not been completely solved. The singing or non-singing dichotomy suggested by Newell's and Brewster's works is no better than other proposed systems that separate games of boys from those of girls, or indoor from outdoor games, or games of different age groups. One writer suggests grouping games into four classes depending upon the elements of competition, chance, mimicry, or vertigo (motion alone, i.e., teeter-tottering). But these categories are too broad for classification purposes, and it is not clear that the last two represent games at all. A better grouping made by anthropologists classifies games according to their requirements for either physical skill, strategy, or chance. This has proved meaningful for studying the relationship of games to cultural and environmental factors. But for folklore purposes—especially folklore archiving—a more workable classification might be made on the basis of the primary kind of play activity involved—whether physical action, manipulation of objects, or mental activity.

First, **pastimes** (or "amusements") must be distinguished from true games. A pastime, as the name suggests, is a traditional recreation performed simply to pass the time away. It lacks what true games have—the element of competition, the possibility of winning or losing, and a measure of organization with some kind of controlling rules. Most pastimes are solo activities such as bouncing a ball, juggling, balancing oneself or an object, swinging, walking on stilts, spinning a top, operating a yo-yo, and making "Cat's Cradles" (string patterns on one's fingers). When two or more individuals toss a ball about, they are engaging in a mere pastime as long as they introduce no rules and no way of distinguishing a winner. Yo-yoing, top-spinning, rope-jumping, or other such activities may lead to a contest of skill or of endurance and thus turn into true games. Two people balance on a teeter-totter more commonly than just one (in the middle of the board), and sometimes two may swing together with one seated and the other standing and "pumping"; these activities, however, remain pastimes. There are even four-handed cat's cradles in which the ever-changing design in the string loop is passed back and forth from one person to another.

A solo recreation, on the other hand, may be a game—"Solitare," for instance, is played against an imaginary opponent, and the player may win, or (more commonly) lose. Puzzle solving is something of a game if one thinks of "winning" by finishing the picture or word pattern in a specified time with no outside help. We even bribe ourselves to finish unpleasant or tiresome tasks by "making a game of it" or by promising ourselves a reward upon completion. Evidently problems such as the range of different folk recreations and the extent of oral tradition involved in them remain unsolved.

Games of physical action may be subdivided by the principal action involved. There are *hopping games* ("Hopscotch"), *chasing games* ("Red Rover"), *hiding games* ("Hide and Seek"), *battle games* ("Prisoners' Base"), and *dramatic games* ("Farmer in the Dell"), to list only the major kinds. At their simplest level, such games are merely outlets for high spirits and a means of getting lively exercise. They provide healthy competitions in strength and skill between individuals or teams. Games like running races, "Leap Frog," "Tag," "Johnny on the Pony," and "King on the Hill" satisfy these needs, but they have other dimensions too. In "Tag," for instance, if "it" is thought of as a fearsome aggressor, possibly the Devil, the safety gained by touching iron (long used to avert evil spirits) or wood (the cross), and the truce cry "King's-X" (royal pardon plus the cross) are all readily understood. (Probably the game as well as the basic symbolism is pre-Christian.) Any doubts that children's games might contain such underlying themes are shaken by the actual appearance of the names "black man" or "Devil" for "it" in many games still in current circulation. Also, hopscotch patterns that have "Heaven" at one boundary and "Hell" at the other are not unusual.

Some types of hiding games illustrate the variety of play that is possible on the basis of one simple concept. In many of these all but one player hide and the person who is "it" searches; various rules govern "it"'s activities while finding other players. In other games one person hides and the others search, and in one ("Sardines") the searchers join the hider one-by-one as they discover him until all are crammed into one hiding place. Still other varieties of hiding games involve a whole team of players hiding and another team searching, or an object or objects are hidden and the players search. Truce terms and sanctuary terms differ from game to game and region to region.

Most of the active games involve a certain amount of mimicry of life situations, although it is only the most complex of these recreations that are usually called "dramatic games." Little children play a game that begins with all but one player in a "jam pile"—everyone falls down in a heap with limbs tangled. Then they cry "Doctor, doctor, we need help!" and the remaining child hurries to untangle them. The game is a simple, playful enactment of a horrible scene that might occur in accidents. In "Mother May I?" the "it" player (who may be male or female) assumes the role of a demanding "mother" who allows movement toward a goal only using types and numbers of rather grotesque steps which "she" dictates, and then only if the children remember to say "May I?" and "Thank you." Cheating, however, is a regular feature of the game. The game of "Fox Hunt" (or

"Hare and Hounds") imitates hunting, with bits of scattered paper instead of a scent as the trail. The city child's counterpart game, "Arrow Chase" (or "Chalk Walk"), is an adaptation for sidewalk playing with detective-like overtones. Nineteenth-century children, girls especially, enjoyed courtship games such as "Knights of Spain" or "Here Come Three Dukes A-Riding," but these have mostly died out now as the more aggressive kissing and party mixer games (discussed below) flourish. Many courtship games, as well as others that involve singing, are related to the play-parties discussed in Chapter 15.

Battle games, like "Cops and Robbers" or "Cowboys and Indians," are dramatic imitations of adult conflicts that have survived even in the age of space exploration. Children have also been reported playing a game with as old-fashioned a title (perhaps learned from TV) as "Wells Fargo." Here the "Indians" are identified by strips of adhesive tape on their foreheads. When they storm the office or stagecoach, they may be "killed" by yanking the tape away.

That children are imaginative and have extremely good memories for the things that interest them is demonstrated by the fanciful forfeits sometimes proposed in games like "Tappy-on-the-Icebox" and the complicated dialogue preserved in one like "The Old Witch." That children have boundless stamina is shown by the hours they will spend in snowball fighting or playing a chasing game like "Fox and Geese" over a pattern stamped in the snow. And that children are adaptable was strikingly demonstrated after the devastating Alaskan earthquake on Good Friday, 1964, when, only a few days later, the children of Kodiak were playing new games called "Earthquake" and "Tidal Wave" amid the wreckage.

Games involving manipulation of objects might be classified by the objects that are used, whether "found" items like stones, sticks, and plants, or manufactured objects like marbles, jacks, balls, and knives. In these games, strategy or dexterity is usually more important than physical strength. Some of them involve trading and winning the objects used in the game. The most fully collected aspect of games with objects is their terminology, which may be both elaborate and lengthy. The games played with marbles, for instance, have given rise to such terms as *fudgies, stickies, changies, roundsies, clearsies, lagging, steelie, dogob, vint, one knuckle down,* and *cateye.* Jacks players use terms such as *pig pens, around the world, taps, baskets,* *behind the fence,* and *lefties.* All too often collectors stop with such vocabulary, failing to document the rules and customs of play sufficiently. Thus we have no full descriptions of knife games beyond the familiar "Mumbletypeg" (others include "Baseball," "Territories," and "Chicken"), and we have little data on the age groups, seasons, regions, and individual places where such games are played, or about the different rules or equipment appropriate for each.

Another area of equipped folk games little studied as yet is that of variations of organized sports. Baseball or softball, for instance, in folk groups are seldom played with full teams, game officials, standard-size playing fields, and the like, Little League notwithstanding. Instead, neighborhood children will use their baseballs, bats, and gloves for games like "Flies and Grounders," "Scrub," "Work-up," and "Stickball," adapting the rules to the terrain available and to the prevailing customs. Similarly in driveway and backyard basketball games, there is only one basket, not two, and the game may range all the way from simple basketshooting and scrambling for rebounds to elaborate spelling or mathematical contests controlled by the drops of shots into the basket. ("C-o-w" is used for a short game, "h-o-r-s-e," for a medium-length one, and "M-i-s-s-i-s-s-i-p-p-i" for a long one.) The influence of playground supervisors may be felt on group ball games such as "Dodge Ball," but there are other games such as "Anthony Over" (or "Anti Over," "Rain on the Roof," etc.) played by opposing "sides" (teams) of from one on up which are completely traditional.

The survival of older folk games in play equipment now produced by manufacturers also deserves study. "Checkers," "Pachisi," and other board games; "Darts," "Beanbags," and other target games; and most card games have traditional ancestors on their family trees. The game of "Tiddlywinks," now a commercially produced one, probably had its origin in earlier play with homemade equipment. A counterpart folk game is still played by little girls in India with broken fragments of glass bangles (worn in bunches as bracelets) which they find washed out of the village dust after rainstorms, and which they gamble with, attempting to win by snapping each other's bangle fragments out of a circle scratched in the ground. "Marbles" and "Jacks," on the other hand, are folk games played now with factory-made equipment. The former, moreover, has increasingly been normalized and regulated in organized tournaments by contest officials.

Games of mental activity are characterized by guessing, figuring, choosing, and the like, although, of course, they usually also involve some physical action as well, and often manipulation of objects. It is difficult to classify a game like "Lemonade" (also called "New Orleans," "Dumb Trades," "The Dumbies' Trade," etc.) that involves dialogue, acting, guessing, and chasing. But the heart of the game, emphasized in several of the variant names for it, is the procedure of one team acting out a kind of work and the other team *guessing* what it is. When the correct trade is named, the guessers chase the actors, and the game continues with different trades being imitated until all players have been caught. The game of "Statues" is a similar active-mental combination game. A leader whirls and releases each player who must then "freeze" in whatever posture the motion leaves him or her in. Then the leader selects the best "statue," or the funniest, to be next leader.

A few other games of mental activity are played outdoors—"Stone School" on the front steps of a house, for instance, with each child advancing up through the grades (i.e., a step) by guessing which of "teacher's" hands holds a stone. But most are indoor games, frequently what are called *parlor games* or *party games*. "Charades" and "Twenty Questions" are two of these which eventually found their way into television "game shows," but a more complex one in folk tradition is "Botticelli," often played by college students or faculty. It requires a leader to give the initials only of a personality, recent or past—real or fictional—in art, music, literature, history, etc. The group guesses at his or her identification by listing credentials that fit such figures with the same initials. Each time the leader cannot come up with the name that another player has in mind, he or she must answer truthfully a direct "yes or no" question about the person he is thinking of. Another popular guessing game is based on a kind of story riddle sometimes termed "logic problems." These are often mini-murder-mysteries "solved" by spotting such slips in the story as the murderer buying a round-trip ticket for himself and a one-way for his victim, or using an icicle for a weapon that will melt without a clue. (So he thinks; it leaves a tell-tale puddle).

Games involving drawn diagrams are usually called *pencil-and-paper games*, although they may occasionally be played on a blackboard or even scratched into the earth or sand. "Tic-Tac-Toe" is the simplest and best known, and is often played as a triple contest, each player recording the games won as well as those that went to "the old cat" as ties. Another similar game is "Squares" or "Completing Squares"; the players alternate connecting dots in a pattern, and they win a point for each square they complete and initial. The game of "Battleship" is similar, but requires two diagrams containing various hidden "ships" which the players attempt to "sink" by calling out the grid coordinates where they believe they are located. (This game has lately been adapted for commercial sale and mass production.) Another game, "Hangman," ends when one player has been "hanged" by missing a guess (usually of letters in a person's name) for each line of a stick-figure drawing of a hanging man.

Traditional letter and number puzzles, tricks and amusements (such as those discussed in Chapter 6) occasionally come close to being games. Those played in automobiles, for example, have rules and winners—the child wins who sees a whole alphabet in initial letters of words on billboards, or who sees the most distant state license plate. (No fair counting except on your own side of the car!) A similar adult amusement is the popular office game of "Pay Check Poker" (or cribbage) in which the "kitty" (cash) goes to the person whose paycheck serial number represents the highest-scoring hand of cards.

Several kinds of folk recreations will not fit clearly into any of the above categories and must simply be grouped last. These include practical jokes, kissing games, and drinking games.

Practical jokes do not qualify as true games because, in Richard S. Tallman's definition, they consist of "a competitive play activity in which only one of two opposing sides is consciously aware of the fact that a state of play exists. . . . the unknowing side is made to seem foolish or is caused some physical and/or mental discomfort." Usually practical jokes require that all participants but one be in on the joke. The unsuspecting dupe may be told that the group is going to play a game called "Barnyard Chorus"; each player is assigned the name of a farm animal whose sound he is to imitate loudly when a signal is given. What the dupe does not know is that everybody else will keep silent, and he alone is left calling out his animal sound—the bray of a donkey. Sometimes this trick is set up with the players blindfolded and assigned the animal sounds in pairs. Then when all of the others have found their partners and removed their blindfolds, the poor "donkey" is still lonesomely braying and stumbling around the room. Other similar practical jokes are "Trip to the Dentist," during which the dupe receives a dash of pepper in his open mouth, and a mock-contest involving a nickel balanced on the forehead, which is supposedly to be flipped down into a funnel stuck into the pants. The victim receives a glass of water poured into the funnel.

Many popular practical jokes take the form of the "fool's errand"—the newcomer to a job is sent searching and asking for a variety of nonexistent tools, materials, or other items. Among the best known of these "beguilers" are the "left-handed monkey wrench," the "sky-hook," and the pilot's "bucket of prop-wash." Other terms suggest a more advanced technical knowledge of a trade: the typesetter's "italic periods," and the banker's "key to the clearinghouse," for example.

One of the most venerable pranks is the "Snipe Hunt," an age-old routine which is still a successful trick on an occasional youthful camper or club member. The other hunters explain the habits of the elusive snipe—prowling nocturnally for food and responding to a soft call or whistle. The victim is to hold a bag open and make the proper sound (sometimes also hold a flashlight or lantern), while the others will fan out to drive the snipe toward him. But all the tricksters simply go home, leaving the poor hunter dolefully "holding the bag" until he realizes he has been fooled. Other old practical jokes are begun as elaborate ceremonies of initiation. In "Introducing to the King and Queen," the butt of the joke is solemnly presented to a boy and girl who are seated on two chairs placed a chair's-width apart and covered with a blanket or sheet. When the dupe is invited to sit between them, the royal figures rise, dropping their guest to the floor or into a tub of water.

Some practical jokes are individual gags pulled by a "trickster" on an unsuspecting audience, and only a few of these may be traditional. One prank that seems to be traditional is the "surprising drink" gambit. The prankster writes for a long time in a crowded library reading room, dipping his steel pen into a supposed well of ink (really grape juice). Suddenly he is seized with a fit of coughing so severe that it seems he will strangle unless he has a drink. Without blinking an eye, he takes up the "ink" and drinks it down. Or the trickster may carry his sample of urine (really ginger ale) into a doctor's waiting room. He examines it critically, then remarks, "Looks a little thin; I'll run it through again," and drinks. Whatever their forms, pranks and practical jokes seem to have created another traditional form, the "practical joke story" which describes past pranks and pranksters. Any of these might be analyzed, using Tallman's adaptation of the outline developed by Oliver H. P. Ferris, in terms of The Actors (prankster or pranksters versus victim or victims) and The Action (nature, intent, and result of the prank).

Kissing games take three different forms, *chasing kiss games* (like "Kiss in the Ring") in which the kiss is a reward for catching a partner; *mixing kiss games* (like "Post Office") in which pairing of couples occurs temporarily during the course of the game, and *couple kiss games* (like "Flashlight") in which couples are established beforehand and the game allows them to kiss each other repeatedly (partner exchanging may occur later in the game). The popularity of these three types with different age groups is roughly equivalent to the first with secondary school pupils, the second with junior and senior high school students, and the third with senior high school and college students. "Flashlight" (or "Willpower," "Spotlight," etc.) illustrates the most actively companionable level of such games. "It" is seated in the center of a room holding a flashlight, and couples sit all around the darkened room. When "it" flashes the light on, he points it to a couple, and if they are *not* kissing, he changes places with the appropriate member. A few kissing games are more like couple amusements than true games. In "Perdiddle," for instance, the boy may kiss his girl companion if he sees a car with one headlight burned out and says "perdiddle" first. If she wins, she slaps him. In "Show Kiss" a boy and girl attend a movie with a love plot, and every time the screen characters kiss, they do too.

Drinking games are highly popular in many college- and high-school party groups, but they seldom surface for any public recognition, either by school administrators or folklorists. Only the gag sweatshirts lettered "Olympic Drinking Team" and the red-eyed students in early-morning classes allude to them. Most drinking games are transparent excuses to "chug-a-lug"—that is, to down a drink of beer or liquor in one draught. The players supply themselves with drinks and then go through a complicated routine of some kind involving numbers, a speech, a series of actions, or a rhythmic chant. Whoever misses must chug-a-lug, refill his glass, and start over. The more often one misses some requirement such as saying "Buzz" for all sevens and multiples of seven ("Buzz-buzz" for seventy-seven, etc.), the more he drinks, and the more he tends to go on missing. Among the popular drinking games are "Categories," "Cardinal Puff," and "Colonel Powwow"; in the latter two, a mock title is conferred upon the player who successfully completes the game.

The first students of American children's folk games—who would have been scandalized at the idea of drinking games—believed that they were rescuing the last remaining fragments of an "expiring custom," as W. W. Newell expressed it. Newell wrote regretfully in his 1883 introduction:

> The vine of oral tradition, of popular poetry, which for a thousand years has twined and bloomed on English soil, in other days enriching with color and fragrance equally the castle and the cottage, is perishing at the roots; its prouder branches have long since been blasted, and children's song, its humble but longest-flowering offshoot, will soon have shared their fate.

Newell's explanations of the origins of children's games were typical of late nineteenth-century folklore theories. He regarded them as belonging to the peasantry recently, but earlier descended from an upper-class source; they came, "from above, from the intelligent class." He also believed, somewhat contradictively, that some games contained survivals of ancient rites and customs. Thus he singled out eleven for special discussion as "mythological games." The familiar "London Bridge," for example, was not only "a representation of the antagonism of celestial and infernal powers," but also an enactment of the human sacrifice once practiced to placate "the elemental spirit of the land, who detests any interference with the solitude he loves,

[and] has an especial antipathy to bridges." (Newell's counterpart in
England, Lady Alice B. Gomme, went even further with a survivals
explanation for "London Bridge," comparing several foundation sacri-
fices in the "actual facts of contemporary savagery" to traditions about
London associated with the game.) But despite the romanticism of
Newell's attitude toward games, the frills in his writing style, and the
doubtful nature of his theories, the texts and notes of American children's singing games which he published were the groundwork for
later studies.

In analyses of children's games, American folklorists seem to have
bypassed the stage that was so important in folktale studies—that of
historic-geographic studies. There are no monographs on American
games to compare with one by a Finnish scholar on the European
"Game of Rich and Poor" that was done according to the classic
"Finnish-method" of Aarne and Krohn. Instead of this, folk game
scholars in the United States have proceeded directly from classification and annotation to studies of the meaning, function, and structure
of games. Some investigators have begun quite simply by asking
children what their games mean to them and why they like them—
always an interesting line of inquiry. In general it appears that what
many children like most about games is the dramatic element. They
tend to identify with the situations and characters represented in
games, and they especially prefer games that suit their own personalities best. Often the children's comments will be gems of analysis in
themselves. One shy child wrote for a folklorist who visited her class,
"The game which I love best is grean gravel because it is not plaid
ruffly." Another, responding to the delight of a collector in a rare
game, said quietly, "I like this one best because *you* like it."

The game preferences of American children since the 1890s have
been fairly closely documented in folklore studies. One survey covering the years 1895 to 1944 for the city of St. Louis pointed out the
gradual disappearance there of the older English games, the increasing influence of school games, and the occasional invention of new
folk games. A more recent study extended the data in both time and
space including surveys from 1896, 1898, 1921, and 1959 in Massachusetts, South Carolina, San Francisco, and Ohio respectively.
Fully 180 different games or pastimes were involved, and conclusions

were drawn concerning changing boy-girl game preferences and the changes in types of games played. One interesting finding in the study was that girls have definitely tended toward the traditional male roles in games (perhaps to match the emancipation of women in American society). At the same time, boys have tended increasingly to reject roles in games that they feel smack of femininity ("Hopscotch," "Jacks," "Jump Rope," etc.), retreating instead to the rougher masculine sports where girls could traditionally follow only as cheerleaders or spectators. Another suggestion of the study was that formal games of a traditional nature may at last be dying out as the organized and commercialized distractions of American society take over.

The structural movement in folktale studies has begun to influence game studies. The suggestion is made that a folktale may be described as "a two-dimensional series of actions displayed on a one-dimensional track," and a game is "structurally speaking, a two-dimensional folktale." In other words, the hero and villain "motifemes," which are simply narrated one at a time in a folktale, are assumed as dramatic characterizations in many folk games and then acted out to a conclusion. But whereas in tales the hero always wins, in games either side may conquer. Interestingly, there are also parallels in special forms of tales and games, for example, the cumulative tale has its counterpart in a game like "Link Tag," and the trickster tale is reflected in practical jokes.

Another recent development in game studies comes from what has been called the behavioral or contextual approach to folklore. Expressing the dissatisfaction of some folklorists with "merely collecting and annotating [game] texts and studying them within diffusionist and survivalist frameworks," and so drawing instead upon "the work of social scientists who are interested in dynamic processes," Robert A. Georges proposes using behavioral models as a device for a holistic analysis of what he prefers to call "traditional play activities." Postulating that such activities are social events involving person-to-person communication as well as cognitive experiences that are clearly recognized by all players as "play," Georges has drawn up three proposed models to represent schematically some kinds of communication and interaction that occur during play; for example:

One social entity encodes
and transmits to the other(s)
a message, indicating his or her
desire to engage in a
particular traditional
play activity. (The
outside arrows represent general
social rules; those marked
"R" are specifically "play
rules" which define this particular
play activity.)

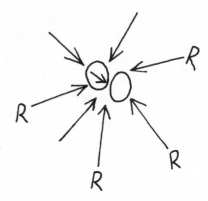

The above may seem like an overly jargonistic and complex way of representing a common situation, such as when one child says to others, "Hey, let's play 'Kick the Can'!" It should be remembered, however, that such "game models" are only analytic devices drawn up in hopes of understanding the much more complex nature of traditional play itself. They serve as analogies or schematic representations of patterns of social interaction that constitute a clear basis for comparisons and further analysis. Also, such analyses utlimately derive from the same basic field and reference work in folklore as did earlier studies; as Georges puts it, his data are from "personal observation . . . participation . . . [and] printed descriptions and texts of traditional play activities." But whether viewed from a comparative, psychological, structural, or behavioral approach, certainly folk games still offer a fertile and partly untilled field for folklore collectors, classifiers, and analysts.

BIBLIOGRAPHIC NOTES

The "New and Enlarged Edition (1903) of W. W. Newell's *Games and Songs of American Children* became the standard one. It was reprinted in paperback in 1963. Lady Alice B. Gomme's important collection *The Traditional Games of England, Scotland, and Ireland,* published in two volumes in 1894 and 1898, was also published in paperback in 1964 (both the Newell and Gomme paperbacks are Dover books). The introductions by Carl Withers for Newell and Dorothy Howard for Gomme are important essays on game study.

Paul G. Brewster's article "Games and Sports in Sixteenth- and Seven-

teenth-Century English Literature," *WF* (1947), 143–56, helps to give historical depth to studies of modern games. Brewster's work in collecting, classifying, and annotating games has been prolific and important, especially in his
book *American Non-singing Games* (Norman: University of Oklahoma Press,
1953), and his editing of the games in the *Frank C. Brown Collection of North
Carolina Folklore* (1: 29–159). A varied and well-annotated collection in a
folklore journal is Warren E. Roberts's "Children's Games and Game
Rhymes," *HF* 8 (1949), 7–34. Iona and Peter Opie's book *Children's Games in
Street and Playground* (New York: Oxford University Press, 1969) contains
British children's games, many of which have parallels in the United States.

Several scholars have proposed sweeping theories concerning games and
the impulse to play. Outstanding among them is Roger Caillois, editor of
Diogenes, who published in that journal "The Structure and Classification of
Games," 12 (1955), 62–75, and "Unity of Play: Diversity of Games," 19 (1957),
92–121. Both articles were stages leading up to his book *Man, Play, and
Games* (New York: Free Press of Glencoe, 1961). An anthropological approach is represented in John M. Roberts, Malcolm J. Arth, and Robert R.
Bush's, "Games in Culture," *AA* 61 (1959), 597–605. Roberts collaborated
with Brian Sutton-Smith and Adam Kendon in a special application of this
theory in "Strategy in Games and Folk Tales," *JSP* 61 (1963), 185–99. Starting
with the observation that "conflicts induced by child training . . . lead to involvement in games . . . which in turn provide[s] . . . learning important
both to players and their societies," these scholars confirmed their hypothesis
that "folktales with strategic outcomes would be found in the same cultural
setting as games of strategy." They did this by comparing games and tales
from several cultures, sorted on the basis of whether strategy was present,
and correlating these with other data on the cultures.

Pastimes have seldom been treated in separate folklore studies. For articles
on "Cat's Cradle" we must turn to British publications—W. Innes Pocock's
article in *Folklore* 17 (1906), 73–93, and 351–73; and Dorothy Howard's in the
same journal, 72 (1961), 385–87. A fascinating little booklet, Kathleen Haddon's, *String Games for Beginners*, first published in 1934, was still in print
recently. The 40-page pamphlet contains descriptions of twenty-eight string
figures from various native cultures, with instructions for learning them, and
even a piece of string with which to practice. The pamphlet is published by
W. Heffer and Sons, Ltd., Cambridge, England. The 1906 book by Caroline
Furness Jayne, *String Figures and How to Make Them*, with an introduction
by A. C. Haddon, was republished in paperback by Dover Books (New York,
1962). See also Lyn Harrington, "Eskimo String Figures," *School Arts* 50
(May 1951), 319–21, which has some good photographs, although rather limited discussion.

Ray B. Browne's article on California jump-rope rhymes, cited in the notes
to Chapter 7, analyzes the various *actions* of this popular pastime, as well as
the rhymes that are chanted with them. The pastime called "Chinese Jump
Rope," which had started to be popular in the United States about 1963, has
been described in Ruth Hawthorne's, "Classifying Jump-Rope Games," *KFQ*

11 (1966), 113–26, and Michael Owen Jones's, "Chinese Jumprope," *SFQ* 30 (1966), 256–63. The pastime is performed with two players holding a long elastic loop stretched between their ankles while a third player jumps in and out of it, stretching it into patterns with her toes as she does so. The same pastime with the same name ("Kinesersjip") was reported from Copenhagen; see Erik Kaas Nielsen's, *Det lille Folk* (Forlaget Fremad, 1965). Roger Welsch discussed a group of "Nebraska Finger Games," [mostly pastimes] in *WF* 25 (1966), 173–94.

A fascinating window into the past is opened by E. Leslie Gilliams's article "Folk-Lore of Children's Games" published in *The Peterson Magazine*, n.s. 5 (Nov. 1895), 1184–92, a reference almost impossible to come by nowadays, worthy of reprinting, if only for its excellent photographs of children at play. A good survey of some older games is found in Mac E. Barrick's chapter "Games from the Little Red School House" in *Two Penny Ballads and Four Dollar Whiskey*, edited by Kenneth S. Goldstein and Robert H. Byington (Hatboro, Pa.: Folklore Associates, 1966), pp. 95–120.

Various games of physical action are described in Eugenia L. Millard's "Racing, Chasing, and Marching with the Children of the Hudson-Champlain Valleys," *NYFQ* 15 (1959), 132–50. Vance Randolph and Nancy Clemens's article, "Ozark Mountain Party-Games," in *JAF* 49 (1936), 199–206, describes a variety of guessing games, forfeit games, courtship games, kissing games, and active games in a regional folk culture. John Harrington Cox printed forty texts of singing games from West Virginia with bibliography and musical notation in *SFQ* 6 (1942), 183–261. Active games of city children were early collected by Stewart Culin in "Street Games of Boys in Brooklyn, N.Y.," *JAF* 4 (1891), 221–37. Excellent candid photographs of New York City children playing five popular street games were published in "Youths' Concrete Joys," *Sports Illustrated* (August 17, 1959), pp. 18–22.

Some games of racial and ethnic minorities are studied in Bessie Jones and Bess Lomax Hawes, *Step it Down: Games, Plays, Songs and Stories from the Afro-American Heritage* (New York: Harper & Row, 1972); Margaret K. Brady, " 'Gonna Shimmy Shimmy 'Til the Sun Goes Down': Aspects of Verbal and Nonverbal Socialization in the Play of Black Girls," *Folklore Annual* 6 (1974), 1–16; and Clement L. Valetta, "Friendship and Games in Italian-American Life," *KFQ* 15 (1970), 174–87.

A reminiscent essay on a game played with objects is J. W. Ashton's "Marble Playing in Lewiston [Maine] Fifty Years Ago," *NEF* 3 (1960), 24–27. A more rigorously statistical article along the same lines (but concerning New Zealand) is Brian Sutton-Smith's "Marbles Are In," in *WF* 12 (1953), 186–93. (This essay is reprinted in Sutton-Smith's *The Folkgames of Children*, mentioned below, pp. 455–64.) An extremely thorough study of the history of one ball game in Erwin Mehl's article "Baseball in the Stone Age," *WF* 7 (1948), 145–61, supplemented by further notes in *WF* 8 (1949), 152–56.

Games based on mental activity are seldom treated separately from other games. One exception is Eugenia L. Millard's article "A Sampling of Guessing Games," in *NYFQ* 13 (1957), 135–43. An interesting popular piece is Martin Gardner's "Mathematical Games. A Bit of Foolishness for April Fools' Day," in *Scientific American* 208 (April 1963), 156–66.

Practical jokes have attracted several studies. Anne Penick described six favorite pranks in "Look Out, Newcomer!" *MF* 4 (1954), 239–43. Kelsie Harder discussed "Introductions to the King and Queen" under the title "The Preacher's Seat," in *TFSB* 23 (1957), 38–39. The prank called "Going to See the Widow" has been the subject of several notes, which were consolidated and supplemented by Wayland D. Hand in *WF* 17 (1958), 275–76. An interesting example of a practical joke apparently growing out of a folktale was described by James Ralston Caldwell in "A Tale Actualized in a Game" in *JAF* 54 (1945), 50. Some pranks involving use of the telephone are discussed by Norine Dresser in *NYFQ* 29 (1973), 121–30; others concerning automobiles may be found in *NYFQ* 30 (1974), 44–65, in an article by M. Licht. A special issue of *SFQ* edited by Richard S. Tallman devoted to studies of practical jokes contains a note and five extended essays on such subjects as definitions of the genre, wedding pranks, and summer-camp pranks; see the December 1974 issue (38: 251–331).

A number of important studies by Brian Sutton-Smith, a leading student of children's games, have been reprinted in the AFS Bibliographical and Special series (No. 24) as *The Folkgames of Children* (Austin: University of Texas Press, 1972). Among these is his 1959 essay "The Kissing Games of Adolescents in Ohio" which furnished the terminology used in this chapter. Richard M. Dorson discusses college drinking games in Chapter 7 of *American Folklore*, pp. 265–66.

The historic-geographic study of the dramatic European "Game of Rich and Poor" was published by Mrs. Elsa Enäjärvi Haavio in *FFC* no. 100 (1932). An important early study of American children's games and the attitudes of their players was made by Jean Olive Heck: "Folk Poetry and Folk Criticism, as Illustrated by Cincinnati Children in their Singing Games and their Thoughts about these Games," *JAF* 40 (1927), 1–77. Leah Rachel Clara Yoffie published her study "Three Generations of Children's Singing Games in St. Louis" in *JAF* 60 (1947), 1–51; Brian Sutton-Smith's more comprehensive article along similar lines was the 1961 publication "Sixty Years of Historical Change in the Game Preferences of American Children," reprinted in *The Folkgames of Children*, pp. 258–81. Alan Dundes, who proposed the structural approach to folktales, has applied his theories to games in "On Game Morphology: A Study of the Structure of Non-Verbal Folklore," *NYFQ* 20 (1964), 276–88, reprinted in *Analytic Essays in Folklore*, 80–87. Robert A. Georges outlines a contextual-behavioral approach in "The Relevance of Models for Analyses of Traditional Play Activities," *SFQ* 33 (1969), 1–23.

IV · MATERIAL FOLK TRADITIONS

❍❥❍❥❍❥❍❥❍❥❍❥❍

The concept of "folklife," introduced in Chapter 14 in connection with customs and festivals, offers a most promising area for original research in American folklore. Offsetting generations of literature-oriented folklore studies, the students of American folklife are now beginning to examine the whole range of traditional verbal lore, behavior, and material creations in folk circulation, especially the latter two categories, which have previously received relatively little attention in the United States. Until recently Americans were backward in developing folklife studies, lagging at least fifty years behind European scholars. Lately, however, American folklife studies have been increasing and improving.

Essentially, the order of subjects presented in this book follows the general history of studies of American oral traditions, from the folk*lore* interest begun in the late nineteenth century, to the emerging folk*life* studies of today. These final chapters deal with material folk traditions, which constitute the largest part of the field of folklife, and, in the United States, the least-studied but perhaps fastest-growing branch of folkloristics. Material folk traditions are too diverse to be effectively summarized in a few pages, and studies in this field have not advanced far enough to provide a systematic theoretical framework for discussion. Therefore, the following chapters are mainly an outline of materials and a summary of what present studies suggest, along with some technical guidelines on recording, documenting, and analyzing material traditions. The areas surveyed are folk architecture, folk handicrafts and art, folk costumes, and folk foods.

18

Folk Architecture

Before we can survey a branch of material folk tradition—folk architecture—it is necessary to clarify further our usage of the larger inclusive category, **folklife**. A confusion in basic terminology is immediately evident. At least in theory, the term "folklore" is synonymous with "folklife," and, in fact, many American folklorists and their publications (including this book) employ the terms in this way—"folklore," in its flexible connotation taking in *all* folk-cultural products. But changing usage is evident; for example, while Alan Dundes's book *The Study of Folklore* (1965) contained chapters on verbal lore as well as on hex and marks and water witching, Richard M. Dorson's *Folklore and Folklife* (1972) used both terms in the title in order to embrace the same spectrum of verbal, customary, and material folk traditions. Possibly the time is ripe now to retitle the present textbook *The Study of American Folklife*, taking our lead from Don Yoder, who has written, "I prefer to follow [others] in subsuming *folklore* (defining it after William Bascom as the verbal arts of a society) under *folklife*, as only one aspect of folk culture." However, an argument against this change is that American folklorists *as a group* have not yet adopted "folklife" full scale for their journals, scholarly societies, and teaching. So we follow current usage, still defining "folklife," as Yoder says, "by default," to mean only customary and material folk traditions, even though there is good reason to substitute the word immediately and permanently for the much-abused term "folklore."

Another preliminary problem is the lack of accepted procedures and theories for American folklife studies, most of which so far have been simply descriptive approaches to individual artifacts or artisans. Again, Don Yoder offers guidance, identifying "three essentially different approaches": (1) Historical Folklife Studies, (2) Folklife Studies and Survivals, and (3) Folklife Studies and the Ethnographic Present. An example of the first approach is that of Theodore Blegen's documenting of the "grass roots history" of Norwegian-American folk culture; of the second, the efforts to preserve examples of Early American architecture; and of the third, questionnaire surveys of existing traditional crafts, such as quilting.

Perhaps the best direction to look in for a model of folklife studies is to Europe, especially to Scandinavia, where systematic research began. In Sweden, folklife study dates from the end of the nineteenth century with the establishment of museums of folk architecture and folk artifacts. The distinctive Scandinavian format became the open-air collection of old farmhouses and out-buildings, the earliest one being *Skansen* park near Stockholm, which was shortly imitated in Norway, Denmark, Finland, and eventually in many Central and Eastern European countries. In 1937 the Swedes formally launched their term for the whole field by beginning publication of the journal *Folk-Liv* with articles printed in English. The Swedish classification system for archiving folklife was soon widely imitated. The most convenient sources in English based on the Swedish pattern deal with Irish folklife. The official collectors' guide used in Ireland, *A Handbook of Irish Folklore* (reprinted in 1963), summarizes all the materials to be investigated, while a book like E. Estyn Evans's *Irish Folk Ways* (New York, 1957) gives a systematic discussion of the findings of fieldwork and research.

The principle of classification for folklife materials developed in Sweden and followed in Ireland and elsewhere in Europe is by the *use* to which customs and artifacts are applied, beginning with land use, cultivation, housing, settlement, and subsistence crafts, and proceeding through furniture, domestic handwork, leisure-time handicrafts, decorative arts, representational art, musical instruments, folk toys, and the like. Basically, it is an arrangement of traditional customs and materials ranging from the necessities of life to the pleasures.

For the purpose of a systematic presentation of the kinds of folklore, we have already dealt briefly with the customary traditions in Section III. The study of material traditions (*folk artifacts*) presents special problems, however, which are best taken up separately. When studying them, researchers will still collect, classify, and analyze data (see Chapter 2), but must also learn some new techniques. Folk artifacts must be photographed or sketched, even if they are going to be brought in physically from the field for an archive or museum. For most fieldworkers, then, this means the ability to make simple measured drawings and the acquisition of at least the rudiments of good documentary still photography.

Probably the best type of camera for all-around folklife fieldwork is a good single-lens-reflex (SLR) model taking 35 mm. film, with a built-in coupled exposure meter. Such cameras are available at a wide range of prices and with a variety of attachments and accessories. Their chief advantage is that one sights on the subject directly through the camera lens, thus seeing at the time exactly what will be in the picture. Since lenses in all but the cheapest SLR models are detachable, and the metering system is either wholly automatic or read directly through the focusing and viewing window, this camera system offers great flexibility and ease of operation at fairly moderate costs. (The automatic electronic models are somewhat more limiting, but faster to use.) It is by no means necessary to master the technical details behind the inner workings of such a camera to use it well— setting the exposure, for example, is usually just a matter of centering an arrow across a circle in the viewfinder. But if photographers acquire the rudiments of photographic theory (as contained in the owner's manual, for example) their results will be far superior to those obtained with any fixed-focus snapshot camera. Whatever the camera used, one should practice with it and see the results at home before using it for fieldwork.

The 35 mm. film size, of course, is the standard one for transparencies, from which color prints of publishable quality may also easily be made, if desired. Black-and-white 35 mm. negatives, even on the sensitive film (such as Kodak Tri-x) now available, are also sufficiently free of "grain" (image coarseness) to make excellent enlargements. Since both slides and monochrome prints are useful for different purposes, and since 35 mm. film comes only in twenty- or thirty-six-exposure rolls, field photographers should acquire as soon as they can afford it two identical SLR camera bodies on which they may interchange their basic lenses.

Besides the "normal" lens supplied with the camera, the two most useful extras are a wide-angle lens and a zoom-telephoto lens. The former can be used when walls, shrubbery, or topography prevent getting far enough back to take the subject in with the normal lens. One must be careful, however, with a wide-angle lens not to tip the camera off a straight vertical plane; this introduces distortion. The zoom lens offers in a single accessory a range of possibilities for magnifying a selected portion of the subject. Such shots are useful, not only for bringing in distant buildings, but also for permitting close detail shots of remote features like chimney tops or cornice mouldings, and with this lens the camera may even be used as a telescope to scout distant features on the landscape in order to see if they are worth hiking over to, for close examination.

Both black-and-white and color films nowadays are produced with sensitivities to accommodate the existing illumination in most field conditions on relatively light days. For unusually dark conditions or subjects, the photographer should have a supplementary flash unit, such as the small electronic flash sold as an accessory with most cameras. The only other basic pieces of equipment needed are a medium-yellow filter, for darkening sky tone in black-and-white photography, and a tripod, for any exposures slower than $1/60$ of a second, particularly telephoto shots. A cable release should be used for tripod shots, or the photographer may set the camera's self-timer to take the picture, in order to avoid camera movement and achieve maximum sharpness.

Sharp, clear, and well-exposed pictures rather than artistic compositions or "trick" shots are needed for documentary purposes. Generally one should take *many* pictures, following the reasoning that film is cheaper than travel, and that the building or other artifact of interest may not be in existence even if one does return to the spot someday. Furthermore, black-and-white 35 mm. film and processing are quite inexpensive, especially if photographers learn to "roll their own" film from bulk rolls into cartridges. (Home processing of film, also quite cheap and simple, is the next step.) Long, medium, and close-up shots should always be taken, along with an indicator of scale in some pictures—a yardstick, ruler, pencil, hand, or person at one side of the shot for size comparison. Other "in-frame documentation" might include a meaningful inscription or sign, the informant demonstrating use of the artifact, or the tools and ingredients for a subject. For any traditional process for steps of construction, a series of pictures illustrating the sequence should be taken.

Negatives, slides, and prints should be systematically filed and carefully preserved after they are processed. The 35 mm. size allows for easy printing of one full black-and-white roll on a single 8 × 10 proofsheet and subsequent filing of these proofs, plus the negatives (in strips of five or six frames), in loose-leaf binders. Photographers or their helpers should have kept a log of data on all shots taken, information which is used to label and annotate the picture file. It is essential at the time of taking pictures to ask all persons appearing in them to sign a release form allowing possible later publication.

Folk architecture and other artifacts should be measured carefully, and the materials from which they are constructed must be identified. Maps and atlases should be made up for recording the locations of finds. Sometimes it is desirable and possible to collect the artifact itself—a complex task when buildings, fencing, farm equipment, and the like are involved. Artifacts may need repairs before they can be moved or studied, and large-scale restoration and reconstruction may be necessary, using historical records or old plans as guides.

Preserving diverse material objects is much more complicated than filing manuscript sheets or tape recordings in an archive. The usual archive for manuscript folklore can adequately accept photographs, sketches, or descriptions of material traditions, but museum facilities and techniques are required for storing and displaying the objects themselves. Classification and analysis of folk artifacts require first that the truly traditional variations be distinguished from individual innovations that are not transmitted, and secondly that the significant traditional variations that define classes and subclasses be identified.

Students of American material folk traditions have fewer indexes and bibliographies to guide them than does the folklorist working with verbal or customary lore, although this situation is rapidly improving. They will also have to become familiar with a large number of foreign folklife studies, and they will have to search for descriptions of earlier American folk artifacts in non-scholarly publications and in local histories, diaries, collections of letters, travelers' accounts, and pioneer reminiscences. Regional literature may yield folklife data too, such as this brief description of a log stile from Mark Twain's *Adventures of Huckleberry Finn:*

> A rail fence round a two-acre yard; a stile, made out of logs sawed off and up-ended, in steps, like barrels of a different length, to climb over the fence with, and for the women to stand on when they are going to jump onto a horse. (Chapter XXXII)

The ideal institution for carrying on folklife studies is a combination museum and research-center, such as the Norwegian Folk Museum at Bygdøy, near Oslo, the Nordic Museum in Stockholm, or the Village Museum in Bucharest, Romania. The closest American equivalent to these is the Farmers' Museum in Cooperstown, N.Y., with its related American folk art collection, annual summer seminars on American Culture, and Master of Arts degree programs in History Museum Training and American Folk Culture. The museum itself is a fine re-creation of an early nineteenth-century New York farm and village. Other notable American folklife museums, also built around a village reconstruction, are old Sturbridge Village, Massachusetts; the Stuhr Museum of the Prairie Pioneer, Grand Island, Nebraska; Old Mystic Seaport, Connecticut; and New Salem Village, Illinois. Oriented more to town life than rural folk culture are such establishments as Colonial Williamsburg, Virginia; and Greenfield Village in Dearborn, Michigan. Other notable collections are in the Shelburne Museum, Burlington, Vt.; the International Folk Art Museum, Santa Fe, N.M.; the Norwegian-American Museum, Decorah, Iowa; the Du Pont Museum in Winterthur, Delaware, and many others. "Living Farm" museums exist near Des Moines, Iowa; Minneapolis, Minn.; Atlanta, Ga., and elsewhere. An accurate reproduction of "Plimoth Plantation" as it was in the early seventeenth century has been constructed in Massachusetts, and leading up to the United States Bicenntenial many similar projects and existing museums received grants to establish or expand facilities. Some Canadian folklife museums are Black Creek Village and Upper Canada Village in Ontario and Pioneer Heritage Park in Calgary, Alberta. To some degree in such institutions the casual visitor may observe displays of artifacts often housed in traditional buildings and see demonstrations of traditional work techniques, while a visiting scholar has access to stored collections of objects and to reference sources.

Since no unified approach to American material traditions has been established, each museum, publication, or research project tends to have its own emphasis and its own peculiarities. Many people conducting research that falls into the field of American folklife are apparently unaware of similar European studies. And even those who know the work in Europe find that European methods are not fully adaptable to American materials because there are certain special conditions here that are not found overseas. To some extent, these are the same conditions that tend to distinguish American folklore generally. For instance, here we have no single national culture, but instead a merging of numerous foreign elements. The pioneering period put European-Americans into a unique relationship with the wilderness continent, but technological change has been so rapid during the short history of the United States that pioneer methods and materials were either lost entirely or changed drastically before there was any interest in studying or preserving them. The social equality, political democracy, and economic opportunity of the New World, with the resulting effects on labor and crafts, were unparalleled in the Old World.

Despite these conditions, the key to studies of American folk artifacts remains the same as for all folklore—it is *tradition*. We may investigate in artifacts, as well as in texts of verbal lore or descriptions of customs, the kinds of things that are transmitted casually by word of mouth or by demonstration. We may attempt to discover how traditional materials originated, how changes occurred, and in what manner traditional variants related to the rest of the folk culture from which they came. We can recognize in material traditions not only survivals from the past, but also recent folk creations, and we should be prepared to admit that traditional "folk" methods of work may be followed by professional craftsmen and artists as well as by amateurs. Above all, we should not be misled in our studies by the notion that *every* artifact that is rural, or old-fashioned, or handmade is a piece of three-dimensional folklore, any more than we think that every amateur poem is a *folk* poem, or that every picturesque remark is a *folk* saying.

Folk architecture, sometimes called "vernacular architecture," includes all traditional nonacademic building types. In particular, these consist of cabins, houses, barns and other agricultural outbuildings, some taverns, shops, offices, churches and other meeting houses, and numerous minor building types such as smokehouses, wash houses, summer kitchens, spring houses, carriage houses, sheds, garages, hunting blinds, ice houses, boat houses, mills, covered bridges, and privies. Folk architecture, and especially folk housing, is the most basic aspect of traditional material culture, being both a three-dimensional product of folk-cultural concepts and an important continuing influence on these same concepts. The placement of the traditional buildings in relation to one another and to the landscape, their floor-plans and heights, the volumes enclosed in them, the light admitted and views afforded by them, the materials of their construction and decoration, their functional qualities, and many other factors all constitute statements of certain human values, and at the same time they are pervasive forces preserving these values. Not only the physical needs for heat, shelter, storage, and uses provided by these buildings, but also the spiritual values they sustain are important to the study of traditional buildings, a field that is just opening up in this country.

Folk architecture in the United States was typified during the settlement period by the use of the most easily available local materials for building in inherited traditional forms. The teepees, wigwams, and lodges of the Indians, the first log houses in the Eastern half of the country, the forts, dugouts, and lean-tos of explorers and home-steaders, the sod houses of the Great Plains, the adobe houses of the Southwest, and other forms all followed this principle. Henry Glassie's study, in Appendix C, of cabin types in the southern mountains is a prime example of how detailed and careful the analysis of only a single kind of dwelling in one region may be. It demonstrates the application of the general theory and method for folklife fieldwork outlined in this chapter and deals specifically with problems of tracing national origins of American building designs and techniques. Furthermore, Glassie's sketches and field data, map, statistics, and bibliographic documentation are all fine examples of the effective presentation of folk architectural research. For all of these reasons, we will refer much of the following brief discussion to this base reference, which should be studied at the same time.

Folk tradition may be evident in the form, the construction techniques and materials, and the uses of buildings, but it is only the first of these criteria—form—which can serve to identify genuine folk architecture and establish its types and subtypes. In other words, a log cabin is "folk" not because it is log, but because it is a traditionally laid-out cabin, "a single construction unit . . . less than two stories high" (page 394). While a true folk cabin may be made of many kinds or combinations of material (as Glassie shows), other non-folk house types (that is, nontraditional forms) might be constructed out of logs joined in traditional ways—a lavish private hunting lodge or a motel, for example. By the same token, there might be traditional or nontraditional uses of buildings, such as holding an art show in a pioneer cabin or a fiddling contest in a football stadium. Form alone defines a building itself as belonging to a culturally viable "folk" tradition.

Since form is the basic criterion, close description and measurement are the chief objects of folk architectural field work. A building under study as an artifact of folk architecture should be measured carefully along each outside wall with a long tape measure, measured again inside from the corners up to and then across each opening, and finally measured for height and for the thickness of walls. A drawn floorplan should indicate the placement of all openings, chimneys, and stairways, besides giving either an accurate indication of scale (see Glassie's floorplans) or the measurements themselves. An "elevation" drawing, also showing scale, or else a photograph can document the building's height and roof shape. It is important to remember during such fieldwork to include all additions to the basic house (porch, shed, "wings," etc.) in the documentation, but during analysis to disregard all but the essential construction unit itself in the establishment of types. The level of further details to be taken down in fieldwork will depend upon the needs and interests of the researcher, but a good general rule is to "keep track of everything," insofar as the time and the facilities allow.

The specific data of field observations and measurements are combined and generalized in order to describe the patterns of folk housing. Glassie speaks of the southern cabins' *primary characteristics* (approximate height, shape, general floorplan, etc.) and their *secondary characteristics* (exact measurements, construction details, interior partitions, etc.) on pages ooo–oo. In general for all folk architectural analysis it is the floorplan and the height of the building that are the prime considerations. The placement of doors and chimney are considered primary, but placement of windows and stairs, being more variable, are secondary to classification. One advantage of our major concern with the building's essential form rather than with other criteria is that whatever the additions to or the condition of a structure, the form remains; asbestos shingle siding and galvanized metal roofing may effectively disguise the log and wood-shingle construction of a cabin, but they cannot hide the square shape or the gable-end chimney of the original.

It should be emphasized that the folk builders were really following traditions; they could just as well have followed a circular floorplan (like that of a Navajo hogan), built an L-shaped house, or placed the chimney centrally in the floorplan or away from a gable end; yet, very seldom did they vary cabin design even to the point of exceeding the typical dimensions of cabins. Nor were these sizes merely dictated by the length of available tree trunks, for approximately the same size cabins reappear in all regions, whatever their forest resources, and even in frame and adobe. Furthermore, logs were often spliced together for larger structures than cabins.

Glassie's analysis (verified by other studies) reveals only two basic cabin forms beneath the many surface features and appendages that individual cabins have. There are the square cabin and the rectangular cabin, both of which have external centered gable-end chimneys and at least one dimension very close to sixteen feet. Thus, the kind of old homemade family housing most traditional in the area surveyed is characterized by a small, neatly square-cornered, single unit (or "single pen," as the log structure is called) with very specific and quite limited variations in the placement of openings. It is a conservative and functional kind of housing with little relationship to the vast areas of American landscape nor to any sense of separation from other family members.

The two-room southern house types which Glassie alludes to on page 404 follow a similar strict pattern, with additions usually built only at the gable end and generally in the same traditional proportions as full cabins have. When a "double-pen" house is formed by addition to the chimney end, it is a "saddlebag" house; when the addition (with a second chimney) is to the opposite end and a breezeway is left open, it is a "dogtrot" house. (Both of these house types were constructed separately, not necessarily just as additions to existing cabins.) The "dogtrot" house, despite the folksy ring of its name (also sometimes "possum trot" or "turkey trot") seems to be descended from a one-story, central-hall, two-chimney frame house type called the "hall and parlor" rather than being simply the result of inventive pioneers individually enlarging their domiciles.

Larger traditional houses often repeat and extend the square and rectangular principles underlying these cabin plans. The "I house," said to have been identified as a traditional type in states beginning with I, (but also said to be shaped like an I at the gable ends), is two stories tall, one room deep, and two rooms wide. In New England it had a central chimney, in the Mid-Atlantic region two inside chimneys at the gable ends, and in the South usually two external gable-end chimneys. The four basic interior volumes of an I house are the identical square or rectangular units of traditional cabins. However, under the influence of the academic architectural mode called "Georgian," I houses and other folk houses acquired a central hall and often Greek Revival trim (such as "return cornices"). From the I house base, one possible variation is "two-thirds of an I house," the equivalent of removing one square or rectangular unit of the floor-plan, leaving only one main room (with chimney) and the "hall." Another possibility, which enlarged the house, was the "four-over-four" design, which simply doubles the house size, usually also retaining the Georgian central hall and with either central or end, internal or external chimneys, depending upon the region. When the roof height of such a house is two stories in front and slopes down as a "lean to" or "shed" to one story in the rear, the form is called a "salt box" (characteristic of, and often named for, New England, but by no means original or peculiar to that region).

Surprisingly, even some traditional barns seem to conform to these patterning principles of American house types. A basic barn type is the double crib design with two cabin-like units side-by-side, joined by one roof, and with gable ends closed and the main doors on the long side. These barns could be covered over with siding, and barns of the same proportions were built as large single units. A four-crib barn has two such structures side by side under a single roof, possibly with doors on all four sides. A transverse-crib barn is just a four-crib barn with doors aligned straight through the center from one gable end to the other. Sometimes these larger barns had more than two "cribs" to a side, and often they were entirely sided over or (as with double-crib barns) could be built as one large unit. Any of these barn types (like the cabin types) might have lean-to appendages, usually extending from the long sides, but sometimes even on all four sides.

Some house and barn types, usually of regional or ethnic origin, stand apart from these general patterns. Examples are the "Cape Cod" house, an English derivative, which has two front rooms on either side of a central chimney and a row of three or more rooms along the back; the Southern "shotgun" house, possibly an African derivative, which has a gable-end entrance and is one room wide and three or more rooms deep; and the Mormon "polygamy house," which served to provide "equal comforts" for several wives of one man. Special barn types include the "English barn," a three-bay structure with stables, hay mow, and a central threshing floor; the "bank barn," with a supported or overhanging bay extending out over a hillside; and various round and polygonal barns.

While construction techniques and materials are not used to identify traditional architectural types, they certainly should be investigated as interesting in themselves, as well as important for determining the national origins and paths of diffusion of folk buildings. American log construction (see page 398) is typified by horizontal placement of hewn logs fitted at the corners with V-notch, half-dovetail, and dovetail joints, and finished with "chinking" between the logs and clapboard siding (almost always original to the building). The antecedents of these construction techniques are Pennsylvania German (ultimately Central and Eastern European), not English (where log construction is not traditional) nor Scandinavian (where logs are shaped and more tightly fitted without chinking and have their notched logs extending at the corners rather than being trimmed off square). Some cabins and most houses are built with so-called "balloon framing," siding over a lighter framework than was used for old barns.

Popular fashions in architecture tend to reject some of the functional qualities of folk architecture. Sod houses, for example, despite some obvious disadvantages, were cheap, fireproof, and well insulated. Log houses are stronger, simpler to build, and better insulated without any special materials than are most balloon-framed houses, but they are considered rustic and outmoded nowadays. As a result, people who still live in log houses often paint or shingle them as a kind of disguise. Log dwellings are sometimes preferred, however, for their same rustic quality as summer cottages or vacation resorts. Newly constructed log buildings or park structures of log often are made (for reasons of pure nostalgia) out of round logs—an earlier style later replaced in traditional building by the more efficient square-hewn logs that fit more securely together and need less chinking. The most degenerate stage of this revival is that which simply consists of false half-logs attached to the outside of a balloon-framed building. Such structures are available as prefabricated houses.

As close studies of folk architecture in specific regions are finished it becomes possible to describe characteristic regional distributions of building types and to chart the culture contacts which they represent. Henry Glassie's book *Pattern in the Material Folk Culture of the Eastern United States* (1968) identifies the most typical house and barn types (among other artifacts) as they appear in four folk-cultural regions, the Mid-Atlantic, Upland South, Deep South, and North. There are, of course, many sub-regional distinctions to be made, as well as studies of the other major sections of the country where various ethnic or sectional "islands" of folk architecture may exist. The Mormon settlers of Utah, for instance, brought with them as cultural baggage mainly the forms of traditional Eastern American architecture, but these houses were constructed of local materials such as adobe, mud concrete, and various stones. Some were made by immigrant craftsmen who had been converted to Mormonism. Thus, what are called in Utah "Old Mormon Houses" may simply be variations of traditional Eastern central-hall plans constructed of locally quarried stone by a Welsh stonemason and enhanced by a modest addition of Greek Revival trim or sometimes an indigenous Utah "Alpine" decor.

While we have looked in considerable detail at some major American folk architectural forms, we have still really only scratched the surface. The principles set forth, however, should enable beginning students to begin making field studies of their own. Left out of consideration here have been such technical matters as chronologies of nails and other hardware, methods for raising houses or barns and roofing them, cutting (or "riving") shingles, building stone chimneys, making adobe, and decorating the interior. We need to study the social contexts of traditional housing expressed in folk speech, folk narratives, folksongs, and other genres. There are also a number of "exotic" traditional building materials, including hay bales, railroad ties, bottles (set in concrete-filled forms), and ammunition cases. Even pretentious nineteenth-century urban houses may have traditional elements associated with them, such as hand-cut scrollwork, sometimes called "Carpenter's Gothic." And in modern building the essential construction jobs such as excavating, stone-work, carpentry, masonry, plastering, plumbing, and roofing could be investigated in detail for traditional elements. Practitioners of these jobs, or new ones, such as installing electrical wiring, automatic heating, or air-conditioning, may have a traditional vocabulary or retain some folk techniques in their work.

BIBLIOGRAPHIC NOTES

There have been appeals for many years for scholars to devote more systematic attention to American folklife. See, for example, two by Norbert F. Riedl, "Folklore vs. *Volkskunde:* A Plea for More Concern with the Study of American Folk Culture on the Part of Anthropologists," *TFSB* 31 (1965), 47–53, and "Folklore and the Study of Material Aspects of Folk Culture," *JAF* 79 (1966), 557–63. An important guide for such studies is Robert Wildhaber's "A Bibliographical Introduction to American Folklife," *NYFQ* 21 (1965), 259–302. Wildhaber mainly lists books, and he includes works on folk architecture, furniture, "imagery and popular painting," tools and utensils, wood carving, metalwork, pottery, glassware, signs, and scrimshaw.

An indication of progress in the decade since these works is W. F. H. Nicolaisen's report "Surveying and Mapping North American Culture," *MSF* 3(1975), 35–39. This article furnishes the background of efforts to establish an American Folklore Atlas, which will begin with a pilot study of foodways.

The volume of essays *American Folklife* (Austin: University of Texas Press, 1976) edited by Don Yoder (several times quoted in this chapter) contains important historical and theoretical statements as well as several excellent studies. Contributors discuss anthropological, esthetic, historic, and geographical perspectives; the subjects of specific studies include folk boats, coil basketry, log architecture, tollgate lore, ethnic lore, and folk customs and rituals. In particular, Warren E. Roberts's report "The Whitaker-Waggoner Log House from Morgan County, Indiana," (pp. 185–207) is a model of folk architectural documentation.

Most American folklore journals have not in the past published much on material tradition, but useful semi-scholarly articles may be found in periodicals such as *Ozark Guide, Mountain Life and Work, Antiques,* and *Hobbies.* Folklife studies are sometimes also published in the journals of historians and geographers. An important journal for studies of American material traditions is *Pennsylvania Folklife*, published quarterly under that name since 1957, but preceded by other variously titled publications of the Pennsylvania Folklife Society. Articles in this journal go beyond Pennsylvania German material, and they are generally well documented and always excellently illustrated. An important survey is Don Yoder's "The Folklife Studies Movement," *PF* 13 (July 1963), 43–56. For further references to works on Pennsylvania German folklife, see Wildhaber's bibliography.

As an introduction to European folklife studies, besides works mentioned in this chapter, one should consult such journals as *Scottish Studies, Ulster Folk Life, Folk-Liv*, and the English *Folk Life*. Sigurd Erixon's study "West European Connections and Culture Relations," *Folk-Liv* 2 (1938), 137–72, is a basic one. Specifically, for the British backgrounds, see Ronald H. Buchanan's "Geography and Folk Life," *Folk Life* 1 (1963), 5–15; Alexander Fenton's "An Approach to Folklife Studies," *KFQ* 12 (1967), 5–21; and the essays gathered in *Studies in Folk Life*, edited by Geraint Jenkins (New York: Barnes & Noble, 1969). Richard M. Dorson was the special editor of an issue of *JFI* 2:3 (1965), 239–366, devoted to "Folklore and Folklife Studies in Great Britain and Ireland." R. W. Brunskill's *Illustrated Handbook of Vernacular Architecture* (New York: Universe Books, 1970), clarifies the architectural terminology and has some direct relevance to American houses, although its scope is mostly British.

A most interesting early survey of American folklife is found in *Lewis Miller: Sketches and Chronicles. The Reflections of a Nineteenth Century Pennsylvania German Folk Artist* (York, Pa.: Historical Society of York County, 1966). Some 160 selections from a total of about 2,000 drawings and watercolors are reproduced, illustrating many diverse aspects of everyday life. Perhaps a comparable effort, documented with camera and sketches, is the series called *Foxfire* (Garden City, N.Y.: Doubleday, 1 [1972], 2 [1973], 3[1975]) edited by Eliot Wigginton, a Georgia high-school teacher who inspired his students to study the folk culture of their own region, and who parlayed a small periodical into book-length publications, government grants, and many spinoff *Foxfire*-like projects. Log cabin building is covered in the original *Foxfire Book*, and a subject index is included in *Foxfire 3*.

The particular approach of cultural geography to American folklife materials may be seen in such works as Amos Rapoport's *House Form and Culture* (Foundations of Cultural Geography Series; Englewood Cliffs, N.J.: Prentice-Hall, 1969), and in such regional surveys as Peter O. Wacker's *The Muconetcong Valley of New Jersey: A Historical Geography* (New Brunswick, N.J.: Rutgers University Press, 1968), and Malcolm L. Comeaux's *Atchafalaya Swamp Life: Settlement and Folk Occupations* (Geoscience and Man, vol. 2; Baton Rouge: Louisiana State University, 1972). Milton B. Newton, Jr., a geographer, has published a useful booklet as *Mélanges*, no. 2 (Museum of Geoscience publication) *Louisiana House Types: A Field Guide* (Baton Rouge: Louisiana State University, 1971). Another example of folk architecture discussed by a geographer is in Joseph E. Spencer's "House Types in Southern

Utah," 35 (1945), 444–57. Two good studies of folk architecture appear in the "Material Culture in the South" special issue of *SFQ* (39 [Dec. 1975], 303–406).

Austin E. Fife is a leading advocate and practitioner of folklife studies in the West. Two of his important survey articles are "Folklore of Material Culture on the Rocky Mountain Frontier," *ArQ* 13 (1957), 101–10; and "Folklore and Local History," *UHQ* 31 (1963), 315–23. Austin and Alta Fife, together with Henry H. Glassie, edited *Forms Upon the Frontier: Folklife and Folk Arts in the United States,* containing several papers on Western folk architecture and folk arts and crafts from a conference held at Logan, Utah (*Utah State University Monograph Series* 16 [April 1969]).

For American folk architecture generally, see Wildhaber's bibliography. Everett Dick's *Sod-House Frontier,* cited in the notes to Chapter 14 above, includes one chapter on building and maintaining the sod house. Roger L. Welsch discussed "The Nebraska Soddy" in *NH* 48 (1967), 335–42; his extended study is *Sod Walls: The Story of the Nebraska Sod House* (Broken Bow, Neb.: Purcells, Inc., 1968). Many of the same sod-house photographs are reproduced in John I. White's "Pages from a Nebraska Album: The Sod House Photographs of Solomon D. Butcher," in *TAW* 12 (1975), 30–39. Good photographs and a bibliography accompany Tim Turner's article "Sod Houses in Nebraska," *Association of Preservation Technology Bulletin* 7 (1975), 20–37. Another plains building material is presented in Roger Welsch's "Sandhill Baled-Hay Construction," *KFQ* 15 (1970), 16–34. A useful "Adobe Bibliography" by Mark R. Barnes appears in the *Association of Preservation Technology Bulletin* 7 (1975), 89–101. John F. O'Conner's *The Adobe Book* (Santa Fe, N.M.: Ancient City Press, 1973), although oriented mainly to the contemporary builder of modern adobe houses, has very good practical information and fine photographic details.

Henry Glassie's notes to his study in Appendix C list numerous references on American log architecture. See also his important theoretical and regional work *Pattern in the Material Folk Culture of the Eastern United States* (Philadelphia: University of Pennsylvania Monographs in Folklore and Folklife no. 1, 1969). A useful and well-illustrated general survey is C. A. Weslager's *The Log Cabin in America From Pioneer Days to the Present* (New Brunswick, N.J.: Rutgers University Press, 1969). Peter O. Wacker and Roger T. Trindell studied "The Log House in New Jersey: Origin and Diffusion," in *KFQ* 13 (1968), 248–68, demonstrating effective use of maps, plates, and historical citations. Log cabins from the upper Midwest are illustrated in Paul W. Klammer's "Collecting Log Cabins: A Photographer's Hobby," *MH* 37 (1960), 71–77. A portfolio of excellent photographs of log buildings in Jackson Hole, Wyo., was printed in *TAW* 1 (1964), 21–30. Another attractive nontechnical publication is Clemson Donovan's *Living with Logs: British Columbia's Log Buildings and Rail Fences* (Saanichton, B.C., Canada: Hancock House, 1974).

Stone houses of northern Utah were surveyed in an article of that title by Austin E. Fife in *UHQ* 40 (1972), 6–23. Teddy Griffith covered one community in the same region in "A Heritage of Stone in Willard," *UHQ* 43 (1975), 286–300, and Richard C. Poulsen turned to a community farther south in Utah in his study "Stone Buildings of Beaver City," *UHQ* 43 (1975), 278–85. On Utah folk architecture in general, see Jan Harold Brunvand, "The Architecture of Zion," in *TAW* 13 (1976), 28–35.

For studies in American traditional house designs beyond the simplest cabin forms see William R. Ferris, Jr., "Mississippi Folk Architecture: A Sampling," *MSF* 1 (1973), 71–83; James R. O'Malley, "Functional Aspects of Folk Housing: A Case for the 'I' House, Union County, Tennessee," *TFSB* 38 (1972), 1–4; Henry Chandlee Forman, *Early Nantucket and its Whale Houses* (New York: Hastings House, 1966); and Henry Glassie's brilliant study *Folk Housing in Middle Virginia: A Structural Analysis of Historic Artifacts* (Knoxville: University of Tennessee Press, 1975).

Barns, among farm buildings, have been studied in such works as Wilbur Zelinsky's "The New England Connecting Barn," *GR* 48 (1958), 540–53; Henry Glassie, "The Variation of Concepts Within Tradition: Barn Building in Otsego County, New York," in *Man and Cultural Heritage: Papers in Honor of Fred B. Kniffen, Geoscience and Man* 5, ed. H. J. Walker and W. G. Haag (Baton Rouge: Louisiana State University School of Geoscience, 1974), 177–235; and two essays by Roger L. Welsch, "The Nebraska Round Barn," *JPC* 1 (1967), 403–9, and "Nebraska's Round Barn," *NH* 51 (1970), 49–92. A fine survey of barn types (including ethnic examples, round barns, and polygonal barns), barn construction details, and barn-building tools and materials appeared in a special section by Lee Hartman, "Michigan Barns, Our Vanishing Landscape" in *Michigan Natural Resources* 45 (March–April 1976), 17–32.

In a unique folklife study John M. Vlach made a detailed survey of two Parke County, Indiana, covered bridge builders' works (36 out of Indiana's 130 examples) which was published in *IF* 4 (1971), 61–88.

19

Folk Crafts and Art

Even before the word "folklife" entered the vocabulary of American folklorists, there were a considerable number of what might be termed folklife studies done from the point of view of art history in the United States and centering on folk crafts and folk art. Even now, some art historians continue to use the term "folk art" in a special sense. An important task of American folklife research, then, is to locate, evaluate, and synthesize these studies in order to establish a critical biliography for the field and to determine what genuinely traditional material has already been described. The beginning student must recognize that not every publication about handicrafts or "folk art" takes a folkloristic approach; indeed, some folklorists now prefer to ignore terms like "folk" and "tradition" in their studies of objects that ordinary people create and embellish in their own individual ways. A review of two representative older publications—one a period survey and the other concerning a particular group—illustrates some of the differences between these writings and modern folklife research on similar material.

To a degree the popular interest in folk arts and crafts that arose in the 1920s and '30s may have been a reaction against nonrepresentational modern art, but at the same time, ironically, the modern art movement claims folk art as part of its own background. in 1932 the New York Museum of Modern Art arranged an exhibition called *American Folk Art* in which two typical attitudes toward the subject were revealed in the subtitle: *The Art of the Common Man in America, 1750–1900*. The implications were that "folk art" must be the work of "common" men, or as the text explained, "people with little book learning in art techniques, and no academic training," and that the golden age of such art in America extended from the middle of the eighteenth century to the beginning of the twentieth. Further, the classification of the works by media (oil, pastel, water-color, velvet painting, wood sculpture, metal sculpture, etc.) suggested that folk art, like academic art (as it is usually distinguished from "design"), should be viewed as being mainly "creative" rather than utilitarian. That is, the artifacts chosen for display were judged significant for their decorative, not their functional, qualities. Yet many of the works illustrated were definitely useful (and, it may be hoped, effective)—weathervanes, advertising symbols (like cigar-store Indians), and signs. So it seems that once these kinds of things were admitted as "art," the door should have been opened for needlework, quilting, basketry, pottery, toymaking, and many other crafts now studied by folklife scholars, and valued (by both folk and folklorists) for both their beauty and their utility. In any case, it seems highly doubtful that the media and period divisions of typical art histories serve any useful purpose in folklife studies.

Numerous books and articles have been based on a similar conception of American folk art, although there is much diversity in the examples to which they refer. A broader scope is found in works on folk groups and their artifacts, such as the studies of Pennsylvania German (or "Dutch") material traditions. All the distinctive forms of building, handicrafts, and decorative art in this interesting regional-immigrant group have been the subject of attention, but the approaches and findings here are usually not directly applicable to other American folk groups. Few other American groups have the regional, linguistic, and general cultural unity of the Pennsylvania Germans, and few but other religiously circumscribed groups go to the lengths they do to preserve old ways of life. The very impressive fruits of Pennsylvania German folklife studies inspire the student of Anglo-American materials, but, as our second example shows, they cannot tell him much about what he will find elsewhere or how he should approach it.

One basic survey in this field is Frances Lichten's *Folk Art of Rural Pennsylvania*, published in 1946. The subject matter is "rural," and it flourished, according to Lichten's discussion, from the middle of the eighteenth century to about 1850. "Art" here is taken to include such disparate items as coverlets, butter molds, stove plates, and decorated barns. The arrangement of items is that of artistic media again, but now it is keyed to the close relationship of old-time farm life with the land itself—its raw materials, its crops, and its supported animals.

Such a classification brings together some odd combinations: stone houses or foundations for houses are with gravestones ("from beneath the surface of the earth"); wood houses are with cabinet-making and ornamental carving ("from the woodland"); and thatching is with basketry ("from the surface of the earth"). The whole book, with its numerous good illustrations, presents a nostalgic picture of the arts and crafts of a special group in a bygone era, but a different presentation will be required for scholars who want to begin investigating American folklife more generally, particularly if they intend to study contemporary instances of material folk creation.

The artifacts of American folk design and creation are certainly an engaging and worthwhile subject for study, but a unified theoretical basis for such study is difficult to formulate. Perhaps even more so than with other types of folk tradition, it seems extremely problematic to categorize traditional artifacts themselves as being "folk" or "non-folk," and their production as being "craft" or "art." How can one distinguish the impulse to create and to decorate objects as essentially any different in a *folk* sense from a "higher" *art* sense? Where does a utilitarian *craft* leave off and an *art* begin? The usual assumptions underlying studies in this infant science of folklife are not much help. **Folk crafts,** for instance, are usually thought of as amateur labor resulting in traditional homemade objects that are primarily functional. But these items may also be made by professional or semiprofessional artisans well aware of their creative abilities, and often the artifacts are decorative as well as useful.

Fencing, for example, is a necessary stage in settlement, and pioneer fences, like houses, were at first made from the nearest resources of the local region. Thus we find stone fences, wooden fences, hedges, and ditches to be common in different parts of the country. The proper construction techniques for each type were traditionally passed on, along with such variant names as "snake fence," "worm fence," or "zig-zag fence" for those made of interlocking split rails. The simplest fences, usually also the earliest, were rows of the waste material generated from clearing land for cultivation—brush, stones, or stumps (generally interwoven into a "rip gut" or "bull" fence). Such fences were fairly functional, but were unattractive and wasteful of land. Later, as time permitted and esthetic considerations prevailed, more attractive rail or "post and rider" fences were put up, and these were often contracted for with local builders or carpenters. Solid, well-aligned, and often painted wooden fencing is still a high-prestige consideration for many property owners, both rural and suburban. Even when barbed wire became generally available for fencing, devices employing the levering principle were invented that became traditional for tightening the strands, and rock-filled frames were made for supporting posts in hard ground where they could not be implanted.

Gates and stiles in fences range from the level of just removing some rails or leaving a small crack to slip through, to elaborate arrangements that permit opening the gate from horseback or in a buggy and that have an automatic self-closing feature. American fence and gate makers demonstrated their taste and ingenuity in the uses to which they put old wagon wheels. Some are lined up in rows as the fence itself; others may appear as the pivot point of a gate or are just fastened to the gate as decoration. The theme is carried indoors when a wagon wheel is used as a chandelier, or its hub alone becomes a lamp base. Form and function are barely distinguishable here.

Stands for rural mailboxes, located near a home's front gate, show similar patterns of development. The basic needs to support the box at a suitable level and to identify its owner can be solved simply by nailing the box to a post and painting a name on it. But people have gone to great lengths to improve on this solution with handcrafted, and often quite decorative, traditional devices made of welded chain links, bent pipes, driftwood, and other materials. A favorite American mailbox stand is the plywood Uncle Sam who holds the box in his hands and is painted red, white, and blue. Another is the old piece of discarded farm equipment—milk can, cream separator, wagon wheel, hand plow, or the like—or a pot-bellied stove. The last sometimes appears supporting a box marked "mail," the smoke pipe marked "newspapers," and the door to the stove itself marked "bills."

In folklife studies, **folk art** is usually thought of as the purely decorative or representational items produced by traditional means. But much folk art is very close to handicraft, and it is not worthwhile to attempt to distinguish the two fields too finely. Stenciling, for example, was once a favorite decorative medium for house floors and walls. But except for the original creative cutting of the design in the stencil pattern, the application of it to a surface was a mere mechanical matter of moving it along, holding it down, and applying paint to the cutout opening. Fancy sewing, quilting, and weaving also satisfy the creative urge and go beyond just holding textiles together or making coverlets warm; they might be considered both folk craft and art.

As with building trades and handicrafts, mere amateur status does not define the folk artist, for traditional creations have come from many professional artists—portraitists, carvers, calligraphers (expert handwriters), metal workers, and the like. In fact, only artisans or artists producing things solely for their own or their family's use can, strictly speaking, be called amateurs. But the vast majority of such creators are specialists who produce only one kind of artifact and then sell or barter it with others; professionalism is the rule, not the exception, in folk crafts and arts.

The particularly loose terminology of many folk art studies further confuses the matter of definitions. We find "primitive art," "popular art," "schoolgirl art," "provincial art," and several other terms in use for essentially the same materials. The most consistent use of the term "folk art" is for untrained ("nonacademic") representational artists, primarily painters, who worked with traditional subjects in traditional styles. Some, but not all of them, were itinerant artists, but *none* of them (at least it has never been proved) painted bodies on canvases all winter and traveled around adding the heads of their customers in the summer. This notion is merely a folk legend of considerable tenacity.

More broadly conceived, by folklorists, American folk art can take in a variety of miscellaneous decorative traditions. In a drowsy schoolroom, for instance, children may amuse themselves by tracing repetitious looped patterns on scratchpaper or on flyleaves of books. Little boys like to carve a checkerboard pattern down the length of a new pencil and all the way around it. Some people fold long paper chains out of gum wrappers or one-dollar bills. Others specialize in carving wooden chains or a "ball in cage" from one piece of wood. Cattails, dried milkweed pods, and other weeds may be gathered and painted for decorations. Plastic bleach jugs, tin cans, and cardboard milk cartons are turned into baskets, banks, or toys. Wreaths are woven of wool, feathers, or human hair and may be fashioned of coat hangers and plastic bags. In one western sawmill, the "chopper sawyers," whose job it is to cut knots out of second-grade to fourth-grade lumber, specialize in decorating knots with a pencil or pen and sending their artwork down the line for the other men to admire. The drawings may be animal figures, caricatures of fellow workmen, or pictures.

One American folklorist who has given these matters a great deal of thought, Michael Owen Jones, in a study of Kentucky chairmakers, proposes this definition of folk art:

> skill in the making or doing of that which functions as (among other things) a stimulus to appreciation of an individual's mastery of tools and materials apparent in what he has made; the output of that skill; and the activity manifesting the use of that skill. . . . [art] is something thought to be special (usually because of the skill required), generating an appreciative, contemplative response in the percipient.

In practice, Jones's informants recognized both the functional and the esthetic qualities of well-made objects; one man referred to the "beauty part" and the "lasting part." Following this lead, then, we may use the terms "craft" and "art" synonymously when studying traditional artifacts. Consequently, the goals for fieldwork in folk artifacts (in common with those for folk architecture) require several different kinds of data: careful description and picturing of the items themselves, facts about the raw materials used and the stages of construction, information about how the skills were acquired and to what uses the finished items are put, psychological profiles of the builders and the users, and statements by the individual makers and their community regarding the "esthetic" appeal of the finished products. However, these are the ideal dimensions of a study, seldom realized; the balance of this chapter merely describes further materials available for analysis.

Traditional handcrafted devices for home, farm, and ranch are numerous, and many are still being constructed and are in regular use. Outside the house proper, there are weathervanes, door knockers, wells, and yard ornaments to investigate. Another interesting category is the identification devices for dwellings, including signs for family and residence names (especially on ranches and summer cottages). The central-western hay derrick was investigated by Austin and James Fife in an outstanding example of an American folklife study that considered the classification and distribution of the objects, the need for them, and their probable history. When they realized that light rainfall in the region allowed for the year-round storage of hay outdoors, Great Basin pioneer farmers created devices to stack their hay into high, compact formations that would shed what rain did fall. First they just dragged the hay up by means of a rope rigged to a "flagpole," but soon they constructed more complex derricks with pivoted booms and sometimes even wheels for moving them from job to job. Neighbors borrowed ideas from one another as the hay-derrick idea spread through the region, and so successful was this traditional manufacture that only recently have any mass-produced devices begun to replace the homemade ones.

Similar studies might be made of traditional fruit-boxing equipment, berry pickers, rat traps, harvesting tools (corn knives, husking pegs, etc.), rope twisters, bits, spurs, rawhide equipment, scarecrows, and other agricultural artifacts. Homemade hunting, fishing, and camping equipment may also be traditional. These include shelters, boats, traps, animals calls, fishing lures, some trout flies, decoys, and camp lanterns, all of which are commercially produced in great variety, but which also linger in some folk forms. A good example of a recent folk invention is the fishing lure made from the aluminum snap-top of a beer or soft-drink can; these appeared in the West for steelhead fishing only about one year after the pop-top beverage can was introduced to the market.

Household or domestic crafts form another large category; either their pursuit has been entirely lost, or some are practiced now only as recreational pastimes rather than subsistence crafts. Spinning, dyeing, weaving, braiding, quilting, sewing, and candle-making were all traditionally learned necessary housekeeping jobs in pioneer times. Only quilting has been the subject of much study, partly because the picturesque names for the many colorful quilt patterns provide both linguistic and artistic matter for consideration. As Austin Fife has pointed out, these names may be simply *descriptive* ("Turkey Tracks"), or they may be *romantic* ("Steps to the Altar"), *biblical* ("Jacob's Ladder"), *ancestral* ("Grandmother's Fan"), *exotic* ("Arabic Lattice"), or *evocative of the pioneering experience* ("Road to California").

A large number of professional crafts with formal apprenticeships provided useful objects for the home and farm through much of the nineteenth century. The list would include woodworking, cabinet-making, furniture making, blacksmithing and other metalworking, glazing and glass blowing, pottery, basketry, and broom making. Such production has largely been transferred to factories now, although small-scale individual-shop manufacture does continue, and in the case of some crafts, like stained-glass making, it has begun to flourish again in recent years.

Baskets, rather than being commercially produced, have been largely replaced by other kinds of containers; thus, whatever baskets are still made almost invariably are folk products. And there are several good practical reasons for the continuing production of baskets: they are durable, inexpensive, light for their strength, reusable, and are constructed in a variety of pleasing shapes and handy sizes. American baskets are usually made of splints (or "splits") of pliant wood, such as white oak or ash woven around bent wood hoops or ribs. Different sizes and shapes of baskets are made for marketing, food harvest or storage, or for use as picnic baskets, magazine baskets, fishing creels or pack baskets. Afro-American basketry is of the "coil" type, made from bundles of "sweet grass" and long-leafed pine needles coiled around and upwards to form the bottom and sides, and sewn together with thin strips made from fronds of palmetto trees.

Folk pottery making, widely practiced in the United States, is a more complex and diversified craft involving chemistry and physics, special equipment, numerous designs, and different marketing traditions. The investigator must study the raw materials (clays and glazes), equipment (wheels, mills for grinding materials, kilns), the potter's shop layout, decorative elements (colors, shapes, handles, lids, inscriptions, etc.) and the great variety of artifacts produced, which include syrup jars, whiskey jugs, pickling crocks, bowls, mugs, plates, and churns. The craft of barrel making no longer exists with individual "coopers" turning out the entire barrel, but traditional work methods persist in the remaining modern cooperages which supply the relatively few wooden vessels of staves and hoops that are still in use. While barrels and kegs were once commonly employed for flour, crackers, nails, lard, gun powder, wine, beer, and many other commodities, and coopers also made tubs, buckets, and churns, nowadays the principal use for barrels in the United States is for aging bourbon whiskey. This industry's need for tight, charred, white oak barrels keeps the craft alive; modern coopers face the same problems of shaping their staves, "raising" a barrel, fitting the hoops and heads, and assuring its tightness as their predecessors did.

The traditional craft of hand-making skis in the United States would provide for an interesting study. It would require a great deal of searching through early accounts of life in northern parts of the country, including Alaska, for evidence, and making careful distinctions between skis and snowshoes, both of which were frequently called "snowshoes" in some regions in the nineteenth century. A character called "Snowshoe" Thompson, for example, wore long, homemade skis when he carried mail in the California mountains in 1856. A Colorado minister in the 1860s wrote in his autobiography:

> I made me a pair of snow-shoes, and, of course, was not an expert.
> . . . [they] were of the Norway style, from nine to eleven feet in length, and ran well when the snow was just right, but very heavy when they gathered snow. I carried a pole to jar the sticking snow off.

A man who settled in Boise, Idaho, in 1869 referred to homemade skis in his reminiscences as "Idaho snowshoes." Were such skis made in other regions, and were they called "snowshoes" or something else there? Does the term "Norway style" indicate that Norwegians taught others to make skis in this country? What materials and techniques were used to make skis? How were they employed? The answers to such questions might well be found in a thorough research project.

Folk toys existed in the past and still exist in great variety. They are made both by parents and by children themselves. Some are made from natural materials (willow whistles, cornstalk "fiddles", burr baskets, and dandelion chains), while others begin with manufactured items (clothes-pin dolls, spool window-rattlers and "tanks," and tobacco-can "harmonicas"). A whole family of toys is made simply from folded paper—"cootie catchers" (a toy for the mock capture of "cooties" from a person's scalp), airplaines, noise-makers, and hats—while toy weaponry forms another large class (slingshots, hairpin launchers, pea-shooters, and rubber-band guns with spring-clothes-pin triggers). Some children make an effective—and dangerous—substitute for fireworks by screwing a machine bolt half way into a nut, filling the cavity with tips cut from wooden "kitchen matches," and the screwing a second bolt in from the other end. The device is thrown into the air so it will come down on a sidewalk or pavement, and when a bolt head strikes, the whole arrangement blasts apart with a loud report.

Musical instruments of folk construction have benefited from the widespread interest in folk music in this country and thus have received considerably more study than many other kinds of material tradition. A number of very simple instruments are found in Afro-American tradition—a "rattler," made of bottle tops loosely nailed to a paddle; "quills," or the panpipe, fashioned of hollow reeds tied together; the "jitterbug," a single string stretched along a board, broom, or house wall; and the slightly more elaborate washtub bass. Much more highly developed, both physically and musically, from African roots in the American five-string banjo. The unfretted fifth string on the folk banjo contributes a drone sound in some strumming styles and takes a more active role in finger-picking. Another distinctive American instrument is the southern-mountain plucked dulcimer. Enjoying a great revival today, the plucked dulcimer is not to be confused with the much rarer (and usually German or East European) hammered dulcimer. The plucked dulcimer derives from the European family of folk instruments that includes the Norwegian *langeleik*, the Swedish *humle*, the German *Scheitholt*, and the French *espinette des vosges*, all instruments with drone strings that are played while being rested horizontally on a table or on the lap. The American mountain dulcimer generally has three strings—a melody string and two drones—and it is shaped in graceful curves along the sides, with sound holes (often heart-shaped) on the top surface. Traditionally, the dulcimer is played with a quill or "feather pick."

Aspects of purely decorative and representational American folk art already mentioned include whittling, needlework, stenciling, and painting. Other examples are scrimshaw (carving and decorating objects of whale bone or ivory), tattooing, gravestone carving, and what have been called "dendroglyphs" (patterns, inscriptions, and pictures carved on trees), particularly common on the white bark of birches and aspens. Folk artisans sometimes make special "art" objects, such as face mugs and figurines by potters and toy furniture or miniature farm equipment by woodworkers. In Afro-American folk art, alligators, heads, and grotesque skulls are found in clay sculpture and wood carving. Even the making of snowmen and other snow sculpture may be considered a folk art form.

Just as musical expression has been identified at folk, popular, and art levels, comparisons might be made of such forms as portraiture, still life, the grotesque, or caricature as they appear in folk art, popular art, and "high" art. Or a historical subject, such as "Custer's Last Stand," might be compared in American folk expression, in popular media such as magazine illustrations or Currier and Ives prints, and in serious academic art. Some scholars, however, argue against the utility of identifying such "levels" of art, and they prefer to drop the terms "folk and primitive art" in favor of something like Michael Owen Jones's formulation "units or structures of expressive behavior learned and manifested primarily in situations of firsthand interaction." Still, some kind of esthetic and comparative evaluations of art levels seems necessary, if only to provide a good foundation for supporting or rebutting such provocative generalizations as these from an art historian:

> Folk art is naïve, crude, clumsy and old-fashioned, popular art often skillful and technically apt, though vulgar, subject to superficial and rapid transformation, but incapable of achieving either more radical change or finer discrimination. Genuine art is used up, disintegrated, and simplified by folk art; it is watered down, botched and bowdlerized by popular art.

BIBLIOGRAPHIC NOTES

The following are general older surveys of American handicrafts, all containing some illustrations and useful descriptions, although their analyses are out of date: *Hands That Built New Hampshire*, published by the Works Project Administration Writers' Program (Brattleboro, Vt., 1940); Ella Shannon Bowles, *Homespun Handicrafts* (Philadelphia, 1931; reissued, New York: Benjamin Blom, 1972); Allen H. Eaton, *Handicrafts of the Southern Highlands* (New York: Russell Sage Foundation, 1937; paperback reprint, New York: Dover Publications, 1973); Rollin C. Steinmetz and Charles S. Rice, *Vanishing Crafts and their Craftsmen* (New Brunswick, N.J.: Rutgers University Press, 1959); and Erwin O. Christensen, *American Crafts and Folk Arts*, America Today Series, no. 4 (Washington, D.C.: Robert B. Luce, 1964).

Mamie Meredith collected "The Nomenclature of American Pioneer Fences" in *SFQ* 15 (1951), 109–51. Two studies with more depth are H. F. Raup's

"The Fence in the Cultural Landscape," WF 6 (1947), 1–12; and E. C. Mather and J. F. Hart's "Fences and Farms," GR 44 (1954), 201–23. A unique fence, "the lopped tree fence" was described by Mary Catharine Davis in SFQ 21 (1957), 174–75.

The Fifes's hay derrick study was published in WF 7 (1948), 225–39, with addenda in WF 10 (1951), 320–22. A distributional study of a particular type of homemade hair- or rope-twister is Fred Kniffen's "The Western Cattle Complex: Notes on Differentiation and Diffusion," WF 12 (1953), 179–85. On a related craft, see Robert and Martha Cochran, with Christopher Pierle, "The Preparation and Use of Bear Grass Rope: An Interview with Robert Simmons, Mississippi Folk Craftsman," NYFQ 30 (1974), 185–96. An interview with a Finnish "tie-hacker" of McCall, Idaho, was published by H. J. Swinney in WF 24 (1965), 271–73. On traditional blacksmithing techniques, see Mody C. Boatright, "How Will Boatright Made Bits and Spurs," JAF 83 (1970), 77–80; and John M. Vlach, "The Fabrication of a Traditional Fire Tool," JAF 86 (1973), 54–57. The Colorado skiing minister quoted in this chapter was Rev. John L. Dyer, whose autobiography, The Snow-Shoe Itinerant, was published in Cincinnati in 1890. "Idaho snowshoes" were described by Thomas Corwin Donaldson in Idaho of Yesterday (Caldwell, Id.: Caxton Press, 1941).

Two studies that relate folk craftsmanship to larger-scale production are Carlos C. Drake, "Traditional Elements in the Cooperage Industry," KFQ 14 (1969), 81–96; and Robert S. McCarl, Jr., "The Production Welder: Product, Process and the Industrial Craftsman," NYFQ 30 (1974), 243–53.

Several books offer general illustrated surveys of household and farm crafts. Jared van Wagenen, Jr., in The Golden Age of Homespun (New York: American Century Series, 1963), provides "a record of the lore and the methods by which our forebears lived upon the land" in upper New York State from the Revolution to the Civil War. Several works by Eric Sloane are beautifully illustrated with line drawings of museum pieces. These include American Yesterday (New York: W. Funk, 1956); The Seasons of America Past (New York: W. Funk, 1958); and Diary of an Early American Boy: Noah Blake, 1805 (New York: Funk & Wagnalls, 1962; repr. Ballantine paperback, 1974).

Special studies of particular crafts are becoming increasingly more common in American folklore journals. See the following, for example: Mac E. Barrick, "Pennsylvania Corn Knives and Husking Pegs," KFQ 15 (1970), 128–37; Henry Glassie, "William Houck, Maker of Pounded Ash Adirondack Pack-Baskets," KFQ 12 (1967), 23–54; Howard Wight Marshall, "Mr. Westfall's Baskets: Traditional Craftsmanship in Northcentral Missouri," MSF 2 (1974), 43–60; Sylvia Ann Grider and Barbara Ann Allen, "Howard Taylor, Cane Maker and Handle Shaver," IF 7 (1974), 5–25; James R. Dow, "The Hand Carved Walking Canes of William Baurichter," KFQ 15 (1970), 138–47; Beulah M. D'Olive Price, "Riving Shingles in Alcorn County," MFR 6 (1972), 108–14; David J. Winslow, "New York Duck Decoys," KFQ 17 (1972), 119–32; Robert Atkinson, "The Kreutz Brothers: Craftsmen in Glass," NYFQ 25 (1969), 100–18; and John A. Burrison, "Alkaline-Glazed Stoneware: A Deep-South Pottery Tradition," SFQ 39 (1975), 377–403.

A general list of household handicrafts was given in the article by Afton Wynn cited in the notes to Chapter 14. Paul Brewster included information on quilt patterns, dyeing, and folk toys in volume 1 of *The Frank C. Brown Collection of North Carolina Folklore.* For related studies, see Annie Louise D'Olive, "Folk Implements Used for Cleaning," *MFR* 2 (1968), 125–34; and Annelen Archbold, "Percy Beeson, A Kentucky Broommaker," *MSF* 3 (1975), 41–45.

There are several books on quilt patterns, most of them offering instructions for making quilts and providing historical notes. A good one is Carrie A. Hall and Rose G. Kretsinger's *The Romance of the Patchwork Quilt in America* (Caldwell, Id.: Caxton Press, 1936; reissued, New York [n.d.]). Carrie Hall's large collection of quilt patches and patterns is deposited in the Museum of Art at the University of Kansas in Lawrence. Commenting on a list of quilt-pattern names submitted by Paul Brewster to *CFQ* 3 (1944), 61, Wayland D. Hand pointed out the interplay of folk and commercial patterns fostered by companies that sold quilt battings wrapped with advertising for their own lines of quilt patterns; see *CFQ* 3 (1944), 151–52. Useful for further studies are Andrea Greenberg's survey "American Quilting," in *IF* 5 (1972), 264–79; and a bibliography of American quilt making compiled by Susan Roach and Lorre M. Weidlich and published in *FFemC* 3 (Spring 1974), 17–28. For the work of individual artisans, see Joanne Farb, "Piecin' and Quiltin': Two Quilters in Southwest Arkansas," *SFQ* 39 (1975), 363–75.

Michael Owen Jones has written a number of important studies of American furniture making, such as "The Study of Traditional Furniture: Review and Preview," *KFQ* 12 (1967), 233–45; " 'They Made them for the Lasting Part': A 'Folk' Typology of Traditional Furniture Makers," *SFQ* 35 (1971), 44–61; and " 'For Myself I like a *Decent,* Plain-Made Chair': The Concept of Taste and the Traditional Arts in America," *WF* 31 (1972), 27–52. Jones's work in these and other articles is incorporated into his book *The Hand Made Object and Its Maker* (Los Angeles: University of California Press, 1975).

American folk toys have been included in general books on folk crafts, but have had little individual scholarly treatment. A popular, nostalgic book that deals largely with simple folk toys is Robert Paul Smith's *How to Do Nothing with Nobody, All Alone by Yourself* (New York: W. W. Norton, 1958). An article describing a small local industry for manufacturing copies of folk toys if Henry B. Comstock's "Folk Toys Are Back Again," in *Popular Science* (March 1960), 144–47. Two instruction books on folk-toy making are Joan Joseph's *Folk Toys Around the World and How to Make Them* (New York: Parents Magazine Press in cooperation with the U.S. Committee for UNICEF, 1972); and Dick Schnache, *American Folk Toys: How to Make Them* (Baltimore: Penguin Books, 1973). Roger Welsch discussed "The Cornstalk Fiddle" (a toy, not an instrument) in *JAF* 77 (1964), 262–63. Another widely distributed folk noisemaker is described by John C. McConnell in "The Dumbull or Scrauncher," in *TFSB* 25 (1959), 89.

Louise Scruggs gave a brief and sketchy "History of the 5-String Banjo" in *TFSB* 27 (1961), 1–5. More detailed studies are Gene Bluestein's "America's Folk Instrument: Notes on the Five-String Banjo," *WF* 23 (1964), 241–48;

C. P. Heaton's "The 5-String Banjo in North Carolina," *SFQ* 35 (1971), 62–82; and Jay Bailey's "Historical Origin and Stylistic Developments of the Five-String Banjo," *JAF* 85 (1972), 58–65. Information on an even simpler class of traditional stringed instruemnts is given by David Evans in "Afro-American One-Stringed Instruments," *WF* 29 (1970), 229–45. Charles Seeger submitted "The Appalachian Dulcimer" to a full historical treatment in *JAF* 71 (1958), 40–51; and S. E. Hastings reports on one notable old instrument in his article "Construction Techniques in an Old Appalachian Mountain Dulcimer," in *JAF* 83 (1970), 462–68. A good regional survey is Charles W. Joyner's "Dulcimer Making in Western North Carolina: Creativity in a Traditional Mountain Craft," *SFQ* 39 (1975), 341–61. Other useful information on dulcimer playing in the Southern mountains is found in the following popular works: John F. Putnam's "The Plucked Dulcimer," *MLW* 34 (1958), 7–13; Putnam's booklet *The Plucked Dulcimer and How to Play It* (Berea, Ky.: Council of the Southern Mountains, 1961); and Jean Ritchie's *The Dulcimer Book* (New York: Oak Publications, 1963). S. J. Sackett discussed "The Hammered Dulcimer in Ellis County, Kansas," in *JIFMC* 14 (1962), 61–64. A study of the folk use made of a commercial musical instrument is A. Doyle Moore's "The Autoharp: Its Origins and Development from a Popular to a Folk Instrument," in *NYFQ* 19 (1963), 261–74.

There are numerous books and publications on folk art, using either that term or one of the others listed in this chapter. Two important exhibition catalogs that are available are *The Abby Aldrich Rockefeller Folk Art Collection: A Descriptive Catalog, by Nina Fletcher Little* (Colonial Williamsburg, Va., 1957); and Agnes Halsey Jones and Louis C. Jones, *New-Found Folk Art of the Young Republic* (Cooperstown, N.Y.: New York State Historical Association, 1960). Among well-illustrated works on nonacademic representational and decorative art are Janet Waring, *Early American Stencils on Walls and Furniture* (1937; reprinted by Dover Publications, New York, 1968); Jean Lipman, *American Primitive Painting* (London and New York: Oxford University Press, 1942); Henry J. Kauffman, *Pennsylvania Dutch American Folk Art* (1946; revised and enlarged edn., New York: Dover Publications 1964); Alice Ford, *Pictorial Folk Art: New England to California* (London and New York: Studio Publications, 1949); and Nina Fletcher Little, *American Decorative Wall Painting 1700–1850* (Sturbridge, Mass. and New York: Old Sturbridge Village and Studio Publications, 1952).

An important picture book on American folk crafts and art is Erwin O. Christensen's *The Index of American Design*, published by the Smithsonian Institution (Washington, D.C., 1950). The Index was part of the Federal Art Project of the 1930s and is now housed in the National Gallery of Art. It includes photographs and drawings of designs, weathervanes, utensils, costumes, and pictorial art. Some good examples of its riches are used as illustrations in Duncan Emrich's article titled "America's Folkways," in *Holiday*, 18 (July 1955), 60–63 and following.

Jean Lipman's book *American Folk Art in Wood, Metal, and Stone* (New York: Pantheon, 1948) is another well-illustraded survey volume, as is her work done in collaboration with Alice Winchester, *The Flowering of Ameri-*

can Folk Art (1776–1876) (New York: Viking Press, 1974). The book *America's Arts and Skills*, published by the editors of *Life* (New York, 1957), although neither wholly art nor folk, contains some folk art, and is magnificently illustrated. It surveys American popular art and design from Colonial times to the present, as do several similar works produced to commemorate the United States Bicenntenial.

Some byways of folk art are charted in articles such as Geoffrey Cortelyon and Kathleen Green's study "Pop Owen," concerning an amateur artist in rural New York state, in *KFQ* 28 (1972), 293–304; Alan B. Govenar's "Leonard Ł. 'Stoney' St. Clair, Tattooist," *JOFS* 3 (1975), 9–14; and E. N. Anderson, Jr., "On the Folk Art of Landscaping," *WF* 31 (1972), 179–88. Kenneth S. Goldstein published an important article concerning his discovery, "William Robbie: Folk Artist of the Buchan District, Aberdeenshire" in *Folklore in Action*, pp. 101–11.

Michael Owen Jones has published a number of thoughtful studies of methodology and analysis of American folk arts and crafts, beginning with "Two Directions for Folkloristics in the Study of American Art," *SFQ* 32 (1968), 249–59. Jones's other work has appeared in *SFQ* 36 (1972), 43–60; *JPC* 4 (1970), 194–212, and 6 (1973), 794–818; *KFQ* 16 (1971), 39–48; and *WF* 30 (1971), 77–104, and 32 (1973), 19–32. A related essay is Elizabeth Mosby Adler's "Direction in the Study of American Folk Art," *NYF* 1 (1975), 31–44.

Three studies of the whalers' art of ivory carving are the following: Marius Barbeau, "All Hands Aboard Scrimshawing," *The American Neptune* 12(1952), 99–122 (reprinted by the Peabody Museum of Salem, [Mass.], 1966); Walter K. Earle, *Scrimshaw: Folk Art of the Whalers* (Cold Spring Harbor, N.Y.: Whaling Museum Society, Inc., 1957); and Edouard A. Stackpole, *Scrimshaw at Mystic Seaport* (Mystic, Conn.: The Marine Historical Assoc., 1958). A brief note on a domestic art/craft form is Ila A. Wright's "Hair Watch Chains and Flowers," *WF* 18 (1959), 114–17.

American gravestones as folk art have been treated in a number of illustrated books of various degrees of scholarly merit and in such articles as Phil R. Jack's "Gravestone Symbols of Western Pennsylvania," in *Two Penny Ballads and Four Dollar Whiskey*, ed. Kenneth S. Goldstein and Robert H. Byington (Hatboro, Pa.: Folklore Associates, 1966), pp. 165–73; and Beulah M. D'Olive Price, "The Customs of Using Portrait Statues as Gravestones," *MFR* 3 (1969), 58–64, 112–20. The journal *AFFWord* published a series of articles on cemeteries and their decoration beginning with the issue (vol. 1) for July 1971; the traditions touched on included Papago, Mormon, Chinese, Polynesian, and Mexican-American. Sara Clark described "The Decoration of Graves in Central Texas with Seashells," in *PTFS* 36 (1972), 33–43.

Black American folk art has recently had some special study in such works as William R. Ferris, Jr., "Vision in Afro-American Folk Art: The Sculpture of James Thomas," *JAF* 88 (1975), 115–31 (which expands upon a 1970 article); and David Evans, "Afro-American Folk Sculpture from Parchman Penitentiary [Miss.]," *MFR* 6 (1972), 141–52. Both writers provide good bibliographic guidance for background reading in this area.

A previously unnoticed form of regional folk art—designs carved by western sheepherders on aspen trees—was documented with photographs by Ansel Adams and Paul Hassel in *TAW* 1 (Spring 1964), 37–45. Since then such studies have appeared as Jan Harold Brunvand and John C. Abramson, "Aspen Tree Doodlings in the Wasatch Mountains: A Preliminary Survey of Traditional Tree Carvings," in *Forms Upon the Frontier*, ed. Austin and Alta Fife and Henry H. Glassie, Monograph Series, 16:2 (Logan, Ut.: Utah State University, 1969), pp. 89–102; and James B. DeKorne, *Aspen Art in the New Mexico Highlands* (Santa Fe, N.M.: Museum of New Mexico Press, 1970). Other obscure folk-art expressions are depicted and discussed in a general way in Avon Neal and Ann Parker, *Ephemeral Folk Figures: Scarecrows, Harvest Figures, and Snowmen* (New York: Clarkson N. Potter, 1969).

The closing quotation in this chapter is from Arnold Hauser's "Popular Art and Folk Art," *Dissent* 5 (Summer 1958), 229–37, reprinted in *The Philosophy of Art History* (New York: Knopf, 1959), p. 347.

20

Folk Costumes

Traditional costumes hold a prominent place in European folklife research, and consequently they are often featured there in publications, archives, museums, and folk festivals. Vestiges of folk costume still linger in the everyday life of some rural regions in almost all European countries, and many city people occasionally put on national or regional garb at festive occasions. Americans have become familiar with these and other foreign folk costumes through such means as folksong and dance groups from abroad, publications and television broadcasts, and travel. We easily recognize certain clichés of clothing as being nationally symbolic—the German in *lederhosen,* the Scot in kilts, and the Russian in a fur cap and high boots, for example. But we tend to assume that the United States really has no distinctive costume traditions, recognizing, perhaps, only a comical American tourist stereotype of a man in shorts, a loud sport shirt, sandals or tennis shoes, and a baseball cap, with a camera dangling around his neck; or an Indian chief with fringed buckskins and full headdress.

The few studies of traditional American clothing that have appeared give the impression that native Indian dress and vestiges of European costume among religious sects constitute the whole subject. In the *Journal of American Folklore,* for example, all of the major references to costume in the published index refer to that of Indian tribes. Most of the monographs and book-length studies have dealt with sectarian costumes, generally those of Pennsylvania-German Protestant groups. But there are many other traditional aspects of clothing in the United States that deserve study.

Despite the pervasive influence of international fashion and the easy accessibility of ready-made mass-produced clothing, some traditional influences continue to be apparent both in *what* Americans wear and *how* they wear it. While we have never had a peasant class with distinctive folk attire, and mobility and mass communications have wiped out many regional clothing styles, some folk-group differentiation is effected as much by costume choices as by folk speech, customs, beliefs, or other forms. Examples include special clothing, such as a tennis or ski "outfit"; holiday costumes, such as for Halloween or the custom of wearing green on St. Patrick's Day; and "dressing up" for special occasions, such as first communion or marriage. Just as with folk music, where traditional material mingles with commercialism, fashion leaders have borrowed ideas from folk practice and exploited them. For instance, recently a style called "folkloric" was introduced which (supposedly) took elements from European peasant costumes to produce and market for the middle-class masses. But since there is considerable published work on cycles in the history of fashionable and popular styles, we will confine ourselves here to outlining only some possibilities in traditional American dress, very few of which have so far been studied.

Folk costume research involves identifying and classifying details of *traditional* dress and adornment among the standardized general aspects, relating these traditions to the larger structure of folk group behavior, and interpreting the meanings of these patterns. Probably in clothing research we will have even greater problems sorting out folk, popular, and elite influences than with any other aspect of folklore. Clothing manufacture, after all, is a gigantic international industry which is quick to respond both to the dictates of "high fashion" or to hints of future fads in current folk practices. So rapid are these changes that to cite specific examples risks dating this chapter; I take a chance mentioning just two styles prominent in store displays at the time of this writing. These are platform shoes, dictated by fashion despite their awkwardness and even health hazards, and, in a style based on traditional practice, "cut-off" shorts with ragged unhemmed lower edges, now available as ready-made garments.

One useful avenue of approach to American folk costume research is the historical, tracing the development of today's clothing styles out of the medley of national and ethnic styles that settlers brought to the new world. We may identify historical differences and developments in costume according to age, sex, national origin, region, occupation, economic and social status, and whether people are dressing for every day or a special occasion.

The first settlers, of course, came to the New World wearing the ordinary clothes of their homelands and bringing whatever fine clothes they could, according to their wealth and social status. Colonial costume, as historical research reveals, preserved considerable diversity in dress, depending upon the national origins, religions, occupations, and other cultural traits of the settlers. Soon, however, modes of dress more appropriate for a frontier society developed, influenced by the physical environment, the available raw materials and means of production, and to some extent by the Indians' example.

The characteristic frontiersmen's outfit—a distinctive American costume—was made from the typical native material, buckskin, right down to the moccasins. The trousers were close-cut without cuffs, but sometimes had long fringes down the sides; the upper garment was a tunic, slit part way down the front and laced, with a sort of cape-shawl shoulder piece. The sleeve edges and cape were also fringed. A coonskin or other fur hat topped the rig, and a belt—usually worn with buckle to the rear to prevent sun glare or snagging—completed it. The explanations offered for the fringing on the outfit sound suspicious. One is that the longer the fringes, the better rain water would drip off a man. Another story is that the fringes were there to provide a ready source of buckskin thongs for tying. Cases are also on record of Mountain Men deriving nourishment, or at least believing that they did, from chewing the fringes from their clothing. Probably the fringe came first as a mere decorative device, and its various practical uses developed later and were orally transmitted.

The settlers that followed the trail blazers on the Great Plains and beyond were farmers from "back East" who wore the homemade clothing common to all of the settlements. As Francis Parkman described them in *The Oregon Trail*, from his observations in 1846, the men wore broad-brimmed hats and "their long angular proportions [were] enveloped in brown homespun, evidently cut and adjusted by the hands of a domestic female tailor." The women wore homespun or "linsey-woolsey" dresses, sometimes supplemented by an apron or shawl, and sunbonnets. A fine description of part of the process of a family making most of its own clothing is included on the Library of Congress recording "Jack Tales told by Mrs. Maud Long of Hot Springs, N.C." (AAFS L47):

It would be on a long, winter evening when, after supper, all of us were gathered before the big open fire, my mother taking care of the baby or else the baby was in the cradle very near to mother, and she would be sewing or carding.

My father would be mending someone's shoes or maybe a bit of harness. The older girls were helping with the carding or the sewing. And all of us little ones would either have a lapful or a basket full of wool out of which we must pick all the burrs and the Spanish needles and the bits of briars and dirt against the next day's carding.

For my mother wove all of this wool that had been shorn from the backs of our own sheep—raised there on the farm that was in the heart of the Great Smoky Mountains in North Carolina—into linsey-woolsey, for hers and our dresses, or into blue jeans for my father's and brothers' suits, or into blankets to keep us warm, or into the beautiful patterned coverlets, to say nothing of all the socks and stockings and mitts and hoods that it took for a large family of nine children. And so she needed every bit of the wool that she could get ready.

As settlers became adjusted to the far West they modified their costume. Mark Twain described himself in miner's garb in *Roughing It*, only a year after he had arrived there in 1861 as a typical greenhorn, being "rusty looking . . . coatless, slouch hat, blue woolen shirt, pantaloons stuffed into boot-tops, whiskered half down to the waist, and the universal navy revolver slung to my belt." The blue or red color of the shirt was evidently a traditional touch; an 1859 guidebook for overland travel advised that "the shirt [should be] of red or blue flannel, such as can be found in almost all the shops on the frontier." Bandanna handkerchiefs, too, were until recently made only in blue or red, and the L. L. Bean Company of Freeport, Maine, long-time outfitter of hunting, fishing, and camping parties, long advised in its catalog "A good blue flannel shirt cannot be beaten for all around wear."

The changes in Mormon pioneer dress during their first thirty-odd years of settlement in the West illustrate a unique case of adaptation of imported styles. The Saints numbered among them midwesterners and easterners, as well as many European converts, all of whom brought elements of their clothing traditions with them to Utah when they first began to arrive there in 1847. But in their eagerness to become "real Americans," most immigrants quickly discarded peasant styles. (One exception may be the Mormon pioneer men's "barn door trousers," possibly developed from North European peasant breeches; these had a front-buttoned flap, somewhat like that on the traditional sailors' pants.) The American fashions of the time influenced women to create substitutes for starch or the whalebone stiffeners used in bonnets or skirts out of pasteboard, folded newspaper, or wooden slats. The climate in the mountain settlements dictated warmer clothing than was common back East, which included quilted petticoats. The desire for adornment on clothing was filled partly by weaving straw flowers out of native grasses and making dyes from wild plants. Special religious rituals and beliefs led to the everyday wearing of sacred underclothing ("Temple Garments") and to robes used exclusively in temple ceremonies. Unlike several other American sects, however, the Mormons developed no uniform outer clothing as a mark of membership and piety, although a women's work costume with wide pants, a short skirt, and a wide-brimmed straw hat ("The Deseret Costume") was proposed at one time. Currently in Utah many of the ethnic groups, whether Mormon or not, are returning to national costumes for festive occasions, and the Mormon women and girls have a strong preference for long "Pioneer style" dresses to wear for church or going out. An LDS (Latter-day Saint) splinter group, The Order of Aaron, has adopted a conservative sectarian costume for general everyday use.

Most early American occupational groups had traditional costume elements, such as a leather apron for a cobbler or blacksmith, a miller's smock, or the nineteenth-century farmer's outfit with its heavy shoes, vest, suspenders, and wide-brimmed hat (later replaced by denim bib-overalls, and still later by matching pant and shirt sets in green, blue, or gray). Merchant sailors of all nations tended to have some distinctive garb, just as different navies of the world still do. American loggers wore checkered shirts, pants that were "stagged" (cut off above the cuffs), sometimes a sash around the waist, and always hob-nailed and well-greased boots. The cowboy's distinctive outfit, much improvised upon, has become a national symbol. Originally it was characterized by the smooth leather (later sometimes fur) "chaps," a dull-colored shirt set off by a red scarf, vest, gunbelt, gloves, high-heeled boots, and wide-brimmed hat. Some of the cowboy-hat styles first associated with different parts of the West are still named for these regions and sell better in some places than others. The first cowboy trousers were usually of brown or naturally-colored canvas, but the blue Levi's were introduced by the eighteen-sixties, and the copper rivets at stress points arrived in 1872 or '73, although cowboys declined to accept them until about the 1890s. Other occupational traditions in dress may be distinguished, as well as the prestige values of different modes, as suggested in such verses from folksongs as this:

> I would not marry the farmer,
> He's always in the dirt;
> I'd rather marry the railroader,
> Who wears the striped shirt.

The later immigrants to the United States and Canada from southern and eastern Europe repeated even more rapidly the earlier settlers' practice of discarding native styles in preference for Westernized fashions. They sensed at once as they mingled with their new countrymen how clearly one's clothes projected a personal image, identifying the outsider as a foreigner. M. E. Ravage, a Romanian-Jewish immigrant, arrived in New York City in 1900; he commented frequently on his awareness of clothes making the man in his book *An American in the Making* (1917). He soon discovered that many of his fellow Romanians mixed their clothing styles as badly as they did their languages; some he saw were "clad in an absurd medley of Rumanian sheep-pelts and American red sweaters." *Real* Americans, he felt, showed more taste and "obvious wealth (judging from their clothes)." It amused him to recall that in his home village in Moldavia "none but young ladies of marriageable age wore gloves; for any one else the article would have been regarded as silly dandyism." But in New York, he wrote, "even teamsters and street laborers wore gloves at their work, to preserve, I supposed, their dainty hands." After many rebuffs during his first job-seeking, Ravage mustered up the courage to ask a potential employer what was lacking in him:

> He looked me over from head to foot, and then, with a contemptuous glance at my shabby foreign shoes (the alien's shoes are his Judas), he asked me whether I supposed he wanted a greenhorn in his store. . . . In order to have a job one must have American clothes, and the only way to get American clothes was to find a job and earn the price.

Ravage finally managed to break out of this vicious circle by borrowing money and some articles of clothing to create a better appearance and win a position. With his first earnings he purchased a new suit, new shoes, and a derby hat; thus (in about three months' time) began to evolve an "American in the making." Ironically, now, descendents of immigrants with experiences like this have formed folksong and dance groups and like to put on a semblance of national costume. And when I traveled in Romania in the early 1970s American tourists were often judged conspicuous for their shoes (usually tennis sneakers), and embroidered Romanian "peasant shirts" were popular souvenir items. The Romanian villagers themselves, however, were often anxious to trade parts of their folk costumes for Western blue jeans or panty hose.

Besides historical developments in traditional dress and the special garb of a few nationality or sectarian groups, other possibilities exist for research in traditional American costumes. Standardized uniforms (as for monastic orders, military units, or bands) are not folk costumes, but probably less formal dress markers indicating one's role or status are, such as the medical student's lab coat, the chef's tall white hat, the motorcyclist's leather jacket, or the ballet dancer's favorite tacky warm-up clothes. The sense of what constitutes "dressing up" in what were once referred to as "Sunday go-to-meeting" clothes, and which occasions call for such garb, would seem to be a traditional matter with variation from one period to another and from region to region. Or people may deliberately "dress down" to show rejection of society's clothing standards and to signal their alliance with like-minded individuals, whether "hippies," "freaks," defenders of the ecology, or others. (These examples illustrate that even within non-conformity there is conformity with another set of standards. Some dissident youth—often dedicated anti-militarists—favor old military uniforms as their badge of rebellion.) Patchwork and embroidered decoration on denim clothing and the modification of jeans and bib overalls into other garments has developed as a modern clothing craft of great variation and popularity. The supposed and actual dress of homosexuals might be studied. The degree of belief and practice involved with lucky clothing, for which basketball coaches are notorious, is another open question, as is the symbolic use of certain garments. For example, the native American coonskin hat was an effective political trademark for Senator Estes Kefauver of Tennessee, then briefly a fashion in children's wear. The popularity of "Come-as-you-are" or period-dress parties could be studied, as could the visual clichés of pioneer costume concoted for use in local historical parades and pageants. Even *not* wearing something—going braless, shoeless, or tieless—constitutes a statement about a tradition made via one's mode of dress, and there are traditional associations between age of a person and what he wears. Some metaphoric proverbial language refers to clothing: "to give the shirt off one's back," "to bet one's boots," "to throw one's hat in the ring," "if the shoe fits, wear it," and "to beat the socks off someone" are examples. Perhaps a good beginning for costume research would be simply to inventory one's own wardrobe to see what traditional elements are present, then to look more closely at one's friends and acquaintances for a time, to see what their clothes seem to be saying about them and to what degree these are traditional statements or are made by some traditional means.

BIBLIOGRAPHIC NOTES

Since there are very few studies in American folk costume, two survey articles by Don Yoder that refer to what little bibliography there is, are especially valuable. One is "Sectarian Costume Research in the United States," in *Forms Upon the Frontier*, ed. Austin and Alta Fife and Henry H. Glassie, Monograph Series, 16:2 (Logan, Utah; Utah State University Press, 1969), 41–75; the other is Yoder's chapter "Folk Costume," in *Folklore and Folklife: An Introduction*, edited by Richard M. Dorson (Chicago: University of Chicago Press, 1972), pp. 295–323. Robert Wildhaber's bibliography (mentioned in the notes to Chapter 18) has a short section on costume and textiles. Some studies of *customs* (see Chapter 14) touch on *costumes* as well.

The following are general histories of American dress that contain good illustrations and some discussion: Douglas Gorsline, *What People Wore: A Visual History of Dress from Ancient Times to Twentieth-Century America* (New York and London: B. T. Batsford, 1952); R. Turner Wilcox, *Five Centuries of American Costume* (New York: Scribners, 1963); and Edward Warwick, Henry C. Pitz, and Alexander Wyckoff, *Early American Dress: The History of American Dress*, vol. 2 (New York: B. Blom, 1965). Many illustrated works on American occupations and trades (cattle raising, railroading, seafaring, farming, etc.) are good sources of information on distinctive forms of work costume and uniform.

The article "Fashion on the Frontier" by Hazel Stein in *SFQ* 21 (1957), 160–64, is undocumented and of little scholarly value. Much better is Fairfax Proudfit Walkup's study "The Sunbonnet Woman: Fashions in Utah Pioneer Costume," *UHR* 1 (1947), 201–22, which is carefully documented and well illustrated.

A rare book-length study of an American costume tradition, Melvin Gingerich's *Mennonite Attire Through Four Centuries* (Breiningsville, Pa.: The Pennsylvania-German Society, 1970), is highly detailed and very well illustrated.

The advice quoted in this chapter about buying red or blue shirts for Western travel was given in Randolph B. Marcy's *The Prairie Traveler: A Handbook for Overland Expeditions* (1859; republished by West Virginia Pulp and Paper Company, 1961). This book contains other interesting references to clothing and food for Western living, as well might other such works. The quotation from L. L. Bean is from the Spring 1966 catalog, but the Navy Blue Shirt is now carried only in the Fall catalogs. In 1976 an executive of L. L. Bean wrote me, "Traditionally red-blue is worn out of doors and these colors do not show the dirt as do tans."

21

Folk Foods

Folk foods are unique as the only traditional product to be quickly and wholly consumed, usually in a short time after preparation. Folk songs and stories may be forgotten, traditional houses deteriorate and burn down, and folk costumes eventually wear out or are discarded, but only folk foods disappear regularly with such speed and completeness. The study of folk foods, therefore, should include the entire process of traditional food handling and consumption: what is eaten, how and when it is eaten, food preparation and preservation, seasoning and serving food, ethnic and regional foods, religious food taboos and other requirements, food terms and beliefs, kitchens and cookware, table manners, and so forth. Such studies, as with most folklife subjects, are far more advanced in Europe than in the United States; European foodways specialists have prepared atlases of food traditions, studies of national and festival foods, films on food preparation, and since 1970 have gathered at international conferences of "Ethnological Food Research" or "Ethnogastronomy" in order to plan and coordinate such research. (Other suggested names for folk-foods research are "Folk Cookery" and "Ethnocuisine.") It is clear that anything as basic as eating, with so many traditional attitudes and techniques associated with it, is highly deserving of serious study. Lately, American folklorists have got the message and have begun to produce good folk-foods research of their own.

As with American folk costume, a historical approach to national food traditions is a good place to start, although only a brief sketch is possible here. The first settlers took some hints from the Indians about how to use the resources of the new land. As we have seen in earlier chapters, American Indian culture had a negligible influence on settlers in terms of verbal folklore, but for solving the practical problem of subsisting in a wilderness, it contributed more. For example, the very term "Indian corn" that the Englishmen used for *maize* (the Spanish-derived word for it) indicated a debt to the natives, as do the Indian-derived names for some corn dishes, such as corn *pone, hominy,* and *succotash.* Traditionally, in the northern states the European peasant staple-food oat or wheat porridge was modified into corn mush (called hasty pudding); in the South corn was traditionally preferred processed into hominy, or processed further as grits.

White trappers and hunters learned from the Indians how to prepare lightweight survival rations like pemmican and "jerked" beef. The Mountain Men of the Western fur trade developed tastes for the Indians' favorite wild meats—both cooked and raw—and even for dog meat. A rendezvous feast of buffalo meat has been described in these terms:

> . . . the Mountain Men often began their repast by drinking some of the blood, which reminded them of warm milk. Then the liver was eaten raw, flavored with the contents of the gall bladder. If the cow buffalo was pregnant they savored one of the trappers' most exotic luxuries: the raw legs of unborn calves. . . . After these delicacies, the trappers were ready for their feast. This always included the hump ribs, which were pulled away by hand and the fat meat gulped down, while grease dripped over the face and clothing. These might be alternated with strips of the tenderloin, partially roasted or boiled, or by chunks of the tongue. Another prized portion was the "fleece," the inch-thick layer of fat that lay just beneath the buffalo hide. Scarcely less tempting were the intestines, or *boudins,* which were roasted, in the fire until puffed with heat and fat, then coiled on a blanket and gulped down without chewing. On such an occasion two trappers would start on the opposite ends of a pile of intestines and work their way toward the middle, each eating faster and faster to get his share, and shouting to the other to "feed fair."

In the Northeast, as late as the 1850s, Henry David Thoreau learned from an Indian companion how to make tea from the "creeping snowberry"; it was "better than the black tea which we had brought," he wrote in *The Maine Woods.* Thoreau mused in his journal in 1859: "I think that a wise and independent self-reliant man will have a complete list of the edibles to be found in a primitive country or wilderness. . . . He will know what are the permanent resources of the land and be prepared for the hardest of times."

If not from Indian lore or systematic study of the wilderness, at least from their own ingenuity and desperation, the tamers of the American frontier sooner or later ate every kind of meat that the land offered. An examination of the literature of early western exploration and travel turned up reports of eating not just the standard fare of game animals, but also badgers, coyotes, insects, lizards, prairie dogs, skins and pelts (either as soup or simply chewed upon), wolves, many other beasts, and even, in extreme circumstances, human beings. One western army veteran wrote that when his unit was out of provisions and forced to devour the mules one by one, a bit of extra flavor could be added to the unseasoned meat by burning the mule steaks on the outside and sprinkling gunpowder over them.

Among these vanguards of the frontier the diet prescribed by available resources and field expediency became, to a degree, traditional. From such practices perhaps we might trace at least part of the modern American's continued passion for hunting wild game and for liking meat cooked rare and served in large portions. Also the early use of such a variety of animals for food probably underlies the current humorous folklore of mock recipes for preparing tough or undesirable game. The cook is directed to put the meat on a plank, season it well, cook it carefully and slowly, and then to discard the meat and eat the plank. Related items are the jesting recipe for "Shadow Soup," which is supposedly made from only the shadow of a fowl that is hung over the cooking pot, and the "Soup Stone" of traditional folktales.

The food of typical frontier occupations developed along traditional lines, limited by what was most readily available and what could be preserved easily. Native folksongs contain some records of these menus; in "The Buffalo Skinners" (a parody of "Canaday I O"), for example, the singer complains,

> We lived on rotten buffalo hump and damned old iron-wedge bread,
> Strong coffee, croton water to drink, and a bull hide for a bed.

In another version the fare is, "old jerked beef, croton coffee, and sour bread." ("Croton water" is probably a reference, surviving from the older song, to water coming from the Croton River in Westchester County, New York, first tapped for the New York City water supply in 1842; various early references to "Croton water" show that there was some difference of opinion then about its drinking qualities and appearance. One writer referred to the New York City town pumps, located at street corners, "so that no person who is athirst need perish. . . . If he stand in need of physic at the same time, the pump will furnish that also." Perhaps the suggestion in the song is just "river water," or the cathartic "Croton oil" may be implied.)

The housekeeping of a "Lane County [Kansas] Bachelor" is described in a song of that title that is also known as "Starving to Death on a Government Claim."

> My clothes are all ragged, my language is rough,
> My bread is case-hardened, both solid and tough . . .
>
> The dishes are scattered all over the bed,
> All covered with sorghum, and government bread.
> Still I have a good time, and I live at my ease,
> On common sop sorghum, an' bacon an' cheese.

What the bachelor yearned for in the song was a home elsewhere and three square meals every day, prepared by someone else:

> Farewell to Lane County, farewell to the West,
> I'll travel back East to the girl I love best,
> I'll stop at Missouri and get me a wife,
> And live on corn dodgers, the rest of my life.

"Corn dodgers" (a term applied to a variety of corn-meal cakes) represent relative luxury in other songs, too, but the long-term bad effect of the unbalanced diet is pictured in "The State of Arkansas" or "An Arkansaw Traveler":

> He fed me on corn dodger that was hard as any rock,
> Till my teeth began to loosen and my knees began to knock.
> And I got so thin on sassafras tea I could hide behind a straw,
> You bet I was a different lad when I left old Arkansaw.

Another popular folksong that pictures the crudeness of bachelor life on the frontier is directed as a warning to young ladies not to marry Kansas boys, Cheyenne boys, Mormon boys, boys of many other places, and in the following version, "Texan Boys":

> Come all ye Missouri girls and listen to my noise;
> You must not marry these Texan boys.
> For if you do your portion will be
> Cold johnnycake [corn bread] and venison is all you'll see. . . .

> When the boys get hungry they bake their bread.
> They build up a fire as high as your head,
> Shovel up the ashes and roll in the dough;
> The name that they give it is dough, boys, dough!

On the nineteenth-century American sailing ships, as described in R. H. Dana's *Two Years Before the Mast*, the diet was a tiresome repetition of meals consisting mostly of weak tea, tough salt beef, and hard biscuits. The shipboard meat barrels were picked over for the officers' meals first, so the ration that reached the crew was bad enough to inspire a chant, called "The Sailor's Grace," which began "Old horse! old horse! what brought you here?" A rare treat was "scouse," made of pieces of salt beef boiled up with pounded biscuits and a few potatoes. Pudding, or "duff," made of flour, water, and molasses, with a little dried fruit added for Christmas, was an occasional dessert treat.

American cowboys and loggers ate a little better than this, although still without much variety. A local song from Maine describes the food supplies of a typical camp in these terms:

> They tote in all their flour and pork
>   their beans, oat, peas, and straw,
> Their beef it comes from Bangor, boys,
>   and some from Canada;
> They haul it to our good cook Lou
>   who cooks it in a pot
> And serves it on the table
>   when it is nice and hot.

Staples of the cowboy diet were similar, although not usually stewed. The westerners consumed large meals of fried steak, sourdough biscuits, and strong coffee, with canned or dried foods included if available. Although one verse of the widely sung "Old Chisholm Trail" declared "Oh it's bacon and beans 'most every day,/I'd as soon be a-eatin' Prairie hay," the cowboys appreciated their cooks' good efforts and got what they could when they could from the countryside to vary the diet. They traded beef for vegetables, fruit, or melons whenever possible, hunted up wild birds' eggs, tried to shoot game, and if nothing else were available just referred to their bacon as "fried chicken" and gulped it down. There seems to be no truth to the story that in logging and cow camps the men took turns being amateur cooks, each being replaced whenever a man complained, and the complainer taking over. (One punchline of this story is, "That tastes like moose turd pie, and by God I *like* it!")

The Dutch oven (a cast-iron kettle with a heavy lid), which allowed controlled baking to be done by an open fire or over a bed of coals, saved cowboy cookery from the tyranny of the frying pan and the stewing pot. A good-food company was sometimes referred to as "strictly a Dutch-oven outfit," and its cook could be counted on to prepare dried-apple pies regularly, and other kinds of treats when supplies were on hand. (The term "Dutch oven" is probably a national slur, like "Dutch treat.") Sourdough cookery, about which a whole book might be written concerning both its cowboy and many other western specialists, provided a staple for the menus of all meals, only occasionally varied with salt-rising bread. The latter, one cowboy commented, "tasted mighty good, but smelled something like old dirty socks."

American men's cooking in their own work camps always concentrated on solid fundamentals that stuck to the ribs. As women settled on the frontier they began to exercise their talents to supply the frills, often having no more to work with than the foods that would keep or could be gathered from the land. Their traditional recipes were passed on from mother to daughter or exchanged with neighbors. Frontier men had already learned to settle for substitutes when supplies ran out—"Horsemint tea" for coffee, or shredded red-willow bark for tobacco. But it took women to invent a way of stretching the coffee supply by baking corn meal in molasses and stirring it into the grounds. Another method was to burn coffee dregs for re-use, and, in fact, nearly every berry, grain, weed, or seed which could be roasted and ground seems to have been tried at one time or another as a substitute for coffee. Sweetenings, always in short supply and expensive, were another challenge to housewives. Sugar, maple sugar, sorghum, and honey were used when readily available, and when they were not, the cook fell back on corncob syrup to stretch the supply of sweetening, or watermelon syrup to replace it. Other ingenious culinary gimmicks included "Lengthened Eggs" (with milk and flour) for breakfast omelets, "Mock Strawberries" made from chunks of peaches and apples, and "Casserole of Rabbit," which was designed to make something worthwhile out of those pesky creatures. (The recipe was revived during the Dust-Bowl period.)

It was with the "Nothing-in-the-house Pies" that the early American housewife showed her best form, and some of her creations are still favorites. These were either concocted from otherwise insipid fruits—green currants or elderberries, for instance—or from unlikely ones such as grapes. The out-and-out "mock" pies required the greatest daring—crushed crackers could be made to taste like an apple filling, with the proper seasoning, and cream pie flavored with either vinegar or field-sorrel might pass for lemon. One mock mincemeat pie was made from green tomatoes, and another from rolled crackers and raisins properly seasoned. It is apparent in such examples that the frontier settlers were intent upon serving the status foods associated with eastern or Old-World menus, even in preference to some of the succulent wild fruits and berries that the new land provided. (By the same reasoning, few white settlers really seemed to relish the Indian foods they tried, and ate them only during periods of shortage.) In some families there was a traditional pie-top design, often a monogram, that was cut or punched into the top crusts as a last flourish, another pie tradition still preserved by some cooks.

Apart from frontier food traditions, there are many other historical foodways that might be studied, only a few examples of which can be cited here. These include wild food gathering (greens, honey, maple sap), traditional food processing (syrup and sorghum-making, moonshining), and several kinds of food preservation (smoking, pickling, salting, drying, canning, and freezing, plus boiling fruit down into "butter"). Studies of American festival foods need to be done, including those eaten at the present time for birthdays, weddings, or other special occasions. Ethnic foodways, among a few groups have been largely maintained, but in most immigrant groups are relegated to special occasions; studies so far also suggest that there is little interpenetration of ethnic recipes, even in situations of intermarriage. The development of regional food specialities and preferences deserves study. The identification of baked beans with Boston, one kind of clam chowder with New England and another with Manhattan, black-eyed peas and fried chicken and many other foods with the South, corn-on-the-cob with the Midwest, and Mexican specialities with the Southwest are partly traditional matters, especially in a day and age in which any region's food can be delivered to any other region with ease, and in which one can declare that chicken cooked anywhere (and in several ways) is "southern fried."

The varying names for similar foods in different regions have folkloristic overtones, too. When the columnist Allan M. Trout of *The Courier-Journal* of Louisville, Kentucky, described a traditional stew made at hog-killing time, his readers wrote in to say that it was called "Pluck" (or "Pluck and Plunder") "All Sorts," "Scrapple," "Liver Mush," "Giblets," and "Monroe County Stew." Doughnuts are variously termed "Fried Cakes," "Crullers," and "Ginger Nuts," in different parts of the country. Green beans may be called "String Beans" or "Snap Beans," and pancakes appear on menus across the land as "Hotcakes," "Griddle Cakes," "Flapjacks" or "Wheat Cakes." Some similar situations occur with soft drinks ("soda," "pop," "soda-pop," "tonic," etc.). Also from our regional cooks have come terms like "Hopping John," "Snickerdoodle," "Hush Puppies," "Apple Slump," "Cinnamon Flop," "Red Eye Gravy," and "Red Flannel Hash."

The basic characteristics of the American folk meal seem to be large quantities, great variety, and the use of regional specialties. This is true whether it is a family meal, a "company meal," or the fixin's for a special festival or gathering that is described. Descriptions of the varied offerings at gargantuan American feasts have been a commonplace of our literature since the Pilgrims' "First Thanksgiving," and the following two are merely a pair of less familiar examples. From Kentucky, this is given as an everyday meal at about the turn of the century:

> The meat was fried old ham, with red gravy. Also on the table were chicken and dumplins, corn, beans, sweet potatoes, okra, candied apples, sliced tomatoes, potato salad, miscellaneous pickles and relishes, hot chess pie topped with whipped cream, and chocolate pie with deep meringue.

And this one is from Oregon from a novel set in 1905:

The supper was all everyday victuals, but there were plenty of them. There was fried deerliver with onions, a little greasier than it needed to be; beefsteak, excellent cuts but infernal cooking, with all the juice fried out and made into flour-and-milk gravy; potatoes, baked so the jackets burst open and showed the white; string beans, their flavor and nutritive value well oiled with a big hunk of salt pork; baked squash soaked in butter; a salad of lettuce whittled into shoestrings, wilted in hot water, and doped with vinegar and bacon grease; tomatoes stewed with dumplings of cold bread; yellow corn mowed off the cob and boiled in milk; cold beet-pickles, a jar of piccalilli, and a couple of panloads of hot sourdough biscuits. For sweets there were tomato preserves, peach butter, wild blackcap jam, and wild blackberry and wild crabapple jelly. For dessert there was a red-apple cobbler with lumpy cream, and two kinds of pie, one of blue huckleberry, the other of red. The country fed well, what with wild game and livestock and gardens, milk and butter and orchards and wild fruits; and no man was ever liable to starve in it unless his digestion broke down from overstrain.

The same American tendency to dream of much good eating is reflected in traditional songs such as "Big Rock Candy Mountain," the metaphorical suggestions of "Pie in the Sky," (labor organizer and martyr Joe Hill's famous parody of "In the Sweet By and By") and in stanzas from hillbilly favorites such as the following:

> Bile 'em cabbage down;
> Bake 'em hoecake brown.
> The only song that I can sing,
> Is "Bile 'em cabbage down."
>   *
> Gonna buy me a sack of flour,
> Bake me a hoecake every hour,
> Keep that skillet good and greasy all the time.

Other appearances of this theme occur in the phrase "chicken every Sunday," and the political slogan "A chicken in every pot."

Modern American foodways offer a real challenge to the folklife scholar: while there are traditional qualities in virtually every aspect of eating and drinking, the most obvious factors influencing these acts are now commercial and professional ones. For instance, ethnic and regional tastes are reflected in many of the fast-food chains (e.g., Taco

Bell and Kentucky Fried Chicken) and even in TV dinners; mixtures of traditions are apparent in such restaurant names as "Mexican-American Smorgasbord" or "Der Wienerschnitzel" (which serves mostly varieties of hot dogs). The foods people prefer for breakfast, while mainly of commercial origin, group themselves in traditional ways: Continental breakfasts, hot versus cold foods, meat versus cereals, fruit and sweets for breakfast, pie for breakfast, side dishes of potatoes or grits, and so forth. The names, timing, and foods considered appropriate for other meals and snacks, as well as for camping or picnics, could be studied. Foods for backpacking range from the commercial freeze-dried products to homemade jerky and pemmican; "natural" or "organic" food devotees, similarly, may either produce their own foodstuffs or buy them in special shops. The concept of "soul food"—including both what is eaten and how it interrelates with other traditional aspects of a subculture, would be a useful piece of research.

Kay Cothran viewed "participation in tradition" with regard to the food preferences of Deep South (pineywoods) "cracker culture"; the four categories of foods she identified were 1) those appropriate whenever eating itself is, 2) those which follow "situational food rules" (e.g., curative foods), 3) foods to be avoided in certain circumstances (e.g., just after childbirth), and 4) things *never* to be eaten (some regarded by her informants as "nigger foods"). Such food rules could be studied much closer to home, and the results would likely involve taboos against talking with one's mouth full or wasting and playing with food, and attitudes toward mixing certain foods in one meal or even mixing them up on one plate.

Probably any American could add something to the following list of other prospective subjects for studies of traditional eating and drinking in the United States: folk speech references to food, such as "in apple-pie order," "not worth his salt," "to eat crow," and "in a stew"; traditions of the "potluck" or "pitch-in" dinner; varieties of alcoholic mixed drinks and ice-cream sundaes; dandelion and other homemade wines; rhymed recipes; "Tuna Wiggle," "Barf on a Board," and other traditional names for institutional cooking; "Adam and Eve on a Raft" and other hashslingers' terms; hobos' recipes; and superstitious food taboos. No folklorist need starve for ideas when so many juicy tidbits remain.

BIBLIOGRAPHIC NOTES

The study of American foodways (ethnocuisine, ethnogastronomy, etc.) got a good early start among folklorists but was a long time developing, finally coming into its own as a viable subspecialty of research recently. The only full-length article on food published so far in *JAF* is John G. Bourke's "Folk-Foods of the Rio Grande Valley and of Northern Mexico," in *JAF* 8 (1895), 41–71. A good indication of progress is the "Special Food Issue" of *KFQ* with five articles edited and introduced by foodways specialist Jay Anderson, *KFQ* 16 (1971), 153–214; it contains studies of foodways research, Indian foods, soul food, and the organic foods movement, plus a report on an international ethnological food research symposium.

Cookbooks and popular works on American foods may be useful in research. *The American Heritage Cookbook and Illustrated History of American Eating & Drinking* (New York: American Heritage Publishing Co. and Simon and Schuster, 1964), for example, is well written, informative, and also magnificently illustrated in both black and white and color. A similar publication is *American Cooking*, by Dale Brown (New York: Time-Life Books, 1968), particularly its chapter "Two Hundred Years in the Kitchen," pp. 184–99.

The description of mountain men eating buffalo meat quoted in this chapter is from Ray Allen Billington's *The Far Western Frontier, 1830–1860* (New York: Harper, 1956; Harper Torchbook paperback edition, 1962), p. 51. Martin Schmitt surveyed western food traditions in " 'Meat's Meat': An Account of the Flesh-eating Habits of Western Americans," *WF* 11 (1952), 185–203. My note on a western tradition of "Mock Recipes for 'Planked' Game" appeared in *WF* 21 (1962), 45–46.

The frontier folksongs referred to in this chapter appear in many collections. Several of these texts are from H. M. Belden's *Ballads and Songs Collected by the Missouri Folk-Lore Society*, University of Missouri Studies 15 (Columbia, 1940). Logger's stew is described in "The Depot Camp" quoted in "Folksongs from Maine," *NEF* 7 (1965), 15–22. Roger L. Welsch gives a number of folksong references to frontier foods, plus other interesting data, in his article " 'Sorry Chuck': Pioneer Foodways," *NH* 53 (1972), 99–113. The food of sailors and cowboys was compared in my own article "Sailors' and Cowboys' Folklore in Two Popular Classics," *SFQ* 29 (1965), 266–83. Edward Everett Dale's *Frontier Ways: Sketches of Life in the Old West* (Austin: University of Texas Press, 1959), has chapters on "Cowboy Cookery" (pp. 25–42) and "Food of the Fronier" (pp. 111–31). An extended study of the former topic is Ramon F. Adams's *Come an' Get It: The Story of the Old Cowboy Cook* (Norman: University of Oklahoma Press, 1952; reissued, 1972). Rose P. White discussed that staple of western cooking in "The Sourdough Biscuit" in *WF* 15 (1956), 93–94; Peter Tamony explored the terminology, mystique, and history of "Sourdough and French Bread" in his Western Words section of *WF* 32 (1973), 265–70. A revealing project which suggests other possibilities with other groups is Charlie Seemann's paper

"Bacon, Biscuits, and Beans: Food of the Cattle Trails as Found in American Cowboy Songs," *AFFWord* 4 (Oct. 1974), 24–39.

Three early notes in *JAF* concerned recipes for substitutes. These were "Traditionary American Local Dishes," *JAF* 13 (1900), 65–66; "Some Homely Viands," *JAF* 13 (1900), 292–94; and "Blood-root 'Chocolate,' " *JAF* 19(1906), 347–48. Miriam B. Webster's "Maine Winter Menus: A Study in Ingenuity," *NEF* 1 (1958), 7–9, has some similar recipes, as do several of the works on pioneer foods mentioned previously.

A query for variant terms and shapes for doughnuts was published by Charles Peabody in *JAF* 18 (1905), 166, but apparently no responses were ever printed. The subject may be pursued, however, in several studies of folk dialect.

B. A. Botkin has sections on regional foods in *A Treasury of New England Folklore* (New York: Crown, 1947), and *A Treasury of Southern Folklore* (New York: Crown, 1949). Southern traditional recipes were discussed by George W. Boswell in two articles appearing in *MFR* 5 (1971), 1–9; and *MSF* 3 (1975), 13–20. Early American recipes from New York and elsewhere in the East are given in articles by Janet R. MacFarlane in *NYFQ* 10 (1954), 135–40 and 218–25, and in *NYFQ* 11 (1955), 305–9. The latter contains one rhymed recipe.

The description of a Kentucky meal in this chapter is quoted from Allan M. Trout's *Greetings from Old Kentucky, Volume Two* (Frankfort, Ky. 1959), p. 71. Another food note from that same state is William E. Lightfoot's " 'I Hardly Ever Miss a Meal Without Eating Just a Little': Traditional Sorghum-Making in Western Kentucky," *MSF* 1 (1973), 7–17. A food item from other Southern states is described in James W. Byrd's "Poke Sallet [a dish made of pokeweed greens, bacon drippings, and eggs] from Tennessee to Texas," *TFSB* 32 (1966), 48–54. Paul Brewster includes cooking, preserving, and beverage making in volume 1 of the *Frank C. Brown Collection of North Carolina Folklore*, pp. 266–75.

The description of the Oregon meal in this chapter is quoted from H. L. Davis's novel *Honey in the Horn* (New York: Harper, 1935; Avon paperback edition, [n.d.]), p. 19. Some Utah folk foods are included in Jan Harold Brunvand, *A Guide for Collectors of Folklore in Utah* (Salt Lake City: University of Utah Press, 1971), pp. 118–19. Marjorie Sackett has discussed Kansas folk recipes in *Kansas Folklore*, edited by S. J. Sackett (Lincoln: University of Nebraska Press, 1961), pp. 226–38; in *MF* 12 (1962), 81–86; and in *WF* 22 (1963), 103–6.

Ethnic American foodways offer many good subjects for study. Three fine examples of published work are Don Yoder's articles "Sauerkraut in the Pennsylvania Folk-Culture," *PF* 12 (Summer 1961), 56–69; "Schnitz in the Pennsylvania Folk-Culture," *PF* 12 (Fall 1961), 44–53; and "Pennsylvanians Called it Mush," *PF* 13 (Winter 1962–63), 27–49. Other studies are Elaine J. Abboud and Jean A. Sarrazin, "New Orleans Lenten Recipes: A Multi-Ethnic Sampling," *LFM* (April 1970), 55–69; Janet Langlois, "Moon Cake in Chinatown, New York City: Continuity and Change," *NYFQ* 28 (1972), 83–117; and Craig Soland, "How to Make a Sve-te-Saba [Serbian food]," *AFFWord* 3 (Spring 1974), 1–7. Marjorie Sackett investigates "the recipe as a measure of the extent to which neighboring cultures influence each other" in her note "Folk Recipes as a Measure of Intercultural Penetration," *JAF* 85 (1972), 77–81.

Since 1971 when the journal began publication, *AFFWord*, the organ of the Arizona Friends of Folklore has periodically had an "Ethno Cuisine" Section. The subjects have included western cooking techniques (Dutch ovens, the goat roast, pit barbecue), food specialties (flour tortillas, son-of-a-bitch stew, cactus jelly), ethnic foods (Norwegian, Serbian, Flemish, Mexican, German of Transylvania), and even pseudo-recipes or food hoaxes (rattlesnake steak).

A good example of modern foodways research merging with recent folklore theory is Kay L. Cothran's thought-provoking article, "Talking With Your Mouth Full: A Communications Approach to Food Rules," *TFSB* 38 (1972), 33–38. An extended summary of an important piece of European food research is provided by Roger L. Welsch in *KFQ* 16 (1971), 189–212; the work is Gunter Wiegelmann's *Alltags- und Festspeisen: Wandel und gegenwartige Stellung* [Daily and Festival Foods: Migration and Present Situation] (Marburg: N. G. Elwert Verlag, 1967).

APPENDICES

❖❧❖❧❖❧❖❧❖❧❖❧❖

Four Sample Studies
in American Folklore

The four studies that follow were prepared especially for this book in order to demonstrate how some of the materials and concepts discussed in it may be applied in a scholarly manner by folklorists. These studies are written and documented in the style of the academic folklore journals, and each one represents something of an innovation in American folklore scholarship.

My own study of a branch of oral folklore takes as its point of departure my earlier historic-geographic study of an Aarne-Thompson folktale type (see footnote 1). The Taming of the Shrew tale is widely distributed in numerous oral and literary versions, and it undoubtedly influenced Shakespeare's comedy, from which it takes its conventional title. But my focus here is on the updated American joke subtype that has a vigorous life both orally and in the mass media. By examining such contemporary offshoots of ancient traditions, we can see how the present adopts and adapts the folklore of the past, and how even jokes in oral lore may belong to a long cultural tradition.

Barre Toelken, the founding editor of *Northwest Folklore,* and editor of the *Journal of American Folklore* from 1974 to 1976, discusses the oral and customary folklore of a group seldom studied. This is, as he writes, the "academicians on both sides of the podium" in American high schools and colleges. Drawing a wide range of examples from his own student and faculty experiences at Utah State University, the University of Utah, Washington State University, and the University of Oregon (where he received his Ph.D. and now teaches), Toelken presents a convincing argument for the serious evaluation of this modern folklore of academe. His collecting methods, and his discussion of diffusion, structure, function, and other matters illustrate principles introduced throughout this book. In addition, several types of folklore only mentioned in passing earlier are here set in their proper group context and analyzed. This study, as a result, might encourage the reader to attempt further "the folkloristic examination of his own culture."

Henry Glassie is one of the first systematic tillers of the field of material folklore in the United States, especially in the area of folk architecture. One of the first Master's Degree recipients of the American Folk Culture Program at Cooperstown, New York, Glassie supports his considerable fieldwork experience in the Southern Appalachians and elsewhere with a solid theoretical basis and an excellent grounding in the international bibliography of folklife scholarship. (For its bibliography of traditional architecture alone his essay is invaluable.) His present study proceeds from fieldwork and the description of the cultural setting of his collected materials, to the crucial stage of classification. The essentially simple system that he offers for placing in order widely varying artifacts demonstrates very effectively how theoretical concepts in folklore may arise out of a bewildering mass of data. Professor Glassie's fine drawings not only clarify his explanations, but also show what a "collection" of buildings might consist of in a country that does not have any extensive "folk museums" of traditional artifacts. Henry Glassie received his Ph.D. in folklore from the University of Pennsylvania, and has been editor of *Keystone Folklore Quarterly*, published by the Pennsylvania Folklore Society. He was the first State Folklorist in charge of the Ethnic Culture Survey for the Pennsylvania Historical and Museum Commission, and has been on the faculties of Pennsylvania State University and Indiana University. In 1976 he was appointed chairman of the Department of Folklore and Folklife at the University of Pennsylvania.

David Evans's essay on blues structure and meaning was written especially for the second edition of this book in order to provide a sample of folk musical analysis in a performance context. It brings to bear the experience of many years of fieldwork and study upon eight specific examples of folk blues collected by the author from black performers. Besides demonstrating admirably how text and music may be analyzed technically by a specialist, the study gives rich insights into blues performance styles, the context of blues singing, the interplay with commercial musical trends, and characteristic attitudes of blues singers toward their traditional art. Particularly important in this study is the rebuttal—via blues scholarship and analysis—of racist arguments of earlier writers on black traditional blues lyrics. David Evans is Associate Professor of Anthropology at California State University, Fullerton, and Record Review Editor of the *Journal of American Folklore*. Beginning as an undergraduate classics student at Harvard (A.B., 1965), Professor Evans's interest in black folk music led him to a career in folklore. He received two degrees in folklore and mythology from the University of California, Los Angeles, the

M.A. in 1967 and the first and only individual Ph.D. awarded in folklore by U.C.L.A. in 1976. He has done fieldwork in black folk music since 1964 and published his findings in a number of folklore journals. The photographs accompanying his essay are by his wife, Cheryl Evans.

APPENDIX A

❂❁❂❁❂❁❂❁❂❁❂

The Taming of the Shrew
Tale in the United States
by Jan Harold Brunvand

The humorous folktale entitled "The Taming of the Shrew" in the Aarne-Thompson index (Type 901) has been collected in some 300 texts from about two dozen national groups which extend from India to Ireland and to the New World. A historic-geographic study established the general pattern of development from a simple anecdote in the Middle East that had passed into southern Europe by the Middle Ages, to a longer and more detailed story that was well distributed in northern Europe by at least the sixteenth century.[1] The essence of all versions is contained in Motif T251.2.3. *Wife becomes obedient on seeing husband slay a recalcitrant horse*, except that the animal punished is not always a horse.

In order to place a representative text before the folklore student, as a frame of reference for the discussion of this interesting tale, I am citing in full the following literal translation of an unpublished Icelandic text of Type 901:

Harkalegt raö
(Doing Things the Hard Way)

It is said that once upon a time there was a girl who was unusually domineering. Many people predicted that she would not be easy to deal with if she ever got married and that her husband was not a man to be envied. At last, however, a young man asked for her hand and he was accepted. Their wedding took place a short time later, and the bridegroom gave his bride a horse on which she rode home from church. It could hardly have been a worse one—an old nag, not worth much of anything.

On their way was a quagmire which was difficult to get over. The bride's horse sank down to its belly and could not stir, and the bride jumped off and stood there at the edge of the mud, her dress dirty and disordered. She did not know what to do. The bridegroom pretended to be very angry and spoke sharply, then quickly drew his sharp knife, ran towards the horse and cut its throat. He ordered his wife to take the saddle and carry it the rest of the way up to the farm. His behavior had such an influence on her temper that she took it without saying a word and put it on her back.

Many years went by, but the evil prophecies about her marriage were not fulfilled. To the contrary, it became proverbial how fine that marriage was and how obedient the wife was to her husband in all respects.

Once the couple went to a party in the neighborhood. After eating, the gentlemen and the ladies went into different rooms. They talked about many things, and finally the farmers started to talk about who had the best wife; each of them boasted about his own wife, and our man was not better than the others. At last he said, "Let us call for our wives, and she who obeys first is the best." This was agreed upon, and the farmers called for their wives. When the ladies were called for, our woman was talking to her sister, but she stood up quickly. Her sister said, "Don't be in such a hurry," and she asked her to stay for a while longer. She answered immediately, "No! You have not carried the saddle like I have." ("*Ðú hefur ekki borið söðulinn eins og ég.*")

So she was the first to come to her husband, and so she proved that he was right.[2]

In what appears to be the oldest layer of the tradition, at the southeastern corner of the area of distribution, a newlywed man subdues his ill-tempered bride by strangling her pet cat in a pretended fit of rage.[3] In the famous medieval Spanish literary version by Don Juan Manuel, the husband violently slays a dog, a cat, and a horse, all of whom had refused to fetch water for him.[4] And in many European folktale versions a dog is slain as well as a horse (or other beast of burden) to frighten the bad wife, who must then carry the saddle or pull the buggy (wagon, sleigh, etc.) home. In northern Europe the story was elaborated with these additions: (1) several details about the bridegroom's uncouth behavior at the wedding, (2) a series of three absurd statements to which the wife is forced to agree, and (3) a wager among three husbands over which one has the most obedient spouse. This "Northern-European Elaborated Subtype," [5] possibly in oral form, must have influenced Shakespeare, whose comedy *The Taming of the Shrew* (ca. 1596) cannot be traced to any known printed source. In the play, however, the mistreatment of an animal is suppressed, while the husband's cruelty toward his wife after they get home is emphasized.

With this summary of matters that I have taken up in detail elsewhere as background, we may examine the tradition of Type 901 in the United States and see what is suggested about folktale transmission and variation.

About fifty New World texts of "The Taming of the Shrew" have been collected, but most of them are brief and undistinguished; the long European tale has not been strongly established here. The best versions are decidedly foreign in character. They are three unpublished French-Canadian versions [6] (ultimately of Scotch-Irish origin) that bear striking similarities to the one that must have influenced Shakespeare, and one good Spanish-American version recorded in New Mexico about 1940.[7] Don Juan Manuel's literary reworking of the tale has, of course, been read by generations of beginning students of Spanish, having appeared in English and American anthologies almost beyond counting (including a recent appearance in a "bedside book" [8] provided for guests in Hilton hotels), but the oral folktale versions in this country have not been affected by it. The bulk of the American texts seem to have an English—or at least a Germanic—background in oral tradition.

Four stand out from the rest because they are the longest and because they contain certain significant details. The first of these texts was collected by Vance Randolph in Farmington, Arkansas, in 1941 (and the informant remembered learning it in the early 1900s).[9] The second was collected by David S. McIntosh in southern Illinois in 1947.[10] A third was collected by Richard Chase in Clintwood, Virginia, and published in 1956,[11] and I collected the fourth in 1959 from an informant living in Bond, Kentucky.[12] The Illinois text is the longest and best, but unfortunately it has the most obscure background. Professor McIntosh secured it first orally and then in writing from a student of undetermined national background in an extension course of Southern Illinois University taught in Pinckneyville. The student wrote: "It is an old story my mother tells, told to her by her mother." As in many European folktale versions, there are several daughters, of which one is shrewish. Despite her father's warning, a man takes her for his bride, and he appears in somewhat uncouth array for the wedding. On the way home he kills his dog and his horse for disobedience, and then forces his wife to carry the saddle. There is a fragment of the wager motif when the reformed shrew abruptly leaves the company of her sisters when her husband calls her, replying to their astonished questions by saying, "*You* haven't packed the saddle."

The general pattern of this version matches numerous northern European ones, and even better evidence for this direct origin of the text is provided by the fact that only seven other known versions conclude with the girl applying a saying about carrying the saddle. These seven come from Iceland (2), Denmark, Sweden, Swedes in Finland, and Finland (2). The line is *Ni har inte burit sadeln* in Swedish, *De havde ikke baaret paa Saddel* in Danish, both sayings conveying basically the same meaning as the corresponding line in the Illinois version. This American informant also remarked: "The last phrase . . . has been used in our family for many years to calm the younger folk when we got to expressing ourselves too forcefully as to what we would or wouldn't do." Similarly, a Finnish informant is quoted: ". . . and that's where the saying 'You haven't carried a saddle' comes from." Finally, we can note that the Illinois student's family name is "Keeling," which may be related to the nautical term *keel* that descended from the Middle English *kele* and was derived from such Scandinavian roots as the Old Norse *kjölr*. The -*ing* family names are frequently Scandinavian, like "Quisling," for instance. All of this evidence points to a direct Scandinavian family background for this particular text.

The long versions from Virginia and Kentucky bear traces of the older general-European story, but they are already well on the way to being transformed to the typically American "joke" form of Type 901. Neither of these texts has more than a bare suggestion of background details for the action, but rather they advance quickly to the taming scene. However, both of them do end with the wife carrying the saddle home, a trait not found further in American tradition. The flavor of these backwoods American versions may be judged from the following verbatim transcript of the Kentucky text from my tape recording of Mr. Pleas C. Wilson of Bond, Kentucky, in 1959:

> The first story is concernin' the ill-tempered young lady that lived in pioneer days, in the country. All the boys seemed to be scared, 'fraid to be henpecked. And there lives an old pioneer, cross the country back in a clearing, needed him a wife. So he decided to go see the young lady, and they talked up a wedding. So he went on his horse and they married; set her up behind him, and they started home. (So if you notice in the story now, he intended to teach her a lesson now, right off'n the reel.)
>
> Well, they were riding along, and the old horse stumbled. He looked at the horse's head right ill and says, "That's once!" They gone on a piece further, and a rabbit run across the road and he shied. Looked at him ill again and he said, "That's twice!" They came to a ford in the creek. The old horse balked and didn't want to ford the creek. So he looked at him and said, "Now that's three times!" Told his wife to get down. *He* gets down, takes the saddle off

and sets it on the ground. And, stepped off a few steps, shot the old horse between the eyes with his rifle. Killed him!

And so his wife began bawling him out for killing the poor old horse. She just kept storming and storming at him, but he didn't say a word, just kept loading this old muzzle-loading rifle. So she finally wearied herself out and hushed, and he looked at her and he said, "Now that's once!" Now he said, "We better get going, I guess." Man says, "Pick up that saddle and let's go!" She hesitated to pick up the saddle and carry it. He looked at her ill again, and said, "That's twice!" Well, she picked up the saddle on her shoulder and away they tuck. Went home, and she made him a good wife.

The Arkansas text collected by Vance Randolph may represent a survival of a more ancient form of the tale, for here it is specifically the wife's favorite pet (in this instance a dog) that is slain by the husband. In all four of these American versions there is a sequence of warnings by the husband to the animal— "That's the first . . . second . . . third time," or "That's one . . ." or "That's once!" And in all four the husband addresses the same warnings next to his wife, or at least he addresses the first and sometimes the second warning to her. The third one is never needed, for she always obeys him thereafter.

"That's once!" as we may call the story now, is the modern Anglo-American adaptation of the old Indo-European narrative tradition of Type 901. The tale has taken on here the most popular format to be found in contemporary urban storytelling. It is brief and pointed, having only one major episode, and it concludes with a "punchline." I have seen only one other version (from Illinois) with any suggestion of a warning to suitors about the shrew in it, and this and only one additional version (from New York) hint that the wife carried some baggage home. One text alone (from Kentucky) has the nonstandard punchline, "Miss Lady, for you that is number one." All other American versions are highly standardized.

The "That's once!" joke form of Type 901 has been collected in many texts since about 1950. I get it annually from my own folklore classes, and it is frequently sent to me by foklorists in other colleges and universities across the country.[13] Although most of the texts themselves are very much alike, their minor details, as well as background information and the side comments that informants make, cast more light on the tradition. For example, several situations and settings have been invented to account for a man and his wife riding home horseback or in a horse-drawn vehicle after their wedding. A common solution is to set the story in the pioneer period, giving the impression, perhaps, that this is a typical piece of American frontier humor. Another frequent opening attributes the tale to a supposedly backward region, such as Vermont, the Ozarks, or West Texas; one telling is set in Italy. The shrewtamer is often said to be a hillbilly, a farmer, or a rancher, depending on the place where it is told. In one version he is said to be a Quaker, and in another text he is a westerner who has married a mail-order bride. One American variant describes a mild-mannered man who is so pestered by a fly buzzing around him while he is eating that he warns it three times and finally swats it, splashing mashed potatoes and gravy all over his wife. She is quieted with the standard punchline.

Several versions put the story in the mouth of an oldtimer who has been asked by someone, usually a newspaper reporter, for the secret of his long and happy married life. Although this detail seems to typify a modern journalistic query, it is interesting to note that a similar opening was used with several Old World texts, including one collected in Persia in 1827.

A contemporary coed began her version by saying, "A guy and his girl were out on a date riding in a buggy . . . ," but why anyone would be riding in a buggy in this day and age was not explained. So far no collected versions have been attributed to the religious sects in this country that still *do* use horse-and-buggy as their regular means of transportation.

The varied situations in which informants recalled learning the joke demonstrate how thoroughly it has been absorbed into the contemporary American scene. Several people said it was told by ministers, either from the pulpit or to a couple just before their marriage. Fathers are reported telling the joke to their newlywed sons, and husbands to their brides; college professors tell it to students, military officers tell it to their men, and in one instance a teacher reported it told as a platform anecdote by a school official at an orientation session for new faculty. Two sources, one from the Midwest and one from the Northwest, said it was acted out as a skit, once at a Boy Scout meeting and once for a church youth group. One student collector heard the story told during a bridge game, and found out about my interest in the tale the very next morning in class.

Even though more than half of the American informants claimed to remember a direct oral source for the story, several of them thought they had also seen it in print or heard it on the radio or on television. Three television personalities were credited with telling the story—Groucho Marx, Jack Paar, and Tennessee Ernie Ford—and, although no informant has provided an exact text or reference from TV, one can imagine how each of these comedians might adapt it to his own style. The continuing circulation of the story among show business personalities is indicated in the following item from the Leonard Lyons column "The Lyons Den" in a *New York Post* of September, 1967:

> THREAT: Jay Harrison tells of the bride who bought [sic] her
> pet dog on their honeymoon. The dog growled at the groom, who

said "That's one" . . . The dog growled again, and the groom said,
"That's two" . . . The dog growled a third time, the groom killed it
with a pistol shot . . . The bride asked him, "Why did you do such
a terrible thing?" . . . "That's one," the groom replied.

Printed sources mentioned ranged from *Playboy* magazine to several local
newspapers; three actual versions from the popular press have been found. In
1952 *The Emancipator* of San Antonio, Texas, carried the tale[14] and credited
it to *The Scandal Sheet* of Graham, Texas. In 1958, when the rage for "sick
jokes" was on, the story appeared in a booklet called *Sick Jokes, Grim Cartoons & Bloody Marys*,[15] where it was only slightly altered from the usual oral
form with the addition of such lines as "You're a sadist, that's what!" In the
October, 1958, issue of *Boys' Life*, on the jokes-from-readers page, the following capsule version was attributed to a lad in Minneapolis:

> A newly married couple were leaving the church they were married
> in, in a horse-drawn carriage. The horse stumbled on a rock. "That's
> one," said the groom. Later on the horse stumbled again. "That's
> two, he said. A while later the horse tripped on a rock. "That's
> three," the man said as he pulled out a gun and shot the horse. His
> wife said he was too cruel. "That's one," said the man, and they
> lived happily after.

Perhaps the most interesting developments in the American tradition of
Type 901 are the passage of the native American joke subtype to Europe, and
the transmission of the American joke in Spanish across the Texas-Mexico
border. In the first instance a text was printed in Ireland in a popular English-
language magazine called *Ireland's Own* (October 31, 1953). This was the
140th text of Type 901 catalogued by the Irish Folklore Commission. The version begins: "An American farmer, who had just celebrated his golden wedding anniversary, was asked for some advice on how to achieve a happy
married life." And the story concludes with the line "That's once!" The new
Spanish-American variant is current in Texas, but it has also been reported by
folklorist Américo Paredes as told to him by a bilingual American citizen who
was in Mexico on vacation when he heard the story told by a Mexican who
spoke no English. The ending, "That's once!" which never appears in native
Spanish texts of Type 901, has been supplied here.

Finally a new literary treatment of Type 901 may be reported from the
United States. There is some chance now that we are dealing with the sort of
thing that Daniel J. Boorstin has labeled a "pseudo-event,"[16] for this version
derived in part from my own research on the folktale tradition. However, it is
particularly interesting because it involved a highly tradition-directed

group—the Mennonites—in a debate on the appropriateness of this particular folktale to their way of life.

In 1960 I enlisted the help of a friend familiar with Low German dialects to translate some texts of The Taming of the Shrew received from archives in northern Germany. My translator, Warren Kliewer, is a writer, and he decided to use the folktale as the basis for an episode in a short story he was then writing. His story, "The Death of the Patriarch," appeared in the Ball State Teachers College *Forum* for Winter 1962–63 (volume 3), Kliewer drew on his Mennonite upbringing in Minnesota for suggestions of setting and character. His story concerns the family death-watch over Ezra Wiehens, a stubborn old German farmer, in a community called "Waldheim," which is established to be probably in Manitoba because of references in the story to Winnipeg.

The climactic episode of Kliewer's story is recalled to the narrator's mind when his eyes fall upon the wedding portrait of Ezra and Anna Wiehens. Here is where Type 901 enters. As people still told the story in Waldheim, Ezra, long fond of hunting, and the possessor of fine hunting animals, had come to his wedding driving a buggy pulled by his favorite sorrel gelding and followed by his best Irish setter. After the marriage he commanded the dog three times to fetch the buggy to him; then he coldly shot it between the eyes. Twice he commanded the horse (which was tied up) to come forward; then he shot it, too. The episode concludes:

> Ezra reached into his coat pocket and pulled out another cartridge which he slid into the chamber. "Wife," the groom said turning to his bride, "you're smarter than both of them. I have to tell you only once. Go hitch yourself up to the buggy."
>
> Anna stood without moving, her eyes and mouth open wide, her hands shaking aimlessly before her body. Someone in the crowd, a man I suppose, said, "Well, he's going to wear the pants in the family." And then Ezra clicked back the hammer of the rifle.
>
> "Faster," he shouted after his wife as she trotted to the fallen horse, stripped the traces off, and pulled the buggy to the church steps by holding to the ends of the shafts. Leaping up and standing in the buggy, Ezra cracked the whip above his wife's head, and they drove out of the churchyard.

It does no justice to an author's work merely to summarize it, but even so it should be clear that Kliewer has realized a believable character here from the bare hints provided in the folktale. By presenting the episode as a local legend and by implying that there were different versions of it in Waldheim, he is true to the nature of oral tradition, and he also has cushioned the reader's shock at the bridegroom's violent behavior. The reader then can allow a little for the villagers' creative imagination over the years. Even so, considering other authoritative acts attributed to Ezra, the wife-taming is not too farfetched for his character. Thus, although Type 901 has apparently not been attributed in oral tradition to Mennonites and similar sects, Kliewer seems to have made it fictionally "right" that it could be.

It must be pointed out that "The Death of the Patriarch" ought to be studied in the context of its reprinting in Kliewer's 1964 collection, *The Violators*.[17] Here his imaginary, remote, and deeply conservative village of Waldheim is enlarged upon in nine further stories that are peopled by, as one Mennonite reviewer indignantly put it (referring specifically to "The Death of the Patriarch"), "fortune-tellers, perverts, idiots, fools, reprobates, and lesser twisted souls,"[18] *The Violators* caused something of a stir in the Mennonite press, to which, however, Kliewer has been and continues to be a popular contributor. He commented recently in a letter to me, "All the reviews in Mennonite publications were polemical, some for, some against."

Two important factors seem to have been operating on these reviewers. They insisted in general upon reading the stories as sociological documents instead of fiction, and usually they failed to recognize the taming episode as a traditional story. The extremes of opinion were represented in one issue of *Mennonite Life* magazine. In a short essay on *The Violators,* one well-informed reviewer mentioned Mr. Kliewer's earlier publications, praised him as a "growing writer," and commented upon some details of his new work, including the remark that "In 'The Death of the Patriarch' he takes the familiar old folk tale of the 'most obedient wife' and transfers it into the Waldheim setting."[19] But following the review a Mennonite reader in Minnesota published a letter branding Kliewer's writing as the "voice of an outsider," and complaining that he gave an unbalanced picture of Mennonite character and social life, allowing "glaring inconsistencies" in his portrayal of Canadian Mennonites.[20] In the *Mennonite Weekly Review* a book reviewer complimented Kliewer's writing style, but objected to the "odd characters, the like of whom I have never met among the thousands of people I have learned to know fairly well." Concerning the stories as a group, this reviewer said, "No doubt, each one makes a point but the bizarre characters in them make one wonder if this can be reality."[21] A third Mennonite publication, *Christian Living,* contained very strong criticism, both of the book and of its author. This reviewer found "The Death of the Patriarch" to be particularly "puzzling." "Puzzling!" he repeated, "not in the sense of hauntingly provocative, but irritatingly weird."[22]

To return to a broader view of the career of this folktale, so far as it has been worked out, we should ask what generalizations may be formulated about such transplants, adaptations, and mutations. Several conclusions seem obvious, although whether they apply only to funny stories, or only to northern European tales, or only to jokes about married couples, it is impossible to say at this time. It does, however, appear likely that similar principles operate in other European narrative traditions that were carried to the United States. The conclusions, briefly stated, are as follows:

Full and relatively complex versions of European tale types will survive best in the United States, if at all, in the traditions of individual families, among relatively homogeneous ethnic groups, or in somewhat isolated regions. Whenever such a story *does* pass into the mainstream of Anglo-American narrative folklore it is likely to be adapted to the "joke" form—that is, the characters become popular comic stereotypes, the plot is abbreviated, and the story develops a "punchline" ending.[23] This joke, then, if it survives for very long, will be adapted to the new time and place, as well as to narrators' various needs or uses for that particular story. Print and broadcasting help greatly to circulate such traditionally based "jokelore," and probably also contribute considerably to the stereotyping of the texts.

Also, some methodological generalizations may be made for the study of such tale-borrowings. Of first importance to folklorists, if they wish to study the careers of such tales, is the necessity to collect systematically not only the best, fullest, and most distinctive oral versions, but also the repetitious retellings of the same joke, fragments, garbled reports, offhand remarks of narrators, hints of printed and broadcasted versions, clippings, and so forth. Further, collectors must realize that tiny details in a text may be revealing (wording, facts in informants' backgrounds, names, descriptions of storytelling situations, etc.) and that there is an international traffic in folk and popular humor, both printed and oral, that is worth looking into.[24] Finally we may emphasize that a literary adaptation of a folk narrative cannot adequately be understood if readers do not approach the work itself in *literary* terms (not as social document). Further, if critics do not recognize direct borrowings from folklore when they encounter them, they may miss just such points as they should be able to clarify; in this instance, however, it must be admitted that had Mennonite reviewers recognized Kliewer's story as a folktale, they could have used a telling argument against it, namely, "It wasn't *really* a Mennonite folktale!"

NOTES

[1] See my unpublished dissertation (Indiana University, 1961), "*The Taming of the Shrew:* A Comparative Study of Oral and Literary Versions."

[2] This text was collected from Hallbera Halldórsdóttir from Selfoss, a town that lies

southeast of Reykjavík, Iceland. The collector, Þórzur Tómasson of Vallnatúni, Iceland, read it on an Icelandic radio program early in 1960. A manuscript copy was deposited in the national folklore archive, from which a literal translation was made for me by the Swedish folklorist Bo Almqvist. I have made only a few stylistic changes in his translation. Two published Icelandic versions of Type 901 are analyzed in my dissertation.

[3] A good version of this "cat-killed" type is found in Sir John Malcolm's *Sketches of Persia, from the Journals of a Traveler in the East*, 2 (London, 1827), pp. 54–58. Other texts come from India, Turkey, and Burma.

[4] *El Conde Lucanor*, ed. by Hermann Knust (Leipzig, 1900), tr. by James York, *Count Lucanor: or the Fifty Pleasant Stories of Patronio* (London, 1888), Chapter 35.

[5] This subtype and its relation to Shakespeare's play are discussed in my article "The Folktale Origin of *The Taming of the Shrew*," *Shakespeare Quarterly* 17 (1966), 345–59.

[6] From manuscript collections in the Archives de Folklore de l'Université Laval (Québec), supplied to me by Professor Luc Lacourcière. Collected 1953, 1955, and 1957.

[7] Juan B. Rael's *Cuentos Españoles de Colorado y Nuevo Méjico*, 2 (Stanford, California: Stanford University Press 1957), pp. 563–65. Two other supposed Spanish-American variants of Type 901 do not belong to the type. These are in Howard T. Wheeler's *Tales from Jalisco, Mexico*, Memoirs of the American Folklore Society 35 (Philadelphia, 1943), 91–92, and Franz Boas's "Tales of Spanish Provenience from Zuñi," *Journal of American Folklore* 35 (1922), 74–76.

[8] *The Hilton Bedside Book*, vol. 6 (New York: Hilton Hotels Corp., 1964), pp. 198–201.

[9] *Sticks in the Knapsack and other Ozark Folk Tales* (New York: Columbia University Press, 1958), pp. 71–73.

[10] "You Haven't Packed the Saddle," *Illinois Folklore* 1 (1947), 17–19; reprinted in Richard M. Dorson ed., *Buying the Wind: Regional Folklore in the United States* (Chicago: University of Chicago Press 1964), pp. 351–54.

[11] *American Folk Tales and Songs* (The New American Library: New York, 1956), pp. 226–27; recorded as told by Richard Chase on an LP recording of the same title issued by Tradition Recordings (TLP 1011).

[12] "Folktales by Mail from Bond, Kentucky," *Kentucky Folklore Record* 6 (1960), 69–76.

[13] Besides the three texts already referred to, twenty-four more were listed in my dissertation, coming from West Virginia, Michigan, Ohio, Indiana, Iowa, Kansas, Missouri, Arkansas, and Texas. I also have four texts collected in Idaho in 1963 and 1964. Two further versions from Texas have been published: Stanley W. Harris's "Stories of Ranch People," *Publications of the Texas Folklore Society* 30 (1961), 175; and Theodore B. Brunner's "Thirteen Tales from Houston County," *Publications of the Texas Folklore Society* 31 (1962), 21–22.

[14] Vol. 15 (Sept. 1952), 5.

[15] Editor Max Rezwin (New York: The Citadel Press, 1958), p. 14.

[16] See Professor Boorstin's book, *The Image: or What Happened to the American Dream* (New York: Atheneum 1961).

[17] (Francestown, New Hampshire, Marshall Jones Company: 1964), pp. 79–97.

[18] Review by Omar Eby in *Christian Living: A Magazine for Home and Community* (Scottdale, The Mennonite Publishing House, Pa.: January, 1966), pp. 32–33.

[19] Review by Elaine Sommers Rich in *Mennonite Life*. (Oct. 8, 1965), p. 189.

[20] Letter from Victor A. Dirks of Savage, Minnesota, pp. 189–190.

[21] Review by Melvin Gingerich in issue of July 1, 1965.

[22] The review by Omar Eby cited above, p. 32.

[23] I discussed a similar adaptation of Type 660 in my article "Some International Folktales from Northwest Tradition," *Northwest Folklore* 1 (1966), 7–13.

[24] A page-one feature by Edwin A. Roberts, Jr., in *The National Observer* 5:39 (September 26, 1966) described the "Armenian Radio joke" current in the Soviet Union. They follow the pattern of American "elephant jokes" and "Polack jokes," and they play on the ethnic slur of the latter.

APPENDIX B

❖❥❖❥❖❥❖❥❖❥❖❥❖

The Folklore of Academe

by Barre Toelken

The traditions of high school corridor and college campus have not yet received from folklorists the close scrutiny and analysis common in most areas of folklore study today, and probably the chief reason has been that even among folklorists themselves folklore has been viewed generally as a thing of the past, a phenomenon which no longer exists except in badly deteriorated remnants, and at that among poorly educated or illiterate people. Such a notion has little or no currency among modern folklorists,[1] but the concept has shaped several generations of scholars whose approach to folklore was exemplified by an earnest combing of the outlands in an attempt to collect and preserve old ballads and tales lest they die out through exhaustion in the combat with creeping literacy.

The gathering of "survivals" and "antiquities," coupled with a myopic view that the terms "superstition," "custom," and "folklore" denote the beliefs of less advanced people ("religion," "science," and "politics" denoting *our* beliefs), generally resulted in the serious investigation only of those things which lay comfortably beyond the folklorist's own nose. Today, one can find a plethora of detailed studies concerning riddles among New Guinea head-hunters, sexual taboos of the Pacific Islanders (island by island), ballads of the isolated Ozarkers, marriage and funeral customs of various immigrant groups, barn styles among the Amish, jump-rope rhymes of small children, hay-derrick construction in certain farming communities, and oral tales from innumerable American Indian tribes—all topics which are closely associated with the concepts of illiteracy, "primitiveness," geographical distance and lack of societal sophistication (taken, of course, from the urban point of view). Only recently, say in the past ten or fifteen years, has there been any attempt to study the traditional materials being passed orally by contemporaneous, urban, educated people.

If, as some astute anthropologists have observed, in a nonliterate society *all* things are oral (and thus presumably of interest to the folklorist), does it not stand to reason that as literacy develops, oral traditions will become useless and die out? And would not this be especially true of a highly literate, well-educated, often sceptical group such as one might find on a college campus? Surprisingly but clearly, the answer is no, and for at least two reasons. First of all, the spread of literacy has discouraged neither oral expression nor the oral dissemination of such expression (the widespread currency of the joke would, by itself, support this). As a matter of fact, it may very well be that the ubiquity of things in print has caused many people to feel an even greater necessity for expressing their chief concerns orally. Secondly, and probably of greater importance to the folklorist, in spite of high literacy rates, most groups which have any appreciable cohesiveness can be observed to share a living, chiefly oral culture, not a printed one.

The cultural elements which bind college students together as an identifiable group have almost nothing to do with the college catalog, the rules list, or the mimeographed directives of Dean and Professor. Rather, they derive from a shared series of live experiences, common fears, hopes and frustrations, all of which are difficult if not impossible to express in essay form (though they do occasionally appear anonymously on desk-tops and rest-room walls [2]). In this sense, then, high school students, or college students, can be seen as members of a folk group, separately literate but communally aliterate. That is to say, while they do know how to read, their cultural expressions (insofar as they represent the academic experience) do not ordinarily come forth through the agency of the printed word. We will find that in these groups traditional materials are far from dead or even anemic; in point of fact, the folklore of Academe is widespread and viable, and reveals with great vividness the traditional concerns of academicians on both sides of the podium, expressed in many of the same genres as folklore is found to take among other folk groups.

The present essay will attempt to provide a general survey of the topics and genres of high school/college lore based primarily on the author's own observations and experiences as a member of both student and faculty camps, as well as on surveys made in high school and college classes by himself and a number of his colleagues. The study is thus one of breadth rather than depth, and will suffice only as a background upon which certain observations will be made by way of precaution and critical stricture on the study of folklore among literates. The student who carries on his own investigation will, of course, want to focus on a far more restricted area and study the characteristics of oral traditions within the context allowed by his own carefully gathered and carefully evaluated data.[3] Furthermore, even in the few years since these data were first gathered, the author has noticed some of the beliefs and expressions changing, disappearing, being replaced by others. The student will do well to take this dynamic state of flux as a basic component of academic folklore.

The primary distinction between faculty and students goes much deeper than the superficial fact that one group is presumably engaged in saying something of importance to the other group, which, in turn, is presumably listening. The faculty at any high school or college not only share in a "great enterprise" which accords them a certain status (if not money), but often see themselves as aligned against a common foe which is willing to use the most devious tactics to win out. Their stories and legends abound in accounts of what other faculty members do, or have done, to quiet a noisy class, to wake up one sleeping student or to squelch the amorous advances of another. According to one typical story, a professor threw a piece of chalk at a sleeping boy to wake him up, but it entered his wide-open mouth and lodged in his throat, nearly choking him to death (in some versions of the tale the boy is still recovering in a nearby hospital and the professor or teacher has been assigned to other duties). A professor is visited by a girl who announces with a blush that she will do anything for a good grade in his class. "Anything?" he asks in mock disbelief. "Anything. I must get a good grade in order to stay in the sorority." "Anything?" he asks again softly, swinging the door closed. "Anything," she replies, eyes downcast. Then, whispering into her ear, "Why don't you try studying?" Still another professor gains traditional fame when he becomes upset at the many students who are bringing tape-recorders to class: he sends an assistant in his place who plays tape-recorded lectures.

Common in both the United States and England is the story of Professor Jenkins, a teetotaler, who is a visiting lecturer on leave from a religious college. At a reception given by his chairman in his honor, sherry is passed, at which Professor Jenkins exclaims, "Why I'd as soon commit adultery as take a drink of wine!" "So would we all, Mister Jenkins," says his host, "So would we all." A Milton professor walks into the classroom on the first day, runs his eyes along the front row, then asks the girls to cross their legs. "Now that the gates of Hell are closed," he says, "we may safely begin our consideration of *Paradise Lost*." The reader no doubt can supply many more examples of the same sort, for they are not restricted in their transmission to faculty members. Yet the faculty tells them usually as tales which reveal "our situation," while the students tell them to show what odd folk the faculty are.[4] Judging from their folklore, faculty members seem to see themselves as benevolent patriarchs whose words are needed, but most often unheeded, by their clients; they reveal a faith in their attractions to the opposite sex, but demonstrate a remarkable dedication—bordering sometimes on raw heroism—to keeping a proper professional distance from their numerous besiegers. When not beset by amorous students, the professors of tradition turn their attention to the vampiric hordes of congenital liars who surround them in every class before each vacation and after each exam. In odd moments they brood about the kindly contempt of colleagues who have seemed, perhaps, a little cool in their reception of the latest scholarly offering before the academic altar.[5]

Since working people in more "practical" jobs may think professors are unrelated to the real world, academicians spice their language with terms and metaphors which are calculated to suggest sweat, technology, and exactitude to outsiders. Books are "tools of the trade"; doctoral degrees are "union cards"; we hear of the "mechanics" of writing and about the "technical aspects" of dramatic composition. We teach "workshops" in poetry; we write of "tension" and "torsion" in literary criticism; we entertain "visiting firemen" instead of official observers or potential candidates for academic positions; our librarians use "trucks" to push books around on, and place the books in "decks" and "stacks" more often than on floors and shelves. And the departmental supervisor is probably a Head rather than a Chairman, but the janitorial tenor of this term may be coincidental.

The student, on the other hand, tells stories about fellow students who outsmarted the teacher, relates "real" instances of eccentricities among instructors, reminisces about obscene remarks made by professors in class, recalls the actions and philosophies of prudish Deans (no red dresses, no patent leather shoes, no girls to sit on boys' laps without the interposition of telephone book or pillow), and describes in detail what other students will do or have done for a grade.[6]

One friend has a music professor who climbed out of the grand piano the first day of class; another friend knew someone who witnessed the "Gates of Hell" remark in Milton class; someone else has it on good authority (i.e., heard from a friend) that an English professor concluded a mid-campus conversation with a student by asking "Which way was I going when we stopped?" and on being told, answered, "Oh, then I *have* eaten lunch."

Last year, one hears from reliable friends, an easily embarrassed biology teacher got rid of all the girls in class by writing an obscene word on the board before taking roll, or by asking an ambiguous question of a blonde in the front row ("Can you tell me, Miss, what part of the body expands to three times its normal size when properly stimulated?" After the girl walks out the instructor shrugs, "What's so bad about the pupil of the eye?").[7] Folk traditions reveal the student as a person who feels unfairly beset by a System which imposes on its prisoners too many unwanted instructors and too much unneeded homework; the student is served incoherence and obscenity in class, inedible food in the dormitory (rumor has it that flies avoid the garbage cans in back of the dorm); and gets poor grades because "The Curve" was unfair (a phenomenon usually attributed in legends to the erratic correction procedures of the professor or to the flagrant currying of favor by some attractive person in the front row).

Students thus feel a certain amount of paranoia to be obligatory and a certain amount of rebellion against their oppressors justifiable. They "cut class" as often as possible, do only enough work to satisfy requirements, and engage in activities which challenge the naïve ideas they are certain their teachers passionately believe in. Their code of class behavior permits, even encourages, them to make academic gains through wit, stealth, or late and reluctant spurts of energy ("out-foxing the prof," "cribbing," "cramming"), but prohibits the exercise of personal charm, amiability, or good looks ("brown-nosing"); protracted and serious academic work is not entirely taboo, but usually results in the label "drudge," a socially serious blemish which must be balanced or expiated by the exercise of other socially acceptable qualities (such as extreme good looks, or talent on the football field). The traditional materials and attitudes transmitted through both faculty and students are based in such concerns as these, and thus the folklore of Academe is seen to grow out of, as well as to reflect, the preoccupations of each group with its own problems (and the concern of both groups with the vagaries and treacheries of the Administration). Moreover, since each group defines itself by contrast to the other, a knowledge of both sets of folklore is required in order to make sense of either one.

In addition to the traditional jargon and popular beliefs of Academe, there exists a seemingly endless supply of traditional materials in the more artistic genres of song and story. Stories told in oral tradition on the college campus are very much in the genre of the *sage*, now receiving closer attention of the folklorists in the form of the urban belief tale. Indeed, many urban legends now in circulation throughout the United States are found to be current as well in Academe; the cement truck driver who fills a supposed rival's car with concrete, the new car for sale cheap because it has a death smell, the man who is thrown nude out of his camper into the streets of Pleasantville, the woman who is forced to pay an outlandish price for a recipe given by a restaurant chef, are all known and actively passed on by the students and faculty. In addition to these, there are a number of tales which have themes of particular applicability to college and high school situations, and these are so widely popular among students as to be current virtually everywhere one can find students. One particular version of the Vanishing Hitchhiker tale (Motif E332.3.3.1), for example, depicts a driver in his teens who picks up a hitchhiking girl in the rain one evening. He lets her off at her house wearing his borrowed sweater, and when he returns to retrieve it he is told by her mother that the girl died in an accident after a prom some twenty years before, and that someone has reported having picked her up at that place on the anniversary every year thereafter. Checking on the story, the young man visits the graveyard and finds her gravestone—with his sweater wrapped around it. Not only did this legend inspire the composition of at least two pop-rock songs during the 1970s, but it relates to some of the Three Nephite stories from Utah. Obviously, the image speaks strongly to something in American life, but what is it specifically? As widespread is the tale of the high school girl who keeps passing out in class (usually a class attended by a friend of the narrator) and is finally taken to the hospital in a coma. There a small spider is seen darting into her highly lacquered bouffant hair-do, and the nurses pursue it, only to find a whole nest of black widow spiders in the girl's hair, which, of course, was hospitable to them because it had never been combed for a year. In some versions she recovers, in others she dies, but the tale is so seriously told and received that students now report having heard the tale told by a teacher (usually a girls' gym instructor or a Health and Hygiene professor) as a true story of what can happen to a girl who does not regularly comb her hair.

Just as current are a number of tales which deal with ghostly or ghastly phenomena encountered in the vicinity of lovers' lanes. Salt Lake City high schoolers of the 1950s and 1960s watched carefully for the Hopping Lady of Memory Grove, the unfortunate and apparently jealous wraith of an old maid whose legs had grown together. She was seen hopping about a small memorial park scratching on the windows of parked cars, sometimes attacking the occupants if their windows were open (one's car could be made Hopping-Lady-proof only by parking it crossways in the road and allowing its high beams to shine for a specified time on an old house in the vicinity, just before entering Memory Grove on amorous business). Both high school and college students tell of a couple parked in a local lane who hear an announcement over the car radio that a dangerous convict (sometimes a lunatic) has escaped from the state prison and can be recognized by a hook on his arm. The girl is sure she has heard a metallic noise against the side of the car and insists on being driven home. Her date complies, in considerable dudgeon, and when he yanks her door open to let her out at home, a hook and an arm-cup fall off the door-handle. In some versions the girl's hair turns white at this juncture—a theme encountered so commonly that it has its own motif number (Motif F1041.7). Boys report telling this story to their dates in order to encourage them to "move over closer," while girls and parents admit telling it to inhibit careless parking. Yet, even though the legend has these rather pragmatic functions, it remains true that the story is generally believed to have happened. In these stories, as with most urban legends, there is an attempt to authenticate the incident by making reference to the source of the story, usually a trusted friend who knows one of the people to whom it happened.[8]

Less structured than these legends but just as current are the countless anecdotes told by students about their professors.[9] They may be distinguished from the narrative legends, for purposes of convenience in study, because they do not seek to tell an engaging story in an engaging way; rather, their aim is to impart in as few words as possible a simple "fact" about someone. Since here the story *qua* story is less important than the "information" itself, we may call these items traditional incidents or legend cores. For example, one hears tell of a professor who writes equations so rapidly on the board that a graduate assistant must follow and erase the board behind him. Since the student erases faster than anyone can take notes, most of the material is irretrievably lost. A similar one simply tells us that there is another professor who writes on the board with his right hand and erases as he goes with his left; anyone who cannot take immediate notes is lost, but since the professor has given the same final examination for twenty-three years, everyone always gets an A. One professor wears the same suit every day for a whole year; another wears a variety of suits, but wears the same trenchcoat, rain or shine, and always forgets to take it off in class; another sometimes leaves the room during a lecture to get equipment or books he has forgotten, but since he keeps lecturing while gone and since he is often out for more than five minutes, his topic is always different when he re-enters. One professor lectures only to the best-looking girl in class, looks only at her, and checks her face after every attempt at humor and on making every point (of course, she nods constantly throughout all lectures, to show that she understands everything he is saying). One day, late in the quarter, however, she is absent. The professor enters, opens his book, puts on his glasses and looks out over the class to her empty seat; after a puzzled moment he asks, "Where is everybody today?"

In contrast to the official anthems imposed on students by their school (most of them composed to a nineteen-thirtyish pseudo-ragtime tune) are the many traditional songs which spring up, usually among the "Greeks," the participants at beer-busts, and the members of specialized clubs (e.g., The Foresters, The Engineers). As one student observed to the author, the most popular kind of songs are those to which the participants can add other verses, and those which allow for accompaniment by physical actions, in both cases the ones which remain in oral circulation for very long must be humorous or risqué, preferably both. Needless to say, such songs are not customarily sung where outsiders may collect them, or Deans break in and hear. Since many of these songs would be classed as obscene if they appeared in ordinary printed media, they are encountered chiefly in oral form; thus their status as folklore is assured largely through their own topics and wording. Two songs, both from college sororities, appear below as moderately safe examples of the type, though the reader should not take them as an indication that girls' songs are less prurient than the boys' in general.

VIOLET TIME

Violate me in the violet time
In the vi-o-lest way that you know;
Ravish me savagely, simply lavish me,
On me no mercy bestow:
For the best things in life are the obvious, oblivious;
Oh, give me a man who is lewd and lascivious.
Oh, violate me in the violet time
In the vi-o-lest way that you know.

FASCINATING BITCH

I wish I were a fascinating bitch:
I'd never be poor—I'd always be rich.
I'd live in a house with a little red light,
I'd sleep all day and work all night,
And once a month I'd take a little trip
And drive my customers wild.
I wish I were a fascinating bitch
Instead of an innocent child.

Many songs are sung by the members of one fraternity in order to cast a goodnatured slur on the members of another. Such rivalry songs are common on all campuses, and, as one would expect of traditional songs, considerable variation comes into play. Representative are the following:

A garbage can, a garbage can,
Upon a field of blue
A closer look revealed to me
The crest of Sigma Nu.

Adam was a beta boy,
Job went Sigma Chi,
Moses was an S A E
But Jesus was a Phi.

From the sororities:

How'd you like to be an Alpha Sly? [10]
To live and love and drink your whisky dry,
To wear your skirts way up above your knees
So everyone can see
You're from the University;
My dearie, come and join the best sorority,

Come and gain your notoriety,
You will lose your sweet virginity
And be an Alpha Sly.

*

I am a dirty D G [11]
A dirty little D G,
I spread a reign of terror where I go;
My chief delight is stirring up a fight
And I beat little kids on the head til they're dead.
For I am a D G, a dirty little D G,
I put poison in my mother's shredded wheat;
I am a blotch on the family's scotch,
And I eat—raw—meat.

The Greek system also serves as nucleus for a number of collegiate practices and stories about those practices. "Goat Weeks," "steals," initiation procedures among the fraternities, as well as corollary customs among other student groups make up a goodly part of college folklore, much of which may be entirely legendary. Initiations and other similar exercises do go on, of course, often in spite of university disapproval. Student informants who are members of the system report such experiences as having to down fourteen raw eggs in fifteen minutes, being paddled with a variety of instruments, having to eat mentholatum sandwiches, playing hair-pulling games with fellow pledges, and being treated to dinners secretly loaded with laxatives. One Western sorority holds its initiation in the rented recreation room of a nearby church. Blindfolded pledges grope into toilet bowls to encounter bananas, are subjected to a number of embarrassing inquisitions, are given off-color or obscene nicknames, and are at length required to enact the giving of birth to a nation, or to imitate the flushing of a toilet. Finally, they are placed one by one in a coffin, shut briefly in, and then allowed to get out, having been "reborn" as active members of the chapter.[12] More commonly encountered are stories and legends told by non-Greeks (barbarians?) about the terrible and frightening excesses of the initiation procedures used by the fraternity system. The point seems to be that *we* would not want to join a group characterized by pledges dying of fright during ghastly initiation ceremonies (Motif N384.4). Thus, the exclusiveness sought by the Greeks is countered by a strongly vituperative exoteric tradition among those who are excluded, or who want to exclude themselves from the ranks of the Chosen.

Members of such secular clubs as the Foresters tell of outlandish pranks played on their campus rivals. In the usual manner of the *sage*, the occurrences are alleged to have happened in the recent past, and the stories usually consist of adventures like bricking up the entrance of the Engineering Building during class hours, engaging in gun battles with the campus police, leading well-fed farm animals into the offices of faculty members at night, rolling huge logs downhill at a particularly offensive campus building, and so on. In reality, a good many pranks—including head-shaving, practiced on captured opponents—do occur during the friendly rivalry of such clubs, and there is ample reason to believe some of the more spectacular stories about pranks played during the club's Mythic Age; nonetheless, even the casual collector of such tales will begin to perceive a general thread of repetition on campuses across the country that testifies to the traditional diffusion of the materials.

Nearly every fraternity or club has or has had a brother who was able to perform a more obscene act in public than his rival in another fraternity,[13] most fraternities and sororities have had presidents who were kidnapped (either by pledges or by rivals) and left handcuffed, nude, tied to a tree in the wilderness, to the gatepost of a nearby university, or suspended from a construction derrick; many fraternities tell of having had a horse shot in their basement (during a dance or a vacation) which developed rigor mortis before it could be evacuated and consequently had to be dissected for removal; most groups have had at least one dance in the past where the centerpiece at the head table was a hand (head, foot, etc.) borrowed from the Medical School anatomy lab (Motif N384.0.1.1). While such happenings may or may not have been actual events, they are more commonly found in oral tradition than in daily experience. Of course, the fact that any item is found in oral circulation does not show that it is historically inaccurate, either; rather, since the folklorist is neither a rationalizer nor a debunker, he simply uses such data to show what things have been popular enough to pass into a viable oral form. In these and other examples of student folklore we may observe in addition the embodiment in expressive form of many private and social "repressions"—actions or words which a student might consider taboo or socially dangerous if actually performed or stated in the normal course of events, but which may be released safely as verbal or pictorial entities of anonymous origins.[14]

Though college songs and tales have been familiar for many years, it comes as a surprise to some that popular belief (superstition), ritual, and traditional custom are as common among highly literate college students as among primitives. To some observers of the collegiate scene it comes as proof of a long-smoldering suspicion about students; to the folklorist, it shows that the uncritical acceptance of certain beliefs passed orally by one's culture is not limited to illiterate savages. Commonly, the beliefs and customs of the campus are analogous to the rites of passage found in the beliefs of any folk group which sees itself as drawn up against an unpredictable world: initiation rituals (already mentioned above), ceremonies concerning love and marriage, magical means of passing final exams, particular modes of behavior toward one's professors, are all part of the students' traditional system.

For an interesting example of ritual on campus, one might investigate the pinning or engagement ceremony.[15] It usually takes place in the dormitory or the sorority house of the girl who intends thereby to reveal her recent engagement. The girl, or more usually one of her close friends, arranges the details of the ceremony, which occurs after supper. During the meal, certain traditional signs (usually the passing of candy) are given that the ritual will take place, but no one—ideally, at least—knows at this point who the engagee is. After the meal the girls adjourn to stand in a circle in the semidarkened living room. A candle is introduced which is often situated in the middle of a large plate and surrounded by rose-buds, or fruits such as oranges and apples, or vitamin pills, or cookies; sometimes the candle has no accompanying paraphernalia at all, beyond a small ribbon or tiny bouquet; usually the engagement ring is tied to the candle or placed over the candle's tip.

The candle is lighted, then passed slowly from girl to girl around the circle, while the girls sing softly an appropriate lovesong. On the third pass, the engagee reveals herself by blowing the candle out, whereupon the rest of the girls rush at her with great screaming and general commotion, apparently by way of congratulation. It is significant to note that few, if any, girls seem to know the older traditional association of the candle, ring, rose-buds, fruits, the chanting circle of women, and the blowing out of the candle [16]; rather, these old elements are probably retained because they have "always" been associated with the customs surrounding the revealing of a coming marriage. The modern girl thus sees the ceremony not as the exercise of a fertility cult, but simply as a dramatic and socially acceptable—perhaps expected—way in which to reveal the exciting news of one's engagement. Both the engagement and the means of its revelation are important to the girl, however, and for this reason the ritual's function is far more important than a mere game.

Thus, the ceremony is a serious traditional ritual, but in dealing with it, we must not fail to keep in mind that the functional properties ascribed to it by those who practice it today are not necessarily the same as those which might have occasioned a similar ritual in another age. These considerations are obligatory throughout the study of folklore, and an unwillingness to exercise them led many students of popular belief, especially at the turn of the century, into embarrassing dead-ends.[17]

Another group of traditional beliefs and practices clusters about the taking of exams. Of more than six hundred students responding to a questionnaire, more than four hundred reported that they engaged in certain customary practices during finals weeks that they did not engage in during the rest of the term.[18]

Probably the most common practice, based on these responses, is the wearing of "grubby" clothes—not simply informal dress, but decidedly and intentionally rumpled and dirty. Other practices mentioned by numerous students include the following: eating raw meat, fasting, abstaining from sex during the exam period, taking a good-luck amulet or a toy to the exam, wearing lucky undergarments (girls), hoping the hardest exam will fall on a lucky date (usually the 7th, 14th, 21st, or 28th), not combing or setting hair (girls), and growing a beard for the week. (This last intentional exercise has become less marked as beards have become more common: does it indicate that some exam customs are meant as a rejection of that authority which occasions the exam? Clearly, what is considered "outlandish" or "antisocial" behavior changes with the times.) While in general the students were reluctant to term these practices "superstitions," they did admit that these were not simply occasioned by lack of time during exams; these clearly are actions taken with the direct purpose of affecting one's ability at the exam.

It probably need not be mentioned that such practices as fasting, eating certain foods, abstinence from sex, wearing of certain clothing, carrying of lucky items, not washing or shaving, and so forth, are customs found more or less typically among a number of relatively primitive clutures who attempt by such measures to effect their futures by ensuring a good hunt. It would be possible, thus, to see the modern student as a moderately literate savage on that account if one were to ignore functional considerations. In this case, the observances are strikingly similar, and they may very well suggest to us that, faced with certain kinds of pressure, humans are likely to attempt to affect the future by magical means requiring the suspension of ordinary modes of behavior and by using everyday items in unusual ways. As fetching as the similarities in practice may be, however, the traditions themselves will remain distinguished by the simple fact that the primitive hunter is usually faced with hunger—if not starvation—if the hunt does not succeed, while the student is faced at most with embarrassment and the bother of re-taking the class if he fails his exam.

One of the most widespread and seriously practiced beliefs among college students is that a class must wait a certain number of minutes for professors when they are late to class. One form of the code usually allows a wait of five minutes for an instructor without Ph.D., ten minutes for an Assistant Professor, fifteen minutes for an Associate Professor, and twenty minutes for a full Professor. There is a good deal of confusion in the system, however, for a significant number of students do not understand the academic ranking: some, for example, report that they must wait ten minutes for an instructor, but twenty minutes for a "doctor" (two different and sometimes overlapping categories); others have a regular progression of times to wait but have the ranks in the wrong order; some think the term "assistant" means a graduate assistant, and would thus wait longer for a graduate student, thinking him a professor, than they would for a full-time instructor.

In spite of occasional aberrations in the system, however, the students do illustrate pretty well some generally accepted folklore theories by their traditional beliefs in this category. Out of more than six hundred students polled in 1965–67, only one reported never having heard of a rule for waiting; not surprisingly, it was found that this student lived off campus, was unaffiliated with any campus social group, ate and studied off campus, and was, in short, not a participating member in the folk group. Although students gave a number of different answers on the obligatory length of wait, more than 78 per cent gave one answer, based on one consideration: the student must wait ten minutes for a non-Ph.D., fifteen for a Ph.D. This illustrates that a specifically formularized belief is held by a small majority; the rest of the members are familiar with the belief and are in the habit of observing it, but are not entirely clear about the details—a condition which may very well be typical of the acceptance/practice rate of any traditional belief, and one which, regularly measured over a large enough sample of a folk group, could reveal the rate of development or deterioration of a particular traditional item within the group. As might be expected, the more impressionable, more frightened freshmen and sophomores exhibit a higher rate of belief in the obligatory wait than do students in the upper classes, which may suggest that as students mature and become more agnostic about the intricacies of college life they either find out that there is no formal waiting period dictated by their college, or continue to accept the fact that there is one but decide not to observe it.[19] Most of the students giving the most common answer (ten minutes/fifteen minutes) are, as one would expect, complete members of the folk group: that is, they not only attend classes together, but they live, eat, and study on campus, thus participating as fully as one can in the specialized community of Academe and sharing continually in its specialized pressures.

When asked why they observe the waiting period, the students generally answer that it is a college rule (though they have heard it only from each other), and that observance of it will provide them with a structured mode of conduct which releases them from responsibility in the event they do leave the classroom. The first part of their answer indicates the uncritical aspect of their belief—an element found organically in superstition; the second part shows that they do have, however, a good sense of how this particular belief functions for them within their culture. It is important to note that in the 1970s, a mere ten years after these figures were first obtained, students reported that although they still recognize the custom, they feel less obliged to honor it. Of course, folklorists must always exercise caution when getting explanations of customs from informants who are believers, but they should never on that account ignore the fact that an informant can often supply commentary on the function of a belief or practice which would otherwise come to the investigator only in fragmentary form or through divine inspiration.

In the closer investigation of academic folklore, then, students must keep in mind a number of distinctive categories which will enable them to see more clearly and thus to evaluate more reliably the functions, the actual working characteristics, of the various traditional modes and genres. In addition to the basic division between students and faculty, for example, one ought to consider other differences, such as age and sex of the believer, and possible differences in the currency of the materials themselves (for example, the distinction between old traditions remaining vestigially in memory versus those current, viable, and in wide circulation). The latter consideration is especially valuable, for a number of studies have been made to show the modern degeneration of older traditions,[20] but there has been comparatively little emphasis on the distinct possibility (suggested strongly by the very existence of urban and academic folklore) that while one tradition dies out because it is out of fashion or confused, other traditions arise to take its place which are quite applicable to the contemporary concerns of the host group.

When asked to list a cure for warts, fewer than half of the students polled could put down anything, and most of those insisted that they had only heard of the treatment (or read about it) and had never practiced it. Asked what one does with spilled salt, about two-thirds answered to the effect that it must be thrown over the shoulder, while one-third (roughly 200 students) had never heard—or remembered—anything on the subject. Of those who did answer the question, the stipulation of the left shoulder was made chiefly by females. It is probably safe to conclude, even on these scanty figures, that among the academic folk group wart cures are vestigial; not many people remember them, and almost no one practices them. If Academe were a self-contained community we might postulate that in two or three generations wart cures would be almost unknown. Yet, since Academe draws its members from other groups which may still have a higher rate of belief in wart cures than that found in the academic world, it will actually be a considerably long time before such items disappear from memory. In the case of salt, the belief seems more familiar, but the specific details are still remembered chiefly by those members of the group who traditionally would have been most concerned with the storing and using of salt, namely the women; significantly enough, some members of the student group, about 10 per cent and mostly women, still actually practice the custom of throwing spilled salt over the left shoulder.

When asked a question which comes closer to their own current frame of concern, however, students reveal a much higher rate of familiarity and practice in traditional beliefs. In addition to customs directly conneted with academic dilemmas, such as the obligatory wait mentioned above, almost all college students possess a sizable body of beliefs which reflect and grow out of the more general conditions of student social life; one example would be the hangover cure. The most commonly stated remedy is the ancient "hair of the dog," which a majority of the students polled understood properly to mean another drink of the same liquor that made one drunk. The complete phrase ("a hair of the dog that bit you") of course suggests homeopathic medicine— "like cures like"; but unfortunately the whole phrase is seldom used anymore, and some few students who thus cannot see the point of the analogy take the statement literally: one wrote, "Well, you're supposed to get some hair off some kind of dog, but then I forget what you're supposed to do with it," while another wrote, "You ask for the lock of hair from the dog [i.e., girl] you were with the night before, but I don't see what good that would do for you if you really had a good hangover." [21] Of course, most students do not believe in homeopathic magic as such, and they are thus at some pains to support this old custom by reference to a supposedly reliable body of underground information on body chemistry.

Again, in areas of concern which deal primarily with attractiveness to, of success with, the opposite sex, college students show a statistically high and consistent rate in their acceptance of tradition. More than 80 per cent can list several foods to take in order to enhance virility and fertility (even though college students do not care in general to engender progeny, they apparently relate their own attractions to the *ability* to do so); the typical single answer is the familiar "seafood," which, like the hair of the dog, seems to have been adopted by this folk culture from outside sources because it serves to express a traditional concern, not limited to the group, which is still current. Similarly, among high school students there exists a large and unexplored area of lore which might be termed folk contraception, featuring varied, often bizarre (and patently unreliable) methods which high schoolers at least claim to believe in.

One might easily mention a great number of beliefs and observances or academic tales such as those discussed above, but the point should be clear: on traditional matters which have been in the past very widely passed in American culture but which have no direct bearing on life in Academe, the rate of familiarity among the college group is usually 50 per cent or less, with those actually believing or practicing the custom almost nil; on traditional items which grow out of concerns still felt by the student, both rates are much higher (75–85 per cent); in those areas most closely and distinctively academic, traditions are familiar to, and practiced by, a powerful majority (usually more than 90 per cent), with a sizable majority within that group agreeing quite specifically on the nature and the details of the observance.

There is often a sharp distinction between males and females, especially in traditional jargon and terminology, and in those rituals and observances connected specifically with the aims and problems of each sex: courtship, love divination, pinning, etc., in which the female's reactions are, or are expected to be, different from the male's. When age and sex are considered together, some interesting facts emerge. When a college class was asked in 1967 what word they used to denote a fellow student who curries favor with the teacher: students under 30 years of age usually answered "brown-nose," or "brownie," the boys' etymology relating the term to a particularly offensive anatomical contact, the girls' to the practice of Brownie scouts of working for merit points. Of the students whose ages are 30 to 45, the men almost all answered "brown-nose," but women nearly all gave "apple-polisher." Of students over 45, men and women gave "apple-polisher" almost without exception (one occasionally found an older student who had picked up "brown-nose" from his own children and used it to show he was up to date). Such an observation helps us see in a rather general way how recently the term came into use, and allows us to surmise that originally it was used by men, that the term itself may no longer be "taboo" for a woman, but that most women are not familiar with its original imagery (or else that they still feel constrained by other taboos not to mention it).

Still other useful considerations about language, custom, superstition, even social psychology, are possible to extrapolate from academic folklore as long as the student keeps such classifying distinctions in mind. An example would be the shift in folklore that occurs between high school and college. Here, age again plays an important role, but in this case, the *particular* age is significant. High school traditions (other than official games and exercises instigated by principals, coaches, and other chaperons) reflect with some accuracy the fears and frustrations of that onerous task of being teen-aged: games such as spin-the-bottle, or "perdiddle" (pop-eye, padiddle, perdido) function as external means of establishing that moment when a young man may kiss a girl; "queer day," usually Thursday, on which students wear or avoid certain colors (yellow, green), allows certain repressions and concerns about sex and about being different to take form within a legitimate—but confined—mode; euphemisms like "It's snowing down south" (your slip is showing) and "She's off the floor" (this is her menstrual period) allow girls to transmit information to and about each other which might cause embarrassment if stated openly. It is not surprising, considering the teenage dilemma, that many—if not most—of these high school traditions seem to mirror the teenagers' acute and often frightened awareness of their own emerging sexuality.

By contrast, college students seem more sophisticated, but a closer look at their folklore shows that it is simply because they have traded some of their puerile fears for adult ones. He no longer must spin the bottle or say "perdiddle" in order to get his kisses, and she hardly remembers when she last referred to snow in the south. Their traditions are now full of stories, customs, remedies and rituals which run high with concern over pinning, engagement, finding a mate, virility and contraception—not necessarily in that order—as well as with problems connected with the impossible daily load of reading, lectures, and homework.

Along with all the distinctions mentioned here, a constant attention must be given by the folklorist to the difference between current *talk* of a belief and the actual practice of it. On most college campuses there is a traditional means of discovering a virgin: statues stand up or speak when she walks by, fixed gates close, stone animals twitter and roar, paintings and statues of angels blow horns and flap wings ("and the last time it ever happened was in the nineteen-thirties, when Shirley Temple visited campus"). "Beliefs" of this sort are just about as common as the belief in the obligatory wait, but there is one obvious distinction: these are jocular in nature and exist only in the telling, and while they may certainly reflect a serious concern for virginity or the supposed rarity thereof, no one can be found who *really* believes the statue of the Pioneer Father will whistle when a virgin walks by. However, the belief in the obligatory wait is perfectly serious, and even the student who has reservations about it will practice it just to be safe. Members of the academic folk group know the difference between these usages, moreover, and would consider anyone naïve and humorless who objected, "Oh, I really don't believe that statue could stand up," and would think a fellow student foolhardy if he walked out of class after a five-minute wait.

Similarly, graduating students wear black robes at commencement exercises because they have become customary and are thus the only thing available; yet a traditional item circulating among some college girls avers that these are black robes of mourning, imposed as a species of penance on those who have not succeeded in getting married during their four years of college. An incautious folklorist/anthropologist from another culture might easily use traditional items such as these to show that in spite of a vigorous technological system, the Americans are highly superstitious, being even so naïve as to believe that statues will speak if presented with a virgin; that in spite of lip-service to equality, the Americans force unsuccessful candidates for marriage to walk, to the accompaniment of a dirge, in robes of mourning to an open field where they are lectured by senile priests who tell them they must now become the servants of their more successful colleagues. Such a statement seems ludicrous to us because we are close enough to the system itself to see the "errors" in theory as they relate to what we know the practice to be; yet a good many anthropological and folkloristic theories have been constructed which are based on the same inability to distinguish between what might be called artistic superstition (beliefs which are passed because they—or the way they are stated—may appeal somehow humorously or esthetically to the group) and religious superstition (beliefs and customs which are taken seriously and are considered to one degree or another obligatory to members of the group). While realizing that people are not always in a position to evaluate themselves clearly, one wonders what the reaction would be of loggers, American Indians, black jail-gangs, and cowboys to articles and books published which attempted to study their cultural traditions without seeing this distinction.

The view of academic folklore given in the present study has been necessarily general and superficial. Students will find, in following some of these threads further in their own research, that the careful folkloristic examination of their own culture will lead not only to valuable considerations about the operation of traditional modes in general, but to the realization that their own traditions include complexes of customary belief which are significant and absorbing in and of themselves. Perhaps most importantly, students will find that folklore is far from dead, and far from being buried by the purveyors of mass folkiness, for folklore is more than the chance survival of antique oddments: it is an informal but viable form of cultural expression which embodies those psychological, social, biological and artistic elements which lie at the heart of human expression.

NOTES

[1] See, for example, the editor's introductory remarks in Alan Dundes's *The Study of Folklore* (Englewood Cliffs, N.J.: Prentice-Hall, 1965), pp. 1–3.

[2] See Jan H. Brunvand's "Desk-Top Inscriptions from the University of Idaho," *Northwest Folklore* 1 (Winter 1966), 20–22; also Allen Walker Read's *Lexical Evidence from Folk Epigraphy in Western North America: A Glossarial Study of the Low Element in the English Vocabulary* (Paris: privately printed, 1935).

[3] In addition, the student should consult Richard M. Dorson's *American Folklore* (Chicago: University of Chicago Press, 1959), pp. 254–67, on college folklore, as well as such articles as the following: Martha Dirks's "Teenage Folklore in Kansas," *Western Folklore* 23 (1963), 89–102; Richard M. Dorson's "The Folklore of Colleges," *American Mercury* 48 (1949), 671–77; Marilyn Ruth Schlesinger's "Riddling Questions from Los Angeles High School Students," *Western Folklore* 19 (1960), 191–95; Betty Suffern's " 'Pedro' at California," *Western Folklore* 18 (1959), 326; Francis Very's "Parody and Nicknames among American Youth," *Journal of American Folklore* 75 (1962), 262–63.

[4] For a thoroughly convincing delineation of the in-group vs. outsider complex as it relates to the study of folklore, see Wm. Hugh Jansen's "The Esoteric-Exoteric Factor in Folklore," *Fabula: Journal of Folktale Studies* 2 (1959), 205–11 (reprinted in Alan Dundes's *The Study of Folklore*, pp. 43–51).

[5] For an engaging account of the methods used by some academicians to overcome such local reactions, see Alan Dundes's "Chain Letter: A Folk Geometric Progression," *Northwest Folklore* 1 (Winter 1966), 14–19.

[6] For stories about cheating on examinations see Lew Girdler, "The Legend of the Second Blue Book," *Western Folklore* 29 (1970), 111–13.

[7] Brunvand discusses such items briefly in two notes on "Sex in the Classroom," *Journal of American Folklore* 73 (1960), 250–51, and 75 (1962), 62–63.

[8] Linda Dégh and Alan Dundes both discuss functions and meanings of such stories in their contributions to *American Folk Legend: A Symposium,* ed. Wayland D. Hand (Berkeley and Los Angeles: University of California Press, 1971).

[9] See Bruce Jackson, " 'The Greatest Mathematician in the World': Nobert Wiener Stories," *Western Folklore* 31 (1972), 1–22; and James T. Bratcher, "The Professor Who

Didn't Get His Grades In: A Traveling Anecdote," *Publications of the Texas Folklore Society* 36 (1972), 121–23.

[10] Alpha Chi Omega.

[11] Delta Gamma.

[12] Inside informants on these and other esoteric customs among the campus tongs have asked to remain anonymous for obvious reasons.

[13] See Anonymous, "Scatalogical Lore on Campus," *Journal of American Folklore* 75 (1962), 260–62.

[14] William R. Bascom, discusses this and related concepts in "Four Functions of Folklore," *Journal of American Folklore* 67 (1954), 333–49; reprinted in Dundes, *The Study of Folklore*, especially pp. 287–91.

[15] As Michael J. Preston has done in "The Traditional Ringing at Temple Buell College," *Western Folklore* 32 (1973), 271–74.

[16] Even those who are familiar with the old song "Blow the Candles Out" do not associate the metaphor—used there to denote sexual intercourse—with their own practice. For a discussion of some fruits and flowers in connection with the processes of sex in traditional metaphor, see J. B. Toelken's " 'Riddles Wisely Expounded,' " *Western Folklore* 25 (1966), 1–16.

[17] Richard M. Dorson mentions a number of them in "The Eclipse of Solar Mythology," *Journal of American Folklore* 68 (1955), 393–416; reprinted in Dundes's *The Study of Folklore*, pp. 57–83.

[18] The statistical observations here following, and those implied throughout this study, are based on a number of brief, limited studies and on a list of questions given to a total of 627 students at four western United States colleges: the Universities of Oregon and Utah, Portland State, and Reed College. Since the classes in which these questions are administered were of different sizes (ranging from eleven to forty-seven), since there was some regional complexion to the answers, and since all students did not respond to all questions, the specific statistics are not consistently reliable except to indicate generally that a particular traditional item is current, or well known in detail, or in disuse. In a few instances where enough clear answers were given, the author has felt it possible to make some tentative evaluations on the quality of belief a given custom may enjoy. For high school customs, beliefs, terminology, etc., the author is indebted to numerous public school teachers in Portland, Pendleton, and Eugene, Oregon, and in Salt Lake City, Utah; he is equally obliged to a number of his own students in various college folklore classes who have offered valuable considerations on college lore. Especially helpful in the compilation of the data presented here were Penelope Diumenti, Lily Uno Havey, Saundra Keyes, Carolyn Middlemiss, Lee Newcomer, Brenda Russell, and Ralph Wirfs.

[19] To be sure, many professors make their own rules about how long a class ought to wait before abandoning the room; however, in most cases the professors themselves give the traditional formula—depending on their degree—and introduce it to their class, saying, "It is customary at this university for the class to wait. . . ." The author has conducted an ardent but thus far fruitless search for the college or university which prescribes in its written codes how long a class must wait for a tardy professor.

[20] See, for example, Herbert Passin and John W. Bennett's "Changing Agricultural Magic in Southern Illinois: A Systematic Analysis of Folk-Urban Transition," *Social Forces* 22 (1943), 98–106; reprinted in Dundes's *The Study of Folklore*, pp. 314–28.

[21] The remedy is discussed at some length by Frank M. Paulsen in "A Hair of the Dog and Some Other Hangover Cures from Popular Tradition," *Journal of American Folklore* 74 (1961), 152–68.

APPENDIX C

◊〉◊〉◊〉◊〉◊〉◊〉◊

The Types of the Southern
*Mountain Cabin**
by Henry Glassie

The study of which this paper is a part began in 1961 as a rambling field survey of the folk architecture of the upland South, stretching from eastern Pennsylvania through western Arkansas.[1] From this large area a smaller one emerged which seemed to be central to the understanding of the traditional architecture of those areas initially settled from either Pennsylvania or the tidewater South. This area (Fig. 1) is only a part of the Southern Appalachian

* This paper is a survival from an earlier day in folkloristic studies of architecture. Its basic historical assertions, that there are two Southern Mountain cabin forms, one English (the square), one Irish and west British (the rectangular); and that log construction has a Germanic provenance, have held together fairly well over the decade since the article's composition. Other things have changed. Much more information is in, both European and American, and the paper's cultural conclusions can be refined. Many people have turned and are continuing to turn to folk architectural—or "vernacular" architectural—research. The static, classificatory mode of vision presented as the "methodology" of the piece has been replaced by more dynamic and true, tougher, deeper approaches to manmade realities. And most importantly, the period of collection and annotation has passed. Studies of material manifestations of culture have caught up. Data have accumulated. It is time to talk about bigger matters, matters of structure and function, meanings and values. The reader wishing to become more up to date, bibliographically and conceptually, is referred to my own overly recondite but earnest book, *Folk Housing in Middle Virginia: A Structural Analysis of Historic Artifacts* (Knoxville: University of Tennessee Press, 1976); see pp. 43–46, 51, 75, 80–85, 88, 104–6, 117–8, 148–52, 200–3 for later thinking on the cabins; see pp. 223–27 for more recent writings on folk architecture; see Chapter 3 for field methods, Chapters 3–5 for more modern ways to the analysis of form, Chapters 6–8 for more speculative and probing interpretive possibilities.

FIGURE 1. AREA OF THE SOUTHERN MOUNTAIN FOLK ARCHITECTURAL COMPLEX.

region; it includes the Blue Ridge from northern Virginia to northern Georgia, including the Great Smokies and their foothills; the southern and central Valley of Virginia; and the eastern escarpment of the Alleghenies in Virginia and West Virginia. It does not include the Cumberlands, the south-ern tail of the Blue Ridge, and most of the Tennessee Valley, as these Appala-chian areas received less direct Pennsylvania German influence and are a part of a different architectural complex, which is comparatively southern in orien-tation. This area is not lacking in either historical or topographical continuity, but it has been established not by geography but by architecture: there are folk architectural elements which are common in the areas adjacent to the one under study but which are rare or peripheral within it; examples include the flue-curing tobacco barn,[2] square and diamond notched corner-timbering on log buildings,[3] and the dog trot house.[4] It is no accident that this is the same area which continues to yield up an amazing quantity of European-American folklore, for just as songs and tales which were probably common in other areas may now be found with regularity only in the mountains, construction techniques and building forms (including the cabins with which this paper deals) once usual but now rare in southeastern Pennsylvania and the coastal South remain common and vital in the Southern Mountains.

It is only within this area that the field survey was intense and systematic; however, those areas which contributed to the mountain culture and to which the mountain culture contributed were also sampled. All kinds of structures—not only houses, barns, and other outbuildings, but fences, bridges and haystacks as well—were entered in the field notes.

Once a ponderous bulk of field material has been accumulated the problem of what to do with it arises; to let it lie unorganized in a closet would be selfish. The usual collections of American folksong or tale include all of the items (or at least those which are intuitively folk) which were collected. The great amount of field material available to the student of folk architecture and necessary for his study to be significant normally precludes the publication of a description, drawings, and photograph of each building. The student, therefore, must order his examples into reasonable types, and, after the conclusion of his fieldwork, the establishment of these types is the first, the most important, and the most often misdirected step of his study.

The study of American material folk culture is so young (if, indeed, it is born) that a well classified study could be of value, and one of the few solid works on American folk architecture, Charles H. Dornbusch's *Pennsylvania German Barns*,[5] is simply a classification. Generally, the folklorist goes beyond this stage and, by adding bibliographical notes at the heads or feet of his collectanea, suggests the spatial and temporal patterns which include his material. It may be that the study of some aspects of folklife—Child ballads, for instance—is moving past the collection-classification-and-annotation phase, but the study of material culture in America has not, and cannot for many years.

The following treatment of the cabins observed within the area sketched above is offered in order to give some idea of how folk architecture may be classified and annotated. The characteristics which most cabins share will be considered first, and, then, the formal, historical, and distributional aspects of the cabins which separate them into two basic types—the square and the rectangular—will be outlined.[6]

These two basic house types are classified as cabins because both are com-

FIGURE 2.   CROSS-SECTIONS THROUGH SOUTHERN MOUNTAIN
CABINS.

A. Half-dovetailed, rectangular log cabin situated south of Del Rio, near Nough, Cocke County, Tennessee (May 1966). B. V-notched, square log cabin situated near Woodville, Rappahannock County, Virginia (May 1963).

posed of a single construction unit and both are less than two stories high.[7] Americans often find it difficult to say "cabin" without prefixing it with "log," [8] but, because house types can move through environmental zones with the same facility that tale types can, cabins were built of stone in Pennsylvania,[9] of brick in Virginia,[10] of log in Texas,[11] of frame in Louisiana,[12] of mud in Ireland,[13] and adobe in Utah.[14] Further, in areas where log construction was common, such as the Southern Mountains, it was employed not only on cabins, but also on bridges and turkey traps and buildings ranging from a four-by-six-foot corncrib to barns and mills measuring over fifty feet in length.[15]

In the building traditions of Scotland and Ireland houses less than two stories high had the floor joists of the loft framed in at the top of the wall or at the plate—the horizontal beam at the top of the wall on which the rafters of the roof rest. A few Southern Mountain cabins were similarly constructed (Fig. 2A), but the great majority had the floor joists of the loft framed in three to five feet—two, four or, usually, three logs in cabins of log—below the plate, affording considerably more headroom (Fig. 2B). Some one-story houses were so constructed in England, particularly in those areas in which

stone construction predominated,[16] but they were not usual in the English colonies of the New World,[17] and it seems likely that the height of the usual mountain cabin is the result of Pennsylvania German influence, for the characteristic German cabins in Pennsylvania were constructed in the same manner.[18]

The cabin loft is usually unheated, though a small fireplace has been observed in a few (Fig. 5C); it is used for the storage of trunks, medicinal herbs, dried fruits, smoked meat and odd "plunder," such as old harness and license plates; formerly the spinning was often done in the loft. Only the older children sleep in the loft; their parents sleep in a low bed in a corner of the ground floor room. The room generally contains, in addition to the bed, a table, a cupboard, a bench, perhaps a "boughten" couch (used at night as a bed, just as the bed serves as a couch during the day), and a great many chairs (usually mule-eared, slat-backs with seats woven of hickory splints or strips of inner tube) which spill out the front door onto the porch or into the bare front yard. The interior walls are whitewashed, papered (ceiling as well as walls) with newspaper, or covered with planed boards usually nailed on vertically. On the walls are hung clothes and firearms, framed oval daguerreotypes of stern and startled ancestors and bright prints (acquired, probably, as a part of a bargain package from WCKY or WWVA) of The Last Supper or Christ in the Garden.[19] In a few cabins the loft is reached via a ladder, and in a very few the floor is an earth one, such as was very common in Ireland and throughout Britain.[20] But, usually, a "boxed in" late medieval [21] stair leads to the loft. The stair, which often has the cabin's only closet under it, is built in a corner or along one wall, usually that opposite the fireplace (Fig. 3). And the floor is almost always composed of boards nailed over "sleepers"—logs hewn flat only on the top—framed in between the sills—the large squared beams placed at the bottom of the front and rear walls (Fig. 2).

FIGURE 4.   EXTERNAL CHIMNEYS IN ENGLAND, THE TIDEWATER, AND THE SOUTHERN MOUNTAINS.

A. Sussex, England; after W. Galsworthy Davie and E. Guy Dawber, *Old Cottages and Farmhouses in Kent and Sussex* (London: Batsford, 1900), plate 49. B. Gloucestershire, England; after Charles Holme, ed., *Old English Country Cottages* (London, Paris, New York: Studio, 1906), p. 85. C. Tidewater chimney situated in Port Royal, Caroline County, Virginia (July 1963). D. From a V-notched rectangular cabin situated southwest of Millboro Spring, Bath County, Virginia (July 1964). E. From a weatherboarded rectangular log cabin, situated south of Marion, Smyth County, Virginia (July 1964). F. From a vertical boarded rectangular frame cabin situated in Dunn's Rock Community, Transylvania County, North Carolina (August 1964).

A   B   C

D   E   F

Both of the mountain cabin types have an external chimney in the center of one gable end (Fig. 4). External chimneys were not unknown in Switzerland,[22] and it is conceivable that this continental tradition trickled through Pennsylvania and Maryland into the north-western Valley of Virginia; [23] the predominance of the external chimney in the Southern Mountains, however, is owed to English influence. The external chimney was primarily a Mediterranean tradition [24] and was taken at an early date, possibly with the Normans,[25] from France to England (Fig. 4A, B). Though found in many sections of England, it is most common in the West Midlands and on both sides of the Welsh border.[26] It became standard in the coastal regions of the South (Fig. 4C) during the earliest period of settlement and was carried from the Chesapeake Bay westward by settlers of English background and contributed to the predominantly German and Scotch-Irish architectural tradition in the upland areas of Maryland and Virginia. The chimneys in the Tidewater were brick; in the mountains they usually are of "rock" mortared with mud (Fig. 4E, F), although a few, particularly in eastern Tennessee, were built entirely of brick, and many were built of stone to the top of the fireplace, or to the shoulders (Fig. 4D), with the remainder of brick. The fireplace (Fig. 5) had a shallow "fire-box" to throw the heat out into the room, and, like hearths throughout the British Isles,[27] an iron pole was placed across it (Fig. 5A) or a swinging crane was placed at one side on which kettles were hung. The cabin chimney does not have a built-in bake oven, for the mountain people, like the Irish and Scots and unlike the English and central Europeans,[28] traditionally do not bake in ovens, but rather make bread in a pot, on a flat board, stone, or skillet, or in a bed of ashes beside the fire.

The basic cabin types share with the other Southern Mountain house types certain characteristics of construction. Until World War I—the great folk cultural watershed—most of the cabins were built of horizontal log, though a few of the oldest cabins extant are of frame. In the past half century most have been built of frame and only a few of log. Southern Mountain log construction (Fig. 6L-N) is characterized by logs, usually hardwood, hewn flat on the front and back, or, less commonly, split in half and then hewn on the outside.[29] Although the logs employed in the construction of outbuildings are often left in the round, less than 3 percent of the over five hundred log houses surveyed within this area were built of unhewn log.[30] Wide interstices were left between the logs, which were "daubed with mud," "chinked" with mud and stones, shingles or rails, or covered with boards. The interstices were often finished off with a layer of lime plaster. Two major methods were used to join the logs at the corner; both were used throughout the area, but one, V-notching (Fig. 6K, N) predominates in Virginia, and the other, half-dovetailing (Fig. 6G, L, M) in Tennessee and North Carolina. These two types of corner-timbering are closely related: both are notched on only the bottom of

FIGURE 5.   FIREPLACES OF SOUTHERN MOUNTAIN CABINS.

A. After Morley, *The Carolina Mountains* (Boston and New York: Houghton Mifflin 1913), facing p. 186. B. From a V-notched rectangular log cabin, situated east of Etowah, Henderson County, North Carolina (June 1963). C. From the loft of the frame square cabin pictured in Fig. 7B, situated between Crozet and Whitehall, Albemarle County, Virginia (August 1964).

the log, and in both the ends of the logs are cut off flush producing a box corner (Fig. 6E).

Log construction was unknown in England [31] and, excepting only military construction,[32] in the English colonies.[33] It was employed during the seventeenth century by the Swedes on the Delaware, and the early scholars, hindered by a sketchy picture of European traditions, guessed that American log construction had its source in the tiny settlement of New Sweden.[34] Scandinavian log construction (Fig. 6A-C) is characterized by logs, usually pine, left in the round, or hewn to a square or hexagonal shape; by the absence of interstices between the logs; by the fact that the logs are notched on the top

or both sides of the log; and by the fact that the ends of the logs extend a uniform distance beyond the corner of the building.[35] On each point, then, Scandinavian log work is markedly different from the American tradition.

Log construction in Europe is not confined to Scandinavia; it is also common in some of the several areas from which the Pennsylvania Germans came. In Switzerland and Germany dovetailed log construction with box corners (Fig. 6D), as well as construction of the Scandinavian type (Fig. 6F), is usual.[36] Similar dovetail construction was also known—but known rarely—in Scandinavia; [37] however, the Scandinavian and Swiss-German dovetailing lacked the chinked interstices so characteristic of American construction, and it is in Bohemia, western Moravia, and Silesia (what is now northwestern Czechoslovakia) that log construction of exactly the American type can be found (Fig. 6G-I).[38] Immigrants came to Pennsylvania from these areas and, though it is difficult to state why from a distance of 250 years, their construction (not that of the numerically dominant Swiss, and surely not that of the little group of Swedes who were becoming acculturated Englishmen) came to

FIGURE 6.   HORIZONTAL LOG CORNER-TIMBERING.

A. After Boëthius, *Studier i den nordiska timmerbyggnadskonsten,* Fig. 117, p. 126. B. View from above of the corner of a log building with the ends of the logs extending beyond the plane of the wall as is usual in Scandinavian tradition. C. After Erixon in *Folkliv,* 1937:1, plate II, 1, p. 18. D. After *Schweizer Volkskunde* 47:5–6 (1957), Fig. 5, p. 73. E. View from above of the corner of a log building with the ends of the log cut off flush producing a box corner, as is usual in central European and American tradition. F. From a photograph taken in the Canton of Zug, by Henry H. Glassie Sr. in the autumn of 1964. G. After *Slovenský Nárdodopis* 9 (1961), p. 522. H. After *Český Lid* 50:4 (1963), photos after p. 224. This corner-timbering is comparable to V-notching. Several outbuildings, though no houses, have been observed in the North Carolina Blue Ridge constructed with exactly this form of corner-timbering. I. After *Etnographica* 3–4 (1961–62), plate 60. J. Full-dovetail corner-timbering from a house near Pine Grove, Schuylkill County, Pennsylvania (July 1962). Full-dovetailing appears also in the northwestern Valley of Virginia. K. V-notching from a house situated near Mount Nebo, Lancaster County, Pennsylvania (July 1963). L. Half-dovetail corner-timbering from a house near Bald Creek Community, Yancey County, North Carolina (June 1963). Half-dovetailing is found commonly also in central Pennsylvania. M. Half-dovetail corner-timbering from a house situated near Zionville, Watauga County, North Carolina (July 1963). N. V-notching from a house situated between Rock Oak and Rio, Hardy County, West Virginia (June 1964).

predominate in Pennsylvania, and from Pennsylvania it was carried, beginning in 1732, into the Southern Appalachian region.

In central Europe, southeastern Ireland, and the Scottish Highlands the small houses often had hipped roofs, but in the mountains, as in medieval England, eighteenth century Scotland, and northern and western Ireland,[39] the small houses have gable roofs. The cabin's gable roof is formed with simple rafters butted at the ridge—the "comb"—either on each other or on a plank ridge pole; both of these roof framing methods were common in medieval England; the latter was usual in Scotland and Ireland, the former in Germany and throughout the American colonies.[40] Over the rafters horizontal roofing boards were nailed and to them were nailed split shingles, called "shakes" [41] in the North but just "boards" in the mountains. Such split shingles were very common in England until the end of the fourteenth century; at the time of the first settlement of America they were still being employed in southern England and the English planted areas of Ireland.[42] They remain common in central Europe,[43] and were employed until the mid-nineteenth century throughout the eastern United States [44] and nearly to the present in the Southern Mountains. The gable ends of the cabin were not built up of succeedingly smaller logs,[45] as was usual in Scandinavia, but are covered with vertical boards (Fig. 9D) as in central Europe and southeastern Pennsylvania,[46] or, more commonly, with horizontal, overlapping weatherboards (Fig. 7C, 9B) nailed to vertical studs framed in between the top log in the end wall and the end pair of rafters.

The cabins, like the other mountain house types, were often enlarged by traditional additions. These additions may be viewed either as appendages to a basic type or as creating new types.[47] Cabins very often have a shed or lean-to addition, which almost always serves as a kitchen; it is usually built onto the rear of the cabin (Figs. 7C, 9B-D), but may also be placed on one end (Fig. 7B). This form of addition is distinctly British; it is particularly common in western England [48] and was usual in the early English colonies.[49] Frequently a front porch (Fig. 9B, 9D, 10C) balances the rear shed and provides what, in the summer, amounts to an additional room. Much less usual than shed additions or porches, are ells, gabled wings added at right angles to the rear of the cabin. A rare form of addition, which has been observed only at the southern end of the North Carolina Blue Ridge, consisted of a separate cabin built immediately behind the original cabin so that their ridges were parallel. These additions should be considered appendages to a basic type, not altering the classification of the example, for houses did not become consistently built as a whole composed of a cabin in combination with any one of these features. The addition of a gabled room onto the end of the existent house was the most usual form of addition through most of Europe; in some parts of Ireland it was thought to mean death to add elsewhere.[50] Gabled end additions were often

FIGURE 7.   SOUTHERN MOUNTAIN CABINS OF THE SQUARE TYPE.
A. V-notched cabin situated south of Fletcher, near Hood, Greene County, Virginia (July 1963). By May 1966 this cabin had fallen to ruins. B. This cabin was built of balloon (light, sawed, nailed together) frame covered with vertical boards. When the shed was added to the chimney end both parts were covered with weatherboards. It is situated between Crozet and Whitehall, Albemarle County, Virginia (August 1964). C. V-notched cabin with rear shed addition situated north of Boones Mill, Roanoke County, Virginia (August 1965). The rear door was apparently cut through when the shed was added, for it swings outward rather than in. This is the largest square cabin that has been observed in the Southern Mountains.

made onto mountain cabins; the resultant two-room house types—two types depending upon whether the addition was made onto the chimney end or the end opposite the chimney—came to be constructed commonly as wholes throughout the South, so, while these types were an important part of the survey of mountain architecture, they lie outside the narrow scope of this paper.

The two basic cabin types which share the characteristics discussed thus far, now will be established:

The Square Cabin

The floorplan of the square cabin is roughly sixteen feet square, though the square proportions are more significant than any specific size. The most usual dimensions are 16' X 16' and 16' X 18'; other dimensions include 14' X 16', 15' X 15', 15' X 17', 18' X 18', 21' X 21'. It has a gable roof and an external chimney in the center of one gable end. Only very rarely is it partitioned into two rooms (Fig. 7C). The front door is located near the center of the front wall or is displaced on the front wall away from the chimney end of the house (Fig. 7A). Occasionally, there is a second door in the gable end opposite the chimney (Figs. 7A, 11B). Characteristically there is no rear door. It very often has a shed addition on the rear (Fig. 7C), and occasionally on one end (Fig. 7B); ell additions are not usual. There may be a second large external chimney built onto the addition. Front porches are not very common.

It has often been written that the sixteen-foot unit—the bay—originated during the Anglo-Saxon period as a response to the stabling requirements of oxen,[51] and it is possible that the square proportions are the result of the squaring off of the Neolithic British hut circle;[52] be that as it may, it is enough to say that the sixteen-foot bay had become traditional by the Tudor period, and that it was employed commonly in the construction of English cottages, many of which were composed of one room, roughly sixteen feet square, with a loft above (Fig. 8A).[53] The most usual one-room house throughout the English colonies consisted of the traditional single bay.[54] The small square cabin is no longer commonly found in the tidewater of the South, but a few examples have been observed up on the coastal plain (Fig. 8B) and into the Piedmont, from where it was carried into the Virginia Blue Ridge. The only difference between the Tidewater-Piedmont and the Blue Ridge examples are that the pitch of the roof on the mountain cabin is less than that, and the loft higher than that, found farther east; that the eastern examples occasionally have internal rather than external gable end chimneys (as in Fig. 8A); and that the mountain cabin is usually log with a stone chimney, whereas the Piedmont examples are usually weatherboarded frame with a

FIGURE 8.   ANTECEDENTS OF THE SQUARE CABIN.
A. Square stone English house; after Wood-Jones, *Traditional Domestic Architecture in the Banbury Region,* Fig. 51. B. Frame cabin of the type found in the coastal regions of the South; situated between Orchid and Gum Spring, Louisa County, Virginia (July 1963). This cabin was built into the end of a large frame house subsequent to its initial construction.

brick chimney (Fig. 8B). Folk architectural patterns, however, are not simple, and in the Piedmont of southern Virginia and northern North Carolina the square cabin is often of log, and several frame square cabins have been found in the mountains (Fig. 7B).

The square cabin is extremely common all along the eastern slopes of the Blue Ridge in Virginia. It is found only occasionally in the Valley of Virginia and the Blue Ridge of Tennessee. It is also found occasionally in the Cumberlands and the Tennessee Valley, and, of either log or frame, in both the piney woods and river bottoms of the Deep South.

The Rectangular Cabin

The most usual dimensions of the rectangular cabin are 16′ X 22′ and 16′ X 24′; others include 14′ X 23′, 15′ X 20′, 15′ X 24′, 16′ X 26′, 17′ X 24′, and 18′ X 23′. It has a gable roof with an external chimney in the center of one gable end. It may consist of only one room, but is frequently divided by a light partition into two rooms, the larger of which contains the fireplace and front door (Figs. 9C, 11D). Rarely there are two internal partitions producing a narrow central passage (Fig. 9D). The front door is located near the center of the front wall or is displaced on the front wall towards the chimney end of the house (Fig. 9A). There is characteristically a rear door in line with the front door. Shed additions are common; they are almost always built onto the rear (Fig. 9B-D). Ell additions and front porches are more common than they are on square cabins. There is not usually a large chimney built onto the addition.

When the Scotch-Irish arrived in America it was natural that they should build cabins of the type they had known in northern and western Ireland.[55] The cabins of Ulster, Connaught and west Munster were composed of a single construction unit, measuring in the vicinity of 12′ X 20′, 13′ X 19′, 13′ X 22′, 14′ X 24′, or 18′ X 27′. They were usually partitioned into two rooms, the larger of which contained the hearth and front door; had an internal gable end chimney; and opposed front and rear doors (Fig. 10A).[56] The traditional stone and mud construction of the Scotch-Irish [57] proved impractical in the New World forests and they quickly adopted the log construction of their German neighbors. As a result, cabins very similar to those in Ireland may be found—though far from commonly today—in southeastern Pennsylvania and north-central Maryland built either of stone (Fig. 10B) or log (Fig. 10C). Although somewhat similar cabins may be found in southern Ireland,[58] in Scotland,[59] England [60] and, particularly, Wales,[61] it seems that the Ulster-Connaught, gable-chimney cabin, with only a change to the English-Tidewater external chimney, became the rectangular cabin type of the Southern Mountains.[62] This hypothesis is buttressed by two major formal characteristics the rectangular cabin shares with the cabins of northern and western Ireland, but which are not typical of the essentially English square cabin. The first is that this cabin, while one construction unit, is, like the Irish and Scottish, often divided by a light partition into two rooms, the larger of which contains the fireplace. In the mountain cabins these partitions are almost always built of vertical boards and whitewashed. The second characteristic is the opposed front and rear doors. Such opposed doors may be found widely in western Europe,[63] but are usually part of a complex structure, such as the Welsh longhouse; [64] whereas, in Ireland, as in the mountains, they are found on one-room houses. These doors represent a survival from the period when the gable-chimney house type sheltered the farmer, his family and cattle; they facilitated the movement of stock and probably served to produce a draft for threshing and fire-building.

The rectangular cabin appears most commonly in those areas in which the Pennsylvania influence was greater than that of the Tidewater. It is found occasionally through the Valley of Virginia and the eastern Alleghenies, and is very common along the Blue Ridge of North Carolina and Tennessee and into the upland Piedmont of North Carolina.

The great majority of the cabins observed within the area of this study conformed very neatly to one of these two basic types; there are, however, a number which vary from the basic type in some significant feature. The most usual variant is of precisely the form of one of these types except that it lacks the chimney. These are very recent cabins, usually—but not always—frame, which have a stove for heating and cooking rather than the traditional chimney. The stove is served by a narrow brick flue usually built against the inside or outside of one gable wall. Another area of variation is in the doors. The square cabin typically has no rear door, though a few were observed which did have one; this rear door was not always in line with the front door (Fig. 11A), but in a few cases it was (Fig. 11B). This could be the result of influence from the Scotch-Irish rectangular cabin, although square cabins in the English-Tidewater tradition did occasionally have rear doors (Fig. 11C).[65] Similarly a very few of the observed examples of the rectangular cabin had no rear door (Fig. 11D). A few of the observed rectangular, stone cabins with internal gable end chimneys in southeastern Pennsylvania also lacked the rear door (Fig. 11E, F). In southern Ulster and adjacent Leinster,[66] the gable-chimney houses, possibly as a result of English influence,[67] often had no rear door (Fig. 11H). Further, the tradition of the opposed doors has been moribund in other parts of Ulster since before 1800 (Fig. 11G),[68] so that the American rectangular cabins lacking the rear door may represent a minor strain in the northwestern Irish gable-chimney house tradition, rather than a nontraditional, individual innovation.

FIGURE 9.   SOUTHERN MOUNTAIN CABINS OF THE RECTANGULAR TYPE.
A. Half-dovetail cabin located west of Allen Gap, Greene County, Tennessee
(August 1964). This is one of the few observed mountain cabins that has an
earth floor. Like many other early log houses, this cabin has been converted
into a tobacco barn. B. Half-dovetail cabin with front porch and rear shed addition situated in the Shelton Laurel area north of Marshall, Madison County,
North Carolina (June 1963). In the front corner at the fireplace end of the
cabin there is a trap door in the loft floor to give access via a ladder to the loft.

The proportions of the floorplans of the cabins—square or rectangular—very rarely presented a problem. The rectangular cabins were always
twenty or more feet in length and almost always over five feet longer than
wide. In the Valley and Blue Ridge of Virginia a few cabins were measured
which, while they appeared to be square cabins, were slightly more rectangular than usual. All of them were roughly sixteen feet long but were less than
sixteen feet in width; almost all of them measured 17′ X 14′ and none was

C. Weather-boarded frame cabin with late rear shed addition, situated west of Allen Gap, Greene County, Tennessee (May 1966). A cupboard is built into the partition. This cabin has Greek Revival trim of the type very common in the rural North during the second quarter of the nineteenth century (see Talbot Hamlin, *Greek Revival Architecture in America* [New York: Dover, 1964, reprint of 1944], generally pp. 258–310), but rare in the Southern Mountains. While built by a carpenter who had some awareness of the non-folk architectural mainstream of his period, this is a perfect example of the rectangular cabin type. D. V-notched cabin with front porch and rear shed addition, situated north of Fairfield, Rockbridge County, Virginia (July 1963).

more than three feet longer than wide. In England the single bay houses were generally about sixteen feet in length but were often less wide than long,[69] so that these cabins follow in the English tradition and should be regarded as variants of the square cabin, particularly because all of their other characteristics—absence of the rear door, displacement of the front door away

from the chimney end of the house—are the same as those of the square rather than the rectangular cabin.

From a study of this kind two sets of conclusions may result. The first is methodological. For analysis any example or type must be broken down into its components; houses, while they appear as wholes, are combinations of separable parts. The mountain cabins are relatively simple house types but any attempt to understand the cabin's history by considering only, as has been usual, its construction,[70] or only the shape of its floorplan would yield a faulty picture. Once the components of a type have been recognized they must be grouped into primary and secondary characteristics. For the mountain cabins the primary characteristics which define the type are: approximate height, shape and general size of floorplan, placement of doors and chimney, and form of roof. The secondary characteristics which do not help to define the type, but which are still culturally significant are: exact height, construction of walls, type of roof framing and covering, precise size of floorplan, interior partitions, placement of windows and stairs, and types of appendages.

The second set of conclusions is cultural. Both of the mountain cabin types reflect some English influence in the external chimney, and, possibly, some Pennsylvania German influence in the usual height. One is basically English in origin; the other is basically north Irish. The techniques used to construct the cabins were mainly Pennsylvania German, in log examples, and Anglo-American, in frame examples. To place these two types in a larger folk architectural context: the other Southern Mountain house types to which a European provenance can be surely assigned (some of which are more common than the cabins) are all English. The types of the Southern Mountain barns, fences, and outbuildings are mostly Pennsylvania German, or derived from

FIGURE 10.   ANTECEDENTS OF THE RECTANGULAR CABIN.

A. Stone cabin with internal gable end chimney from County Kerry, Ireland; after O Danachair in *Ulster Folklife* 2 (1965), Fig. 1, p. 25. The partition is formed by a dresser and a cupboard. B. Stone cabin with internal gable end chimney located west of Monkton, Baltimore County, Maryland (August 1965). C. V-notched log cabin with internal gable end chimney, front porch and rear shed addition, situated between Kingsville and Bel Air, Harford County, Maryland (July 1962). During the spring of 1966 this house partially burned. Some folklorists wish their informants to be sociopolitically aware; graffiti scribbed on the plastered wall of this cabin reflect the attitudes of the American countryman better than any "protest song": "Balto Co Politicians to do dam dirty work/cominist unions/UnGodly people They are a discrase to our cuntry/ all so aganst non union people/ Dont want the poor old time people to make a living/ money hogs."

German originals, with a few of English origin. Southern Mountain folk architecture is, then, predominantly Tidewater-English and Pennsylvania German; [71] yet, the majority of the mountain people are of Scotch-Irish ancestry and those Southern Mountain folk cultural elements which have received attention, most notably songs, seem to be a part of a north British, north Irish tradition. Architecture, therefore, tends to balance the picture of the mountain culture and indicate that the search for the origins of other elements of the Southern Mountain folk culture—such as pottery, tales, vehicles, food, quilt patterns, dance tunes, and firearms—should be carried on in central Europe and southern England as well as in the Lowlands of Scotland and northern and western Ireland.

FIGURE 11.   GROUND FLOOR PLANS OF VARIANT CABINS WITH
THEIR ANTECEDENTS.

A. V-notched square log cabin situated between Whitehall and Crozet, Albemarle County, Virginia (May 1966). A frame addition was built onto the end of this cabin opposite the chimney, but it has since fallen in. B. Half-dovetail square log cabin situated in the Shelton Laurel area, north of Marshall, Madison County, North Carolina (June 1963). Note that this cabin has three doors but no windows. C. Frame cabin after Forman, *Tidewater Maryland Architecture and Gardens*, p. 67. D. Half-dovetail rectangular log cabin situated between Earlysville and Free Union, Albemarle County, Virginia (August 1964). Of all observed Southern Mountain cabins this was the most difficult to classify: it lacks a rear door like the square cabin; it is more square (four feet longer than wide) than the usual rectangular cabin and more rectangular than the usual square cabin. It is situated in an area in which square cabins are very common. Probably it is a rectangular cabin that has been influenced by the square cabin. E. Stone cabin situated southeast of Honey Brook, Chester County, Pennsylvania (May 1966). F. Stone cabin situated north of West Chester, Chester County, Pennsylvania (October 1965). G. From County Londonderry, Northern Ireland; after McCourt in *Gwerin* 3:4 (1961), Fig. 1, p. 169. At the rear of the kitchen is a "bed outshot," a feature that does not seem to have been transplanted to America; for it see Caoimhin Ó Danachair's "The Bed Out-Shot in Ireland," *Folk-Liv* 19–20 (1955–56), pp. 26–29; and Desmond McCourt's "The Outshot House-Type and its Distribution in County Londonderry, *Ulster Folklife* 2 (1956), pp. 27–34. H. From County Wicklow, Ireland; after O Danachair in *Béaloideas* 5 (1935), facing p. 211.

NOTES

¹ An earlier form of this paper was read before the American Folklore Society in Denver, Colorado, November 20, 1965. I am indebted to Professors Fred Kniffen, E. Estyn Evans, and Bruce Buckley for help at various stages of the project.

² The flue-curing tobacco barn is common through the southern Virginia and North Carolina piedmont immediately east of this area; see: John Fraser Hart's and Eugene Cotton Mather's "The Character of Tobacco Barns and Their Role in the Tobacco Economy of the United States," *Annals of the Association of American Geographers,* 51 (1961), 288–93.

³ Square notched corner-timbering is common in the Valley of Virginia north of this area, through the Virginia and North Carolina piedmont, and is found also in eastern Kentucky. A few, generally late, examples have been observed within this area, particularly in the Smokies. Diamond notched corner-timbering is common east of this area in Virginia and North Carolina; only one diamond notched building has been observed within the area. For these types see: Fred Kniffen's and Henry Glassie's "Building in Wood in the Eastern United States: A Time-Place Perspective," *The Geographical Review* 56 (1966), 53–65.

⁴ This type is found in the northern North Carolina piedmont, in southeastern Kentucky, in the mountains of Alabama, the Tennessee Valley and throughout the Deep South. A vew few examples have been observed in the Blue Ridge of North Carolina and Tennessee. For this type see: Edna Scofield's "The Evolution and Development of Tennessee Houses," *Journal of the Tennessee Academy of Science* 11 (1936), 229–40; and Martin Wright's "The Antecedents of the Double-Pen House Type," *Annals of the Association of American Geographers* 48 (1958), 109–17. The conclusions of both of these papers are questionable, but both present good material on the type.

⁵ The Pennsylvania German Folklore Society 21 (1956), (Allentown, 1958).

⁶ A bibliography of material on Southern Appalachian cabins would include the following. While their quality is very uneven, all of these works contain an interesting note or two, and most include valuable photographs: Henry Howe's *Historical Collections of the Great West* (New York: George F. Tuttle, and Cincinnati, 1857), 2, 193–94, 262, 308; Frederick Law Olmsted's *A Journey in the Back Country* (New York: Mason Brothers, 1860), pp. 230–31, 237–38; James Lane Allen's "Through Cumberland Gap on Horseback," *Harper's New Monthly Magazine* 73 (June 1886), 61–62; John Fox Jr.'s *Blue-Grass and Rhododendron* (New York: Charles Scribner's Sons, 1901), pp. 10–11; Ellen Churchill Semple's "The Anglo-Saxon of the Kentucky Mountains: A Study in Anthropogeography," *The Geographical Journal* 17 (1901), 596–98; Samuel Kercheval's *A History of the Valley of Virginia* (Woodstock, 1902), pp. 151–52; John Water Wayland's *The German Element of the Shenandoah Valley of Virginia* (Charlottesville: author, 1907), pp. 190–91; Margaret W. Morley's *The Carolina Mountains* (Boston and New York: Houghton Mifflin, 1913), pp. 184–85; John Preston Arthur's *Western North Carolina A History (from 1730 to 1913)* (Raleigh, 1914), pp. 258–60; John C. Campbell's *The Southern Highlander and His Homeland* (New York: Russell Sage, 1921), pp. 73, 87–89, 143, 195–97; James Watt Raine's *The Land of Saddle-bags* (New York: Council of Women For Home Missions and Missionary Education Movement of the United States and Canada, 1924), pp. 13, 74, 208–10; Horace Kephart's *Our Southern Highlanders* (New York: Macmillan, 1926), pp. 76, 82, 110–11, 216–17, 314–17, 322–23; Robert Lindsay Mason's *The Lure of the Great Smokies* (Boston and New York: Houghton Mifflin, 1927), Chapter 9; Margaret A. Hitch's "Life in a Blue Ridge Hollow," *The Journal of Geography* 30 (1931), 312, 315; Mandel Sherman's and Thomas R. Henry's *Hollow Folk* (New York: Thomas Y. Crowell, 1933), pp. 1, 5, 49–50; J. Wesley

Hatcher's "Appalachian America," in *Culture in the South*, ed. W. T. Couch (Chapel Hill: University of North Carolina Press, 1935), pp. 382, 387; Jack Manne's "Mental Deficiency in a Closely Inbred Mountain Clan," *Mental Hygiene*, 20 (April 1936), 269–70; Allen H. Eaton's *Handicrafts of the Southern Highlands* (New York: Russell Sage, 1937), pp. 41–43, 47–54, 256–57; Laura Thornborough's *The Great Smoky Mountains* (New York: Thomas Y. Crowell, 1937; Knoxville: University of Tennessee Press, 1962), pp. 95–96; Edwin E. White's *Highland Heritage* (New York: Friendship Press, 1937), pp. 31–32; Clark B. Firestone's *Bubbling Waters* (New York: Robert McBride, 1938), pp. 8, 12, 17, 47, 84; Works Projects Administration, *North Carolina: A Guide to the Old North State* (Chapel Hill: University of North Carolina Press, 1939), p. 124; Works Projects Administration, *Tennessee: A Guide to the Volunteer State* (New York: Viking, 1939), pp. 155–56; Works Projects Administration, *West Virginia: A Guide to the Mountain State* (New York: Oxford University Press, 1941), p. 161; Charles S. Grossman's "Great Smoky Pioneers," *The Regional Reviews*, 7:1, 2 (July–August 1941), 2–6; Alberta Pierson Hannum's "The Mountain People," in *The Great Smokies and the Blue Ridge*, ed. Roderick Peattie (New York: Vanguard, 1943), pp. 140–41; Elizabeth Skaggs Bowman's *Land of High Horizons* (Kingsport, Tenn.: Southern Publishers, 1944), pp. 36–37; Muriel Earley Sheppard's *Cabins in the Laurel* (Chapel Hill: University of North Carolina Press, 1946), pp. 52–53, 67, 156–57; J. Paul Hudson's "Appalachian Folk Ways," *Antiques* 57 (May 1950), 368–69; Inez Burns's "Settlement and Early History of the Coves of Blount County, Tennessee," *East Tennessee Historical Society Publications*, 24 (1952), 54–55; North Callahan's *Smoky Mountain Country* (New York: Duell, Sloan, and Pierce, and Boston: Little, Brown, 1952), pp. 9–11; Wilma Dykeman's *The French Broad* (New York and Toronto: Rinehart, 1955), pp. 52–53; Esther Sharp Sanderson's *County Scott and its Mountain Folk* (Huntsville, Ala.: author, 1958), pp. 56–57; Marion Pearsall's *Little Smoky Ridge* University, Ala.: University of Alabama, 1959), pp. 25, 82–86; Harriet Simpson Arnow's *Seedtime on the Cumberland* (New York: Macmillan, 1960), pp. 256–76; Joseph S. Hall's *Smoky Mountain Folks and Their Lore* (Asheville, N.C.: Great Smokey Mountains Natural History Association, 1964), p. 48.

[7] There are two-story one-room houses in the Southern Mountains; these have floorplans of the same proportions as the cabins but usually have larger dimensions. They seem to be the result of the English tradition of the two-story, one-room house; for examples: Rowland C. Hunter's *Old Houses in England* (New York: John Wiley, and London: Chapman and Hall, 1930), plate 16; the references under footnote 53; Henry Chandlee Forman's *Early Manor and Plantation Houses of Maryland* (Easton, Maryland: author, 1934), p. 189; J. Frederick Kelley's "The Norton House, Guilford, Conn.," *Old-Time New England* 14 (January 1924), 122–30; and Arthur Kyle Davis's *Traditional Ballads of Virginia* (Cambridge, Mass.: Harvard University Press, 1929), facing p. 244.

[8] In 1803, a traveler in the Alleghenies, Thaddeus M. Harris, distinguished between cabins and houses on the basis of their construction; a "log cabin" has round logs, a "log house" hewn logs. Harris has been consistently followed by historians. Even if his distinction did represent a traditional usage it does not hold within the area of this study, where one-room houses of hewn log, round log, or frame are generally called "cabins"; for a much more important reason than this, however, his distinction must be abandoned: house types cannot be established or named even partially on the basis of their construction. Within the area of this study the smallest houses and outbuildings were built of hewn log, where in the Deep South even a large two-story house might be built of round logs; for an example: Wilbur Zelinsky's "The Log House in Georgia" *The Geographical Review* 43 (1953), 174–75, 177 fig. 3.

[9] Eleanor Raymond's *Early Domestic Architecture of Pennsylvania* (New York: William Helburn, 1931), plates 72–77.

[10] A one-room brick house of exactly the same proportions as the square mountain cabin of log or frame was observed in Middleburg, Loudoun County, Virginia (August, 1964).

[11] Fred R. Cotten's "Log Cabins of the Parker County Region," *West Texas Historical Association Year Book* 29 (1953), 96–104; Seymour V. Connor's "Log Cabins in Texas," *The Southwestern Historical Quarterly* 53 (1949), 105–16. Cotten's paper represents a careful, local, untheoretical study of the type needed currently in folk architectural studies.

[12] Fred Kniffen's "Louisiana House Types," in *Readings in Cultural Geography* eds. Philip L. Wagner and Marvin W. Mikesell (Chicago: University of Chicago Press, 1962; reprinted from *Annals of the Association of American Geographers* 26 [1936], 179–93), pp. 159–61, 164. This is the classic culturogeographic study of architecture.

[13] Patrick Duffy's "The Making of an Irish Mud Wall House," (with comment by Pádraig MacGréine), *Béaloideas* 4 (1933), 91–92.

[14] J. E. Spencer's "House Types of Southern Utah," *The Geographical Review* 25 (1945), 450.

[15]. Charles Morse Stotz's *The Early Architecture of Western Pennsylvania* (New York: William Helburn, 1936), pp. 269, 276–77, reports a mill built of logs measuring 54′ 9″. In the Southern Mountains and central Pennsylvania several log barns have been measured which are over seventy feet in length.

[16] M. W. Barley's *The English Farmhouse and Cottage* (London: Routledge and Kegan Paul, 1961), p. 106.

[17] Thomas Tileston Waterman's *The Dwellings of Colonial America* (Chapel Hill: University of North Carolina Press 1950), p. 245. For examples of one-story houses with the joists of the loft framed in at the plate from both the North and South, see: Addison F. Worthington's *Twelve Old Houses West of Chesapeake Bay*. The Monograph Series (Boston: Rogers and Manson, 1931); and Ernest Allen Connally's "The Cape Cod House: an Introductory Study," *Journal of the Society of Architectural Historians* 19 (1960), 47–56.

[18] Robert C. Bucher's "The Continental Log House," *Pennsylvania Folklife* 12 (Summer 1962), 14–19.

[19] The interiors of the cabins in the Southern Mountains and in Ireland seem to be very similar, particularly in such matters as furnishings, the use to which the loft is put, and the whitewashing and decorating of the walls. For a few of the many good descriptions of Irish interiors see: Dorothy Hartley's *Irish Holiday* (Dublin: Browne and Nolan 1938), pp. 238–248; Robert Lynd's *Home Life in Ireland* (London: Mills and Boon, 1909), pp. 17–19, 30, 291; Robin Flower's *The Western Island or The Great Blasket* (New York: Oxford University Press, 1945), pp. 43–47; and Eric Cross's *The Tailor and Ansty* (New York: Devon-Adair, 1964, originally published 1942), Chapter 2.

[20] For assorted references to earth floors in folk houses in Ireland and Britain see: Walter Gregor's *An Echo of the Olden Time from the North of Scotland* (Edinburgh, Glasgow: John Menzies, and Peterhead: David Scott, 1874), pp. 18, 36; Peter F. Anson's *Scots Fisherfolk* (Banffshire: Saltire, 1950), pp. 14–15; J. C. Atkinson's *Forty Years in a Moorland Parish* (London: Macmillan, 1891), p. 19; A. K. Hamilton Jenkin's *Cornish Homes and Customs* (London and Toronto: J. M. Dent, 1934), pp. 17, 36–37; Thomas Roscoe's *Wanderings and Excursions in South Wales* (London, n.d., probably c. 1855), p. 43; Edward MacLysaght's *Irish Life in the Seventeenth Century: After Cromwell* (London: Longmans Green, 1939), pp. 111, 333.

21 Nathaniel Lloyd's *A History of the English House* (London: The Architectural Press, and New York: William Helburn, 1931), p. 451. For good American examples see Don Blair's *Harmonist Construction.* Indiana Historical Society Publications, 23 (Indianapolis: Indiana Historical Society, 1964), pp. 67–70, plate VI.

22 C. Gillardon's "Das Safierhaus," *Schweizerisches Archiv für Volkskunde,* 48 (1952), pp. 201–32.

23 An early log house was observed between Broadway and Edom, Rockingham County, Virginia, which had an external chimney different in profile from the usual English-Tidewater chimney, and rather like the few published photos of the Swiss chimneys (June 1964).

24 Sigurd Erixon's "West European Connections and Culture Relations," *Folkliv* 2 (1938), 165–66.

25 Cf. C. F. Innocent's *The Development of English Building Construction* (Cambridge: Cambridge University Press, 1916), p. 269; Margaret Wood's *The English Mediaeval House* (London: Phoenix, 1965), Chapter 20.

26 Barley *op. cit.*, pp. 98, 112, 145, 156, 221; Joscelyne Finberg's *Exploring Villages* (London: Routledge and Kegan Paul, 1958), pp. 134–136. Sir Cyril Fox's "Some South Pembrokshire Cottages," *Antiquity* 16 (December 1942), 307–19.

27 Arthur R. Randell's *Sixty Years a Fenman,* ed. Enid Porter (London: Routledge and Kegan Paul, 1966), p. 65; Michael J. Murphy's *At Slieve Gullion's Foot* (Dundalk: Tempest, 1945), pp. 23–24; Kevin Danaher's *In Ireland Long Ago* (Cork: Mercier, 1964), pp. 20–21; F. Marian McNeill's *The Scots Kitchen Its Traditions and Lore With Old-Time Recipes* (London and Glasgow: Blackie, 1937), Chapter 4, particularly p. 49; Alwyn D. Rees's *Life in a Welsh Countryside* (Cardiff: University of Wales, 1950), pp. 43–44.

28 Caoimhín Ó Danachair's "Bread," *Ulster Folklife* 4 (1958), 29–32. For the English tradition see George Ewart Evans's *Ask the Fellows Who Cut the Hay* (London: Faber and Faber, 1962), Chapter 4. For the Pennsylvania German tradition: Amos Long, Jr.'s "Bakeovens in the Pennsylvania Folk-Culture," *Pennsylvania Folklife* 14 (December 1964), 16–29. Some of the traditional mountain recipes may be found in *Mountain Makin's in the Smokies* (Gatlinburg, Tenn.: Great Smoky Mountains Natural History Association, 1957).

29 The traditional log construction must not be confused with the nonfolk "rustic" log construction of which hunting lodges and park structures are built. This type of construction, based vaguely on Scandinavian rather than American traditions, may be found in Chilson D. Aldrich's *The Real Log Cabin* (New York: Macmillan, 1928); William S. Wicks's *Log Cabins and Cottages: How to Build and Furnish Them* (New York: Forest and Stream 1929); *Building With Logs,* Miscellaneous Publication No. 579 U. S. D. A. Forest Service (Washington, D.C., 1945); William E. Petty and Clayt Seagears's "Log Cabin," *The New York State Conservationist* 6 (December-January 1951–52), 20–21. Such construction is to traditional log work as a Brooklyn folknik is to a traditional ballad singer from Newfoundland.

30 The approximate number five hundred represents those houses on which the log construction could be examined. The majority of the log houses of the Southern Mountains are covered over with boards or asbestos, and their construction cannot be inspected. Only a little over 30 per cent of the log buildings surveyed within this area are houses; most are barns and other outbuildings.

31 H. L. Edlin's *Woodland Crafts in Britain* (New York: Batsford, 1949), pp. 136–37.

32 Stuart Bartlett's "Garrison Houses Along the New England Frontier," *The Monograph Series* 19, 33–48; also in *Pencil Points* 14 (June 1933), 253–68.

418   THE STUDY OF AMERICAN FOLKLORE

³³ Harold R. Shurtleff's *The Log Cabin Myth*, ed. Samuel Eliot Morison, (Cambridge, Mass.: Harvard University Press, 1939). His thesis is stated on pp. 3–8, 51–56, 186–87, 209–15.

³⁴ This idea was put forth by Henry C. Mercer in "The Origin of Log Houses in the United States," *Collection of Papers Read Before the Bucks County Historical Society* 5, 568–83; and in *Old-Time New England* 18 (1927). It was followed with reservation by Shurtleff (p. 209), but has been wholeheartedly adopted by both historians and architectural historians; it appears, for example, in these two standard and generally excellent texts: James Marston Fitch's *American Building* (Boston: Houghton Mifflin, 1948), p. 8; and Hugh Morrison's *Early American Architecture* (New York: Oxford University Press, 1952), pp. 12–13, 504–6. For a more complete treatment of log construction see Kniffen and Glassie, *op. cit.*

³⁵ For Scandinavian log construction: see Sigurd Erixon's "The North-European Technique of Corner Timbering," *Folkliv* 1937, 13–60; Gerda Boëthius's *Studier i den nordiska timmerbyggnadskonsten från vikingatiden till 1800-talet. En undersökning utående från Anders Zorns samlingar i Mora* (Stockholm: Fritzes, 1927), pp. 50–91.

³⁶ Richard Weiss's *Häuser und Landschaften der Schweiz* (Erlenbach-Zurich and Stuttgart: Eugen Rentsch, 1959), pp. 40–43, 54–57.

³⁷ Kristofer Visted and Hilmar Stigum's *Vår Gamle Bondekultur* (Oslo: J. W. Cappelens, 1951), 1, p. 54.

³⁸ There are many articles on and photographs of northwestern Czechoslovakian log construction scattered through the Czech folklife journals: *Slovenský Národopis, Český Lid, Sborník Slovenského Národného Muzea Etnografia,* and *Etnographica.*

³⁹ Innocent, *op. cit.,* p. 90; Alan Gailey's "The Peasant Houses of the South-west Highlands of Scotland: Distribution, Parallels and Evolution," *Gwerin* 3 (1962), 227–42; E. Estyn Evans's *Irish Heritage* (Dundalk: W. Tempest, 1963), pp. 58–60, 84–85. For roof types see Aymar Embury 2d's "Roofs!" *The Monograph Series,* 18:1 (1932), pp. 250–264.

⁴⁰ Innocent, *op. cit.,* pp. 13–14, 82–85; I. F. Grant's *Highland Folk Ways* (London: Routledge and Kegan Paul, 1961), pp. 144, 149; Alan Gailey's "Two Cruck Truss Houses Near Lurgan," *Ulster Folklife* 8 (1962), 57–59; Morrison *op. cit.,* p. 27.

⁴¹ Bradford Angier's "Shake Roof," *The Beaver* 293 (1963), 52–53.

⁴² Innocent, *op. cit.,* pp. 184–85; Harry Batsford and Charles Fry's *The English Cottage* (London, New York, Toronto, and Sydney: Batsford, 1950), pp. 20, 65; W. H. Crawford's "The Woodlands of the Manor of Brown Low's-Derry, North Armagh, in the Seventeenth and Eighteenth Centuries," *Ulster Folklife* 10 (1964), p. 60.

⁴³ H. Bichsel's "Das Schindeln," *Schweizer Volkskunde* 30 (1940), 1–3; Štefan Apáthy's "Sindliarstvo v okolí Bardejova," *Slovenský Národodpis* 2 (1954), 65–93.

⁴⁴ Marcus Whiffen's *The Eighteenth Century Houses of Williamsburg* (Williamsburg, Va.: Colonial Williamsburg, 1960), p. 69; J. Frederick Kelley's *The Early Domestic Architecture of Connecticut* (New York: Dover, 1963, reprint of 1924), pp. 49, 84–85, 133–34; Henry C. Mercer's *Ancient Carpenters Tools* (Doylestown, Pa.: Bucks County Historical Society, 1960), pp. 11–14 (also in *Old-Time New England* 15–19).

⁴⁵ A few minor outbuildings in the North Carolina-Tennessee Blue Ridge were constructed with purlin roofs in this manner. The Walker Sisters cabin in the Smokies, which is pictured in several of the publications listed under footnote 6, was also built with a purlin roof, but this survey uncovered no other examples.

⁴⁶ G. Edwin Brumbaugh's "Colonial Architecture of the Pennsylvania Germans," *Pennsylvania German Society Proceedings* 41 (1933), 23, plates 14, 23–26.

⁴⁷ Cf. Sidney Oldall Addy's *The Evolution of the English House* (London: Swann Sonnenschein, 1898), p. 42.

⁴⁸ Barley, *op. cit.*, pp. 115–16, 134; Raymond B. Wood-Jones's *Traditional Domestic Architecture of the Banbury Region* (Manchester: Manchester University Press, 1963), p. 218.

⁴⁹ Henry Chandlee Forman's *The Architecture of the Old South* (Cambridge, Mass.: Harvard University Press, 1948), pp. 37, 90–93, 147–49; Norman M. Isham and Albert F. Brown's *Early Connecticut Houses* (New York: Dover, 1965; reprint of 1900), p. 268.

⁵⁰ E. Estyn Evans's *Irish Folk Ways* (New York: Devin-Adair, 1957), pp. 41, 45.

⁵¹ Addy *op. cit.*, pp. XXII–XXIII, 66–69, 200; Allen W. Jackson's *The Half-Timber House* (New York: McBride, Nast 1912), pp. 4–5; Reginald Turnor's *The Smaller English House 1500–1939* (London: Batsford 1952), p. 12.

⁵² At Skara Brae, a Neolithic settlement in the Orkneys culturally related to East Anglia, have been found several houses which seem to be transitional between round and square. The one in the best state of preservation, house number seven, is internally seventeen feet square, but the outer wall, which varies from three to eight feet thick, gives it a round appearance. See V. Gordon Childe's *Ancient Dwellings at Skara Brae* (Edinburgh, 1956), and Childe's *The Dawn of European Civilization* (New York: Alfred A. Knopf, 1958), p. 333.

⁵³ Batsford and Fry, *op. cit.*, pp. 16, 36, 87; Barley, *op. cit.*, pp. 46, 48, 59, 142–43, 162–63, 250, fig. 36 Coningsby (B); Wood-Jones, *op. cit.*, Chapter 8 and pp. 197, 199; Sydney R. Jones's *English Village Homes and Country Buildings* (London: Batsford, 1947), pp. 89–90, plan A; Anthony N. B. Garvan's *Architecture and Town Planning in Colonial Connecticut* (New Haven, Conn.: Yale University Press, 1951), pp. 82, 105–6.

⁵⁴ Morrison, *op. cit.*, pp. 21, 65–67, 136; Henry Chandlee Forman's *Virginia Architecture in the Seventeenth Century* (Williamsburg, Va.: Virginia 350th Anniversary Celebration Corporation, 1957), pp. 23, 37–39; Forman's *Architecture of the Old South*, pp. 15, 36–41, 113, 121; Frances Benjamin Johnston and Thomas Tileston Waterman's *The Early Architecture of North Carolina* (Chapel Hill: University of North Carolina Press, 1947), p. 26.

⁵⁵ Some early historians—Charles A. Hanna's *The Scotch-Irish* (New York, 1902), 1, 163, for example—maintained that the Scotch-Irish culture was purely Scottish, and that the period the Lowland Scots spent in Ulster did not affect them; in this regard it is interesting to note that the Scotch-Irish cabin is Irish, not Scottish.

⁵⁶ For the gable-chimney Irish house see: Åke Campbell's "Irish Fields and Houses: A Study of Rural Culture," *Béaloideas* 5 (1935), 57–74; Campbell's Notes on the Irish House," *Folkliv* 1937:2–3, pp. 205–34; Canoimhín Ó Danachair's "Three House Types," *Ulster Folklife* 2 (1956), 22–26; Ó Danachair's "The Combined Byre-and-Dwelling in Ireland," *Folk Life* 2 (1964), 58–75; E. Estyn Evans's "The Ulster Farmhouse," *Ulster Folklife* 1 (1955), 27–31; Evans's "Donegal Survivals," *Antiquity* 13 (June 1939), 209–20; Evans's *Irish Heritage*, Chapter 7; Evans's *Irish Folk Ways*, Chapter 4; and the references under footnotes 66 and 68.

⁵⁷ Caoimhín Ón Danachair's "Materials and Methods in Irish Traditional Building," *The Journal of the Royal Society of Antiquaries of Ireland* 87 (1957), 61–74.

⁵⁸ Kevin Danaher's "Old House Types in Oighreact Ui Chonchubhair," *The Journal of the Royal Society of Antiquaries of Ireland* 68 (1938), 227–29, plate XXVIII, 1.

⁵⁹ Colin Sinclair's *The Thatched Houses of the Old Highlands* (Edinburgh: Olive and Boyd, 1953), "Dailriadic Type." John Dunbar's "Some Cruck-Framed Buildings in the Aberfeldy District of Perthshire," *Proceedings of the Society of Antiquaries of Scotland* 90 (1956–57), p. 82; Grant, *op. cit.*, Chapter 7.

⁶⁰ Basil Oliver's *The Cottages of England* (New York: Charles Scribner's Sons, and London: Batsford, 1929), pp. 23–24; Addy, *op. cit.*, pp. 38–41.

⁶¹ Iorwerth C. Peate's *The Welsh House* (Liverpool: Hugh Evans, 1946), pp. 88–111,

plate 36; Sir Cyril Fox's and Lord Raglan's *Monmouthshire Houses* (Cardiff: National Museum of Wales, 1953) 2, 43₇; Fox's and Raglan's *Monmouthshire Houses* (Cardiff: National Museum of Wales, 1954) 3, 38, 40; Fox, *op. cit.*, pp. 307–14.

[62] Cf. E. Estyn Evans's "Cultural Relics of the Ulster Scots in the Old West of North America," *Ulster Folklife* 11 (1965), 34.

[63] Peate's *The Welsh House*, p. 144.

[64] For the Welsh long-house, see the following articles in I. Ll. Foster and L. Alcock, eds., *Culture and Environment Essays in Honour of Sir Cyril Fox* (London: Routledge and Kegan Paul, 1963); J. T. Smith's "The Long-House in Monmouthshire, A Reappraisal," pp. 389–414; P. Smith's "The Long-House and the Laithe-House: A Study of the House-and-Byre Homestead in Wales and the West Riding," pp. 415–37; and Iorwerth C. Peate's "The Welsh Long-House: A Brief Re-appraisal," pp. 439–44.

[65] For examples: Henry Chandlee Forman's *Tidewater Maryland Architecture and Gardens* (New York: Bonanza, 1956), p. 67; Henry Lionel Williams and Ottalie K. Williams's *Old American Houses 1700–1850* (New York, 1957), p. 71.

[66] Caoimhghín Ó Danachair's "Old Houses at Rathnew, Co. Wicklow," *Béaloideas* 5 (1935), 211–12.

[67] Cf. Evans's "The Ulster Farmhouse," p. 29.

[68] George Thompson, Desmond McCourt, and Alan Gailey's "The First Ulster Folk Museum Outdoor Exhibit: The Magilligan Cottier House," *Ulster Folklife* 10 (1964), 29; Desmond McCourt's "Cruck Trusses in North-West Ireland," *Gwerin* 3 (1961), 168–73.

[69] See Addy, *op. cit.*, pp. 32–34; G. E. Fussell's *The English Rural Labourer* (London: The Batchworth Press, 1949), pp. 10–12; and the references under footnote 53.

[70] Mercer's "The Origin of Log Houses," (see footnote 34) guessed that because log construction was Swedish the whole cabin must be Swedish, and he had been generally followed. A somewhat more modern view, which still fails to completely separate construction and form, holds that the Southern Appalachian cabin is a Pennsylvania German log house which has undergone some change through Tidewater influence; see Henry Glassie's "The Appalachian Log Cabin," *Mountain Life and Work* 39 (Winter 1963), 5–14; and Fred Kniffen's "Folk Housing: Key to Diffusion," *Annals of the Association of American Geographers*, 55 (December 1965), 561.

[71] Unfortunately the only works on mountain architecture to which the reader can be referred are my own: "The Smaller Outbuildings of the Southern Mountains," *Mountain Life and Work* 40 (Spring 1964), 21–25; "The Old Barns of Appalachia," *Mountain Life and Work*, 40 (Summer 1965, 21–30; "The Pennsylvania Barn in the South," *Pennsylvania Folklife*, 15 (Winter 1965–66), 8–19; 15 (Summer 1966), 12–25; "Southern Mountain Houses: A Study in American Folk Culture," Master's Thesis, American Folk Culture Program, Cooperstown, State University of New York College at Oneonta (1965).

APPENDIX D

◦)◦)◦)◦)◦)◦)◦)◦)◦

Structure and Meaning in the Folk Blues
by David Evans

Since the beginning of the twentieth century over fifty thousand performances of blues have been recorded or collected on paper. The bulk of this vast documentary enterprise has been carried out by commercial phonograph companies, beginning in 1920. Even before this, in 1912, blues had begun appearing in sheet-music form. In origin, however, blues were a noncommercial form of folksong performed by southern blacks. This folk blues tradition has continued to the present time, carried on by mostly obscure performers little known outside their own communities, while the rest of the world has come to know the blues mainly through its more commercialized forms popularized by phonograph records and other mass media.[1]

Such a broad variety of settings is indicative of the extraordinary importance blues have had for black Americans. These songs have commented on almost every major aspect of daily life for blacks as well as a great number of personal and topical subjects of special interest to individual singers. For many years blues were one of the few forms of artistic expression available and open to large numbers of blacks. As a result, many of the finest musical and lyrical creations of black culture in America have been expressed through the medium of the blues.

There have been many thousands of blues singers in all sorts of community settings from southern plantations and small farm areas to towns and urban ghettos. Some of the more popular commercial performers have made a good living as professional musicians, but the great majority of blues singers have been semiprofessional at best, having to supplement what little money they might make from music with income from other, steadier forms of work.

Despite the humble status of most black blues singers, the form of music they created has exerted enormous musical influence both among blacks themselves and in a much wider community. By the end of World War I, blues had become the predominant form of black secular folk and popular music. Even earlier than this they had begun to enter the southern white folk music tradition. By the 1920s they had become an important part of commercial "hillbilly" music, and they have continued to influence various forms of "country and western" music.[2] Also by the 1920's, blues had entered the mainstream of American popular music. Many white vaudeville singers performed blues, and instrumental blues formed a large part of the repertoire of dance orchestras. Blues were fundamental to the development of jazz and swing music during the 1920s and 1930s, and still, today, whenever jazz musicians want to return to their musical roots, they generally turn to the blues. In the 1950s blues again affected American popular music through the medium of rock 'n' roll. For the first time large numbers of American whites began listening to authentic black blues singers. White rock 'n' roll singers, like Elvis Presley, also featured blues in many of their performances. British and American rock groups, like the Rolling Stones and the Grateful Dead, gave young people yet another strong taste of the blues in the 1960s, and popular singers and composers continue to use the blues form for a large number of their songs. Blues are now known internationally and can be heard as part of the popular music of many countries. Thus, although blues began and have continued as a form of regional black American folklore, they have also gained worldwide recognition and helped to change the course of popular music both in America and abroad.

With so many recorded examples and such a long history, blues naturally exhibit a great variety of characteristics, making it difficult to arrive at a concise definition. Nevertheless, there are certain traits that recur in the majority of blues, so that the form is capable of being described and one can recognize a blues and distinguish it from other song forms. The following traits are the most characteristic and distinctive ones for the blues, especially the folk blues.

Blues singers themselves generally describe the blues as a worried feeling, a description that differs little from the long-time standard English usage of the word. Indeed, blues songs deal with a wide range of life's problems as they are experienced by generally lower class blacks. But blues, despite their name, can also treat life's joys and successes. Basically, blues celebrate life itself with all its ups and downs, treating their subjects dramatically and often with striking imagery. Their style is lyric rather than narrative, stressing the subject's emotional dimension from a first-person point of view. They are usually sung in a highly emotional and animated manner, as if the singer were describing his personal feelings and experiences. Most singers, in fact, claim to have experienced or at least witnessed the things that they sing about. But their subjects are also typical, even universal, experiences, well known to their audiences. Thus not only can blues function as self-expression, catharsis, and therapy for the singer, but they also fulfill the same needs for the audience. In fact, if they fail to fulfill these wider needs, the singer will find himself without an audience.

All of the subjects that blues singers deal with are potential problem areas of life. For the most part blues singers are content to describe the dimensions of their subjects, taking the situation as given and not likely to be altered significantly in the long run. No real solutions to major problems are proposed in the blues. At the same time, however, small temporary successes and failures are constantly noted, often in a highly exaggerated manner. Self-pity and grandiose fantasy, abuse and praise alternate throughout blues lyricism. The man/woman relationship is by far the most important subject in the blues, probably because this area of life is most susceptible to daily fluctuation. Blues are also frequently sung in a social context of dancing and partying where relationships between the sexes are being formed, broken, strengthened, or strained. A closely related theme is travel and wanderlust. Blues singers often express an intention to "leave town" or "catch the first thing smoking," presenting themselves as victims of mistreatment or unfaithfulness by a lover. Sometimes the singers claim to be returning to a faithful lover back home or a former lover, an "old-time used-to-be." Sometimes travel or hoboing is undertaken simply for its own sake, the consequence of the singer having "a rambling mind." The more active blues singers, in fact, frequently are ramblers, going from town to town in search of musical jobs and better times. Additional themes in the blues are farming and its problems, industrial work, poverty, alcohol and drugs, sickness and death, gambling, voodoo and magic, crime and prison, the color hierarchy within the black community, natural disasters, racism, and topical events that affect the singer and his community. Often the man/woman and travel themes are worked into other themes.

The majority of blues utilize a twelve-measure stanza structure like that printed below in Example 5. The verses usually have an *AAB* pattern, the first line being repeated once while the final line adds to or comments upon the first two. Usually the lines rhyme or display assonance. Each line of text lasts approximately two and one-half measures and is followed by an instrumental response lasting about a measure and a half. The most common accompanying instruments in the folk blues are the guitar, piano, or harmonica, usually played by the singer himself, to which may be added one or more instruments played by others. Female singers accompany themselves less often. The accompaniment usually creates or suggests a standardized harmonic pattern. This consists of a chord based on the tonic note for the first four measures (line 1). Although the vocal melody of line 2 is usually the same as that of line 1, the harmony of the accompaniment switches to a chord based on the subdominant for measures 5 and 6, returning to the tonic for measures 7 and 8. For the third line the accompaniment moves to the chord based on the dominant for measure 9, changes to the subdominant for measure 10, and returns to the tonic for measures 11 and 12. Many folk blues, however, depart somewhat from this standardized pattern, often by adding or subtracting a few beats from the twelve measures or altering the harmonic pattern of the accompaniment. Examples 1, 4, 5, 7, and 8 below all contain slight modifications of this sort in some of their stanzas. Other blues utilize two-line, four-line, and other patterns. Eli Owens's "Ways Like the Devil" (Example 6), for instance, is made up of four-line stanzas formed by repeating the final line of the standardized *AAB* pattern. Charlie Taylor's "Annie Lee" (Example 2) also has a final four-line stanza, while Bessie Mae Charleston's "Water Boy" (Example 3) with its long moaning lines could be considered almost free form. Improvisational variation, in fact, both in the vocal melody and the instrumental accompaniment, could be considered a regular feature of the blues. In some cases singers actually employ alternate strains in some of their stanzas or a quite different accompaniment part, particularly when playing instrumental choruses or (borrowing the jazz term) "breaks."

Several stylistic features of blues performance serve to create a type of musical tension that matches the lyric tension or ambivalent mood so characteristic of blues texts with their celebrations of life's vicissitudes. For one thing, the instrumental phrase at the end of each line serves as a "response" to the "call" of the vocal. Often the instrument also punctuates the vocal lines with notes or phrases that answer other notes or phrases in the singing. In creating this pattern of call and response, the performer frequently develops a rhythmic tension between the voice and accompaniment or between two or more musical lines in the accompaniment. This tension often takes the form of duple and triple rhythms performed simultaneously. A further melodic tension is found in the use of neutral tones or "blue notes." The most common of these occur at the third and seventh degrees of the scale and are pitched approximately midway between the major and minor of those degrees. In staff notation blue notes are often indicated by arrows (↑ and ↓) printed above the note on a staff or above a sharp or flat in the key signature to indicate that the note is slightly raised or lowered. From the point of view of the blues singer, of course, blue notes are not tension-producing per se but are rather a normal part of the blues scale. They do, however, create a sense of melodic tension when they are sounded against the notes of an instrument played in a Western scale (which lacks blue notes). And if the performer wants to produce blue notes on an instrument of Western origin, such as a guitar, piano, or harmonica, he must use special playing techniques like "choking" or "worrying" the guitar strings or "bending" notes on the harmonica.

As noted earlier, the blues developed around the beginning of the twentieth century as a form of folksong among mostly rural lower-class blacks, but it soon became popularized and commercialized, especially in the cities. Popular blues, as exemplified by the majority of blues issued on commercial phonograph records, usually contain original lyrics composed by the performer or a professional songwriter, unless the piece is a recreation of some earlier commercially recorded blues. They also tend to adhere quite closely to the *AAB* or some other standardized stanzaic pattern. Their lyrics are usually thematic in the sense that from listening to the text it is possible for one to reconstruct a coherent story or visualize a scene clearly. Each blues, then, treats one particular aspect of one of the typical blues themes.[3] The earliest folk blues, on the other hand, relied mainly on traditional verses that the singers would recombine in a number of different ways in the processes of learning and composing their songs.[4] The traditional verses and stanzas served as formulaic building blocks that could be recombined in a limitless number of ways to construct new texts. These traditional elements are still used by many folk blues singers in composing and performing their songs. The texts of these blues are often nonthematic in the sense that a single theme is not maintained throughout and the listener cannot reconstruct a coherent story or visualize a single scene clearly. On the other hand, as the commercial recording of popular blues has increased over the years, many folk blues singers have been influenced by blues that they hear on records and have begun to compose blues of their own in the manner of the more commercialized pieces. Thus some folk blues today continue to be nonthematic textually, while others are thematic. The following examples illustrate the variety of approaches to composition that can be found in folk blues.

"Monday Morning Blues" is a good example of the more modern type of folk blues modeled on the thematic approach of popular blues. Its singer and composer, Ira Coney, was born in 1933 and has been more influenced in his style and repertoire by phonograph records than have the other artists represented here, all of whom were born around the beginning of the century and compose blues in older styles. Indeed, his "Monday Morning Blues" borrows much of its melody and text from a commercial recording made in 1946 by Lowell Fulson, "Trouble Blues" (Big Town 1074). The scene that Coney's text describes is easy to visualize, as it is presented in the form of a dialogue between the singer and his woman. In fact, the text comes close to being a narrative in its logical sequencing of stanzas, but it lacks the sequence of scenes or episodes that characterizes a narrative text in the strict sense. The continuity between stanzas is aided by Coney's spoken remarks (in italics), and even his guitar helps in presenting the song's message, as Coney makes the strings "moan" by bending them and playing many blue notes. Although most of the verses are traditional and used by other blues singers in different combinations, the song as a whole is obviously a very deliberate and carefully worked-out composition. Coney even has a story about how he came to compose this piece: "We have a lot of rough weekends, you know. I be feeling bad some Monday mornings, have to get up and go to work. So I thought that over, and so I put one together on that. It goes something like this right here."

Example 1. "Monday Morning Blues." Ira "Tiny" Coney, vocal and guitar.[5]

1. Now now, when I wake up some Monday mornings, blues and
       trouble around my bed.
   Now, when I wake up some Monday mornings, blues and trouble
       around my bed.
   You know, I never will forget the words I heard my baby said.
   What'd she say?

2. She say, "I'm gonna leave you in the morning, and your crying
       won't make me stay."
   Yes, I'm gonna leave you in the morning, and your crying won't
       make me stay."
   "Only thing I can say, little girl, that I'll meet you again some
       day."
   *When I told her that, it hurt her. She had to moan one time. She
       said. . .*

[Guitar chorus—guitar moans.]

All right!

3. *When I told her,*
   I said, "If you is got to go, I hope to meet you again some day.
   Oh, if you is got to go, I hope to meet you again some day.
   Oh, when I do, little girl, you'll be changed of your evil way."

Charlie Taylor's "Annie Lee" shows yet another form of influence from popular blues. In fact, it is loosely based on a record of the same title (Aristocrat 2301) made by Robert Nighthawk (Robert Lee McCollum) in 1949. Taylor sticks more or less to Nighthawk's melody, while his brother attempts to imitate the record's guitar part, but the singer makes the song his own by departing considerably from the text of the record. This is done by composing original lines in a stream-of-consciousness manner, sacrificing the ending rhymes in order that the song's composition may be simultaneous with its performance. This is a compositional technique that Taylor and many other folk blues singers favor, though it is rarely recorded commercially, since such pieces often betray the looseness of hasty improvisation and are so highly personal as to be obscure in their meaning. Taylor's piece, however, is a well-structured folk blues, and by basing it on a popular record he can be certain of gaining the audience's interest. The text is thematic, clearly presenting a scene of the singer begging Annie Lee to return to him, though at the same time he appears to be having second thoughts about the relationship. The scene is not developed, however, by having the stanzas follow each other in a logical sequence. In fact, from a purely logical standpoint the song would make better sense if the stanzas were sung in reverse order. As the text stands, Taylor says in his opening stanza that he is going to quit calling Annie Lee, but then he goes on to sing about her for another five stanzas. In the song's final line he states that he is going to talk about Annie Lee and then ends his singing abruptly, letting the guitars finish out the line. But by using this reverse logic Taylor is able to increase the song's dramatic power enormously, letting the singer's plight gradually unfold to its full dimensions, rather than stating the problem's outlines at the beginning and then filling in the details. Taylor opens the song with statements about how he loves Annie Lee and is constantly calling her (Stanzas 1–2). Then he appears to be addressing her directly, begging her to return (Stanza 3). Next we learn that the singer has been "running around," probably the cause of Annie Lee's leaving him (Stanza 4). Finally we are told that she is not nearby but that the singer must call her on the telephone and that she is so far away that they are not likely ever to get back together again (Stanzas 5–6). By gradually building up to this dramatic climax, Taylor is able to increase the sense of tension in his song. He does this even further by shifting between addressing the song to Annie Lee and to his predominantly male audience ("boys"). This alternation must be viewed as symbolic of the tension between the singer's devotion to Annie Lee (begging her and calling her name) and the audience's ideal of unconcerned masculine behavior (letting her go). This basic tension is not resolved in the song, as is true of most folk blues, but the performance itself helps to define the dimensions of a typical problem and make such problems more bearable by providing a catharsis for both the singer and his audience. This process is all the more remarkable when one considers the fact that the text was composed spontaneously and that its structure was developed unconsciously.

Example 2. "Annie Lee." Charlie Taylor, vocal and guitar; Willis Taylor, guitar.[6]

1. Annie Lee, Annie Lee, darling, I swear I keep on calling Miss
   Annie Lee.

> I said, I'm calling Miss Annie Lee, darling; I swear I call Miss
> Annie the whole night long.
> I'm gonna quit calling Miss Annie Lee, now darling; I think I'll let
> Miss Annie Lee even go.

2. I love Miss Annie Lee, darling; I loves her all the time.
   I said, I love Miss Annie Lee, boys now; I swear I love Miss Annie
   Lee, boys, all the time.
   I'm gonna stop talking about Miss Annie Lee now; I ain't gon' say
   no more.

3. I'm begging Miss Annie Lee. Annie Lee, please ma'am, come
   back home.
   I said, I'm begging Miss Annie Lee now, darling. Annie Lee,
   please ma'am, come back home.
   I want you to come back now, darling; baby, please don't leave no
   more.

4. I love Miss Annie Lee, darling; she keep me crying, boys, all night
   long.
   I said, I love Miss Annie Lee, boys now; I swear she keeps me
   crying all night long.
   I'm gonna quit my way of running around, boys now; won't have
   to cry no more.

5. I'm gonna call Miss Annie Lee. I'm gonna call up over the
   telephone.
   I'm gonna call Miss Annie Lee, boys. Believe I'll call up over the
   telephone.
   I'm gonna call up to Atlanta, boys now. Lord, let Miss Annie Lee
   even go.

6. Looka here, Miss Annie Lee, what are you trying to do?
   Go on and leave me, Miss Annie Lee. Say, you ain't gonna leave
   me no more.
   I says, I love Miss Annie Lee, boys, love Annie Lee the whole
   night long.
   I'm gonna talk about my loving Annie Lee now. Yeah . . .

The two blues that we have examined so far are both thematic. Both suggest a clear and consistent scene in the minds of listeners. They also display the original creative powers of their composers, "Monday Morning Blues" through its tightly constructed combination of sung text, spoken comments, and guitar figures, and "Annie Lee" through its spontaneous dramatic development of a scene from life. Many other folk blues contrast with these by utilizing almost exclusively traditional textual elements, combining them in such a manner that nonthematic texts are produced. As we have observed, most of the earliest folk blues were traditional and nonthematic, and today this approach is mainly used by older performers, having been largely supplanted by original thematic composition among younger singers under the influence of more than fifty years of commercially recorded blues.

A number of prominent writers on blues have criticized the reliance on traditional verse material by folk blues singers. Samuel Charters, for instance, has labeled these traditional elements "undistinguished," "overly familiar," "conventional," and "derivative." [7] Paul Oliver has stated of them that "for the minor singer with small creative talent they are an indispensable substitute for original thought; for the more inventive bluesman they are sometimes too easy a solution for the verse problems posed by his own song." [8] Such assertions, however, often fail to take into account the fact that artfully constructed blues can be created from traditional elements combined in an original manner. Often the traditional verses contain remarkable poetic imagery, and many blues singers must be applauded for their excellent taste in selecting these verses and keeping them alive in tradition. [9] Originality of composition cannot in itself be said to have greater merit than borrowing from tradition. Instead each piece must be judged objectively on its own merits. The examples which follow all rely heavily, almost exclusively, on traditional textual elements, yet they display some remarkable poetic qualities.

Some traditional blues, although textually nonthematic, do present a general consistency of mood or setting while their specific subject shifts in successive stanzas. Bessie Mae Charleston's "Water Boy" is an example of such a blues. [10] It is the lament of a prisoner on a chain gang, drawing heavily on the tradition of verses developed by countless singers in southern jails, prison farms, and levee camps. [11] The moaning and long, gradually descending lines of the melody serve to link this blues with the unaccompanied hollers sung by black workers in these and other settings, a style which can be traced back to the slavery period. [12] Charleston, in fact, normally sings this piece unaccompanied, though on this recording a friend strummed simple guitar chords behind her singing. After setting the scene of the chain gang in Stanza 1, she goes on in the rest of the song to depict three different incidents in the typical daily life of a prisoner. Each incident involves water in some form (rain, ice, drinking water). Normally one might think of water as something soothing in the context of a chain gang, but in each of the last three stanzas a mood of dissatisfaction is actually expressed, culminating in the singer's grumbling against the water boy, who has a lighter task than the other prisoners. The im-

Bessie Mae Charleston and Matt Willis PHOTO BY CHERYL EVANS

agery of Stanza 3 is especially striking. This song, then, displays a well-developed structure, even though it is not thematic in the manner of the first two examples.

Example 3. "Water Boy." Bessie Mae Charleston, vocal; Mott Willis, guitar.[13]

1. Mmmm, captain, captain, mmmmmmmmmmm.
   If I had a' listened what my mother said,
   I wouldn't a' been wrestling with the ball and chain.
   Mmmmmmmmm, mmmmmmmmm, mmmmmmmmm,
     mmmmmmmmm.

2. Captain, captain, it's started raining.
   I asked for shelter.
   "Pick up your pick and shovel, just keep on working."
   Mmmmmmmmm, mmmmmmmmm.

3. Aaaaaaaaah, ooooh.
   I asked for a pillow. He gave me a block of ice.
   Mmmmmmmmm, mmmmmmmmm, mmmmmmmmm,
     mmmmmmmmm.

4. Water boy, water boy, pass your water 'round.
   If you ain't got no water, set your bucket down.
   Mmmmmmmmm, mmmmmmmmm.

Many other nonthematic folk blues lack even the degree of textual consistency found in "Water Boy." Often such blues jump from one subject to another and even make contrary statements in successive stanzas. These characteristics have led many writers to label such blues 'incoherent" and the products of poor compositional skills on the part of their singers. As early as 1911 the folklorist Howard W. Odum noticed this tendency in many blues, attributing it to the mingling of stanzas that originally belonged to two or more separate songs, each of which was presumably a more coherent composition.[14] Odum failed to realize that the singers were actually drawing from a mental reservoir of traditional lyrics that they could use in building any number of songs, and that most of these traditional lines and stanzas did not belong to any particular song in the singers' repertoires. A few years later another folklorist, Dorothy Scarborough, sought a racial explanation for this practice, stating: "The colored mind is not essentially logical, and the folk-song [*i.e.*, blues] shows considerable lack of coherence in thought. Unrelated ideas are likely to be brought together, as stanzas from one song or from several may be put in with what the singer starts with, if they chance to have approximately the same number of syllables to the line." [15] Although some writers have attempted to defend this textual inconsistency,[16] the overwhelming opinion in print has been negative. Charters has called one example "confused." [17] John Fahey has noted "disconnection, incoherence, and apparent 'irrationality' of the stanzas" as an outstanding characteristic of the blues of singer Charley Patton.[18] Stephen Calt states that another singer is "struggling with two separate stories " and characterizes folk blues in general as "jumping capriciously from subject to subject." [19] Even some blues singers themselves have criticized the lack of apparent continuity in many folk blues, such as Brownie McGhee, who states: "I always believed in telling a story without getting lost on three or four different subjects." [20]

While many of the blues to which these writers refer are indeed superficially inconsistent, a closer examination reveals that they are hardly products of illogical or confused minds but rather that they often reveal a tight underlying poetic structure. Let us look at "It Won't Be Long," a blues by Charley Patton that Fahey has called an example of "extreme incoherence" and "non-sensical." [21] Patton was one of the greatest and most influential of the early Mississippi folk blues singers. Born sometime in the 1880s, he is one of the few representatives of the first generation of blues singers to make commercial recordings. He recorded this piece at his first session in 1929, taking the tune and most of the lyrics from the common repertoire of traditional elements.[22] Mengelwood, in Stanza 2, was a logging camp a few miles outside of Memphis.

Example 4. "It Won't Be Long." Charley Patton, vocal and guitar.[23]

1. I believe sweet mama gonna do like she said, baby.
   I believe sweet mama gonna do like she said, baby.
   She gon' cook my supper, Lord, put me in her bed.

2. You ever go to Memphis, stop by Mengelwood, baby.
   You ever go to Memphis, stop by Mengelwood, baby.
   You Memphis women don't mean no man no good.

3. She's got a man on her man, got a kid on her kid, baby.
   She's got a man on her man, got a kid on her kid, baby.
   Done got so bold, Lord, won't keep it hid.

4. Ah, rider, ain't gonna be here long, baby.
   Well, ah, rider, ain't gonna be here long, baby.
   Well, ah, rider, daddy ain't gonna be here long.

5. I believe sweet mama sure was kind to me, baby.
   I believe sweet mama sure was kind to me, baby.
   She's up at night like a police on his beat.

6. I'll tell you something; keep it to yourself, baby.
   I'm gonna tell you something; keep it to yourself, baby.
   Please don't tell your husband, Lord, and no one else.

7. She is a long tall woman, tall as a cherry tree, baby.
   Got a long tall woman, tall as a cherry tree, baby.
   She gets up 'fore day and she puts that thing on me.

Although the song is ostensibly addressed to the singer's baby," it would be a mistake to view this as a unifying element in the text. This is simply a literary convention of the blues and has no more semantic significance than the interjection "Lord" in the last line of several stanzas. The key element to an understanding of this text is the second stanza with its implied contrast between the women of Memphis and Mengelwood. Although the precise basis for the contrast is not made clear in this stanza, the remainder of the stanzas, in fact, can be grouped into two sections depicting contrasting relationships with women. Stanzas 1, 3, and 4 form the first section, while Stanzas 5, 6, and 7 form the other. Stanzas 1 and 5 both describe women who treat the singer right, but in 1 the singer is obviously visiting the woman at her home, while in 5 the woman is walking out at night, evidently to visit the singer. Stanzas 3 and 6 continue the contrast. Stanza 3 describes a woman who openly consorts with two husbands and two boy friends ("a man on her man, a kid on her kid"), while Stanza 6 is the singer's plea to his woman not to tell her husband or anyone else about their relationship. The final contrast consists of the singer's bidding farewell to a woman in Stanza 4 and a woman discreetly ("fore day") coming to visit the singer in Stanza 7. Patton does not make clear which woman he prefers, for both apparently treat him well (Stanzas 1 and 5). Stanza 2 does not make clear which woman is from Memphis and which is from Mengelwood. This ambiguity is probably deliberate, for the function of Stanza 2 is not to identify the "actors" but to set the framework of contrast into which the other stanzas can fit. The basic message of this blues that the singer presents to his audience is a dilemma. One type of woman entertains many men openly and is visited for brief periods by the singer. Another type of woman sneaks away from her husband at night to visit the singer secretly (presumably returning to her husband before he awakes). Both types of woman are capable of satisfying the singer, yet there is a note of uneasiness expressed in Stanza 2 that some women "don't mean no man no good." In fact, it is quite obvious to anyone that both types of relationship that Patton describes can lead to trouble. Ambivalence and contrast, then, are at the heart of this blues, and its text is well structured to express this fact.

It is impossible to know whether Charley Patton consciously conceived of the contrastive structure of the text of "It Won't Be Long." This type of structure is quite common in folk blues that make use of traditional textual elements, but the singers are rarely articulate about their processes of composition except usually to say that their songs just "come to them" or are "in the air." [24] The chances are, however, that contrastive structural patterns are an unconscious product of the singer's imagination. Many of the blues that employ traditional elements are composed at the time of performance with the singer spontaneously calling forth verses and stanzas from his mental storehouse and setting them to his chosen melody and instrumental accompaniment. A blues of this sort is never repeated the same way again, although all of its separate elements are used by the singer in other performances. Since such performances are unique and not planned in advance, whatever structure they display must be considered unconscious.

Roosevelt Holts's "I'll Catch the Train and Ride" is a good example of a spontaneously composed blues constructed from traditional elements. This was the first piece I recorded from Holts in a four-day series of sessions with him. All of its textual and musical elements were used by him in various other blues during this period except for the first stanza, though he also used this stanza in blues recorded on other occasions. Like the previous example, it displays a contrastive structure. Stanza one is an expression of regret by the

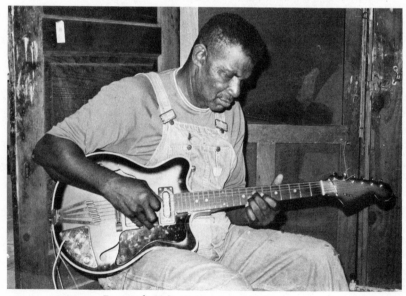

Roosevelt Holts PHOTO BY CHERYL EVANS

singer for his lifestyle, while the next stanza is a ringing affirmation of the free, rambling lifestyle. The third and fourth stanzas also present contrasting images, one of loneliness and the other of intimacy. In addition to *contrast*, this blues displays another important structural principle of traditional non-thematic blues, the *association* of related ideas. The two contrastive pairs of stanzas are linked to form a tightly constructed blues by the association of ideas of catching a train in Stanza 2 and drifting like a ship in Stanza 3. (The music of Stanza 2 is printed here as an example of the standardized twelve-measure *AAB* stanza pattern.)

Example 5. "I'll Catch the Train and Ride." Roosevelt Holts, vocal and guitar.[25]

1. Crying, Lord, have mercy, baby, on my bad-luck soul.
   Lord, have mercy, baby, on my bad-luck soul.
   Well, that Good Book teach you, gonna reap just what you sow.

2. Well, I'll drink my whisky, I'll catch the train and ride.
   Lord, I'll drink my whisky, I'll catch the train and ride.
   Yeah, when I find me a sweet little woman. I'm gonna pin her to my side.

3. Well, I'm drifting, I'm drifting like a ship out on the sea.
   Lord, I'm drifting, I'm drifting like a ship out on the sea.
   Well, I ain't got nobody in this world to care for me.

4. Well, the sun's going down; know what you promised me.
   Lord, the sun going down; know what you promised me.
   Well, you promised me something the poor boy really need.

Not all blues that use traditional elements are composed at the time of performance. Some of them are largely or entirely set pieces, offering little or no room for improvisation at the time of performance. Their relatively fixed form may be due to the fact that they were learned from other performers whose creations have been respected and left intact, or they may simply represent combinations of traditional elements created by their current performers which constitute for them satisfactory finished products, ones that they see no need to alter in subsequent performances. In the latter case the structure of such pieces may be developed consciously by the composer, although an unconscious process is equally possible.

An example of a relatively fixed blues made up of traditional lyrical and musical elements is Eli Owens's "Ways Like the Devil," also called by him "Commissary Blues." Owens stated that the piece properly contained four stanzas, though in five performances recorded in the span of five days he

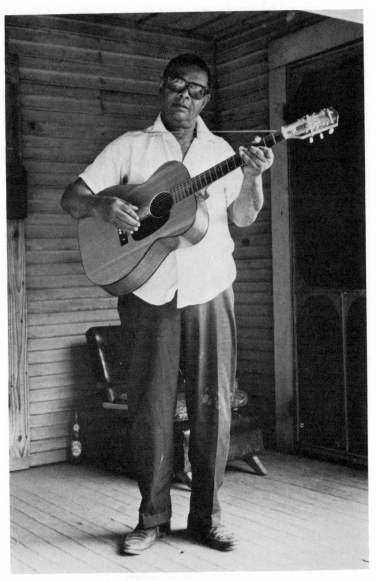

Eli Owens PHOTO BY CHERYL EVANS

never sang a complete version. Nevertheless, he sang only four different stanzas altogether, so that these can probably be considered the ones that belong in a complete version by him. This piece is probably such a stable item in Owens's repertoire because he associates it with another blues singer, Harrison Lee Bridges, from whom he learned it in the 1920s in Oak Vale, Mississippi. Owens respected Bridges as a musician and has apparently been reluctant to change the piece. In Stanza 1 of the version transcribed below the term "monkey men" means fools, especially in the sense of men who put complete trust in the fidelity of their women. Stanza 3 should be interpreted in the sense that the singer's woman has run up a large bill at the commissary where he trades. Many employers on large plantations, levee camps, and lumber camps used to operate a general store or "commissary" where their employees could obtain food and other goods on credit against their payment at the end of the work period. Many black workers often found themselves broke or in debt to the company store at "settlement time," frequently through such causes as low wages, high prices at the store, a dishonest boss, or extravagant purchases on credit (in this case made by the singer's woman).

Example 6. "Ways Like the Devil." Eli Owens, vocal and guitar.[26]

1. I got ways like the devil born in the lion's den.
   I got ways like the devil born in the lion's den.
   Well, my daily occupation, taking women from the monkey men.
   Yeah, my daily occupation, taking women from the monkey men.

2. Don't the moon look pretty shining down through the tree?
   Don't the moon look pretty, woman, shining down through the
     tree?
   Oh, I see my baby when she don't see me.
   Yeah, see my baby when she don't see me.

3. I went to the commissary laughing, where I come away crying.
   Went to the commissary laughing, where I come away crying.
   Well, that dog-gone woman, she done took up all my time.
   Yeah, that dog-gone woman, she done took up all my time.

[Guitar chorus.]

In two of his other versions Owens inserted the following stanza after the first stanza above:

My baby got ways like a fox squirrel in a tree.
My baby got ways like a fox squirrel in a tree.
Oh, she see me coming, she go hide from me.
Yeah, she see me coming, she go hide from me.

Adding this stanza, we again have a blues that displays a contrastive structural pattern. The stanzas numbered 1 and 3 above represent the song's outer framework. In the first stanza the singer boasts about how he can steal women away from their foolish husbands or lovers, while in the final stanza the singer himself has been made a fool of by his woman, quite likely with the consent of his boss who runs the commissary, the "other men" in this case. The two interior stanzas present images involving a tree, but they contrast scenes in which the singer and his woman look on each other unobserved. This blues, then, deals with the problem of trust and faithfulness, doing so with a nonthematic text and a contrastive structural pattern.

The last two examples above were both constructed out of traditional textual and musical elements. One was put together at the time of performance, and the other was a relatively stable item in the performer's repertoire. Some traditional blues, however, represent a compromise of sorts between these two approaches to composition in that they contain some elements that constitute a stable *core* that does not vary from one performance to another, while the other elements are added to the core at the time of performance. Usually a blues core consists of a vocal melody, an instrumental part, and a single stanza or line of text. To this are added additional stanzas sung to the same melody and accompaniment, chosen during the performance itself. The line or stanza of text that belongs to the core usually contains a striking image or figure of speech that helps to make the core memorable both to the singer and his audience. In fact, many blues cores become traditional fixed musical/lyrical combinations, utilized by a number of blues singers, each of whom adds his own set of traditional stanzas to the core during performance.

"Canned Heat Blues" by John Henry "Bubba" Brown is an example of a blues constructed from a core. In this case the core consists of the piece's melody, guitar part, and the line "canned heat's killing me." Brown learned this blues core from Tommy Johnson in Jackson, Mississippi, who composed and recorded "Canned Heat Blues" in 1928 (Victor V-38535).[27] "Canned Heat" is a type of cooking fuel made by the Sterno Company. During Prohibition some people drank this cheap and readily available alcoholic substance along with such other unwholesome products as denatured or rubbing alcohol ("alcorub"), hair tonic, liquid shoe polish, and extract of Jamaica ginger. Tommy Johnson was addicted to canned heat and these other drinks and spread their use along with his song to many others in Mississippi over the course of a long blues singing career that lasted until his death in 1956. His recipe for preparing the drink has been described by his brother:

> That canned heat, you know, it was red. It was in those little old cans. When you open it, take the top off the can. He'd strike him a match and burn it, burn the top of it. And he'd put it in a rag and strain it. It's got juice in it. Squeeze the juice out of it into a glass.

And then get him some sugar and put it in there. And then some water. And there he'd go.[28]

Canned heat and similar substances not only produced inebriation, but often they also produced a permanet disability known colloquially as the "limber leg" or "jake leg" (after jamaica ginger).[29] The effects of such drinks became the theme of many other blues besides Johnson's, indicating that the subject was well known to blues singers.[30] Remarkably, Tommy Johnson himself did not seem to suffer any consequences from his lifelong addiction. He died of a heart attack at the age of sixty! [31]

Although the version of "Canned Heat Blues" that Tommy Johnson recorded commercially in 1928 was a thematic blues, "Bubba" Brown says that in person Johnson would sing "most anything" in it. Evidently he means that Johnson performed the song's core, adding to it additional stanzas at the time of performance, probably to produce a nonthematic blues. Certainly this is the practice that Brown himself follows, as his two versions printed below demonstrate. Other singers who learned the piece from Johnson also perform the song's core while adding other stanzas different from those on Johnson's recorded version.[32] Brown's first version is as follows. He states that some of his verses besides the core verse were ones that Johnson sometimes sang in this piece.

Example 7. "Canned Heat Blues." John Henry "Bubba" Brown, vocal and guitar.[33]

1. Oh well, I drink so much canned heat 'til I walked all in my sleep.
   Says, I drink so much canned heat, I walked all in my sleep.
   Says, I had to drink that canned heat. Lord, I didn't have nothing
       else to eat.

2. Says, my dog, he jumped a rabbit, and he run him a solid mile.
   Says, my dog jumped a rabbit, and he run the rabbit a solid mile.
   Well, he seen he couldn't catch the rabbit; he sit down and cried
       just like a child.

3. Says, I'm going to Memphis, from there to Baltimore.
   Says, I'm going back to Memphis, boys, from Memphis back to
       Baltimore.
   'Cause when I was around your place, you drove me 'way from
       your door.

4. Says, now I done drinked so much canned heat until that canned
       heat's a' killing me.

Well, I done drinked so much canned heat, babe, 'til canned
   heat's a' killing me.
I'm gonna get me a train; I'm going back to Memphis, Tennessee.

5. Says, and my dog, he jumped a wild fox, and he run him 'round in
      front of my door.
   And my dog, he jumped a wild fox; he brought him right in front
      of my door.
   I says, "Just looky here, dog, don't run no chicken-eater up here
      no more."

The above text apparently does not develop a single theme. In fact, it seems
to contain three different themes: the singer's drinking and health problem,
his desire to travel, and his dog's inability to hunt properly. This text, then,
might seem to confirm Brown's observation that "Canned Heat Blues" was
a song in which one could sing "most anything." Yet, though the stanzas do
not represent a single definite underlying story or scene, they do maintain a
consistency of mood, somewhat in the manner of "Water Boy" (Example 3).
The singer depicts himself as addicted to canned heat and ruining his health
(Stanzas 1 and 4). This and the fact that his friends (or possibly his lover) have
driven him away (Stanza 3) can be taken as the reasons for his desire to travel
(Stanzas 3 and 4). The stanzas about the singer's dog (2 and 5) again present
an image of a lack of success. Possibly the dog is even to be taken as symbolic
of the singer himself, in which case we might compare Stanzas 3 and 5, in
which the singer and the dog are driven away from their companion's door.
The general mood of this piece, then, is one of regret and self-pity.

A little over a month later Brown recorded another version of "Canned
Heat Blues," this one very different in mood though still employing the same
core.

Example 8. "Canned Heat Blues." John Henry "Bubba" Brown, vocal and
guitar.[34]

   1. Says, I tell you baby, canned heat's a' killing me.

   2. Well, I drinked so much canned heat 'til it made me weak in my
         knee.
      Says, I drinked so much canned heat 'til it made me weak all in my
         knee.
      Well, I'm gonna drink my canned heat just as long as I can live.

   3. Says, I'm going to Memphis, from there to Birmingham.
      Says, I'm going to Memphis, from there back to Birmingham.
      'Cause I'm gonna make my home way down in good old Alabam'.

4. Says, I drinked so much canned heat 'til it made me weak all in my
knee.
Says, I drinked so much canned heat 'til it made me weak all in my
knee.
I'm gonna drink my canned heat; you can say just what you please.

Here the mood is not one of regret and self-pity but rather one of boasting
and determination to survive. The travel theme in Stanza 3 seems more an affirmation of a life style of drinking and rambling than a desire to escape or a
feeling of rejection. These two examples, then, of "Canned Heat Blues" by
the same singer show that a blues core is a very flexible compositional device
that can be used to help generate texts that are otherwise very different from
each other. Although most folklorists would probably consider these pieces to
be variants of each other or of a common song type, the pieces obviously can
have quite different meanings.

The eight examples printed above should demonstrate the flexibility and
variability in folk blues. They can be thematic or nonthematic; deliberately
composed prior to performance, improvised during performance, or partly
improvised and partly composed deliberately (the core technique); and they
can be either original compositions of the singer, arrangements of traditional
material, copies of phonograph records, or even combinations of material
from all of these sources. Folk blues also may or may not be the direct personal expressions of their singers or composers, though from their vivid first-
person style of delivery they usually appear to be such. Most of the blues
printed here, however, did not represent the current or the former conditions of their singers. "Bubba" Brown was never a canned heat drinker or a
rambler. In fact, he retired on a pension after working thirty years for the
same company. He associated "Canned Heat Blues" with his friend and
fellow blues singer Tommy Johnson, whose music Brown greatly admired.
Although Roosevelt Holts sang "I'll drink my whisky, I'll catch the train and
ride," he was a teetotaler at the time of recording, and if he rode anywhere it
would have been in his Chrysler. Bessie Mae Charleston was definitely never
a chain-gang prisoner, and in her song, in any case, she adopts the persona of
a male convict. Charlie Taylor's "Annie Lee," although highly personal in
style, was ultimately a reworking of a phonograph record of the same title. Eli
Owens lived in town at the time of recording, nowhere near a commissary,
nor was he in the habit of stealing women from "monkey men." In any case,
he learned his song from another singer. And Ira Coney, despite the picture
of marital dissolution in his "Monday Morning Blues," was a happily married
man and father of nine who performed the piece in front of his wife and family.

Most blues singers employ a variety of the approaches to learning, composition, and performance described above, relying to a greater or lesser extent in each individual performance on such factors as originality, tradition, personal experience, improvisation, and so forth. No folk blues singer familiar to me uses only one of these approaches exlcusively. Yet the singers do recognize one criterion that should be common to all blues: that they tell the truth.[35] Obviously this truth need not be literal or autobiographical.[36] Instead the performer must sing something that is true to life, something that represents a typical experience or thought for people in the singer's community or audience. All of the texts printed above are filled with such typical experiences or thoughts. Thus, even if the words of a folk blues represent a fantasy for their singer, they are reality for someone else close to the singer or a fantasy in which others can easily share. Folk blues do not deal with unique or remote experiences that only the singer could understand or with the experiences of people unlike the singer and his audience. These songs, then, serve as a means of self-expression for the blues singer but also indirectly for the audience around him. The blues singer becomes their spokesman, the organizer of their thoughts, opinions, and fantasies.

If the folk blues singer must be conscious of his audience, we should look again at the contexts of these songs. Of all the social situations for blues performance described at the beginning of this article, probably the most common are the house party and the gathering at the local juke joint. These situations are usually characterized by dancing, drinking, a great deal of noise besides the music, and a variety of other distractions from the music, such as conversation, gambling, and watching the dancers. In some of the larger affairs there may even be two competing sources of music, one of which may be a record player, juke box, or radio. In any case the blues singer must compete with his context as well as perform within it. The attention span of people in this kind of audience tends to be short. Frequently they do not listen closely to an entire performance even if they are in close enough range to the singer to hear it clearly. Thus only one or two stanzas of a song might actually register on a typical member of a folk blues audience. If a song is well structured as a total composition, this fact is not likely to be perceived during its performance except possibly by the blues singer himself. Under these circumstances, then, such devices as nonthematic composition, improvisation, and textual structures based on the principles of contrast and association of related ideas prove to be great advantages for the blues singer in reaching his audience and fulfilling his function as their spokesman. They provide the singer the opportunity to develop ideas succinctly, appeal to a variety of interests, and express contrasting sides of common problems, thus maximizing his appeal to various members of his audience. The blues singer can have something for everyone. Frequently members of the audience will respond to an individual line or stanza with a shout of encouragement or agreement with the singer or banter directed toward a statement expressed in one of the verses.[37] Rarely are comments made on the song as a whole.

But folk blues are not always sung under such hectic circumstances. Charley Patton's "It Won't Be Long" (Example 4) was sung in a commercial recording studio, while the other examples printed here were sung in the singer's or a neighbor's home, either with an audience of family and friends or strictly for the collectors. In fact, these pieces would have been difficult to record at a juke joint or house party because of the noise, crowded conditions, and sometimes rowdy behavior of the participants.[38] Although the conditions of the natural context can influence the content of a blues performance, and although some of these conditions were lacking in the examples presented here, these examples still give a true picture of the variety of styles used by folk blues singers in composing and performing their songs, for the singers are so used to performing under hectic circumstances that they simply retain the same approaches in more relaxed ones. It is only when singers begin to become more self-conscious about their roles as popular artists for a mass audience or when they realize that they can reach a mass audience with their thoughts through phonograph records and other mass media that they make a major shift in their approach to composition and performance. Records can be contemplated by their audience at leisure and under controlled circumstances, and a popular singer on a stage performing through a public-address system can be heard over the noise of his surroundings. Under these conditions blues usually contain thematic texts with a single idea more fully developed than in the folk blues. Popular blues texts are usually more original and deliberate compositions than folk blues texts, which are frequently traditional and improvised at the time of performance. These developments must not be taken as indications of progress, however. They simply represent equally suitable responses to different social circumstances.

NOTES

[1] For a good history of the blues see Paul Oliver, *The Story of the Blues* (London: Barrie & Rockliff, 1969). Blues singers themselves discuss their music and careers in Paul Oliver, *Conversation with the Blues* (New York: Horizon, 1965), and Robert Neff and Anthony Connor, *Blues* (Boston: David R. Godine, 1975). Blues recordings through 1966 are listed in two important discographical works, John Godrich and Robert M. W. Dixon, *Blues & Gospel Records 1902–1942* (London: Storyville, 1969), and Mike Leadbitter and Neil Slaven, *Blues Records: 1943–1966* (London: Hanover, 1968). The earliest substantial collection of folk blues was made by Howard W. Odum early in this century in Mississippi and Georgia and published in "Folk-Song and Folk-Poetry As Found in the Secular Songs of the Southern Negroes," *Journal of American Folklore* 24 (1911), 255–94, 351–96. This article was reprinted with few changes in Howard W. Odum and Guy B. Johnson, *The Negro and His Songs* (Chapel Hill: University of North

Carolina Press, 1925). For a more recent large collection of folk blues see Harry Oster, *Living Country Blues* (Detroit: Folklore Associates, 1969). Some early blues sheet music has been reprinted in *Blues, An Anthology*, ed. W. C. Handy, with a historical and critical text by Abbe Niles, revised by Jerry Silverman (New York: Mcmillan, 1972). Collections of blues texts from commercial phonograph records are printed in Paul Oliver, *The Meaning of the Blues* (New York: Collier, 1963); Eric Sackheim, *The Blues Line, A Collection of Blues Lyrics* (New York: Grossman, 1969); Stefan Grossman, Hal Grossman, and Stephen Calt, *Country Blues Songbook* (New York: Oak, 1973); and A. X. Nicholas, *Woke Up This Mornin': Poetry of the Blues* (New York: Bantam, 1973).

[2] On black-white interchange in the blues see Tony Russell, *Blacks, Whites and Blues* (New York: Stein and Day, 1970).

[3] On the folk/popular distinction in the blues see David Evans, "Folk, Commercial, and Folkloristic Aesthetics in the Blues," *Jazzforschung* 5 (1973), 11–32. On the attitudes and activities of the songwriters, commercial record companies, and their blues artists see W. C. Handy, *Father of the Blues* (New York: Collier, 1970); Perry Bradford, *Born with the Blues* (New York: Oak, 1965); "Quality in 'Blues'," The *Metronome* 39 (Sept. 1923), 140; "Origin of 'Blues' Numbers," *Sheet Music News* 2 (Oct. 1923), 8–9, 41; Robert M. W. Dixon and John Godrich, *Recording the Blues* (New York: Stein and Day, 1970); Mike Seeger, "Who Chose These Records? A Look into the Life, Tastes, and Procedures of Frank Walker," in *Anthology of American Folk Music*, ed. Josh Dunson and Ethel Raim (New York: Oak, 1973), pp. 8–17; David Evans, "An Interview with H. C. Speir," *John Edwards Memorial Foundation Quarterly* 8 (1972), 117–21; Lester Melrose, "My Life in Recording," in *The American Folk Music Occasional*, ed. Chris Strachwitz and Pete Welding (New York: Oak, 1970), pp. 59–61; Norman Cohen, " 'I'm a Record Man': Uncle Art Satherly Reminisces," *John Edwards Memorial Foundation Quarterly* 8 (1972) 18–22; Kip Lornell, "Living Blues Interview: J. B. Long," *Living Blues*, no. 29 (Sept.–Oct., 1976), 13–22; Charles Keil, *Urban Blues* (Chicago: University of Chicago Press, 1966), pp. 69–95; Mike Leadbitter, *Crowley, Louisiana Blues* (Bexhill-on-Sea, England: Blues Unlimited, 1968); and Mike Leadbitter and Eddie Shuler, *From the Bayou* (Bexhill-on-Sea, England: Blues Unlimited, 1969).

[4] These processes are identified and described in David Evans, "Techniques of Blues Composition among Black Folksingers," *Journal of American Folklore* 87 (1974), 240–49. For a more detailed discussion see David Evans, "Tradition and Creativity in the Folk Blues," unpublished Ph.D. dissertation (University of California, Los Angeles, 1976).

[5] Recorded near Portal, Georgia, January 15, 1976, by David and Cheryl Evans.

[6] Recorded in Crystal Springs, Mississippi, August 31, 1970, by David Evans.

[7] Samuel Charters, *The Bluesmen* (New York: Oak, 1967), pp. 73, 133, 134, 209.

[8] Paul Oliver, *Screening the Blues: Aspects of the Blues Tradition* (London: Cassell, 1968), pp. 90–91.

[9] On poetic imagery in the folk blues see especially Odum and Johnson, pp. 269–96; Sterling A. Brown, "The Blues As Folk Poetry," in *Folk-Say, A Regional Miscellany: 1930*, ed. B. A. Botkin (Norman: University of Oklahoma Press, 1940), pp. 324–39; Sterling A. Brown, "The Blues," *Phylon* 13 (1952), 286–92; Samuel Charters, *The Poetry of the Blues* (New York: Oak, 1963); Oster, pp. 61–95; Stephen Calt, "The Country Blues As Meaning," in Grossman, Grossman, and Calt, pp. 8–35; and Paul Garon, *Blues and the Poetic Spirit* (London: Eddison, 1975).

[10] For analyses of other blues of this sort see Charters, *The Poetry of the Blues*, pp. 23–26.

[11] For an important study of the southern black prison song tradition see Bruce Jackson, *Wake Up Dead Man: Afro-American Worksongs from Texas Prisons* (Cambridge,

Mass.: Harvard University Press, 1972). For prison blues see Oliver, *The Meaning of the Blues*, pp. 231–58; and Oster, pp. 305–46.

[12] On the "holler" tradition see Harold Courlander, *Negro Folk Music U.S.A.* (New York: Columbia University Press, 1963), pp. 80–88. On the relation of the holler to the blues see Charters, *The Bluesmen*, pp. 27–28; Oliver, *The Story of the Blues*, pp. 17–25; Oster, pp. 11–13; John A. Lomax and Alan Lomax, *Folk Song U.S.A.* (New York: New American Library, 1966), p. 70; and Alan Lomax, *The Folk Songs of North America* (Garden City, N.Y.: Doubleday, 1960), p. 573.

[13] Recorded near Crystal Springs, Mississippi, July 14, 1971, by David and Cheryl Evans.

[14] Odum, "Folk-Song and Folk-Poetry," pp. 260, 268.

[15] Dorothy Scarborough, *On the Trail of Negro Folk-Songs* (Cambridge, Mass.: Harvard University Press, 1925), p. 272.

[16] Francis Lee Utley noted the "masterful poetic logic" of one such blues in "The Genesis and Revival of 'Dink's Song'," in *Studies in Language and Literature in Honor of Margaret Schlauch,* ed. Mieczysław Brahmer, Stanisław Helsztyński, and Julian Kryzyżanowski (Warsaw: Polish Scientific Publishers, 1966), pp. 457–72. Oster, pp. 76–87, also attempts to explain several such blues.

[17] Charters, *The Bluesmen,* p. 121.

[18] John Fahey, *Charley Patton* (London: Studio Vista, 1970), p. 60.

[19] Calt, pp. 20, 21.

[20] Barry Elmes, "Living Blues Interview: Sonny Terry & Brownie McGhee," *Living Blues,* no. 13 (Summer 1973), 20. For other similar opinions of blues singers see Bruce Iglauer, Jim O'Neal, and Bea Van Geffen, "Living Blues Interview: Lowell Fulson," *Living Blues* no. 6 (Autumn 1971), 18; and Charters, *The Poetry of the Blues,* p. 20 (quoting Furry Lewis).

[21] Fahey, pp. 60, 63.

[22] Related blues by Memphis groups are "Minglewood Blues" (Victor 21267; recorded 1928) by Cannon's Jug Stompers, reissued on *Cannon's Jug Stompers,* Herwin 208, 12″ double-LP; and "New Minglewood Blues" (Victor 23266; recorded 1930) by Noah Lewis's Jug Band, reissued on *The Great Jug Bands,* Origin Jazz Library 4, 12″ LP.

[23] Recorded in Richmond, Indiana, June 14, 1929; issued on Paramount 12854; reissued on *Charley Patton, Founder of the Delta Blues,* Yazoo L-1020, 12″ double-LP.

[24] David Evans, *Tommy Johnson* (London: Studio Vista, 1971), pp. 91, 99; David Evans, "Booker White," in *Nothing But the Blues,* ed. Mike Leadbitter (London: Hanover, 1971), pp. 253–54; Valerie Wilmer, "Blues People: Fred & Roosevelt," *Jazz Journal* 19 (Aug. 1966), 24; Al Wilson, "Robert Pete Williams, His Life and Music," *Little Sandy Review* 2 (July 1966), 21; Oster, p. 4.

[25] Recorded in Bogalusa, Louisiana, August 24, 1970, by David Evans. Issued on *Roosevelt Holts and His Friends,* Arhoolie 1057, 12″ LP.

[26] Recorded in Bogalusa, Louisiana, August 26, 1970, by David Evans. Issued on *South Mississippi Blues,* Rounder 2009, 12″ LP.

[27] Johnson's version is printed and discussed in Evans, *Tommy Johnson,* pp. 56–58, 93–94. For more information on Brown see David Evans, "Bubba Brown: Folk Poet," *Mississippi Folklore Register* 7 (1973), 15–31.

[28] Evans, *Tommy Johnson,* p. 57.

[29] Kelsie B. Harder, "The Jake Leg," *Tennessee Folklore Society Bulletin* 27 (Sept. 1961), 45–47.

[30] Among the other blues on this theme are Tommy Johnson's "Alcohol and Jake Blues" (Paramount 12950; recorded 1930; no known copy extant); Ishman Bracey's

"Jake Liquor Blues" (Paramount 12941; recorded 1930); Keghouse's "Canned Heat Blues" (Vocalion 1239); "Sloppy" Henry's "Canned Heat Blues" (Okeh 8630; recorded 1928; Will Shade's "Better Leave That Stuff Alone" (Victor 21725; recorded 1928); and Willie "Poor Boy" Lofton's "It's Killing Me" (Decca 7010; recorded 1934) and "Jake Leg Blues" (Decca 7076; recorded 1934). Bracey and Lofton were friends of Tommy Johnson, although their songs are unrelated except in theme.

[31] Evans, *Tommy Johnson*, pp. 85–87.

[32] K. C. Douglas, "Canned Heat," issued on *K. C. Douglas, A Dead-Beat Guitar and the Mississippi Blues*, Cook 5002, 12″ LP (recorded 1956); K. C. Douglas, "Canned Heat," issued on *K. C. Douglas, Big Road Blues*, Bluesville BV 1050, 12″ LP (recorded 1961); Houston Stackhouse, "Canned Heat," issue on *Mississippi Delta Blues*, vol. 1, Arhoolie ST 1041, 12″ LP (recorded 1967).

[33] Recorded in Los Angeles, California, June 9, 1967, by David Evans and Marina Bokelman. Issued on *The Legacy of Tommy Johnson*, Matchbox SDM 224, 12″ LP.

[34] Recorded in Los Angeles, California, July 17, 1967, by David Evans and Marina Bokelman.

[35] Evans, "Folk, Commercial, and Folkloristic Aesthetics in the Blues," 13–15; Charters, *The Poetry of the Blues*, pp. 11–14; Oliver, *Conversation with the Blues*, pp. 23–25.

[36] On the question of "autobiography" in blues see Rod Gruver, "The Blues As Dramatic Monologues," *John Edwards Memorial Foundation Quarterly* 6 (1970), 28–31; Jeff Titon, "Autobiography and Blues Texts: A Reply to 'The Blues As Dramatic Monologues'," *Ibid.* 6 (1970), 79–82; and Rod Gruver, "The Autobiographical Theory Re-Examined," *Ibid.* 6 (1970), 129–31.

[37] On the role of the audience at blues singing events see William Ferris, Jr., *Blues from the Delta* (London: Studio Vita, 1970), pp. 61–86; and Wiliam R. Ferris, Jr., "Gut Bucket Blues: Sacred and Profane," *Jazzforschung* 5 (1973), 68–85.

[38] On this point see David Evans, "Fieldwork with Blues Singers: The Unintentionally Induced Natural Context," *Southern Folklore Quarterly*, in press.

Index

Note. In this index, as in the text itself, major terms are emphasized where they are first introduced and defined by means of boldface or italicized type; generally these page references appear first in an analyzed index heading. The separate chapter-length discussions of basic folklore genres are not indexed, nor are individual titles or examples of these types. Such subjects are easily located with the Table of Contents; however, references to the basic genres outside these special chapters have been indexed. The index gathers references to all non-folklore details—personal names, cities and states, regions, institutions, publications, nationalities, theories, etc. Especially, it brings together references to *approaches to the study of folklore* (see, *e.g.*, Analysis of folklore, Attitudes, Structural analysis, Contextual analysis and Style) and to *bodies of folk tradition* (see *e.g.*, Children's folklore, College folklore, Immigrant folklore, Military folklore, Negro folklore, Occupational folklore, and Regional folklore).

Customs, 1, *4*, **244–45**; dance and, 260; folk gestures compared with, 277; folk gestures compared with, 277; in games, 288; drinking games as expiring, 293; *See also* Death (and funeral) customs

Cycle: of legends, *106*, 107, 110, 119; of jokes (*see* Joke fads)

Dahomean Narrative (F. S. and M. J. Herskovits), 106

Dalhart, Vernon, 157,

Dana, R. H., Jr., 348

Dance songs, *261*; in play parties, 263–65

Darling, John, 113

Darwin, Charles, 104

Davidson, Levette J., xi–xii

Death (and funeral) customs: superstitions attached to, **231–32**; customs associated with, 246, 249–50

Deep South, *see* Southern folklore

Dégh, Linda, 32, 108

Denver (Col.), 31, 112

Derision rhymes, **86**

Desk-top inscriptions (horizontal graffiti), **91**

Dialect, 4, **40–41**; pronunciations in, **42**; vocabulary in, **42–45**; in rhymes, 85; in *Märchen*, 130; in folk music, 209; in games, 287–88

Dialect songs, *165*

Dialect stories, *132*; black, *133*; Jewish-American, *133*; dramatic element in, 266

Dickens, Charles, 53

"Dictionary of American Popular Beliefs and Superstitions" (Hand), 228

Dictionary of American Proverbs, 57

Diddling (chin music), 158, 208

Diedrich Knickerbocker's History of New York (Irving), 280

Diffusion, *103*, 106, 283

Dillinger, John, 113

Disasters: ballads about, 197

Disney, Walt, 129

Doctor Watts, 208

Doolittle, General, 113

Dorson, Richard M., ix, 2, 14, 15, 110, 114, 119, 274, 302

Dramas, *4*, **267–69**; as extinct, 27; dances and, 259; in games, *285*

Dramatic element in folklore, **265–67**

Drinking games, **293**

Droodles, **69–70**

Dundes, Alan, x, 44, 58, 72, 143, 222–23, 302

Durante, Jimmy, 114

Easter: superstitions related to, 233; customs associated with, *251*; folk dramas of, 267

Edwardsville (Ill.), 265

Egypt: as region in Illinois, 28

1812, War of: ballads from, 193

Einstein, Albert, 115

Elephant jokes, 134

Elite traditions: transmission of, 3

Elizabeth II (Queen of England), 281

Emerson, Ralph Waldo, 58

Emida (Idaho), 118

Emotional core of ballads, 176, 183

Endless tales, *138*

Engagement, *see* Courtship (and engagement)

English and Scottish Popular Ballads, The, 199

English Riddles from Oral Tradition (Taylor), 64

Epic poetry: folk roots of, 12

Epitaphs, **90**

Ethical dimension of folklore collecting, 16

Ethnic groups (nationality groups), *4*, 28, **31–32**; classification of categories, 17; dialect vocabulary of, 43–44; foods of, 350; jokes about, 134; *See also folklore of specific ethnic groups; for example:* Black folklore

Ethnocentrism: defined, **246**

Ethnogastronomy (ethnological food research), 344

Ethnography, **245**

Ethnology, **245**

Ethnomusicology, **206**

Etiological narratives (explanatory narratives), *99–100*

Eton College, 133

Euhemerism, 105

Euhemerus, 105

Evans, David, viii

Evans, E. Estyn, 303

Explanatory narratives (etiological narratives), *99–100*

Fables (moral tales) 52, **129**; *cante*, *139–40*, 149

Fairy tales: as folktales, 125–26

Faith healers, 230

Fakelore, 2, 8

Family stories, *114*

Farmers' Museum (Cooperstown; N.Y.), 307

Father's Day: customs associated with, *251*

Fences: making of, as folk craft, 321–22

Ferris, Oliver H. P., 292

Festival of American Folklore, 254

Festivals, *4*, *245*, **252–53**; dances in, 259; foods in, 350

Fiddle tunes, 207, 209, 262; play parties and, 263; dramatic skits with, 266

Fife, Austin, 324, 325

Fife, James, 324

Fifth Symphony (Beethoven), 280

Finger rhymes, 80

Finger-and-toe counting rhymes, 81

Finglish, 28, 44

Fink, Mike, 113

Finnish-American folklore: Finnish-Americans as folk group, 28; of Astoria (Ore.), 31; dialect pronunciation in, 42; dialect vocabulary in, 44

Finnish method, *see* Historic-geographic method

First-person reminiscences, *114*

Fishing and hunting: superstitions attached to, **234**; customs in, 250–51

Florida, 31

Flyleaf inscriptions, **90–91**

Folk: concepts of, 27; lack of sophistication associated with concept of, 222

Folk architecture (vernacular architecture), 5, **308–15**; analysis of, 18

Folk Art of Rural Pennsylvania (Lichten), 320